DATE DUE		

Crisis in Economic Theory

Crisis in Economic Theory

A Study of Monetary Policy, Analysis, and Economic Goals

by

William J. Frazer, Jr.

University of Florida Press   /   Gainesville   /   1973

Library of Congress Cataloging in Publication Data

Frazer, William Johnson, 1924–
    Crisis in economic theory.

    Bibliography: p.
    1. Money. 2. Money—Mathematical models.
    3. Monetary policy. 4. Economics. I. Title.
    HG221.F84   332.4   73–16273
    ISBN 0–8130–0392–X
    ISBN 0–8130–0445–4 (pbk)

PRINTED BY
STORTER PRINTING COMPANY, INCORPORATED
GAINESVILLE, FLORIDA

TO

N.W.L.

and

Lulu Slaton Thompson

Contents

Preface

THIS BOOK emphasizes monetary policy and a crisis in economic theory. The focus on monetary policy and theory is one way of questioning the empirical content and relevance of economic theory. In the initial period of the impact of the modern computer, delineated in the text as the 1960s, the outpouring of statistical results accelerated. In the end, this onslaught—as augmented by the issues provided by the inflationary episodes of the mid-1960s through the early 1970s—was more than received doctrine in economics could handle. The accelerated pace of change gave enlarged emphasis to behavioral notions, state-of-mind variables, and the like.

As the literature of the 1960s evolved, all the main topics of monetary economics were introduced in discussions of policy and goals. This focus provides a theme for an otherwise fragmented set of topics, but the changes in this highly important area of study have broad implications. They are shown to extend to the theory of relative prices and an exchange economy.

Behavioral propositions have been apparent in monetary economics—at least since the work of Keynes in the 1930s and, to some extent, Irving Fisher just before him—and a relatively abundant supply of data was available for analysis, as evidenced by the lengthy appendices in the monthly issues of the *Federal Reserve Bulletin*. Thus the prospect of testing theories and their policy implications attracted the modern analysts to statistical tools and computers. It is a thesis of this book that their results accelerated the pace of change in a major segment of economic theory, and hence the crisis.

The impact of the computer has been phenomenal. The new-found capacity to promptly analyze masses of data evoked stronger demand for more timely and verifiable explanations of policy actions and inactions. Notions encouched in the banking view of the Federal Reserve's approach to policy were torn asunder. Relatively static analytical devices were shown to be less relevant to the real world. Relevant dynamic and behavioral notions rose, but the transition and the demands for methodological sophistication imposed by the computer overwhelmed the analysts. They were less certain of the directions in which their new capacities and information would lead them.

This book is about these changes and their methodological underpinnings. It consists of seven parts, divided into chapters with occasional appendices. The appendices on selected methodological topics are mainly guides for the reader less familiar with econometric models and methods. The book is partly a survey of selected papers, mostly from the 1960s and early 1970s, with some empirical orientation. Ramifications of the various papers, comments, and controversies advance the themes of the book. But it is more than a review; events are interpreted, redirection and changes are called for, original notions emerge. An emphasis on the further introduction of probability into economic analyses appears.

There are divergent and even inconsistent explanations of phenomena, some even supported by statistical results from analyses of the same data. This book tries to achieve consistency in explanation and in empirical facts; statistical results and logic are the criteria for assessing the relevance of explanations and for retaining the most relevant explanations in an otherwise fragmented literature. As one writer said in an early 1969 book review, "professional opinion within the field is so fragmented that an uninitiated reader is likely to feel he has been abandoned in a jungle of anarchy without anyone to help him find his way out."

This book was written for the benefit of a rather broad audience of analysts, government and bank officials, and academic economists operating in the sphere of national economic policy. A reader has suggested "those already sophisticated in the book's subject matter," "professional economists, mostly those in the field of money, either in universities, research organizations, or government agencies."

The possibility of such a volume occurred to me in early 1968, when I first published the overview that appears in Chapter 2. Initially I thought of reprinting a collection of papers juxtaposing the conflicting interpretations of evidence, to bring out the themes of the present book. However, the reproduction cost of these specialized and voluminous materials is prohibitive.

A number of individuals were helpful in the preparation of the book, including two whose names appear later, William P. Yohe and Robert E. Weintraub. Howard S. Ellis, formerly of the University of California at Berkeley, graciously read and commented in detail on an initial draft.

Among the others who read parts of the book, I wish to single out William Fellner, also formerly of the University of California at Berkeley and later Yale, for his helpful and encouraging comments about advancing some probabilistic aspects of the analysis of economic behavior. Carter C. Osterbind, of the University of Florida's Bureau of Economics and Business Research, consoled and encouraged the author. Robert E. Williams, Michael A. DiSalvo, and Derriel B. Cato, all graduate students, provided stimulating association and comments during the period in which the book took shape.

W.J.F.

Gainesville, Florida

Part I

Introduction

1

A Renewal of Interest in Monetary Policy and Issues

1.1 INTRODUCTION

THIS CHAPTER introduces some of the many players and contrasting ideas about monetary policy, as variously defined. It also sketches some historical changes in views about the effects of monetary policy, including in relation to fiscal policy (defined as the shaping of government revenues and expenditures with the view to achieving national economic goals).

Empirical data have played a role. Sir John Hicks, the reviewer of Keynes' *General Theory* [229][1] for the *Economic Journal*, notes that some of the key ideas in Keynes' thinking soon took a secondary role in interpretations because of certain findings [201, pp. 308–11]. Hawtrey had questioned on empirical grounds whether the central bank could control the long-term interest rate as Keynes presumed (Ch. 7). A summary of replies to an Oxford questionnaire about the lack of the influence of the interest rate on business decisions had appeared in a 1938 publication [260]. The data and analyses were crude by present standards, but apparent failures of monetary policy cleared the way for the "Age of Fiscal Policy."

Fiscal policy became the focus of illustrations of the Keynesian investment multiplier [323, pp. 289–92]. The singularity of this emphasis on fiscal policy began to reverse itself in the 1960s. Again there were results from analyses of data, but under the impact of the modern computer the outpouring of results was overwhelming. There were difficulties and issues concerning the selection of a policy indicator (Ch. 10), the point of entry for the central bank (the Federal Reserve in the United States), and the relationships between monetary and real variables. The evolution of these

---

1. Throughout the book, numbers in brackets are used to refer to references at the end of the book. Sometimes page numbers are included in the brackets. Parentheses will be used for references to other chapters and sections of the book.

difficulties and issues and some resolutions of them are discussed in this book.

Even casual observations of empirical data have had impact, but economists of the archaic pre-computer days abstained from empirical testing on the large scale of the 1960s. They did not try to capture the essence of the processes revealed in data ordered as time series and at a moment in time (on a cross-section basis), often saying others could do the testing and pointing to the complexity of the task. There were certainly enclaves and centers of research with an empirical orientation (Chs. 5, 18), and these were destined to become more prominent during the crises in economic theory.

In what Joan Robinson [310] has referred to as the first crisis in modern economic theory (immediately preceding the appearance of the *General Theory*), casual observation called attention to the incompatibility of the persistent state of unemployment with the accepted theory. In Joan Robinson's and some others' view [201, pp. 3–5], this set the stage for new work. As viewed by others [358] and in this book, crisis in theory came in the late 1960s, but this later crisis was less tractable from only casual observation.

In the late 1960s one could point to such subtle, empirically demonstratable phenomena as the "inflationary recession," the expected rate of change in prices as a component of interest rates, and the presence of planning in the New Industrial State (especially to avoid tight credit conditions). "Inflationary recession" is a label for an admixture of emphases: on the one hand, on the interaction between interest rates and price expectations; and, on the other hand, on cost-push inflation (price increases due to rising wages, other costs, and sluggish productivity) and management's necessary cessation of reasonable featherbedding whenever profits are squeezed. The persistence of inflation and unemployment from the late 1960s through 1971 led to crises in the balance of payments and monetary arrangements, internationally, and to the introduction of non-market controls on wages and prices, domestically. These were ominous for the future of the economy and of an economics that posits competitive labor and product markets and flexible prices. Presently, however, emphasis is placed on economic analysis of stabilization and money, and extends to the theory of relative prices and exchange. Hence the crisis in economic theory is broadly viewed. One might say of this particular crisis [310] that it is simply a renewal of the first crisis.

For Keynes, money was the link between the present and the future; its role was both illuminated and clouded by him, and obscured more in the decades immediately following him. Economics works best when the economic subjects lack the capacity to remember and learn, when there is no yesterday and only a certain or given tomorrow. Anticipations—and, to a degree, planning—introduce special time dimensions to economics. Received doctrine has not coped well with these.

The resistance of economists to the introduction of these phenomena was increasingly weakened, both by developments in the 1960s and by the enhanced ability of more economists to analyze more numbers in more combinations than had been dreamt possible. The role of the future was always troublesome, but it proved especially troublesome for the orthodoxy of the 1950s and 1960s (Chs. 5, 7), and for analyses that emphasized equilibrium as a balancing of weights (Sec. 2.2). The computer accelerated the growth of large structural equations models (Ch. 14) and gave rise to evaluations of them and their methodological underpinnings in the light of empirical findings.

A reaction to Keynesian economics was inevitable in the 1960s, simply because it had become orthodox when unmanageable problems persisted and rapid changes were occurring in economics under the impact of the modern computer. Some economists wrote and spoke of a "Keynesian Counter-Revolution" and "Monetarist Counter-Revolutions" [201]. (Economists at times show considerable inclination to split hairs in distinguishing parochial stances. One finds references to "monetarists," "weak monetarists," "Friedmanians," "modern Keynesians," and so on, as defined later.) But such labels are less encompassing than the present reference to the "initial impact of the modern computer." The contributors to the changes in economics have constituted a broader group than just monetarists, and empirical economics and the computer have influenced emerging monetarist and other views as well.

Some personages.—In the 1960s period of turbulent developments in analysis and policy, important players included Paul A. Samuelson, Milton Friedman, Arthur F. Burns, Walter Heller,[2] and numerous others. Through his textbook on economics [317, 320, 323], Samuelson was a principal expositor of notions subsequently identified as "Keynesian" (as distinct

2. These individuals are contemporaries, but the list might be extended to include Irving Fisher (1867–1947), one of the most original U.S. economists. He was associated with Yale University from 1890 to 1935. He started his teaching career as a tutor in mathematics and employed his mathematical skill in his teaching and writing of economics. The high distinction he attained in economics diminished somewhat following the Great Crash of 1929. That autumn he said, "Stock prices have reached what looks like a permanently high plateau." However, in the 1960s his name regained prominence with the rise of interest in monetary economics.

from Keynes' notions). Over 2 million copies of the book were sold from its first edition in 1948 through its seventh in 1967. In 1970, he received the second Nobel Prize in economics.[3]

Milton Friedman founded a school of thought to which the label "monetarists" [309, pp. 4–5] has been applied. He has been a principal contributor to the revival of belief in the potency of monetary policy, in part fostered by his first National Bureau book with Anna Schwartz [155, Ch. 7] which reevaluated the role money played from 1929 to 1933. Arthur Burns was an associate of Friedman at the National Bureau, the nonprofit organization for empirical research in economics. Burns' relations to major publications and the empirical interests of Friedman are discussed later (Secs. 5.1, 3.2, Appendix to Ch. 8). In February 1970, Burns became Chairman of the Board of Governors of the Federal Reserve System.

Walter Heller was the astute political economist in the executive office during the 1961–65 term. Heller's term as Chairman of the President's Council of Economic Advisors accompanied increased public interest in economics and epochal emphasis on fiscal policy. He is identified with the "New Economics," which represents the concerns of Keynesians in the 1960s, during the presidencies of John Kennedy and Lyndon Johnson.

Reactions.—Friedman's presidential address to the American Economic Association in December 1967 [140] reflected the revival of interest in monetary analysis as it relates to policy. He chose to oppose two policy objectives: (1) the early post-World War II idea of pegging interest rates through open-market operations and "announcements" about policy, and (2) the state of employment in the short run. In attempts to peg rates, the growth of the money stock must ultimately accelerate and change the demand for money via the expectation of price-level changes. Once expectations change, pegging is impossible (Sec. 1.4).[4]

Friedman objected to the use of the state of employment as a policy criterion because a "natural" percentage of unemployment is consistent with price-level stability and wage increases of a given percentage per

3. The Academy of Sciences of the Nobel Foundation emphasized Samuelson's actions to "raise the level of scientific analysis in economic theory," and pointed to his *Foundations* [325] as his best known work and to his specific contributions (as may be found in his collected papers [321, 322]). Even so Samuelson's case is a paradox since he advanced the Keynesian emphasis on fiscal policy as a means of achieving economic stability and high levels of employment, and the prize in economics was funded in 1968 by the Central Bank of Sweden. The occasion for the funding was the 300th anniversary of the Bank of Sweden, the oldest of present-day central banks.

4. This conclusion is also drawn by Gibson in a paper relating to aspects of Friedman's work [167, p. 34].

annum. These wage increases are equivalent to the percentage increase in productivity per annum, caused by technological change and improvements in capital equipment. Unemployment may be reduced in the short run below the natural level, but this reduction is traded off for an increase in the price level and additional wage increases, since wages must rise faster to keep real wages unchanged. The price-level changes then set in motion a cycle so that the short-run unemployment target cannot be maintained. This analysis centers around the Phillips curve (Sec. 1.3).

Friedman compares the belief that "the state of employment itself should be the proximate criterion [ultimate goal] of policy" to "gap-closing and growth" as a main objective of policy changes, rather than the smoothing of the business cycle. As Walter Heller has said [191, pp. 64–67], "we . . . adopted as our fiscal gauge the 'full employment surplus,' the excess of revenues over expenditures which would prevail at 4 percent unemployment [as a percentage of the labor force]."[5] This 4 percent figure was to be reset at a lower level, following a reduction in the structural component of unemployment (unemployment due to a mismatching of labor skills and job vacancies).

Friedman's reference to "fine tuning" also applies to the "New Economics" of the Kennedy–Johnson years. The terms, as used in those years, suggested a rather specific and persistent attainment of maximum employment, production, and purchasing power such that cyclical change in time-series simply merges into smooth measures of economic growth.[6] The dis-

---

5. The "full employment surplus" was to reflect the budget surplus that would result with an increase in employment and tax revenues (especially the progressive income tax). The notion was used in the early 1960s in defense of a tax cut proposal for consumers as a means of achieving full employment and a budget surplus. In reviewing the episode, Turgeon [358, p. 65] points out that "In the third and fourth quarters of 1965 . . . when the economy was supposedly near full employment and 'overheated,' the federal budget was still showing deficits." He then notes that "the concept has now been rechristened as the 'full employment balance' with no reference as to whether or not a surplus would be forthcoming."

6. Cyclical changes are changes in business conditions as defined later (Chs. 3 and 4) and changes in time-series exclusive of their seasonal, secular, and random components. In fact, such cyclical changes may be viewed as variations about a growth curve. Growth curves themselves are exponential curves, sweeping upward when the growth rate is positive. Acceleration in the growth of some variable such as $Y(t)$ means that the curve for a given rate of growth takes on a greater slope at a given time. A common form of growth curve may be illustrated by an equation $Y(t) = ae^{(k/g)t}$, where the only variables are income (Y) and time (t), and where initial time is zero.

Recession in the foregoing context is simply a retardation of growth. By the latter criterion a mini-recession occurred in the United States in 1966–67, although it did not show up in the reporting of recessions by the National Bureau. Recom-

tinguishing feature of the "New Economics," according to Heller [191, p. 59], is that it "pressed into the public service the lessons of modern economics—of Keynes and the Classics—" to achieve material betterment, rising quality of life, and growing equality of opportunity. Burns has characterized the central doctrine of the "New Economics" [56, pp. 31–32]:

> That the stage of the business cycle has little relevance to sound economic policy; that policy should be growth-oriented instead of cycle-oriented; that the vital matter is whether a gap exists between actual and potential output; that fiscal deficits and monetary tools need to be used to promote expansion when a gap exists; and that the stimuli should be sufficient to close the gap—provided significant inflationary pressures are not whipped up in the process.

1.2 MONETARY STUDY AND SOME ELEMENTS OF ANALYSIS

In the 1960s the increased interest in the interrelated areas of the demand for money and monetary policy paralleled the increased use and availability of the modern computer for monetary research. Efforts in the demand for money area have been directed toward the identification of empirical demand functions for money or toward establishing the validity of economic relationships implicit in analyses of the demand for money. A frequent objective is the establishment of a relationship between variables such that the manipulation of one—say, by the monetary authorities—might control another, and thus help the monetary authorities to achieve certain goals. A similar objective has been common in monetary policy studies; the establishment of "linkages" or causal sequences that follow from a directly controlled variable to some ultimate economic goal.

The difficulties inherent in such studies have been severalfold: (1) statistical analyses of data in these areas need to be combined with monetary theory or analysis to establish causation; (2) there are complicating interrelationships between monetary and real variables; and (3) the pervasiveness of the influence of expectations (beliefs and views about the

---

mendations have been made to advance the Bureau's reporting of recessions along such lines [274]. The recommendations will likely become increasingly appropriate as success is attained at "fine tuning," at eliminating cyclical changes in time series.

In the 1960s and earlier, a recession was thought of as being "a sustained decline in aggregate economic activity lasting at least six months." The National Bureau's dates for peaks and troughs in business cycles are so widely accepted that Fels uses them in scoring the accuracy of forecasters. In other words, he has the forecasters attempting to identify what the National Bureau will subsequently date as a cyclical peak or trough [112]. On the dating of turning points specifically see Fels and Hinshaw [112, n. 2, pp. 3–4].

future) on economic variables. Analysts frequently fail in attempts to estimate and find stable parameters for equations and to test hypotheses (statements about parameters) under two interrelated approaches: (1) static analysis in which expectations are taken as data (assumed to be zero elastic or not to operate); and (2) the laboratory approach to analysis implicit in the term *ceteris paribus*. Both approaches—and thus much of received economics as it relates to monetary policy—are inadequate to shed light on policy problems and influences in a world where the unavoidable psychological effects of changes occur. These effects are often pervasive and interfere with the presumed independence of variables.

Ceteris paribus and expectations.—The technique of *ceteris paribus* (a presumed laboratory) is old in economics, including Keynesian economics. It is of a hammer and tongs variety, symbolizing an effort—as if by some Procrustean process—to force viable economic phenomena into a laboratory mold. It permits a bastardly use of mathematics in areas of economics where such use is inappropriate and leads to a misguided tracing out of causal forces.

To illustrate the problem, consider four variables, X_1, X_2, X_3, and X_4, which are related in some way. Without defining specific relationships the present ones may be denoted: $X_1 = f(X_2, X_3)$, $X_2 = g_1(X_4)$, and $X_3 = g_2(X_4)$. Here the variable X_1 is dependent on X_2 and X_3, and X_2 and X_3 are each influenced by X_4 in some fashion. In anticipation of subsequent constructs, one may think of X_4 as an expected rate of inflation, X_2 as the cost of funds for capital expenditure (or interest rate), X_3 as the rate of return on capital outlays, and X_1 as the amount of capital expenditures. Now, if X_2 and X_3 are both influenced by X_4, and if X_4 is operating, then only a misleading interpretation of the cause(s) of observed changes in X_1 can result from, say, impounding X_4 in *ceteris paribus* (treating it as a constant as if in a laboratory experiment). Proper mathematical analysis will call for the use of the function of a function rule which would bring out the dependence of X_2 and X_3 on some common force.

This problem is carried over to the classical least squares statistical method. Employing that method, one may wish to estimate parameters and view X_1 as dependent on X_2, X_3, and X_4. But the *ceteris paribus* assumption is intrinsic in the assumption of zero covariance or correlation[7] be-

---

7. The common-sense interpretation of independence is analogous to that of zero covariance or correlation. For instance, a formula relating the covariance between X_2 and X_3 to their correlation coefficient is

$$\rho = \sigma_{23}/\sigma_2\sigma_3$$

where ρ is the correlation coefficient, σ_{23} is the covariance, and σ_2 and σ_3 are standard deviations for X_2 and X_3 respectively.

tween any two of the so-called independent variables. The problem in statistical method is that of multicollinearity, as discussed in the appendix to Chapter 1. In the presence of multicollinearity, analyses of data are not useless, but they require a different interpretation.

Keynes, Keynesians, and expectations.—Keynes' *General Theory* was rich in ideas about expectations, wealth effects, instability in a market economy, and means of stabilizing it. Hicks views Keynes and Hawtrey as being in agreement on certain issues leading up to the *General Theory*, [201, p. 308]: "the doctrine that a free market is not automatically self-righting." Stability in the monetary unit is determined by the "carryover of memory," but this, though it "prevents prices from moving erratically, does not prevent a continual slide in one direction or the other." As Hicks views the thoughts of the period [201, p. 308], the "psychological" effect of a price movement is a key principle: "As soon as prices move sufficiently for people to extrapolate—to base their expectations of future prices not upon current prices but upon the way prices have been changing—a destabilizing force is set up."

This adaptive expectations notion may be denoted as

$$(\text{Price expectations})_t = f(w_o\,P_t + w_1\,P_{t-1} + w_2\,P_{t-2} + \ldots + w_n\,P_{t-n})$$

where price expectations at the current time (t) are said to depend on current and past prices (P_t, P_{t-1}, . . . , P_{t-n}), each multiplied by some weight (w_o, w_1, w_2, . . . , w_n). As the analysis is developed later (Chs. 7, 8, 12, Appendix to Ch. 1), the stronger the effect of the more distant past and its extrapolation into the future, the larger the weights for past prices in relation to more recent prices, and the less the past is extrapolated into the future, the weaker its effect. As the lyrics of the song say, "Yesterday is dead and gone, and tomorrow is out of sight."

As Hicks concludes [201, p. 313], Keynes' explicit introduction of expectations was praiseworthy. But what Keynes gave with one hand he took away with the other, for expectations mainly appear as given conditions. Hawtrey was apparently more systematic in the treatment of expectations. He identified, Hicks says, "an element [expectations] that ought to come into any monetary theory." Samuelson says [326], "As for expectations, the *General Theory* is brilliant in calling attention to their importance and in suggesting many of the central features of uncertainty and speculation. It paves the way for a theory of expectations, but it hardly proves one."

What evolved from the *General Theory*—particularly in the hands of the American translators—was a set of building blocks, referred to as the income-expenditure model. They have been summarized by the Hicks-Hansen IS-LM apparatus as presented in Chapter 4. Expectations enter as underlying conditions.

1.3 THE BUILDING BLOCKS AND THEIR KEYNESIAN ATTRIBUTES

The building blocks include the aggregate supply and aggregate demand block (or its saving, investment counterpart), the liquidity preference block, and the investment demand block. In the first, there is the notion of aggregate consumption as an increasing function of income. As income increases, consumption expenditures increase, but by a smaller amount; the slope of the function is less than one. To consumption one may add investment, broken down to include private investment, government expenditures, and net foreign investment. Even so, these additional expenditures are treated as being less affected by income than is consumption. They bear a weaker relationship to income so that the relationship between the aggregate of expenditures and income is characterized by the consumption function.

The income received by wages, interest, rents, dividends, and so on and in exchange for the total of output (or supply) may be viewed as going entirely into either consumption or saving (also encompassing direct investment). In any event, viewing the total supply in relation to aggregate income (in relation to itself, as consumption and saving have been defined), supply increases as income increases and by the same amount. This increase suggests a slope (or derivative) of one, whereas the aggregate demand relation has a slope at a point of less than one. The relationships intersect to determine the levels of aggregate supply and aggregate demand.

The liquidity preference building block centers around the demand for and supply of money. Money is demanded to satisfy various motives including the transactions (and precautionary) and the speculative. The first motive concerns holding balances to effect transactions, the second suggests the need for balances to deal with uncertain and unforeseen developments, and the third centers around speculation over bond prices and interest rates. In the most Keynesian contexts [320, Appendix to Ch. 18], a rise in the interest rate provides an inducement for switching out of money balances relative to income and into marketable bonds. Thus, the quantity of money demanded bears an inverse relationship to the interest rate, where the rate is that on long-term government bonds. The money supply, on the other hand, is unaffected by the interest rate—bearing a zero relationship to the interest rate and being controlled outside the block or by the monetary authority. Thus, the supply of and demand for money intersect to determine the interest rate, since the two reflect different relationships to the interest rate.[8]

The last of the three blocks, the investment demand block, concerns expenditures for real capital: plants, equipment, and inventories. The rate of return on these expenditures relates the anticipated stream of returns to their supply price or cost. As the amount of the expenditures increases, the anticipated streams are thought to increase less than proportionally; returns per unit diminish as investment increases. The result is an inverse relationship between the rate of return and the capital expenditures. Since the rate contains some risk element, it must be adjusted downward to achieve a certainty equivalent, a comparison with the interest rate viewed as the riskless rental value of money. The interest rate is determined from the liquidity preference block, so it bears a constant relationship to investment. Given the notion that investment will expand until the interest rate and the rate of return (its certainty equivalent) are equal, the level of investment is determined by the building block. The prospective streams of returns are assumed to be given (constant expectations), so there is the prospect of control over the level of investment (and thus over aggregate demand, since investment is a component) by the authority that controls the interest rate.

Control over the interest rate, moreover, is control over the value (or demand price) of existing assets. This includes equities (stocks) as well as real assets, where the Federal Reserve's presumed control over the interest rate varies inversely with the values of existing assets [249, pp. 157–68], given prospective streams of returns. Thus inducements for additional investment are suggested by imbalances in values (demand prices) and costs (supply prices). Here is the further notion of one whole class of goods (bonds and equities) in which the separate goods are treated equally as far as inducements to invest are concerned.

The notion of a schedule or relationship in the foregoing passages is that of a relationship at a moment in time. The consumption-income relationship, for example, may potentially be obtained empirically from a study of household budgets at a given date—from a cross-section study of the ex-

8. The banking community is said to accept the inverse relationship between money and interest rates as do Keynesians, but for different reasons. By buying government securities in the open market to expand the money supply, there is the view that their price will rise (and therefore yields will decline, since the serial returns and maturity price are contractually determined). Academic economists and the financial community alike, says Friedman [140, p. 6], "see, in their mind's eye, a negative sloping liquidity preference schedule."

penditures and incomes of households at a given time. If some of the behavioral relationships are stable over time, they may be viewed as prevailing, as some of the controlled measures are varied to yield a set of points (solutions) over time. For example, there is the notion that by varying interest rates—and hence investment and aggregate expenditures—a consumption-income relationship may be identified from time-series data.

The foregoing is called statics, before time is introduced; it is called something else after time is introduced, after so-called controlled variables (or constant relationships) are permitted to vary. Some call this dynamics; a form of dynamics called comparative statics when one is mainly concerned with tracing out the changes from one solution (so-called equilibrium) point to another. Leijonhufvud, as reviewed later (Ch. 7), suggests that it should be called the disequilibrium state, the true dynamics in which Keynes was interested.

Once underlying conditions are permitted to change arbitrarily in the building blocks, the blocks become very flexible and useful in communicating some widely accepted analytical notions. What is presently of concern is their special Keynesian attributes. These may be listed as (1) the investment multiplier with emphasis on fiscal policy, (2) the liquidity trap, and (3) the inelasticity of investment demand. To this list, one may add the Phillips curve. The IS–LM summary of the income expenditure model said nothing about prices on the output of goods and services at levels below full employment. In the high pressure years of the 1960s, the Phillips curve was added to reintroduce the determination of price. Defending a less vulgar or "modern Keynesian" position, Teigen reviews the price-level as being endogenous. "In other words," he says [347, p. 15], "rather than assuming that prices are fixed as a means of making the simple static model determinate, modern Keynesians introduce an aggregate labor market and production function into the analysis." This will be discussed later (Ch. 5), however, because further elaboration soon takes one into a consideration of special time dimensions and into a more modern Keynesian emphasis on large-scale, structural equations models.

In the Keynesian framework, the multiplier adds potency to fiscal policy, and the trap and inelasticity of investment demand weaken the case for monetary policy. As stated by Samuelson in an early edition [323], "usually it [monetary policy] is regarded as at best a supplement to other stabilization policies, such as fiscal policy." The limits on monetary policy's potency include:

1. The trap: "Changes in the amount of money may have very *weak effects on the rate of interest* if rates are already very low and if people are quite indifferent between holding bonds and holding money."

2. Inelasticity of investment demand: "Even if there are some changes
in the rate of interest, the rate of *investment spending may turn out
to be relatively little affected by changes in interest rates.*"

The reader is warned by Samuelson [323, p. 394] against relying on the
knowledge of fiscal policy. There are questions about the planning of
public-works projects and about their timing [323, p. 399]. There is the
question [323, p. 400] of whether "private investment is frightened off by
government expenditure or by the deficit." The answer is obtained, perhaps
correctly, by noting that "the cash register calls the tune."

The investment multiplier.—The investment multiplier was originally
introduced as the sum of terms of a geometric progression suggesting the
effects of public works expenditures on income. Thus a multiple effect (the
product of the multiplier and the public works expenditure), rather than
just a pump-priming type effect, is obtained from the injection of expenditures [323, p. 401, n. 1]. The multiplier is equal to one over one minus the
slope of the consumption function, as in the income expenditure block.

The liquidity trap.—The liquidity preference demand for money, reviewed earlier, entails an inverse relationship between the interest rate and
the stock of money demanded. It may exist as a relationship with unit
interest elasticity at its various points, as long as percentage changes in the
money stock parallel percentage changes in the interest rate, expressed
absolutely, or as long as percentage changes in the interest rate parallel
percentage changes in the income-money stock ratio. However, if the inverse relationship kinks—if large percentage changes in the money stock
parallel small or almost zero percentage changes in the interest rate—then
there is the prospect of a liquidity trap.[9] Intuitively, the trap idea implies
that the demand for money balances cannot be fully satisfied at very low
interest rates. Efforts to lower the interest rate by monetary means become
ineffective. Keynesians were inclined to posit that such a trap existed in the
1930s, as in the United States. However, studies and controversy in the
early 1960s over the trap notion [126, Ch. 4] failed to confirm the notion
of a trap or kink in the liquidity preference demand curve for money.

9. The liquidity preference model is commonly shown in a geometric form.
There the demand for money (M_d) is a function of the interest rate [$f(i, \overline{Y} =$
const.) or, in equation form, $M_d = a\overline{Y} + b/i$, with $a\overline{Y} =$ const.]; the money supply
is exogenously determined ($M_s = \gamma$); and the intersection of the supply ($M_s = \gamma$)
and the demand schedules [$f(i, \overline{Y} =$ const.)] yields an equilibrium interest rate $(\overline{i})$.
The neighborhood of the liquidity trap is identified as the segment of the demand
function where $| (\Delta M / M) / (\Delta i / i) | \to \infty$. An empirical question is whether
low interest rates follow from shifts in the function or from movements along the
function in the neighborhood of the trap.

The inelasticity of investment demand.—Inelasticity of investment demand is somewhat analogous to the liquidity trap. If accelerating bank credit and the money stock serve to entirely satisfy an enhanced desire for money balances, then there is no extra expenditure—just as there is no effect in the trap contexts. To the extent that there is a small percentage change in interest rates and none in investment expenditures, interest elasticity of investment demand approaches zero.[10]

The Phillips curve.—The Phillips curve relates the rate of change in the price level, $(1/P)$ (dP/dt), to unemployment as a percentage of the labor force. The percentage of the labor force unemployed is thought to vary inversely with the rate of change in the price level within the neighborhood of stable prices and full employment (defined as about 4 percent unemployment for reasons of friction in the system and movements from job to job).[11] Thus to reduce unemployment below 4 percent would necessitate some constant rate of inflation. Keynesians have been inclined to accept this inflation in exchange for temporary reductions in unemployment. A difficulty with the analysis, as Burns points out [56, pp. 54–57, 144], is that the curve is merely a record of short-run responses. The system adjusts to the stimulus from a given rate of change in prices, and a higher rate is called for to get the same stimulus.[12]

An empirical study by Lucus and Rapping [252, pp. 342–50][13] leads to rejection of the long-run Phillips curve and some support for the expecta-

10. A statement of the hypothesis in different terms is that the interest elasticity of investment (I) is zero; $|\ (\Delta\ I\ /\ I)\ /\ (\Delta\ i/\ i)\ |\ \to\ 0$.

11. A typical Phillips curve emphasizes a relationship between the rate of change in the price level $[(1/P)\ (dP/dt)]$ and unemployment as a percentage of the labor force, and also concerns the annual rates of changes in wages per hour $[(1/W)(dW/dt)]$. At stable prices $[(1/P)\ (dP/dt) = 0]$, wage increases are at a given percent per annum. The rates of change in prices and wages respectively are shown on parallel vertical axes. As both rates rise, unemployment declines, and vice versa.

12. Commenting on the gradual adjustment to inflationary episodes, Hicks says [202, pp. 162–63]: "Inflation does give a stimulus, but the stimulus is greatest when the inflation starts—when it starts from a condition that has been non-inflationary. If the inflation continues people get adjusted to it, when they *expect* rising prices, the mere occurrence of what has been expected is no longer stimulating. Nor can the fade-out be prevented by accelerating the inflation, for accelerating the inflation can be expected too. It is perfectly possible to have an 'inflationary' equilibrium, in which prices go on rising, even for years, more or less as they are expected to rise; but then there is no stimulus."

13. Lucus' and Rapping's study contains a bibliography on the Phillips curve. Turgeon [358, pp. 65–66] elaborates on one of the changing conditions underlying the Phillips curve. He sees a change from a demand-pull inflation to a cost-push one (emanating from the supply side of the market) as one in which "overall price increases tend to be of approximately the same magnitude even though un-

tions view: "the inflationary-unemployment trade-off is a short-run phenomenon, or that sustained inflation will make *no* contribution to the
permanent lowering of unemployment rates." In his eighth edition [317, pp.
810–12], Samuelson himself says "the measured Phillips curves represent
short-term relationships."

1.4   A CATALOGUE OF SIMPLE MODELS

Some simple models of assets—or assets and liabilities, more broadly
viewed—may be sketched to indicate the essence of some of the explanations and policy prescriptions implicit in various points of view. They are ad-
mittedly oversimplified, but they shed some light.[14] Their essential attributes
come up in the discussion of the routes via which the Federal Reserve influences expenditures, and the ratio of income to the stock of money.

The first model in our catalogue is Keynes' model. It brings out the fact
that the central bank must control the interest rate directly without influencing expectations in order to achieve its prescribed effects. The Keynesian
model and the same model with a Friedmanian twist are presented to emphasize their particular adjustment paths. The question of central bank
entry and control arises in the case of other models also, including a Fisher
model, the liquidity-financial intermediaries model (plus a "New View"),
and an alternative. Wealth-induced effects figure in the discussion of two of
these models. They are defined and treated separately, to juxtapose them
with expectations-induced effects.

In some respects the oversimplified models do not conflict. Two—the
Fisher model and an alternative—emphasize firms that invest in capital
goods. The liquid asset model, may apply to households without applying
to the overall economy or to business firms in particular, in contrast to the
emphasis some place on the so-called liquid asset model [309, pp. 24–25].
Furthermore, the role of relative returns on assets—as discussed under a
"New View"—need not be excluded from the adjustment process in the
formulation labeled "an alternative." To be sure, returns on assets come to
the forefront as the role of expectations advances and that of wealth-
induced effects recedes.

Further attention should be directed to the fact that in Keynes' short-run
analysis (with constant expectations) the price level is a mythical level. It

---

employment rises." In other words, for Turgeon the curve becomes "horizontal"
or flattens out over a longer stretch as the rate of price increases declines as unemployment decreases.

14. On aggregation and simplification, see Leijohnufvud [249, Ch. III].

is identified with capital goods values rather than with the supply price (or cost) of capital goods and it varies inversely with the interest rate. The concept of a mythical price level for values is potentially useful, however, especially when expectations are permitted to change and interest rates are potentially constant or rising, rather than declining. It is useful because one may readily introduce effects similar to those associated with an increase in the expected rate of change in prices (the average of prices on goods and services) as in Friedman's analysis, even when the measured average of prices is stable or increases only at a constant rate. In empirical data, one finds sharp and distinct effects of changes in expectations when prices are rising in the ordinary sense, but these are harder to identify when prices are stable or rising at a constant rate, even though some expectational effects remain. Such effects operating on prospective returns are considered broadly later (Chs. 2, 8). The rate of change in the price level is one of the factors influencing prospective returns.

Keynes' model.—Keynes' model for diagnosing the economy's ills, as determined by Leijonhufvud [249, pp. 130–56], consists of two classes of assets, money and nonmoney. Money includes short-term financial assets (short-term government securities). Nonmoney assets are long-term, including both capital goods and bonds. The streams of returns from both classes may be discounted by the interest rate but, as widely known, the longer the time to maturity the greater the inverse effect of a given interest rate change on the bond values (and capital values as well), all with the given state of expectations. The interest rate is simply and directly controlled by the monetary authority, though in practice this control may be questioned (Ch. 7).

The point, however, is that a change in the interest rate causes expenditures and the ratio of expenditures (or income) to the money stock to change. A decline in the interest rate raises capital goods values (some level of mythical prices) and, as the latter exceed the supply price (or cost) of capital goods, there is an increase in expenditures on capital goods and the turnover of money (income or expenditure velocity) increases. It is also presumed that the expenditures can be financed at the lower interest rate which is unaffected by any change in expectations.

The Keynesian model again.—The Keynesian model emphasizes two assets—money and bonds [249, p. 147; 274, pp. 46–49; 388, pp. 79–80]. These are close substitutes. The asset holders respond to an increase in the money stock by purchasing bonds; and via a supply-demand-quantity mechanism, the increase in the quantity of bonds demanded raises their price and thus lowers the interest rate. The lower interest rate then stimulates investment, depending on the interest elasticity of investment demand. In Leijonhufvud's treatments of the Keynesian model [249, pp. 135, 147], consistent with the interest inelasticity of investment demand, capital goods are viewed as short-lived just like commodities. The Keynesians also introduce questions about the availability of funds through bank loans [317, pp. 294–95; 309, p. 49].

Questions of inelasticity aside, if spending and income increase enough the demand for money can rise, possibly enough to raise interest rates and induce further demand for bonds in relation to money and income. A higher interest rate can cause the velocity of money (the ratio of income or expenditure to the money stock) to rise. In some expositions, expectations and "momentum" may be brought in to fit the situation [309, pp. 46, 54, 68, 72] and the definition of the short run is not tied to constant expectations [309, p. 37].

The Keynesian model with a Friedmanian twist.—Friedman takes the liquidity preference building block and offers an explanation of how interest rates ultimately rise and how the economic system tends to "overshoot" in response to accelerated growth in the money stock. In doing this he introduces distinctions and interrelationships between Wicksell's "natural rate of interest and Fisher's real rate."

Wicksell's natural interest rate may be defined as the rate on loans "which is neutral in respect to commodity prices, and tends neither to raise or to lower them." According to Wicksell [371, p. 233], "it comes to much the same thing to describe it as the current value of the *natural rate of interest on capital*."[15] It may also be thought of as equivalent to the rate that would prevail if income, saving, investment, and the money stock all achieve sustainable rates of growth (Ch. 2).

Next, Fisher distinguishes between the nominal and the real rate of interest, such that

$$ i = r + \left(\frac{1}{P}\frac{dP}{dt}\right)^* $$

where *i* is the nominal interest rate, *r* is the real interest rate (approximately

15. Hicks defines the natural rate [203, Ch. VI, esp. p. 59]: "The natural rate is strictly to be interpreted as the rate of exchange between 'wine' now and 'wine' a 'year' hence; or since relative prices are unchanging, between any good now and the same good a 'year' hence. It is only when we impose the extra condition that money prices should be unchanging that it becomes necessary to equate this natural rate of interest to the market rate (which is the rate of exchange between money now and money a 'year' hence). Equality between market rate and natural rate then emerges as a condition of price stability."

the rate which would prevail in the absence of expected price changes),[16] and $\left(\dfrac{1}{P}\dfrac{dP}{dt}\right)^*$ is the expected rate of change in prices. Expected price changes are reflected directly in the nominal interest rate, but Friedman views Fisher as emphasizing a secular or long-run price expectations effect. In the conventional liquidity preference framework—with interest elasticity of the demand for money and a negatively sloping liquidity preference schedule— accelerated growth in the money stock might be expected to lower the interest rate below the natural rate and to contribute to inflation via an accelerated rise in the flow of capital expenditures. Friedman accepts this, but once inflation is anticipated—as in Fisher's distinction between the nominal and real interest rates—the nominal natural interest rate rises, and this requires a faster increase in the money stock (inflation) to hold down the market interest rate.[17] There is need for a distinction between a short-run effect (the effect via a negatively sloping liquidity preference schedule) and a long-run effect via expected price changes.

The effect of the money stock changes on expectations must operate with a long lag to be consistent with Friedman's statement about the monetary officials' ability to lower the interest rate in the short run. Here the position is analogous to the short-run one Leijonhufvud attributes to Keynes. Even so, if there is inflation, and an accelerated rate of increase in the money stock is thought to contribute to it, then it might be expected that further acceleration in the money stock could not reduce the nominal interest rate as Friedman has suggested. There are also questions about the use of the actual rate of change in prices as a surrogate for the expected rate, and about the possible lag in the effect of such rates on nominal interest rates. The lagged effects of price-level changes are discussed in Chapter 13, but the more methodological aspects of it appear in an appendix to this chapter.

When interest rates decline in the short run and then rise, some analysts call it a whiplash effect, but Friedman gives it a special analytical under-

16. Technically, another term may be added to the right hand side of the Fisher equation. This third term is the interest that could be earned (or foregone) on the increment (decrement) in the nominal interest payment due to the price adjustment. For the complete derivation of the equation, see Irving Fisher [113, pp. 8–11, 66–67].

17. A rising interest rate, such as may accompany a rise in prices, may be illustrated by shifting the demand schedule (n. 9) to the right at a faster rate than the supply schedule as the inflationary component of income $(\overline{Y})$ increases. It could also be illustrated by defining the money balances demanded as real balances $[M_d/P = f(i)$ where P is the price level] so that as the price level increased, the interest rate would be pushed upward along the demand schedule.

pinning in his presidential address [140], in a 1968 Savings-and-Loan proceedings paper (Ch. 3), and in his essay on the optimum quantity of money [138, pp. 8–14].[18] Accelerating the growth of the money stock would raise the growth rate for nominal income and prices (assuming real income constant). The equilibrium paths for prices and nominal income are exponential or logarithmic curves that shift with the growth rate of the money stock.[19] The transition process is crucial, for during the transition the average rate of price rise exceeds the equilibrium rate. To each individual it looks as though "by reducing his cash balances" he can increase his consumption. Prices start to rise, the depreciation cost of holding money increases, and thus the individual will try to hold a smaller real quantity of money and thereby contribute to further price increases.

In the transition from the initial to the final long-term equilibrium, the rate of price rise must overshoot its long-term equilibrium level. Initially, "it takes time for people to catch on to what is happening . . . they let actual balances exceed long-run desired balances." Then there is overshooting. In the liquidity preference framework cited earlier, the overshooting takes the form of an overshooting of nominal income and a rise in interest rates.[20]

Fisher's model.—Fisher's model had a classical emphasis on money and capital goods. Expanding the money supply had an immediate and direct effect on the purchase of goods. Prices on these goods rise, but by only a fraction of the amount needed to restore some previous equilibrium. Zwick

18. Friedman's "Optimum Quantity of Money" comes up later in the discussion of monetary rules (Sec. 16.1). In essence, when cash balances are reduced because of the depreciation cost of holding money, means of reducing cash with higher cost of production from the point of view of society overall are employed. For example, an errand boy can be used to take large bills to the bank to get change. It turns out, in Friedman's framework, that the optimum stock of money is one that contributes to a declining price level and an appreciation from holding money.

The essay in question has been widely reviewed and criticized. Stein devotes an entire article to it [343]. The essay is pure theory (at least as pure as theory can be in economics). It is only touched upon because of the inclusion of assumptions that are foreign to an analysis of expectations, and because he does not advocate that the optimum quantity policy be implemented.

19. For example, a relation between ln P (prices) and time (t) may be denoted in log-linear form. A higher Greek mu (μ) which is the rate of growth would shift upward the line defined by the equation. Note that the equation for the relationship is of the same form as that in n. 6. The only difference is that instead of income one has prices, instead of the constant a one has P_0, and instead of the constant $\overline{k}/g$ one has μ. Taking the logarithm of both sides of the equation in n. 6 would yield an equation similar to that suggested in this note.

20. In reference to the equations given in n. 6 ($M_d = a\overline{Y} + b/i$ and $M_s = \gamma$), the constant $a\overline{Y}$ would increase more than the constant γ.

says [388, p. 80], "Because of the lag in the adjustment of prices, an excess demand for goods results, causing inventories to fall and businessmen's expectations about future sales volume to rise." The expectation of increases in sales "causes loan demand by business firms to rise not only in equal proportion but in greater proportion than the initial increase in the supply of bank credit." Zwick [388, n. 6], citing Fisher, mentions "the slow revision of the interest charges to business firms by banks."

Elsewhere, Fisher held an inequality of foresight view—the expectations of borrowers were more attuned and sensitive than those of lenders. Subsequent work questions this (Ch. 13). Even so, Fisher had the money stock working directly on expenditures with a positive rather than an inverse effect on interest rates.

Non-bank intermediaries, and the "New View" of money and liquid assets.—John G. Gurley and Edward S. Shaw advanced some speculative views about the role of the liabilities of (or claims against) non-bank financial intermediaries as near-monies in the asset structures of the holders of such claims. They did this in a 1960 publication, *Money in a Theory of Finance.* Intermediaries (life insurance companies, savings and loan associations) are so-called because they intermediate the flow of saving (receive it) into investment (extend credit for expenditures). In the Gurley-Shaw view the relatively liquid claims were substitutes for money. They thought that the growth of near-monies weakened the effects of monetary policy—since the near-monies were not controlled by the Federal Reserve—and contributed to a post-World War II rise in the velocity of money. This latter notion has been widely discussed and evaluated with respect to analyses of data [126, Ch. 9; 309, Ch. 10]. The notion comes up later in this book (Chs. 4, 6).

The notion of additional liquidity in the form of near-money assets, however, has been further discussed [108, pp. 578–81; 328, pp. 262–67] as a part of a "New View" of money as presented by Tobin [328]. Elements of this "New View" are relevant to a discussion of wealth effects especially, but its expositor has explicitly viewed it as a "prolegomena to future work" [108, p. 580] rather than as a basis for conclusions about policy [355]. The "New View" treats money as one among a number of other assets. The transmission of changes in the money stock occurs through changes in the relative returns on assets, rather than through the more classical price-induced wealth effects that create imbalances in the demand for money. The role of such a wealth effect is clarified below. However, one of its fundamental tenets is that banks are not different from other financial institutions in any important respects. Banks obtain funds through the sale of liabilities (time deposits) and use these funds to purchase assets.[21] Analysis of the sources and uses of funds is the same as for any other financial institutions.

The commonly exposited and recognized money and credit creating powers establishing the uniqueness of commercial banks are deemphasized in the "New View." The parent of the "New View" wishes to construct a theory wherein banking firms are profit maximizers with behavior analogous to other firms. This may shed light on behavior that does not involve the unique money and credit creating powers of commercial banks.

An alternative balance sheet model.—Two classes of assets and their liability counterparts are recognized as a final alternative balance sheet model [126, Ch. 7]. The two classes are (1) assets with a contractual or fixed claim in dollar terms against future income, and (2) assets with a residual claim on income, such as plants and equipment or securities of the equity type. To some this represents a pre-Keynesian Cambridge tradition [249, pp. 143–44], at least as far as assets go, but there is more to it.

Policy factors—such as announced changes in the tax credit on capital investment or recognized increases in the growth of the money stock—contribute to a change in expectations, and the model reacts to these. Consider, for example, an expected rise in the price level for goods and services, or consider a tax credit that has the same effect on prospective returns and thus their discounted value. The inducement, for firms investing in plants and equipment, works through the residual claim portion of assets. There is an incentive to accelerate the growth of these residual claims and thus increase them relative to total assets and to accelerate the growth of liabilities needed to support the assets. In price inflation, there is the special prospect of repaying loans with lower purchasing power dollars. Banks—and other institutions specializing in debt financing and constrained by their specialties—can accommodate some of this financing. In such a context, the liquidity of firms may be broadly viewed as including a portion of liquid assets and an absence of claims, say, by the bank (having an unused line of credit) in relation to total assets, as discussed in Chapter 15.

The question is raised—in the context of the foregoing model and in subsequently discussed policy functions—of the need to abstract from the noise, from the random and seasonal changes, in order to focus on cyclical stabilization. Should monetary analysis distinguish between "defensive," "seasonal," "road-clearing," arbitrage operations in the money market by the Federal Reserve and cyclical or seasonally adjusted changes in policy

---

21. The term "funds" should be defined. It simply refers to bookkeeping entries. An entry increasing a liability is a source of funds, and an entry increasing an asset account is a use of funds.

indicators? This question is raised in part by the nature of the control mechanism, and in part because cyclical and secular movements contain more of the smoothness required for the extrapolation into the future of current and past changes. Firmness is needed in direction and beliefs for any change to have its clearest influence on expectations, as brought out analytically in Chapter 8.

Wealth effects and expectations.—Some economists have complained that the Keynesians lack rigor in relying on assertions about sticky prices [249, pp. 7, 394] and in denying the prospect of price-induced wealth effects [293, pp. 23, 28–29]. Leijonhufvud—as reviewed later (Ch. 7) and introduced above in reference to Keynes' model—revived the interest-induced wealth effect: a decline in the interest rate raises values (increases wealth) and induces an upward shift in the consumption function.

Pesek and Saving [293] focused on the price-induced wealth effect: given money (currency, and deposit liabilities of commercial banks) as a part of the net wealth of society, a downward adjustment of the price level made wealth-holders feel wealthier and thus made them increase consumption. As is well known—commercial banks aside and other things being equal—a deflation (decline in the average of prices on the current output of goods and services) affects lenders favorably and debtors unfavorably to the extent that debtors repay loans with deflated dollars. Thus if the lenders' assets and the debtors' liabilities are equal—as in the bookkeeping sense where debits and credits are offsetting—the effect of a deflation (or an inflation) is symmetrical with respect to debtors and creditors. One effect offsets the other. But Pesek and Saving argue that in a special economic sense the liabilities of commercial banks are not truly anyone's debts because of the special monopoly and money and credit creating powers of the banking system. The liabilities of the banking system, they said, are a part of the net wealth of the community.

In both instances—Keynes' case and Pesek and Saving's—the effects depend on the impoundment of expectations. But additional difficulties arise in Pesek and Saving's case. As prices move enough for the public to extrapolate into the future, a counter and possibly overwhelming destabilizing force is set up. One could argue that letting prices slide is not really necessary, but the prescription is to induce wealth by increasing the money stock. Even here expectational forces may be set in motion so that they overwhelm or are indistinguishable from the wealth effects, at least over short periods of time. Wealth effects may be a longer period phenomenon.[22]

22. A second difficulty arises from the critics of Pesek and Saving. Ahmad [1] points to technical aspects of their analysis. He says (1) that, under the conditions

1.5 SUMMARY

There was a revival of interest in monetary policy in the 1960s following a Keynesian era. In the monetary sphere the focus was on the interest rate. With expectations constant, the central bank was viewed as controlling the interest rate directly. Through a reduction in it, capital values (mythical prices) were thought to increase relative to supply prices (costs). For Keynes there was the prospect that the rate could not be influenced adequately, and for the Keynesians there were the notions of the liquidity trap and interest inelasticity of investment demand. From some research by Friedman and others on the role of money, however, followed a reevaluation of the effectiveness of monetary policy and the implication of a policy for a longer run, as over a business cycle.

In Friedman's assessment of data, the interest rate has been said to vary inversely with changes in the rate of change in the money stock in the short run, as in the Keynesian model. There are delayed changes, too, resulting in a secular price expectation, as in a Fisher relation. These delayed changes, in the case of acceleration in the money stock, cause interest rates to rise. In Fisher's model of firm behavior, on the other hand, the acceleration of the money stock works directly on the purchase of goods and expected sales. The effect is slower and there is overshooting, but interest rates do not decline in the interim.

In other ideas, prospective returns may be influenced by a variety of prospects, including those for sales, inflation, and the fiscal actions and inactions of government. The money stock may work as in Fisher's model of firm behavior, but other factors may work too, including an increase in a tax credit by the government. One effect may be an imbalance between

---

presumed, the issue of extra money adds as much disutility to the issuer as it adds wealth to the private holder, and (2) that the authors forgot ("as Adam Smith did, but less excusably so") that value is determined by the marginal and not total utility.

Continuing, Ahmad says, "in equilibrium money like air adds a great deal to total utility, but, like air again, it is not part of the net wealth in the economic sense."

Friedman and Schwartz also refer to the Pesek-Saving work and note the point about value and marginal utility [154, pp. 112–13]: "We value items by market price, which corresponds to marginal utility, not average utility; hence, a reduction in scarcity may reduce the total value . . . that we attach to the total quantity. In the extreme, a free good will have an aggregate value of zero, yet it clearly contributes more to total utility than a lesser amount would."

There are other comments especially directed by Friedman and Schwartz at efforts by Pesek and Saving to define money on a prior grounds [154, Ch. 3]. This question of definition comes up again (Appendix to Ch. 7).

capital values (mythical prices) and observed prices. An upward impetus to spending in the case of an increase in the credit may come about without actual price level changes. Positing an excess of mythical prices over observed prices may be simply another way of describing various influences: a regressive pull influence toward more normal conditions as conditions move toward the norm, a push away from the norm as conditions move away from the norm, and a pull influence toward normality when the market interest rate is below the natural rate.

There are still other notions in this chapter. They concern the demand for money, its velocity, interest rates, and the liabilities of non-bank financial intermediaries. In the Keynesian model a rise in interest rates results in an increase in velocity because of the inducement to hold less money and more bonds relative to income. In a Gurley-Shaw view, the growth of non-bank intermediaries has raised velocity by causing an increase in holdings of near money assets and a decline in money holdings, both in relation to income. There are two other prospects: that interest rates and velocity may respond to similar forces, such as the expected rate of change in prices, and that only some sectors—such as households—reflect aspects of the Gurley-Shaw world, while others respond more predominantly to factors impinging on prospects, more or less certainty and so on. All of these will be discussed further.

2
Policy, Operations, and Goals
An Overview

2.1 INTRODUCTION

A VOLUMINOUS LITERATURE leads up to the issues and policy problems dealt with in this book. Some is cited in this chapter. In some respects, the literature is an outgrowth of certain special studies and reports, notably Milton Friedman's early paper on time lags and the monetary and fiscal framework [148, pp. 245–64], J. Tinbergen's studies of economic policy generally,[1] and the reports of the Royal Commission on Banking and Finance in Canada [398], the Commission on Money and Credit in the United States [403], and the Radcliffe Committee in Great Britain [404].[2] These and other works on monetary policy tend to focus on the notion of goals or targets at various levels, the interrelationships between tools and goals, and questions about time lags—the time between the need for a policy change and the recognition of the need, between the recognition and the implementation of the change, and between the implementation and the effect of the change—as considered further in Chapter 10. If the lags were long, monetary policy was thought to be ineffective as an instrument for economic stability. There were also questions about the substitution of "rules" for discretion in the conduct of monetary policy (Chs. 16, 17) and about the traditional Federal Reserve emphasis on money market and credit conditions.

*A 1968 paper [120, pp. 1–41] provides the basis for this chapter. Many of the original references are retained, partly because they are portions of the literature giving rise to the book.
1. References concerning these studies are found in Frazer [120, n. 4] and in Frazer and Yohe [133, Ch. 25].
2. The "New View" of banks, as dealt with by Tobin (Sec. 1.4), has been said to have incorporated the Radcliffe hypothesis [108, p. 580]; that the effects of changes in the quantity of money may be offset by changes in other liquid assets, or "that money is just one of many liquid assets."

Brunner and Meltzer [46, pp. 15–16] were particularly critical of the Federal Reserve officials' focus on money market and credit conditions as distinct from relations between such variables as the money stock and national economic goals. The Federal Reserve's central policy-making group—the Federal Open Market Committee (FOMC)—responded to its critics by specifying in its directive that some aggregate monetary measures should behave in a particular way. Some difficulties were encountered, however, in the diversity of the behavior of the desired credit conditions and aggregate monetary measures, and a "proviso" clause was added to the FOMC's directive in mid-1966 to give operating personnel a chance to change desired measures between the FOMC's meetings.[3]

In early 1970—following Arthur Burns' arrival as chairman at the Board (Sec. 1.2)—the FOMC began stating more directly its desires with respect to the aggregates for bank credit and the money stock, rather than "referring to them in the form of a proviso clause" [392, p. 83]. Market conditions were still considered relevant, particularly over short periods of time, and the time horizon for a path of credit and monetary aggregates was viewed as encompassing a longer period [392, p. 86]. "Long-run paths" have been emphasized as providing "the Committee with a means for focusing on the emerging trend of growth in the money supply or in bank credit." At a January 1972 meeting, the Committee indicated greater reliance upon the course of total reserves as a guide to open market operations, more specifically upon member bank reserves available for private nonbank deposits (RPDs). RPDs are a reserve aggregate, defined as total member bank reserves minus reserves required against U.S. Government demand deposits and net interbank deposits.

The difficulties of relating the day-to-day conditions to the aggregates did not vanish, nor is understanding of the shorter-run interrelationships entirely obvious. This is [392, p. 95] indicated (1) by the fact that the desired targets "may sometimes turn out to be in conflict," and (2) by the need to adjust day-to-day operations "in line with the sense of priority among operating objectives given by the FOMC." Even so, the emphasis shifted and an overall approach surfaced that is consistent with the original paper [120] underlying this chapter. Specifically, a 1971 Staff Paper on the policy

---

3. The difficulty causing the need for the "proviso" clause apparently also caused the rejection of an hypothesis posed by Anderson and Levine about monetary management [9, pp. 41–49]: "A change in money market conditions, usually expressed in terms of the degree of pressure in the money market, induced by Federal Reserve actions has a predictable effect on short-run changes in money, bank credit, and long-run interest rates." Carlson [63, pp. 347–49] comments on the Anderson-Levine paper, from a rather inoperative *ceteris paribus* point of view.

and instructions aspects of the FOMC directive [392, pp. 80, 84] emphasized that in framing policy they should consider (1) influences on financial conditions, interrelationships with the real economy, and "expectation factors," and (2) money and credit market conditions and long-run growth in the money and credit stocks. Developments in January 1972 (release dated April 10) indicated an interest in the long-run growth of total reserves.

This relatively eclectic approach—with some allowance for the growth of monetary aggregates and for expectations—is a departure from the banking and Keynesian views (Chs. 5, 8). On the other hand, the approach does not give sole emphasis to the rate of change in the money stock, as some monetarists and advocates of traditional rules might wish (as Brimmer has pointed out [33]). As mentioned in Section 2.2, and on numerous occasions in this book, expectations phenomena (as illustrated by the relation between interest rates and anticipated inflation, introduced in Ch. 1) are very troublesome for broad portions of received theory, including Keynesian theory and theorems centering about the notion of equilibrium.

Some academic and Federal Reserve economists have focused on even narrower areas of study than market conditions. This area is that of monetary policy "actions." There also has been emphasis on so-called "linkages" or causal sequences, beginning with some action such as a discount rate change or an open market transaction. Lurking in the background of these studies was the problem of operationally defining the term "monetary policy."

This chapter is about monetary policy and the preceding study areas and questions. It focuses on the difficulty of relating goals for credit conditions to goals for the money stock, at the operating level. Special ideas that emerge and reappear later in the book include: (1) an equality of foresight principle in which lenders and borrowers show a common responsiveness to factors influencing economic prospects, (2) the vanishing (zero) short run of Keynes, (3) an interrelationship and parallel movement in credit conditions and business conditions, (4) the probabilistic weighting of prospective returns and the discounting or slanting of probabilities, (5) the need for an abstraction from seasonal and defensive operations in establishing a clear direction to policy changes with respect to the stabilization of business conditions, (6) an interrelationship between monetary and fiscal policy, (7) the partial dependence of a lag in the effect of a policy on the definition of policy, and (8) the concept of a policy over an entire cycle.

The analysis in this chapter is constrained by certain facts or prospects that have appeared and reappeared, especially since the initial impact of the modern computer. In broad outline these are that: (1) cyclical peaks (troughs) in the interest rate coincide roughly with similar peaks (troughs) in business conditions; (2) cyclical peaks (troughs) in the velocity of money coincide roughly with peaks (troughs) in business conditions; and (3) the interest rate and the velocity of money are not strongly related causally but respond to similar changes emanating from other sources.[4] Evidence and explanations bearing on the velocity-interest rate association are reviewed primarily in Chapter 4. Present analysis anticipates such an association, although there are allowances and exceptions. First, the presence of non-market restraints, such as the administered ceilings on interest rates for home and municipal financing, must be acknowledged. Second, any major changes affecting the definition of the money supply (currency in circulation outside the banking system plus demand deposits other than U. S. Government and domestic inter-bank deposits) and the ease of effecting payments must be allowed for, most likely in their effect on the velocity ratio. Such changes could come about through changes in the payments mechanisms and the synchronization of receipts and expenditures, as under the future impact of the computer, and in the use of overdraft facilities, as under some credit card arrangements.[5]

The present approach to large structural equations models differs considerably from the approach which emerged in the mid-1960s. Then the emphasis was on introducing so-called policy variables, such as the discount rate in Fromm [156], aimed toward simulating the effect of changes in specific instruments.[6] It was hoped that this would help the policy-maker

4. For evidence on post-World War II turning points for interest rates, velocity, and business conditions in the United States, see Frazer [123, pp. 28–29]. Reviewing such evidence over longer periods for interest rates and business activity, Cagan [59, pp. 219–44] finds that changes in the turning points for interest rates conform well with changes in business activity on the whole, although there are discrepancies at times.

The failure of interest rate changes and National Bureau measures of changes in business activity to conform perfectly could be due to institutional changes in financial markets and instruments and to the imperfect nature of National Bureau estimates of cyclical turning points. The 1966 period in the United States provides an example of the failure of the respective sets of turning points to coincide, although Cagan recognizes interest rate measures as providing one of the most useful bodies of evidence on cycles. In September 1966 in particular, the widely cited interest rates reached peaks, and numerous analyses dealt with a business adjustment following that date, but the National Bureau did not report a cyclical peak. The period had symptoms of a business adjustment, but large increases in military, defense, and other government expenditures offset possible adjustment changes in some series. (Compare Ch. 1, n. 6)

5. Ritter and Atkinson [308] speculate about prospective changes in the payments system and their effects.

6. Fromm [156] defined simulation as a "solution to the system changing some set of conditions from those which would otherwise prevail, e.g., a shift in the discount rate."

to assess the effects of the uses of the instruments. The structural equations models and the more specialized policy models are dealt with in Chapter 14.[7] Monetary policy emerges as more than policy with respect to the use of instruments of credit control. In combination with the broader view of policy, possible diverse effects of simultaneous changes in the flow of bank credit and in the rate of change in the money stock, and the tendency for monetary and real variables to be highly interdependent all complicate the usefulness of econometric models of the 1960s. Their usefulness is affected unless there is explicit allowance for the need to change parameters to accommodate shock effects of certain events and pronouncements. Instead of the econometric view with fixed parameters, there is the present view that policy indicators reflect shock effects, responses to exogenous factors, and either inactions or actions of the policy-makers. In fact, actions or inactions in response to events are viewed as primary functions of the policy-makers.

2.2 Some Elements of Analysis

Elements of analysis form the foundations of this chapter and other parts of the book. They include notions of equilibrium, aspects of the general theory of choice and general equilibrium analysis, a relationship between income and wealth, and elementary Keynesian analysis. There are numerous instances of notions of equilibrium: the classical balancing of weights (as drawn from mechanics), a solution to a system of equations (as in the intersection of two lines in a simple supply-demand sketch), an underlying trend or exponential growth path about which the system varies in response to "push" and "pull" effects with shifting weights (Ch. 8), and Friedman's notion of such a growth path with a tendency for oscillations about the path to be damped (Ch. 5).

Neutral credit and monetary conditions are characterized by a constant income velocity of money and by equal percentage changes in broad aggregates in the form of stock and flow variables. These indicate constant business conditions, while differential changes in the growth rates for the respective stock and flow variables indicate changes in business conditions. The changes in the credit and monetary conditions and those in business conditions are related by definition and indicated by changes in the same set of conditions. There is emphasis on expectations, probabilistic views of the future, and the exogenous determination of some variables. Factors

7. For early references on the interpretation of statistical evidence, small- and large-scale models, and the interdependence of variables and causation, see Frazer [120, n. 4, n. 15].

affecting expectations are treated in a variety of mechanical forms, as well as in terms of "shock" effects. Shock effects and exogenous factors are introduced to bring to the forefront some crucial changes with which monetary authorities should deal in the conduct of credit and monetary policy.

Efforts to suppress the destabilizing role of expectations, or to capture their essence through reliance on anticipatory series, have not resulted in sufficiently operational analyses. Reviewing the Friedman-Schwartz analysis of economic stability, for example, Meltzer notes [270] that "transitory" changes in income are excluded from analysis by the use of concealing measurement procedures such as that for permanent income, and that special factors are unsystematically used to explain special developments. As widely discussed [123], a Friedman hypothesis about the wealth (or income) elasticity of the demand for money called for a secular decline in the velocity of money over the post-World War II years. As matters turned out, the average growth rate in the money stock was less than the assumed rate and the income velocity of money underwent a secular rise. Greater certainty about the future, the phenomena with which operating officials must deal as a routine matter, was consequently invoked to explain the decline in the public's holdings of money balances in relation to income.

The theory of choice.—The general theory of choice by economic units envisions maximization of the flow of returns from holding assets subject to a constraint, such as the size of total assets. In particular—from the point of view of this book—it yields sets of equilibrium conditions whereby absolute returns are maximized when the rates of return from additions to alternative classes of assets are equal (Sec. 1.4). Differential changes in the rates of return constitute imbalances. These coincide with differential changes in the rates of change for the alternative classes of assets, and differential changes in the rates of change constitute equilibrating adjustments. The process of adjustment and readjustment is continuous. The economic subjects are searching for equilibrium, but economic changes have a tendency to overshoot also. Equilibrium with respect to assets or wealth is emphasized, but the analysis may apply to liabilities as well. In fact, a special part of analysis in this book centers around a liquidity hedging motive for holding assets, namely the motive for holding money (or assets fixed in money terms, such as bonds) as a store of funds for meeting a future need, such as to repay bank loans, effect planned capital outlays, or discharge liabilities.

Liquidity preference and some exogenous factors.—To further introduce some relevant, aggregative measures and provide a mechanism for illustrating the response of both the interest rate and the income velocity of money to selected factors, Keynesian building blocks (Sec. 1.3) are brought forward:

$$\text{Demand:} \quad M_d = c\overline{Y} + \frac{b\overline{Y}}{i}, \, b > 0$$

$$\text{Supply:} \quad M_s = \gamma\overline{Y}$$

$$\text{Equilibrium:} \quad M_s = \overline{M}_d$$

$$\text{Interest rate:} \quad \overline{i} = \frac{b\overline{Y}}{\gamma\overline{Y} - c\overline{Y}}$$

where $Y = C + I$, and where $c\overline{Y}$ is the proportion of money balances held to satisfy the precautionary and transactions motives, $b\overline{Y}$ is the proportion held to satisfy the speculative motive, M_d is the quantity of money demanded, M_s is the stock of money supplied by the monetary authorities, $\overline{i}$ is the interest rate, I is the flow of investment, Y $(=Y_d)$ is income received in the form of payments to the factors of production, Y_d is aggregate demand, and $C(Y)$ and $S(Y)$ are consumption and saving as respective functions of income.

In the liquidity preference model and the equilibrium value for the interest rate $(\overline{i})$, in particular, equal percentage changes in the flow of income (Y) and in the money stock (γY) leave the interest rate (i) and the velocity of money (Y/γY) unchanged. (Other stock and flow quantities in the economic system, of course, are presumed to vary in equal proportions also.) A 100 per cent increase in the interest rate and velocity of money parallels a doubling of income in relation to the balances (bY and cY) for satisfying the various motives; in general, as a simple first approximation:

$$\frac{d \ln V_y}{d \ln i} = 1$$

where $d \ln V_y$ ($\times 100$) is a percentage change in income velocity and $d \ln i$ ($\times 100$) is a percentage change in the interest rate.

Equal percentage changes in all of the stock and flow variables, with velocity and interest rates constant, yield neutral credit and monetary conditions.[8] Now, proceeding from the neutral position of equal percentage changes in the stock and flow variables, tax (and fiscal policy) factors may be introduced to cause differential percentage changes. These may include

8. This definition of neutral credit conditions is the same as the "rough" definition employed by Johnson and Winder [212, p. 13], although in the latter view deviations from the neutral position are in terms of changes in the money supply series.

such diverse changes as those in income tax rates and in a tax credit [133, pp. 366–67, 428]—a credit against income tax payments amounting to some percentage of capital expenditures. In the case of a tax cut for consumers—as in 1964 in the United States—the flow of consumption expenditures shifts upward from its growth path and the rate of change in income increases. These cause the interest rate and the velocity of money to increase, given a constant rate of change in the money stock with the monetary authorities controlling Y. In the case of the tax credit, an increase would accelerate the flow of investment and therefore income, and would also affect the rate of return on the flow of capital outlays. This operates in the capital value, supply price framework:

$$CV = R_1/(1 + i) + R_2/(1 + i)^2 + \ldots + R_n/(1 + r)^n$$

$$C = R_1/(1 + r) + R_2/(1 + r)^2 + \ldots + R_n/(1 + i)^n$$

where CV is the value at time zero of a given flow of instrumental capital (or the mythical price level for that flow, as attributed to Keynes in Sec. 1.4), C is the cost or supply price of a given instrumental flow at time zero, $R_1, R_2, \ldots, R_n$ is the stream of prospective returns per annum from the flow of instrumental capital after allowance for risk and liquidity elements, and r is the rate of return on the flow of capital outlays. An increase in a factor—such as a tax credit for expenditures on instrumental capital—has a shock effect on expectations. It increases R_1 above, $i =$ constant and $C =$ constant momentarily, so that $r > i$ and $CV > C$. One would have the inducement for expanding the flow of investment. The movement is toward equilibrium ($r = \overline{i}$) with the velocity of money and the flow of investment rising, and with the monetary authorities responding by going along with increases in velocity and the interest rate.

Another factor is the expected rate of change in prices, $(1/P)$ (dP/dt) (Sec. 1.4). It would cause the Rs above to increase, as well as the rate of return (r) and the interest rate, especially in the earlier contexts. Only now there is no Keynesian short run (defined as a time span with constant expectations). As matters turn out [131 and Ch. 13], the return on capital is clearly affected by factors affecting prospects, but the interest rates are also affected. There is the idea, embellished later (Ch. 13), that interest rates are set to some extent by traders in securities and that considerable adjustments in rates can be independent of changes in the quantity of securities (a demand for funds) being brought to the market and in the quantity being withdrawn (a supply of funds). Lenders and traders may adjust rates in response to the same factors that influence, say, manufacturing corporations in establishing a rate of return, by conscious estimation or by implication. What moves the economic situation forward is a thrust or buoyancy, identified later (Chs. 8, 13) as an extrapolative push effect. Shock effects and policies are also relevant. Temporary imbalances in the relations between the interest rate and the rate of return, value (mythical price) and cost, and desired and actual balances (as implicit in changes in velocity) are the imbalances relating to changes in the flow of investment and changes in monetary and credit conditions. The main factors causing changes in the rate of change in the above stock and flow variables are obviously operating from outside the framework consisting of the preceding elements of analysis. These outside operators involve changes in credit conditions, the tax credit (also related to credit conditions), and so on. They are factors impinging on expectations, the prospective streams of returns, degrees of certainty about the future, and so on. In particular, (Ch. 8) the prospective returns may be viewed as utilities or simply as dollar amounts—especially after excluding non-monetary rewards or penalties—and these in turn may be viewed as being weighted by probabilities.

Expectations.—Expectations enter the above relations and models in a variety of ways other than the shock effects of non-repetitive exogenous factors. For one, wealth (W) is the capitalized value of the prospective stream of income, Y/r. A given flow of investment is the discounted value of a prospective stream of returns. In the first instance expectations are sometimes viewed as determined by past and more recent values (Sec. 1.2). Such a view has led to Friedman's definition of permanent income as some function of a weighted average of current and past incomes [126, pp. 142–43]. The average of past values, however, cannot forecast all of the customarily experienced changes in prospective income, nor embody all of the short-run or even secular effects of factors impinging on expectations of future income. In particular, the discounting or slanting of probabilities allows for vague and elusive beliefs and controversial evaluations (Ch. 8), and the averaging process may even conceal some of the short-run effects on expectations that contribute to instability in expenditures. For example, Meltzer [270, pp. 404–22; 126, Appendix to Ch. 6] points out that Friedman's use of the permanent income measure leads to the exclusion of "transitory" changes in income. Meltzer says "transitory" is another name for the business cycle.

Expectations also enter the above relations and models in the preference for money balances in relation to other classes of assets, including assets with a residual claim against future income such as inventories, plants and equipment, and other goods. Prospective price-level increases on goods and services, for example, increase the prospective returns from the residual-claim assets and reduce the prospective purchasing power of money balances, as well as the power obtainable from assets with a fixed income stream and maturity value such as bonds. Consequently, prospective price-level changes affect the cost of holding money balances and bonds. To deal with these prospects, some analysts introduce the rate of change in prices as a measure of the opportunity cost of holding money. Supposedly a prospective increase in the price level affects the fixed-claim assets adversely and contributes to declines in such assets as proportions of total assets, wealth, or income. At least this possibility exists for firms with assets in monetary and real form, such as manufacturing corporations. Other institutions, such as commercial banks, are more constrained by laws and traditions to other investment opportunities. In the face of expected inflation they may simply continue to expand debt assets and adjust interest rates upward in anticipation of declining purchasing power dollars, at least as long as the Federal Reserve provides the necessary reserves. The creators of debt assets have an inducement to expand as manufacturing corporations expand, even though they are not favored in the same way by the prospects.

In the latter instance, prospective changes in the average of prices are thought to be influenced by rates of change in current and lagged prices. Factors other than prospective price-level changes, however, can affect the value of inventories, plants, and other goods, in relation to the value of money balances and other fixed-claim assets. The tax credit was introduced above as one such factor. Greater certainty about the future is another, since it weakens the motive for holding money balances and those assets commonly ranked on a balance sheet as being more liquid. In the present framework, allowance has been made for the introduction of mythical prices in some instances, and changes in these may also be extrapolated and exert influence on prospects.

Changes in velocity and interest rates reflect changes in prospective prices,[9] degrees of certainty about the future, the tax credit, and so on. They also involve another form of switching of assets, notably between cash and bonds. To assign probability values to the liquidity preference demand function for money and to explain the shape of the demand function for money [129, pp. 70–78], interest rates are expected to decline (rise) and the value of bonds rise (decline) when the interest rate (i) is above

---

9. Jorgenson [214, pp. 151–52], commenting on the Keynesian investment demand model, says that the "criterion for optimal investment behavior . . . is inconsistent with maximization of the present value of the firm" unless "the rate of change of the price of investment goods varies with the rate of interest."

(below) the normal rate.[10] The prospect of a rise in interest rates then contributes to a switching from bonds to money balances as a proportion of assets; the proportion subsequently switches out of money balances, since the same factors affecting the cost of holding bonds are affecting the so-called opportunity cost of holding money balances. The various changes are developed with respect to selected changes in prices, values, degrees of certainty, interest rates, and velocity, but the overall analysis also applies when the converse changes are being discussed. This particular formulation of liquidity preference operates when expectations are being permitted to change and allows for the introduction of notions concerning subjective probability. As brought forward later (Ch. 8), the formulation is contrasted with Tobin's which depends on a constancy of expectations, a more restrictive set of axioms, and an introduction of probability in terms of the variance of returns.

Cyclical and secular changes, and business conditions.—The present analysis involves growth rates, exponential curves, and changes in the growth rates (or slopes of the curves). The average growth rates and their corresponding curves provide the base around which cyclical fluctuations or changes in economic or business conditions occur. The average growth rates of secular trends themselves may change, but the secular changes are still analytically distinct. Equal percentage changes in all stock and flow variables leave the interest rate and the income velocity unchanged (roughly, as a first approximation) and differential percentage changes in selected stock and flow variables involve changes in interest rates, income velocity, and business conditions.

The terms "economic activity" and "business conditions" are used interchangeably. The former term suggests the hours of work, the number of people working, and so on. Economic activity may be constant and still coincide with an exponential growth in output and income (in constant prices) per annum; it may decline without output and income per annum declining; and it may increase with the result that the growth curve for output and income simply takes on a greater slope.[11] "Economic activity"

10. The normal rate is subjective, as discussed later (Ch. 8). For a discussion of a method for estimating a normal "rate" or "level" see Modigliani and Sutch [281, pp. 185–87].

11. Culbertson and Friedman [145, pp. 447–48, 452–54] entered a controversy on the question of the adequacy of lag measures based on the "timing" of peaks and troughs in general business. The controversy centered on what was meant by the "level of business." References in the present chapter are to a constant level of business and secular growth, and business cycles (changes in business conditions and changes in the growth rate or the slope of an exponential growth curve). Friedman's discussion amounts to about the same thing. He says [145, p. 452] "the

or "business conditions" suggests a built-in dynamic, "a tendency for output to grow in an economy with a constant level of employment, given a neutral monetary policy (presently denoted as a constant rate of interest)." Technological change has been said to displace some workers such that their re-employment constitutes a source of growth in output with a neutral monetary policy, under reasonable competitive conditions at a given level of employment.

The money stock: exogenously determined variables.—The preceding liquidity-preference model includes the money stock as an exogenously determined variable. In a priori constructs of the foregoing type, this means that it is determined outside of the model, as by the monetary authority, although there has been considerable speculation about the definition of an exogenous variable (Ch. 5). Even so, the assumption is quite common in monetary analysis and no alternatives have been proven superior in facilitating operational analyses.[12] Analysis treating the money stock as an exogenous variable, of course, must occasionally be modified by incidental remarks and by the recognition of a shock effect of specific conditions on the liquidity preference demand by banks for excess reserves [282].[13] In his book *The Neutralized Money Stock* (Homewood, Ill.: Richard D. Irwin, Inc., 1968), Hendershott attempted to argue that the money stock was endogenously determined because its determinants in the bank-reserve equation sense (as defined shortly) were simply responding to other changes in the system. By extracting these influences, a neutralized money stock and an unbiased measure of Federal Reserve actions were to be achieved. But the suggestion has not held up well to scrutiny [224] as a measure of monetary influence on the economy or as a satisfactory basis for evaluating Federal Reserve actions. It was argued that since the Federal

---

rate of change in the stock of money . . . has the same dimensions as the so-called level of business." Further, he recognizes the difficulty "in principle" of selecting turning points in general business, but as a practical matter he chooses to use National Bureau reference cycle dates. Objecting to the use of simple ups and downs in selected series, Friedman points out that some series rise during expansions and contractions in general business.

When analysis shifts from levels to rates of change for stock and flow variables, much is gained but errors in the data for the transformed series became more relevant. On the difficulties of using currently issued data, especially where estimates are sought in the rate of change, see Frazer [120, n. 10].

12. Research on supply equations has been conducted in a variety of quarters, as discussed by Meltzer [268, pp. 169–82].

13. Brunner and Meltzer [47] also outline a rationale for banks' demands for excess reserves and refer to a "probability distribution summarizing a bank's uncertain prospects with respect to the flow of reserve funds . . ."

Reserve reacts to the conditions of the economic system in setting the money supply, the money supply is a totally endogenous variable. But this would seem to be an especially hollow argument. In any equation system a controlled or policy variable must be changed in order to change the system.

One of the grave difficulties encountered in monetary policy analysis is the recognition that monetary authorities have influences on the demand side of the markets for bank reserves and money, other than those they exert on bank credit through changes in bank reserves. "Announcement effects" have been mentioned, and the growth of the money stock has also been brought out in this respect.

Teigen has objected to the view "that the Federal Reserve System can set the money stock at any desired level," as have some others (Sec. 2.3). He views the question as empirical, apparently to be answered by the methods of regression analysis [349, pp. 284–85]: "to what degree are the monetary authorities able to influence monetary variables through their manipulation of the instruments of monetary policy, and how stable are these relationships through time?" In the 1960s, research involving the classical methods of regression analysis—including restrictive assumptions involving their use—did little to answer Teigen's questions. Quite commonly the assumptions about the uses of the tools ignore the way they are used in Federal Reserve operations [126, pp. 290, 291, 310]. Teigen [349, pp. 284–85] has also been critical of the assertion "that the simple money multiplier [the reciprocal of the reserve requirement] is merely modified in a predictable way by the operations of commercial banks, and that the link between reserve operations and the money supply remains unique and dependable."

The equilibrium state.—As pointed out, some aspects of general equilibrium analysis underlie parts of this book. These include (1) a form of optimizing behavior tending to bring about the equality of rates of return from additions to various classes of assets, (2) the recognition of n-1 goods and services plus money (with money serving as a link between the present and the future), and (3) the equality of the number of unknowns and equations (Appendix to Ch. 14). These aspects of analysis may be brought forward—all without accepting the necessity of a full employment outcome as Teigen suggests that one must [347, p. 15], without limiting money to its unit of account function only, without accepting the notion of a stable equilibrium (the "balance" notion, especially in terms of levels rather than rates of change in stock and flow quantities), and without restricting treatment to the perfect competition of Walras' model. A looser idea of competition will do [330, pp. 974–75]. Mainly the behavioral units must be able to adjust their asset holdings—subject to an asset constraint, as in a Lagrangian function, and to the laws and customs governing behavior, all over a period of time as long as that identified with phases of post–World War II business cycles.

The introduction of aspects of general equilibrium analysis is intended to bridge a gap between the study of the behavior of the economy as a whole and the study of behavioral units. In the one instance, there are index numbers and aggregates, and in the other there are individuals, business firms, and groups of individuals and firms. In focusing on the whole, however, the equilibrium notion of general equilibrium theory gets translated into underlying, exponential trend paths about which changes occur. Even "modern Keynesian analysis" (as defined later, and mentioned by Teigen [347]) has not gone this far. Teigen does say [347, p. 19] that "the economy is always in transition, moving toward resting points, which themselves are repeatedly being disturbed." Instead of "resting points" with repeated disturbances, the alternative—the main body of analysis in this book, bearing on the short- or trade-cycle (or countercyclical stabilization goals)—is one in which economic conditions tend to exhibit "push" effects.

However, the introduction of such tendencies, particularly where associated with expectational phenomena, holds special consequences for the existence of a general competitive equilibrium [16, Ch. 14] in an economy with a past and a future and with prices and most contracts quoted in nominal money terms. In Chapter 8, expectations intervene so that all economic agents do not take prevailing market prices as data, as posited by general competitive analysis.

2.3 DEFINITIONS OF CREDIT AND MONETARY POLICIES

There are many works purporting to be about monetary policy and its effects, and, by contrast, definitions of the term "monetary policy" are exceedingly few.[14] This is bewildering in view of the obvious difficulties inherent in discussing the effects of monetary policy without defining it in reasonably operational and precise terms. Even so, the term "monetary policy" has been used in different ways, some of them quite common. It has been used to mean almost everything done by a central bank, exclusive of bank and personnel administration. The term has also been widely used to imply the use of the tools of monetary and credit control such as the discount rate, and in the mid-1960s one increasingly encountered the use of

---

14. For a list of such works see Frazer [120, n. 39].

the phrase "monetary policy actions" to refer to actions involving the tools. Some serious works purporting to deal with monetary policy actually deal with "monetary policy actions" [173, pp. 1–2, 4–5, 63, 98, 102, 114, 130, 174–75, 195–96]. One encounters the further distinction between policy actions and possible indicators such as free reserves (the excess reserves of banks, less borrowings from the Federal Reserve), the money supply, and interest rates [190, pp. 299–303].

The subject of indicators becomes involved (Ch. 10). One dimension of it seeks, for example, to distinguish between policy actions and forces other than policy actions influencing interest rates, and to distinguish between policy actions and forces other than policy actions influencing the money stock. In the latter instance there is the neutralized money stock [192, 193, 224]. In these instances, however, so-called monetary policy is related only to the policy actions portion of an indicator. The usual statistical problems concerning the interdependence of economic variables arise in efforts to extract non-action influences, and there are also questions about the prospect of controlling the broader measures and about the actual responsibilities of the Federal Reserve. These questions are considered further only after a review of some common usages of the term "monetary policy." The definition of credit or monetary policy one adopts is crucial to the conclusions one makes about the effects of policy and the lags in the effects, as Section 2.4 reveals.

Some definitions of credit and monetary policies.—The term "monetary policy" is commonly used as a synonym for "credit policy" and "credit" and "monetary conditions" [375; 376, pp. 64–75]. In these instances, interest rate changes are cited as indicators of changes in money market and credit conditions, as the "tone" and "feel" of the money and credit markets. A short-term rate such as the interest rate on Federal funds (essentially a rate on the use of the reserve balances of one bank by another on an overnight basis) or the 3-month Treasury bill rate may be cited to indicate money market conditions. A rate such as the rate on prime business loans (loans to the best business risks) at banks may be cited as indicating credit conditions, but the rates will tend to rise and fall together, making allowances for the prime loan rate as a more administered rate (at least prior to the tendency in the early 1970s to tie it to other market rates). In any event, as introduced in the next section, there are complications in equating credit and monetary policy, due mainly to some differential effects of common factors on the stock of bank credit and the money stock (defined as currency plus demand deposits adjusted). Nevertheless, in broad outline there is a close relationship.

If by credit policy or conditions one means the cost and availability of credit as reflected in some fundamental interest rate and if by monetary policy or conditions one means the policy with respect to the stock of money in relation to income, then one is led to expect a very close relationship between the respective policies, at least in the analytical framework of Section 2.2. There one is led, in particular, to see a very close relationship between the interest rate (i) and the income velocity of money (V_y), so that percentage changes in one coincide with percentage changes in the other. The average of the rate of change in the interest rate and the rate of change in the velocity of money could be viewed as a measure of the change in credit and monetary conditions. In such a context, credit is "easy," "neutral," or "tight" when the interest rate is declining, continuing unchanged, or rising, respectively. The corresponding monetary conditions are the reverse of the credit conditions. For example, interest rates and velocity vary directly, but tight credit (rising interest rates) corresponds with easy money (rising velocity) in the sense that actual balances exceed desired balances. In the latter instance, velocity is rising as a result of efforts by the holders of money balances to create an equilibrium between desired and actual balances; they try to reduce balances in relation to income by increasing the flow of expenditures. Credit is tight when velocity is rising, but the credit is being sought as a liability and a source of funds for increasing assets, rather than as a means of achieving larger holdings of money balances in relation to income or assets.

Adopting the preceding measures as indicators of credit and monetary policy, respectively, one could distinguish between random, seasonal, cyclical, and secular changes in policy, in view of the tendency to make such distinctions in analyses of time series. A number of writers speak of a distinction between long-run movements in interest rates and a cyclical policy,[15] and Sayers [329, pp. 711–24]—emphasizing the growth of money in relation to other assets and liabilities—reminds one that in the long run the public chooses what it will accept as money. Monetary policy may be varied and restrictive, but excessive and prolonged restriction or expansion of money and credit will ultimately decrease the importance of bank deposits as money, although there are complexities (Ch. 1, n. 18; Appendix

---

15. Axilrod and Young [17] emphasize that "To understand the behavior of interest rates, it is important to distinguish the long-run trend in rates from cyclical and other short-run variations in rates. In practice, of course, what we call long-run forces are always present and they influence short-run changes, while the effects of short-run forces may also ramify into the future."
Cagan [59, p. 230] also speaks of the need to distinguish trend factors.

to Ch. 7). This suggests a "natural economic limit" on the expansion of bank credit and deposit liabilities.

Tools and targets.—A policy is a chosen course toward desired objectives. In this sense, a policy implies a target or goal. In the case of the Federal Reserve, there may be a variety of policies on a variety of matters: the administration of the discount windows at the respective Federal Reserve banks, the administration of the System's trading desk at the Federal Reserve Bank of New York, the rate of change in aggregate bank credit, the rate of change in the stock of money, and so on. There may be policies at different levels (operational, intermediate, etc.), with those at one level initiating the implementation of a policy at another level.

Emphasis has commonly been placed on three different levels—operational, intermediate, and ultimate—as reviewed elsewhere [133, pp. 564–66]. At the operational level, bank reserves have been emphasized as a target, as in the context of the bank reserve equation. Credit and money market conditions, as previously defined, have been viewed as goals at the intermediate level. The ultimate goals have been and remain the commonly cited ones—maximum employment, production, and purchasing power (stable averages of prices on current output). International or balance of payments objectives are also considered. The goals or targets of a preceding level may be the tools or instruments for achieving goals at the next level. As an operational matter, however, the bank reserve and money market conditions goals have been somewhat combined, and longer-run goals for the growth of bank credit and money have been brought to the operations level too. These together bear on the achievement of overall economic goals [392, pp. 84–85, 94]. Even so, by focusing on the bank reserve equation, some perspective is provided (1) on the role of actions with respect to the discount mechanism and open market operations, and (2) on the situation faced by the account manager and the FOMC generally. Essentially one sees that, in the implementation of policy, consideration must be given to a variety of variables and their effects—offset or reinforced, entire or partial. The quality or softness of current information at the operating level and day-to-day shifts in market conditions must both be faced [392, pp. 81, 83, 91, 93]. Clear indications must be abstracted from a good bit of "noise."

The bank reserve equation is[16]

$$R + G + C_T - C_S - T_C - F - R_M = 0$$

or

$$R + G + C_T - C_S - T_C - F = R_M$$

16. The equation is set forth and related to balance sheet items in Frazer and Yohe [133, pp. 215–21].

where R is Federal Reserve credit, G is monetary gold stock (or this stock plus its counterpart since January 1970, in the form of the monotized special drawing rights or SDRs of the International Monetary Fund), C_T is Treasury Currency, C_S is currency in circulation (net), T_C is Treasury cash, F is foreign and other Federal Reserve deposits and miscellaneous accounts, and R_M is member-bank reserves (exclusive of member-bank vault cash). Further, the variables may be rearranged, as placing currency on the side with member bank reserves yields the monetary base. The bank reserve equation is an identity, but a goal at the operational level may be viewed as member-bank reserves (including vault cash). The main variable controlled by the Federal Reserve in the equation, however, is Federal Reserve credit (R), although the level of the required portion of member-bank reserves is limited by the Federal Reserve's control of reserve requirements. Other variables in the equation may be viewed as residuals over which the Federal Reserve has little direct control, and among these the monetary gold stock (G) has been of particular historical importance in the magnitude of its influence on reserves of commercial banks.

Federal Reserve credit in the bank-reserve equation results from discounts and advances made through the discount windows of the respective Federal Reserve Banks and from open market transactions in securities for the open market account. The Federal Reserve controls Federal Reserve credit (R) by varying the size of the open market account and by other ways, but member-bank reserves can undergo substantial changes without any changes in open market operation, administration of the discount window, or the required reserve ratio.[17]

As far as money and credit market conditions are concerned, short-term rates—such as the Federal funds rate or the Treasury bill rate—are usually emphasized, but long-term rates are also relevant. The short-term rates have large variance, possibly due to the predominating influence of more recent economic changes, and the long-term rates have relatively less variance, possibly due to the constraining influence of conditions in the more distant past [131]. The longer term yields seem to reflect more fundamental influences. Evidence suggests, however, that the more basic yields—such as those on government securities—reflect the influences of the past and the expected future rates, as well as the underlying flow quantities of securities coming on the market (a demand for funds) and securities being withdrawn from the market (a supply of funds). One may say that the rates are determined by the interactions of familiar supply and demand schedules, but

17. For a discussion of the control over member-bank reserves, see Dewald and Gibson [91, pp. 143–50].

the schedules themselves are subject to shifts in response to changing expectations.

The schedules would include (1) the liquidity-preference demand for money and the supply of money, and (2) the liquidity-preference demand for bank reserves and the supply of bank reserves as discussed later (Ch. 11). In the first of these instances, as emphasized earlier (Sec. 2.2), changes in the supply of money affect the interest rate directly and may affect imbalances in desired and actual balances simultaneously which further affects the interest rate and the income velocity of money. In the second instance the central bank may influence the supply (R_M in equation form) and contribute to rates of change in bank credit (the aggregate of commercial bank loans and investments) and the money supply, depending on changes in currency holdings of the public in relation to deposits and on changes in the division of deposits between demand and non-demand deposits.[18] However, the preference of commercial banks for excess reserves (reserves in excess of legally required reserves) or net excess reserves (free reserves, a net reserve surplus, or excess reserves less borrowing through the discount windows of Federal Reserve Banks) may also influence the supply of credit and money.

Much of what has been said in the foregoing framework may be summarized in the simple relationship

$$M = mB$$

where M is the money stock, m is a money multiplier, and B is the monetary base. The monetary base is allied with member bank reserves. The Federal

18. The changes in question involve money (credit) multipliers and currency and time deposit drains [133, pp. 39–48]. A number of writers deal with the drains and with the question of central bank control over the quantity of money.

In particular, Gramley and Chase [177, pp. 205–13] give special emphasis to the time deposit drain. Dewald [90, pp. 512–13] also emphasizes that "the public and bank-desired holdings of various assets clearly are vital determinants of the quantity of money or of interest rates," as well as the constraints imposed on the money supply by required reserve ratios and the level of bank reserves. Assuming no excess reserves and "a given distribution of currency and deposits subject to different required reserve ratios, he calculates the maximum money supply as (actual money/required reserves) × (actual reserves), and finds "that 94 percent of the quantity variation in changes in the quantity of money from 1948 through 1965 [in the United States] was attributable to changes in maximum money." He interpreted this to suggest "that the constraints of required reserve ratios and bank reserves could not easily be ignored" as determinants of the money supply. Dewald cites other works dealing with maximum money or bank credit measures, and with some controversy between economists favoring actions to control the money supply versus actions to control the rate of interest.

Reserve controls this by effecting desired changes and offsetting undesired changes. The money multiplier herein allows for any switching between time and demand deposits and reflects the reciprocal of the sum of three ratios: required reserves to demand deposit liabilities, the public's desired currency holdings to demand deposit liabilities, and excess reserves to demand deposit liabilities. Just as the Federal Reserve can offset undesired changes in the member bank reserve equation, it can vary the legal required reserve ratio to achieve the desired money multiplier. Empirically, however, the money multiplier has been shown to fluctuate over a narrow range and to be predictable, and the trend rate of growth of the money stock has been dominated by the trend rate of growth for the monetary base [344, pp. 3–6].

The Federal Reserve is presently viewed as giving effect to member bank reserves through a combination of actions and inactions, and as having diverse influences on credit conditions. The analysis of these influences and conditions is complicated by developments on the demand side of the respective markets for funds and money balances, by allowances for special effects of changes in the rate of change in the money stock on imbalances between desired and actual balances, and by allowance for the rationale of parallel movements in income velocity and the interest rate.

Monetary policy, fiscal policy, and the independence of the central bank.—The preceding measures and reviews of credit and monetary conditions (and policies) give the Federal Reserve responsibility both for its actions with its tools—open market operations and so on—and for the impact of other factors on the interest rate. Responsibilities for contributing to the achievement of national economic goals have been recognized, but the Federal Reserve's responsibilities for countering or reinforcing the effects of some fiscal or tax measures have also been shown by demonstrating the impact of some changes in tax measures (Sec. 2.2) on the interest rates and by defining credit conditions in terms of the interest rate. Such a relationship of fiscal policy to monetary policy is emphasized by Wilson [376]:

> Just what should be included by the term "monetary policy" is exceedingly difficult to define. It might be extended to comprehend any action that is concerned to influence the volume and character of the flows of money and of money substitutes throughout the economy. On a strict interpretation, this would embrace much of fiscal policy also, since action concerned with the raising and expenditure of the public revenues obviously has monetary effects.

In addition to the general relationship of fiscal to monetary policy, there is a special kind of long-run relationship between fiscal (and tax) policy

and policy with respect to bank credit and the money stock, given the prospect of a secular rise in prices and the Federal Reserve's assumption of
price-level stability as an ultimate goal. The Federal Reserve can expand
credit and money at faster rates and assure adequate growth of the banking
sector without sacrificing price-level stability, if an incomes policy (Sec.
18.6), fiscal policy, and moral suasion on the part of the executive branch
of government assume a larger part of the burden of controlling price-level
increases and assuring adherence to guidelines for wage increases.[19] In the
long run, bank credit and the money stock should grow at sufficient rates to
assure the continued acceptance of bank deposits as money, and the avoidance of the acceptance by the public of other sorts of assets (particularly
real goods) as money in view of the immense convenience and economy in
using bookkeeping entries as money.

In the short run, the monetary authorities in the United States have some
special protection from political pressures in money and credit policy matters. This is provided by a form of independence within the structure of
government, but it is presently matched by a degree of responsibility implicit
in the definitions of credit and monetary policy. The independence allows
the monetary authorities to pursue an unpopular cause—such as restricting
the growth of bank credit—when it would aid the attainment of ultimate
goals. On the other hand, the definitions of credit and monetary policy imply
a responsibility to reinforce or offset effects on the interest rate arising from
other quarters. Reuber deals with the political difficulties raised by independence and the justification for it [306, p. 41]:

> Independence, apart from the political difficulties it raises, may create
> unnecessary additional conflicts among objectives and among instruments
> which means that a less favorable combination of objectives will be at-
> tained than in the absence of such independence. Independence can never
> improve on a fully coordinated approach to policy unless one is willing
> to assume that an agency having such independence is both willing and
> able to accept as one of its objectives the goal of compensating for errors
> being made by other policy makers.

2.4   LAGS AND ALTERNATIVE CONCEPTS OF MONETARY POLICY

Possible lags between the need for and the initiation of a change in monetary policy, and between the initiation and the effect of change were outlined by Milton Friedman in a 1948 article [148]. Since then monetary
policy lags have been discussed by Friedman [145, pp. 446–47], Culbertson

19. On moral suasion and the chief executive, see Romans [311].

[80, pp. 467–77; 79, p. 374], Mayer [259, pp. 358–74], White [368, pp. 142–47], Sprinkle [341, pp. 333–46], Johnson and Winter [212], Brunner and Meltzer [48, pp. 36–50], Kareken and Solow [222, pp. 14–96], Dewald and Johnson [92, pp. 171–89], Reuber [305, 306], Hendershott [195, pp. 519–23], Willis [375], and Jorgenson and Stephenson [217], among others. The lags dealt with have included the *inside lag* and *the outside lag*. The *inside lag* consists of a *recognition* and *action lag*; the lag between the need for actions and the recognition of this need and the lag between recognition of the need for action and the action. Overall, the *inside lag* is said to be implicit in estimates of "the time elapsing between changes in the indicators of a need for policy changes and the actual responses of policy" [306, p. 143; 212, pp. 116–17]. Among the estimates of such a lag are those resulting from regressing single monetary policy indicators, such as the nominal stock of money, on indicators of economic performance, such as prices and the percentage of unemployment [92, 47]. Some other estimates involve other methods, including the measurement of the average lag time between turning points in selected time series [145].

The *outside lag* is the lag in the effect of a change in policy. Jorgenson and Stephenson [217, pp. 16–27] emphasize such a lag in their concern with the "time structure" of the relationship between investment behavior and its determinants. In their analysis, the time structure encompasses the average length of the lag between changes in a policy instrument and its effects, and the form of the lag—whether the form of the lag is geometric, Pascal, inverted-V, or some arbitrary distribution. On the length of the lag, they note that a long lag suggests a possibly adverse effect of an intended policy of stabilization on investment behavior. On the form of the lag, they note that a high concentration of effects in time calls for a precise control of the timing of policy measures and that a distribution of effects over very substantial periods of time calls for a less precise control.

The difficulties with such lag studies are severalfold. A lag relation between two series does not necessarily imply complete dependence or any clear-cut linkage mechanism, in part because of the prospect of some common response in economic time series to forces such as the thrust and momentum of the economy or expected inflation. More fundamentally, however, even the measured lags can be misleading since they are averages. And these—as Yohe's and Karnosky's study (Appendix to Ch. 1) suggests—are subject to possible variation when the sample period is split.

Estimates of the presence of lags are dependent on the use of definitions and the selection of indicators of changes. Earlier (Sec. 2.2), the prospect of covariation in the income velocity of money and the interest rate was introduced. Business conditions were then identified with changes in income velocity and the interest rate, and definitions of credit and monetary conditions (Sec. 2.3) were reviewed and equated with changes in the interest rate. Consequently, viewing the change in business conditions as an indication of a need for change in policy and viewing a change in policy as a change in credit conditions, analysis leads to the prospect of an inside lag time of approximately zero. Similarly, if one views cyclical changes in the rate of change in the money stock $\left(\frac{1}{M}\frac{dM}{dt}\right)$, with maximum rates occurring in an expansion phase of business activity and minimum rates in a recession phase, and if one views an increasing (decreasing) rate as causing an increase (decrease) in economic activity, then policy is at times procyclical rather than countercyclical (as in the case of interest rates) and one is led to expect a relatively long lag in the effect of monetary policy.

A zero inside lag.—The idea that changes in credit conditions coincide roughly with cyclical turning points is borne out by several analyses, including a Brunner-Meltzer analysis [48]. It relates turning points to statements from the record of each meeting of the FOMC concerning credit ease and credit tightness in the 1952–62 period. Summarizing the results in one of their tables, they suggest that the recognition and action lags are comparatively short, approaching a zero inside lag.[20]

Dewald and Johnson have also found a close relation between credit conditions and business conditions. They reported on regression results involving credit condition (interest rate) variables, the money stock as alternative target, the timing of changes in policy, and a variety of business condition variables. They found a closer relationship between the credit condition and business condition variables, including the percentage of unemployment, real GNP in billions of dollars, the consumer price index, and the balance of payments deficit. They concluded [92, p. 189]:

> The monetary authorities appear to react more quickly to changes in the environment if they are assumed to aim at controlling money market conditions than if they are assumed to aim at controlling the quantity of money. The former assumption is probably more consistent with generally accepted views of how monetary policy is conducted in practice than the latter, and adoption of it leads to conclusions about the flexibility of monetary policy much more flattering to the monetary authorities.

Analysis in Section 2.2 suggests that changes in credit conditions are such a fundamental part of changes in economic activity that it is impossible in a

20. Specific conclusions arrived at by Brunner and Meltzer are listed in Frazer [120, n. 66].

properly functioning, peacetime, market economy to alter the timing of changes in interest rates in relation to changes in economic activity. Indeed, some analysis leads to the belief that the Federal Reserve influences changes in economic activity itself and that interest rates are only one manifestation of those changes. Suggested below is the concept of a stabilization policy over an entire cycle in which the Federal Reserve is determining within limits the timing of peaks and troughs in business conditions to achieve national economic goals.

A Friedmanian analysis of the effects of monetary policy.—Friedman's analysis of the effects of monetary policy—conducted in some instances with Anna Jacobson Schwartz—involves emphasis on special elements of monetary analysis and an empirical study of cyclical changes [145, pp. 446–47; 126, pp. 139–85]. Reports on the latter led Kareken and Solow to conclude [222, pp. 14–18] (1) that Friedman's reporting of cyclical patterns suggests a long *outside lag* in the effects of monetary policy, (2) that a change in monetary policy—as viewed by Friedman—is a change in the money stock (ΔM, not $\frac{1}{M}\frac{dM}{dt}$), and (3) that the lag in the effect of a change in the rate of change in the money stock is measurable, in an expansion phase of business conditions, from the peak rate of change in the money stock to the peak in business conditions.

Friedman does view changes in monetary policy in terms of changes in the rate of change in the money stock, as have others, but the lag in the effect is not as long as some assert.[21] There is a long lag when measured from peak rates of change in the money stock to their corresponding peaks in business conditions, but this analysis is of overall cyclical patterns of changes in economic variables rather than of a lag in the effect of a given change in the rate of change in the money stock. The overall cyclical analysis provides support, in Friedman's view, for stabilizing the rate of change in the money stock $\left(\frac{1}{M}\frac{dM}{dt}\right)$.

Elements of analysis emphasized by Friedman include: (1) the notion of an imbalance between desired and actual money balances, such that an excess of the latter gives rise to an increase in the velocity of money; (2)

---

21. Friedman views holders of money balances as able to readily adjust their balances to a desired level by increasing expenditures (measured as the product of the average of prices and output) and pushing prices upward if necessary. The adjustment by holders of money balances to changes in the money stock and imbalances between desired and actual money balances is relatively rapid. Allais [2, pp. 1137–38, 1150–51, 1154] assumes "that the discrepancy between the actual and desired value of money holdings is always relatively small."

the notion that a prospective change in prices, as indicated by the rate of change in prices, affects interest rates, the cost of holding money, and the velocity of money; and (3) the notion that changes in the rate of change in the money stock affect the rate of change in prices and the balance (or imbalance) between desired and actual money balances.

Friedman begins with changes in the rate of change in the money stock because of their theoretical appeal. He says that it is "theoretically appealing to regard the 'normal' or secular monetary base around which cyclical fluctuations occur as described by a constant percentage rate of change in the stock of money and to regard changes in the percentage rate of change as the feature of monetary behavior that contributes to the generation of cycles." On the roles of the rate of change in prices, imbalances between desired and actual money balances, and further changes in prices, Friedman may be quoted as follows [145, p. 455]:

> The percentage rate of change in prices itself is the opportunity cost of holding money rather than goods. An unanticipated change in the rate of change of the stock of money would then produce a deviation of the actual from the desired stock of money for two reasons: initially, it would make the actual stock deviate from the expected stock and therefore from the desired stock; subsequently, by altering the cost of holding money [presumably via expenditures and further influence on prices], it would change the desired stock of money itself. These discrepancies will set up adjustments that may very well be cyclical, involving overshooting and reversal. It is therefore theoretically appealing to regard the 'normal' or secular monetary base around which cyclical fluctuations occur as described by a constant percentage rate of change in the stock of money and to regard changes in the percentage of change as the feature of monetary behavior that contributes to generation of cycles.

In the context of his cyclical analysis of the lag between peaks (troughs) in the rate of change in the money stock and business conditions, Friedman concluded [145, p. 449] that "Changes in the behavior of the stock of money (A) exert an important independent influence on the subsequent course of events with a lag that is (B) on the average sizable and (C) highly variable, relative to the usual length of cyclical movements."

Part A of the conclusion is developed as follows:

> The direction of influence between the money stock and income and prices is less clear-cut and more complex for the business cycle than for the longer movements [secular movements] ... Thus changes in the money stock are a consequence as well as an independent cause of changes in income and prices, though once they occur they will in their turn produce still further effects on income and prices.

Parts B and C of Friedman's conclusion deal with the difficulty of anticipating developments a year or so ahead, as would be required for effective stabilization. Other analysis (Sec. 2.2) suggests that imbalances in the desired and actual money stocks may arise from sources other than changes in the rate of change in the money stock. In this context, discretionary changes in the rate of change in the money stock may be desirable to counter destabilizing imbalances in the desired and actual stock of money. Friedman has not entirely approved of this.[22] But it might be added that increasing the emphasis in the directive (Sec. 2.1) on longer-term growth in the credit and money stocks probably adds some stability to short-run policy changes. As brought out on other occasions, this would be consistent with views advanced by Friedman.[23]

The concept of a policy over a cycle.—As introduced in Section 2.2, average growth rates in stock and flow variables provide the base around which cyclical fluctuations or changes in economic or business conditions occur. These changes in business conditions coincide with changes in the interest rate and the income velocity of money, and they reflect adjustments in response to imbalances in desired and actual money balances. They also reflect adjustments in various classes of assets (and liabilities) via differential rates of changes in response to the impact of outside factors on the prospective returns from the alternative classes of assets. The outside factors include the determination of the rate of change in the money stock, some shock effects such as a change in the tax credit, and others contributing to degrees of certainty about the future, price-level changes, and so on. Friedman emphasizes the rate of change in prices as the major determinant of the "opportunity cost of holding money," changes in the velocity of money, and the rate of expenditures on goods and services. Also, an increase in the rate of change in prices, or the prospect of a rising price level, results from a rise in the rate of change in the money stock.

The present analysis allows for a wider variety of factors impinging on expectations. It suggests that expectations be treated more systematically in monetary analyses, and that monetary policy and the responsibilities of officials be viewed broadly to encompass allowances for shock effects, responses to exogenous factors, and the role of policy inactions as well as actions. Prospective price-level changes—as distinct from changes in the

22. Some reasons are cited in Frazer [120, n. 79].
23. The 1971 Staff Paper cited earlier says [392, p. 86], "But the benefits that might be expected from an increased degree of emphasis on monetary aggregates in the conduct of open market operations relate to the question of monetary control under conditions of uncertainty."

value of additions to alternative classes of assets (changes in mythical prices)—are not the only prospective changes that can give rise to changes in business conditions, as some analyses imply. Consequently, business conditions are subject to changes other than changes in the rate of change in the money stock, and the monetary authorities are left with something to stabilize, even if they were to effect a constant growth rate in the money stock.

As factors have differential effects on alternative classes of assets and on the value of goods and services, differential changes occur in the rates of change in the various classes of assets, in terms of changes in business conditions. For some institutions, such as banks, these changes occur in various time-to-maturity classes of debt assets and in the relation between loans and investments, with the flow of business loans by banks depending more on business conditions than on bank liquidity. For non-financial business firms, relative changes in asset and liability accounts involve broader classes—the fixed-claim assets and liabilities such as government securities and bank loans, and the residual claim assets such as plants, equipment, and inventories. The behavior, financing, and expenditures of these firms are considered later (Ch. 15).

For the present it is simply noted that large firms account for a major portion of capital outlays. These firms are characterized by planning for the future. Liquidity is built up in anticipation of future outlays and these are influenced primarily by probabilistic beliefs about the future, as outlined later (Ch. 8). Concepts exist of an exponential locus of points toward which unsustainable rates of change must regress. Approaching an upper turning point, a liquidity change—possibly of the nature of a crisis—reflects an anticipated reversal in business prospects. Adjustments take place in balance sheet items and expenditures. The declining phase of business conditions is a readjustment, partly in response to the presence of sustainable conditions in the first place.

Suggested decision rules.—The above review and earlier analysis suggest certain rules for stabilizing business conditions. One is to accelerate an expansion (contraction) of business activity, creating (a) the prospect of an improvement (a slowdown) in such activity, (b) imbalances between supply prices and mythical prices, and (c) the prospect that interest rates will rise (decline) in the future. A second suggestion is to constrain an expansion in business conditions as a means of sustaining the expansion, mitigating the duration of the succeeding adjustment, and mitigating the overall variance of changes in rates of change about their trend values. The first set of changes would be influenced by announcements of policy changes and by clearly discernable changes in the rates of change in bank credit and the money stock. In order that these changes be clear, they should be averages, exclusive of seasonal and day to day operations. These are present in the nature of the controls, particularly with respect to bank credit and money supply goals. The second rule follows from the recognition of a regressive pull effect of normality (subjectively viewed) on expectations, and from the identification of recessions with readjustments to sustainable or normal conditions. The readjustments themselves have an extrapolative influence on expectations.

What is said about the pattern of expectational influences in relation to capital expenditures, their financing, and liquidity relates as well to analysis of expectational influences on the term structure of interest rates (as defined later).

2.5 SUMMARY

In monetary policy study, questions arise about the definition of the term "monetary policy," about the lag between recognizing the need for and effecting a change in policy, about the lag in the effect of a change in policy, and about the traditional emphasis by central bankers on conditions of the credit and money markets as distinct from the relationship between central-bank operations and ultimate economic goals. Defining "monetary policy" is more than an idle exercise, since the definition one adopts affects his views about lagged relations and other matters. Studies attaching a conventional meaning to the term—as, say, a synonym for "credit policy"—reveal an inside lag of approximately zero. Other studies—most notably, those by Milton Friedman—focus on the rate of change in the money stock and find a long lag in the effect of policy. In measuring the lag in the effect of policy, Friedman considers the time dimension between extreme values for the rate of change in the money stock and their corresponding turning points in business conditions. A change in the rate of change in the money stock—operating via imbalances between desired and actual money balances and adjustments in responses to imbalances—has a rather rapid effect on expenditures and prices in Friedman's analysis, as in others, but Friedman's view of the lag in the effect of monetary policy involves a broader concept.

In some instances, credit and monetary policies have been distinguished where the former refers to the conditions surrounding the cost and availability of bank credit and the latter refers to the rate of change in the money stock in relation to the rate of change in income. Here the focus is on the tendency for the interest rate and the income velocity of money to vary directly over time and for the two to vary in analytical contexts—responding similarly to changes in the same sets of conditions, tax factors, expected rates of change in prices, and so on. Indeed, viewing differential rates of change in stock and flow variables as causing interest rate and velocity changes and as causing fluctuations about secular changes, the changes in the interest rate and velocity may be viewed as indicators of changes in credit and business conditions. Adopting the common definition of "credit conditions," then, credit conditions (as indicated by the interest rate) are related to business conditions (as indicated by the velocity of money). In effect, different names apply to similar phenomena, although some changes could affect the two measures differently. These might include changes in the payment mechanism as under the future impact of the computer and changes in the use of overdraft facilities.

In broad outline, the likely similar impact of expected increases in prices on the financial sector (on the rates set by lenders), and on the real goods sector (on the prospective returns by investors) suggests an equality of foresight principle. And the role of expectations in such a context suggests elimination of the notion of the short run (constant expectations) as defined by Keynes. The role of the probabilistic weighting of prospective returns also enters, and suggests an analysis in which expectational forces sometimes play a crucial role in creating changes in economic variables. Simple functional relationships and schedules—of a variety common in received economics—serve to remind economists of the presence of additional notions, but the results obtained with their strictest uses may be misleading. Expectational phenomena need to be allowed for, especially in considering the role and effects of monetary policy. The imprecision and inclusiveness surrounding the relationship between money market conditions and monetary aggregates in the very short run suggest a need to abstract from the noise and defensive aspects of monetary and credit policy in focusing on economic or cyclical stabilization. The need for clear direction in the changes in policy comes to the forefront when one wishes to speculate about "pronouncement effects," a positive role for policy in stabilizing conditions reflecting expectational forces.

The Federal Reserve has been criticized for focusing excessively on money market and credit conditions as indicators of policy changes. However, the emphasis began to shift in the mid-1960s. And following Arthur Burns' arrival as chairman at the Board in early 1970, the FOMC directive focused more directly on a longer-run path for credit and monetary aggregates. The change in the directive suggested more emphasis on changes in money market and credit conditions relative to underlying and stable changes in monetary aggregates.

Part II

Banking, Monetarist, and Other Views

3
Some Views and Analysis

THE TRAINS of thought and analysis introduced in this chapter and running through Part II are complicated. Some of the most fundamental issues of economics are involved, especially as they relate to behavior over time, patterns of relationships between time series, causation, state-of-mind variables, simple models, and simple equation and structural equations models.

In the context of a modern industrial society, behavior gives rise to many time series. These may be classified as to whether they lead, lag, coincide, or display no regularity with respect to changes in business conditions. Economists construct models, attempt explanations of economic behavior, and seek consistency between the models, explanations, and observations. Other sorts of evidence (as from cross-section data) may be invoked, but inconsistency with time series evidence requires the rejection of hypotheses.

Among the issues that arise are: (1) whether some leading series such as the rate of change in the money stock via some stock adjustment mechanism, or such as the interest rate, explains almost singularly ensuing changes in economic time series; (2) whether, as a matter of dominant first order approximation, time series for real and financial variables may be mainly responding to some common influences operating on, say, the participants' anticipations about the future; (3) whether imbalances between possibly fictitious distinctions (such as that between "desired" and "actual" money balances or that between "the rate of interest" and "the rate of return") and the notion of ensuing adjustments between these imbalances in response to certain other changes will best explain the relationships between time series; and (4) whether the influences of recent and more distant changes as well as learning and the coalescing of opinions about future conditions, in the contexts of group situations, are also required to explain the varying patterns of relationships among time series.

Some simple and complicated explanations of economic behavior are examined. A historical banking view is mentioned in two chapters (4 and 7). Here control over business conditions is thought to result from a particular linkage mechanism and control over certain money market variables. In Chapter 7, this view is identified with a Keynesian view and the income expenditure model. On the other hand, a monetarist view has particular emphasis on the importance of the money stock as a causal force, with other characteristics, as in Section 3.2 below. Milton Friedman and his closest followers are often identified with such a view [318, pp. 7–8; 309, pp. 43–46]. Whatever the case, by 1970 the co-called monetarists were not always placing as much importance on the money stock as some had anticipated.

3.2   THE MONETARIST ("EMPIRICAL") REVOLUTION

Attributes of modes of thought and theory have been mentioned and variously identified. The Keynesian mode was introduced as the orthodoxy of the 1950s and early 1960s (Secs. 1.1, 1.2) against which the rapid changes brought on by the modern computer could be contrasted. These Keynesian attributes continue to appear and reappear throughout the book. There is, however, a positive side—notions that emerge from the apparent empirical onslaught of the 1960s. Many have attempted to identify it as a Friedmanian or monetarist revolution [39, 210], and textbooks in economics have come to introduce Friedman along with Keynes as an authority for arbitrating the correctness of an economic point of view.

This book deals with the rise of monetarism as only a part of the initial impact of the modern computer and the empirical onslaught. Friedman certainly played a major role, partly because of his prior empirical orientation (Sec. 5.1).[1] The timing of his rise which coincided with the computer's must be emphasized. There are other aspects of the economics and sociology of his rise, as treated by Johnson [210, pp. 6–9]. (1) The early Keynesians became senior economists, but continued to trade on their foresight for having participated in a revolution. This was to the detriment of

---

1. Friedman and his associates were primed for the computer, as indicated by the volume Friedman edited in 1956 (*Studies in the Quantity Theory of Money*, University of Chicago Press, 1956) when his associates were still using hand calculators. With the aid of the computer, Friedman and his associates contributed to a redirection of monetary economics.

their juniors, but in the United States—"where institutional competition prevents centralized control of professional advancement"—junior professionals could dissent and still advance. (2) The fields of theorizing opened up by the Keynesian revolution ran into diminishing returns. (3) Keynesian economics came to suffer from the same defect as the orthodoxy Keynes attacked—"the attempt to explain essentially monetary phenomena in terms of a mixture of real theory and *ad-hoc-ery*." (4) The growing professionalization of economics and the rise of the United States as a world power facilitated an interest in scientific issues, exclusive of any visible interest on the part of the general public. (5) The emergence of inflation as both a U.S. and a world problem in the mid- to late-1960s provided an opportunity for new modes of thought. Inflation was the monetarist issue "that Keynesian theory was least well designed to deal with." (6) Keynesian economics tended to "proliferate into larger and yet larger models of the economic system, a tendency which sacrificed theoretical insights to the cause of descriptive realism and which had the incidental but important detractions of demanding large sums of scarce research money available only to senior economists and of turning young economists into intellectual mechanics." In contrast, the revolution held some offering for the small-scale intellectual.

Johnson finds some similarities in the conditions surrounding the Keynesian and monetarist revolutions, and speculates about the engineering of such a revolution [210, p. 3]. Nevertheless, in addition to the role of the computer, there is a difference in the respective chief protagonists. Keynes was an aristocrat, a man of affairs with artistic temperment, and an economist in a world where economics was not especially professionalized. (He did not even have an earned doctorate.) Friedman, in contrast, was born in New York City and rose to prominence in a highly organized, professionalized setting. His rise and ultimate impact required organization, mainly in relation to empirical economics and the modern computer. This he partly developed at his home institution and partly found ready-made at the National Bureau for Economic Research (Secs. 5.1, 18.3). His success and that of the computer in economics was a triumph for the Bureau and empirical economics.[2]

2. As reviewed by Rader [296, pp. 8–18], Friedman and the Bureau are brought together. The Bureau's early emphasis under the guidance of Wesley Mitchell was on the simple collection and publication of economic facts. Arthur Burns (Sec. 1.1) succeeded him, and provided the link to Friedman, as pointed out later (Sec. 5.1). With Friedman one finds some relation to a more contemporary scientific view as

The framework of Friedman's monetary analysis as presented by him in early 1970 [136] is reviewed in Chapter 5. Even so, some attributes of monetarist thought as seen by Teigen [347], Brunner [39], and Rasche [300] may be listed for further introduction. Teigen draws primarily on Friedman [136] and Brunner [39], and mentions additional themes which characterize monetarist writing. First, monetarists have emphasized equilibrating price-level adjustments rather than the output adjustments attributed to Keynesians [347, p. 12]. Friedman has subsequently stressed the need to consider both types of adjustments (Sec. 5.4), but the adjustment feature is also tied in with matters concerning time spans [300, pp. 26, 28; 347, pp. 12, 16, 18]. Monetarists have focused at times on long-run movements where real variables such as output are less influenced by monetary forces. In the long run in Brunner's review of monetarism [39, pp. 13–14], underlying growth paths for the money stock exert relatively little influence on the underlying growth rate for output, but variations in the rate of change in the money stock about its underlying growth path do. In this long-run view as reviewed by Teigen [347, p. 12], there is full employment, since all markets, including the labor market, have adjusted to policy shocks [300, p. 28]. In the short-run Keynesian view, the labor market remains in disequilibrium [300, p. 28; 347, p. 15]. The Keynesians see some short-run instability built into the private real sector of the economy or occurring in response to swings in anticipations of the business community, all independent of major policy events [39, p. 6]. "Keynesians," Teigen points out [347, p. 16], "are more concerned with short-run analysis (for instance, that related to counter-cyclical stabilization)."

Another monetarist attribute is the money stock, portfolio transmission mechanism [347, pp. 12, 17]. An increase in the money stock causes an excess of actual over desired balances and this imbalance works itself out in changes in relative prices and spending on other financial and real assets. The spending causes the market value of specific assets to change. The Keynesians may also view a portfolio, but their emphasis has been on the investment demand building block (Sec. 1.2), with an imbalance between the interest rate and the rate of return leading to a change in investment, although there are questions about the inelasticity of investment demand.

---

summarized by Rader [296, p. 8]:
> "The dominant opinion found in recent work on economic methodology is that of logical positivism, which says that economics is an empirical science that must be analyzed by logical means to explain events (more properly, to coordinate simultaneous and sequential observations). Again, science should be judged by the extent to which it 'fits the facts' and economics should become a positive science."

This, of course, can lead to a Keynesian emphasis on fiscal policy and the investment multiplier as introduced earlier (Sec. 1.2). Questions then arise about the stability of the money demand relation, the demise of the interest rate as a determinant, and the correspondence to experience of such central concepts as the money and investment multipliers.[3]

The former questions are taken up in Chapter 4. The extensive literature on the money and investment multipliers comes up in Chapter 5. The money relation in the monetarist framework focuses, with some exceptions, on demand rather than supply (Appendix to Ch. 7) because the public is thought to be able to adjust its holdings of real balances (deflated for price-level changes) by simply spending more or less and thus influencing the price level and the real balances held. Hence, there is a reference in the Rasche title [300] to "demand management."

Friedman can also employ the Keynesian liquidity-preference building block, as reviewed in Chapter 1, in discussing monetary and price anticipatory influences on interest rates. Teigen and Rasche concede the Keynesian's failure to deal with the price anticipatory influences [347, p. 14; 300, p. 27], and Teigen [347, p. 20] attempts to show how they can be introduced in the Keynesian IS–LM model (Ch. 4). One may recognize in Teigen that Keynesian mechanics can be manipulated to achieve some inflationary anticipation, when special assumptions are made about relative speeds of adjustment in various markets.

As already noted in Johnson's review of the economics and sociology of the revolution, the monetarists have tended to favor small-scale models. They suggest an emphasis on matters of first order importance, and they charge [347, p. 13], that "The Keynesian position is that knowledge of allocative detail (e.g., substitution relationships between various financial assets) is necessary for the proper understanding of policy processes, implying a need for complex structural models."[4] There is a relaxation of the

3. The references to the money and investment multiplier call attention to a further way of delineating the monetarist position [347, p. 13]; "Monetary impulses are the dominant factor in explaining changes in the pace of economic activity, in contrast to the Keynesian position which assertedly takes real impulses as primary."

4. In defending against this, Teigen [347, p. 21] reverts to the old argument (Sec. 2.2) that "monetary policy is carried out through the traditional instruments . . . and not direct manipulation of the money stock." Rasche [300, pp. 27–28] sees these large-scale models as an attempt to deal with the limitations of highly aggregative framework, but then concedes that the econometric problem of estimating distributed lags has proven particularly difficult and that the timing of responses to actions found in the models is a major area of difficulty. Rasche concedes further that "monetarist models have to date established a forecasting record which is credible when compared to the more entrenched income determination approach."

ceteris paribus notion (Sec. 1.2) as the structural equation method and the significance attached to allocative detail give rise to larger structures, and there is an increased reliance on the highly restrictive ceteris paribus notion and substitution measures as expectational phenomena get impounded.[5]

One might say that the monetarists deal with phenomena that introduce shifts in the schedules of the standard IS–LM summary of the income expenditure model [39, pp. 4, 20, 23]. In contrast, the Keynesians have relied upon the slopes attributed to the respective schedules. The short-run shifts or instabilities in the system have been attributed by monetarists to the government sector, to the monetary and fiscal policies [39, p. 6]. These policies become a source of shocks that influence economic prospects; there is the prospect that much would be stable if the policies were stable. However, in this book shocks, other expectational influences, and systematic knowledge of the formation of expectations are important, partly because of the presumed troublesomeness of such phenomena even in the absence of policy-engendered instability, and partly because of the presumed role of economics as a guide to the policy-maker. There is a convergence of expectational aspects of Keynes economics (Ch. 8), of phenomena treated unsystematically or impounded in ceteris paribus by Keynesians, and of elements found in the monetarist literature.

In the early 1970s the Keynesians of the 1950s and 1960s and the monetarists of the 1960s tried to accommodate each other. This accommodation may be viewed partly as a concession for the survival of the best of the two schools and partly as a concession to the advancement of economics along empirical grounds. Friedman himself initially sought to emphasize differences that could be reconciled empirically. Nevertheless, underlying differences in methodologies continue to arise and may persist for some time (Secs. 18.1–18.3). Traversing the issues continues to seem worthwhile as a means of improving conceptions of the past and paths of the future.

An emphasis on expectations and the tastes and preferences of behavioral units (mainly households, Ch. 5) emerges from Friedman's work in par-

---

5. Teigen himself introduces a "partial" and a "systematic" elasticity [347, pp. 16, 24–25]. A partial elasticity is the traditional one calculated along a function of one independent variable, while impounding other forces in ceteris paribus. It may be called a "Marshallian elasticity." A systematic elasticity in Teigen's exposition would be a priori, but one that allowed for the response of one quantity (output) to another (money) when the response of the entire system is taken into account. This "system" is not "the" economic system, but rather a system of equations.

ticular. In dealing with the long run and related notions such as that of permanent income (Sec. 2.2), account is taken of the influence of the more recent and distant past on the current outlook.

The degree of certainty about the future of economic conditions became very important (Ch. 4) when the luxury goods hypothesis failed to forecast the post–World War II rise in the income velocity of money. The idea of a change in an anticipated norm for interest rates became a basis for questioning the existence of a liquidity trap. Though not original with Friedman, the attention directed toward the price-anticipations component of interest rates (Appendix to Ch. 1) was certainly advanced by him. The need to introduce expectations into economic theory in a relevant, systematic, and serious way is thought to have emerged as part of the empirical onslaught, beginning mainly about 1960.

Many have contributed to the crisis in theory, to changes in analysis, and to empirical findings. Some of the attributes of analysis and theory that emerge in this book are: (1) an equality of foresight principle which holds that numerous factors simultaneously influence the expectations of financial markets participants and non-financial decision units alike; (2) an expectations theory of interest rates that does not require major reliance on changes in the quantities of securities offered (amounts of funds sought) or sought (amounts of funds supplied), as in the received expectations theory of the term structure of interest rates; (3) an explanation of turning points in business conditions that involves probabilistic slanting and group decision-making; (4) an equilibrium notion that centers about underlying growth paths, changes in rates of change in stock and flow quantities, and changes in a balancing of weights with respect to the recent and more distant past, all without the presence of a priori prescription of time paths as being damped, oscillatory or explosive; (5) a vanishing short-run with respect to Keynes' theory, such that liquidity preference is given a different orientation from that contributed by James Tobin; (6) a distinct treatment for bank credit and the money stock, such that an increase in the amount of credit sought may coincide with a weakened preference for money and an increase in the velocity of money; (7) a treatment of the demand for non-cash forms of liquidity by business firms that subordinates the notions of transactions demands and related economies of scale, as a means of explaining changes in the turnover of cash balances; and (8) the notion that the extent of planning—and particularly planning to avoid tight credit conditions—imparts a different time dimension to the influences of monetary policy.

3.3   Monetarist-Keynesian Controversy in the Early 1960s

A controversy over the relative real world relevance of a simple quantity theory of money model and a simple Keynesian model evolved as part of the monetarist-Keynesian controversy in the early 1960s. The question was whether money or "autonomous" expenditures is a better variable to explain consumption expenditures. It eminated from a 1963 paper by Milton Friedman and David Meiselman (Ch. 5).

The simple models controversy took several twists and bore certain fruit. Among the twists (Secs. 5.3, 5.4) was its reappearance in a significant effort by Friedman to set forth his theoretical framework [136], and in Tobin's use of the simple model strategy to bring out or expose certain characteristics of Friedman's position and approach to monetary economics. The early part of the controversy gave rise to the statement of an autonomous variable as an exogenous variable. There were excursions into aspects of single and structural equations models and into autocorrelation (Ch. 5).

Several characteristics of Friedman's position are brought out in his theoretical-framework statement (Sec. 5.3) and in the Tobin exchange (Sec. 5.4): (1) a general equilibrium model underlies his overall approach: (2) he draws on Leijonhufvud in discussing the Marshallian ordering of price and quantity adjustments; (3) he relies on Tobin in bringing forth a statement on Keynes' liquidity preference model; (4) he prefers to view the demands of firms for money as a part of a production function in lieu of a utility analysis; and (5) his primary objective and that of his associates has been empirical rather than theoretical in nature. The first characteristic is quite common among monetary economists (Secs. 1.4, 2.2). The second is treated in reviewing Leijonhufvud's book (Ch. 7). The basis for Friedman's reliance on Tobin is questioned, but, in addition (Ch. 8), the ties between Keynes' liquidity preference model and his early interest in probability are viewed as evolving in different directions from those introduced by Tobin. Tobin's widely cited and accepted analysis is reviewed as depending on constant expectations, the strenuous utility axioms from game theory, and an independence (zero covariance) between the current and expected interest rate, among other things. The fourth characteristic prohibits Friedman from employing neo-Bayesian methods to explain the behavior of decision-making units of large firms, because such an analysis combines probabilities with utility analysis rather than with traditionally viewed production functions.

Friedmanians have placed great store in the money stock as a causal factor. Others have done so to a lesser extent, introducing other determinants of business conditions. In the post–World War II years another explanation of the determinants of expenditures relative to the stock of money arose—"the substitution hypothesis of Gurley and Shaw."

3.4 THE SUBSTITUTION HYPOTHESIS

The main thesis of Gurley and Shaw—introduced earlier (Sec. 1.4), reviewed in various sources, and quoted and paraphrased by T. H. Lee—may be restated briefly. The growth of financial intermediaries (life insurance companies, savings and loan associations, and savings institutions generally) and their liabilities (money substitutes) has been a major contributor to the post–World War II rise in the income velocity of money in the United States; the growth of intermediaries and their competition with one another for the savings of households and other economic units contributed to a rise in interest rates; and these in turn contributed to a switching out of cash relative to income (or assets) into money substitutes such as the liabilities of financial intermediaries.

The Gurley-Shaw thesis is repeated (Chs. 4, 6), but others have sought different explanations of the post–World War II rise in the velocity of money. One early explanation (Ch. 4) was that the interest rate and the income velocity of money were responding to roughly the same factors, such as those operating to weaken the need for money balances for speculation and unforeseen contingencies and those to increase the certainty of prospective returns from real capital. At about the time of the appearance of this explanation, Friedman and Schwartz posited independently that the post–World War II rise was not causally related to the rise in the interest rate and that the rise in velocity was due to greater certainty. Friedman and Schwartz were observing the postwar rise after Friedman's luxury goods hypothesis (Sec. 2.2) and earlier studies had led him to predict a decline. In these contexts they brought in the role of uncertainty as the explanation.

T. H. Lee became a primary spokesman and defender of the Gurley-Shaw position in a series of papers, including a paper in the *American Economic Review*, December 1967. (Gurley was the managing editor at the time.) Sam Peltzman later (March 1969) tested Lee's position against the uncertainty type of explanation, mainly with reference to Friedman and Schwartz. He found that something of the nature of uncertainty is required to explain the post–World War II rise in the velocity of money. Jaffee comments on Peltzman's paper and brings forth additional empirical results. The uncertainty view prevails. All of this comes up in more detail in Chapter 6.

3.5   A BANKING VIEW

In Part II there is no extensive discussion of papers espousing an essentially banking view of the workings of monetary policy. Good examples of a banking view are presented separately by Warren Smith [337, 338] and Paul Samuelson [317, 318].[6] Both have referred to their views in the monetary policy area as "neo-Keynesian" or "post-Keynesian." Samuelson has discarded earlier references to a liquidity trap and the inelasticity of investment demand, as discussed along with the Keynesian building blocks (Sec. 1.3). Both Smith and Samuelson emphasize the availability of funds[7] and the velocity-interest rate relationship of the Baumol-Tobin type [337, p. 115; 317, p. 309] discussed in Chapter 4. Even so, both rely on the Keynesian investment demand mechanism.[8]

There is a tendency to illustrate the effects of changes in credit policy with special references to housing [337, pp. 108–9; 317, p. 295] and local government to some extent, despite the rather unique institutional arrangements on which the effects depend. Samuelson [317, p. 295] suggests an analogy between the interest rate and availability effects on households and industrial concerns. Smith leaves the question of the effects more open-ended, as on the new industrial corporations. But in no case are the effects on such concerns dealt with except by indirection. Their problem, consequently, would seem to be that the modified Keynesian explanation does not fit the crucial sector, so there is resort to explaining effects in the very sectors that may call for a sheltering from the effects.

Essential elements of the causal nexus as outlined by Smith [337, pp. 106–7] are: (1) the central bank intervenes through an open market purchase of short-dated governments to lower the Treasury yield curve (as

6. Ritter and Silber [309, p. 4] refer to Samuelson as a Keynesian, and they use the term to encompass the so-called neo-Keynesian views.

7. The availability of funds may be in relation to the amount sought (Ch. 15), since bank credit and especially loans tend to expand more when interest rates are rising. The availability doctrine that evolved in the early 1950s, however, holds that a rise in interest rates parallels a reduction in the availability of bank credit, widens the margin of unsatisfied borrowers, and results in the nonprice rationing of the limited supply of credit to customers by the credit-granting institutions. This latter conception of availability characterizes both Smith [337, pp. 106–7] and Samuelson [317, pp. 294–95, 314–15].

8. The mechanism is that given with reference to the capital value (mythical price) and supply price (Secs. 1.3, 2.2). It is a common part of the banking view and used readily in Federal Reserve publications to illustrate the effect of the interest rate [402, pp. 135–37]. An essential ingredient in the Keynesian and banking contexts is the assumption of a zero covariance between expected returns and the interest rate, presumably as controlled by the Federal Reserve.

defined in Sec. 7.4), given an arbitrage mechanism and a "chain of port-folio substitutions"; (2) bank credit expands and yields decline as a result of this expansion; and (3) the lower yields raise the demand price for capital goods relative to their supply price and result in the production of new capital goods. As outlined by Samuelson, the essential elements involve the Keynesian building blocks [347, pp. 313–27] and five steps by which the Reserve authorities affect spending [317, pp. 294–95]. His "majority eclectic view" [317, p. 309; 318, p. 12], the one he favors, holds "(1) that *both* fiscal and monetary policy matters much, (2) that the velocity of circulation of money is induced to increase systematically when interest rates rise and make it economical for people to turn over their cash balances more rapidly, and (3) that open-market purchases which create new M for the community have their stimulating effects on spending somewhat offset by the reduction in liquid interest-bearing government bonds now held by the community." The second part of this view is found in the work of Baumol, Tobin, and T. H. Lee.

The interest rate is a focal point, and changes in its level are the means of exerting control. The money stock enters as the means of controlling the interest rate particularly in Samuelson [317], but the interest rate has a more independent existence in Smith [337, 338], all in contrast to Chapter 2. The question of whether the interest rate or the money stock is the appropriate control variable has involved Smith and some others in discussion about the exogenity or endogenity of the respective variables.[9] In his earlier discussion Smith [338, pp. 45–46] implies that there is something in nature that determines the endogenity or exogenity of a variable, whereas in fact the applicability of the terms depends on analysis distinct from the real world—unless the model or analysis is thought to capture the essence of some natural process. In the second of his proceedings papers [337, p. 116], he does not use the term "endogenous," but the implications are clear. The Federal Reserve controls the interest rate fairly directly in his short-run, banking framework. The money stock, on the other hand, is highly endogenous as it responds to changes in interest rates. Wallich comments on Smith's choice of targets [364, p. 129]:

9. George Horwich attempts to argue that money is the most endogenous variable because observed changes in money stock are affected by factors other than Federal Reserve actions. This paper, "Money is the Most Endogenous of Variables," was read before the money and banking breakfast of the Midwest Economics Association in Minneapolis, April 19, 1968. In the paper, Horwich is reviewing Hendershott's book (Sec. 2.2).

I note his ringing declaration that he prefers interest rates to money supply. I find myself of two minds, although I think I can sort out these two
minds. The argument that interest rates are the right target to look at because that is how the transmission mechanism works is not compelling.
If interest rates are highly endogenous, if money is less endogenous, then
money may be the better target. At first sight, one would think that interest rates are extremely endogenous, money less so. This is not quite
certain, however. If the Federal Reserve can be expected to respond as
a policymaker to conditions in the economy, then everything the Fed does
becomes endogenous.

Smith's positions on the endogeneity of the money stock and the interest
rate's effect on home construction are also outlined in his textbook [336,
pp. 233–34, 295, 306, 308, 319–20]. His argument on the endogeneity of
the money stock would follow very much that attributed to Hendershott
(Sec. 2.2), and his position on policy actions and instruments [336, p. 295]
is essentially the earlier one of Teigen (Sec. 2.2) and Goldfeld (Sec. 2.2).
Without defining "Keynesianism," Smith says the textbook is "unabashedly
Keynesian" [336, p. ix]. Examination of it reveals a predominantly Keynesian stance and common Keynesian attributes. One finds the Keynesian
building blocks as outlined earlier (Sec. 1.1), and analysis of these leads to
the IS–LM model. Even when more elaborate treatment is given to compensate for the "shortcomings" of the model [336, pp. 316–22], the contribution is essentially Keynesian. Monetary policy works mainly through the
interest rate, with a decline following from an increase in the money stock
or open market purchases [336, pp. 236–37, 317–18]. There are "feedback" effects [336, pp. 237, 246, 321], with a rise in income causing interest rates to rise, but only a part of the decline in interest rates is counter-
acted, as in a similar treatment by Teigen [347, pp. 19–20]. Even the
Keynesian inclination toward a large-scale, structural equations model of
the Federal Reserve–MIT vintage (Ch. 14) is present [336, pp. 204–5, 316
(n. 34)]. One finds an a priori argument suggesting little interest elasticity
of investment demand and even a liquidity trap [336, pp. 117, 204, 226,
234, 236, 260–61, 307, 316–22, 333–36], but when the Federal Reserve
model is introduced with lags, then interest rate effects are found [336, pp.
204–5].

Work by Hamburger of the Federal Reserve Bank of New York (Sec.
15.2) is cited on lagged interest rate effects [336, p. 318 (n. 38)]. The
interest rate effects, as just described, work through portfolio adjustments
[336, pp. 317–18], with an emphasis on switching between money and
bonds. There is the entire Baumol-Tobin emphasis on an economy of scale

in transactions and the interest rate as a determinant of the demand for money and thus the velocity of money [336, pp. 205, 219–22, 227, 228–34, 261]—all as critically reviewed in Chapter 4.

On other occasions in Smith's textbook, levels are treated rather than rates of change in stock and flow quantities, and the term "equilibrium" (Sec. 2.2) means nothing but a mathematical solution to an equation system, whatever may have been intended about the existence of any balancing of forces [336, pp. 10, 92, 102, 175, 236, 238, 249, 252, 254, 268]. In addition, autonomous investment and the multiplier play traditional Keynesian roles [336, pp. 236, 240], and adjustments occur in output rather than prices [336, pp. 91, 317, 114]—all as considered in Chapter 5.

Finally, expectations about future economic conditions come in, but there is an absence of any price expectations effect on interest rates, especially simultaneously on interest rates and the marginal efficiency of capital. The role of expectations in a discussion of the term structure of interest rates is lucidly presented [336, pp. 280–93]. Nevertheless, there is no evidence that the managerial units share in the formation of these expectations. Despite numerous references to expectations [336, pp. 110–13, 171, 222, 234, 242, 252], they are simply independent of the fabric of analysis.

3.6   AN IMPACT OF THE COMPUTER

The impact of the computer as a device for analyzing masses of data is everywhere evident in a redirection of monetary economics in the 1960s. It might be characterized by an increased emphasis on potentially verifiable relationships involving state-of-mind variables, behavioral relationships, and the general study of expectations. Simple income expenditure and quantity theory mechanics were initially emphasized in the early empirical work of the 1960s; but by the late 1960s an emphasis on changes in rates of change, probabilities, extrapolative "push" effects, pull toward normality, common trend, and so on was widely evident. Nevertheless, the subject is an overwhelming one, and the simple constructs may linger on, suggestive of partial relationships in a complicated world or as aids to our memory. This would be instead of serving as explanations of some crucial aspects of economic behavior, at least from a policy point of view. In emphasizing anticipatory aspects of economic behavior (Ch. 8), rates of change in the money stock and related aggregates are especially relevant, but the money stock hardly appears as a single determinant of business conditions. Rather it seems to operate along with other factors by some expectational mechanism, such as is illustrated by its possible tie with rates of change in prices and the influence of the latter on interest rates and prospects concerning the flows of returns from capital expenditures.

Explanations of business conditions phenomena—with emphasis on anticipatory aspects of economic behavior—stress the use of neo-Bayesian methods and the introduction of probabilistic weighting schemes (Ch. 8). General equilibrium theory, money, the consumption function, the investment multiplier; these are all present. However, the "push" effects that series share, pulls toward normality, subjective probabilities, probability weighting schemes for group decision-making situations, learning from the past and changes over time, and notions about probability weights and coalescing of opinions; these are all introduced. The latter are especially important in explaining turning points in business conditions and the varying duration of expansion phases of business conditions.

Learning, along with the mechanism whereby opinions become more reinforcing as they coalesce, provides some explanation of the speed with which some anticipatory series adjust. The learning and coalescing mechanism also provides some explanation of the timing of the adjustment of some anticipatory series relative to other measures of business conditions. Entire cycles, phases, or even trends may be anticipated and learning may occur, such that adjustments take place that are more complicated than quarter-to-quarter responses to imbalance between "actual" and "desired" magnitudes or imbalances in "supply" and "demand" prices for capital goods.

Insofar as long adjustment or cyclical phases are concerned, these adjustment mechanisms imply the prospect of either a relatively quick reversal of the direction of changes or a sluggishness in the ability of economic units to give effect to their desires. Neither may be sufficiently characteristic of the real world to serve as a guide to policy formation. For example, there is the prospect that the policy-maker simply may decelerate the growth of the money stock relative to the desired stock, and thus redirect business conditions in some fixed lag pattern, without influencing the desired stock. Another prospect is that the direction of the flow of capital outlays may be changed by raising (lowering) the interest rate and thus raising (lowering) the demand price for capital goods relative to the supply price, without simultaneously affecting the supply price. There is more about lags in policy and its effects in Parts III through V.

3.7 SUMMARY

These questions are raised for resolution in later chapters. Nevertheless, there are suggestions concerning their resolution. Monetarists like Friedman do not always place as much reliance on the money stock as some believe, and the more contemporary Keynesians are not as simple-minded about the role of fiscal policy and interest rates as some others believe. Friedman's research objectives and those of his associates were more largely empirical than some anticipated. They were primed for the impetus given to empirical work by the modern computer. Under its impact, state-of-mind explanations begin to come to the forefront. One—greater certainty about the future as an explanation of the post–World War II rise in velocity—conflicts with the substitution hypothesis of Gurley, Shaw, and Lee. Quite possibly there is a middle ground between the household sector and the more industrialized sector. Even so, Friedman's introduction of Tobin's liquidity preference model seems rather strained, particularly in view of its reliance on constant expectations (Keynes' short run).

In the modern period, the strictest Keynesian view relying on the liquidity trap and the interest inelasticity of investment demand gets modified. Essential aspects of the Keynesian (or banking) view linger on, such as the focus on the interest rate and the supply side of bank credit and money. Modifications include an emphasis on the availability of credit, explanations of effects on housing and municipal government sectors, and the Baumol-Tobin explanation of the velocity-interest rate association. These efforts at bolstering the Keynesian mechanism simply strain it. There is no positive approach to the effects of policy on modern industrial concerns with emphasis on planning. Here anticipations and their probabilistic weighting come to the forefront. Simple rises and declines in interest rates in the Keynesian (or neo-Keynesian) framework are inadequate to explain parallel movements in the velocity of money, the variation in the duration of expansion phases, and turning points in business conditions.

4

Some Aspects of the Demand for Money

4.1 INTRODUCTION

As STATED in Section 1.2, two areas of monetary economics have received particular attention since the dissemination of the modern computer: the demand for money and monetary policy. The two are interrelated but the former and the velocity-interest rate association provide the theme for this chapter. The explanations for the association have some basis in the catalogue of models in Section 1.4. Two of the main potentially conflicting classes of explanations of the post–World War II rise in velocity—the financial intermediary and expectational classes—are re-examined in Chapter 6. Earlier evidence from investigations is cited now and some later evidence is reviewed in Chapter 6.

The precomputer studies of the demand for money include those by A. J. Brown, Avram Kisselgoff, and Henry Latané [126, pp. 7–8]. Those of the first two appeared in 1939 and 1945, respectively, and were motivated mainly by Keynesian liquidity preference analysis (Sec. 1.3). Indeed, Keynes' liquidity preference building block is important in most of the studies of the demand for money.

The Brown and Kisselgoff studies reported a direct relationship between the velocity of money [the ratio of income (Y) to the stock of money (M), usually defined to include currency and demand deposits adjusted] and the interest rate, as implied by Keynesian analysis (Sec. 1.3). That is to say, given the money stock as constant (or as controlled by the monetary author-

Note: This chapter is based on a lecture given at Clemson University and published in their *Review* [118, pp. 1–29]. It drew mainly from an earlier book, *The Demand for Money* [126], where over one hundred references on the subject may be found. The original book is frequently cited, a few references in the original lecture are brought forward, and a few references are added.

ity) a rise in the interest rate induces a greater effort on the part of economic units to reduce money balances in relation to income, such that income and therefore the income velocity of money increases along with the interest rate. Brown and Kisselgoff, as did Martin Bronfenbrenner and Thomas Mayer after them [126, Ch. 4], seemed to suggest that they had actually identified a liquidity preference function—that is, that observations of values for the money stock (M) and for the rate of interest (r) were such that the fit of a line to coordinates for the observations revealed a decreasing demand function for money balances [M = f(r), df(r) / dr < 0]. Brown also introduced other possible determinants of the demand for money, including the preceding year's change in the price average as a measure of the expectation of appreciation or depreciation in the purchasing power of money. Irving Fisher and others had earlier speculated about the effect of price-level changes on interest rates, and the role of price-level changes has received considerable attention since then, during the revival of interest in monetary policy [140, 141, 169].

Latané, in the first of two related papers, avoided any sort of explanation for the velocity-interest rate association and simply reported results from two regressions. First he regressed proportionate cash balances (M / Y) on the reciprocal of the interest rate (1 / r) and then he reversed the regression. He later extended his results [126, Ch. 5] and the form of the regression changed somewhat. Even so the net result indicated that the velocity of money and the interest rate are closely associated and percentage changes in the one variable parallel approximately equal percentage changes in the other. Still later Latané updated his results in two sources [245, pp. 408–9; 246, pp. 333–35]. Using his equation from earlier work, he estimated yields on Aaa corporate bonds and noted a continuation of a close relation between his estimated yields and actual yields, except for some noticeable departures in the early and late 1960s. In the early 1960s observations were below the estimates and in the late 1960s observations were above estimates.

As cited elsewhere [126, p. 112; 246, p. 334], Carl Christ replicated Latané's earlier results about 1963. He said, "as the years went by, I plotted the new data on Latané's graph, and something happened that is very remarkable in the brief history of econometric equations: the new points were closer to the regression line than the points of the sample period." Christ even suggested a causal relationship,

(1.1)
$$\Delta r \rightarrow \Delta \left(\frac{Y}{M}\right)$$

Defining a change in monetary policy as a change in the interest rate (Δr), he suggested that with the money stock constant the monetary authorities could increase velocity (and thus income) by increasing the interest rate.

There have been two schools of thought about the relationship between money and interest rates in the Keynesian tradition. One is the relationship between the interest rate and velocity as introduced above. The other, as set forth in greater detail later, is analysis in the Keynesian tradition, with a traditional banking view, whereby the sequence of causation runs from an increase in the money stock to a decline in interest rates to a rise in income,

(2.1) $\Delta M \rightarrow - \Delta r \rightarrow \Delta Y$

In the one instance, an increase in the interest rate causes an increase in income in relation to the money stock. In the other, a decrease in the interest rate causes an increase in income. These conflicting thoughts appear later in this chapter. They gain significance when one recognizes that (1) changes in the interest rate and the velocity of money parallel one another over periods of changing business conditions, (2) turning points in the interest rate and the velocity of money roughly coincide with one another and with turning points in business conditions, and (3) the most rapid increases in the money stock have occurred during periods of rising interest rates, at least before the changes coinciding with Arthur Burns' arrival at the Board (Sec. 2.1).

Christ has noted that Latané's statistical results implied a demand function for money such as,

(3.1) $M = f(r, Y)$

This is a common way of denoting the Keynesian demand function, but discussion of it usually proceeds in very "slippery" *ceteris paribus* terms, in which the several variables are not changing simultaneously as in the real world. Furthermore, the velocity-interest rate relationship may be more completely specified as follows:

(3.2) $\ln \left(\dfrac{Y}{M} \right) = \alpha + \beta \ln r$

where ln denotes a natural logarithmic transformation of variables (and a change in the transformed variable times 100 is a percentage change) and where, in accordance with statistical results, $\beta \approx 1$, and the variation in either of the variables accounts for 86 percent or more of the variation in the other. Equation (3.2) may be rewritten, after taking the logarithm of the velocity ratio and rearranging terms,

(3.3) $\ln M = \beta_0 + \beta_1 \ln Y + \beta_2 \ln r$

Multiple regression results for equations of the latter form have been surveyed elsewhere [126]. They are said to be consistent with the velocity-interest rate association and with the notion that percentage changes in velocity roughly parallel percentage changes in the interest rate. In view of occasional covariation in income and the interest rate as formerly surveyed, allowances for such variation must be made in assessing the meaning of the values for the regression coefficients. Even so, previous results would seem to be consistent with the notion that as a first approximation the regression coefficients in equation (3.3) are approximately one, after the allowance for the distorting results from covariation in the "independent" variables. This is also called the problem of multicollinearity (Appendix to Ch. 1).[1]

Numerous statistical results support the notion of a strong velocity-interest rate association [126]. These follow from analyses of (1) aggregate data, (2) annual data, (3) quarterly data, and (4) sectoral data. The association is perhaps among the few in economics that approaches the scientific status of an empirical law. One can even take a relationship such as (3.2) and perform numerous algebraic operations. For example, both income and money stock can be divided by population to get per capita income and per capita money balances, both income and money balances may be divided by the price level to get measures for real income and the real money stock, various averaging procedures may be applied to the variables, and logarithms of quotients and products may be taken to get various multivariate equations. Perhaps a chief merit of statistical results for equation (3.2) in such transformed fashion is the additional support they provide for the velocity-interest rate association, although some of the transforming operations will alter regression coefficients if not the high coefficients of determination.[2]

1. Occasions may also arise where the role of special institutional changes will need to be assessed. For example, the nature of the money supply may change, and controls over interest-rate ceilings on non-demand deposits may distort the otherwise routine patterns of shifting between demand and other deposits as well as shares in savings and loan associations.
2. Lee's *American Economic Review* study is an example of such additional support for the velocity-interest rate association. See the upper half of his Table 1 [247, p. 1172].
An additional study by Starleaf [342], involving the exotic demand-supply partial adjustment models and the use of distributed lag formulations, also seems to reaffirm the velocity-interest rate association. For example, Starleaf concludes [342, pp. 158–59] that (1) the usual formulation of the money demand-supply partial adjustment mechanisms make no sense, since "in the short run, the demand for money changes by a multiple of a change in the money stock," (2) thus, models

Variables other than income and the interest rate have been introduced in money demand functions. There has been some discussion of which interest rate should be included in the demand function. With respect to a Friedman demand relationship, Allan Meltzer concluded that population was a poor predictor [126, pp. 132–34]. Also, Meltzer and Richard Selden —Friedman's own student—have concluded [126, pp. 130–34, 141–49] that Friedman's luxury-goods hypothesis as applied to the demand for money is a poor predictor of the post–World War II rise in velocity. The luxury-goods hypothesis suggests that money is a luxury for which quantity demanded increases more than in proportion to income or wealth (income velocity declines).

In their defense of the luxury-goods hypothesis, Friedman and Anna Jacobson Schwartz say that greater certainty about the future (a weakening of the motive for holding money as means of dealing with unforeseen circumstances) could explain the post–World War II rise in velocity [126, pp. 118–21]. They say, further, that Latané's interest rate explains too much and that the post–World War II rise in interest rates may have reflected expected changes in prices. Later, in his presidential address and a related paper, Friedman emphasized rates of change in prices (an expectations surrogate) to explain changes in interest rates of the cyclical and post–World War II secular variety [140, 141]. In the analysis, Friedman introduces the variant of Keynes' liquidity preference building block (Sec. 1.4) and becomes partly Keynesian in that an acceleration of the growth of money stock initially lowers interest rates [compare sequence (2.1)] and, following some lag in its effect over time, contributes to the prospect of inflation, and thus to a rise in interest rates.

Warburton [365] is also among those who have attributed the post–World War II rise in the velocity of money (his "rate of use of money") to influences on expectations. He makes special adjustments in his measures for income and the money stock (Sec. 10.4) and relates the rise in velocity from 1950 to 1965 to inflation (and to the absence of cyclical downswings in final product prices). In particular, Warburton [365, p. 130] expresses the view that the Employment Act of 1946 and the alertness of the Government in dealing with recessions affected the attitude of business policymakers. "That," he says, "has been described as looking over the valley,

---

are reformulated and tested along with distributed lag models, and (3) test results indicate that "the demand for money is a function of past as well as current values of income and interest rates." Now, since money itself can be shown to be a function of its current and past values, one is left with results very suggestive of equations (3.2) and (3.3).

and to an accentuation of the tendency (previously observed) for business executives to be complacent about a decline in sales and output believed to be temporary and therefore uninclined to take compensatory action by offering better terms to customers." Reactions to initial final product prices, moreover, compound price changes. "Demands of organized labor in contract negotiations, and adjustment of various annuity and pay scales to cost-of-living index" are noted.

Other works appearing in the 1960s [120, 126] mention the prospect of factors operating simultaneously on both the interest rate and the velocity of money. These correspond to such expectations variables as (1) certainty about future development, (2) prospective price-level changes, (3) other factors affecting prospective returns such as the tax credit and accelerated depreciation. In such a framework of simultaneous effects, accelerating the growth of the money stock may mitigate a decline or contribute to a rise in both velocity and the interest rate but does not necessarily require a greater percentage change in income than in the money stock. There are still lags in relations between time series, but they may be adjustments to sustainable growth rates for the stock and flow variables in question rather than or as well as lags in the reaction responses to money stock changes. Hence, some differences come to the forefront and are brought out in Section 4.2 in a review of some alternative theories.

The money demand equations have had great appeal. For example, they suggested the prospect of reducing the demand for money by increasing the interest rate (with the money stock constant), so as to bring about increases in velocity and income (and thus, the level of employment, and so on). The following question arises, as in the case of Christ's discussion: how could the monetary authority change the interest rate without changing the rate of change in the money stock? To answer, one may suggest the following factors, all of which would operate on other variables as well as the interest rate: (1) an "open mouth" policy (announcements), (2) reports giving rise to the prospect of inflation or deflation, and (3) actions and reports conducive to a feeling of greater certainty about future development.

Much discussion has centered about the appropriate interest rate to be included in the money demand functions [126, pp. 87–89]. Some analysts have emphasized the role of the long-term interest rate as on government or corporate Aaa rated bonds. These emphasize the additional relationship to real capital investment and the greater prospect of capital gains and losses on long-term securities. Others emphasize a short-term rate or point to a vector of all interest rates as being most ideal. Lee has even emphasized a differential between the yield on savings and loan association shares and the yield on money such as demand deposits ("the negative of service charges" on demand deposits), although this differential is probably highly correlated with the yield on the shares and other comparable rates. Still another analysis [120; 126, Ch. 11] has emphasized changes in the level of rates (as indicated by a long-term rate) and changes in the structure of rates (as indicated by the spread between the short- and long-term rates and as discussed in Ch. 13), particularly as a surrogate for changes in the relationship between present and expected rates. In view of strong interrelationships between the market rates and the tendency for turning points in the structural changes to coincide with turning points in velocity and long-term rates [120, n. 28], the selection of any particular rate is probably of no great empirical matter as far as the velocity-interest rate association is concerned, since changes in one rate can be translated in terms of another.

The notion of simultaneous effects on the velocity of money and the interest rate may be enlightening and useful for policy purposes. Nevertheless—given the analysis and the interrelationships between changes in variables, changes in the structure of interest rates, and reinforcing ideas about expectations, corporate liquidity, and capital budgeting [119]—the idea of simultaneous effects and accompanying analysis brings to the forefront a specter of multicollinearity. The specter looms especially large as it may relate to the development of more complicated, multi-equation, least-squares regression, special-purpose models. The Federal Reserve–MIT model [85] has been such a model, at least in its initial conception. In addition to other complications as noted later, reinforcing ideas about planning and capital budgeting by industrial corporations and differences in their liquidity structure have created difficulty for the analysis of related time series and ideas about simple linkages between the time series. These and other matters are dealt with in additional detail in Section 4.3. The monetary research and policy implications of the analysis of the velocity-interest rate association and of setting it side by side with analysis concerning a Federal Reserve–MIT model are set forth in Section 4.4.

4.2   EXPLANATIONS OF THE VELOCITY–INTEREST RATE ASSOCIATION

In the mainstream of the economic literature there have been two principal explanations of the velocity-interest rate association: one following from the Keynesian liquidity-preference building block or from the Hicks-Hansen IS–LM analysis, and the Tobin or Baumol-Tobin explanation centering about economies in the transactions demand for money. To these some may add a third, the substitution hypothesis of Gurley and Shaw [247, p. 1169]:

"that liquid assets such as savings deposits at nonbank financial institutions are close substitutes for money and, therefore, that the demand for money depends on interest rates on nonbank intermediary liabilities." A fourth explanation lurks in Milton Friedman's analysis of factors affecting the interest rate [140, 141], and a fifth alternative is implied in still other sources [120, 126].

Outlines of these various explanations follow in this section. First, however, the Keynesian building blocks (Secs. 1.3, 2.2) are drawn upon.

A sequence of causation has commonly been associated with these building blocks;

$$(4.1) \qquad \Delta M \rightarrow - \Delta r \rightarrow \Delta I \rightarrow \Delta Y$$
$$\underset{\Delta B_c}{\uparrow} \qquad \nearrow \quad \nearrow$$

where ΔM is a change in the money stock, Δr is a change in the interest rate, ΔI is a change in investment, ΔY is a change in income, and ΔB_c is a change in bank credit (a change in the total of bank loans and investments). This sequence, especially as amended with the change in bank credit, has characterized economic thinking about monetary policy and has characterized a banking view of linkages with respect to monetary policy. As modified, the sequence shows bank credit and money both changing with the change in money, and it shows possibly the changes in bank credit and money operating simultaneously to lower the interest rate and subsequently raise income. The bank-credit appendage to the sequence suggests that changes in bank credit as well as the interest rate may influence investment expenditures by business firms, in accordance with a traditional banking view.

The sequences shown thus far are adequate for illustrating the direction and thrust of changes. As shown, however, they are not adequate either theoretically or practically as representative of changes in the real world. There, as introduced in Section 2.2, one may concern himself with rates of change in the stock and flow quantities and with changes in the levels for interest rates and prices, except in special instances where the price-level changes may serve as surrogates for expected price-level changes. Using rate of change notation as suggested, sequence (4.1) would more appropriately be denoted

$$(4.2) \qquad \Delta \frac{1}{M} \frac{dM}{dt} \rightarrow - \Delta r \rightarrow \Delta \frac{1}{I} \frac{dI}{dt} \rightarrow \Delta \frac{1}{Y} \frac{dY}{dt}$$

Hicks-Hansen IS–LM analysis.—The Hicks-Hansen IS–LM analysis has been presented in numerous sources. The present source is Samuelson's

Economics [320, Appendix to Ch. 18], because of the role attributed to
him earlier (Secs. 1.1, 3.4). As the label suggests, the analysis consists of
an investment-saving (IS) curve and liquidity-money (LM) curve. These
are set out on an income-interest rate plane, with income on the horizontal
axis. The IS-curve slopes downward and to the right, so that when the
interest rate is lower investment and income [and therefore saving, recall
$S(Y)$] increase. An autonomous shift in investment (Sec. 5.2) is a shift in
the IS-curve. The LM-curve slopes upward, so that when the interest rate
is higher behavioral units are "coaxed" more into securities, so that income
rises in relation to a constant money supply, as suggested by liquidity
preference analysis.

Now, an increase in the money supply will shift the LM-curve to the
right so as to lower the interest rate ("initially" the text says) and raise
income. Factors contributing to increases in investment and expenditures
generally will shift the IS-curve in the same direction, and quite possibly
from a 1960s vantage point inflationary prospects from accelerating the
growth of the money supply may shift the IS-curve in such a direction. To
be sure, the IS–LM analysis synthesizes many things, and Samuelson's text
says it provides "a definite and general theory of the velocity of money."
The theory is general, but a commonly accepted assumption is that a rising
interest rate on bonds or debt assets contributes to a rise in velocity, as by
coaxing "people more into securities and out of money."

Thus many analysts have viewed a direct variation in velocity and bond
yields as confirmation of a testable hypothesis implicit in Keynesian, IS–LM
or Hicks-Hansen analysis [126, Chs. 4–8]. Many also have noted negative
interest-rate coefficients and positive income coefficients in a regression
equation of the form of equation (3.3) as confirmation of such an interest
rate effect.[3] Such evidence is insufficient for two reasons: (1) the multiple
regression coefficients add nothing more than a reaffirmation of what is
already known about parallel movements in the velocity ratio and interest
rates, even after the performance of certain operations on the numerator
and denominator of the ratio; and (2) the theory calls for switching into
debt assets (or non-cash form of liquidity) in relation to income (or assets)
as well as out of money balances in relation to income. Where such evidence has been examined, as in Chapter 15 in the case of the important
sector of manufacturing corporations, rising interest rates have not been
accompanied by an increase in non-cash forms of liquidity.

The Baumol-Tobin explanation: economies in the transactions demand

---

3. For an example that is not covered in Frazer [126], see Lee [247].

for money.—The Baumol and Tobin analyses are in complicated static form [126, Ch. 8]. In most discussions or applications of them, business firms have been emphasized. Potentially empirically verifiable notions that have been associated with them are: (1) as economic units increase in size, economies in the transactions cost of bonds (or similar non-cash liquid assets) occur such that money balances are reduced in relation to sales (the sales-to-cash increases) or asset size, and non-cash liquid asset holdings increase in relation to size; (2) as interest rates rise there is further inducement to buy bonds, and hence an increase in the sales-to-cash ratio (a surrogate for income velocity in the case of business firms).

The first notion has been used in testing to mean simply that sales-to-cash ratios will rise as sales (or asset size) increase at a moment in time, as in the case of the analysis of cross-section data for business firms. The second has been interpreted to mean that the velocity of money (or sales-to-cash ratios) will parallel movements in interest rates over time, as in the liquidity-preference analysis. More recently Lee [247] finds negative interest rate coefficients and positive income coefficients, after analyzing time-series data and, in effect, using an equation of the form of equation (3.3), and after performing certain averaging operations on variables and the numerator and the denominator of the velocity ratio implicit in the equation.[4] He concludes [247, p. 1169], "the present study also reveals a plausibility of the Baumol-Tobin-Whalen hypothesis . . . of economies of scale in holding cash for transactions and precautionary purposes."[5]

Quite certainly there are economies in large transactions that can be determined by observing data for cost by size of transaction. There are other economies in the management of cash balances and non-cash sources of liquidity that would follow from the notion that firms must reach a certain size to justify the employment of an expert financial manager. Moreover, as manufacturing corporations increase in asset size beyond 10 million dollars, sales-to-cash ratios rise, government security holdings (or non-cash liquid assets) increase more than in proportion to size, and bank loans (a liability) increase less than in proportion to asset size (Ch. 15).

However, the objections to the Baumol-Tobin hypothesis or previous tests of the hypothesis from cross-section data are severalfold: (1) the tests do not distinguish between economies in transactions costs and those in the more rapid turnover of money balances (high sales-to-cash ratios);

4. Lee's principal interest rate measure is the yield on savings and loan association shares minus the yield on money (the negative of service charges on demand deposits at commercial banks).
5. E. L. Whalen has been a principal spokesman for the Baumol-Tobin approach.

(2) estimates show that the costs of non-cash forms of liquidity far exceed the economy from faster turnover of balances [119]; and (3) tests have not recognized relatively low levels of bank indebtedness as a source of liquidity and as a determinant of the demand for money, as emphasized elsewhere [119] and in the alternative model of Section 1.4.[6] All of these difficulties abound in tests of the Baumol-Tobin hypothesis [119; 126, Ch. 7]. In a recent study, Vogel and Maddala [342] conclude that "a strong argument can be made for economies of scale in money demand." Moreover, in focusing on the transactions demand for money and the Baumol-Tobin analyses specifically, Sprenkle [340] makes several points: (1) differences in the decentralization of cash management and the timing of receipts (or payments) make large differences in optimal cash holdings; (2) large balances are held to pay for bank services; (3) cash balances of large firms vary with economic conditions and with the least lag (in comparison with the balances of households); (4) the received transactions models explain very little.[7]

In addition to the difficulties with Lee's tests and conclusions with respect to time series and the Baumol-Tobin hypothesis, there is the major objection mentioned earlier—that the theory calls for switching into non-cash forms of liquidity in relation to income (or sales or assets) as well as out of money balances. In this respect, non-cash forms of liquidity have grown less than in proportion to sales over the post–World War II years as interest rates have risen, at least as far as manufacturing corporations are concerned (Ch. 15). There was the prospect of some switching between kinds of non-cash liquid assets as interest rates on non-demand liabilities of banks increased in the 1960s, which would be especially germane to Lee's thesis, but Lee does not consult such evidence from the time series.[8] There

6. Relatively low levels of bank indebtedness, with unused lines of credit and so on, permit the use of bank loans as a source of funds on short notice. Such a source is a substitute for holding relatively large sums of government securities as a source of non-cash liquidity.

7. There is a segment of literature on transactions cost and the demand for money that differs substantially from that presently criticized (that which treats the greater turnover of cash balances as an attempt to economize on cash as interest rates rise and provide alleged inducement for holding more bonds). It does concern, however, the interrelationship between the real and monetary sectors of the economy, and in one instance offers reinforcing notions about the turnover of money balances, expectations and uncertainty, about the public's willingness to accept bank deposits as money, and about the immense convenience and economy in using bookkeeping entries as money (Sec. 2.3). This literature is treated later (Appendix to Ch. 7).

8. Papers by Lee have appeared prior to the one listed below [247]. These earlier papers are discussed elsewhere [126, pp. 274–84].

is even the prospect that the household sector of the economy is especially sensitive to yields on shares in savings and loan associations (possibly in conjunction with the advertising of those yields),[9] but Lee does not make an explicit distinction between the behavior of the broad groups implied in his analysis of aggregate data.[10]

Friedman and the interest rate.—Attention has previously been directed toward pro-cyclical movements in the velocity of money and the interest rate. Now an additional set of changes from Section 2.4 may be introduced, along with an analytical notion of Irving Fisher's introduced in Section 1.4. In the first instance, turning points in the rate of change in the money stock have historically led turning points in business conditions and thus in interest rates—on the average and before Burns' arrival at the Board (Sec. 2.1)—with the cyclical downturn lagging the maximum and the upturn lagging the minimum rate of change in the money stock. Fisher's notion is that the nominal interest rate is the sum of a natural rate and the expected rate of change in prices.[11]

Now with the foregoing facts and the analytical notion, a regression of the rate of change in interest rates would be expected to yield the best fit for lagged values of changes in the rate of change in the money stock, at least as far as the relationship between the rate of change in the interest

9. One may be inclined to agree with the view of Lydall, a Britisher, in assessing the sensitivity of households (as distinct from the expert cash managers of large firms). With reference to households and his fellow Britisher, Lydall said [253, p. 9], "I think Keynes was inclined to assume that his own speculative interests were shared by all relatively well-to-do persons. Such evidence as we have, however, suggests that the great majority of owners of assets have no speculative reactions to changes in the rate of interest, or indeed, to other aspects of the situation."

10. After emphasizing cash management of a type that characterizes the modern industrial corporation, Lee asserts—on the basis of what amounts to no evidence at all—the following [247, n. 13]: "Friedman et al. explain the postwar rise in velocity with the ad hoc argument of the public's favorable economic expectations. . . . Instead, it can be argued that a more efficient cash management with the increasing attractiveness of non-bank intermediary liabilities is responsible for a reversal after the war of, what Friedman et al. call, the secular velocity decline."

A specific objection to these comments is that the sector most typified by expert cash management has not experienced a rise in non-cash liquidity as required by Lee's thesis, even during the period to which he confines his study [119, 120, 126].

11. Fisher was analyzing the Gibson paradox [169, pp. 13, 22–23], so-called after an early analyst rather than the Gibson cited in the references. Both were concerned with the empirical tendency for prices and interest rates to move together. The covariation was thought to be paradoxical because the theory prevailing at the time held that interest rates must be low to stimulate investment spending and a higher level of prices. The term "Gibson paradox" is said to have been coined by J. M. Keynes. The phenomenon of rising interest rates and prices is said to have been called the "Ricardo-Tooke conundrum" before Keynes.

rates and the change in the rate of change in the money stock is concerned. Indeed, such are the findings of William Gibson from regression analyses of monthly data for the post–World War II period [169].

Drawing on the above facts, the Fisher notion, and Gibson's and others' results, Friedman concludes [140, 141] that the acceleration in the money stock following the minimum rate of change during the contraction of business activity causes first a decline in the interest rate and then, after a three-to-nine or average six-month lag, a rise in the interest rate. The rise follows because of an expected rate of change in prices of goods and services. Accelerating the growth of the money stock is then said to contribute to a rise in contrast to traditional analysis [compare with sequences (2.1) and (4.1)].

Friedman translates the conclusions above into a Keynesian liquidity preference framework (Sec. 1.4). In particular, real balances (M/P) demanded are said to be a decreasing function of the interest rate [141, pp. 14–15]. As the price level (P) rises the real balance ratio declines (with the money stock constant) and the interest rate is pushed upward along the liquidity preference function. Gibson achieved the same effect by retaining nominal balances in the conventional liquidity preference model and requiring that the liquidity preference schedule shift further to the right than the money supply schedule to achieve a higher interest rate.[12] Carrying the analysis in this direction, even after dividing both the money stock and income variables by the price level, also suggests a parallel movement in interest rates and the velocity of money. The growth of income at a faster rate than the money stock provides for the shift in the liquidity preference function and the increase in the interest rate.

There is no criticism of the mechanics of these relationships, but two other points are involved. Friedman refers to open market purchases, as does Gibson [169, pp. 11–12], to illustrate that with an increase in the demand for money-market instruments their prices would be bid up and interest rates would decline.[13] But this simple open market operations approach to determining interest rates was questioned earlier (Ch. 2) and

12. The exercise in question appeared in the June 1967 version of Gibson's paper as it was presented at the Federal Reserve Bank of Chicago. In his later version [169, pp. 17–18] Gibson has the liquidity-preference curve and the money stock shifting by equal amounts so that the income effect "obviously just balances the liquidity effect." The latter exercise would appear to be inconsistent with the facts about the velocity-interest rate association, but one cannot be sure about the way in which income enters the implied equation for the liquidity-preference curve.

13. This would be in view of the well known inverse relationship between the prices of non-new issues of bonds and market interest rates.

even the notion of a determination of yields by a simple supply-demand quantity mechanism is challenged later (Ch. 13). Also, when velocity is declining, as in a recession, the decline is characteristically described as caused by an excess of desired over actual balances. The idea is that adjustments are taking place in the portfolio positions or asset structures.

Thus the criticisms of the analysis are as follows.[14] When the Federal Reserve intervenes in the market with open market operations they may also be conducting defensive and arbitrage operations, buying a little and selling a little to achieve a market condition. These defensive operations may be considered exclusive of or in combination with cyclical stabilization objectives. If you have portfolio imbalances at the time of intervention in the adjustment processes, then these must be considered in lieu of arbitrary assumptions about static conditions. If desired balances are already in excess of actual balances, increasing the actual balances should mitigate the decline in income velocity and interest rates. Friedman's lags in effects may be too long in this type of consideration and in Fisher's model below. In addition, publicity attached to changes in the rate of change in the money stock in the present-day economic environment is likely to shorten the effects on expectations. Some have said that the behavioral units are good quantity theorists and readily extrapolate announcements of excessive growth in the money stock into a future of rising prices. George Mitchell notes that "some of the monetary lags are short," and "the effect on expectations is immediate." Friedman too says that an "announced" jump in the rate of change in the money supply could possibly have an immediate effect on interest rates [141, pp. 16–17].

A substitution hypothesis.—Tong Hun Lee cites evidence resulting from regression analyses of annual data. This, he says [247, p. 1179], supports "the substitution hypothesis of Gurley and Shaw." The analyses in question are linear, following logarithmic transformations. Logarithms for annual averages of monthly data for the money stock (defined, first, as per capita currency and demand deposits in real terms and, then, as the latter plus commercial banks time deposits in real terms) are regressed on logarithms for a variety of averages; an average of per capita net national income, and such yields as those on savings and loan association shares and four-to-six month commercial paper, each minus the yield on the money serving as the regressor. In addition to the income measure and, later, a lagged value for the money stock, regressions include each of the average yields separately, in pairs, and then all together.

---

14. See comments on Friedman's paper [141, pp. 47–48].

The growth of savings and loan associations in the 1950s and early 1960s has been widely publicized, but this would not necessarily be reflected from a comparison of regression coefficients, even for uncorrelated interest rates. The interest sensitivity of households to yields on savings and loan shares in relation to other yields, as suggested by Lee, could be affected by the publicity given to such yields and the public's access to the savings and loan associations. Possibly households do find savings and loan shares better substitutes for money than commercial paper and common stocks, but these concessions to Lee's evidence from the time series are not the same as the acceptance of interest rate changes as a major cause of changes in the demand for money. There is more on this later (Ch. 6).

An alternative explanation.—As brought out later (Ch. 15), facts about the behavior of some time series for manufacturing corporations include the following: (1) sales-to-cash ratios (a surrogate for the corporate manufacturing sector's contribution to the income velocity ratio for the whole economy) and yields such as those on high grade corporate bonds are highly correlated; (2) the regression of the sales-to-cash ratio on the bond yields, following the logarithmic transformations of data, results in a regression coefficient such that percentage changes in the ratio roughly parallel percentage changes in the bond yields; (3) the regression of the ratio of non-cash liquid (marketable) assets to bank loans (another potential source of funds on short notice) on the bond yields fails miserably to reflect increases in non-cash liquidity as interest rates rise; and (4) average growth rates for sales, money balances, and non-cash liquid assets, over years as recent as the 1953–66 period of rising interest rates, reflect increases in the sales-to-cash ratio and declines in non-cash liquid assets and bank loans as a source of funds on short notice in relation to sales and/or total assets. Facts about the liquidity structure of firms at moments in time (from analysis of cross-section data) include these [119, 126]: (1) cash balances and bank loans increase less than in proportion to asset size; (2) non-cash, marketable liquid assets increase more than in proportion to asset size; and (3) sales and asset size are highly correlated with sales increasing in proportion or more than in proportion to asset size.

Now, both of the above sets of facts are significant because they suggest that parallel changes in the time series for the sales-to-cash ratio and bond yields are not linked simply and directly, with the latter causing the former, and that the rise in the yields on bonds (or debt assets generally) does not contribute to switching, as from cash to government securities. These suggestions contrast with notions emanating from conventional liquidity-preference analysis, and with explanations or remarks by Baumol and Tobin,

Gurley and Shaw, and Tong Hun Lee. In other words, some firms hold more cash in relation to sales (or size) than others, others hold more liquidity in non-cash forms in relation to sales (or size), so that parallel movements in the sales-to-cash ratio and rates on debt assets are inconsistent with the widely stated idea that the sales-to-cash ratio rises predominantly because of a form of switching from cash to interest-yielding, non-cash forms of liquidity.[15]

So much for the present for the foregoing inconsistency! So much too for the previously mentioned explanations for parallel movements in the velocity of money and interest rates as they apply to the important corporate manufacturing sector! The presently noted inconsistency, of course, would not apply to the Friedman explanation outlined earlier which depends on expectations about price-level changes and lags in responses to changes in the rate of change in the stock of money. The alternative to all of the foregoing explanations has been developed mainly as it would apply to manufacturing corporations, but it is suggestive of somewhat similar behavior for households, at least as far as the velocity-interest rate association is concerned.

Features of the alternative explanation are varied. For one thing, expectations theories account remarkably well for changes in the structure of interest rates, as emphasized later (Chs. 12, 13) and as indicated by the spread between the yields on long- and short-term rates of interest. Also, as emphasized later (Chs. 13, 15) and as embodied in a principle labeled equality of foresight, the expectations of the managers of industrial corporations are responding with the same sensitivity to the same factors that shape expectations in the financial markets, only the prospects of business firms concern prospective returns on additional capital outlays and variations in the proportions of broad classes of assets such that the sales-to-cash ratio (a velocity of money component) is the counterpart to the interest rate in the financial markets. Business firms maintain liquidity and vary it in response to degrees of uncertainty about unforeseen needs, in response to prospective price-level changes and such, and in response to the anticipated need for funds to carry out planned capital outlays (Ch. 15). Some firms, depending mainly on their size, plan more for future needs and conditions and maintain more liquidity than others. Liquidity is a luxury in the sense that it costs firms more to maintain relatively high levels of liquidity than to earn returns on additional capital. The more liquid firms have

15. Similar cases [119] have been made for parallel movements in inventories and bank loans, and for parallel movements in government security holdings (or non-cash marketable-type liquid assets generally) and federal tax liabilities.

higher sales-to-cash ratios at a given time, but the dollar and cents savings from turning over cash more rapidly are more than offset by the cost of maintaining additional liquidity, that is, holding additional non-cash liquid assets and so on. Even so, liquidity has its advantages and those of relatively larger asset size who can afford it do maintain it.

There is abundant emphasis on expectations as determinants of interest rates, and on the ratio for the income velocity of money as mentioned above and on later occasions. Friedman has emphasized expected price level changes as a determinant of interest rates. He and others have also related greater certainty about the future to the turnover of money balances. The present analysis emphasizes greater certainty, expected price level changes, tax credits, and so on as determinants of both the velocity of money and the interest rate. For example, both the prospect of inflation and an increase in the tax credit (the government credit against tax liabilities for expenditures on additions to plants and equipment) increase the prospective returns on additional capital expenditures, and both contribute to higher interest rates. The prospect of inflation contributes to higher interest rates because the market discounts rates of changes in prices in determining market rates, and the tax credit contributes to higher rates because it creates the prospect of higher returns on capital and therefore on the means of financing capital expenditures.

Statistical results from regressing the velocity of money on the interest rate or from regressing the money stock on income and the interest rate, following logarithmic transformations of the data, reflect very high correlations and excellent linear fits. They cannot reflect a simple and direct causal relationship between money demand and interest rates for reasons given. Quite likely both the velocity of money and interest rates are responding in large part to the same factors. Some of these are shocks from outside factors (such as changes in the tax credit or the outcome of a presidential election with accompanying prospects of more or less inflation) that operate, say, after the sample period for estimating regression coefficients. The effect of these factors would ordinarily nullify the applicability of the estimates to a future or prediction period, but amazingly the outside factors have maintained some stability in the relationship in question. This is amazing on two counts: (1) it is consistent with the present analysis of the demand for money, and (2) the analysis poses serious difficulties for certain types of econometric models, as introduced below (Sec. 4.3) and as reviewed in Chapter 14.

Keynesian and Fisherian adjustment processes.—While not dealing with the demand for money directly, Zwick [388] deals with aspects of the adjustment path and process of adjustment of the economy to monetary changes. There are some complications, mainly as brought out in the appendix to this chapter. The market and demand for bank credit may be distinguished from that for money, although money arises in the process of expanding bank credit [120, n. 11].[16] Zwick benefits from making this distinction at times, but when convenient he makes it obscure. However, his conclusion is of interest in the context of this chapter.

Although focusing on the supply of and demand for bank credit, Zwick seeks to distinguish two effects: (1) a direct effect of an expansion of bank credit on interest rates, and (2) an indirect effect working via an increase in the demand for bank loans. The first effect is said to be Keynesian, and pushes the interest rate downward. Zwick sees it as working through an expansion of the money stock in the IS–LM model. The second effect is said to be Fisherian, as in Fisher's two asset model (Sec. 1.4), and the credit expansions alter prospects to increase the demand for bank credit in the form of loans (money?) and to raise interest rates. Zwick's final interpretation [388, pp. 93–94] is that both direct and indirect responses are present. Credit expansion and the accompanying expansion of the money supply do not necessarily reduce the interest rate.

The decline in interest rates works from an expansion of the money stock and a substitution of bonds for money (as switching into additional bonds at the margin). The Fisher effect would operate simultaneously to thwart the decline in the interest rate. Thus, the decline would never show up in the data that are needed to estimate the presence of the effect. On the other hand, the Fisher effect would presumably not thwart the switching into bonds, since a rising rate coaxes switching into bonds in the IS–LM analysis.

The effect of an increase in the supply of money in the Fisherian framework on output and prices is direct.[17] Prices lag in their upward adjustment and this—rather than an imbalance with the mythical prices of Sections 1.4 and 1.5 and any strengthening of the push effect—gives rise to the excess in demand for goods, "causing inventories to fall and businessmen's expectations about future sales volume to rise." Continuing, Zwick says [388, pp. 80–81], "the lag in the adjustment of prices . . . causes loan de-

16. The motive for wishing to increase and carry an additional liability in the form of bank credit is not the same as that for wishing to hold a larger money balance. As emphasized in the appendix, in obtaining credit, money may arise coincidentally and strictly as a medium for exchanging an acquisition of credit for the acquisition of a non-money asset.

17. Some readers may wish to compare Zwick's interpretation of interacting Keynesian and Fisherian analyses with the analysis of firms' demands for securities and bank loans in Frazer [126, pp. 212–13].

mand by business firms to rise not only in equal proportion but in *greater* proportion than the initial increase in the supply of bank credit." Interest rates are said to rise above the initial level because "the percentage increase in the demand for loans exceeds the percentage increase in the supply of loans."

As brought out later (Ch. 15), changes in bank reserves and bank credit in no way follow in phase with changes in bank loans by significant groups of manufacturing corporations. The role and pattern of bank loans to business firms and the demand for bank loans seem to have changed considerably from Fisher's day and from the analysis posited by Zwick. Even so, the analysis of the direct effect of credit and money stock changes on output and prices is relevant.

4.3   THE FEDERAL RESERVE–MIT MODEL AND THE VELOCITY–INTEREST RATE ASSOCIATION

Research involving large scale structural equations models was made especially enticing by the initial impact of the modern computer, which is examined in Chapter 14. This section simply poses the possible conflict between aspects of analysis in this chapter and in the early structural equations models. To some extent the section also anticipates discussion of exogenous variables and structural equations in the appendix to this chapter and in Chapter 5.

The main structural equations model with a policy emphasis that emerged under the initial impact of the computer was the Federal Reserve–MIT model. In its January 1968 form [85] it contained sixty-five equations. A forerunner to it contained fifty equations. Both models had as their special objectives the quantification of the effects of changes in monetary policy (or monetary policy instruments) on the economy. The idea, as expressed in a preliminary paper by Ando and Goldfeld, was to establish linkages and trace out effects resulting from such policy measures as "open market operations of the traditional type," changes in the "reserve base," and changes in required reserve ratios. As stated later by De Leeuw and Gramlich [85, p. 11], "the major purpose is to be able to say more than existing models about the effects of monetary policy instruments—both in themselves and in comparison with other policy instruments." Most of their efforts have been concentrated "on the treatment of financial markets and on the links between financial markets and markets for goods and services."

Such linkages research with so-called "structural equations" models has seemed ambitious, given (1) the unsatisfactory state of estimation techniques when applied to economic time series, particularly intercorrelated series of the type discussed in this chapter and (2) the emphasis by some on research with respect to operations in the tradition of the "art of central banking" as a means of better understanding the influences on price-level expectations of market participants, and influences on "state-of-mind" variables generally. Thus, this section deals with the idea of a large-scale, special-purpose, policy model—as distinct from an actual model of the Fed–MIT type with all of its special problems and uses of estimation techniques. In doing so, the idea of such a model is contrasted with the monetary policy and methodological implications of the analysis of the velocity-interest rate association thus far.

A structural equations model.—A structural equations model contains more than one equation. It should be expected to have as many endogenous variables as behavioral equations, and a sufficient number of exogenous variables. The endogenous variables are determined within the model—that is, a solution to the system of equations (or a reduced form) may be obtained for any of the endogenous variables in terms of the estimated parameters of the models and the exogenous variables. An exogenous variable (one not determined by the model proper)[18] can be controlled, as in the case of a given change in member-bank reserves, to contribute to a change in an endogenous variable. Such a change operates through a given reduced form with estimated parameter values and exogenous variables. In general, the parameter values are assumed to be independent of one another (have zero covariance, as in Ch. 1, n. 7), with no outside factors operating to change them or the probability structures associated with them, as time passes from the estimation period to the forecasting period. Such presumably is the nature of linkages between changes in policy instruments and changes in endogenous variables (including goals or targets of policy changes).

Single equation models or single equations of the structural equations model may also be used when the value of a "dependent" variable is predicted from changes in the so-called "independent" variables, given estimated coefficients. In tracing out causal linkages, the estimated coefficients are assumed to be given along with their probability structures, as in the case of the reduced form equations for the structural model. Equally important for policy purposes, the estimated coefficients in the right-hand member of the regression equation [note equation (3.3) in Sec. 4.1] are

18. The definition of an exogenous variable is actually quite restrictive in terms of the strenuous assumptions it makes about the stochastic structures implied by least-squares regression analysis [71, pp. 156–57].

assumed independent of one another. In other words, the variables accompanying the coefficients are uncorrelated and have zero covariance. This, however, is a strenuous requirement in light of what has been said about covariation in the variables discussed in this chapter. In fact, the endogenous variables of a structural equation model are themselves "jointly dependent" and special methods must be used to deal with covariation in the variables, as noted below.

Models for policy purposes may be used for tracing out causal linkages (forecasting the effects of a particular policy change) or for forecasting generally. The first makes greater demands on a model, notably that of stability in the underlying probability structures and zero covariance in the "independent" variables in the case of the single equation model. In that case, the policy use of the model requires that the regression coefficients in an equation such as (3.3) be read as if they actually reflect the separate effects of the accompanying variables. The covariation or correlation in the so-called independent variables may not interfere with forecasting generally. At least this would be true when the same forces are operating in the estimation and prediction periods, and as long as no separation of specific effects is sought.

The simple equation for the velocity-interest rate association.—A relationship between the income velocity of money and the interest rate is discussed throughout this chapter. Changes in the two variables are said to reflect responses to common factors, in large part. Moreover, the respective variables are said to relate to a whole host of other changes. The changes in velocity, for example, are related to financial planning, capital budgeting, capital expenditures (and therefore national income and employment), the demand for money, and changes in non-cash forms of liquidity, including marketable security holdings and bank loans (as indicated in Ch. 15). Changes in the interest rate are related to changes in the structure of interest rates, expectations theories about changes in the structure, shock effects, and changes in state-of-mind variables such as uncertainty and prospective inflation. Consequently, intercorrelation in the velocity of money and the interest rate can be viewed as relating to intercorrelation in a whole host of time series. The analysis then holds serious implications for the prospect of separating effects of policy instruments on other variables when there is so much outside interference and intercorrelation.

An objective with a single equation or a structural equations model is to add enough equations and enough variables to assure that the endogenous variables are determined within the model, given fairly reliable coefficients in the reduced form equations. More equations are called for when endogenous variables are responding to shocks from outside the systems. The process of adding equations can be endless [71, pp. 157–58], given the state of methodology in the 1960s and an economy responding to factors of the type emphasized in this chapter.

The problem of multicollinearity may arise in either a single or a structural equations model. In the first instance, two or more of the so-called "independent" variables are correlated. This problem may be dealt with by adding equations and variables to account for the covariation in the independent variables, since the covariation or multicollinearity implies that additional variables are at work. In either instance, the method calls for reduced form equations for the particular interrelated variables. Parameters in the reduced form equations with exogenous ("predetermined") variables are then estimated and the equations are used to estimate new series for the intercorrelated variables. The new estimated values are then used in the analyses rather than the original observed series. Such a method is known as that of two-stage least squares [71, pp. 432–46]. The application of the method, however, involves strenuous assumptions, and, unless these are satisfied, the method may not remove the initial deficiency. In discussing the demand for money, de Leeuw has reported that "ordinary least squares and two-stage least squares often seem to give similar relationships for results."

4.4   SUMMARY

A number of interrelated themes have been stressed, including: (1) the demand for money with emphasis on a single-equation model (or variants of that model); (2) the prospect of roughly simultaneous changes in the velocity of money and the interest rate in response to common factors, including changes in "state-of-mind" variables such as the uncertainty of future prospects and expected price-level changes; (3) the notion of lagged relationships in economic time series that may result from the destabilizing effect of unsustainable growth rates in the stock and flow variables such as money and income (and therefore unsustainable levels in interest rates, prices, and employment); and (4) the presence of differences in the liquidity structure of firms such that parallel movements in their sales-to-cash ratios and in interest rates on debt-type financial instruments cannot be said to be causally related. However, the stressed themes also include: (1) the demand for money with emphasis on regression results for a single-equation model and a causal sequence such that accelerated growth in the money stock causes interest rates to decline, presumably exclusive of seasonal and defensive operations on the part of the Federal Reserve; (2) the notion of a fixed lagged response such that the acceleration of the growth of the money stock would exert a price-expectations effect only after a lag of three to six months; (3) the problem of viewing the regression coefficients of a single-equation model as a reflection of the separate effects of changes in inter-related "independent" variables; (4) the need for the enlargement of a single-equation policy model when multicollinearity exists; (5) a possible means of separating the effects of intercorrelated variables in structural equations and other models; and (6) the use of "large" policy models in establishing causal linkages as distinct from their use in forecasting.

In effect, the two preceding groups of interrelated themes are juxtaposed. Analysis and facts concerning the first group suggest impediments to the successful use of the methods implicit and explicit in the second group. For example, the possibility of shock effects operating on a host of interrelated real and "state-of-mind" variables suggests the presence of multicollinearity in single equation models of the demand-for-money type, and it suggests the difficulty of obtaining a large econometric model with sufficiently stable underlying probability structures to facilitate an accurate tracing of causal sequences. Conversely, the likely presence of multicollinearity in single equation models and the likely presence of unstable probability structures and the need for an increasingly large number of equations in the large, special-purpose, policy model, all suggest support for the validity of the first group of themes.

5
Simple Quantity Theory and Income Models

5.1 INTRODUCTION

FRIEDMAN AND MEISELMAN (hereafter, on occasion, FM) presented one of a number of papers initiated by the Commission on Money and Credit (CMC) in the late 1950s [153].[1] The paper was a product of studies at the University of Chicago (Workshop in Money and Banking) started almost a decade earlier. It used simple models to emphasize the essence and relevance to the real world of one approach as distinct from another, and the CMC paper precipitated widespread controversy. With the passage of time and probably an increase in the capacities of economists, the level of methodological discussions was escalated, as indicated in this chapter.

The simple models seemed to be useful in emphasizing the main aspects of an approach or point of view. In fact, they were used by Friedman in a major 1970 paper [136] in which he states his approach to monetary analysis, shows diverging aspects of quantity theory and income expenditure models, and introduces unresolved problems and an approach to their solution. The simple model technique was also used by James Tobin in a 1970 paper [353] to bring out certain characteristics of Friedman's approach.

The widespread controversy precipitated by the initial FM paper had some interesting side issues and revealed some tangible evidence of the impact of the modern computer on economic analysis. The side issues centered about (1) the evolving distinction between single (and reduced form) equations and structural equations, and (2) a definition of an auton-

---

1. The CMC was established in 1957 as a private, nongovernmental organization to initiate studies of the United States monetary and financial system. The studies were later published for the Commission by Prentice-Hall, Inc. The volume cited in the text is one among a number of volumes containing the CMC studies.

omous variable. The relevance of money in economic analysis was demonstrated and later viewed on a more equal footing with fiscal policy.

The Friedman paper [136] setting forth his approach is important and is relevant to our study for a variety of reasons. Some economists have doubtlessly searched the literature to learn more about the position of an economist of the prominence of Milton Friedman. Those who have done so have probably noticed the inevitable absence of a complete theory, as had Allan Meltzer.[2] There were other such critics. Friedman said that his 1970 article [136] was largely a response to them.

The article and the controversy surrounding it [135] and related papers still reveal gaps, but some aspects of Friedman's position are more definite. The fragmentary—and at times almost inconsistent—nature of the theory is also brought out on occasions, including an encounter with Tobin [137, 353, 354] and other critics [135]. On the positive side, Friedman's 1970 paper indicates areas in which effort may be directed to fill gaps in existing theory, and he draws distinctions between Keynes and Keynesians, as mentioned earlier (Secs. 1.3, 1.4). He also points out a need to switch emphasis from changes in levels to some combination of changes in levels and rates of changes, as in Section 2.2.

Despite his distinctions between Keynes' work and that of Keynesians, however, Friedman draws on the work of James Tobin, a presumed Keynesian, in discussing Keynes' liquidity preference model and its ties with probability. This position of Friedman's is emphasized again—in Chapter 8, the analysis introduced by Tobin is shown to have had different origins from Keynes' probability, and to depend on cardinal utility axioms.

Also in Chapter 8, probabilities are combined with utilities in discussing the behavior of firms. Friedman views firms in the perspective of production functions and the ultimate owners of wealth. Theses matters centering about the saving-investment sectors are regarded by Friedman as "unfinished" business [135, p. 919].

Another point brought out in Friedman's 1970 paper and in Tobin's and others' encounters with him is the largely empirical character of Friedman's orientation toward monetary economics. On occasions Friedman has described himself as essentially an empirical scientist. This is not surprising, although some economists have persistently questioned it, possibly in part because of their view of Friedman's early interests in the Marshallian demand curve [147, pp. 47–94], fully flexible exchange rates [147, pp. 157–

---

2. See a discussion of Meltzer's review and Friedman's theory in Frazer [126, Appendix to Ch. 6].

203], and the theory of price.[3] Apparently, what separates Friedman and his more vociferous critics is the absence of a common methodological point of view [135, pp. 906–7, 908, 921, 925, 933] as elaborated in Section 18.3. In part because of this absence, this book gives special attention to methodological distinctions. They are crucially related to one of the theses of the book—that the empiricists were to carry the day in the 1960s in economics, largely under the initial impact of the modern computer.

Some of Friedman's asides on methodology bear listing [135, pp. 908, 920, 921, 925]:

> Keynes was no Walrasian seeking . . . a general and abstract system of all-embracing simultaneous equations. He was a Marshallian, an empirical scientist seeking a simple, fruitful hypothesis.

> In this view [Marshall's] "Economic Theory . . . has two intermingled roles: to provide 'systematic and organized methods of reasoning' about economic problems; to provide a body of substantive hypotheses, based on factual evidence, about the 'manner of action of causes.' In both roles the test of the theory is its value in explaining facts, in predicting the consequences of changes in the economic environment. Abstractness, generality, mathematical elegance—these are all secondary, themselves to be judged by the test of application."

> From a Walrasian approach, "abstractness, generality, and mathematical elegance have in some measure become ends in themselves, criteria by which to judge economic theory. Facts are to be described not explained . . ."

> The long-run equilibrium in which, as I put it, "all anticipations are realized" and that is determined by "the early quantity theory plus the Walrasian equations of general equilibrium," is not a state that is assumed ever to be attained in practice. It is a logical construct that defines the norm or trend from which the actual world is always deviating but to which it is tending to return or about which it tends to fluctuate.

The empirical emphasis helps explain Friedman's rise to prominence in the decade in which the modern computer was exerting its initial impact on monetary analysis. The empirical emphasis is also consistent with Friedman's long-standing ties with Arthur F. Burns and the National Bureau of Economic Research,[4] and with Burns' work on business cycles in particular.

3. For an outgrowth of this early interest, see Friedman [144].
4. Friedman was a member of the research staff at the National Bureau as early as 1937. Burns was an associate of the Bureau's founder, and was the Bureau's Director of Research (1945–53), President (1956–67), and Chairman of the Board (1967–68). He had a long tenure as a professor at Columbia University, and served as Chairman of the Council of Economic Advisors in the 1952–56 period. In 1970 he became Chairman of the Board of Governors (Sec. 1.1).

An essential feature of Friedman's research on money, according to him, is an explanation of the tendency for the economic system to overshoot, to generate cycles in business conditions.

5.2   MONETARY VELOCITY AND THE INVESTMENT MULTIPLIER

The initial paper and others bearing on the controversy precipitated by FM are reviewed here and in the next section. They center about three independent studies appearing in 1964–65, and a fourth appearing in the early 1970s [237]. One of the studies in the first group was by Donald D. Hester [198], another was by Albert Ando and Franco Modigliani [14] (hereafter, on occasion, AM), and another by Michael DePrano and Thomas Mayer [87] (hereafter, on occasion, DM). These studies and the discussions surrounding them reflect what one may call a first generation impact of the computer. As Section 5.3 reveals, the discussion escalates to one about structural equations models and fairly exotic bits of method. This may be viewed as a second generation impact.

In their first jointly authored paper, FM [153] set out to test a simple version of the quantity theory of money against a simple version of Keynesian income expenditure theory. The procedure was (1) to regress consumption expenditures on the money stock (C = a + bM), as indicative of a simple quantity theory model; (2) to regress consumption expenditures on autonomous expenditures (C = a + bA), as indicative of simple Keynesian income expenditure theory; and (3) to compare the results to determine the extent of the correspondence of the central concepts of the two theories to experience. There were also multiple regression analyses with both the money stock and autonomous expenditures as "independent" variables to facilitate a comparison of partial regression coefficients.

The correlation coefficient for the simple consumption-money stock relation for the entire 1897–1958 period was 0.98, and for the consumption-expenditure relation it was 0.76. Annual data were used for this longer period, and quarterly data were used for the postwar period, 1946–58. Conclusions were based primarily on results for short sub-periods. FM, as later revealed, had experimented with lagged as well as contemporaneous relationships, and with first differences for the variables as well as for their levels. The first-difference correlations were later brought forward and published in the FM reply to Donald Hester [152].

A major part of the controversy over the FM study centered about the definition of autonomous expenditures and the merits of testing such simple models. These aspects of the controversy and related methodological issues are reviewed below. In particular, Hester, AM, and DM all appeared to hold and defend more moderate Keynesian positions than the one tested by FM. During the period of controversy all generated additional statistical results. The overall results of the analyses of data and the controversy would appear to give support to the FM position that the consumption-money relation was more relevant to experience and more stable.[5]

FM recognized that all economists embracing a Keynesian approach might not place the same emphasis on monetary and real phenomena, and consequently on the simple money and income expenditure approaches. Thus, they note that the issue is empirical. It concerns judgments [151, p. 761; 153, pp. 168–69] about "which set of relations in the more generalized theoretical system is (a) critical in the sense of being in practice the primary source of changes and disturbances and (b) stable in the sense of expressing empirically consistent relations which can be depended on to remain the same from time to time."

FM appear to be justified in advancing their version of the simple income expenditure approach and in focusing on the empirical question, which is the second of the foregoing issues. They are supported by the increasing recognition of the breadth of views about Keynes' work and by the distinction drawn between Keynes' economics and Keynesian economies (Secs. 1.3, 3.2; and Ch. 7). As indicated (Secs. 1.3, 3.2), the Keynesian model is characterized by the income expenditure, fiscal policy, liquidity trap oriented model found in U.S. textbooks in the 1950s and 1960s.

FM described a central feature of simple income expenditure models [151, p. 767]:

> The central feature of simple income expenditure models is that they distinguish between two categories of expenditures entering into the income stream: [1] expenditures that are closely linked to (induced by) current income flows, and [2] expenditures that are autonomous, not in the sense of being random or arbitrary or unexplainable but simply in the sense of not being determined by current income flows. This distinction between induced and autonomous expenditures—not that between consumption and investment—is fundamental. The tendency has arisen to use the term "consumption" as synonymous for "induced" because of the empirical judgment that consumption (or, better, changes in consump-

---

5. In their final rejoinder, AM do not concede this conclusion [13, p. 768], but they note agreement on two conclusions: (1) that the simple correlation tests could not be expected to throw light on the relative importance of variables in question in the determination of output and employment; and (2) that the outcome of the tests did not indicate greater stability for either the consumption-money or consumption-autonomous expenditure relation.

tion) is predominantly induced and, conversely, that the bulk of induced expenditures consist of consumption.

The simple aggregate-supply-demand building block of the Keynesian tradition may be stated as follows, using symbols for induced (U) and autonomous (A) expenditures:

Aggregate
demand: $Y_d = U + A, U = f(Y)$ A = const.

Aggregate
income: $Y \equiv U + S, S = f(Y)$ $\dfrac{dY}{dY} = 1$

Equilibrium: $Y = Y_d$ or $U + A = U + S$

Investment (A)
equals saving (S): $A = S$

Now the movement in the equilibrium point (denoted by coordinates $\overline{Y}_d$, $\overline{Y}$) and changes in income (changes in Y) result from shifts in investment (shifts in the constant A), so consumption (induced expenditures, U) may be treated as a function of income [$U = f(Y)$] or as a function of autonomous expenditures [$U = f(A)$].

If one views consumption (U) as a simple linear relationship with income (Y), then

$$U = \beta + \alpha Y, 0 < \frac{dU}{dY} = \alpha < 1$$

Substituting for U in the demand equation,

$$Y_d = \beta + \alpha Y + A$$

Then, given the equilibrium condition,

$$Y = \beta + \alpha Y + A \qquad \overline{Y} = \frac{\beta + A}{1 - \alpha}$$

By the quotient and other rules,

$$\frac{dY}{dA} = \frac{1}{1 - \alpha}, \alpha = \frac{dU}{dY}$$

This is the formula for the sum of an infinite geometric progression. It is also of the same family as R. F. Kahn's famous public works or employment multiplier [218], and the inspiration for Keynes' multiplier (Sec. 1.3). A change in autonomous or government expenditures was supposed to have a multiple effect on income. However, simply to estimate a correlation coefficient for income (Y) and autonomous expenditures (A) was to correlate a part of a variable with itself, (since $Y = U + A$). So FM choose instead to correlate consumption (the induced or U portion of income) with autonomous expenditures.

As FM assert in their reply in the *American Economic Review*, no essential complications are introduced by further subdividing the autonomous component of income in the above equations. They also show that the demand equation above and the consumption relation can be viewed as reduced form expressions for more complicated models [151, n. 18 and p. 768]. According to FM the situation becomes more complex if there are different income totals and if different components of consumption are "induced by different income totals which themselves differ by non-induced components."

The impact of the computer.—The original FM paper and related papers provide another example of the initial impact of the computer on economics. In comparing the benefits and costs of the theoretical and empirical viewpoints, one might say that the computer sharply reduced the previously enormous cost of obtaining empirical information.

The FM and related papers run a "gauntlet of tables" of statistical results that would have been impossible to produce before the computer. In attempting to define "autonomous expenditures" or pin the concept down empirically, more measures were produced than there were participants in the controversy. All this was evidence of the looseness and imprecision of what had gone before. Finally, as FM appeared to suggest, they were led by the overall controversy to formulate more explicitly the income expenditure model of their analysis and to clarify the requirements for a comparison of the simple velocity and multiplier models.

The trend toward empirical study, as brought about in part by the computer, involves several aspects of study. Theories must be expected to generate testable hypotheses. The compatibility of a variety of theories with the same set of observations is indicative of the need to introduce more discriminating restrictions on some or more of the theories. As these aspects of study imply, the economics of an earlier time may have been accepted with greater tolerance of vagueness, emptiness of empirical content, and lack of applicability and relevance. This would partly explain why FM could label as Keynesian the crude multiplier version they choose to test and why so much controversy ensued over their study.

The definition of "autonomous expenditures."—Alvin Hansen—an early
mentor of Paul Samuelson[6] and one of the foremost American figures in the
interpretation of Keynes for the American audience—offered a concluding
word about autonomous and induced investment in a 1951 volume [186,
pp. 190–94]:

> Autonomous investment springs notably from changes in technique.
> Autonomous or independent investment (more or less independent of
> *current* sales) is opened up by inventions, new discoveries, new products,
> and new processes. Induced investment, on the other hand, is the result
> of an increase in final demand or sales volume. . . .
>   Autonomous investment is typically the spark plug that starts an up-
> ward business movement. And it has a magnified effect on income via the
> multiplier. . . .
>   A full employment boom, once achieved, rests precariously on a high
> volume of autonomous and induced investment. When autonomous in-
> vestment fades away, income falls not only by the amount of the auton-
> omous investment but also by the falling away of the induced consump-
> tion. . . .

Fiscal policy could also be brought into play to exert countercyclical, multiplier effects on income.

In defining autonomous expenditures, the narrowest concept FM considered in their initial paper was [153, p. 246]: "A = Net private domestic
investment plus net foreign balance plus government deficit on income and
product account." There were other principal alternatives considered, but
all of FM's critics objected. Hester restricted his criticisms to the simple
correlations and to the definition of autonomous expenditures. He said,
FM "have represented the autonomous expenditure theory in very unortho-
dox form." Hester then noted that FM were "fully justified in attacking the
lack of a precise definition of autonomous expenditures in most discussions
of this model."

AM said that FM failed to provide a relevant criterion to distinguish
between "autonomous" and "induced" expenditures. The criterion suggested by AM [14, pp. 697–98] was "whether or not the variable is supposed to be correlated with the error terms of the test equation to be
estimated." This seems to suggest that autonomous expenditures exert a

---

6. Hansen arrived on the campus at Harvard as Littaur Professor in the fall
following the appearance of Keynes' *General Theory* and he soon had a marked
influence on Paul Samuelson (Sec. 1.1). Samuelson [322, pp. 1123–24] lavishly
credits Hansen for the background work underlying the combined multiplier and
accelerator mechanisms. In December 1960, Hansen introduced Samuelson as President of the American Economic Association.

"shock-type" effect, and that any covariation between the error term and an "independent" variable would disqualify the "independent" variable as a proper definition of autonomous expenditures. AM repeat their specific definition in their rejoinder to FM [13, p. 787]. They say their method of specifying autonomous variables is "well known to those familiar with econometric literature." Here they were introducing the idea of a structural equations model with rank and order conditions for identification satisfied.[7] In such a context they viewed autonomous expenditures as an exogenous variable.[8]

DePrano and Mayer, like AM, tended to view autonomous investment as an exogenous variable [87, pp. 734–37], outside of a structural equations model. Investment that can be determined within the model is endogenous by definition and consequently depends on the model. A part of DM's procedure was to correlate components of the FM definition of autonomous expenditures with consumption and to show that the correlation falls as so-called "endogenous" components are added. Thus DM claimed that the success of the money-expenditure relationship in the FM tests was due to their particular definition of autonomous expenditures.

In their final reply, FM conclude [151, p. 764] that "If the concept of 'autonomous' expenditures is to be useful as something more than an incantation for the faithful and an empty box for our ignorance, then there must be some objective and operational criteria for giving it empirical content." Meiselman mentions the definition in a later paper [263]. He says, " 'autonomous' spending is understood to originate outside the usual economic calculus—a Vietnam, or perhaps a burst of spending for capital goods following technological innovation, or a change in tax rates following a conversion to a new economic ideology."

---

7. The conditions for identifying a structural equations model are highly restrictive. The whole idea is quite idealistic. The order (necessary) and rank (sufficient) conditions for identification may be briefly stated as follows [71, p. 300]: (1) Order condition—"*To be identified, an equation in a model of G linear equations must exclude at least G-1 of the variables* [including both endogenous and exogenous variables] *that appear in the model.*" (2) Rank condition—"*An equation in a linear model of G equations is identified if and only if at least one nonzero determinant of G-1 rows and columns is contained in the array of coefficients formed as follows: Starting with the row-and-column array of coefficients in the model, omit all columns not having a prescribed zero in the equation in question, and omit the row of coefficients of that equation.*"

8. The definition of an exogenous variable in the context of structural equation models is given by Christ [71, p. 156]: "*An exogenous variable in a stochastic model is a variable whose value in each period is statistically independent of the value of the random disturbances in the model in all periods.*"

Overall results, removing trends, and measures of goodness of fit.—Overall results indicated a relatively stronger consumption-money relationship. Some important evidence to the contrary, however, was provided by AM for different concepts of autonomous expenditures and for periods since 1929 taken as a whole. These included the exceptional years 1929–39, originally noted by FM as the period "that gave rise to the income expenditure theory in its present form." FM also noted that AM emphasize a long period and analyze data for 25-year periods, 1929–41 and 1947–58. FM concluded that Keynesian analysis is a short-period analysis and that results for the 25-year periods are dominated by trends, as indicated by the differences between the means for the two periods.

In their reply to FM, AM [13] (1) report results for the separate periods, 1929–41, 1947–58, and 1929–41 plus 1947–58; and (2) use "the ratio of the standard deviation of the residual error term [squared error variance, S_e^2] to the mean of the dependent variable, as suggested in FM's reply." AM preferred the squared standard error of the estimate over the correlation coefficient as a measure of goodness of fit. Also they referred to lagging the dependent variable as a means of removing trend rather than using first differences, but FM [151, p. 759] view the lagged-variable technique as less illuminating than splitting the sample and obtaining results for different periods.

On AM's use of the squared standard error of the estimate, FM comment [151, p. 759]:

> *When the dependent variable is the same*, the squared standard errors for different sets of independent variables are directly proportional to squared correlation coefficients. . . . Hence, substitution of squared standard errors for the correlation coefficients we presented would have changed nothing of substance. When the dependent variables are not the same, both correlation coefficients and standard errors are likely not to be comparable. That is precisely why we insisted that every comparison between the alternative theories should involve the identical dependent variable, both in concept and in years covered.

DePrano and Mayer presented another variety of results from analyses of data. They used different definitions for autonomous expenditures, performed regressions for levels and for first differences, and split the sample for various sub-periods of the 1929–63 period. They reported the following summary of their results [87, pp. 741–42]:

1. For the whole period excluding the war years, both autonomous expenditures as we define them and money give good fits, with money somewhat better.

2. Including the war years lowers the correlation coefficient for money to some extent and reduces the correlation coefficients for our autonomous expenditures much more.
3. For the periods before and after the war, our autonomous expenditures do better than money for first differences, while the results are mixed when the levels of the data are used.
4. For the sub-periods which include the war, money does much better than our autonomous expenditures.
5. In all periods fixed private domestic investment plus exports do extremely well. . . .
6. FM's concept of autonomous expenditures, with few exceptions, does worse than any of the other variables.

A methodological issue: single versus structural equations models.—
Hester, AM, and DM were all critical of the single equation models of FM and alluded to structural equations models. The discussion of and experience with such models, however, was more evident in the late-1960s than in the mid-1960s when Hester, AM, and FM were writing.

Aspects of structural equations models were introduced in Section 4.3. In such a context, the so-called "independent" variables in a single equation model are all exogenous in the sense that they are determined not by the model, but outside it. Whenever the error term in a single equation model is correlated with lagged values of itself, there is evidence that a more careful search will permit the introduction of one or more new variables in the equation and thus leave the error term to behave in a random, unsystematic fashion. Moreover, the variables in a reduced form equation are supposed to be free of correlation with one another if the structural equations implicit in the notion of a reduced form equation satisfy the proper restrictions. The reduced form equation consists of parameters that embody combinations of parameters from the structural equations and of exogenous and predetermined variables.

A single equation may be a reduced form or a single equation in a structure. In the latter case, there are equations for each endogenous variable as mentioned earlier (Sec. 4.3). Ideally, new variables and new equations might be added until all interrelationships in the structure are accounted for and the structural parameters are stable from period to period and thus free of shocks from outside the system, including shocks that may change two or more parameters simultaneously. There are other problems, such as may be dealt with by two-stage, least squares (Sec. 4.3).

The idea, at present, is that the methodology becomes quite complicated and success with the structural equations models may not be achieved in any ideal sense, though some [237] seem to come closer than others. One uses method as best he can, allowing for all aspects of it. To begin with, every use of regression analysis need not attempt to identify or set forth a complete system of structural equations. Often theories in economics cause one to expect certain variables to behave in certain ways or in relation to other variables. Consistency with such prospects and observations should be expected. But there is evidence of an awareness in the literature that econometric-theoretic rules need to be modified and accompanied with a priori considerations outside of econometric theory in analysis of economic behavior.

From one point of view, simple regression models may be more satisfactory, at least in providing limits to some "time" regression coefficient. In discussion at a 1968 conference, Friedman [141] posed the issue of taking account of simultaneous equations bias in the method for estimating regression coefficients through viewing a single regression equation as a reduced form equation. Simultaneous equations bias (or false estimation of regression coefficients) arises from inadequate identification of a given relationship in what should be a simultaneous equations model. To deal with irregularities, multicollinearity, or just plain shifts in the parameters of a given equation, some new variables are added and, implicitly or explicitly, some additional equations. The difficulties in this approach are twofold, as mentioned by Friedman: (1) there is danger of improperly specifying a relationship, and (2) the process of adding equations and variables may be endless. To buttress the argument about the difficulty of dealing with simultaneous equations bias, Friedman points out that many attempts to use two-stage or three-stage least squares end with the report that the results are not much affected.[9]

On the side of the single equation approach, Friedman points out that a single equation may be regarded as a reduced form equation (a solution to a simultaneous equations model). Here the identification problem does not arise. In the case of a simple regression equation, some so-called exogenous or predetermined variables may be said to be omitted. But Friedman apparently proposes to get around this and other statistical problems by estimating extreme values for the true regression coefficient in such a model. He says [141, p. 51], "one way in which I have tried to get around it [the simultaneous equation bias] in particular work we are talking about here is

9. Two-stage least squares was mentioned earlier (Sec. 4.2). Three-stage least squares is an attempt at even further improvement in the estimation technique under certain conditions [93, pp. 209–19]. Improvement under these conditions results from using information on the covariance structure of error terms in a structural equations model.

by estimating upper and lower limits rather than single values." One limit is apparently the result of a vertical least-squares fit of a line between two variables, and the other the result of an estimate of a horizontal fit (Appendix to Ch. 1).

5.3   AN ESCALATION OF METHODOLOGICAL COMPONENTS

In reaction to the studies of Section 5.2, Kmenta and Smith [237] ignore what evolved about the definition of an autonomous variable. For them it is simply a variable controlled, as are bank reserves in the bank reserve equation (Sec. 2.3). They present a small structural equations model and introduce a number of relatively exotic aspects of methods, such as impact and dynamic multipliers [93, pp. 508, 521–25] and specification error tests. They sought to estimate particular effects of changes in the money stock and in government expenditures upon the specific movements of GNP throughout a period rather than to give sweeping coverage for an entire period.

The KS findings are quite consistent with themes evolving in this book, as with respect to expectations. There is much evidence (albeit somewhat hidden) of an increased emphasis on the relevance of expectational and dynamic phenomena. This may be viewed as a response to the impact of the modern computer—the effect on the more static and received views of early empirical findings and the enhanced capacity to handle exotic aspects of method more readily. But there are some difficulties in the KS analysis, and these are mentioned below.

The structural equations model and some estimates.—KS's model contains eight equations (five behavioral and three definitional), seven endogenous variables (C, consumption; I^d, producers' outlays on durable plants and equipment; I^r, residential construction; I^i, investment in inventories; r, yield on corporate bonds; Y, gross national product; S, final sales goods and services) and five exogenous variables (G, government purchases of goods and services plus net foreign investment; L, money supply plus time deposits in commercial banks; M, money supply narrowly defined; R, time deposits in commercial banks; and t, time in quarters). The latter reduce essentially to an emphasis on two policy variables (G and M) and time trend.

The sample period for estimating the effect of the two policy variables on the specific movements of GNP is the decade 1954–63, extending from the end of the Korean War to the beginning of serious military involvement in Vietnam. Interest centers upon two equations for GNP: (1) a derived (rather than estimated) reduced form equation with current and lagged endogenous variables in, say, its right-hand member; and (2) a derived "fundamental dynamic equation" with lagged values for GNP itself as well as for the current and lagged values of the exogenous variables. The coefficients for the current values of the two policy variables (G_t and M_t) in the first equation are termed impact multipliers.

The second equation is first used to determine whether the system is dynamically stable (whether its oscillations are damped). It is then used to reveal the influence of the policy variables on the time path of GNP, following the elimination of all but the current values of GNP from the equation. The equation following from this elimination contains coefficients that are called "dynamic multipliers." For the current values of the policy variables, the "dynamic multipliers" are the same as the impact multipliers, but the remaining multipliers for the policy variables are said to indicate delayed effects of each exogenous variable on the time path of GNP. The sum of coefficients for current and lagged values of a policy variable is said to yield "the long-run or equilibrium multiplier for that variable" for a large number of lagged values.

The multipliers estimated as above from quarterly data for the decade 1954–63 are:

	Impact	*Dynamic*
Government expenditures	1.1427	1.8406
Money Supply	0.3649	1.2270
Trend	0.1035	0.6363

In KS's analysis all monetary variables were deflated by the implicit price index for consumption expenditures, but the multipliers just shown are substantially lower than those often estimated in static models or for the investment multiplier of the Keynesian model (Sec. 1.3).

The behavioral equations and some aspects of method.—In setting forth the equations for their model, KS elaborated on some additional underlying equations and reasoning. For example, in deriving their consumption equation for estimation, current consumption was stated as being equal to the sum of some proportion of permanent income, a proportion of liquid assets of the current period less the level desired in the next period, and a stochastic disturbance term. On further assumption (namely that desired liquid assets equal a proportion of permanent income) and substitution, consumption is shown to depend on permanent income, liquid assets (L), and the error term. Permanent income is then defined in terms of an adaptive expectations model, as in earlier contexts (Sec. 2.2). Applying a transformation and substituting appropriately, the consumption function for estimation is obtained.

Investment is designated in three parts (I^d, I^r, I^i)—all combined in the GNP identity ($Y = C + I^d + I^r + I^i + G$) as one of the equations of the model—and a behavioral equation enters for each component of investment. All three are based on a notion concerning the desired level of investment (I^*):

$$I_t^* = a_o + a_1r_t + a_2(S_{t-1} - S_{t-2}) + a_3t$$

Here one may observe the presence of the interest rate (a proxy for the cost of capital as KS view it), a factor emphasizing a change in sales ($S_{t-1} - S_{t-2}$), and a trend term. (An error term should be understood to be present, as in all behavioral equations.) KS view the term $a_2(S_{t-1} - S_{t-2})$, as an accelerator where investment depends on the change in sales of the past period, but it may also reflect an extrapolative push effect of recent changes in sales on expectations about future sales and returns on investment. The trend term is to take account of "autonomously" induced changes in investment, but again it may simply reflect an extrapolation of normality and some pull effect on expectations about a future return to normality.

Continuing with investment, KS assume that only a fixed fraction of the desired adjustment— $\gamma(I_t^* - I_{t-1})$ —is accomplished within a period. Allowing for the impact of this term on the change in investment, substituting the right-hand member of the desired investment equation for I^*, and rearranging terms results in the equation form used for the investment equations.

The fifth and final behavioral equation in the KS model is their demand for money equation. Since they consider the money stock as exogenous, they select the interest rate as the dependent variable:

$$r_t = \gamma_o + \gamma_1Y_t + \gamma_2M_t + \gamma_3M_{t-1}$$

The terms $\gamma_2 M_t + \gamma_3 M_{t-1}$ are thought to capture a commonly held—and, one may add, an equally commonly rejected—notion that households and firms are unable to adjust their money holdings to the desired level, as discussed in Chapter 2 and in Frazer [126, p. 164]. In any event, one observes the main ingredients of the velocity-interest rate association, with the exception of an additional lagged term for the money stock which, presumably, allows for further adjustment to the actual money stock of the last period.

Clearly—as indicated by the role of permanent income, lagged values generally, and allowance for time trend—expectational mechanisms of the type indicated in this book are present in the KS model. They are not given expectational interpretations by KS, but they are present nevertheless.

KS use three-stage least squares method in estimating the coefficients for their behavioral equations, with two exceptions. The adaptive expectations coefficient in the consumption function was obtained with two-stage least squares. An alternative method was also used to estimate the interest rate equation, but the estimates by the alternative methods were similar.

By traditional and other criteria KS's results appear satisfactory. The R^2's were high, and so on. They also used more exotic methods and subjected the model to a predictive test and a specification of error test. In the predictive test, values for the endogenous variables were predicted for eight quarters beyond the 1954–63 period, these were compared with actual values, and tests of the significance of the differences between predicted and actual values were satisfactorily met. An exception was the prediction for consumption in the first half of 1964. The tax cut in early 1964 for consumers was thought to explain the difficulty. The specification of error test used by KS applied to reduced forms. They were designed to uncover errors resulting from the omission of relevant explanatory variables, misspecification of the functional forms, simultaneous equation bias, and heteroskedasticity.

Conclusions and difficulties.—KS drew several conclusions, as already mentioned. The "long run" multipliers were lower than they are often assumed or introduced via static models. The money supply did not appear to be a more important determinant of expenditures than "autonomous" expenditures (government expenditures in the KS case). The effects of both monetary and fiscal policy (changes in M and G, respectively) were often destabilizing, and the record of monetary policy was even poorer than for autonomous expenditures. These latter conclusions were based on a quarter-by-quarter comparison of the effects of changes in the combined monetary variables (L and M) and in government expenditures, in the context of the model. In about half of the quarters the monetary variables had a greater effect, and in about half fiscal variables had a greater effect. Cumulative changes in the policy variables were shown to have sometimes produced procyclical rather than countercyclical effects.

Difficulties in the KS analysis include (1) the notion of a fixed lagged relation, (2) the absence of estimates from splitting the sample, and (3) the idea of an effect on current investment from the current cost of funds. For example, the average lag from a peak rate of change in the money stock to an upper turning point in business conditions may have one dimension, and the corresponding lag between a trough rate of change and a trough in business conditions may have another (Sec. 2.4). Also, the KS model contains an interest rate variable that was earlier shown to respond in a different pattern to the expected rate of change in prices when the sample for the 1952–68 period was split (Appendix to Ch. 1). Further, as brought out later (Ch. 15), a good bit of the corporate planning in the modern industrial state may center about financial planning to avoid the effects on investment of tight credit (high interest rates).

5.4   SOME PROBLEMS OF MONETARY ANALYSIS

In one of his theoretical papers [136], Friedman (1) surveys aspects of quantity theory and income expenditure models, including price-quantity adjustment and liquidity aspects; (2) summarizes key points of his survey by setting forth a highly simplified aggregate model and using the model to indicate major unresolved problems, as he views them; and (3) sketches a possible theoretical approach to resolving the problems. This section touches on these aspects of Friedman's paper.

The role of the aggregative model attributed to Friedman in this section has been exaggerated by some critics [135, pp. 907–9]. "This model," Friedman says, "was specifically designed to bring out the *defects* in both main approaches [quantity theory and income-expenditure]." Continuing [135, p. 911], he says that the framework in which the model appears implies variability of the lag in monetary policy, and "surely it can be taken for granted that stochastic disturbances must be added to all of the equations before they are used to interpret historical data."

Price-quantity adjustments.—Price-quantity adjustments and expectations in Keynes' liquidity preference model are among the topics of Friedman's survey. His discussion of both draws on Leijonhufvud's analysis, as reviewed later (Ch. 7).

As noted in Section 7.2, Leijonhufvud credits Keynes with reversing Marshall's adjustment process in which prices adjusted more rapidly than quantities. The prices, in fact, adjusted so rapidly that they could be regarded as instantaneous. Friedman describes the process [136, pp. 207–8]:

> An increase in demand (a shift to the right of the long-run demand curve) will produce a new market equilibrium involving a higher price but the same quantity. The higher price will, in the short run, encourage existing producers to produce more with their existing plants, thus raising quantity and bringing prices back down toward their original level, and, in the long run, attract new producers and encourage existing producers to expand their plants, still further raising quantities and lowering prices. Throughout the process, it takes time for output to adjust but no time

for prices to do so. This assumption has no effect on the final equilibrium position, but it is vital for the path to equilibrium.

Carried over to monetary analysis or the Cambridge cash balance approach to the quantity theory, Marshall's price adjustment analysis took a form in which changes in the demand and supply of money were reflected entirely in the price level. Friedman says, further, that "the quantity theorists can be validly criticized for having 'assumed' price flexibility."

Keynes, on the other hand, deviated some from Marshall. Friedman says [136, pp. 208–9] that Keynes followed Marshall in his method but deviated by reversing the roles assigned to price and quantity:

> He followed Marshall in replacing the continuous adjustment by a series of discrete steps ["comparable with approximating a continuous function by a set of straight-line segments"] and so analyzing a dynamic process in terms of a series of shifts between static equilibrium positions. Even his steps were essentially Marshall's, his short-run being distinguished from his long-run by the fixity of the aggregate capital stock. However, he tended to merge the market period and the short-run period, and . . . he concentrated almost exclusively on the short run.

> He assumed that, at least for changes in aggregate demand, quantity was the variable that adjusted rapidly, while prices were the variable that adjusted slowly, at least in the downward direction. Keynes embodied this assumption in his formal model by expressing all variables in wage units, so that his formal analysis—aside from a few passing references to a situation of "true" inflation—dealt with "real" magnitudes, not "nominal" magnitudes.

Friedman is inclined to point to Keynes' reversal of Marshall's price-quantity adjustment as being in accordance with observations in the 1920s and 1930s, however rationalized. He says, "at least in the decade and a half between the end of World War I and the writing of *The General Theory*, economic fluctuations were manifested to a greater degree in output and employment than in prices." Keynes' qualifications are noted [136, p. 210]: "At 'full' employment, he shifted to the quantity theory model and asserted that all adjustment would be in price—he designated this a situation of 'true inflation.' " Friedman points out, however, that "Keynes paid no more than lip service to the possibility" of true inflation. So, says Friedman, "it does not misrepresent the body of his analysis largely to neglect the qualification."

Keynes' reversal of the price-quantity adjustment with emphasis on quantity is seen by Friedman as "the key to the difference in approach and analysis between economists who regard themselves as Keynesians and those who do not." Friedman probably has a point in making this broad distinction, but there is more—as noted in Sections 1.3, 3.2, and Chapter 7. There is the question of the adequacy of the price mechanism as a communications mechanism. The study of communications and control in dynamic systems is mentioned in Chapter 7.

Liquidity preference analysis.—The analysis of the demand for money has evolved as a part of liquidity preference analysis. Much has been said on the subject [126], and Friedman devotes considerable attention to it in interpreting Keynes, and to some extent his followers [136, pp. 212–17]. The subject is important, however, and since Chapters 7 and 8 proceed along different lines, close attention is presently focused on Friedman's remarks.

To formalize Keynes' analysis, Friedman writes the demand function

$$\frac{M}{P} = \frac{M_1}{P} + \frac{M_2}{P} = k_1 y + f(i - i^*, i^*)$$

where nominal money balances (M) are deflated by the price level (P), decomposed into transactions and precautionary balances (M_1) and speculative balances (M_2), and set equal to the sum of some proportion of real income ($k_1 y$) and the function f. The arguments in the function are (1) the spread between the current interest rate (i) and the "expected," "normal" or "safe" rate (i^*), and (2) the expected rate. Adding the expected rate alone as an argument is especially relevant to Friedman's discussion of Keynes' long-run demand. Expectations are constant in the short run in Keynes' analysis so the expected rate (i^*) can be omitted, except insofar as its presence facilitates explanation.

The distinction between the classes of balances [$M_1/P = k_1 y$, and $M_2/P = f(i - i^*, i^*)$] need not be drawn too tightly, but presently attention focuses on the speculative portion of the balances. Analysis of them gives rise to the hyperbolic shape of the function, as described in Chapter 1 (n. 8) and Section 2.2. The "safe" rate is not shown, but, as Friedman says, the expected or normal rate may be thought of as the mean value of a probability distribution.

The choice situation depicted in Keynes' model is one of holding money or bonds (as in Sec. 1.4), and speculation is strictly over the prospect of capital gains or losses from holding bonds. The choice situation may be broadened to encompass assets with a "residual" claim (as distinct from "fixed") against future income (Sec. 1.4). In Keynes' short run (with constant expectations), however, this extension does not follow.

In the narrower choice situation the lower the interest rate (thus the larger the spread between i and i^* with $i - i^*$ negative), the greater the possibility of a rise in interest rates to some subjectively viewed norm and of a capital loss from holding the marketable bond, the value of which varies inversely with the interest rate. This possibility contributes to the demand for a larger quantity of money balances at lower interest rates and to the liquidity trap depicted in Section 1.3. For a higher interest rate, the reverse speculation follows.[10]

There is another explanation for liquidity preference, particularly recognized by Tobin [356, pp. 67–70], whom Friedman cites. It relies on differences of opinion. In brief, the first assumes a given expected interest rate on a long-term bond for individual investors, such that a rise in the current rate above the expected rate results in a switching of the entire portfolio out of cash. Where differences of opinion about the future rate prevail, individual demands are different. Even so, their discontinuous step functions can be aggregated to yield a smooth curve that relates the demand for cash inversely to the interest rate.

Some have said that the explanation of liquidity preference as relying on the normal rate involves an inconsistency—the model assumes constant expectations, but the expectation of a future change in the interest rate varies with the spread between the current and normal rates (with $i = i^*$). The demand for money depends on the extent of the expectation of a change in rates. Tobin thus treats expectations as given, and relies on differences of opinion. Another alternative (Ch. 8) is to remove the constraint imposed by Keynes' definition of the short run. Friedman, however, does not distinguish adequately between the return-to-normality and the difference-of-opinion explanations, but he relies on Tobin's analysis of the elasticity of the demand in discussing Keynes' special twist.

At low levels for current rates relative to the "safe" or normal rate, the prospects of risk in rates and capital losses are great; the demand for cash to satisfy the speculative motive is strong. Increases in the quantity of cash by the central bank would simply satisfy this demand further without leading to interest rate and expenditure changes. This is the "trap" situation as depicted in Section 1.3. Friedman, on the other hand, describes high elas-

10. This return-to-normality explanation, with the liquidity trap and all, may be found in Smith [336, pp. 333–34], where the explanation is offered as a part of Keynesian economics. Smith, one may recall, was described in Section 3.5 as a Keynesian.

Teigen, Smith's associate, suggests [347, p. 15] that Keynesians "today" (presumably, Jan. 1972) should not be saddled with the liquidity trap assumption. He mentions empirical evidence against the existence of the trap, as have others [126, Ch. 4]. Nonetheless, except for the Tobin analysis in the present section, neither the "old" nor the "modern" Keynesians have presented any revision of the liquidity preference model.

ticity of the demand for money with respect to the interest rate at i = i*
[136, p. 214]: "For given i*, he [Keynes] believed that this function would
be highly elastic at i = i*, the degree of elasticity of an observed numerical
value of i depending on how homogenous the expectations of different
holders of money are and how firmly they are held." Friedman cites Tobin
at this point.

For Tobin, any change in the rate (i) away from the expected rate (i*)
resulted in a switch entirely into money or bonds. If opinions about the
future rate were homogenous, this implied an aggregate demand function
for money with high elasticity at i = i*. As Friedman says [136, p. 214],
"Let there be a substantial body of holders of money who have the same
expectation and who hold the expectation firmly, and f will become perfectly
elastic at that current interest rate."

Tobin takes the view that the pull-toward-normality explanation received the greatest emphasis by Keynes, but that the differences-of-opinion
explanation was Keynes' original. Elements of the latter explanation are not
precluded by the former, but Tobin strains to make a distinction between
uncertainty as "disagreement among investors concerning the future of the
[interest] rate" and "subjective doubt in the mind of an individual." This
is apparent partly because Tobin's theory relies on uncertainty as subjective
doubt on the part of the individual investor. The disagreement and subjective doubt, however, may occur together (Ch. 8).

Friedman himself distinguishes most sharply between the short-run and
long-run liquidity traps [136, pp. 214–15]. "In the long run," he points out,
"i must equal i*, so f(i − i*, i*) reduces to a function of i* alone." If the
prospects of returns from capital expenditures are altogether depressed, as
in the 1930s, then the expected rate on assets other than money may become very low, possibly below the market interest rate [136, p. 215]:

> If investment opportunities were sparce, yet the public's desire to save
> were strong, the "equilibrium" rate of interest he [Keynes] argued, might
> have to be very low or even negative to equate investment and saving.
> But there was a floor to the market rate set by liquidity preference. If this
> floor exceeded the "equilibrium rate," he argued, there was a conflict
> that could only be resolved by unemployment that frustrated the public's
> thriftiness.

Friedman sees a fallacy in this argument [136, p. 215]; "The introduction
of money not only introduces a floor to the 'market rate,' it also sets a
floor to the 'equilibrium rate.' " The idea is that the two floors are identical
in the long run, apparently because society will adjust its employment and
expenditure patterns to accommodate the growth rate for the money stock.

One may accept the notion that the possible existence of the liquidity trap is a poor explanation for unemployment, as in the 1930s. Friedman says the failure of central banks in their attempts to peg interest rates at low levels has made that proposition untenable. He apparently has in mind (Sec. 1.4) that ultimately in accelerating the growth of the money stock to lower interest rates, the demand for money relative to income will decline (the liquidity preference curve will shift outward more rapidly than the money stock).

In his day Keynes accepted the notion that the central bank could control the interest rate, except in trap situations. Chapter 7 questions instead whether the central bank controls the interest rate directly or indirectly through its influence on expectations.

Friedman on firms' demands for money.—Friedman has said very little about firms' demands for money and his analyses of the demand for money have usually been highly aggregative, including all economic units. Even so, his comments in his "theoretical framework" paper of 1970 [136] should be noted. Discussing wealth or a total portfolio of assets, he says [136, p. 202], "it is important to distinguish between ultimate wealth holders, to whom money is one form in which they choose to hold their wealth, and enterprises, to whom money is a producer's good like machinery or inventories." This distinction—which Friedman has made before—has never seemed entirely clear, and the analogy to inventories overlooks unique aspects of money and the preferences of some managers for more or less risky ventures and financial structures.

Obviously firms' wealth is largely nonhuman wealth, and money must serve essentially the same functions for households and business firms, apart from differences in the size and sophistication of its management. Friedman's comments seem at times to suggest that money should be an input in a firm's production function, along with labor and capital. He has also said [136, p. 205] that "rates of return on alternative assets are, of course, highly relevant to business enterprises." In his earlier work with Anna J. Schwartz, he referred to firms' demands for money, in the language of consumption theory, as a luxury good. In any event, rates of return on assets of firms can be generated in a conceptual sense by utility analysis (or Lagrangian functions in particular), and such an approach does open the prospect of utilizing notions from modern probability in attempting explanations of the behavior of managers, particularly in the setting of the modern industrial corporation (Chs. 8, 15).

A simplified aggregate model.—To summarize key points about the distinction between simple quantity theory and income expenditure models,

Friedman presents and discusses a simple model that contains the distinct models as special cases. In the form of restatement he is bringing forward models discussed earlier in this chapter (Sec. 5.2). The more recent notation is presently used. The restatements shed minor additional light on the distinction between the two models: the Keynesian model asserts that changes in nominal income will be absorbed by output changes (rigid prices being assumed); the quantity model asserts the supremacy of price changes.

In the simple forms, Friedman favors the quantity theory version. Primarily, however, he views the emphasis on either price level changes alone or output changes alone as shortcomings. He sketches a possible theoretical approach to the adjustment process.

The sketch is intended to show how some gaps (or "unresolved problems") might be filled. The gaps, apart from the price–quantity one just mentioned, are that (1) both models deal with short-run adjustments of shifts from one static equilibrium position to another; (2) both models treat levels of prices and output, rather than changes in prices and changes in the rate of change in output, as in some modern analyses; (3) in the quantity theory model interest rates adjust instantaneously to a saving-investment equilibrium, and in the income expenditure model they adjust to equate the quantity of money demanded and supplied; (4) there is no explicit role given to anticipations, although they are given great prominence in the development of liquidity preference demand; (5) both models, as stated by Friedman, contain a missing equation (the quantity theorists deal with the omission by introducing the Walrasian equations of general equilibrium to explain output, whereas the income expenditure group introduces the more arbitrary assumption of sticky prices); and (6) neither model deals with the division of a change in nominal income in the short run, between prices and output.

Friedman's simple model encompasses the quantity theory and income expenditure models as special cases:

(1.0)
$$\frac{C}{P} = f(\frac{Y}{P}, r)$$

(2.0)
$$\frac{I}{P} = g(r)$$

(3.0)
$$\frac{Y}{P} = \frac{C}{P} + \frac{I}{P}$$

$$(\text{or, alternatively, } \frac{S}{P} = \frac{Y\text{-}C}{P} = \frac{I}{P})$$

$$(4.0) \qquad M_d = P \cdot l \left(\frac{Y}{P}, r\right)$$

$$(5.0) \qquad M_s = h(r)$$

$$(6.0) \qquad M_d = M_s$$

where, the symbols are the same as those set out in Section 2.2, except r is the interest rate and f, g, l, and h simply denote functions. As in equation (5.0), M_s can be set equal to a constant (or exogenous variable) without affecting any of Friedman's uses of the model, at least in the theory paper [136] from which it is extracted.

Friedman refers to equations (3.0) and (6.0) respectively as market clearing or adjustment equations. Equation (3.0) states the equilibrium condition whereby aggregate supply equals aggregate demand, and equation (6.0) states the equality of the quantities of money supplied and demanded. Equation (1.0) is a consumption function with an interest rate variable added. Equation (2.0) implies an investment demand schedule. Equation (4.0) expresses a liquidity preference schedule with the price level factored out of the dependent variables.

As in the FM controversy just reviewed (Secs. 5.2, 5.3), the relevant distinction between consumption and investment is described by Friedman [136, p. 218] as being "between expenditures that are closely linked to current income . . . and expenditures that are autonomous." Friedman says [136, p. 218], "The identification of these categories ["induced" and "autonomous" expenditures] with consumption and investment is our empirical hypothesis." Carrying the empiricism to an extreme, he says, "For theoretical purposes, any part of investment spending that is conditional on current income should be included with C." This of course might result in the classification of a major portion of capital spending by firms as consumption, as suggested by the KS investment relations (Sec. 5.3) where investment is partly correlated with current and past sales. Consequently in studying household and firm behavior others may prefer the "threshold of the household" view in delineating categories.

Friedman notes the presence of seven variables (C, I, Y, r, P, M_d, and M_s) in the six equation model. The way he accounts for the determination of the model by treating first one and then another variable as exogenous provides a distinction between quantity theorists and Keynesians. The simple quantity theory is said to treat income in constant prices [Y/P in equation (3.0)] as determined outside the model ($Y/P = y = y_0$). The simple income expenditure theory treats the price level as determined

$(P = P_o)$. Friedman says [136, p. 220], "It appends to this system an historical set of prices and an institutional structure that is assumed either to keep prices rigid or to determine changes in prices on the basis of 'bargaining power' or some similar set of forces." He points out that developments represented by the Phillips curve (Sec. 1.3) reflect more recent attempts to bring the determination of prices back into the body of economic analysis, to establish a link between real magnitudes and the rate at which prices change.

Substituting the right-hand members of equations (1.0) and (2.0) into (3.0), and rearranging terms creates:

$$(7.0) \qquad\qquad y_o - f(y_o, r) = g(r)$$

Equation (7.0) determines r (let $r = r_o$). Equations (5.0) and (6.0) determine M ($M = M_o$). Thus substituting these determined values in equation (4.0), gives:

$$(8.0) \qquad\qquad M_o = P \cdot l\ (y_o, r_o)$$

This determines P ($P = P_o$), but it also implies the classical quantity equation,[11]

$$(9.0) \qquad\qquad P = \frac{MV}{y}$$

Here with V constant, the price level or nominal income, P_y, is determined. The emphasis is on prices.

The income expenditure solution proceeds differently. Given $P = P_o$ rather than $Y/P = y_o$, and substituting the right-hand members of equations (1.0) and (2.0) into (3.0), gives:

$$(10.0) \qquad\qquad \frac{Y}{P_o} - f(\frac{Y}{P_o}, r) = g(r)$$

Equations (4.0) through (6.0) yield:

$$(11.0) \qquad\qquad h(r) = P_o \cdot l\ (\frac{Y}{P}, r)$$

---

11. Dividing the right-hand member of (8.0) by y_o, and then multiplying that member by y_o, gives

$$M_o = P \frac{l\ (y_o, r_o)}{y_o}$$

Replacing the factor $l\ (y_o, r_o)/y_o$ by its equivalent, $1/V$, and dropping subscripts, gives $M = P_y/V$, and $P = MV/y$.

Equations (10.0) and (11.0) each contain the same two variables (Y and r) and their solution determines them.

If the consumption function, $f(Y/P, r_o)$, is approximated by a linear relation, such as

$$\frac{C}{P} = C_o + C_1 \frac{Y}{P}$$

If the right-hand member is then substituted in equation (3.0), this creates

$$\frac{Y}{P} = C_o + C_1 \frac{Y}{P} + \frac{I}{P}$$

Solving for Y/P gives

(12.0)
$$\frac{Y}{P} = \frac{C_o + I_o}{(1 - C_1)}$$

That is, real income is the product of the Keynesian multiplier and autonomous investment.

Equations (9.0) and (12.0) are currently the important ones. Recognizing that neither model says anything about how a change in nominal income may be divided between real income and prices, one might ask of regression results whether money has more effect on income [Py as in equation (9.0)] or whether autonomous investment has more effect as implied by equation (12.0). For equation (12.0), one would not want to correlate a part of a variable (such as I_o) with itself ($Y = C_o + I_o$), so one ends up with the simple regression equations of Section 5.2.

$$C = a + bA$$

$$C = a + bM$$

A theoretical approach.—There are more unresolved problems than Friedman lists, and one may take various directions to resolve them, depending on the intentions of the analyst. A different direction is suggested in Chapter 8. Friedman himself focuses on adjustment processes that require distinctions between "actual" and "anticipated" magnitudes, such as encountered in the liquidity preference model as a "current" interest rate and a "safe," "normal," or "expected" rate. On other occasions, distinctions have been made between "actual" and "desired" quantities. In the demand-for-money context these have been related to changes in the velocity of money with velocity rising as "actual" exceed "desired" balances. Friedman himself emphasizes that "the excess of nominal balances will therefore tend to be eliminated, even though there is no change in the nominal quantity of money, by either a reduction in the real quantity available to hold through price rises or an increase in the real quantity desired through output increases." In Keynes' and Keynesian analysis, one encounters the notion of imbalances between "the rate of interest" and "the rate of return," but in some instances such imbalances may be viewed as nothing more than fictions employed for analytical convenience. The imbalances are often rationalized as adjusting with varying degrees of rapidity, such as may depend on definitions, measurement techniques, and leading, lagging, and coincidental relationships between series. Indeed, some decision and behavioral units might have vision of entire cyclical patterns of relationships, with recessions serving primarily as adjustments to the excesses of expansion phases.

In Friedman's sketch of a theoretical approach to the adjustment process, "actual" and "anticipated" magnitudes are treated as identical to "measured" and "permanent" magnitudes, although the terms need not be identical in other contexts. At his long-run equilibrium position, "all anticipations are realized, so that actual and anticipated magnitudes, or measured and permanent magnitudes, are equal." He regards "the long-run equilibrium as determined by the earlier quantity-theory model plus the Walrasian equations of general equilibrium." He regards "the short-run equilibrium as determined by an adjustment process in which the rate of adjustment in a variable is a function of the discrepancy between the measured and the anticipated value of that variable or its rate of change, as well as, perhaps, of other variables or their rates of change." Feedback processes are also introduced.

In allocating changes in nominal income to price and output changes separately, two major factors are introduced: "anticipations about the behavior of prices—this is the inertial [pull toward normality] factor stressed by Keynes—and the current level of output or employment compared with the full-employment (permanent) level of output or employment."

All of the six gaps listed earlier are touched upon: (1) adjustments, whether from one static state to another; (2) changes in rates of change rather than just levels; (3) the possible presence of adjustments other than simultaneous ones; (4) anticipations; (5) equations from general equilibrium analysis; and (6) the division of changes in nominal income.

In concluding his paper [136], Friedman emphasizes an instructive point. Rather than the elaboration of a theory, the disentanglement of the systematic from the random and erratic forces in the record has been a primary objective of his studies.

5.5   A TENDENCY FOR THE ECONOMIC SYSTEM TO OVERSHOOT

To clarify the nature of his theoretical approach, Friedman introduces a hypothetical monetary disturbance. The approach itself is set forth in an "incompletely specified system of simultaneous differential equations," and the verbal statement of its solution is apparently impossible. However, enough is given to illustrate the flavor of the adjustment processes Friedman has in mind.

The illustration proceeds along lines introduced earlier (Sec. 1.3) in referring to equilibrium paths. The liquidity preference demand for money is considered first, then the time path of the adjustment to a shift in the rate of monetary expansion. Possible alternatives to Friedman's treatment are mentioned, particularly the tendency for the economic system to overshoot in making adjustments along lines somewhat different from Friedman's, as elaborated in a discussion of expectations, money, and subjective probability (Ch. 8).

Liquidity preference demand.—In his 1968 discussion [141], Friedman referred to empirical work done over the 1965–67 period. Exclusive of long-term movements, the facts with which Friedman dealt were, as in Chapter 2, that (1) interest rates move in phase with changes in business conditions, (2) turning points in interest rates coincide roughly with turning points in business conditions, and (3) turning points in the rate of change in the money stock precede turning points in business conditions. Friedman mentions broad factual evidence; relatively high interest rates and inflation have been found in those countries where the growth of the money stock has been the most rapid (Brazil as contrasted with Switzerland), and interest rates fell most rapidly in the U.S. when the money stock declined.

A variety of theoretical elements are invoked to explain (or rationalize) selected aspects of economic behavior as revealed by the empirical facts. The following elements concern the use of economic statics and lags in responses to certain changes, on one hand, and expectations and the possible immediate effect on expectations of announced changes in certain time series (as in the money stock), on the other.

To explain the main empirical facts, Friedman presents a modified Keynesian, liquidity-preference building block, as mentioned in Sections 1.4 and 4.2. In those sections, more rapid growth in the money stock causes a rise in nominal income after some passage of time. As a result the interest-rate, money-stock relationship shifts to contribute to a rise in interest rates. Once the rise in income starts, there is some "catching up to do"; nominal income must rise faster to adjust to the previously accelerated growth of the money stock. This is one of Friedman's explanations for a tendency to "overshoot."

As indicated in Chapter 4, there are several principal objections to this theorizing. These are exclusive of Friedman's analysis concerning the rate of change in prices and the long-term movements. For one thing, average lag times probably vary with the extent and duration of the cycle. For another, the analysis concerning the initial effect on interest rates from acceleration or deceleration (the liquidity effect) proceeds from an excessive "static state" equilibrium (it proceeds from a condition of portfolio balance and constant interest rates and income velocity). Friedman suggests a simple supply-demand cross in which intervention by the Federal Reserve in an open market purchase reduces interest rates. This suggestion contains the view of open market operations that was rejected in Chapter 2. In the alternative analysis, changes under consideration are essentially cyclical and secular rather than monetary or seasonal. In such a case, interest rates and income velocity tend to be either rising or falling and to reflect portfolio imbalance, and the Federal Reserve is conducting defensive operations in the money market with expectations on the part of dealers serving as a primary short-run determinant of money market rates. The effect of intervening by effecting a stabilizing ("non-defensive") change in the growth of the money stock may be different on a cyclical basis if imbalance exists.

Another principal objection concerns the common explanation apparently adopted by Friedman whereby an increase (decrease) in interest rates increases (decreases) the willingness of economic units to hold less (more) cash and more (less) debt securities, all in relation to the total asset portfolio (or income). The objection here—as stated in Section 4.2 and in Chapter 15—is that one important and potentially interest-sensitive sector simply has not behaved in this way, and that rising interest rates have not contributed to a rise in noncash forms of liquidity. The conventional notions to which Friedman alludes may be applicable in a secondary sense.

In the case of the simple linkage scheme with a change in the money stock operating on the interest rate with some lag, and in the case of the role of expectations and the behavior of noncash forms of liquidity and interest rates, Friedman seems to set forth theoretical elements that meet the criticisms above. He says [141, p. 16], "if it were announced that the jump [in the growth of the money stock from 3% to 5%] was going to occur, it would be plausible that it would have an immediate effect on prices." The means and efficiency in the communication of market changes (including, especially, changes in bank credit and money) are certainly variables in the analysis of lags and changes in expectations.

Time paths.—To illustrate his theoretical approach, the adjustment process, and the tendency for the system to overshoot and thus generate cycles, Friedman starts with a situation of full employment, stable prices, output growing at 3 percent per year, and other assumptions [136, p. 229]:

> Assume that the income elasticity of demand for money is unity, so that the quantity of money is also growing at the rate of 3 percent per year. Assume also that money is wholly non-interest-bearing fiat money and that its quantity can be taken as autonomous.

> Assume that there is a shift at time $t = t_0$ in the rate of growth of the quantity of money from 3 percent per year to, say, 8 percent per year and that this new rate of growth is maintained indefinitely.

With constant 3 percent output, prices according to the assumptions would be rising at 5 percent after the jump from 3 to 8 percent growth in the money stock. Nominal income at first sight would seem to grow at the same rate as money. With the price rise fully anticipated, and the recognized cost of holding money, however, the velocity of money and expenditures would increase, so that the path for expenditures would actually be at a higher rate than that for money at first sight.

There is some question about the effect of inflation on the measurement of income and whether it includes the nonpecuniary services of money, as implied about the services of money and the optimal rate of growth in the money stock in Section 1.4. But this issue aside, via the Fisher equation (Secs. 1.4, 4.2) interest rates would rise to equal the sum of the nominal rate and the rate of change in prices, and the additional cost of holding money may be no more than the 5 percent inflation.

Possible adjustment paths à la Friedman to a shift in nominal income from 3 percent to 8 percent may be shown [136, p. 233]. In such an illustration the derivative of the natural log for income would be a percentage change, and the equilibrium time paths would be shown as horizontal lines or constants with respect to time. With respect to the horizontal line, three adjustment paths may be shown, each of which involves overshooting. These come about because of some need for catching up to a new equilibrium path after the jump in the growth rate for the money stock. In this explanation, there is the idea that some lag is involved in effecting an adjustment to a distinct shift rather than to gradually evolving changes in expectation. To make expenditures catch up to an increase in the growth rate for the money stock, expenditure units must over-spend for a time. There may be other adjustment paths, but damped paths—rather than steadily and repetitively oscillating or even explosive ones[12]—have one feature in common, "the area above the 8 percent line must exceed the area below."

The need to explain cyclical behavior and turning points in business conditions is certainly important in economic theory and is an historical shortcoming of it. In Friedman's framework, the turning points would apparently be explained in terms of acceleration or deceleration in the rate of growth of the money stock. This would seem to be the case, even though Friedman has increasingly mentioned the presence of forces other than money in discussing business conditions.[13]

In Chapter 8, theory is set forth in which the tendency for the system to generate cycles depends on a predominance of "push" effects over "pull" effects, as time series approach a so-called neutral growth position. Turning points in business conditions are explained in terms of these and other expectational forces, and in terms of the role of coalescing opinions in the weighting of possible outcomes of anticipated events.

5.6 SOME KEYNESIAN REACTIONS

James Tobin, pointed to by some as a Keynesian [136, p. 211, n. 11], and Milton Friedman, credited by some with the responsibility for characteristic propositions of "monetarism," both carry forward the controversy precipitated by the early Friedman-Meiselman paper and outlined in Section 5.2. Tobin [353, 354] turns the use of simple models against propositions he attributes to Friedman.[14] He presents what he calls "a version of the

---

12. A catalogue of the possible time paths representing solutions to difference equations may be found in Goldberg's book, along with difference equation counterparts to differential equations [172, esp. pp. 46–47, and 77–86].

13. In his comment on Tobin's attack on the simple money income relation and on the time unit for discussing the relationship, Friedman says [137, p. 319]: "Since there is no unambiguous way to count causes, the only way to assure that changes in the supply of money are *the* 'principal cause,' with no further qualification, would be for them to account for more than half of the variance of all changes in money income—from minute to minute, day to day, month to month, and so on—for periods of all durations. I do believe that changes in the supply of money have accounted for more than half the variance of money income for reasonably long periods and for changes measured over intervals of a year or more. But they certainly have not done so for all periods and all intervals." In his 1968 S-and-L paper, Friedman [141, pp. 26–27] also recognizes factors affecting interest rates in the short run other than rates of change in the money stock.

14. Tobin cites in particular the early FM paper [153] and the Friedman paper, "Lag in Effect of Monetary Policy," discussed in Section 3.4. The latter paper, and two others emphasized by Tobin ("Money and Business Cycles" with Mrs. Anna J.

ultra-Keynesian theory that Friedman is so often attacking," and a Friedman model. Apparent purposes are (1) to have the models generate some leading and lagging relationships between money and monetary income, and (2) to question the use of lagged relations between time series in support of notions about causation. Of possible interest are conclusions and asides about whether timing observations are indecisive on the direction of influence.

Teigen [347], an associate of Warren Smith (Sec. 3.3), has also reacted to Friedman's characterization of Keynesians—or more specifically to their being identified with the simple income-expenditure model and with major emphasis on output rather than price level adjustments. He draws on Friedman's model.

The Friedman-Tobin encounter.—As pointed out in Section 1.1, Friedman was critical of the New Economics of the Kennedy-Johnson years and the Keynesian aspects of it. Tobin himself had been a member of the President's Council of Economic Advisors in 1961–62. In addition, he was the author of an attack on Friedman that appeared in the *Washington Post* (April 16, 1967). The attack was answered by Karl Brunner and Allan Meltzer (April 30, 1967). Tobin considered the implications of Friedman's link between the money supply and economic activity. There is much more to the attack, but especially germane is Tobin's comment on causation:

> Professor Friedman and his school of modern "quantity theorists" do not rely on constant velocity. They now focus attention on the *rate of change* of the money stock rather than on the stock itself. The decisive evidence is supposedly that turning points in the rate of change of money supply usually precede turning points in business activity. Of course they do. The rates of change of all cyclically fluctuating variables generally lead the variables themselves. In booms the economy loses speed before it actually shifts into reverse. The fact that the rate of change of money stock leads, like other rates of change, proves nothing whatsoever about causation. Most likely, money supply and business activity are both the results of a complex economic process.

Tobin's ultra-Keynesian model [353] contains a money demand equation with constraining conditions that make it somewhat unrepresentative of the Keynesians. The money demand is the sum of an asset demand, related to the interest rate and "allocable" wealth, and a transactions demand, proportional to income. The money demand varies inversely with the interest rate, but the authorities are viewed as providing the necessary reserves to

---

Schwartz, and "Monetary Studies of the National Bureau") are reprinted in Friedman [138]. In his comment [137], Friedman cites the later volume and draws on approximately the same studies as those cited by Tobin.

keep it constant and to permit banks "to meet the fluctuating demand of their borrowing customers for credit and of their depositors for money." This condition adds a "positive conformity" of money to business activity, somewhat along lines that Friedman has regarded as "all too common in central banking."

Under these conditions, the ultra-Keynesian model generates changes in the rate of change in the money stock that lead changes in net national product by more than a quarter of a cycle. It leads rates of change in net national product as well. The model generates cycles and leading changes in money of a type attributed to Friedman, and yet money has no causal importance in the model.

The so-called Friedman model as brought out by Tobin [353] is a structural equations model with an equation suggestive of Friedman's permanent income hypothesis about the demand for money.[15] The hypothesis states in effect that money is a luxury good, that changes in money demand increase more than in proportion to wealth (or permanent income measured as an exponentially declining weighted average of income). In the overall model the money supply is autonomous, and demand adjusts to supply. Only current income can adjust, since permanent income is the only variable in the money relation other than money, money supply is autonomous, and much of the permanent income is part history. In the overall model with business fluctuations—including fluctuations in the money stock—the money stock lags income at peak and trough. Thus, the so-called Friedman model fails to generate the empirical patterns that Friedman reports.

An important point of Tobin's exposition of his so-called Friedman model is that in explaining procyclical changes in the velocity of money, something is lost in explaining timing [353].

> There are two Friedmans when it comes to describing the causal mechanism from money to income. One is the Friedman of the permanent income hypothesis. . . . The logic is that the demand for money is quite insensitive to current income, because current income has only a fractional weight in permanent income. This has the virtue of explaining why the monetary multiplier in the cyclical short run is so large and why velocity varies procyclically. But the cost of this explanation, as we have seen, is that it implies an immediate response as well as a powerful response. What is gained from the hypothesis in explaining amplitudes is lost in explaining timing.

Tobin's ultra-Keynesian model in which money has no cause generates leads in the rate of change in the money stock. The model in which money

15. Considerable space is devoted to this hypothesis elsewhere [126, esp. Ch. 6].

has a causal effect fails to generate the leads, but explains procyclical changes in velocity. Friedman denies the relevance of Tobin's exercises. He says that (1) the influence of money on income with the lags he describes is supported by evidence other than timing, and (2) the demand equation for money is but "one element of a theory designed to account for the observed tendency of cyclical fluctuations in income to be wider in amplitude than cyclical fluctuations in money." In other words, the two sets of behavior are rationalized and supported separately.

The foregoing seems to shed some light on Friedman's work. Friedman himself describes the real Friedman [137]:

> The real Friedman has presented the permanent income hypothesis as a partial explanation of one structural equation in a complete model. . . . The real Friedman has emphasized that the "necessity for overshooting in the rate of price change and in the rate of income change (though not necessarily in the level of either price or income) is in my opinion the key element in monetary theory of cyclical fluctuations." And this statement is in a context in which the permanent income element that Tobin extracts is not present in the analysis at all!

The participants in the controversy seem to agree on timing evidence in general. Consistency of a hypothesis with timing evidence is not alone sufficient evidence, but inconsistency requires the rejection of the hypothesis. As Friedman points out, timing evidence may not be decisive since (1) a number of time series may simply be responding to common influences, and (2) what appears as a leading relation of one variable to another may simply be an inverted relation with a lag.

Sims pursues the issue of causation further by introducing a methodological novelty [334, p. 540], "a direct test for the existence of unidirectional causality." According to a variation on a criterion developed by Granger, Sims' test is as follows [334, p. 541]:

> If and only if causality runs one way from current and past values of some list of exogenous variables to a given endogenous variable, then in a regression of the endogenous variable on past, current, and future values of the exogenous variables, the future values of the exogenous variable should have zero coefficients.

After applying the test to post-war, quarterly data for GNP and the money stock, Sims finds that results agree with the hypothesis that causality runs from money to GNP, without feedback. The hypothesis that causality is unidirectional from income to money is rejected. The test is said to have some importance because of questions reviewed above and because "most efficient estimation techniques for distributed lags are invalid unless causality is unidirectional." There are qualifications to the test of causation, however, in that [334, p. 542] "it is possible to construct models in which a money on GNP regression does not yield a causal relation and yet this paper's test would not detect feedback."

Basically Sims is using GNP as a surrogate for business conditions, which is highly questionable (compare Sec. 2.2). He recognizes [334, n. 4] that in such a case there may be no feedback from current dollar GNP to money, despite the presence of a feedback from business conditions to the money stock. Simple reversed causality structures, like the one attributed to Tobin above, "cannot be constructed to give apparent money-to-GNP causality." On the other hand, more complicated structures can be constructed to yield a reduced form showing bidirectional causality except under very special assumptions. For the unidirectional case to surface, the money stock must be "essentially identical to a truly exogenous variable." To illustrate the case where money balances may falsely appear to cause GNP, Sims draws on the more mystical of Keynes' insights to introduce animal spirits, as seems to have become fashionable after the initial impact of the computer. ("Animal spirits" may be defined as a sort of spontaneous, unreasoned optimism—a sort of urge to activity—that at times moves enterprise beyond what is warranted on a reasoned basis and that falters at times, too.) "Thus," Sims says [334, p. 543], "if money has in the sample been passively and quickly adjusted to match the animal spirits of bankers and businessmen, and if animal spirits is a truly exogenous variable affecting GNP with a distributed lag, then money might falsely appear to cause GNP." Continuing, he says "An assumption that future values of money or income cause current values of the other . . . will affect the apparent direction of causality. However, the effect is much more likely to make a truly unidirectional structure appear bidirectional than vice versa."

Teigen's criticisms.—In reacting to Friedman's characterizations of Keynesians, Teigen proceeds from a summary of Friedman's model (Sec. 5.4) and focuses on the price-quantity adjustments controversy and other aspects of monetarism. Those were introduced earlier (Sec. 3.3).

The model is summarized thus [347, p. 11]:

(1) $$\frac{Y}{P} = C(\frac{Y}{P}, r) + I(r) \qquad \text{(IS)}$$

(2) $$M_o = P \cdot l(\frac{Y}{P}, r) \qquad \text{(L-M)}$$

(3) $$Y = Py$$

where the symbols retain their earlier meaning, only the exogenous money supply is M_o and real income (or output) is denoted y. Equation (1) brings together the first three equations of Friedman's model and yields a familiar IS curve (a reduction in the interest rate increases investment and real income, given prices). Equation (2) brings together equations (4.0) and (5.0) of Friedman's model and yields the LM curve (a rise in interest rates contributes to switching from money to bonds but raises income, M = constant). Equation (3) simply defines nominal income as the product of output and the average of prices on current output.

Now, Teigen's equations contain Y, p, r, and y, as endogenous variables. The focus of attention is on the extra variable, which is output in the case of the monetarists. A system of Walrasian demand and supply equations with equilibrium conditions (compare Sec. 2.2) is invoked to determine output. Teigen says [347, p. 12] that this "of course implies that the equilibrium position of the model is one of full employment." The short-run dynamics of Friedman's model are different. With real output predetermined, equation (1) yields a solution for the interest rate and this depends only on real income. Equation (2) yields a solution for the price level and it changes in response to M_o.

Teigen says this short-run version of the model yields the classical dichotomy between the real and monetary sectors. It also illustrates that real income raises interest rates and that an inflationary component of interest rates is impossible in the IS-LM framework, given the slopes commonly attributed to the respective curves.

The monetarist model treats the price level rather than income as being determined outside of the model. Taking the price level as exogenously determined again permits a solution to Teigen's equations without the classical dichotomy. Teigen says [347, p. 12], "All of the variables are now determined jointly rather than recursively."[16]

Teigen would point out that there are aspects of monetarism (Ch. 3) other than the assumptions providing a unique solution to the IS–LM model, but he continues to discuss price-quantity adjustment. He views the "modern" Keynesians as having a more satisfactory explanation of the price level [347, p. 15]:

> Rather, the standard static "complete Keynesian system" is widely recognized to be one in which the general price level is one of the variables determined by the interaction of the system, and hence is free to

16. By this he means that you are not obtaining a solution from one sector of the model or economy and then plugging it into another, and so on to get a solution. Recursive solutions are especially characteristic of the larger structural models (as discussed in Ch. 14).

move, but to be one in which there are imperfections in the labor market
—most typically, a money wage rate which is inflexible downwards. In
other words, rather than assuming that prices are fixed as a means of
making the simple static model determinate, modern Keynesians introduce an aggregated labor market and production function into the analysis. This could be viewed as the Keynesian equivalent of the "Walrasian
system of equations" asserted by Friedman to be the hallmark of the ad-
herents to the modern quantity theory approach. It is of course much less
satisfactory in that all labor market activity and all kinds of production
are aggregated into perhaps as few as two equations (i.e., a reduced-
form labor market equation and an aggregate production function)
rather than having each market and each activity represented by specific
equations. It is more satisfactory on two counts: first, the equations at least
are explicitly specified, and second, these equations do not yield the
full employment outcome, as is typically in case when depending on a
Walrasian system.

Continuing on the price-quantity adjustment, Teigen says [347, p. 16]:

The essential difference in this regard between Keynesians [very "modern" Keynesians] and monetarists therefore would appear to be that the
former view all prices (including wages) as flexible, while the latter
consider all prices except the money wage rate to be flexible (money
wages are viewed as inflexible, at least in a downward direction, due to
such structural phenomena as minimum wage laws, union contracts, and
the like). This distinction has significant implications for the analysis.

It seems Teigen has transformed the price-quantity adjustment matter
into a discussion of the merits of having both wages and prices be flexible,
rather than only prices. On this he concludes as follows [347, p. 16]:

The Keynesian treatment now cannot be said to be fundamentally less
satisfactory than the monetarist one in terms of methodology, except
perhaps on grounds having to do with problems of aggregation . . . Rather,
the difference now lies in the analytic usefulness of the assumptions
themselves. Is it more appropriate to assume that wages and prices are
flexible, or that money wages are sticky while prices can adjust? The
answer to this question depends on the nature of the problem being studied
in any particular case, and this suggests that an important difference between the two schools of thought may be that Keynesians are more
concerned with short-run analysis (for instance, that related to counter-
cyclical stabilization) while monetarist assumptions are more consistent
with long-run analysis.

5.7 SUMMARY

In the late 1950s Friedman and Meiselman presented a paper concerning
the test of a simple Keynesian model against a simple quantity theory model.

One model emphasized a simple consumption-autonomous expenditure relation, with an implicit investment multiplier, and the other emphasized a simple consumption-money relation, with an implicit money multiplier. The ensuing controversy and the modern computer combined to generate a voluminous output. It led to discussion of structural equations models and some agreement about the definition of an autonomous variable, namely that an autonomous variable is an exogenous variable, "whose value in each period is statistically independent of the values of all random disturbances in the model in all periods."

Indeed, the definition was strenuous and would leave little to call autonomous. Thus, in a highly developed state of the controversy, Kmenta and Smith overlooked the major fruitful result and simply equated an autonomous variable with the idea of a controlled variable.

Friedman gives considerable emphasis in his theoretical work to the definition of an autonomous variable as the basis for distinguishing between consumption expenditures and investment, while Kmenta and Smith simply test the principal competing theories by an examination of impact and dynamic multipliers for the money stock and government expenditures. The main results of the entire controversy would be (1) a greater awareness of structural equations models, reduced forms, and the definition of an autonomous variable; (2) the recognition of a more nearly equal relevance of monetary and fiscal policy; and (3) further agreement about the attributes of Keynesian economics. These, as originally introduced in Chapters 1 and 3, include the expenditure multiplier (with a concomitant emphasis on fiscal policy and autonomous investment), the liquidity trap, and a particular treatment of prices. Adjustments in the system are through quantities rather than through prices, but once full employment is reached the price level comes in. In the simple quantity theory model, changes in the money stock are reflected entirely in prices rather than in output. Friedman points to the need to allow for both price and quantity changes, and questions the Keynesian trap hypothesis, as have others. Teigen enjoins Friedman, especially on the price-quantity matter. He says "modern" Keynesians recognize that "the general price level is one of the variables determined by the interaction of the system." It is free to move but is related to imperfections in the labor market. This could be viewed, Teigen says, as the Keynesian equivalent of the Walrasian system of equations. He finds the modern Keynesian approach superior, with its explicitly specified equations (structural equations models?) and short time span (short run?) in which unemployment can occur.

In adopting a positive liquidity preference position, Friedman relies on Tobin. This is shown to be related to the assumption of constant expectations. The Tobin explanation of liquidity preference gets questioned later and probability enters the analysis in more explicit theoretical terms.

Friedman emphasizes a long-run equilibrium (or "neutral") position in terms of some underlying permanent magnitudes (as in the case of permanent income) and the normal or expected interest rate (as in the case of Keynes' safe or normal rate). There is a tendency for changes to gravitate toward such magnitudes, but there is also instability. Friedman sees it in the tendency for the system to overshoot, as in the case of a lagged response to an acceleration in the money stock. The tendency for the economic system to generate cycles is important, but too much depends on the lagged responses. Friedman concedes that a publicized change in the money stock may have immediate effect on spending because of the effect on expectations. Tobin presents a simple model with Friedmanian attributes that fails to generate leads in the rate of change in the money stock, but does explain procyclical changes in velocity. He is able to draw out the fact that Friedman deals with aspects of behavior that are rationalized separately. This is also consistent with an emphasis on aspects of Friedman's empirical work—the disentanglement of the systematic from the random and erratic forces.

Sims pursues the question of the direction of causality, revealed from time series, by suggesting a test of unidirectional causality. There are some complications in applying the test, especially where the anticipated future of one series affects the current values of another. However, focusing on the money stock and GNP as he does, he concludes that "the effect is much more likely to make a truly unidirectional structure appear bidirectional than vice versa."

The tendency for the economic system to overshoot need not rely on Friedman's explanations about lags. Such a tendency may be identified with the extrapolative push effect of recent changes on expected future magnitudes. The Kmenta-Smith study emphasizes the dependence of current magnitudes on lagged values and on changes from one recently past period to another. Such changes—as in the case of the alleged accelerator effect of past sales on capital investment—however, need not represent such mechanical responses to sales. Rather the influence on investment may be through the impact of recent changes on future prospects. This would seem particularly true in an industrial state characterized by an emphasis on planning and anticipations.

6

The Substitution Hypothesis and Greater Certainty

6.1 INTRODUCTION

EXPLANATIONS OF the roughly parallel movements in interest rates and the income velocity of money, and especially of the post–World War II rise in both, have been highly controversial. At one extreme were explanations involving the interest rate as the determinant or causal factor. A popular variant of these explanations has been called the "Gurley-Shaw thesis" or the substitution hypothesis (Secs. 1.4, 4.2). Discussion of it has been vague and ambiguous, but more verifiable statements have been induced by the recognized need for them in empirical work. One such statement is that the growth of financial intermediaries and their offering of a higher price for savings caused a switching from money balances relative to income into the liabilities of financial intermediaries relative to income, and thus contributed to a rise in the income velocity of money.

At another extreme of the explanations of the postwar rise in velocity was one centering about a weakening of the precautionary motive for holding money balances or a greater certainty with respect to the anticipated outcome of economic developments, possibly higher prices, and so on. In these explanations the role of the interest rate as a causal factor was minimized. There was the further implicit or explicit prospect (depending on the particular explanation) that some third force contributed to the rise in both velocity and interest rates. The force mentioned (Sec. 4.2) was greater certainty with respect to economic outcomes and possibly higher prices. This might encompass such factors as acceleration in the depreciation of capital goods, tax credit for capital outlays, the 1964 tax cut for consumers, and actual and anticipated spending on the wars on poverty and in Vietnam, particularly in the second half of the 1960s.

134

This chapter is about the foregoing explanations, with particular emphasis on papers by Lee [248] and Peltzman [291] and related discussions [163, 181, 209, 247]. In the broader literature on the subject of the Gurley-Shaw thesis there have been statements about the absolute increases in the liabilities of financial intermediaries [309, p. 107], improvements in the management of the cash balances of nonfinancial corporations [309, p. 25; 164, pp. 221–22], and the upward movement in velocity and the interest rate [164]. Difficulties with explanations concerning such statements have included (1) the failure to distinguish between levels and rates of growth (as mentioned in Ch. 5), especially in relation to rates for income and surrogates for income such as sales; (2) the tendency to draw conclusions about the trend in the liquidity of nonfinancial corporations without actually examining the data on liquidity, except for the liabilities of intermediaries [as in 164, 309]; and (3) the tendency to arrive at conclusions from data on money balances and interest rates without discriminating between households and firms, which possibly might vary differently. Some of these difficulties are still present in the work examined, but the shift to a consideration of rates of change and of common trends in velocity and interest rates is very obvious.

6.2 THE SUBSTITUTION HYPOTHESIS

If two goods substitute for one another, they are called substitute goods. More formally, if a rise in the price of good X causes a decline in the quantity of X demanded and a rise in the quantity of good Y demanded, and if a rise in the price of good Y causes a decline in the quantity of Y demanded and a rise in the quantity of X demanded, then goods X and Y are substitute goods. These criteria for substitute goods, in the case of financial instruments such as bonds, are usually discussed in terms of yields. (Recall that the prices of outstanding issues of bonds vary inversely with yields.) For example, one may investigate the effect of a rise in the yield on Treasury bills (a decline in the price of the bills) on the quantity of money (currency and demand deposits adjusted) demanded, as one phase of determining whether Treasury bills and money are substitute goods. In this example, some evidence might be expected from dealing with the question of whether Treasury bill holdings increased relative to total assets or income as the yield on the bills increased. Evidence that money balances declined relative to income as the Treasury bill yield increased would be only a part of the evidence.

A formal way of denoting the foregoing competitive quality between financial assets is in terms of cross elasticity [the cross elasticity of the demand for money with respect to savings and loan shares is defined as the ratio of the percentage change in the quantity of money ($100 \times d \ln M$) to percentage change in the yield on S-and-L shares ($100 \times d \ln r_{SL}$)]. Of course, different goods may be substitutes in different degrees, so one may investigate relative magnitudes concerning cross elasticities. But these Marshallian elasticities may be difficult to isolate in the real world.

To deal with the competitive quality of selected financial assets, Lee [248] presented a variety of statistical results. These were obtained by regressing the money stock per capita in real terms (M') on such variables as an exponentially weighted average of past incomes per capita (Y_p), the yield on commercial bank time deposits (r_T), and the yield on S-and-L shares (r_{SL}), where the yields are net of the yield on money, as mentioned in Chapter 4. These kinds of regressions were run to compare the various coefficients and assessments of their significance.

One of Lee's possibly representative regression equations [247, pp. 412–18] is

$$\ln M' = 2.73 + 0.583 \ln Y_p - 0.064 \ln r_T - 0.430 \ln r_{SL}$$
$$(13.60) \qquad (3.31) \qquad (11.48)$$
$$\bar{R}^2 = 0.99, \ DW = 0.763$$

in which Lee made use of quarterly data, 1956–66, after Galper [163] presented results from analyzing quarterly data on S-and-L shares by interpolating semiannual advertised rates. In his own paper, Galper supported some of Lee's earlier conclusions following analyses of annual data [163, p. 406]:

> Lee's conclusions are thus seen to be confirmed. Savings and loan shares appear to be closer substitutes for money than do time deposits, and Friedman's broader concept of money which includes time deposits but not savings and loan shares may be inappropriate, at least for the postwar period. Also, when the interest rate paid on S-and-L shares is used in a demand for money equation, discrepancies between desired and actual money holdings are eliminated more rapidly than when the time deposit rate is used.

In a more controversial tone, Hamburger disputed Lee's earlier evidence [181, p. 407]:

> Lee's findings depend critically on the use of interest rate differentials. Once this procedure is abandoned and the yield on money is introduced

as a separate variable, there is little evidence that savings and loan shares are closer substitutes for money (narrowly defined) than other assets. In addition, the demand for money appears to adjust more slowly to changes in yields on savings and loan shares than to changes in other rates.

In his reply [247], Lee rebuts Hamburger and his alternative methods that were employed in analyses of annual data, 1951–65.

For the period for which Lee, Galper, and Hamburger analyzed data, the relative size and significance of the coefficient for the ln transformed S-and-L yield does not appear to stand out. A more fundamental question, however, is whether the rise in S-and-L yields causes the demand for money to decline relative to some measure of income. Indeed, Lee and others contend that the post–World War II general rise in yields—and particularly those on the liabilities of financial intermediaries—caused the post–World War II rise in the velocity of money. This contention can be disputed by several facts. In general, Lee has analyzed data for the economy as a whole and has failed to discriminate between the behavior of the household and business sectors. Making this distinction would seem necessary in view of the fact, introduced earlier (Sec. 4.2) and brought out later (Ch. 15), that evidence on manufacturing corporations does not support the hypotheses Lee advances.[1] The money balances held by such firms are a volatile and significant component of the income-velocity ratio for the economy as a whole. Further, such firms are not known to routinely hold balances in savings and loan associations.

6.3   THE VELOCITY–INTEREST RATE ASSOCIATION

Studies by Chow and Hamburger have dealt with adjustments in the stock of money actually held to some so-called long-run equilibrium level.[2] A form of the adjustment in the level of money balances to some desired level, however, is through expenditures on goods and services, as for example in the context of the income velocity of money.

There are other ways of adjusting the level of balances, but over an expansion phase of business conditions or over some secular phase, as in the postwar United States, a rising income velocity ratio (Y/M, or E/M in Peltzman's paper) may be viewed as an indication of a desired reduction

---

1. For further background on Lee's work and his special effort to support hypotheses attributed to Gurley and Shaw, see Frazer [126, Ch. 9].
2. The studies mentioned have been reviewed in an extensive review of the pre-1967 demand-for-money literature [126, pp. 164–66, 264–74].

in money balances in relation to income on the part of economic units as a whole. The money stock is controlled by the Federal Reserve (as in Sec. 4.2), so the adjustment is through expenditures on goods and services. In such a setting Peltzman attempts to deal empirically and very formally with the causes of the post–World War II rise in income velocity. He rejects the interest rate as a causal factor.

In reacting to Peltzman's paper, Jaffee comments that a key variable has been omitted from the estimated equations, and that this imparts a downward bias to the possible influence of the interest rate on velocity. He says that including this key variable changes the conclusions. His objective [209, pp. 216–19] is to reconcile Peltzman's findings with previous work, particularly by those who have viewed changes in the interest rate as a significant cause of changes in the velocity of money. Peltzman [290, pp. 220–21] rebuts Jaffee's theoretical points and questions the substance of his findings. Both Peltzman's and Jaffee's points are reviewed later, along with results from analyses of data.

Peltzman's analysis.—Dealing with the conflicting sets of arguments outlined in the introduction to this chapter, Peltzman cites the Friedman-Schwartz argument of greater certainty about the future. In earlier postwar work Friedman advanced his luxury goods hypothesis about money, namely that money balances are a luxury good and that, as the hypothesis requires, the stock of money balances held increases more than in proportion to wealth or income.[3] The hypothesis, which suggests a declining velocity of money, did not fare well as velocity continued to rise after the early postwar years. In such a context Friedman and Schwartz said the cause was greater certainty about the future [126, Ch. 6 and Appendix to Ch. 6]. Peltzman interprets this to suggest that there is an expected reduction in the expected frequency of switching transactions and thus in the total transactions cost of holding non-money assets over time, but greater certainty may relate as well to a reduction in the need for balances for unforeseen transactions and thus to the variance of probable future transactions. In addition, Peltzman supports this broad class of conclusions about the postwar rise in velocity. He even suggests, perhaps correctly, that the luxury goods hypothesis may have still been in operation.

Peltzman denotes that an intended or expected change in velocity is directly related to a discrepancy between "desired" and "actual" velocity, as in his equation

3. For references to the hypothesis and discussions about it see Stroup and Frazer [132, pp. 489–93]. For discussions of the hypothesis as it applies to the business sector in particular, see Frazer [119, Chs. 3 and 4].

(1) $$(d(\frac{E}{M}) \, / \, dt)^* = a[(E/M)^* - (E/M)]$$

where E represents total expenditures, M is the quantity of money, a is a constant coefficient of adjustment, and * denotes expected or intended value. An unanticipated increase in the rate of change in money balances contributes to an excess of "actual" over "desired" balances and thus to an excess of "desired" over "actual" velocity and, hence, an expected rise in velocity. All the variables in equation (1) are then treated as natural logarithms, which permits a rearrangement of terms in the quotient of the left-hand member. Equation (1) is then rewritten as

(2) $$(dE/dt)^* = a[(E/M)^* - (E/M)] + (dM/dt)^*$$

In his equation (2) Peltzman simplifies by assuming that the Federal Reserve, for example, is expected to effect a constant growth rate in the money supply ($[(1/M)(dM/dt)]^* = $ constant). All deviations of the expected rate of change in consumption expenditures, $[(1/E)(dE/dt)]^*$, from the average growth in consumption over a long period of time "are regarded as adjustments to a discrepancy between desired and actual velocity." Desired velocity, $(E/M)^*$, or a form of a long-run equilibrium demand function is then specified in log-linear form as

(3) $$(E/M)^* = b + c(E/P) + ei$$

where (E/P) represents real expenditures, i is the interest rate, and "variables in upper case are natural logarithms, those in lower case are absolute values." This specification is in accordance with theoretical notions whereby, in the particular case, the right-hand member of the equation includes real expenditures and the interest rate. Friedman's luxury goods hypothesis would require that the coefficient c be positive, but it could be zero, and the postwar trend may cause some to make it negative. The widely revealed velocity-interest rate association would require that the coefficient e be positive.

The right-hand side of equation (3) gets substituted into equation (2). In addition, however, Peltzman includes a secular trend term since "factors other than income and interest rates and specific to the postwar period may be responsible for the postwar rise in velocity." According to him [291, p. 131], "first, add a trend term (ft) to the right-hand side of (3), and substitute this expression for desired velocity into (2) to get"

(4) $$(dE/dt)^* = a[b + c(E/P) + ei + ft - (E/M)] + (dM/dt)^*$$

The idea in introducing the trend term is that its coefficient will reflect other factors. As Peltzman concludes, the presence of a significant secular trend in postwar velocity would mean that income and interest rate movements cannot explain fully the behavior of postwar velocity. After regrouping the terms of equation (4) and taking the first derivative, Peltzman gets his equation

$$(4'') \quad \frac{d[(dE/dt)^*]}{dt} = 0 + ac\,\frac{d(E/P)}{dt} + ae(di/dt) + af - a\,\frac{d(E/M)}{dt}$$

Discussing this form he says [291, p. 131], "effects attributable solely to trend are expressed in a constant, *af*, which cannot, of course, reflect movements in the other variables." The constant "*af* should equal zero if postwar movements in velocity can be attributed entirely to movements in income or interest rates; otherwise *af* will be positive."

With equation (4'') Peltzman gets regression results. They will stand on their own, apart from the rationale about the adjustment mechanism, but not apart from the problems of regression analysis of time series such as multicollinearity and serial correlation as discussed in appendices to Chapters 1 and 3. Even so, the Durbin-Watson statistics provided in Peltzman's Table, 6–1, by their closeness to the number two rather than zero or four, would indicate a probable absence of serial correlation.

Results in Table 6–1 are shown for expenditures defined as "consumption" and as "net national product," and for the use of various definitions of money in the velocity ratio. Friedman has emphasized consumption in the money relationship, as discussion of work by Meiselman and Friedman (Sec. 5.2) indicates. But Friedman has also emphasized permanent income in consumption function and in demand for money relations, and Peltzman regards consumption as a proxy for permanent income (for expected income as indicated by a weighted average for current and past incomes).

On the basis of evidence, Peltzman (1) deletes the interest rate from his model as insignificant, (2) notes that 40 to 60 per cent of the effects of money changes are completed in one quarter, and (3) concludes [291, pp. 134–35] that "results do imply strongly that interest rate movements cannot explain the postwar rise in velocity."

Comment and rebuttal.—Attempting to restate the behavioral structure of Peltzman's model, Jaffee [209, p. 216] rewrote the long-run equilibrium demand equation [Peltzman's equation (3)], and the adjustment equation [Peltzman's equation (2)], as

$$(1) \qquad (E - M)^* = a_0 + a_1 T - a_2(E - P)_{-1} + a_3 i_{-1}$$

(2) $\Delta (E - M) = \gamma[(E - M)^* - (E - M)_{-1}]$

where E = logarithm of expenditures in current dollars, M = logarithm of money stock, P = logarithm of price deflator for E, T = linear time trend, i = logarithm of the interest rate, and $*$ = desired value. The time unit is a quarter. (Note that time trend is introduced immediately by Jaffee.) Substituting the right-hand member of equation (2) into equation (1) gives

(3) $\Delta (E - M) = \gamma a_0 + \gamma a_1 T - \gamma a_2 (E - P)_{-1} +$

$\gamma a_3 i_{-1} - \gamma(E - M)_{-1}$

which is the counterpart to Peltzman's equation (4).

The counterpart to Peltzman's equation (4″) is obtained by taking first differences of equation (3) to obtain

(4) $\Delta^2(E - M) = \gamma a_1 - \gamma a_2 \Delta(E - P)_{-1} +$

$\gamma a_3 \Delta i_{-1} - \gamma \Delta(E - M)_{-1}$

where the superscript 2 on the Δ simply signifies that differences are taken for an equation describing changes to begin with. Before estimating this equation Peltzman separates the variable $\Delta^2(E - M)$ into $\Delta^2 E$ and $\Delta^2 M$, but using Jaffee's notation he would also bring forward the asterisk used for the right-hand member of equation (1). He then assumes $\Delta^2 M = 0$. This omission of $\Delta^2 M$ is objectionable from Jaffee's point of view. He says [209, p. 217], "it is unwarranted because this variable will tend to bias the coefficients; more specifically, suppressing $\Delta^2 M$ will impart a downward bias to the interest rate coefficient." He reasons that moving the term $\Delta^2 M$ to the right side of equation (4) will bias the interest rate coefficient downward "since the money stock and interest rate can be expected to be negatively correlated."

To deal with his objection, Jaffee analyzes data with both Peltzman's formulation of the right-hand member of equation (4) and his own formulation. The two forms of equation (4) for which data are analyzed are emphasized in Table 6–2. As shown in the table, equations (A.1), (B.1), and (C.1) are for Peltzman's formulation and (A.2), (B.2), and (C.2) are Jaffee's. The coefficients for the interest rate variable Δi_{-1} increase slightly when the variable $\Delta^2(E - M)$ is used. In all instances, consumption expenditures are used as the measure for expenditures, E, and the Treasury bill rate as the measure for the interest rate, i. "Qualitatively," Jaffee says [209, p. 218], "the results are unchanged if we substitute net national product for E and/or the long-term government bond rate for i."

TABLE 6-1 REGRESSION RESULTS, 1953-I THROUGH 1967-II (58 OBSERVATIONS)

Estimate Number and Description	Constant (×100) (1)	Real Expenditures (2)	Expenditures-Money Ratio (3)	R (4)	s.e. (×100) (5)	D.W. (6)	t for Interest Rate (7)
Expenditures defined as consumption, and money defined as:							
E2: currency plus demand deposits	.750 .149	−.386 .137	−.479 .157	.675	.721	2.19	−0.60
E3: currency plus demand deposits plus commercial bank time deposits	.454 .148	−.421 .126	−.400 .121	.685	.712	2.15	0.02
E4: currency plus demand deposits plus commercial bank time deposits plus deposits at mutual savings banks and savings and loan associations	.261 .183	−.372 .141	−.446 .148	.673	.723	2.19	0.17
Expenditures defined as Net National Product, and Money defined as:							
E5: Currency plus demand deposits	.494 .166	−.097 .184	−.564 .220	.579	1.00	1.99	−1.95
E6: Currency plus demand deposits plus commercial bank time deposits	.121 .169	−.098 .149	−.562 .161	.625	.958	2.17	−1.37
E7: Currency plus demand deposits plus commercial bank time deposits plus deposits at mutual savings banks and savings and loan associations	−.218 .216	.043 .171	−.694 .184	.640	.944	1.89	−1.76

Note: The dependent variable is the quarterly first difference of the quarterly change in the natural log of expenditures. The independent variables are quarterly first differences of the natural log of the indicated variables. All independent variables are lagged one quarter. Coefficients are shown above their standard errors.

R is the multiple correlation coefficient, *s.e.* ×100 is the standard error of estimate in percentage points, *D.W.* is the Durbin-Watson statistic (which indicates no significant serial correlation in the residuals of any regression in the table). The last column gives the ratio of the coefficient of the interest rate variable to its standard error if the regression had been expanded to include it.

Sources of Data: Personal consumption expenditures, net national product, real personal consumption expenditures, real net national product all from *Survey of Current Business.* Money supply data and interest rate (yield of long term government bonds) data from *Federal Reserve Bulletin.* All data are seasonally adjusted with the exception of mutual savings bank and saving and loan deposits; preliminary analysis indicated that neither of these series had any strong seasonal pattern. Flow variables are annual rates.

Source of table: Sam Peltzman, "The Structure of the Money Expenditure Relationship," *American Economic Review,* March 1969, p. 133.

TABLE 6–2—REGRESSION RESULTS, 1953–I THROUGH 1967–II

Money defined as:	Constant ($\times 100$)	$\Delta(E-P)_{-1}$	$\Delta(E-M)_{-1}$	Δi_{-1}	R^2	S_e	D.W.
A. Currency plus demand deposits $= M_1$							
A.1 $\Delta^2(E) =$	.790 (5.8)	−.296 (−2.3)	−.649 (−4.8)	.007 (1.4)	.537	.622	2.04
A.2 $\Delta^2(E-M) =$	.777 (4.9)	−.038 (−.26)	−.967 (−6.2)	.012 (2.2)	.521	.716	2.17
B. M_1 plus commercial bank time deposits $= M_2$							
B.1 $\Delta^2(E) =$	.428 (2.9)	−.416 (−3.3)	−.406 (−3.8)	.009 (1.8)	.480	.659	2.13
B.2 $\Delta^2(E-M) =$	.157 (.79)	−.135 (−.78)	−.717 (−4.9)	.015 (2.1)	.405	.894	2.10
C. M_2 plus time deposits at mutual savings banks and savings and loan associations $= M_3$							
C.1 $\Delta^2(E) =$	.173 (.99)	−.320 (−2.3)	−.522 (−4.0)	.009 (1.8)	.490	.652	2.13
C.2 $\Delta^2(E-M) =$	−.159 (−.75)	−.063 (−.37)	−.781 (−4.9)	.013 (2.1)	.428	.798	2.08

The equations were estimated using ordinary least squares; t-statistics are shown in parentheses and the R^2 is not corrected for degrees of freedom. Data sources are given in Peltzman (Table 1). Data revisions available April 1969 were used.
Source of table: Dwight M. Jaffee, "The Structure of the Money-Expenditure Relationship: Comment," *American Economic Review*, March 1970, p. 217.

The rationale for assuming $\Delta^2 M = 0$ is set forth by Peltzman [290, p. 220]:

> I chose to set the intended expenditure change, the variable of primary interest, equal to the actual change and to set the expected change in money equal to a constant. Jaffee would have me set the latter change equal to its actual value as well. This is unnecessarily restrictive. For the aggregate of money holders, the actual change in money is, after all, largely determined by the monetary authorities. Unless spending units forecast exactly what Federal Reserve monetary policy is going to be over the period for which they are making expenditure plans, the assumption of equality between expected and actual money changes may not be useful. My procedure can surely be improved upon: for example, one might set $(\Delta M)^*$ equal to an empirically determined weighted average of past money changes. But, to assume, as Jaffee has in effect done, that money holders have perfect foresight about Federal Reserve policy raises as many difficulties as it eliminates. For example, suppose money holders do not have such perfect foresight, and the Federal Reserve conducts a counter-cyclical monetary policy. This will introduce a positive bias into the coefficients of $\Delta(E - P)_{-1}$ in Jaffee's Table 1. To illustrate: let the Federal Reserve observe a low (high) value of $\Delta(E - P)$ today and react by accelerating (retarding) the money supply next quarter in an amount not entirely anticipated by money holders. Then $\Delta(E - P)_{-1}$ and $\Delta^2(E - M)$ will tend to move together, without this movement having been intended by the money holders whose behavior the model purports to describe. Indeed, this may explain why the coefficient of $\Delta(E - P)_{-1}$ increases algebraically when Jaffee goes from my model to his version of it.

Jaffee also objects to Peltzman's use of second differences—as in equation (4) above—as a means of avoiding multicollinearity in an equation with trend-like variables. He says [209, p. 218], "Even in general practice this solution may be of limited value since what one gains in excluding multicollinearity is likely to be offset by deterioration in the quality of the data as one uses changes over short periods of time." He finds the case for second differences even weaker [209, p. 218] "because the specification in the first difference form already includes [allowance for] time trend."

As a test of the sensitivity of the results to the use of second differences, and having found time trend less important for broader definitions of money, the equivalent of equation (A.2) in Table 6–1 was estimated in first difference form. The result was

$$\Delta(E - M) = .726 + .414\,T - .109(E - P)_{-1} -$$
$$\quad\quad\quad\quad (2.8) \quad (4.1) \quad\quad (-2.4)$$

$$.407(E - M)_{-1} + .014i_{-1}$$
$$(-4.3) \quad\quad\quad\quad (3.7)$$

$$R^2 = .283 \qquad S_e = .642 \qquad D.W. = 1.70$$

Jaffee says [209, p. 219] that "The impact elasticity of the interest rate remains essentially unchanged, although it becomes still more significant, but the speed of adjustment falls by more than half. This implies that the long-run interest elasticity more than doubles when first differences are used. Furthermore the standard error of estimate is about 10 percent smaller in this case."

In rebuttal, Peltzman accepts Jaffee's version of his model, and makes several points about the substance of Jaffee's empirical results [209, p. 221]:

> What important difference does this [Jaffee's version] really make? Jaffee does indeed report significantly positive interest rate-elasticities of desired velocity. However, note their magnitudes. For all money supply definitions, and in first or second difference form, the estimated interest-elasticity of desired velocity never exceeds .035. I reported a maximum value of .014 (p. 132, fn. 5), in my 1969 article. In this context the difference between .035 and .014 or zero is negligible. Specifically, an elasticity of .035 cannot account for any substantial part of the postwar rise in velocity. Further, Jaffee's estimates for conventional money retain the significant time trend in desired velocity in both first and second difference form. It was precisely my point . . . 'that those who have explained the postwar rise in velocity by interest rate movements have confounded interest rates with some other trend-related phenomena' (p. 136). No substantially different conclusion can be drawn from Jaffee's own results.

Finally, Peltzman agrees with Jaffee's interpretation of the time-trend coefficients for various money definitions, "namely that there has been a secular shift from demand to time deposits." He says [209, p. 221]:

> I made just that point (p. 136, fn. 16). However, one must doubt that rising time deposit interest rates can explain a substantial part of this movement. Time deposit rates have, after all, moved up with other interest rates, and both Jaffee's estimates and mine show interest rates to be of negligible importance in explaining the postwar rise in velocity. Something else, perhaps improvements in the technology of banking or improved expectations about economic stability, must be responsible for this shift from demand to time deposits. The shift to time deposits might then simply be part of an overall shift from money to nonmoney forms of wealth. In any case, since Jaffee's results no less than mine appear to rule out an interest rate explanation for the postwar rise in velocity the task for future research remains to identify empirically the trend-related source of the postwar rise in velocity.

Time deposits and the administration of ceilings on such rates have at times affected the movement of such rates in relation to other rates. This subject comes up on other occasions, as in the Appendix to Chapter 15. It is tangential to Peltzman's final remarks.

6.4 SUMMARY

A fundamental question arising from the Gurley-Shaw thesis is whether a post–World War II rise in yields on S-and-L shares caused the demand for money to decline in relation to income. This is disputed and there are problems in the analysis of data on this question. S-and-L shares are emphasized in assessing the growth of financial intermediaries, but the aggregates used imply that nonfinancial firms show the same interest in such shares that households show. Another extreme explanation centers around greater certainty about economic prospects and possible inflation. Indeed, there is the a priori speculation that velocity and interest rates are responding to some common forces. This follows the results of this chapter, at least for secular changes in the post–World War II years. The velocity and interest rate measures share a common trend. This prospect was mentioned earlier (Ch. 4), particularly as it relates to nonfinancial corporations. The question of the relation between household money demands and intermediaries is obscured, possibly by the absence of analyses of adequate data on households.

7

Keynes' Economics
Some Revisions

7.1 INTRODUCTION

MUCH HAS BEEN SAID about Keynesian economics as the orthodoxy of the 1950s and 1960s, about a crisis in theory, and about a revolt against the orthodoxy with its special attributes (Chs. 1, 3, 4). These attributes have included: (1) a special emphasis on fiscal policy and the investment multiplier; (2) the notion of a liquidity trap and a closely related inelasticity of investment demand; (3) a linkage machanism with special attention to the interest rate as the main control variable relating to capital expenditures; (4) a special emphasis on variability of the interest rate in relation to a constant marginal efficiency of investment (or capital) and, conversely, on autonomous investment and the variability of the marginal efficiency of capital; (5) occasional asides about the influence of credit conditions, mainly with reference to home construction; (6) an emphasis on equilibrating quantity rather than price level adjustments; (7) a summary of the income-expenditure model in the form of the IS–LM model with special shortcomings in the analysis of interest rates and anticipated rates of change in prices; (8) an emphasis on equilibrium levels (rather than rates of change) for stock and flow quantities in combination with a carryover of the classical notion of equilibrium as a balancing of forces to that of a solution to simultaneous equations; and (9) a focus on increasing amounts of Keynesian detail through the construction of a large-scale, econometric model of the economy. Some may add that there was an emphasis on the stabilization of business conditions in contrast to the long-run time dimension of monetarists. This attention to stabilization, however, is not unique to Keynesians. It is brought forward and retained in this book as a goal of national policies, and it was an objective of Keynes, even though the short run in his work was defined as a time span of constant expectations.

Among the first writers to attempt a large-scale accounting of the special attributes of an essentially American, parochial view of Keynes' work was Leijonhufvud [249].[1] He tried to restate and distinguish what Keynes actually said in his writings, mainly *The Treatise on Money* (1930) and *The General Theory* (1936).

Some economists would say that Leijonhufvud read too many of his own or Robert Clower's notions [74] into Keynes' work. Nevertheless, Leijonhufvud's was a needed systematic work. Keynes' main work had come to mean many different things to different economists. There was also need for help in pinning down and restricting hypotheses and aspects of analysis, particularly with respect to their sources.

Leijonhufvud's book (and thus to a secondary extent two earlier articles [250, 251] based on the manuscript) is reviewed in this chapter with special attention to Keynes' economics rather than Keynesian, partly because so much writing has been devoted to Keynesian economics. In fact, some of Keynes' views get revised and updated, and there is a definite change in the approach to the workings of monetary policy.

The distinguishing attributes of Keynes' economics that receive emphasis are (1) unemployment disequilibrium, (2) aggregative structure, (3) the interrelationship between the real goods and financial sectors, (4) uncertainty and the term structure of interest rates, and (5) the point of central bank intervention. Revisions are made in attributes (2) through (5) by letting Keynes' short run (the period of constant or zero elastic expectations) vanish.

Leijonhufvud says [249, p. 391], "Keynes conceived his task to be that of 'analyzing the economic behavior of the present under the influence of changing ideas about the future.' " There was an emphasis on expectations but, as mentioned in Section 1.2, Keynes offered it with one hand and took it away with the other. Expectations return to the forefront when Keynes' short run vanishes. This also entails an equality of foresight principle and

---

1. As early as 1954 Dillard was deploring the tendency for the work of American Keynesians to depart from Keynes' own theory [94, pp. 3–30]. He examines the hypothesis "that the properties of money constitute the ultimate theoretical basis in Keynes' analysis," and discusses some aspects of money dealt with more recently by those cited in the appendix to this chapter. One might even suggest that Leijonhufvud's work accelerated the decline of Keynesian economics by sharpening the distinction between Keynes' and Keynesian economics. This paper by Dillard and one he cites by Abba Lerner ("The Essential Properties of Interest and Money," *Quarterly Journal of Economics*, May 1952) on Chapter 17 of the *General Theory* were influential in shaping the present author's early interest in Keynes' economics and in liquidity.

leads to a special formulation and analysis of the liquidity preference demand for money in Chapter 8, to a re-examination of Tobin's theory of liquidity preference, and to a probabilistic explanation of turning points in business conditions and in interest rates.

The connection between this chapter, the next, and the impact of the modern computer is elementary. The outpouring of empirical results has increasingly reflected (1) the shortcomings of testable notions and policy linkages following from received constructs, and (2) the need to explicitly introduce expectations and probabilistic aspects of economic behavior. Indeed, the mathematical treatment of expectations is integrated with the economic approach to the evaluation of prospective returns.

A part of the economics attributed to Keynes by Leijonhufvud is the price system as a communications mechanism. Keynes, as reviewed in more detail (Sec. 7.2), is said to have recognized the shortcomings of this system, in contrast to his Cambridge contemporaries and immediate predecessors. The particular point about the price system has attracted renewed attention from some economists, mainly Karl Brunner and Allen Meltzer. Brunner [38] is drawn upon in Section 7.2 in an elaboration on the explanation for differential rates of adjustment in output and prices. The two together have been interested in achieving a suitable introduction of the theory of relative prices (micro-economics) into an analysis of aggregates for output and employment, and averages for prices, on the one hand, and with interest in integrating the respective theories of money and prices, on the other. Some work concerning these interests, including especially a treatment of uncertainty in relation to relative prices, is reviewed in the appendix to this chapter.

7.2   UNEMPLOYMENT DISEQUILIBRIUM

Keynes' attack on classical economic theory was "symbolized" by his attack on Say's law (the excess demands for goods exclusive of money sum to zero). It was an attack on (1) the short-run empirical relevance of the "classical" model, (2) the relative unimportance of money in that model of a freely competitive, money-using system, and (3) the communications mechanism envisioned in economic theory. In the first instance, Keynes was interested in a process of adjustment to disturbances and in reversing the ranking of the importance of selected variables in the adjustment mechanism (Sec. 5.3). Current output in money terms (also viewed as income) in Keynes' analysis is more subject to adjustment over a short period of time than individual prices, as a group, and the price-level alone, even in competitive, interrelated atomistic markets. The sluggishness of the price adjustments, according to Leijonhufvud [249, p. 67], however, is due to the inadequacy of the communications mechanism, and not to any classical notions about inflexibility as a result of monopoly elements, as some Keynesian models assume (Sec. 5.6).

It is of no use to counterattack Keynes by introducing Walras' law with money as a good and with a known set of prices. Walras' law, in the sense of Lange, asserts that all excess demands sum to zero, including that for money, but insufficient status is accorded money. Both Say's law and the treatment of money in Walrasian equilibrium analysis fail to recognize the relevance of money as the most liquid of assets, indeed as an asset the speculative demand for which may give rise to changes in aggregate demand for current output.

The price system and effective demand.—In the classical system several assumptions are objectionable as far as communication is concerned. These include the assumption of an immediate adjustment of prices to imbalances in quantities supplied or demanded, that of perfect knowledge about equilibrating prices, and that of the absence of any costs connected with changing prices and output, which would enable traders to detect and move to a new equilibrium. Leijonhufvud notes that Keynes denied the existence of perfect information and invoked uncertain prospective developments as a guide to current production. In particular, in dealing with the questions of communication and the theory of "involuntary" unemployment, Leijonhufvud [249, pp. 81–102] draws heavily on Robert Clower's effort [74] to clarify the formal basis of the Keynesian revolution. Clower distinguishes between excess demand relations of the conventional general equilibrium model and effective excess demand schedules. The first set of trading plans, termed "notional excess demand schedules" by Clower, is drawn up on the basis of an announced set of prices (a vector of prices), and the second takes into account constraints on transactions quantities, particularly the constraint imposed by current income. The first would rule satisfactorily at full employment equilibrium, but following a "shock" to the system, the second set is effective at less-than-full employment equilibrium. The "shock" shifts the aggregate demand schedule and then transactors cut back expenditures as income declines. This cutback may be interpreted as a movement along a consumption function (Sec. 1.3). Unemployed resources emerge, and traders institute a search for proper price and quantity relationships. This takes into account information of "effective" rather than "notional" demands. There are multiple repercussions, in view of the role of the income expenditure multiplier, and the information gathered in the form of announced prices (the "notional" vector) is dated even while the information is being gathered. Feedbacks from initial tendencies toward unemployment to expenditure decisions and attitudes about the certainty of future developments constitute, in a sense, a "cybernetic chain of information feedbacks" [249, p. 102]. Leijonhufvud feels this was the direction in which Keynes was moving, although "the study of communications and control in dynamic systems" was still in the future at the time of Keynes' writing [249, p. 396].

A constrained process is at work in the foregoing analysis. One of Keynes' major contributions—the consumption function—comes to the forefront. Not every household can buy and sell what it pleases. There is prospect of involuntary unemployment (and involuntary under-consumption). Keynes is said to have striven for a general theory that encompasses disequilibrium situations, with the conventional general equilibrium model as a special case. Some of this is "fairly 'modern' stuff" [249, p. 91], but it is offered nevertheless as the sort of thing Keynes had in mind, as indicated by the evidence.

Uncertainty and the consumption function.—As introduced earlier (Sec. 1.2), once business conditions are moving away from normal—say, in a downward direction—the movement may be extrapolated and recent changes create prospects more relevant to the current than to the more distant past and the pull toward normality. Uncertainty also has this effect of giving more emphasis to recent changes, and it is especially related to the demand for money and closely related assets in their unique capacity to lull disquietudes. Keynes dealt with the important question of consumption as an ultimate objective of economic activity and the prospect of "uncertainty" in contrast to the "certainty assumption of metastatic theory" (the needed extension of the perfect market information postulate to a consideration of changes over time, in the context of the static general equilibrium model).[2] In particular, savings could, like money, be held to meet unforeseen developments. Thus greater uncertainty would result in an upward shift in the saving-income relation as well as in the money-income relation (greater uncertainty would result in a decline in the income velocity of money).

---

2. Discussing the consumption function, Leijonhufvud emphasizes its empirical character (that of a psychological law whereby consumption increases less than in proportion to income over short periods of time). He devotes space to indicating practical difficulties in deducing empirically relevant relationships ("operational hypotheses") from choice-theoretic axioms [249, pp. 209, 210, 216], to discussing the unsatisfactory state of capital and interest theory during Keynes' time [249, pp. 212–24], and to reviewing the postulates of metastatics [249, pp. 227–30].

Uncertainty and sticky prices.—Building on Keynes' criticisms of the neo-classical economics of price adjustments, Brunner extends criticism to encompass Keynesian economics and the formulation of price theory since Keynes' work. Brunner [38, p. 49] says that in the Keynesian view the price-theoretical program visualized by Keynes was abandoned, and "a multiplier emerged with no attention to relative price beyond some interest rate responses [imbalance between the cost of funds and the rate of return on new investment]." On standard choice theory, he notes [38, pp. 7–8] the presence of "given endowment and preferences with fully known prices and perfect information about the quality of goods." He then abandons the assumption of perfect information and introduces money as a medium of exchange (partly as a means of reducing the number of price ratios traders must envision in searching out an optimal position).[3] The presence of money reduces some uncertainty about relative prices, but investment in information can also reduce the uncertainty with respect to relative prices, qualities of goods, and market opportunities [38, pp. 7–13]. Money balances, of course, may be used to purchase information as well as to facilitate adjustments in the holdings of other assets or in liabilities.

Information is costly to produce in Brunner's price-theoretical framework. There are two major implications. One concerns the presence of an extra cost element in returns to a seller on the one side of the market and in addition to price from the buyer's side. These marginal cost elements affect adjustments mainly in the "short run." The second major implication concerns the differential rate of price and output adjustments to disequilibrium [38, p. 21]: "The short-run [?] adjustment velocity of quantities exceeds the corresponding velocity of prices in all cases requiring substantial costs of producing information about prevailing market opportunities. Relative short-run price inflexibility thus emerges as a rational consequence of wealth-maximizing behavior in the context of incomplete market information and costly information production."

Monetary impulses modify aggregative measures such as output and employment and more gradually induce adjustments in the price-level. The speed of adjustment in the price level depends on "the load imposed with the impulse and the nature of the cost functions governing production of information and adjustments."

As the appendix to Chapter 7 reveals, Brunner and Meltzer together pur-

---

3. Every item may be quoted as a price relative to money. In its absence, every item is quoted in relation to every other item and there are more relative prices about which information is required.

sue the foregoing line of reasoning to explain the emergence of widely used media of exchange. There are interesting gymnastics, but Brunner maintains [38, pp. 5–7]—and later Brunner and Meltzer together maintain—that aspects of the definition of money and the "motivational classification" introduced by Keynes take the existence of money for granted without explaining its emergence.

7.3   AGGREGATIVE STRUCTURE

Some simple models were catalogued in Section 1.4. One of the features of the models was the classification of assets (or assets and liabilities) which comprise a structure. Such classification is important for it suppresses certain features and implies differences in the substantive aspects of analysis surrounding the models. Leijonhufvud [249, Ch. 3] deals with aggregation in Keynes' and Keynesian models. These matters and models are reviewed and an alternative model (Sec. 1.4) is also brought forward.

In aggregating over transactors, as in the case of a consumption function, the relative incomes (the distribution of income) may be viewed as constant, or the changes in them may be of secondary importance in relation to changes in the level of income. In dealing with the dollar amount of an aggregate of goods, changes in relative prices get subordinated to changes in some average of prices. In aggregation over assets, relations between prospective streams of return become the basis for distinguishing classes of assets. Probabilistic considerations concerning the prospective returns comprising the streams become important, especially as brought out in the next chapter. The returns may include contractual returns and capital gains (and losses) as well. But for the time being—distinguishing the two and thinking of a bond asset—constant expectations and varying interest rates suggest one sort of risk, particularly that of a capital loss or gain from changes in asset values. However, if expectations are thought to vary in response to the same factors affecting interest rates (the rate of change in prices as in Sec. 1.4), then different sorts of risks are suggested and thus different classificatory schemes. The implications of the alternatives are far-reaching and concern even the route via which monetary policy may exercise its effects.

In Keynes' basic model (Sec. 1.4) capital goods and bonds are one aggregate, and stocks (equities) may be included with them. Given the state of long-term expectations, the respective values of bond-streams and equity-streams parallel one another such that their relative value remains constant. Money broadly defined was another aggregate, but in line with rules of classification its value varied out of phase with the capital goods class. As emphasized earlier (Sec. 1.4), given a series of prospective returns (a state of expectations) and a spectrum of maturities for marketable, debt assets, a change in the interest rate results in a greater change in values, the longer the term to maturity. Thus a change in the interest rate parallels an inverse change in capital values of long-term capital assets (bonds and equities). As Leijonhufvud says [249, p. 172], "Knowledge of the value of 'the' interest rate is tantamount to knowing the market price." Such a price was referred to earlier as mythical.

Now over the short period of a change such as the foregoing, the schedule relating the supply price of the assets in question to the stock of capital does not shift, merely the capital value of a given future stream (the schedule relating demand or mythical price to the stock of capital goods). Consequently, a reduction in the interest rate by the monetary officials gives rise to an excess of capital values over supply prices (or, what amounts to the same thing, an excess of the rate of return over the interest rate). The imbalance provides inducement for an increase in capital outlays and sets the stage for capital expansion. In Keynes' model, the overall analysis suggests a fairly high interest elasticity of investment (that a small decline in the interest rate would call forth a fairly significant increase in investment expenditures). This was partly due to Keynes' emphasis on capital goods as being long-lived. The Keynesians viewed capital goods as being shorter-lived than Keynes did.

As Leijonhufvud notes with reference to Keynes' model [249, p. 153], "the interest-elasticity of the present value [price] of a perpetual income-stream is unity; the same elasticity for money of all kinds of deposits is zero; the interest-elasticity of the present value of a short-lived capital instrument or short-lived credit instrument is very low." Given the role of non-money assets (including capital goods), consumer goods and capital goods are distinguished, in view of the implication that the price of capital goods varies in relation to consumer goods. In the next section this classification scheme is related to Keynes' analysis of the term structure of interest rates and the workings of monetary policy.

In the Keynesian model, as Leijonhufvud defines it, (1) the separate financial aggregates include money and bonds, and (2) both consumer and capital goods are included in a single aggregate for output. In the first instance, there is no mechanism for accelerating expenditures as in Keynes' model where capital goods are aggregated with bonds. " 'Autonomous' private-sector investment" and the multiplier and fiscal policy play greater roles. In the second instance, both consumer goods and capital goods can be viewed as a single aggregate because there is no question of the price of one in relation to another varying inversely with the interest rate. Any change in the relative prices is secondary to price-level changes, so far as the over-all behavior of the economy is concerned. This view is probably more nearly correct in modern times because physical capital is more subject to obsolescence and less long-lived, especially under the influence of accelerated depreciation for tax purposes, and because the central bank does not have the type of control over the long-term interest rate that could cause the price of capital goods to vary substantially in relation to consumer goods over a short period of time.

The main difference between the highly aggregative Keynesian model and the present alternative is the variable state of expectations. Sets of factors—such as those affecting prospective changes in prices—operate differently on debt assets as distinct from capital-goods, equity assets. Prospective inflation reduces the value of the debt set and the purchasing power of money balances, and it raises the value of the capital-goods, equity set, so that prospective inflation gives rise to a switching between broad classes of assets and accelerated expansion of capital-goods assets. The income velocity of money would rise, as would interest rates, in view of the anticipated buoyancy in business conditions and/or the inflation. If the inflation were recent and the horizon for its continuation near—so that the anticipation would be less constrained by a return to normality over a longer period—then as velocity and interest rates rose, short-term rates would rise more than long-term rates, as embellished elsewhere [131, Sec. II, n. 9]. Thus, the term structure of interest rates (defined as the structure of yields on financial assets that differ mainly with respect to maturity) would also be brought in.

The vanishing short run and the tendency for capital goods, the investment sector (as suggested by the analysis of the velocity ratio), and the financial markets sector (as suggested by the analysis of the term structure of interest rates) to respond simultaneously to the same factors impinging on expectations are related to the equality of foresight principle, suggested initially in Chapter 2. In contrast, in Keynesian analysis some autonomous factor (new technique, new discovery, etc., Sec. 5.2) could influence investment prospects and the rate of return on capital without affecting the interest rate (or the expectations of lenders), and the unequal effects (or inequality of foresight) became a basis for expansion in business conditions. In a Fisherian framework (Sec. 1.4), businessmen expecting some inflation may increase expenditures and loan demand at prevailing interest rates since lenders (bankers) would be slower to adjust expectations and thus interest rates to the changes taking place.

In the alternative classificatory scheme, expectations are not constant and monetary policy works differently from that in Keynes' model. The existence of rather continuous changes in the term structure of interest rates and the verification for a form of expectations theory concerning it [131] would support the present scheme, as should become more obvious in later chapters (12, 13). In the present scheme, Keynes' and the traditional central banking emphasis on the level of interest rates and simple linkages between expenditures and the banking mechanism recedes, and emphasis on an alternative comes to the forefront. Monetary policy is viewed as operating on a more abstract plane, via expectations and expected changes in interest rates. The crucial set of changes is that in the relationship between prevailing rates and those expected to prevail in the future. Indeed, changes in the term structure of interest rates are even suggested as an indicator of changes in monetary policy. The imbalance between the interest rate and the rate of return, as a condition for changing business conditions, becomes merely a fiction, although a convenient one, since the interest rate and the rate of return move procyclically.

There are other elements to Keynes' and the foregoing alternative analysis. Keynes' short run (the period of constant expectations) vanishes and the focus shifts from so-called defensive central bank operations to an analysis of economic instability as indicated by the short cycle in business conditions. Keynes sought to focus on this economic problem, but he went about it in a more traditional banking way. According to Leijonhufvud [249, p. 183], the inadequate investment of the 1930s was "*a problem of interest rate inflexibility.*" Apparently, by the time of the Great Depression and Keynes' *General Theory* (1936), Keynes began to have doubts "that *conventional* monetary operations could budge the long rate *rapidly* enough to avoid prolonged periods of unemployment." Although Leijonhufvud does not note it, this sort of statement suggests that part of the problem was inadequate understanding by either economists or central bankers of how the central bank controlled the interest rate.

7.4 Monetary Policy and the Integration of the Real and Financial Sectors

An important feature of Keynes' contribution was the integration of the theory of money with that of output. A strengthened demand for money and other liquid assets could result in a decline in the effective demand for output and in a decline in output. As brought out by Leijonhufvud [249, pp. 282–314], a dimension of the relationship between the real goods sector and the financial markets centered about the term structure of interest rates, as reflected in the yield curve or the spread between long- and short-dated securities differing mainly with respect to the dating feature.[4] The analysis centering about the yield curve provided the basis for the introduction of monetary policy and the central bank's influence over capital expenditures.

Keynes' theory of the term structure is considered in this section, and term structure theory relating to an alternative approach is also considered.

Normal backwardation and monetary policy.—Keynes advanced a theory of normal backwardation. It asserts some preference for the certainty of capital over income and a preference for short-dated over long-dated securities, on the grounds that changes in the interest rate affect the value of securities more, the longer the time to maturity. The term "normal backwardation" is equated to liquidity preference theory, but the latter is quite distinct from Keynes' and variants of Keynes' analysis of liquidity preference demand for money (an analysis of a preference for money vis-à-vis other assets). The preference for money relates to the need for cash as a means of dealing with uncertainty over future developments as well as a means of avoiding capital losses and realizing gains via speculation over changes in the level of interest rates. This speculative behavior is usually explicitly related to the so-called liquidity preference building block of Keynes' analysis or to variants of that analysis, as considered earlier (Sec. 5.3) and in the next chapter.

The policy analysis goes as follows. Since there is a preference for short-dated assets, the central bank can vary the supply of short-dated securities on the market, as through open market operations, and thus more or less satisfy the preference. An excess of purchases would drive the price of the securities upward (and thus the short rate downward). The entire curve would shift downward via an arbitrage mechanism[5] as the market adjusted its preference to the altered supply conditions [249, pp. 154, 162, 175, 196, 199, 201, 207, 287]. The decline in the long rate in Keynes' two-asset model (Sec. 7.3) would raise the value or demand price for physical capital, just as it did that for bonds, given the state of long-term expectations.

Leijonhufvud views the foregoing thinking on policy matters as providing

4. The yield curve simply results from fitting a line or curve to a scatter of coordinates (points) consisting of yields and the corresponding maturities for debt instruments that differ primarily with respect to time to maturity at a given time or period.

5. The arbitrage mechanism in question is that whereby securities may be sold in one market segment and others immediately purchased in another. There is the view that such transactions are effected to take advantage of discrepancies that may exist in the structure of interest rates.

the basis for a "bills only" policy on the part of the Federal Reserve in the United States. In the Federal Reserve's view of the post-accord and mid–1950s period, the interest rate could be lowered or raised by effecting open market transactions at the short end of the yield curve. Keynes was skeptical of the latter according to Leijonhufvud, but this book questions whether the Federal Reserve has control over the interest rate via simple supply-demand mechanisms and independent of the influence on expectations. To concede that expectations have a predominating influence is to reject the bankers view of monetary policy linkages, Keynes' model, and the Keynesian model, as outlined by Leijonhufvud.

A difficulty for Keynes' analysis and the banking view is posed by competing theory and the empirical support for it. For example, expectations about future rates may determine the term structure, with or without a preference for short-dated assets as a means of assuring greater capital certainty. The relevant question for operational purposes is which set of forces predominates. In a process of varying the supply of securities in the market, bank credit and the money stock may change simultaneously and affect expectations so that the effect of the latter change dominates over the effect of change in the supply of securities on capital expenditures.

Alternative theory.—Term structure theories have tended to two extremes, as outlined elsewhere [131]. The extremes are characterized by the Meiselman (received) expectations hypothesis and the segmented markets hypothesis. A main attribute of the received expectations hypothesis is that the long-term rate is an average of expected short-term rates. A portfolio manager might choose from a series of n consecutive single-period bonds and an n-period bond, depending on the greater expected return over the entire period. This procedure of choosing via a supply-demand-quantity mechanism leads to an increase in the price (reduced expected return) for securities purchased (or sold) and reduces the price (increased expected return) for securities not purchased (or sold) so that the expected return over n periods is the same no matter which investment pattern is selected.

At the other extreme, the segmented markets theory treats expectations as non-operative (zero elastic). Speculation is minimized and particular maturities of securities are selected to coincide with an anticipated need for funds. Thus the possibility of loss in value from an increase in interest rates is minimized. One might say that a liquidity hedging motive is present. However, the short- and long-term markets are segmented. The prices in one segment are independent of those in another, and the prices depend on the quantities of securities supplied and demanded in the respective segments of the markets.

The backwardation notion of Keynes—like the foregoing term structure notion—relies on a supply-demand-quantity mechanism,[6] but emphasizes the preference for short-dated instruments and interrelated markets. In view of the supply-demand-quantity mechanism, a twisting of the yield curve should be possible, as in the Federal Reserve's Operation Twist which began in early 1961. But the prospect is most related to the market segmentation view. The twist effort was directed toward raising short-term rates and lowering long-term rates by selling in the former segment of the market and by buying in the latter. The objective was to strengthen the U.S. balance of payments position and still encourage domestic investments as in the investment demand building block (Sec. 1.3). Even in this expansion phase of business conditions when an expectations mechanism was operating in the operations favor, however, it could not have been judged a success (as appraised in Part IV).

In the term structure theory accompanying the alternative model of the last section, as set forth by Terrell and Frazer [131], there is liquidity hedging and some preference for short-dated securities as a source of funds for unanticipated needs. The time-to-maturity profiles of the securities held[7] are related in large measure to the anticipated need for funds, but the term structure of rates is released from some of its dependence on strong supply-demand-quantity notions of the other theories. In fact, an important attribute is that interest rates and the structure of rates may change in accordance with expectations, even at times when the relative quantities of the different maturities placed on the market and held by various groups are fairly stable.

In this alternative context, monetary policy exerts its influence on interest rates and the term structure in the same way it exerts its influence on a major segment of capital expenditures. This segment of expenditures is notably that by large manufacturing corporations (Ch. 15) which plan

6. The term "supply-demand-quantity" is used to mean that some quantities of securities must come on or be withdrawn from the market in order for the security prices (and thus yields) to change. The prospect of some adjustments in yields (and thus prices) taking place among traders without accompanying changes in quantities is posed elsewhere [131] and below.

7. These profiles may be described through the notion of a frequency distribution or relative frequency density as in probability theory (131, Sec. III). In such cases, for different institutional groups, time to maturity of different portions of government debt may be thought of as measured along a horizontal axis, and the par value (in dollars) of the debt in each maturity class (or the amount of the security as a proportion of the respective portfolios) may be thought of as being measured on a vertical axis, all at the moment in time.

their expenditures and their financing to be largely independent of the availability of bank credit as usually discussed by Keynesians (Sec. 3.4).

7.5 Summary

Keynes extended economics to include unemployment disequilibrium. Money and closely related liquid assets played a special role; uncertainty could lead to an increase in their demand and a reduction in the effective demand for output. Unemployed resources emerge, and traders institute a search for proper price and quantity relationships. The price system as a communications mechanism is inadequate, however, and there are feedbacks from the tendency toward unemployment to expenditure decisions. Uncertainty with respect to relative prices and market opportunities may be introduced into the price theory prevailing since Keynes' time. Information may be purchased to reduce uncertainty about relative prices, the quality of goods, and market opportunities, but the cost imparts an additional element into the analysis of prices and market decisions. All of this, as brought out by Brunner, suggests one reason why adjustments to disequilibrium may occur more rapidly in output changes and more gradually in relative price and ultimately price-level changes.

The financial and real sectors are additionally related to Keynes' model through theory about the term structure of interest rates. Money and liquid noncash assets are one class of assets, and bonds and real capital are another. With expectations constant, a reduction in the interest rate has the most effect on the value of the assets at the long end of the maturity spectrum. Monetary policy enters in; purchase of securities at the short end of the spectrum may be transmitted to the long end, and a reduced interest rate calls forth additional capital outlays.

Uncertainty, speculative attributes surrounding the demand for money, and changing ideas about the future are involved. Even so, in the short run of Keynes' theory expectations are constant, so all anticipations about the future are secondary. When this short run vanishes, expectations come to the forefront, but the changes call for revisions in aspects of Keynes' analysis. In the case of an expected rate of change in the price level, the main classifications of assets that emerge are those with a fixed claim against future income and those with a residual claim. Also there are factors that impinge simultaneously on expectations about returns from capital outlays and on expectations about interest rates. The real and financial sectors are interrelated, but the relationship differs from that which follows from the treatment of expectations as a constant.

Monetary policy also enters differently; it influences prospects concerning business conditions, inflation, and so on. The prospect of simple and direct control over the interest rate by the central bank comes into question. The contrasting way in which policy is thought to operate calls for an alternative view of the term structure of interest rates. In particular, the view brought forward is one in which yields comprising the term structure are at times adjusted in accordance with changing prospects and without the intervening need for changes in the quantities of securities purchased in one maturity sector or sold in another.

8

Expectations, Money, and Subjective Probability

8.1 INTRODUCTION

THE REVIVAL of an awareness of money and its role has been a theme of previous chapters. In closely related developments, the outpouring of statistical results from the modern computer tended to bring to the forefront the need to deal more systematically with probabilistic aspects of behavior, such as uncertainty.[1] The notions also encompass dynamic phenomena falling within the purview of expectations, such as the "expected rate of change in prices" (Secs. 1.4, 4.2, Appendix to Ch. 1), "extrapolative pushes," "regressive pulls," "shocks," and the dimunition of the slanting of certain prospects as opinions in group situations reinforce one another. The "push" effects are the direct influence on expectations of the thrust and propulsion of current and recent changes. The "pull" effects are attractions toward some subjectively viewed normal rates of change—or levels, in the case of the interest rate. The "shocks" are factors operating outside the usual economic theory, such as announcements of important policy changes or events, a Vietnam, the energy crisis, and change in political administration. The dimunition of the slanting of opinions pertains to the interpersonally controversial character of some decisions.

Keynes himself attributed importance to expectations in the *General Theory*, but proceeded to present an analysis of a period in which expecta-

---

1. The term "uncertainty" is used most often in this book, as in neo-Bayesian analysis, to mean a probabilistic expectation other than certainty, as noted by the assignment of a probability.

Sometimes in economics the term is used to mean incomplete knowledge. Frank Knight restricted the applicability of probability to the rather traditional actuarial problems he termed risk, all as distinct from uncertainty. As Fellner [111, p. 30] and others have said, "He concluded that entrepreneurial decisions and profits belong in the theory of uncertainty, not in that of risk."

tions were constant, as brought out in the previous chapter. A method used there was to let the short run vanish and then to revise aspects of Keynes' economics. In this chapter another part of his early interest is brought out and revised, that relating to subjective probability. It is related to the subject of money. As outlined earlier (Sec. 5.4), Keynes introduced two explanations for the liquidity preference demand for money. One dealt with a regressive pull toward normality and the other facilitated a treatment of demand with constant expectations, particularly as developed by James Tobin [356]. In this chapter Tobin's theory is discussed further and juxtaposed with one in which expectations are permitted to vary.

Among the original notions in the final sections of this chapter, there is an explanation of turning points in business conditions (or interest rates) in probabilistic terms. Some concepts of probability and utility (neo-Bayesian concepts) appear in Section 8.2. There is emphasis on subjective judgments about prior probabilities, and on learning. Neo-Bayesian method [297, 298] and specific propositions attributed to Fellner [111] are used to provide insights into the extent to which behavioral units are guided by possible returns to normal values or by growing deviations from them.[2] Section 8.3 sets out concepts of utility maximization and mathematical expectations in forms that are both consistent with the neo-Bayesian notions and conducive to their subsequent use.

8.2 NEO-BAYESIAN DECISION THEORY

From Bayes' theorem [362, pp. 30–33] one may write, following Fellner [111, pp. 49–56],

$$(1.0) \qquad \frac{P_D(H_1)}{P_D(H_2)} = \frac{P_i(H_i)}{P_i(H_i)} \cdot \frac{P(D/H_1)}{P(D/H_2)}$$

ratio of posterior probabilities	ratio of prior probabilities	represents ratio of likelihood functions

where the P's denote probabilities, H_1 and H_2 are hypotheses about events, posterior means after observing the data (D) [and consequently $P_D(H)$ is the probability of a hypothesis after observing the data], prior means before observing the data, $P(D/H_1)$ is a conditional probability or prob-

2. For annotated bibliography on neo-Bayesian decision theory and related works, see Raiffa [297, pp. 298–300] and Fellner [111, pp. 210–33].

ability of observing a sample given a hypothesis ($/$), and so on.[3] When the hypotheses exhaust the possibilities and their separate probabilities sum to one, then the separate probabilities of the events may be obtained from knowledge of the foregoing ratios.

The ratio of posterior probabilities depends only on the ratio of prior probabilities and the ratio of the likelihoods.[4] The modern Bayesians contend that prior probabilities should be assigned on the basis of initial guesses, hunches, and available information. Forerunners of the modern Bayesians (e.g., Pierre Laplace) and some others have relied on the still useful and relevant principle of insufficient reason, in which equal probabilities are assigned to the states of nature when there is no information about them. In equation (1.0) this means assigning equal probabilities to the priors in the prior probability ratio. In either case, once the ratio representing the likelihood function is found, the problem is solved.

One could continue to gather further information and continue to use the procedure just outlined. The posterior probabilities of the last drawing or sample could be used as prior probabilities in the next sample, and so on. From either the numerator or denominator portions of equation (1.0) alone, a separate equation could be written. As Zellner says of statistical estimation and continuous distributions [387], "*In every instance*, the posterior probability density function (pdf) for parameters is proportional to the prior pdf times the likelihood function with the factors of proportionality being a normalizing factor." This statement of Bayes' theorem is commonly denoted

$$P(\theta_i|X) \quad \propto \quad P(\theta_i) \qquad P(X|\theta_i)$$

posterior probability of parameter	prior probability	represents likelihood function

where a hypothesis in equation (1.0) is represented by a parameter (θ_i), X represents the data, and $\propto$ is the sign of proportionality. In other words,

3. Prior possibilities are initial judgments about the probabilities of events as viewed by a decision-maker or group prior to acquiring new experience or information from data. Posterior probabilities are judgments of probabilities subsequent to acquiring experience or information from data, as incorporated in a likelihood function. A likelihood function is a function expressing the probability of observing a given sample, as some parameter value or given condition varies, e.g., $F(x_1, x_2, \ldots, x_n; \Theta)$ where x's are the given sample and Θ is the variable parameter.

4. The conditional probabilities in equation (1.0) are said to represent the likelihoods, because the likelihoods are related to the conditional probabilities by some factors of proportionality [111, n. 11, p. 50].

the posterior function incorporates all available information, prior and sample. Steps in addition to those just outlined could be taken toward further generalization.

Utility analysis and slanting.—In the neo-Bayesian approach, Bayesian reasoning is combined with utility analysis. Fellner emphasizes [111, p. 56] that it assumes "that a reasonable decision maker maximizes the probabilistic expectation (mathematical expectation) of the *utility* of wealth to him, and thus his probabilistic expectation of the utility of the potential consequences of the acts he is considering." The probabilities or weights in the mathematical expectation may even be viewed as being slanted in Fellner's semiprobabilistic approach [111] to allow for the shakiness of judgments that are unstable in the decision-maker's mind.[5]

The slant in such instances [111, pp. 7–8] "expresses an allowance for a specific type of non-money rewards and disadvantages."[6] It is especially relevant in decisions concerning groups [111, pp. 1, 100, 173, 199], in which there may be special rewards and penalties for making decisions on the basis of firm versus shaky judgments. Thus the Fellner version of subjective probability theory would seem especially relevant to the requirements of a formal theory about economic units that dominate the behavior of overall economic measures in a highly developed industrial state. Such units include large firms and groups of institutional investors. For the most part their behavior reflects the decisions of managers and committees as distinct from owners.

Learning from experience.—There are the subjective probabilities, the slanting to allow for special situations, especially group decisions. There is also the subjectivity embodied in utility functions. From the points of view of positive economics, decision-making, investment, and related behavior, there may be constant changes as a result of learning from experience. In reference to the discussion of equation (1.0), there may be learning from experience in that information from data and initial beliefs

---

5. It is true, as recognized by various writers [111, p. 33], "that many reasonable individuals feel more uneasy about action based on mere hunches—on shaky and highly controversial degrees of belief—than about action motivated by well-established and firmly held numerical appraisals." In controversial situations, "reasonable individuals are entitled to feel *differently* [slant their judgments] about relying on one or the other of these *various types* of judgements."

6. To say that a probability is slanted means that certain prospects are placed at a more or less discount [111, p. 36]. As Fellner says [111, p. 172], "a downward-slanting subject will lower the function of the weighted marginal utility of potential gain for various prospects, and he will raise the function of the weighted marginal utility of potential loss for these same prospects."

or priors combine to yield posterior probabilities, which in turn become the basis for hunches and judgments in the next assignment of probabilities.

Greater certainty.—Especially relevant to changing initial beliefs is the following proposition by Fellner [111, p. 8]:

> *Proposition (1.1).* If judgment is thought to be shaky in the sense of un-certain, "then it seems plausible to expect that in a good many cases the semiprobabilistic slanting inclinations will diminish (though they will not disappear) as the decision maker *gets used* to being faced with some specific type of decision."

Group behavior.—Another plausible effect on judgments by decision-makers concerns their interpersonally controversial character [111, p. 8]:

> *Proposition (1.2).* "Slanting inclinations will diminish . . . wherever large groups of *like-minded* individuals are formed."

This suggests that as opinions about changes coalesce the opinions of market participants and decision-makers generally become reinforcing.

8.3 Fellner's Semiprobabilistic System

The emergence of a formal body of probability theory—namely neo-Bayesian theory with a semiprobabilistic emphasis—contributes to the possibility of broadening the formal structure of economic theory. It can also be made more viable and relevant to aspects of observed economic behavior. With these goals in mind, certain modifications are introduced, presently with respect to Fellner's system and later (Sec. 8.4) with respect to Keynes' analysis.

Neo-Bayesian probability theory—or decision theory, as Raiffa has called it—emerged as a normative theory under the direction of Raiffa, Schlaifer, et al. Fellner introduced it as part of positive economic theory.[7] In the semiprobabilistic form he gave to the theory [111], the theory recognizes real world attributes of decision-makers, investment behavior, groups, and so on. It seems natural to view the approach as potentially useful in posi-tive economics. The relationship would be somewhat similar to that be-tween capital budgeting as a normative subject and a modified version of Keynes' investment demand model as positive theory [133, pp. 359–62].

---

7. The less initiated reader will recall that positive theory in economics is theory about economic behavior rather than a prescription for proper behavior or decision-making. Decision theory under Raiffa et al. emerged as a prescription for logical decision-making by behavioral units.

Selected capital budgeting procedures have been in such wide use by large manufacturing firms that it seemed natural to recognize their presence to try to elucidate a positive theory of the investment behavior of such firms (as in Ch. 15). The modifications to Fellner's system center upon the utility function and the role of mathematical expectations in decision theory.

The utility function and the maximum gain in utility.—As emphasized in Section 8.2, the utility function plays an important role in neo-Bayesian decision theory. Von Neumann-Morgenstern utility axioms are also introduced [111, pp. 81–84] to give a cardinal quality to utility as in their *Theory of Games and Economic Behavior.* Even so, in Fellner's axiomatic system there is less emphasis on independent events, the independence axiom is troublesome [111, p. 162; 165, p. 262], and there is emphasis instead on exchangeable events [111, pp. 77–78, 174]. In drawing on Fellner's approach, however, the strong cardinal utility axioms are not presently essential. The probabilistic and slanting notions may be brought forward and applied in a Hicks-Allen, ordinal utility framework [197, Ch. 2].[8] In such a case, the emphasis shifts from the measurement of utility to simply generating some behavioral notions that are thought to be applicable to the real world with a minimum of constraint being imposed by the axioms.[9] The foundations of the approach include the Hicks-Allen sort of choosing among alternatives with prospective utilities [including the implication about the comparibility of a sure prospect (cash) and an uncertain prospect (a chance at a prize)], requirements for consistency centering about reliance on slanted probabilities [111, pp. 146–55], Bayesian notions [111, pp.

---

8. There is a net gain in this in addition to any reduction in the strenuousness imposed by cardinal utility axioms. In particular, the presence of vagueness in many decisions leads Georgescu-Roegen to question the indifference postulate and the indifference curves present in Hicks-Allen utility theory [165, pp. 254, 255–56], particularly in considering the comparability of two expectations [166] but the aspects of the theory questioned appear to be dealt with by drawing on Fellner's approach. The problem with which Georgescu-Roegen was dealing is suggested by the rhetorical question [166, p. 13]: "How many times do we hear around us that 'this is a difficult decision to make'?" In drawing on Fellner's semiprobabilistic approach of slanting, some system and precision about vague decisions come in to fill a void.

9. The analysis of the independence axiom is crucial here. It leads to two notions: (1) the ranking of preferences is not altered by a linear transformation of the utility function; and (2) the differences between utilities are not altered by a linear transformation. The weaker indifference postulate of ordinal analysis, as in Henderson and Quandt [197, pp. 19–23], permits any monotonic transformation of a utility function to serve as a utility function index. A batch of commodities that maximizes one function will maximize any monotonic transformation of it. In this sense, the ordinal functions are more general than the cardinal ones, but the axiomatic system of ordinal utility will not encompass the case of the measurement of utility.

48–49], and the basic axioms and rules of probability [111, pp. 72–76; 362, pp. 19–22]. These probability axioms may be taken as given (presupposed as a part of the preference structure), or the probabilities as well as the utilities may be derived from the axioms. In the former case, only utilities are derived from the axioms since the probabilities are already part of the axiomatic structure. The latter approach is presently chosen. The warning inspired by Gabriel Cramer [111, pp. 106–8] is relevant: one must allow for the inclinations of many subjects to disregard small probabilities, very small probabilistic differences, and small monetary losses or gains.

Fellner introduces a utility function [111, pp. 96–97] with the variable "wealth minus initial wealth of the present period (gains in dollars)." In encompassing wealth or total assets more generally, as presently proposed, one gets a different aggregate utility. The first utility, as introduced by Fellner, is simply a marginal quantity; it consists of the differential for total utility from wealth, where the variable is the differential for wealth.

So utility is introduced as a function of assets or wealth. In particular, viewing utility as a function of separate assets comprising a total and recognizing the total as a constraint, one may form a Lagrangian function. Of course, the behavioral subjects who are maximizing utility are subject to other constraints on their actual behavior such as may be imposed by laws, traditions, attitudes, and practices, but no formal counterparts for these are introduced in the Lagrangian function. If they were, the function would soon include more constraints than variables and the formal mathematical statement in this case would break down. Apart from this, then, one may conclude from the first order conditions for a constrained maximum that the utility yielded by a given batch of assets is a maximum when the rates of return from additions to each class of assets are equal [126, Ch. 7; 133, pp. 51–57, 367–71]. In traditional utility analyses the utilities may encompass non-pecuniary returns and allowances for risk and liquidity, as do the related rates of return. When probabilities are applied to utilities (or the dollar returns comprising them) as in mathematical expectations, however, an analysis in operational terms may proceed more readily from allowing the probabilities and the discounts applied to them to take on the burden of the more subjective elements under analysis.

In the foregoing approach one may also discuss a cost that is minimized, namely the cost of funds for asset expansion. The minimum cost condition is met when the interest rates from alternative sources of funds are equal. These rates include psychological elements. This equilibrium condition, in combination with that for the maximization of returns, yields a Keynesian equilibrium in which the rate of return from additional assets and the interest rate are equal. The latter equality also relates to a form of profit maximization [133, Appendix to Ch. 17].

These profit and equilibrium conditions are analogous to those in Fellner [111, Ch. 4], only his profit measure is cardinal. There one finds a gain function [111, pp. 111–12], "the *weighted marginal utility of potential gains as a function of the amount to be invested in the project.*" And a loss function [111, p. 112], "the *weighted marginal disutility of potential loss as a function of the amount to be invested.*" The gain and loss functions together yield a maximum profit position or a maximum gain in expected utility [111, Ch. 5]. This maximum profit analysis is analogous to that accompanying the Keynesian investment demand model. From this point of view, one should be able to find counterparts to Fellner's gain, loss, and maximum-gain-in-utility notions. These would include: (1) expected returns per period, $r\,I^e$, (2) expected cost of funds per period, $i\,I^e$, and (3) profits, $r\,I^e - i\,I^e$, where r is the rate of return, I^e is planned capital outlays, and i is the interest rate. Ex post profits are thought of as being maximized by the maximization of expected or ex ante profits.

Mathematical expectations.—The probability notion of a mathematical expectation is not—without modification—immediately related to psychological notions about expectations in general economics, but it can be related.

"Mathematical expectation" is synonymous with "arithmetic mean" and "expected value." In the discrete case, the mathematical expectation is the sum of the products of possible events and their probabilities.[10] In the simplest decision problems, for example, one deals with probabilities that sum to one, and with the occurrence and non-occurrence of an event. Raiffa [297, p. 9] refers to the *expected monetary value* (EMV) of a gamble that results in a payoff of \$0.00 or \$100.00, with equal probabilities of ½:

$$\text{EMV} = \tfrac{1}{2}\,(\$0.00) + \tfrac{1}{2}\,(\$100.00) = \$50.00$$

10. If X is a random variable that may take on the values $x_1, x_2, \ldots, x_n$ with probabilities $p_1, p_2, \ldots, p_n$, then the expected value of X, denoted $E(X)$, is

$$p_1 x_1 + p_2 x_2 + \ldots + p_n x_n = \sum_{i=1}^{n} p_i x_i$$

In contrast to such a measure of the central tendency of a variable, variance is a measure of dispersion—the degree to which the probability distribution of the variable is spread out or centered with a narrow interval. The variance (V) of X is defined as the average square deviation of X from its expected value (E):

$$V = p_1\,(x_1 - E)^2 + p_2\,(x_2 - E)^2 + \ldots + p_n\,(x_n - E)^2$$

A strict EMV'er would accept this gamble at a price of up to $50.00. A non EMV'er might assign less value to the foregoing gamble and prefer a certainty of only $40.00 to the gamble for $100.00, because of an aversion to risk. Fellner deals with such prospects [111, pp. 90–97].[11]

In analyses of simple events, the Raiffa school would insist on the probabilities summing to one [297, pp. 110–14]. The semiprobabilist would be less insistent,[12] or at least he would permit the probabilities to be slanted or discounted even where the undistorted probabilities sum to one [111, p. 64].

The decision theorist tends to labor simplistic decision problems in setting forth his subjects. The problem becomes "horrendous to think about," as the number of possibilities and decisions increases [297, p. 156]. Even so, it is thought advantageous to think systematically about assigning probabilities.

Time is another complicating problem, as when certain and less certain prospects must be discounted for time preference. This occurs in the idea of the capital value, or demand price (CV), of an addition to assets, as the discounted value of prospective returns (R_t, $t = 1, \ldots, n$):

$$(1.1) \qquad CV = \frac{R_1}{(1+i)^1} + \frac{R_2}{(1+i)^2} + \cdots + \frac{R_n}{(1+i)^n}$$

where i is the interest rate for discounting the returns, and where expected returns concern genuine economic expectations as distinct from mathematical expectations. However, for illustrative purposes, if one treats the time horizon as zero or nonexistent, the demand price relation (1.1) becomes

$$(1.2) \qquad CV = R_1 + R_2 + \ldots + R_n$$

and each of these R's could be treated in a simple mathematical expectation framework, with CV being the sum of their expected monetary values.[13] As

11. See Raiffa [297, pp. 60–70] on the shape of indifference curves for risk-averse individuals.

12. Raiffa includes an illustrative footnote on Robert Moses of New York [297, p. 110]. He notes that Moses had appealed to the Weather Bureau at the time of the New York World's Fair to report an 80 per cent chance of fair weather rather than a 20 per cent chance of precipitation. There were two related ideas: (1) emphasizing the positive would improve attendance at the fair, and (2) the sum of the subjective probabilities of the event of rain and not rain were greater than one.

13. Using notation from the body of the chapter,

$$(EMV)_1 = p_1(R_1) + (1 - p_1)(\sim R_1)$$
$$(EMV)_2 = p_2(R_2) + (1 - p_2)(\sim R_2)$$
$$\ldots\ldots\ldots\ldots\ldots\ldots\ldots\ldots\ldots$$
$$(EMV)_3 = p_n(R_n) + (1 - p_n)(\sim R_n)$$

where p's are probabilities, the R's are events, and $\sim R$'s are non-occurrences of events. The $\sim R$'s may be viewed as zeros in the present case.

n approaches 30, relation (1.1) approaches $CV = R/i$, as shown elsewhere [133, p. 55]. Further, $i = R/CV$ and—allowing for the elements composing R as discussed below—the ratio R/CV may be interpreted as the ratio of a marginal utility to its price. The ratio may be obtained from the maximization of an ordinal utility function, subject to a wealth or asset constraint. The probabilistic weighting of marginal utilities then introduces a neo-Bayesian analysis. One characteristic is that the introduction of a variance of an expected value as in the relative frequency approach to probability is no longer necessary. Attitudes toward risk and the reliability of an expected value are now imbodied in the probabilistically weighted utilities. In addition, at equilibrium the rates of return are equal for different classes of assets (e.g., $i_1 = i_2 = \ldots = i_n$, for n classes), and they are also equal to the marginal utility of money as in the theory of an exchange economy (Appendix to Ch. 7). But even with ordinally weighted utilities, one can speak of shifting weights that correspond to a disturbance in the equilibrium and that set in motion an adjustment at the margin toward a new equilibrium.

Elsewhere in the discussion of prospective returns [126, Ch. 7; 133, Chs. 4–5, 17] returns and their corresponding rates have been decomposed into elements, including liquidity elements. Varying such elements—both as they entered into returns and rates for discounting them—has been a way of adjusting for subjective attitudes, particularly those toward risk. Keynes used them in obtaining the certainty equivalent of an uncertain prospect. In the present context, however, adjustments in the liquidity element may be viewed as having a counterpart in a weighting scheme, as in decision theory. With the exception of money—where the flow of returns is mainly in the form of the security and convenience of holding money—the prospective returns in strict dollar amounts could be viewed as weighted. In a high risk venture the weights would be small relative to those in a low risk venture. In the case of greater certainty of returns the weights would increase toward one. They would decrease in the case of a behavioral unit with increasing preference for capital certainty over income, and thus the value or the demand price of an addition to assets would decline for a given interest rate. One may think of liquidity discounts or premiums that are analogous to the discounts and premiums associated with prospective events by Fellner.

The present system would indeed become horrendous to think about in terms of all the detail of decision theory.[14] One must abstract some to introduce decision theory into positive economics.

14. In a brief passage, Raiffa [297, p. 100] says he deals with only a small part of the mammoth subject called "capital budgeting." He says, "The deeper one goes

8.4 EXPECTATIONS AND THE LIQUIDITY PREFERENCE CONSTRUCTS

Some writers have been critical of Keynes in the area of expectations. Among these, Tobin has pursued one line of inquiry. Lawrence Klein says Tobin appears to have fruitfully applied modern theories of portfolio selection to rationalizing liquidity preference theory [233, p. 206]. The development is said to follow "in the tradition of time-honored principles of sound investment counseling—diversification of holdings to minimize risk." Average return and risk are considered separately. Leijonhufvud [249, p. 369] refers to Markowitz in particular in this respect. Klein also traces a line of inspiration to the utility and probability notions in the work of von Neumann and Morgenstern, rather than to Keynes himself. Keynes, however, was an early probabilist with a subjectivist point of view.[15] Thus, the probabilistic line of inquiry is reopened by reviewing Tobin's contribution and Markowitz's mean-variance analysis.

Tobin's theory of liquidity preference.—Tobin recognized in Keynes' work two explanations of liquidity preference: (1) one relying on differences of opinion [356, pp. 67–70], and (2) one relying on the notion of a "normal" long-term rate "to which investors expect the rate of interest to return." Both were introduced earlier (Sec. 5.4). In brief, the first explanation assumes a given expected interest rate on a long-term bond (or consol) for individual investors, such that a rise (decline) in the current rate above (below) the expected rate results in a switching of the entire portfolio into (out of) bonds. Where differences of opinion about the future rate prevail, individual demands are different. Even so, aggregating them provides a smooth curve that relates the demand for cash inversely to the interest rate. Some minor complications affect the slope and position of the curve, but the central bank is thought to be able to intervene through open market operations and achieve specific interest rates by determining the level of the money stock.

In the second explanation of the inverse money–interest rate relationship, there is a "normal" interest rate to which investors expect interest rates to return. The further the current interest rate is, say, below the normal rate, the greater the prospect of a rise in rates (and a loss of value from holding bonds) and the stronger the preference for money.[16]

---

into this area, the harder it becomes to isolate a problem for prescriptive analysis —everything seems to be intertwined with everything else."

15. Raiffa touches on this [297, pp. 275–76, 283–84].

16. This second explanation of the inverse relationship between money and interest rates is embellished elsewhere [129, Sec. 1] and attributed to Keynes. Probabilities are assigned to various prospects of future changes in bond yields (and

Tobin believes the first of the foregoing explanations to be Keynes'
original but recognizes the second as receiving the greatest emphasis by
Keynes.[17] A flaw in Keynes' theory—as seen by Fellner, embellished by
Tobin [356, pp. 70–71], and reviewed by Leijonhufvud [249, pp. 366–83]
—concerns an inconsistency: the varying strength of expectations in the
theory of liquidity preference, and the constancy of expectations over the
short period in the theory generally. As stated by Leijonhufvud, Keynes'
analysis is short-run, and many of his analytical results follow from defining
the short run as one in which expectations do not change (are zero elastic
or inelastic).

Proceeding on this type of criticism, with notions of variance and risk
as found in Markowitz [257], Tobin seeks to develop his own explanation
of "the inverse relationship of demand for cash to the rate of interest." He
uses risk avoidance behavior, and proceeds from the assumption that the
expected value of capital gain or loss from holding interest-bearing assets
is always zero.

It is hard to contemplate just why the expected value of a capital gain or
loss is always zero and independent of the current interest rate, as assumed
by Tobin [356, p. 71]. In its particular context it must satisfy some of
Keynes' critics about the role of expectations in the liquidity preference
model when expectations were being assumed constant in the short run. In
contrast to the regressive pull analysis, the investor in Tobin's analysis [356,
p. 71] "considers a doubling of the rate just as likely when the rate is 5 percent as when it is 2 percent, and a halving of the rate just as likely when it
is 1 percent as when it is 6 percent." Continuing, Tobin [356, p. 85] and
Markowitz [257] say that their approach "has the empirical advantage of
explaining diversification . . . while the Keynesian theory implies that each
investor will hold only one asset [the one yielding the maximum return]."

---

prices) as a means of explaining the shape of the co-called liquidity preference
curve.

17. Elements of the first are not precluded by the second, but Tobin [356, p. 70]
strains to make a distinction between uncertainty as "disagreement among investors
concerning the future of the rate [of interest]" and "subjective doubt in the mind
of an individual investor." This is apparent in part because his own theory relies on
uncertainty as subjective doubt on the part of the individual investor. The disagreement and subjective doubt, however, may occur together. There may indeed be
wide trading in securities, because opinions over the directions of change have not
coalesced, as emphasized later. As in Fellner's analysis [111, pp. 4–5] differences
in degrees of belief by individuals may be the greatest when there is the most doubt
on the part of the individuals. In the pull-toward-normality explanation of liquidity
preference, at the normal rate the probabilities of a rise or a fall in the interest
rate may simply be equal [129, Sec. 1].

In dealing with the above criticism about the short run, one can accept the assumption and revise the theory or one can revise aspects of Keynes' analysis along different lines. The latter course was chosen in Chapter 7. It requires a great deal, including the achievement of consistency with the notion that the central bank does not control the interest rate directly as in Tobin's theory, but rather via expectations, via some influence on, say, the expected rate of change in prices. Tobin's criticism about the investor holding only one asset follows from special emphasis on the difference-of-opinion analysis cited earlier. However, a Keynes liquidity preference model need not rely on such special emphasis, and preferences can be introduced as derived or acquired from the environment of choice.[18]

Markowitz's mean-variance analysis.—In addition to drawing on von Neumann-Morgenstern utility axioms, Tobin [356, pp. 74, 85] introduces Markowitz's "expected return-variance of returns" rule (E-V rule).[19] Markowitz relies on mathematical expectations notions, as in Section 8.3, and rejects the rule that "the investor does (or should) maximize discounted expected, or anticipated return," as in equation (1.1). He notes variations of this rule following Hicks, although not the particular variation outlined in Section 8.3. In any event, he rejects the rule because it does not allow for the "observed and sensible" diversification of portfolios of securities.

In contrast, in the previous section and the one to follow, the approach is to proceed from "prior" distributions of portfolios—or assets and liabilities more generally—with adjustments taking place at the margin in terms of flow quantities. An expected rise in the price level, for example, may contribute to the prospect of an enlarged flow of returns from real property rather than bonds, such that changes occur: real property increases as a proportion of total assets, the marginal utility from the enlarged form of expenditures on real property declines as the flow increases, and ultimately the changes contribute to a new equilibrium distribution. In particular one may view diversification as (1) falling within the subjective purview, and (2) subject to some constraint by the special purposes served through specialization and by statutes governing groups of institutions. Such allowances would encompass savings and loan associations specializing in mortgages, commercial banks specializing in the acquisition or creation of debt instruments as assets, and so on.[20]

18. Diversification can also be explained with an analysis of wants as discussed by Georgescu-Roegen [165].
19. Tobin relies primarily on the notion that risk is associated with variance. For reasons peculiar to his analysis he uses standard deviations [356, p. 72], square roots of variances. (See note 10 above.)
20. This view of diversification is crucial as the range of choice is broadened

Markowitz's E–V rule, which he sees as implying diversification, is simply the following: the investor should want to select a portfolio that gives rise to some combination of expected value or mean (E) and variance (V) such that variance is a minimum for given expected value, and expected value is a maximum for given variance. This seems to suggest a valid form of optimizing behavior. Certainly, however, it is not inconsistent with viewing diversification as outlined above and with weighting prospective returns and then maximizing them or their discounted value. The main difference is that economic situations are amenable mainly to personalistic interpretations of probability and the relative frequency notion of a variance is not brought forward in the neo-Bayesian framework. The notion of repeating an experiment many times under the same conditions and thus obtaining the variance of expected values is dropped in the context of modern decision theory. This variance approach is related to the repetition of an experiment and a relative frequency theory of probability where the probability of an event is the limit of the ratio of favorable outcomes to the number of times the experiment is repeated. Subjective or personalistic probabilities apply in the case of non-repetitive events or repetitive ones occurring under different circumstances. Moreover, subjective variance may be obtained.

Liquidity preference analysis in perspective.—The analysis of the liquidity preference demand for money has taken many turns, as reviewed and outlined in various sources [126, 249]. There is Keynes' model as outlined by Leijonhufvud [249]. There is the Keynesian model [249, pp. 354–68; 126, Ch. 4], which considers the choice between money and bonds whereby a rise in the interest rate induces switching into bonds, and an increase in the money stock lowers interest rates, and so on, all on the ceteris paribus assumption. There are the micro-models which emphasize the transactions demand for cash. as advanced by Baumol and Tobin and criticized by Brunner and Meltzer [126, Ch. 8]. There is Tobin's behavior towards risk

---

to include financial and real assets as well as selected liabilities. In the emphasis on fixed return and residual return assets—with the differential impact of prospective rates of change in prices on the two classes—manufacturing corporations are readily capable of varying assets as proportions of same total and of increasing the use of bank loans as a substitute for reducing the proportion of financial assets in anticipation of inflation. Commercial banks, however, are more restricted in their switching activities, and necessarily so if nonfinancial firms are going to switch assets as described. The banks deal more uniquely with debt assets, and have an inducement to expand even in the face of inflation, since they are prohibited for the most part from making earnings on residual claim assets, and since they can at least adjust their price of credit upward to allow for the effect of inflation on the purchasing power of balances in which they will be repaid.

model as just reviewed. Characteristic of each of these is one of two tendencies: (1) to treat the interest rate as something the central bank simply manipulates, say through open market operations, to control the demand for money and the income velocity of money (the ratio of income to a given money stock), or (2) to treat the money supply directly as a determinant of the interest rate rather than to have expectations intervene. Tobin [356, p. 69], for example, refers to a curve that tells "what the quantity of cash must be in order to establish a particular interest rate."

In all of the foregoing cases, there is a crucial loss of reality, as judged by modern empirical evidence. The central bank in the more industrialized state simply does not control the interest rate so directly [122, Sec. III].[21] A variety of determinants of the interest rate have been mentioned (Chs. 2 and 4), but a very tangible and interesting bit of evidence links the interest rate to the expected rate of change in the price level (Ch. 1, Appendix to Ch. 1). The expected prices in turn may be related to the growth rate for the money stock. Moreover, in the case of the demand price for a capital good [as in equation (1.1)], a central bank's efforts to stimulate investment by lowering interest rates may be secondary to its effects on prospective returns, especially if the efforts contribute to the prospect of inflation. An effort to lower rates via an acceleration of growth of the money stock may, in some settings, contribute to both the prospect of greater returns in the case of variable return assets and the prospect of higher interest rates.

Another loss of reality follows when the liquidity preference models are offered to guide the policy-maker in his quest to stabilize the trade or short cycle. The models unrealistically have the central bank simply intervening in the process of cyclical stabilization without regard to the defensive and seasonal character of many of its operations, as mentioned in Chapter 2 and on other occasions. Simplicity itself is not at issue. Any theory must possess it, but it should serve to shed light on real phenomena, particularly phenomena which cannot be circumvented in empirical investigations.

In summary, the main contrasting characteristics of Tobin's liquidity preference analysis and the alternative with varying expectations are:

21. Tobin even recognized this problem in setting forth his own theory [356]. He said, "By actions and words, the central bank can influence investors' estimates of the variability of interest rates; its influence of these estimates of risk may be as important in accomplishing or preventing changes in the rate as open market operations and other direct interventions in the market."

Difference of Opinions	*Regression Toward the Normal Rate*
1. Constant expectations (the short run of Keynes' economics)	1. Variable expectations (Keynes' short run vanishes)
2. Diversification explained by Markowitz E-V rule	2. Diversification received from the environment of choice
3. Probability from Markowitz (increase in variance means lower probability of achieving expected value, more risk, etc.)	3. Probability from neo-Bayesian decision theory
4. Game theory axioms and the concept of cardinal utility	4. Hicks-Allen ordinal utility, with modifications
5. Present and expected interest rates are independent (zero covariance)	5. Present and expected interest rates are interdependent
6. Federal Reserve has direct control over the interest rate	6. Federal Reserve influences the interest rate through its influence on prospective rates and business conditions, and through rates of change in the stocks of money and bank credit

8.5   DYNAMIC ANALYSIS, COALESCING OPINIONS, AND TURNING POINTS

The term "dynamics" is presently used to suggest a treatment of processes or forces in motion.[22] An approach is proposed characterized by (1) a release of expectations and other peculiar qualities of analysis (such as that restricting the choice to between money and bonds) from their impoundment in *ceteris paribus*, and (2) an effort to allow more systematically for influences operating outside conventional economic theory. In such an approach, the basic building blocks of Keynesian analysis are retained as a first approximation (Secs. 1.3, 4.2), but their roles are somewhat modified by the setting and by an emphasis on broad classes of assets: (1) those with fixed claims (claims with fixed contractual returns) against future income in current prices such as (a) cash and (b) near-money assets and bonds; and (2) those with claims against residual portions of income in current prices such as (a) instrumental capital and (b) equities. Expected rates of change in prices affect the first class unfavorably in one or both of two respects: (1) by reducing the purchasing power of the anticipated payments, and (2)

---

22. "Dynamics" is one of the widely misused words in economics. Sometimes it is used simply to suggest the introduction of time, even as in the comparison of one presumably static state (or set of forces at rest) with another, and sometimes it is used to suggest the introduction of difference and differential equations.

by contributing to an upward adjustment in market interest rates (and thus a downward adjustment in values) on the part of those lenders who seek compensation for the anticipated loss of purchasing power. Expected price increases have a favorable effect on assets with the residual claim since price increases enlarge the residual portions of income. Factors other than expected prices may readily be cited (Sec. 2.2).

The explanation for the inverse relationship in the liquidity preference building block centers about the normal interest rate as a rate toward which the current rate is pulled. The further the current rate is below (above) the normal rate the greater the pull or probability of return to the normal level and the greater the probability of a capital loss (gain) from relatively long maturity bonds during the future. Adding the money stock as a variable constant subject to central bank control (an exogenous variable)—possibly after allowing for a variety of factors and offsetting or reinforcing effects (Sec. 2.3)—the interest rate is determined for a given income. However, having released expectations from their traditionally impounded position, the building block is now more an explanation of bond prices and interest rates than of the stock of money demanded. For example, if interest rates are low in relation to their subjective norm, there is a move at the margin out of bonds relative to income and into nonfinancial assets at the margin and relative to income for behavioral units other than primarily financial ones, since gains are expected on nonfinancial assets for such institutions. The shift at the margin is out of money balances too. All of this is brought about, not by a movement along the simple money-demand schedule, but by the fact that money balances relative to income are declining and thus accelerating the outward movement of the simple schedule relative to the rate of change in the money stock.

For the primarily financial units, such as banks and government security dealers, the range of choice of assets is restricted mainly to debt assets. The restriction is by statute or by the special purpose served by the institution, as mentioned earlier (Sec. 8.4). In many financial institutions the desire to balance security holdings by maturity against an anticipated need for funds may predominate, but there may be more speculative designs, especially in the case of government securities dealers. There may be more switching as traditionally envisioned in the liquidity preference model (Sec. 8.4). Even so, it is definitely secondary to the broader kind of switching in the present interpretation of the central bank control over time series for income, employment, and purchasing power. It is secondary because, as in Section 8.4, the central bank is not thought to control the interest rate directly or even primarily through its open market purchases from dealers or through its linkage as a supplier of reserves and credit to commercial banks rather than via the demand side of the market for credit.[23]

In the simple investment demand building block, the interest rate from the liquidity preference model enters as a variable constant with respect to the flow of investment in capital goods and inventories, but the interest rate is nonetheless exogenous to the simple model. Another of our simple schedules relates the rate of return of the flow of capital outlays to the level of the flow. The interest rate constant and the schedule intersect to determine the level of the flow. However, with factors operating to increase the prospective flow of returns from capital expenditures, the outward movement of the simple schedule in the present building block accelerates even faster than the constant interest rate, so that as the flow of investment increases, the interest rate increases. Here—except for a fictional distinction for analytical convenience—one recognizes the interdependence between the rate of return on the flow of capital outlays and the interest rate. This is in contrast to the traditional tendency to treat the two rates as if they were independent, given the definition of the short run as that in which expectations are constant.

Next, the aggregate supply-demand building block contains its usual 45-degree line, the line relating changes in aggregate income received to itself. Aggregate demand still consists primarily of consumption expenditures as some increasing function of income, with a slope of less than one, plus a variable constant for investment in real capital. However, in the overall model the neutral or basic position, as outlined earlier (Sec. 2.2), is one in which all stock and flow quantities are changing at the same rate. In the aggregate demand-supply construct this means investment is growing exponentially and creating some increase in income and movement along the consumption function. It also implies some upward shift in the consumption function to account adequately for consumption. In other words, there is a push effect on consumption in addition to the current income effect.

---

23. A traditional linkage mechanism and a less traditional one (regarding central bank reserves, bank loans to business, interest rates, and business expenditures) are discussed in Chapter 15.

In the more restricted, money-and-bonds, switching context, when there is a weaker and weaker prospect of a gain from holding bonds—as in anticipation of a smaller and smaller decline in interest rates, as in a recession—the volume of trading in marketable bonds should rise. The forces are working to encourage the realization of capital gains, weaken the motive for holding marketable bonds, and possibly strengthen the motive for holding cash, all at the margin. When there is a stronger and stronger prospect of a gain from holding bonds—as in anticipation of a smaller and smaller rise in interest rates and a possible reversal of their movement—the volume of trading should decline.

This particular combination of effects on consumption could be captured a priori at least by expressing consumption as a function of current income and as a possibly constrained exponentially declining weighted average of past incomes, as discussed on other occasions (Secs. 2.2, 5.3).

The neutral position.—The basic rates of growth for the stock and flow quantities are definable as sustainable rates—rates that can be maintained for a long period of time without undue upward or downward pressure on the price level and unemployment. These growth rates create "push" effects, as already emphasized in the case of consumption, and they also relate to a tendency for the systems to overshoot (Sec. 5.5). At the neutral position, the push effect simply supports the prospect that the growth underlying current business conditions will continue. There is some upward thrust.

This neutral position is consistent with traditional notions that (1) investment as a variable constant is more volatile than the current income-consumption relation, and (2) changes in investment exert influence via the investment multiplier on income and thus on consumption. Analyses of data on the turnover of money balances by the various sectors support such traditional speculations [126], in the sense that the turnover of money balances is more volatile over time for nonfinancial business firms than for households. This neutral position is also consistent with the notion that the expectations of decision-makers in business firms are more sensitive to economic changes than those in households. The consumer sector's traditional modes of life weigh heavily, and get reflected in the shape of the consumption-income relationship.

At the neutral position the regressive "pulls" toward normal behavior are zero for stock and flow quantities, since the subjective norms for the quantities themselves may properly be interpreted as a locus of points forming an exponential growth curve. Moreover, in the income expenditure building blocks (Sec. 2.2), basic growth rates for stock and flow quantities imply constant levels for interest rates, as well as for price, employment, and un-employment levels.

The neutral position as outlined is rather idealistic, even as a first approximation to real trends, and thus one may allow for the need for some modifications. First, some wealth or income effects may be influencing the growth of certain assets, or assets and liabilities more generally. Money balances, for example, have been mentioned as a luxury good by Friedman (Sec. 4.2), and noncash sources of balances on short notice for large manufacturing corporations have been described as being subject to wealth effects, as will be discussed in Chapter 15. Second—from the review in Section 8.2 and Fellner's proposition about facing specific decision problems, and from the preceding outline of the uses of money—there is clearly the prospect of secular changes in the need for money. For example, decision-makers consistently experiencing recovery from short-lived recessions may become accustomed to being faced with such changes. Thus one might expect a secular reduction in the need for money balances relative to income as a means of dealing with the uncertain future. In such cases, the neutral or growth curve for the money stock would sweep slightly less upward. Such a reduced need for money would come about through an increase in the weights applying to returns (a reduction in the slanting of the probabilities for the prospective returns), as in equations (1.1) and (1.2). The returns would be from the more risky assets, such as plants and equipment, and thus through a rise in the rate for relating prospective returns to the supply price for marginal amounts of plants and equipment vis-à-vis money balances.

Shock effects, destabilizing changes and cyclical changes.—Shock effects are generally exerted over a shorter time than the effects just mentioned. They are discontinuous, non-routine, and non-repetitive in most instances. They might be viewed as including changes in a surtax on household incomes or a tax credit for investment by business firms, where an increase in the first reduces expected disposable income and a reduction in the second reduces the returns from selected capital outlays. They include the military involvements—as in Vietnam, Laos, and Cambodia, and earlier in Korea—as well as changes in administration and possibly related changes in ideology. These shocks might change the certainty of some anticipated economic changes, including inflation or deflation. The shock effects may nudge a departure from or toward the basic, secular, or neutral sorts of changes.

Once destabilizing changes are set in motion (once stock and flow quantities are moving predominantly at unsustainable rates, either above or below their neutral position), the motion and the ensuing patterns of developments have effects of their own. For example, there is overshooting (Sec. 5.5), and there are possibly some acceleration effects on expenditures for real capital or inventories, as mentioned in the discussion of work by Kmenta and Smith (Sec. 5.3). These would result from the faster growth rate for sales, as in the crude accelerator models for capital investment [133, Sec. 15.3] or inventories,[24] possibly as modified by some learning process,

24. A common form of the acceleration relationship has two basic relationships: (1) the net flow of investment at time t is set equal to the rate of change in the total stock of capital goods (K) over time, $I(t) = d\,K(t)/dt$, and (2) capital is maintained as a fixed proportion of sales or income (Y), so that $g = K(t)/Y(t)$. The ensuing common form is $I(t) = g\,dY(t)/dt$.

particularly for firms using the cruder models in the management of inventories. As expenditures are accelerated, an initial effect on the part of large manufacturing firms may be a working down of the backlog of planned expenditures itself until time permits an enlargement of the backlog. Some firms plan expenditures and financing more than others (Ch. 15), and the extent of planning affects the patterns of certain series [122, Sec. III], as when inadequate liquidity becomes a constraint on expenditures. Regulations such as those imposing ceilings, although variable, on selected interest rates [122, pp. 182–84], in combination with the limited financial resources of households, impart additional patterns of relationships between time series. There are numerous examples of differential patterns of changes, but ultimately a wide range of time series are classifiable as tending to lead, coincide with, or lag changes in business conditions.

Decision units may be expected to consider these influences and patterns of changes in varying degrees of detail and sophistication as they formulate expectations. The neo-Bayesian framework (Sec. 8.2) with its learning and even subjective ignorance will accommodate the workings of these various influences on expectations.

Among the business conditions there are changes, push effects, and pull effects of the time series, but these alone will not explain turning points in business conditions generally or in a specific series such as that for the yield on long-term government bonds. Presumably expectations may be formed with respect to changes in the direction of a variety of leading, coinciding and lagging indicators. Some, such as interest rates, may play more prominent roles than others. With this in mind, however, the ensuing analysis focuses only on business conditions generally.[25]

Turning points.—The absence of an explanation of turning points and the varying duration of phases in business conditions has been a shortcoming of economic theory and its various constructs.[26] "Push" and "pull" effects are not very helpful in themselves. Accelerated growth in a series suggests a stronger upward thrust of movement, but it is balanced by a

25. For the definition of business or credit conditions, see Section 2.2 and Frazer [122, n. 3, p. 169].

26. The received explanations of turning points have centered about autonomous variables and Keynes' investment multiplier, as discussed with reference to Hansen (Sec. 5.2), or the lagged effect of a change in the rate of change in the money stock, as discussed with reference to Friedman (Sec. 2.4). Difficulties with these explanations include their inability to account for variations in lagged relations and in the duration of cyclical phases (Secs. 2.4, 5.3).

Drawing on the work of Hansen, Samuelson has offered an explanation of turning points in terms of his combined multiplier and accelerator models (compare n. 24 above) [322, Chs. 42–48]. The Nobel Foundation's Academy of Science

stronger pull toward normality. At what stage are such balanced forces turned in one direction or another? Shock effects must play a role by combining either to reinforce the direction of change or to reverse it, but there are other relevant aspects of this theory.

The present explanation of turning points requires recognition of opinions about future business conditions, and recognition of the formation of such opinions as a group activity. Important decision groups include those concerned with the budgeting and financial planning of large corporations. There are smaller decision units functioning outwardly as independent units but also functioning as part of a larger socio-economic complex. The role of individuals (or small units) in a larger group is intimately related to probabilistic slanting in controversial situations, all as outlined earlier. For example, when opinions are almost equally divided on the immediate direction of change in business conditions, then there is considerable slanting of the probability of a change. This occurs along lines set forth in Fellner's semi-probabilistic approach (Sec. 8.2) and by the nature of allowances for controversial matters in group situations. As opinions about the anticipated change coalesce, there is less uncertainty, opinions become reinforcing, and weights shift to favor pull effects rather than push effects. The final and principal proposition is in order.

Proposition (2.1). As opinions about a change in the direction of business conditions coalesce, turning points in business conditions occur.

The proof is straightforward, as suggested by the foregoing comments. By proposition (1.2), as opinions coalesce there would be diminished slanting of the probability of a change in direction of business conditions. Diminished slanting creates a relative strengthening of pull effects. The turning point in business conditions occurs. The proposition follows. Proposition (2.1) and its related proof explain turning points in business conditions as determined in the present framework by the plans and actions based on the expectations themselves.

The role of push and pull effects and the explanation of turning points may be illustrated with a familiar equation for expressing "adaptive expectations" or "extrapolative forecasting" (Sec. 1.2):

$$\dot{Y}_t^e = w_0 \, \dot{Y}_t + w_1 \, \dot{Y}_{t-1} + w_2 \, \dot{Y}_{t-2} + \ldots + w_n \, \dot{Y}_{t-n}$$

---

pointed to this model as among the specific contributions for which Samuelson was awarded the second Nobel Prize in economics. The Academy's announcement was dated October 26, 1970. On Samuelson, see Sections 1.1, 1.3, and 3.4.

where $\overset{\bullet}{Y}{}^e_t$ is the expected rate of change in income at the current time (and a surrogate for expected business conditions), and

$$\sum_{i=0}^{n} w_i \overset{\bullet}{Y}_{t-i}$$

is a weighted average of current and past rates of change in income. [One may write

$$i^e_t = \sum_{i=0}^{n} w_i \, i_{t-1}$$

for the expected long-term interest rate (i^e), and so on for other business conditions indicators].

In the present contexts, as opinions about a turn in business conditions coalesce, the weights for the terms in the more distant past are slanted less than those in the more recent past. The regressive pull toward a more normal state overwhelms the push effect of the more current state in its influence on the expected rate of change in income.[27]

In the neo-Bayesian framework (Sec. 8.2) there is a large role for learning and it relates to the coalescing of opinions. Questioning of the sustenance of a rapid expansion is justified from experience. In keeping with the notion of sustainable rates, a rapid expansion sustains only so long as decision units as a whole refrain from questioning its sustenance. Once decision units begin to question, the opinions coalesce and become reinforcing. A turning point occurs and ensuing adjustments follow. A crucial effect in the termination of a more rapid rise in business conditions is the questioning of its sustenance.

8.6 SUMMARY

Keynes' general theory encompassed the cases of both full and less-than-full employment equilibrium. There was an emphasis on money, but it was neglected in the years immediately following the appearance of *The General Theory*. Possibly this was caused by the failures of monetary policy or the shortcomings of our understanding of monetary policy. In any event,

27. One may denote weighted lag coefficients on a vertical axis and then plot them against lagged time moving to the right from *t–n* on the horizontal axis, all at a moment in time. The effect of the shifting weights as time changes, then, is that the line through the points moves toward a downward sweeping position as the past receives greater weight, and that the line moves toward an upward sweeping position as the past receives less weight. This way the movements of the plotted curves take on characteristics usually associated with changes in the common yield curve (Ch. 7, n. 4).

there was a revival of interest in money and its influences on economic magnitudes in the 1960s under the impact of empirical research and the modern computer. New notions were brought forward and research proceeded in a variety of directions. However, much seems to have been omitted from economic theory that concerns learning, the probabilistic discounting of prospects, and decision-making in group contexts. Following this line of thought, an outline of a theory has been set forth encompassing expectations phenomena. It recognizes the presence of decision-making units that rely on prior experience, make probability judgments on the basis of old and new information, and learn from experience. The theory attributes to economic units a combination of probabilistic reasoning (albeit subjective), utility functions, and optimizing behavior. The attribute of probabilistic reasoning combines readily with theory where money is thought to be relevant because of its role in dealing with speculative and uncertain outcomes or developments.

Keynesian mechanics of the income expenditure model are brought into the present theory and portions of Keynes' economics concerning money and changing ideas about the future come to the forefront. This is achieved in part by letting the short run, as defined in Keynes' works, go to zero. The definition has been viewed as too restrictive in the light of modern notions about central bank control over the interest rate. Letting the short run vanish, moreover, overcomes an inconsistency between the definition and the role of expectations in Keynes' or variants of his liquidity preference building block. Most notably the prospect of an inverse relationship between the demand for money balances and the interest rate was rationalized in terms of the dependence of the demand on the greater or lesser probability of an expected rise in interest rates. This aspect of theory is retained with continued emphasis on probabilistic behavior and increased emphasis on the relationship between bonds and interest rates. It is in lieu of Tobin's model for liquidity preference behavior towards risk.

Heretofore, economic theory has lacked the capacity to explain turning points and indicators in business conditions. This capacity exists in the present approach. Probabilistic slanting of weights attached to possible outcomes in controversial group situations, and the diminution of slanting as opinions coalesce and reinforce one another, both combine to yield insights concerning the extent to which decision units are guided by the expectation of a return to normality or the expectation of continued and growing deviations from normal values. The present approach also takes account of the tendency for the intensity of slanting inclinations to grow or decline as situations become more or less unusual.

Part III

Federal Reserve Behavior, Policy Indicators, and Lags

9
Federal Reserve Behavior
by William P. Yohe

9.1 INTRODUCTION

THE POLITICAL ECONOMY of monetary policy decisions is the topic of this chapter. This was such a new interest in monetary economics in the 1960s that there was not a well-developed literature. What existed was an agglomeration drawn from history, political science, and economics. The modern computer did not make a noticeable impact on the literature of decision-making in the Federal Reserve System, except in a few instances. There was some impact on the broader literature dealing with the recognition and decision parts of the lags in monetary policy—as introduced in Sections 2.1 and 2.4 and as further considered below—and there was some impact on the models of decision-making, also as reviewed below. Further, there has probably been some impact on the desired qualifications of appointees to the Federal Reserve's decision-making bodies, as mentioned elsewhere [122, Sec. II].

An organization like the Federal Reserve System does not itself "behave," but rather the people who exercise power over decisions behave. The central policy-making body in the Federal Reserve is the Federal Open Market Committee (FOMC), consisting of the seven members of the Board of Governors and the twelve Reserve Bank presidents. The committee is empowered by law to direct open market operations and has become by tradition a forum for the discussion of all aspects of system policy. Hence, most of the attention in studies of monetary policy-making has been concentrated on the FOMC. The basic raw materials for such studies are the

Note: Most of this chapter was written while the author was serving as scholar in residence in the Research Department of the Federal Reserve Bank of St. Louis. He is especially indebted to Christopher Babb, Michael Keran, and Keith Carlson for helpful comments.

personal papers of two former governors, the speeches and congressional testimony of FOMC principals, official Federal Reserve publications, the record of FOMC policy actions in the *Federal Reserve Bulletin* and *Annual Report*, and the FOMC minutes for 1936–65, which have been released to the National Archives in stages since 1964.[1] The Federal Reserve publishes extensive financial and business statistics, many of which presumably influence policy deliberations. A number of studies have attempted to draw inferences about the timing of policy actions and the importance of various Federal Reserve goals from the statistical analysis of various time series.

In what follows, some of the historical and descriptive work on Federal Reserve organization and leadership is surveyed (Sec. 9.2), empirical studies of FOMC behavior are reviewed (Sec. 9.3), and more or less explicit models of FOMC decision-making are reviewed (Sec. 9.4).

9.2 FEDERAL RESERVE STRUCTURE AND LEADERSHIP

One of the most striking commentaries ever made on the critical role of a dominant leader in the conduct of Federal Reserve policy was reiterated by Friedman and Schwartz [155, p. 692]: "If Benjamin Strong [Governor of the Federal Reserve Bank of New York, who died in 1928] could 'have had twelve months more of vigorous health, we might have ended the depression in 1930, and with this the long drawn out world crisis that so profoundly affected the ensuing political developments.' "[2] Substantiating this assertion is a major theme of the Friedman and Schwartz account of the early years of the Great Depression.

Barger [22, Ch. 15] has written a brief account of the traditional conflict between the Federal Reserve Bank of New York and the Board in Washington and of the leadership exercised by Strong and his successor at the New York Bank, George L. Harrison, and by later Board Chairmen Marriner Eccles and William McC. Martin. The ability of Chairman Martin to accommodate both Republican and Democratic administrations is the subject of two articles [313, pp. 11–13; 187, pp. 11–14].

Political scientists have paid surprisingly little attention to Federal Reserve organization and functions. Their studies tend to be critical and to propose drastic reforms. Reagan investigated Federal Reserve structure for

---

1. There is a useful compendium of source materials by Easthurn [103]. The 1936–60 FOMC minutes were made available in 1964, the 1961 minutes in 1967, and the 1962–65 minutes in 1970.

2. Snyder [339] made the original statement quoted by Friedman and Schwartz. See also Chandler [66].

the Commission on Money and Credit nearly a decade ago and concluded [302, p. 75]:[3]

> Professionalization means orderly routines in procedure and hierarchy in organization, and an ethical code of commitments to professional standards and to organizational objectives—the characteristic virtues of bureaucracy. The Federal Reserve exhibits these virtues. But in the current context, professionalization also means institutional inbreeding, and, in turn, the growth of dogmas and a tendency to propagandize. The Federal Reserve exhibits these flaws. . . . In the wider political arena the System enjoys the general advantages that go with a reputation for expertise in an occult craft, so long as all goes well.

Studies of Federal Reserve "politics" by economists are more numerous. In 1948, Bach wrote a report on the Board of Governors for the Hoover Commission, out of which evolved a book [19].[4] Many of the issues which Bach initially discussed, such as Federal Reserve "independence" and the lack of statutory objectives for monetary policy, were still current almost twenty years later [122]. Whittlesey [370, pp. 33–34] has examined the effect of important changes in FOMC procedures in 1955 and after, and he concludes that the power of the chairman and the influence of economists has been enhanced. He has also studied [369, pp. 77–87] the origin and nature of Federal Reserve attempts to suppress any rapid and detailed disclosure of its policy actions. One of his principal conclusions [369, p. 87] is that the primary reason for central bank secrecy is "to avoid embarrassment later on in case it appears that a different course would have been wiser."

A few ex–Federal Reserve economists have written critical evaluations of monetary policy-making. The most scathing, perhaps, is "The Mysterious World of THE FED" by Hastings and Robertson [189, pp. 97–104].[5] The authors specify, in descending order, what they regard as the ten "nodes of power" within the Federal Reserve System, with the Chairman of the Board at the top, followed in order by the other governors, Board advisers, and the FOMC. Hastings and Robertson argue that the Chairman's influence is exercised primarily by his ability to determine FOMC decisions, regardless of the views of the majority of its members.

Dozens of Fed "insiders" and "outsiders" participated in the extensive 1964 congressional hearing [400]. A subsequent article [381, pp. 351–62]

---

3. Reagan's research paper for the Commission on Money and Credit has also been published [302, pp. 361–402].

4. See also his later discussion [8, Ch. 7].

5. The study was reprinted in the 1964 Patman *Hearings* [400, Vol. 2, pp. 1519–25].

catalogs the rather diverse views expressed therein on various aspects of
FOMC decision-making. A 1968 Joint Economic Committee report [397]
revealed that the problems enumerated repeatedly in the 1964 hearings re-
mained. Some of the views of participants in the 1968 report are reviewed
later (Ch. 17).

9.3 EMPIRICAL STUDIES OF FOMC DECISIONS

Quantitative work on FOMC deliberations and decisions may be conveniently grouped under three headings: (1) the measurement of decisions
on the policy directive, (2) FOMC voting behavior, and (3) the length of
the "inside lag" in monetary policy.

The principal "output" of FOMC deliberations is the economic policy
directive to the manager of the Open Market Account at the Federal Reserve Bank of New York. For example, the directive[6] issued at the last
meeting in 1970 [392, pp. 103–4] contained three parts: (1) a summary
of recent changes in economic activity, prices, costs, interest rates, bank
deposits, money supply, and bank credit; (2) the policy statement that the
FOMC sought "to foster financial conditions conducive to orderly reduction
in the rate of inflation, while encouraging the resumption of sustainable
economic growth and the attainment of reasonable equilibrium in the
country's balance of payments"; and (3) the charge that this policy should
be implemented by "maintaining the recently attained money market conditions," with the proviso that operations could be modified if growth rates
for money and bank credit were not at least as great as expected.

Note that there are numerous adjectives but no quantitative specifications of the desired changes in ultimate targets, financial conditions, or
policy actions. Two techniques have been used to try to measure the extent
of a directive change. One is to use a quantitative proxy in the form of a
readily available financial indicator that is quickly influenced by policy
actions. Such a procedure is fraught with statistical problems. In addition,
it is tangled up with the issue of what constitutes appropriate monetary
policy indicators, as reviewed in the next chapter.

Another technique is to scale the directive itself to determine the magnitude of the intended policy change. An elaborate scheme for scaling direc-

---

6. This directive touches upon two 1966 innovations: use of the "bank credit
proxy" (member bank deposits) to estimate bank credit changes more quickly,
and the "proviso clause" mentioned earlier (Sec. 2.1). The directive also reflects
an early 1970 innovation (also as mentioned in Sec. 2.1), the more direct statement
of desires with respect to aggregates for bank credit and the money stock.

tives was worked out by Deming [86], an economist who was president of the Federal Reserve Bank of Minneapolis, attended many FOMC meetings, and had access to all of the minutes. The state of monetary policy was scaled from $+3$ (greatest ease) to -3 (greatest restraint), and substantive changes in a directive were considered as movements by one unit along the scale. In addition, he tried to account for "shades" in the directive—the addition of subsidiary instructions involving very slight policy changes without altering the substance of the directive. These were regarded as adding or subtracting a half point on the scale.[7] Unfortunately, Deming left the Federal Reserve before completing this work and never released his scaling of directives for the 1951–62 period.

Brunner and Meltzer, in their 1964 work for the Patman Committee [46, 47, 48]—considered earlier (Ch. 2) in three separate parts—devised a scale for measuring the extent of individual directive changes, rather than the cumulative degree of tightness or ease [48, Appendix II].[8] Such changes were placed on a scale ranging from $+1$ (greatest change toward ease) to -1 (greatest change toward tightness). In the 1970 directive mentioned above, the change would be assigned the value 0. From about 1959 through the 1960s, changes in the directive were infrequent and mostly of an incremental nature, only $\pm \frac{1}{8}$ on the Brunner-Meltzer scale. Several studies by others have used this scale and will be mentioned later. Brunner and Meltzer have used their scalings primarily for work on "inside lags" and for demonstrating the close relationship between directive changes and changes in free reserves, as defined earlier (Sec. 2.3).

Besides a summary of the discussion and the policy directive, the record of FOMC policy actions contains the voting outcome by the governors present and the Federal Reserve Bank presidents currently serving as voting members of the committee. While there is some question about the significance of the formal FOMC voting records [189, p. 101], such information represents the kind of data for which political scientists have developed various analytical techniques. Several of these techniques [380, pp. 396–405] were used to analyze the votes on the economic policy directive over the decade following the committee's reorganization in 1955. The most frequent outcome over this period was a unanimous decision not to change the previous directive. After 1959, policy changes were more incremental

7. For example, if past directives indicated a policy of moderate tightness (-2), then the injunction to maintain an "even keel" during an upcoming Treasury financing would temporarily move the scaling by a "shade" of $+\frac{1}{2}$.

8. For several later studies, Brunner and Meltzer have updated their scaling [267, pp. 28–31].

in nature, and dissent became more frequent as would be consistent with the rapid changes of the 1960s in the monetary area, although few Reserve Bank presidents seemed inclined to oppose Chairman Martin during his tenure.

A collection of hypotheses is presented in the previous study to account for the overwhelming occurrence of unanimous FOMC decisions. Canterbery [61, pp. 25–38][9] has attempted to elucidate the question of the Committee's nature. He specifically identified FOMC members by occupational background ("lawyer-bankers" and "economists"), specified corresponding a priori policy preferences under various economic conditions, and tested the predictions of his model against the actual voting record vis-à-vis contemporaneous economic conditions.

There have been several studies of the "inside lag" in monetary policy over the 1953–60 period. The authors of the two earliest studies [222, pp. 62–97; 47, pp. 37–47] did not have access to the FOMC Minutes; further (and related to this lack of access), they assumed the action lag to be zero, so that their estimates of the inside lag were synonymous with the recognition lag as defined earlier (Sec. 2.4). Kareken and Solow [222] obtained the longest estimates of the lags (8.5 months, on the average, at business cycle peaks, and 3 months at troughs); the excessive length of their lag measures has been attributed to their choosing a monetary policy indicator (potential bank credit) that itself lags the taking of action [374, pp. 591–93].[10] Brunner and Meltzer [46, 47, 48], dating action by policy reversals in the Record of Policy Actions, found average lags of zero months at peaks and four months at troughs.

Three studies of inside lags have used the FOMC Minutes [46–48, 51, 374].[11] Buehler and Fand [51, pp. 21–35], using changes in the intended direction of the free reserves target to time the taking of action, have produced the shortest estimates of the inside lag (an average of two months at troughs and minus one month at peaks). Willes [374] has attempted to disaggregate the inside lags and separately estimate the recognition and action components. His results for the total inside lags are nearly the same as Brunner and Meltzer's [46, 47, 48], but he found two peaks for which

9 See also Canterbery's other work [60, Ch. 12].

10. All of the studies have used NBER turning points for dating peaks and troughs (compare Ch. 2, n. 4).

11. A general discussion of the contents of the FOMC *Minutes* appears elsewhere [399, pp. 3–15]. A monetary historian, Elmus R. Wicker, was working on a detailed study of the *Minutes* in 1971. He presented a preliminary paper, "Reserve Supply Strategy, 1951–1957," at a seminar at the Federal Reserve Bank of Richmond, March 26, 1971.

the action lags were minus five or six months (action was taken considerably in advance of the upper turning points), which yielded slightly negative net lags when combined with positive recognition lags.

Hinshaw [205], on the other hand, sought to assess the forecasting ability of FOMC members vis-à-vis professional business cycle forecasters, by carefully studying the summaries of the remarks of each president and governor in the FOMC *Minutes*. He defined the recognition lag as the time elapsing between a turning point and the committee's assignment of 50 per cent probability to the fact that a turning point had occurred. The "confirmation lag," however, is the time elapsing from a turning point until a 90 per cent (nearly certain) probability is attached to the existence of a turning point. With a "certainty score" for every meeting, Hinshaw was able to relate the timing of policy reversals and major policy changes (using Brunner and Meltzer's scalings) to the committee's degree of certainty that a turning point had been reached. He concluded [205, pp. 120–21] that "the Committee changed policy at the peaks on less conclusive evidence than it required at troughs, and that its decision-making process in the vicinity of peaks proceeded by successive approximations."

9.4   MODELS OF FOMC DECISION-MAKING

The term "model" is used here in the general sense of a logically complete structure for explaining policy actions. The discussion will begin with more or less verbally specified models, proceed to the "reaction function" literature which attempts to infer the impact on policy actions of a variety of policy objectives, and conclude with more elaborate models for explaining Federal Reserve decision-making.

Verbally specified models.—Replying to the frequent charges that the Federal Reserve has "money market myopia" and lacks any explicit analytical framework for making decisions, Koch [238, pp. 3–9, 12–15] of the research staff of the Board of Governors presented complicated flow charts to convey the Federal Reserve's conception of the policy transmission process and the sources of information (or indicators) to which it will respond. On the other hand, Guttentag [179, pp. 1–30], an economist formerly with the Federal Reserve Bank of New York, was a severe critic of the Federal Reserve's alleged preoccupation with a "money market strategy." He has attempted to conceptualize the policy-making process, distinguishing such components as policy determinants, policy formulation, operating targets, strategic (intermediate financial) targets, and a logically complete operating strategy. The "money market strategy" Guttentag asserted to be logically incomplete, since there is no particular conception of the linkages from money market conditions to ultimate targets.[12]

Drawing on his work on the inside lag, Mark Willes [375] has conceived the Federal Reserve as conducting monetary policy within what he called the "cyclical framework." As a consequence [375, p. 6], the Federal Reserve regards "cyclical peaks as signals for the need to begin an expansionary monetary policy and cyclical troughs as signals for the need to begin a restraining monetary policy." Willes proposed an alternative framework that sensitizes monetary policy actions directly to departures from unemployment, price-level, growth, and balance of payments objectives.

The "reaction function" literature.—The most extensive literature pertaining to Federal Reserve behavior concerns the estimation of a great variety of alternative "statistical reaction structures" and related "reaction functions." The U.S. studies stem from the original work done by Reuber for the Porter Commission in Canada [305, pp. 109–32]. A representative list of studies was cited earlier (Sec. 2.4).

The simplest procedure is to select an intermediate financial target that the Federal Reserve presumably regards as critical in its operating strategy (money, bank credit, or some interest rate) and regress it on current values of various ultimate target variables and on the lagged intermediate target. The result is a geometrically decaying distributed lag structure [234, pp. 553–65], with the relative weight of independent variables in the past assumed to be reflected in the coefficient of the lagged dependent variable. The equation may be transformed into a reaction function by setting the lagged dependent variable equal to its current value (a presumed condition for equilibrium) and solving for the intermediate target variable as a function solely of ultimate target variables. It is then possible to calculate implicit "trade-offs" among the ultimate targets—the rates at which changes in the ultimate targets could be exchanged without requiring any change in the intermediate target variable.

Dewald and Johnson [92] did such a study for the decade after the Treasury–Federal Reserve Accord of 1951. They experimented with a number of intermediate financial targets, ranging from free reserves to money and interest rate series, and they used as independent variables ("performance indicators") the real GNP, consumer price index, unemploy-

---

12. Maisel [254, pp. 153–57] has drawn on a "personal construct" and Guttentag's framework to explain the FOMC's early 1969 variant of the "money market strategy"—the linkages from money market conditions (free and borrowed reserves and various short-term interest rates) to the "bank credit proxy" (member bank deposits).

ment rate, and balance of payments deficit. The best statistical fit was obtained with the money supply (currency and demand deposits) as intermediate target. Substantial time lags for most of the responses in the intermediate targets were found in all of the regressions, and the balance of payments was not found to be significant in any of them. Several reaction functions were derived and the implicit trade-off rates among the ultimate objectives were calculated.

All of the subsequent studies involved attempts to overcome serious deficiencies in the Dewald-Johnson (DJ) work. These deficiencies and some of the proposed improvements may be summarized as follows:

1. Any one of the DJ equations may be regarded as a reduced form equation for a (linear) structural model of the economy, combined with a preference function for the policy-maker. The coefficients of the ultimate target variables are thus a composite of the model's structure and the weights attached to each in the preference function.[13] The "trade-offs" calculated from the coefficients do not then reveal anything about the importance of particular objectives unless additional information is provided. Furthermore, it is doubtful that the "true" Federal Reserve preference function contains only current levels of ultimate targets and no deviations of a target's current level from some desired level.[14]

2. The selection of particular intermediate financial targets in the regressions raises the whole question of appropriate indicators for monetary policy, the subject of Chapter 10. Other authors (Havrilesky [190], Buehler and Fand [51], and Keran and Babb [226]) have preferred to use as a financial target a variable more proximate to policy actions than money or interest rates.

3. Not all movements in an intermediate financial target should be explicable on the basis of economic stabilization objectives. Open market operations, for example, are used for "defensive" purposes to offset seasonal and irregular shocks to the reserve base, to assist the Treasury in major refundings and cash borrowings, and to stabilize interest rates. Non-stabilization objectives ought to be more significant for a study using monthly data than quarterly data, but significant effects have also been found in the latter [226, pp. 7–20].[15]

13. The first to raise this argument was John Wood [377], whose work will be discussed below.

14. Havrilesky [190, p. 302], for example, includes the price level in his "policy action function" as the square of the difference between the actual index and a constant base period index. For an introduction to the theory of quantitative economic policy, see Hickman [200, pp. 1–17].

15. Wood's and Torto's works will be discussed below. Equations using monthly

4. Single equations for the entire time period of study [72, p. 467] imply that the monetary authority has "a linear, temporally consistent set of decision rules and relative priorities for the achievement of different objectives."[16] Christian [72] has shown, however, that for subperiods of the DJ study, shifts in the importance of various objectives apparently did occur.

5. There is a presumption of strong multicollinearity among the independent variables in the regressions (movements in the price level, GNP, unemployment, and the balance of payments are not independent of each other). One solution would be to find a proxy variable to represent the state of all of the stabilization objectives. Thus, Keran and Babb [226, pp. 8–9] use free reserves as this proxy, citing the high correlation between changes in this series and changes in intended stabilization policy, as reflected in the FOMC directive. Even if distributed lags had been specified (which is not the case in Keran's and Babb's study), this procedure may obfuscate the use of the resulting reaction structures to provide information about the "inside lag."

Some elaborate models.—A somewhat more ambitious undertaking than estimating single equation statistical reaction structures is an attempt to infer the Federal Reserve's implicit decision rule (or reaction function) within a structural equations model which presumably reflects the policymaker's conception of the linkages connecting policy actions and ultimate targets. Such projects have been completed by Wood [377] and Torto [357]. Wood [377, pp. 135–66] heroically assumes that the Federal Reserve seeks to optimize its policy actions subject to a quadratic preference function[17] containing the usual ultimate targets, short term interest rates, and the Federal Reserve's government securities portfolio. Its conception of the "linear constraint" is represented by a crude model of the economy's structure in which current values of the target variables are determined by extrapolations from past values of the same variables, by current free reserves, and by current government budget and debt variables.

---

data information on the free reserve target from the FOMC *Minutes* have been estimated by Buehler and Fand [51]. There is also a question of whether the use of seasonally adjusted data eliminates most of the defensive operations (Wood [377] argues that it would, while Torto [357] demonstrates that it does not). For separate studies of defensive operations, see Andersen [5, pp. 19–26] and Schotta and Bonomo, [26].

16. Besides an invariant policy-formulating framework, the lack of attention to the stability of regression coefficients in the DJ study carries implications about the linearity of the underlying model and the presumed reliability of the particular lag distributions estimated [72, pp. 465–67].

17. An introductory essay by Theil [351, pp. 18–42] explains the approach used by Wood.

Torto [357] seeks to use a more refined model of the economy (an improved version of Goldfeld's model [173]) in which a behavioral equation for open market operations is specified and simultaneously estimated with the rest of the model, using two-stage least squares. Torto also attempted to distinguish "defensive" from "dynamic" open market operations (those directed toward stabilization). He runs a single equation estimate for open market operations, similar to the reaction structures discussed earlier, and compares the results with an equation simultaneously estimated with the complete model. Interestingly, the coefficients of the variables reflecting defensive operations are somewhat larger in the latter estimates. They are generally comparable to those obtained by Keran and Babb [226].[18]

Using computer techniques for analyzing and simulating sleep, another study views FOMC decisions as part of a stochastic (Markov) process [379].[19] Combined with changes in the domestic economy and balance of payments conditions, decisions on the policy directive comprise sequences of states, which may be tested for "memory" and used in various simulation experiments.

Work has been done on a different model for replicating FOMC decisions on the economic policy directive, based on inputs of a greater number of monthly data series [382, 383]. There the FOMC is conceived as a heuristic problem-solver which employs a network of simple rules-of-thumb to seek, process, and evaluate information about the state of its ultimate target variables and about the response of financial conditions to actions based on past decisions. An extension of the so-called "Carnegie Tech approach" to simulating decision-making by business firms [82], the model contains statements of FOMC objectives that are "satisficing"[20] rather than maximizing, and contains procedures for limited search when conflicts arise between results and intentions and for the assessment of "slack" in the financial system.

18. The equations in the two studies are specified somewhat differently, but the Federal Reserve is found to offset (with changes in government securities holdings), nearly dollar-for-dollar, shocks to bank reserve positions (variously specified).

The decision rule for open market operations derived by Torto also contains as independent variables the loan-to-deposit ratio of member banks and the changes in manufacturers' inventories, both of which are statistically significant. The former may be construed as a separate intermediate financial target, and the latter as a leading indicator of ultimate target variables.

19. A basic reference for this kind of approach is Bartholomew [23].

20. The term "satisficing" is used to indicate that behavior is directed not toward attaining an optimum, the path to which is unknowable, but toward the fulfillment of minimum standards (making ultimate target variables no worse or not so bad as before). For example, the unemployment target is attained so long as unemployment is not high and rising.

9.5 SUMMARY

The study of Federal Reserve behavior ranges from studies of the policy-making personnel and leaders, decision-making, bureaucratization, and Federal Reserve "politics," on one hand, to attempts to infer decision rules implicit in a structural equations model and to distinguish between "defensive" and "dynamic" open market operations, on the other. The first type of study is discussed on various other occasions in the book and elsewhere. The need to distinguish between "defensive" and "stabilization" objectives of policy in analyses is recognized in early chapters (Secs. 1.4, 2.3) and throughout the book.

There have also been studies of the minutes of the FOMC's meetings and the inside lag in monetary policy. In the first, there has been noticeable effort to measure the extent of the change in the FOMC's directive to the manager of the open market account. One procedure has been to use a proxy for the directive changes, but there are statistical problems and controversy over the selection of the appropriate indicator, as discussed in the next chapter. Another procedure has centered about schemes for scaling and measuring directive changes. Brunner's and Meltzer's scheme has been widely cited. It is mentioned on other occasions.

Studies of the inside lag in monetary policy have been made with and without access to the FOMC's minutes, and some have attempted to construct models of FOMC decision-making. Apart from verbal models and the structural equations model mentioned above, attention has been drawn to "reaction functions"and their problems. These have failed to distinguish between "defensive" and "dynamic" objectives, and have presumed multi-collinearity, as dealt with in this book. Further study even attempts to extend a "Carnegie Tech approach" for simulating decision-making to FOMC decision-making in particular.

10
Policy Indicators and Lags
by Robert E. Weintraub and William J. Frazer, Jr.

10.1 INTRODUCTION

POSSIBLE LAGS in recognizing the need for and in effecting changes in monetary policy and in the effects of policy changes were introduced in some detail earlier (Sec. 2.4). The first group was denoted as the inside lag and the second as the outside lag. The first was dealt with along with Federal Reserve behavior (Ch. 9). The present chapter concerns policy indicators and targets of Federal Reserve actions, lags in the effects of policy changes, and thus, to some extent, the outside lag. Two issues stand out: (1) whether the interest rate or the rate of change in the money stock is the best indicator, and (2) whether the Federal Reserve can control the money stock via its policy actions.

In the empirical revolution of the 1960s, these questions seemed quite pertinent to some monetary analysts and observers,[1] including Friedman and his modern quantity theorists, Karl Brunner and Allan Meltzer, and various independent intellectuals. As mentioned on other occasions (Chs. 3, 5, Appendix to Ch. 7) Friedman was predisposed to empirical research and had his ties with the National Bureau. He and the Bureau were elevated to greater prominence by the computer. Brunner's and Meltzer's particular empiricism originated differently, but they too took a stand that was definitely to increase in prominence, as introduced on other occasions (Ch. 2, Appendix to Ch. 7). It centered about the money stock, the supply side of the money supply-demand notion, high-powered money, and later the integration of the theories of money and relative prices. Underlying all of this was a feeling of inappropriateness with respect to a prevailing tendency

---

1. The literature on the questions was voluminous, as indicated earlier (Sec. 2.4), in this chapter, and to some extent in the references.

to erect a "gap" between theory and policy [40, pp. 1–3]. This feeling was a source of Brunner's and Meltzer's particular empiricism.

There were always overtones of empiricism in the monetary policy orientation. Certainly, some academicians and practitioners were always aware of placing constraint on the claimed relevance of theory to monetary policy by insisting on description of certain operations and institutionalized activities. In addition, there was the generally latent belief that good theory had to meet tests of relevance. But Brunner and Meltzer made open issues of the selection of indicators and the explanations of responses to policy changes, and they rose to prominence with them in the empirical revolution of the 1960s. The roots go back a little further, but as early as 1964 they were referring to their continuing project, "Monetary Theory and Monetary Policy," and to financial support from the National Science Foundation. (The NSF provided consistent organizational support for their research in the 1960s and early 1970s).

A 1966 conference on the campus of Brunner's home institution—at the time and beginning in the early 1950s, the University of California at Los Angeles—represented an early assault on the problems of targets and indicators. It resulted in a volume edited by Brunner [40] in which his work was supported by NSF. Many of the authors of papers in that volume (including a survey of the entire discussion by Weintraub [40, Ch. XIII]) also appear in the references underlying this chapter.

Surveying the changes in Section 2.1—from primary reliance on a money market indicator, to the introduction of the "proviso" clause in mid–1966, to the increased reliance on the money stock as a target in 1970, to greater reliance on total reserves—makes some questions of policy indicators seem almost moot, of only historical interest. Whatever the case, it is partly in that interest that the gymnastics, the pros and cons of the issues, are reviewed in greater detail in this chapter.

The succeeding chapter deals with special historical events, "inertia" effects and possible shifts in banks' preferences for excess reserves. These events, effects, and shifts are dealt with to suggest (1) substantially different lags in the effects of a change in excess (or "free") reserves at one time as distinct from another, and (2) the need for substantially larger increases in excess reserves to achieve given increases in bank credit and the money stock at one time as distinct from another.

There are both positive and normative aspects to the subject of indicators and targets. The positive or indicators aspect concerns a variable (or group of variables) that accurately and meaningfully reflects actual Federal Reserve policy as it may be directed toward neutralizing seasonal disturbances, eliminating cyclical changes, or speeding or slowing overall economic growth. The normative or target aspect concerns the variable(s) that the Federal Reserve should be influencing through the use of their tools (mainly discount rate changes, open market operations, and changes in reserve requirements) to achieve ultimate economic goals (maximum employment, production, and purchasing power for the domestic economy, as prescribed by the Employment Act of 1946 and as interpreted since that time). The normative and positive aspects become entwined almost indistinguishably in most discussions.

Time series and the outside lag.—The problem of measuring the outside lag is largely a positive one, though the extent of the lag also depends on the definition of policy one selects, and there are other complications as well. For example, the effect of accelerating the growth of the money stock might begin immediately and accumulate for a time as in some lag patterns. The publicity given the change might have some immediate effects via expectations on, say, interest rates and variables such as the volume of planned capital outlays (Ch. 15). Also, timing of the effect(s) of accelerating monetary growth will vary, depending on whether the economy is taut and operating at a high level of performance, whether it is operating at a low level of potential capacity, and whether behavioral units are sensitive to changes or relatively insensitive. Moreover, economic time series occur in patterns—some lead, others lag, and still others change more or less with business conditions themselves. These changes may reflect a dynamic which is internal to the economic system itself, as with the path of a solution to a growth model with fixed parameters. Alternatively, observed time series patterns may reflect some common response by a number of variables to the same outside force (Sec. 4.3). Still another explanation is that economic changes are characterized by simple extrapolative pushes and regressive pulls; in the first instance, a change in a series or a change in the rate of change creates the prospect of a further change in the same direction; in the second instance, the further a series departs from some average or normal growth path, the stronger is the pull back toward the average or normal growth path (Ch. 8). Most likely, time series reflect all of these forces and factors in some combination. Weights of the importance of each set may vary, and the emphasis on each set may be brought forward for a specific purpose.

A present point and source of difficulty in the analysis of time series is simply that the techniques and methods that were customarily employed in the 1960s and early 1970s in the analysis of interrelated time series are limited in their capacity to extract causal sequences and relationships—

although this limitation was not widely recognized at the time. For example, the time elapsing between a peak rate of change in the money stock and an upper turning point in business conditions may not be identical to the outside lag in the effect of the change in the rate of change in the money stock. A further problem is that the lagged relationship between two variables—as indicated by the use of adjustment coefficients in the application of a regression analysis—is not necessarily that which would occur as a result of the effect of a change in one variable on another.

As previously noted, the length of the outside lag in monetary policy depends on the definition of policy. Using the procedure advanced by Friedman (Sec. 2.4) of measuring the time from a peak rate of change in the money stock to an upper turning point in business conditions, one finds an average lag time of sixteen months. The average from the trough rate of change in the money stock to the trough of business conditions is twelve months, as reported by Friedman. Mayer [258, pp. 324–42] summarizes other studies reporting similar results. Warburton [365] studies variability of the lag, after making special adjustments in the usual expenditure and money stock measures, and after devising his own method of determining turning points in business conditions. Some researchers who view the lag time as indicated by the adjustment of banks to a change in reserves, however, report lags of only a month or two [50, pp. 855–64; 299, pp. 651–54].[2] Still other studies,[3] using a change in interest rates as the point from which to measure the outside lag, report lags varying from three to eighteen months.

The problem of isolating effects and measuring their lags is complicated. Some of these complications are discussed in this chapter by reviewing studies of Warburton and Hamburger.

2. Willes [373, p. 9] describes the methods used by Bryan [50] and Rangarajan and Severn [299]. Bryan describes a familiar stock-adjustment model where the size of the adjustment coefficient determines the lag. He is interested in whether a short time is required for banks to adjust their reserves to a desired position. This is determined in his analysis by a set of variables encountered by banks in the ordinary course of operations. His equation, estimated by ordinary least squares, turns out to include an estimate of the "adjustment" coefficient. It serves as the basis for evaluating the lag time in the adjustment of reserves to a desired level. The existence of a short adjustment lag is supported by Bryan's findings.

Bryan further demonstrates for a selected group of banks in the St. Louis Federal Reserve District that the lag estimate depends on data organization, and that using weekly rather than monthly data reflects more rapid adjustments. Yohe and Karnosky also test this hypothesis about the aggregation of data over longer observation periods [384, pp. 26–28, esp. n. 22], but they get virtually the same lags for quarterly as for monthly data.

3. For a survey of these, see Hamburger [182]. Hamburger's survey is considered further later (Sec. 15.2). He has also made a more contemporary survey [180].

Analysis bears on the problems of extracting from the records information about monetary policy and its effects. It also bears on prescriptions for the appropriate policy in the normative sense of economics. As emphasized earlier (Sec. 2.4), if lags in the effects of policy are so long and undependable that they complicate forecasting, then a counter-cyclical policy should probably not be attempted. This analysis suggests, from a normative point of view, that the monetary authorities should direct policy actions and inactions toward a target which they can change quickly and predictably, and which will exert a known effect on some ultimate economic goal over a short time, although there are problems of distinguishing between defensive and dynamic operations.[4] The choice of a target variable, however, is no less complicated than the positive problem of measuring the outside lag. In addition, there may be various strategies to the target problem as just described.

Policy indicators.—Traditional banking emphasis had been on interest rates, the interrelated "tone" and "feel" of the market, and free reserves, as far as policy indicators are concerned. With the rise of the prominence of the monetarist school (Ch. 3), the money stock began to receive prominent attention. In linkage studies of a type mentioned earlier (Ch. 2) and structural equations models elaborated upon later (Ch. 14), attention focused mainly on policy actions with respect to discount rates, open market operations, and changes in required reserve ratios. A question was raised—what indicator(s) should the Federal Reserve be held responsible for controlling?

At one extreme is the view that the true indicator cannot be influenced by any factor outside the direct and immediate influence of the Federal Reserve. This seems to make the monetary authorities responsible only for variables completely under their control, but others view the range of responsibility more broadly. A common approach, as matters have evolved,

---

4. The term "dynamic operations," with reference to overall Federal Reserve operations (including mainly operations for the FOMC), is subject to varying definitions. The use of the term with reference to Federal Reserve operations originated in a monograph by Roosa [312]. Roosa was describing additional objectives of such operations that had come following the banking acts of 1933 and 1935, and he was distinguishing these from the previous objective of Federal Reserve operations—to provide an elastic currency in the sense of serving as a defense against "cash drains," and otherwise to operate according to fixed rules in the framework of "real bills, gold flows, and so on." This defensive arrangement was consistent with a growth in bank credit and the money stock as a means of accommodating the growth in income [133, pp. 142–59]. Dynamic operations against this background meant counter-cyclical operations, and the term is so used throughout this book unless otherwise specified. Andersen [4, p. 277] is explicit in also using the term in this way (with reference to "operations to exert a contracyclical influence on the economy") and he cites Roosa.

is to focus on a sources-and-uses-of-member-bank-reserves equation of the type introduced earlier (Sec. 2.3) and to note that the level of bank reserves could be controlled sufficiently through the control of one variable, such as Federal Reserve credit. Only a few complications intervene between the control over reserves or the reserve base and control over the money stock (narrowly defined). The main changes occur in (1) currency drains, (2) time deposit drains, (3) Eurodollars,[5] and (4) shifts in the preference of banks for excess reserves,[6] as described especially in the next chapter. The first occurs when the public elects to hold more or less currency relative to deposit liabilities. The time deposit drains in particular concern the adminis- tration of the Federal Reserve's Regulation Q, as discussed from time to time in this book. Eurodollars are dollar balances at foreign banks, for which a strong market developed in the 1960s. Paralleling this development, the larger commercial banks used Eurodollars as a source of funds in the 1966 and 1969 periods of stringent credit. They would transfer the balances from a foreign branch to the parent bank in the United States (effecting an intra-bank transfer), expand credit on the basis of them, and in effect credit "other liabilities" rather than deposits. The actual money supply would consequently be understated. Gaines [161] illustrates that "if Eurodollars were to be treated as time deposits in the completion of the broadly defined money supply, this measure would have shown no change in the first quarter [of 1969] rather than a 2.4 per cent rate of decline."

Indeed, even with the intervening changes between changes in reserves or the reserve base, as defined more specifically below, the relationship be- tween changes in such measures as the monetary base and the money supply is quite strong, particularly in the post–World War II years. The strength of such relationship is indicated in Table 10–1. Note in particular that monthly changes in the base (Δ B) and in deposits of the Treasury at commercial banks (Δ D) account for 80 per cent of the variation in changes in money narrowly defined (Δ M$_1$). Here changes in Treasury deposits are allowed for because they are transfers to or from deposits appearing as a part of the publicly held money supply and because they can be predicted

5. The literature on the origins, evolution, and functioning of the Eurodollar market proliferated rapidly in the late 1960s and early 1970s. In this respect one may wish to see Kvasnicka [240, pp. 9–20], Kolpstock [236, pp. 12–15], and Dufey [99, pp. 19–24]. The latter paper contains additional references, including several to books and monographs on the subject.

6. Changes in the Treasury's deposits with commercial banks also intervene between control of reserves or the reserve base and the money stock, since such changes involve opposite changes in publicly held deposits. But changes in Treasury deposits are transient and hence are ignored here.

Table 10–1

Correlations Between Monthly Changes in "Money" and Some
Explanatory Variables

Time Period	Definition of Money	Explanatory Variables and Their Coefficients (Constant Term Omitted)	R^2
March 1947 to March 1965	ΔM_1	$2.38\ \Delta B_t - .85 \Delta D_t$ (24.6) (−18.0)	.80
March 1947 to March 1965	ΔM_1	$2.23\ \Delta B_t - .74 \Delta D_t + .78 \Delta B_{t-1} - .02 \Delta D_{t-1}$ (26.0) (−17.3) (8.84) (−.58)	.86
March 1947 to March 1965	ΔM_2	$2.15\ \Delta B_t - .82 \Delta D_t$ (17.7) (−14.2)	.70
March 1947 to March 1965	ΔM_2	$1.98\ \Delta B_t - .70 \Delta D_t + .91 \Delta B_{t-1} - .05 \Delta D_{t-1}$ (18.3) − (13.0) (8.15) (−.86)	.77
Feb. 1947 to Dec. 1964	ΔM_1	$1.39\ \Delta B_t$ and 11 dummy variables to adjust for seasonal variation (5.88)	.80

"t" values in parentheses
None of the data were seasonally adjusted
Explanation of Symbols
ΔM_1 = Monthly Change in Currency and Demand Deposits
ΔM_2 = Monthly Change in Currency and Total Deposits
ΔB = Monthly Change in Monetary Base
ΔD_t = Monthly Change in Deposits of Treasury at Commercial Banks
Source: Allan H. Meltzer, "Controlling Money," A statement prepared for the meeting of Treasury Consultants, Washington, D. C., April 3, 1969.

fairly readily. Broadening the definition of money to include total deposits reduces the variance in changes in money (ΔM_2) explained by variance in the explanatory variables.

Equations such as the bank reserve equation may be readily deduced from a consolidated money balance sheet of the Federal Reserve Systems and the United States Treasury [133, Chs. 9 and 10]. One such equation with emphasis on the monetary base has been associated with the prominent work of Karl Brunner and Allan Meltzer, as introduced earlier (Ch. 2, n. 13, and Appendix to Ch. 7). In one statement of the explanation and use of that base [8, pp. 7–11], the monetary base (St. Louis definition) is an adjusted "source base." The "source base" is analogous to the magnitude called "high-powered money" by some and called the "monetary base" by Brunner and Meltzer. The adjustment is simply to reserves, to allow for "the effects of changes in reserve requirements on member bank deposits, and for changes in the proportion of deposits subject to different reserve requirements."

10.2 THE MONEY STOCK AS A CONTROL VARIABLE AND INDICATOR

Attention has been focused on whether the Federal Reserve can control the money supply via control over reserves or base money. There are also closely related questions about the extent of the predictability of variables other than Federal Reserve Bank Credit in such equations as the bank reserve and monetary base equations, about whether income has more influence over the money stock than vice versa, about whether an interest rate or the money stock is a more reliable indicator, and about whether by focusing on "free" reserves in the conduct of defensive operations the Federal Reserve contributed to instability in total reserves. This section deals with these questions.

There are other questions beyond whether the Federal Reserve can control the money supply and whether it is a satisfactory indicator of the "thrust" of policy[7] and of policy actions. These questions center on the interrelationships between different indicators, on whether information about a change in one indicator can be translated into information about a change in another, and on the whole strategy of the Federal Reserve's approach to economic stabilization. The first of these questions is treated in Section 10.3 in the review of a structural equations model on the subject. The question about the overall strategy and approach is the subject matter of the entire book.

Can the Federal Reserve control the money supply?—Whether the Federal Reserve can control the money stock has become an important question in view of rules proposals about its growth, as discussed in Chapters 16 and 17, and in view of its possible use as an indicator (or intermediate goal) of monetary policy.

Studies of the question have focused on opinions, algebraic exercises, analyses of data, and operational matters. Guy E. Noyes [288]—Senior Vice President and Economist, Morgan Guaranty Trust Company, New York— possibly expressed the widespread agreement of the 1960s over the Federal Reserve's ability to control the money stock within a given range, as from

---

7. It is commonly inferred that the term "thrust" means that the authorities are doing something that exerts a force in a given direction. "Thrust" has been a commonly used word since the advent of rocketry and travel in outer space in the 1960s. The thrust is often referred to as easy or loose if the Federal Reserve is thought to be doing something to ease the availability of bank credit to borrowers. It is tight when the reverse condition prevails. In the traditional banking context, an easy policy is thought to have an expansionary effect on business conditions, although—as indicated later (Ch. 15)—the business conditions may have more effect on credit ease than the Federal Reserve effects on the supply side of the market for credit do.

3 to 5 per cent, to allow for imperfections in the control mechanisms and informational systems. He said [288, pp. 181–82],

> I have discovered nothing in my relatively brief experience as a commercial banker that leads me to question the proposition that, with rare exceptions, the Federal Reserve could, by its policy actions, force the commercial banking system to so manage its assets and liabilities as to produce a reasonably stable rate of growth in the narrowly defined money supply in the 3 to 5 per cent annual rate range. Such a policy would only rarely produce acute financial market problems and then with ample warning so that modifications could be made.

In addition, Weintraub [367, pp. 257–70] presented algebraic exercises in terms of bank credit and money multipliers, as well as early empirical evidence, all supporting the prospect of control.[8] Leonall C. Andersen [4, pp. 275–88], a Federal Reserve Bank of St. Louis economist and later vice president, and Sherman J. Maisel [254, pp. 152–84], a member of the Board of Governors of the Federal Reserve System at the time, both focused on operational matters.

In analyzing the prospect of Federal Reserve control over the money stock, Andersen focuses on the effectiveness of the Federal Reserve in controlling variables that are closely related to the money stock, such as high-powered money and the Federal Reserve's holdings of government securities. His study supports the notion that the Federal Reserve can control movements in such variables to a high degree and thus control the money stock.

Maisel gives some idea of the magnitude of the job of controlling the narrowly defined money supply in the short period via control of the reserves available as a base for deposit creation. Even though there are technical problems, the main idea of the magnitude of the control job is conveyed by reference to the irregular movements in reserves—those that must be offset or provided in addition to changes actually required to directly support the desired change in the money supply. Comparing changes in reserves over a month or quarter respectively with underlying trends, he finds [254, pp. 161–70] that the shorter period changes are seventeen (for a month) and six (for a quarter) times as much as the trend changes.[9]

Are interest rates or the money stock a more reliable indicator of monetary policy?—Dealing with such a question in a 1969 paper, Allan Meltzer

8. Weintraub's paper also deals with the effects of changes in the money stock, but these are not presently introduced.

9. The monthly and quarterly changes in reserves were averages for the six-month period November 27, 1968, to May 28, 1969, and the trend or average changes were for the three-year period 1966 through 1968.

[267, pp. 11–31] drew on his work with Karl Brunner on the indicator problem—the problem of selecting the most appropriate indicator of monetary or Federal Reserve policy.[10] As in the case of much of the work on indicators, the focus is on a choice between changes in the interest rate and changes in the rate of change in the money stock. Free reserves, bank credit, and the money base are also considered by Meltzer.

To aid in discriminating between the indicators, a standard hypothesis is emphasized by Meltzer (Sec. 1.4): the nominal interest rate is equal to the real rate plus the expected rate of change in the price level.[11] High (low) interest rates caused by high (low) rates of inflation should not be interpreted as an indication of contractive (expansionary) monetary policy. To use terms sometimes used by others, a model may be implied and in it the interest rate is endogenous.

Also in terms used by others, the money stock is less endogenous. There is a feedback effect through the credit market, but the dominant effect follows from the growth rate of the money base.

To support the contention that the money stock is a better indicator since the interest rate is relatively more misleading, Meltzer examines several bits of evidence. He includes facts about the behavior of interest rates, the money stock, and the monetary base (St. Louis definition).[12] In broad outline, the facts, as described by Meltzer [267, p. 20] are:

> Interest rates and the growth rate of money generally rise during periods of economic expansion and fall during contractions. One of the few exceptions in this century is the expansion of the '30s when interest

10. On the use of the term "indicator" Meltzer says [267, p. 12], "As in previous work with Brunner, I use the term . . . to refer to a scale that permits changes in the thrust of policy to be recognized and permits policies to be compared." On the indicators used by economists he says, "Generally, the indicators used by economists provide relative, not absolute, measures of the thrust of policy and thus permit policies to be compared to previous or alternative policies but not to ideal or optimal policies."

11. On the lagged relation between the market interest rate and the anticipated rate of change in prices, Meltzer comments [267, pp. 19–20], "The empirical work may overstate the length of the lag. I believe skilled market participants form anticipations and, at the margin, adjust the prices of outstanding securities to changes in the anticipated rate of inflation more rapidly than is suggested by empirical estimates of the lag. . . . If I am correct, the marginal effect of actual price changes on anticipated price changes and market interest rates may be larger than is suggested by available evidence. In this case, some part of the cyclical change in market interest rates is attributable to changes in anticipated rates of inflation."

12. Meltzer states [267, n. 4] the St. Louis definition (on the uses side) "as bank reserves plus total currency plus the sum of reserves liberated or impounded by changes in reserve requirement ratios and redistributions of deposits between classes of banks."

rates fell while the stock of money rose. The experience of the '30s provides the main evidence in support of the view that periods of monetary expansion are characterized by low or falling interest rates. During the '50s and '60s, interest rates rose in expansions and fell in contractions, just as they did in the '20s and in many earlier periods.

As Meltzer points out, on a traditional view of credit ease and tightness, the interest rate changes reveal a counter-cyclical Federal Reserve policy. On his interpretation (or his and Brunner's) "the behavior of interest rates during cycles reflects the pro-cyclical nature of monetary policy." In Meltzer's framework this traditional view is due to the presumption of a counter-cyclical policy when in fact the money base is moving pro-cyclically and contributing to higher interest rates via expenditures and expected price level changes.

Referring further to the behavior of the growth rate for the monetary base and alluding to other changes in the postwar years, Meltzer proceeds [267, p. 21]:

> Periods of above-average growth in the monetary base are followed by periods of inflation, as in the middle '50s and in 1966–68. The below-average growth rate of the base in the mid-'40s was followed by a low rate of inflation, and even deflation, in the late '40s. Despite "pegged" interest rates, the price level fell or rose slowly from 1948 to the start of the Korean War. The low average growth rate of the base in the late '50s was followed by a period of sustained expansion and price stability, even after the growth rate of the base rose. Interest rate levels, on the other hand, provide much less reliable information about the future levels of activity and prices. Although high market rates always occur during periods of highest inflation, market rates provide little information about the future rate of inflation.

There is more to Meltzer's paper; some questionable interpretations,[13] and evidence for the period from mid-1964 to early 1969 from a compar-

13. On one occasion in discussing the case for and against interest rates, Meltzer [267, p. 13] mentions widely divergent views about "the reasons rates change" and "the principal sources of instability in an economy such as ours." The two views mentioned include a psychological view and an alternative. According to the alternative, instability arises from lagged effects of past changes in monetary and fiscal policy. Elsewhere in this book these views need not be distinct. The lagged effects might operate via an "expectations" mechanism, and psychological notions are required to explain the timing of turning points in business conditions (Ch. 8).

A final difficulty in Meltzer's paper is the sharp distinction drawn between two reasons often given for using interest rates: (1) the reasoning implied by the income expenditure model and (2) that expressed by the bankers' or central bankers' view. Slightly different perspectives are implied, but the views come to the same thing. As in earlier chapters (Secs. 3.4, 4.2) the central bank in both views changes the interest rate to alter the level of expenditures, depending on interrelated interest

ison of the Federal Reserve's *Record of Policy Actions* and the level of free reserves. This evidence is an up-dating of the Brunner-Meltzer study cited earlier (Sec. 2.4), "The Federal Reserve's Attachment to the Free Reserve Concept." The more recent conclusion is that data support the view that the Federal Reserve continued (at least through early 1969) to use free reserves as a main indicator.

Has the Federal Reserve, in focusing on "free" reserves in the conduct of defensive operations, imparted additional instability in total reserves (and therefore the money stock)?—In a 1970 study, Bonomo and Schotta [26, pp. 659–67] support Meltzer's conclusion about the Federal Reserve emphasis on "free" reserves, but they also present evidence that is inconsistent with another opinion advanced by Brunner and Meltzer in one of their 1964 studies.

On the positive side, Bonomo and Schotta deal in particular with whether defensive open market operations (OMO) are best characterized by focusing on "free" reserves or on total reserves. Using the regression methods they "estimate the fraction of changes in factors other than OMO affecting reserves and free reserves which has actually been offset by contra-disturbance or defensive OMO." Calculating annual values (for 1931–68 of the offset performance) of free reserves relative to total reserves, they report a relatively greater offset in free reserves, particularly since the Federal Reserve–Treasury accord of 1951. Bonomo and Schotta conclude that the defensive actions of the Federal Reserve are best characterized by reference to "free" reserves.[14]

---

elasticities measures for money and capital goods. The so-called bankers' view mainly gives substance to the method of changing the interest rate—given expectations and an arbitrage mechanism, open market operations shift the yield curve.

The older banking view, with the automatic gold standard, precedes the view associated with Keynes (Sec. 7.4). Under the automatic gold standard interest rates played a role, but the primary regulation concerned changes in the price levels of countries relative to one another. Meltzer's discussion omits these. Further, in the United States the central bank did not adopt any "dynamic" view of economic stabilization of the Keynes type until the early 1930s. Under gold standard thinking, the Federal Reserve in the United States was a passive agent, instability was due to malfunctioning of the financial system, and adherence to the rules for discounting commercial paper would give rise to a money supply (currency) that varied with the needs of commerce and trade. The latter and defenses against the seasonal need for currency were to assure stability (133, Chs. 6, 7, and 8).

14. They define "defensive" operations as "those transactions which are designed to offset disturbances in member bank reserves" and they define "dynamic" operations as "those which seek to change bank reserves to permit monetary expansion or contraction." The first definition is satisfactory, but the latter is inadequate by comparison with its counterpart in note 4, above. Even so, no damage is done to their study because they are almost exclusively concerned with defensive operations.

10.3 THE MONEY STOCK VERSUS THE INTEREST RATE: THE STRUCTURAL EQUATIONS APPROACH

Prior to the rise of the monetarists in the 1960s, the Federal Reserve emphasized simultaneous variations in short-term interest rates and the reciprocal of free reserves as being indicative of variations in monetary or Federal Reserve policy. Under the influence of the monetarists, others have suggested the money stock or its rate of change, and some emphasis has been given simply to the aggregate for total reserves (Sec. 2.1). As brought out later, some have questioned the adequacy of any single indicator. For reasons outlined in the previous section, there are arguments for focusing on the money stock that do not in themselves bring into question the existence of any interrelationships between free reserves, interest rates, and the money stock. Implicit in the notion of the existence of such interrelationships is the prospect, say, of a change in the rate of change in the money stock being translated into an interest rate change with one properly adjusted indicator serving as a substitute for another.

In view of what has been said (Sec. 10.2) about the differential extent of outside influences on the different indicators, the translation of the informational content of one variable to another is obviously not easy. Studies of the linkages between Federal Reserve operations and the various indicators have in fact taken a bewildering variety of forms. Even so, in a 1970 paper, Hendershott and de Leeuw [196, pp. 599–613] presented a study citing the linkage approaches and suggesting that the various forms of such linkage studies can be reconciled—"these apparently contrasting approaches are in fact closely related and in some cases equivalent." Having gone through some a priori exercises, they bring forth results supporting their contention from analyses of quarterly data without seasonal data for the 1954 to mid-1967 period. Their approach uses the structural equations model, as introduced in this study (Sec. 4.3) and as will be covered more extensively in Chapter 14.

The empirical results brought out by Hendershott and de Leeuw are presented as equations for only one sector of a larger and unspecified structural equations model. Their statistical approach to estimation is nevertheless the structural equations approach. There are also references to adjustment lags—for example, between a change in excess reserves and interest rates. Such lags in the model are estimated as fixed, all in obvious contrast to the notion of variable lags and effects as introduced at the beginning of this chapter. Even so, their analysis and results do suggest interrelationships between bank operations, free reserves, interest rates, and the money stock (or more narrowly, in their case, simply demand deposits). For estimation they use ordinary least squares and two-stage least squares, as initially outlined in Section 4.3. Their analysis and results are reviewed below.

The several approaches and their basic equivalence.—The several approaches relating Federal Reserve operations to the various indicators have involved, according to Hendershott and de Leeuw [196, p. 599]: (1) "bank adjustment of reserve positions and various banking-system identities," (2) "a direct connection between short-term interest rates and central bank actions," (3) "a flow commercial bank deposit 'supply' function (the relation between changes in commercial bank deposits, central bank activity, and other variables)," and (4) "stock commercial bank deposit 'supply' functions." They begin their analysis by setting out a reserve adjustment relationship, that is—without any transformation—a "free-reserve equation." When combined with a banking system identity, the free-reserve equation "provides one way of estimating the effect of central bank actions on the stock of deposits or on short-term interest rates." By algebraic transformation they show [196, p. 600] that the identity and the equation are equivalent to "(a) an equation 'explaining' the level of short-term interest rates, (b) an equation explaining the change in bank deposits, and (c) an equation explaining the level of deposits."

The reserve adjustment equation and the identity are

(1.1) $\Delta Rf = \Delta\lambda(Rf^* - Rf_{-1}) + \alpha_1 \Delta Rue - \alpha_2 \Delta CL.$

(1.2) $Rf^* = \beta_1 + \beta_2 rdis - \beta_3 rtb.$

where Rf is free reserves, Rf^* is desired free reserves, Rue is "effective" unborrowed reserves, CL is commercial and industrial loans from commercial banks, $rdis$ is the discount rate at Federal Reserve banks, and rtb is the three-month Treasury bill rate. Effective unborrowed reserves (Rue) and commercial and industrial loans (CL) are referred to as "impact" variables ("variables that influence observed free reserves only temporarily"). They are externally determined portfolio items. Continuing and substituting the right-hand member of equation (1.2) in (1.1) gives

(1.3) $\Delta Rf = \lambda\beta_1 + \lambda\beta_2 rdis - \lambda\beta_3 rtb - \lambda Rf_{-1} + \alpha_1 \Delta Rue - \alpha_2 \Delta CL$

This equation can be solved for the treasury bill rate (rtb) by simply rearranging terms.

However, to obtain change-in-deposits and level-of-deposits equations and additional identity, its first-difference form and a definition are needed. In the order mentioned, these are

(1.4) $Ru \equiv Rf + Rr \equiv Rf + qD$

(1.4)' $\Delta Ru \equiv \Delta Rf + q\Delta D + D_{-1}\Delta q$

(1.5) $\Delta Rue \equiv \Delta Ru - D_{-1}\Delta q \equiv \Delta Rf + q\Delta D$

where Ru is unborrowed reserves, q is the average reserve requirement ratio
(the ratio of required reserves, Rr, to total commercial bank deposits, D).
First-differencing equation (1.4) gives (1.4)'. In equation (1.5) a change
in effective unborrowed reserves (ΔRue) is defined as the sum of a change
in unborrowed reserves (ΔRu) plus reserves liberated by changes in reserve
requirements ($D_{-1}\Delta q$) which is negative on the assumption of an increase
in reserve requirements. The extreme right-hand member of equation (1.5)
follows from the definition and equation (1.4)'.

Dividing equation (1.3) through by $\lambda\beta_3$ and setting the treasury bill rate
on the left-hand side gives

(1.6) $$rtb = \frac{\beta_1}{\beta_3} + \frac{\beta_2}{\beta_3}\,rdis - \frac{1}{\lambda\beta_3}\Delta Rf - \frac{1}{\beta_3}Rf_{-1} +$$

$$\frac{\alpha_1}{\lambda\beta_3}\Delta Rue - \frac{\alpha_2}{\lambda\beta_3}\Delta CL$$

Solving equation (1.5) for a change in deposits (ΔD), gives $\Delta D \equiv$
$\Delta Rue\,1/q - \Delta Rf\,1/q$, and substituting the right-hand member of equation
(1.3) into this result gives

(1.7) $$\Delta D = -\lambda\beta_1\frac{1}{q} - \lambda\beta_2\frac{rdis}{q} + \lambda\beta_3\frac{rtb}{q} + \lambda\frac{Rf_{-1}}{q}$$

$$+ (1 - \alpha_1)\frac{\Delta Rue}{q} + \alpha_2\frac{\Delta CL}{q}.$$

Solving equation (1.4) for deposits gives

$$D \equiv Ru\,1/q - Rf\,1/q$$

and adding Rf_{-1} to both sides of equation (1.3), so that its left-hand
member is Rf (i.e., $\Delta Rf + Rf_{-1}$), and then substituting this result in the
deposit identity[15] gives

15. In further relating their equations to others, Hendershott and de Leeuw
show that a portion of Brunner's and Meltzer's non-linear money supply hypothesis
follows from equation (1.8),

$$D = \frac{Ru}{q + \dfrac{Rf^*}{D}}$$

To obtain this from equation (1.8), assume that desired free reserves vary in

(1.8) $$D = \frac{Ru}{q} - \lambda\beta_1 \frac{1}{q} - \lambda\beta_2 \frac{rdis}{q} + \lambda\beta_3 \frac{rtb}{q} -$$

$$(1 - \lambda)\frac{Rf_{-1}}{q} - \alpha_1 \frac{\Delta Rue}{q} + \alpha_2 \frac{\Delta CL}{q}.$$

The exercise above indicates that selected approaches to the linkage between Federal Reserve operations (changes in the rediscount rate, reserve requirements, and effective unborrowed reserves) and indicators (changes in free reserves, Treasury bill rate, and deposits or changes in deposits) are closely related. In fact, after introducing a reserve adjustment equation and an identity, equations (1.3) and (1.6) follow. It is then only necessary to introduce an additional identity and a definition to permit the deduction of equations (1.7) and (1.8). The four equations (1.3), (1.6), (1.7), and (1.8) are in a form for empirical estimation. The counterparts to these equations as estimated by Hendershott and de Leeuw are:

$$\Delta Rf = - .065 + .156\,rdis - .151\,rtb - .337\,Rf_{-1} +$$
$$\quad\quad\quad\quad (.062)\quad\quad (.050)\quad\quad (.044)$$

$$.472\Delta Rue - .0636\Delta CL + \sum_{i=1}^{4} a_i S_i$$
$$(.053)\quad\quad\quad (.0137)$$

$$R^2 = .858 \quad\quad s.e. = .086 \quad\quad DW = 1.870$$

$$rtb = - .544 + 1.14\,rdis - 1.10\Delta Rf - .642 Rf_{-1} +$$
$$\quad\quad\quad (.06)\quad\quad\quad (.37)\quad\quad\quad (.154)$$

$$085\Delta Rue - .0511\Delta CL + \sum_{i=1}^{4} b_i S_i$$
$$(.237)\quad\quad\quad (.0443)$$

$$R^2 = .960 \quad\quad s.e. = .232 \quad\quad DW = 1.130$$

$$\Delta D = .069\frac{1}{q} - .151\frac{rdis}{q} + .142\frac{rtb}{q} + .333\frac{Rf_{-1}}{q} +$$
$$\quad\quad\quad\quad\quad (.061)\quad\quad (0.49)\quad\quad (.045)$$

$$.539\frac{\Delta Rue}{q} + .0661\frac{\Delta CL}{q} + \sum_{i=1}^{4} c_i \frac{S_i}{q}$$
$$(.051)\quad\quad\quad (.0131)$$

$$R^2 = .919 \quad\quad s.e. = .793 \quad\quad DW = 1.875$$

---

proportion with total commercial bank deposits and that "desired and observed free reserves are always equal," that is $\lambda = 1$ and $\alpha_1 = \alpha_2 = 0$.

The Brunner-Meltzer non-linear money supply hypothesis has been the subject of research by others, particularly at the Federal Reserve Bank of St. Louis.

$$D = .015 \frac{1}{q} - .146 \frac{rdis}{q} + .130 \frac{rtb}{q} - .684 \frac{Rf_{-1}}{q} - .473 \frac{\Delta Rue}{q} +$$
$$\quad\quad\quad (.065) \quad\quad (.070) \quad\quad (.085) \quad\quad (.071)$$

$$.0641 \frac{\Delta CL}{q} + 1.004 \frac{Ru}{q} + \sum_{i=1}^{4} d \frac{S_i}{q}$$
$$(.0156) \quad\quad (.018)$$

$$R^2 = .9996 \quad\quad s.e. = .802 \quad\quad DW = 1.877$$

where the $\sum_{i=1}^{4}$ terms represent seasonal dummy variables. Their inclusion lowered the standard errors of the estimates by approximately 8 per cent.[16]

Hendershott and de Leeuw comment on the foregoing results [196, p. 606]:

> Ignoring the constant terms (and this includes the reciprocal of the reserve requirement in the deposit equations), which have no expected sign, every coefficient in every equation has the anticipated sign. Also, the coefficient of the one variable with an expected magnitude, the unborrowed reserves term in the deposit level equation, is very close to the value implied by the derivation— 1.004 versus 1.000. In addition, only three coefficients are not significantly different from zero at the .05 level —the impact variables in the bill-rate equation and the bill-rate coefficient in the deposit-level equation (the latter is significant at the .10 level).
>
> The standard errors of the two deposit equations, $793 million and $802 million, are, not surprisingly, very close, and they are very comparable with the $86 million standard error of the free-reserve equation. The standard error of the bill-rate equation is twenty-three basis points. All of these standard errors are comparable with those obtained in other studies.

Simultaneous-equation bias.—Now using the four equations for which empirical estimates are obtained, one may summarize and compare some implied response measures. Such measures are obtained by viewing the equations as if they were non-stochastic (as if they were exact) and differentiating one given variable with respect to another (as $\partial rtb / \partial Rue$) in each of the four equations, using the method of implicit differentiation. When this is done the partial derivatives or responses are shown to be similar, except for the Treasury bill rate equation. It yielded "markedly dissimilar estimates of the relevant parameters." Simultaneous-equation bias—or

16. In actual analyses of data some special specifications are introduced. Mainly, however [196, p. 605], "Dollar magnitudes are measured in billions of dollars; interest rates are in percentage points."

multicollinearity as defined on other occasions in this book—is offered as an explanation of the discrepancy in response measures.

Simultaneous-equation bias comes from concentration on only one equation of a simultaneous equations model, and from the presumption that the so-called independent variables of the one equation are not truly exogenous or independent. Hendershott and de Leeuw suggest an explanation for their differential response estimates in terms of this bias.

Results using two-stage least-squares.—To obtain reduced form equations for free reserves and the Treasury bill rate, Hendershott and de Leeuw use a three equations model, including equations (1.4) and (1.3):

(1.4) $Ru = Rf + qD$

(1.3) $Rf = \lambda\beta_1 + \lambda\beta_2 rdis - \lambda\beta_3 rtb + (1 - \lambda)Rf_{-1} +$

$$\alpha_1 \Delta Rue - \alpha_2 \Delta CL$$

$$D/Y = \beta_4 - \beta_5 rtb + (1 - \lambda')(D/Y)_{-1}$$

The last equation is a demand for deposits equation with deposits (1) and income (Y) varying proportionately ("deposits are homogenous of degree one in income"). Here the analysts "allow for partial adjustment of deposits to changes in the bill rate (λ' is the speed of adjustment)."

Using the three equation model and solving respectively for free reserves and the treasury bill rate gives

(2.1) $Rf = \gamma_0 + \gamma_1 rdis + \gamma_2 Rf_{-1} + \gamma_3 \Delta Rue - \gamma_4 \Delta CL +$

$$\gamma_5(Ru/qY) - \gamma_6(D/Y)_{-1}$$

(2.2) $rtb = \gamma_7 + \gamma_8 rdis + \gamma_9 Rf_{-1} + \gamma_{10} \Delta Rue - \gamma_{11} \Delta CL -$

$$\gamma_{12}(Ru/qY) + \gamma_{13}(D/Y)_{-1}$$

As outlined earlier (Sec. 5.3), estimates of these constitute the first stage of the two-stage procedure. (As in all of the Hendershott–de Leeuw equations in their present study, the signs of the coefficients are indicated by the signs preceding them.) The results of quarterly estimates for the reduced form equations, again for the 1954 to mid-1967 period, are

$$Rf = .882 - .038 rdis + .679 Rf_{-1} + .496 \Delta Rue - .052 \Delta CL +$$
$$[1.22] \qquad [8.91] \qquad [4.25] \qquad [-3.20]$$

$$1.481(Ru/qY) - 3.908(D/Y)_{-1} + \sum_{i=1}^{4} a_i S_i$$
$$[.33] \qquad\qquad [-.92]$$

$$R^2 = .937 \qquad \text{s.e.} = .086$$

$$\text{rtb} = 3.904 + 1.242 \text{rdis} + .027 \text{Rf}_{-1} + .089 \Delta \text{Rue} - .052 \Delta \text{CL} -$$
$$[15.45] \qquad\quad [.13] \qquad\quad [.29] \qquad\quad [-1.22]$$

$$22.842(\text{Ru/qY}) + 31.838(\text{D/Y})_{-1} + \sum_{i=1}^{4} b_i S_i$$
$$[-1.95] \qquad\qquad\quad [2.84]$$

$$R^2 = .949 \qquad \text{s.e.} = .226$$

On this occasion, "the numbers in brackets below the coefficients are t-ratios." Hendershott and de Leeuw say [196, p. 610], "the only sign contrary to expectations is that of the discount rate in the free-reserve equation, and its coefficient is both small and insignificant."

Using the first stage results, it is now possible to obtain two-stage estimates for the free-reserve and bill-rate equations. The new estimates are shown with coefficients from the ordinary least squares (OLS) estimates juxtaposed in brackets:

(3.3) $\Delta \text{Rf} = -.100 + .191 \text{rdis} - .175 \text{rtb} - .349 \text{Rf}_{-1} +$
$$(.125) \qquad (.107) \qquad (.051)$$
OLS estimate $[.156] \qquad\quad [-.151] \quad [-.337]$

$$.459 \Delta \text{Rue} - .065 \Delta \text{CL} + \sum_{i=1}^{4} a_i S_i$$
$$(.072) \qquad\quad (.014)$$
$$[.472] \qquad\quad [-.064]$$

$$\bar{R}^2 = .836 \qquad \text{s.e.} = .086 \qquad \text{DW} = 1.790$$

(3.6) $\text{rtb} = 0.636 + 1.118 \text{rdis} - 4.59 \text{Rf} + 2.913 \text{Rf}_{-1} +$
$$(0.58) \qquad\quad (1.43) \qquad (1.01)$$
OLS estimate $[1.14] \qquad\quad [-1.10] \quad\; [.459]$

$$1.980 \Delta \text{Rue} - .277 \Delta \text{CL} + \sum_{i=1}^{4} b_i S_i$$
$$(.78) \qquad\qquad (.100)$$
$$[.085] \qquad\qquad [-.051]$$

$$\bar{R}^2 = .952 \qquad \text{s.e.} = .227 \qquad \text{DW} = .822$$

When these results are used to obtain response measures via implicit differentiation, "estimates of interest rate responses, deposit multipliers, and speed of adjustment all fall close together." Hendershott's and de Leeuw's implicit impact response estimates are shown in Table 10-2.

TABLE 10–2

Responses to Changes in Effective Unborrowed Reserves
Two-Stage Least-Squares Estimates

	$\dfrac{\partial \text{rtb}}{\partial \text{Rue}}$		$\dfrac{\partial D}{\partial \text{Rue}}$	
	Short-run	Long-run	Short-run	Speed of Adjustment
ΔRf: Eqn. (3.3)	− 3.09	− 1.99	4.96	.394
rtb: Eqn. (3.6)	− 2.61	− 1.68	5.22	.366

Source of table: Patric H. Hendershott and Frank de Leeuw, "Free Reserves, Interest Rates, and Deposits: A Synthesis," *Journal of Finance*, June 1970, p. 611.

Referring to these estimates they say [196, p. 611] that "The short-run (one-quarter) interest rate response to a change in unborrowed reserves is about minus 3; that is, a billion-dollar open-market purchase holding deposits constant (the classical demand for money) and income constant, lowers the bill rate by three percentage points." They mention two types of lags underlying their model to explain the difference between short- and long-run responses of the bill rate to a change in unborrowed reserves [196, pp. 611–12]:

> First, banks respond to movements in interest rates with a lag (they only partially close the gap between observed and long-run desired holdings). Thus banks tend to increase their holdings of free reserves even further in subsequent periods in response to the initial decline in the bill rate. Banks achieve greater free-reserve holdings by selling securities, raising the bill rate. The second, more generally-noted bank lagged response tends to lower the bill rate in subsequent periods. Banks initially raise free-reserve holdings above their "short-run desired level"; they do not immediately invest the entire portion of the increase in unborrowed reserves that they eventually intend to invest. The subsequent tendency to reduce free-reserve holdings to their short-run desired level entails security purchases by banks, which lower the bill rate. The former lagged response outweighs the latter; the long-run decline in the Treasury bill rate in response to a billion-dollar open-market purchase still holding deposits and income (and thus nonbank security demand and total private security supply) constant, is only two percentage points.

Apparently responding to the feedback and expectations effects attributed to Meltzer in the previous section, Hendershott and de Leeuw conclude [196, pp. 611–12] that "allowing for all security supply and demand responses would reduce the negative bill rate effect, possibly even making it positive." Emphasizing the variety of influences impounded in ceteris paribus in the least squares analysis, they speak of a liquidity trap for bank reserves. In particular, they say [196, p. 612], "the short-run deposit multiplier is in the neighborhood of five; that is, holding interest rates constant [the Keynesian liquidity trap], a dollar open market purchase increases deposits by about five dollars." (The alert reader should notice an inconsistency in the conclusion—the assumption of a liquidity trap for reserves and a simultaneous expansion in the money supply. Such are the pitfalls of the method.)

10.4   DIVERGENT APPROACHES: SOME FURTHER CONSIDERATION

The divergence of approaches in the estimation of lags and the variety of measurement and conceptual problems associated with them are brought into further focus in two papers which appeared in the early 1970s, by Warburton [365] and Hamburger [180]. Warburton uses the method— identified earlier with Friedman (Sec. 2.4)—of measurement from a peak (or trough) rate of change in one variable to a peak (or trough) in business conditions. Hamburger, on the other hand, surveys results obtained with structural equations and reduced form models, as defined in Section 4.3 and as examined in further detail in Chapter 14. This particular review by Hamburger is done "with the objective of examining the factors which account for differences in the results." This is referred to as his second survey, since an earlier one appeared in 1967 [182].

Warburton's variability study.—Warburton makes some rather special definitions. First, there are "final product expenditures"—GNP exclusive of inventory changes and net exports, and after the substitution of business and individual tax payments for government purchases of goods and services. These changes are thought to result in an expenditure measure on which changes in the money stock operate more directly. Erratic and unreasonable variations in the inventory component of quarterly measures of GNP prior to 1939 render poor GNP estimates for use in analyzing business cycle turning points. Second, there is the need for a special concept of the money supply to relate to the special expenditure measure. The concept used is that of money held by business and individuals which excludes "deposits held by States and their subdivisions, and by foreign governments, firms, and individuals." Separate measures of the velocity of money (or its rate of use) follow from the foregoing definitions, once money is introduced with and without time deposits. The price levels of final products and expenditures in constant dollars also enter as separate elements of the equation of exchange.

Warburton's monetary policy data are of two types: policy actions and changes in monetary aggregates. Only the latter are discussed in this chapter. All of the stock and flow data are in the form of quarterly index numbers, "derived from seasonally adjusted data at annual rates." There are separate indexes for the period 1919 to 1947 and for the post–World War II years through 1965. The main monetary measure, in addition to the money supply, is effective bank reserves—"aggregate member bank reserves adjusted for changes in percentage requirements and in the relative amounts subject to differing percentages." The effective bank reserve measures are presented in turn for total reserves and for those applicable to demand deposits (those applicable after allowance for estimated reserves against time deposits).

There are more details on the indexes and measures, and special criteria for selecting peaks and troughs in the indexes. Three sets of data on peaks and troughs in business conditions are used: "final product expenditures," the gross national product, and the National Bureau's reference cycle dates. With special emphasis on the post–World War II years, all three sets identify recessions in 1948–49, 1953–54, 1957–58, 1960–61. And a recession is identified in 1966–67, in the one case where data are available.

With respect to the lagged relationships, some observations may be summarized:

1. There is a substantial range in the lags from peaks in the effective reserve measure to their corresponding downturns (or peaks) in business conditions, with a maximum of eleven quarters in one case, and seven to eight in two others. When money is narrowly defined, there is a central tendency of three to five quarters lag (for five of nine cases) and of two to four quarters lag (for the other four of the nine cases).

2. For upswings in business conditions the lags for both the reserve and money stock measures are much shorter, as Friedman reported. One would expect this from the tendency for expansion phases to be of longer duration than contraction phases (Sec. 2.4).

3. The lag distributions from reserves to the money stock (both definitions) are usually not over one quarter for downswings, nor over two for upswings (though, as commonly noted, banks are responding through changes in their investment portfolios rather than in response to changes in demands for bank loans).

4. After allowance for lags, there are strong covariations between the effective reserve measure and business conditions, and there are also high

correlations between the duration and the magnitude of the respective changes. Continuing, Warburton says, "The correlation between money held and its rate of use (with the latter lagging) can be readily understood as a consequence of the conditions produced by changes in the stock of money, with differences in amplitude influenced by expectational situations."

5. Turning points in purchases of final products, expressed in constant and current dollars respectively, tend to occur in the same quarters in thirteen of the eighteen swings. "However, Warburton notes, "from 1950 to 1965 there are no cyclical downswings in final product prices—that is, there was a continuous upward trend with no interruption longer than one quarter."

This latter aspect of the behavior of prices in the post–World War II years relates to analyses of both expectations and price adjustments, and to the future of monetary, price, and wage controls. These various aspects of analysis are brought together in the final chapter.

Hamburger's second survey.—As reviewed earlier (Sec. 2.4), Friedman has pointed to long lags in the effect of monetary policy. By early 1971, some overly zealous economists [242] were presenting models in which changes in the money supply were having a once-and-for-all effect on the level of GNP in the quarter in which they occurred, and Keynesian structural equations models (as in various versions of the FRB–MIT model) were suggesting long lags in the effects of policy. To account for some of the factors contributing to the results, Hamburger surveys literature on lags in the effect of policy and undertakes some new estimations when they are considered necessary to reconcile different sets of results. Among the factors he considers are the type of estimation model, the choice of the monetary policy variable, the influence of the seasonal adjustment procedure, the choice of the sample period, and the estimation technique (the estimation of lags with and without the use of the Almon lag technique, as introduced in Appendix to Ch. 1).

Structural vs. reduced form models.—Structural equations models may yield reduced form equations and a solution may be obtained in which a key variable is a function of variables exogenous to the model, as introduced earlier (Sec. 4.3). On the other hand, one may proceed directly with the estimation of an equation using variables similar to those found in some structural equations models. Hamburger [180, pp. 290–92] draws on such an equation as presented by de Leeuw and Kalchbrenner [83] and compares its results with separate results obtained from the use of three different versions of the FRB–MIT model.

The form of the equation used by de Leeuw and Kalchbrenner is

(4.1) $\Delta Y_t = a + \sum_{i=0}^{7} b_i \Delta NBR_{t-i} + \sum_{i=0}^{7} c_i \Delta E_{t-i} + \sum_{i=0}^{7} d_i \Delta RA_{t-i} + u_t$

where ΔY = quarterly change in GNP, current dollars, ΔNBR = quarterly change in nonborrowed reserves adjusted for reserve requirement changes, ΔE = quarterly change in high-employment expenditures of the Federal Government, current dollars, ΔRA = quarterly change in high-employment receipts of the Federal Government in current-period prices, and u = random error term. Hamburger reports that in estimating coefficients for equation (4.1), the Almon distributed lag technique is used with a second or a fourth degree polynomial (Appendices to Chapters 1 and 15). The lag chosen in this case, involving the Almon technique in Hamburger's analyses, maximizes the $\bar{R}^2$ (adjusted for degrees of freedom).[17]

In the comparison of the performance of the two types of estimation, attention is focused on the cumulative effects of a one dollar change in nonborrowed reserves on GNP [the sum of the b_i's in equation (4.1)]. These cumulative effects are sketched for the comparison. After the first three or four quarters, the de Leeuw–Kalchbrenner results are reported as well within the range of those results obtained with three versions of the FRB–MIT model. Hamburger concludes [180, p. 292] "that when non-borrowed reserves are chosen as the exogenous policy variables, i.e., the variable used in *estimating* the parameters of the model, it makes very little difference whether the lag in the effect of policy is determined by a structural or a reduced form model. . . . For the purpose of our analysis, this finding implies that the type of statistical model employed to estimate the lag in the effect of monetary policy may be less important than other factors in explaining the differences in the results that have been reported in the literature."

Specification of the policy variable.—To evaluate the relevance of the variable selected to represent monetary policy [180, pp. 292–93], results are compared for several different variables—the money supply (narrowly defined), the monetary base, total reserves (effective nonborrowed reserves plus member bank borrowing), and "effective" nonborrowed reserves (non-borrowed reserves adjusted for changes in reserve requirements). Mone-tarists have emphasized the first two, and "critics of the monetarist approach" (Keynesians?) are said to have often used the effective non-borrowed reserves because it excludes some "nonpolicy" influences. This is

17. In the Appendix to Chapter 15, analyses using the Almon lag technique with second, third, fourth, fifth, and sixth degree polynomials are reported. As reported there, varying the degree of the polynomial in some cases can add more explanatory power than varying the lengths of the lag.

the sort of argument that has surrounded the search for a neutralized money stock (Sec. 2.2) and emphasis on policy actions (policies exclusive of those of inaction). The monetarists are said [180, p. 292] to sidestep the statistical question "of whether the money supply or the monetary base qualify as exogenous variables to be included on the right-hand side of a reduced form equation."

Results for comparison are obtained using parameter estimates similar to equation (4.1). Once again the Almon technique is used. The cumulative results are presented in the experiment as percentage distributions so as to focus on the time required for the total (100% effect) to work out. The total response of GNP to changes in the money supply, the monetary base, and total reserves are reported as working out within four or five quarters. But only 40 per cent of the response of nonborrowed reserves appears in this period, with the full effect distributed over two and a half years. Thus the conclusion [180, p. 293]: "The evidence suggests that the relatively short lags that have been found by the monetarists in recent years depend more on the application of the monetary policy variable than on the use of reduced form equation."

The influence of the seasonal adjustment procedure and splitting the sample.—The influence of the seasonal adjustment procedure came to the forefront in early 1971 when A. B. Laffer, an assistant to White House Advisor George Schultz (later Secretary of the Treasury), presented a forecasting model with R. D. Ranson [316, pp. 13–18; 242]. The model contained three equations, the most important one being [180, p. 294][18]

$$(4.2) \quad \% \Delta Y = 3.21 + 1.10\% \Delta M_1 + .136\% \Delta G - .069\% \Delta G_{-1} -$$
$$\qquad\quad (4.9) \quad (5.5) \qquad\quad (6.9) \qquad\qquad (3.3)$$

$$\qquad\quad .039\% \Delta G_{-2} - .024\% \Delta G_{-3} - .046 \Delta SH +$$
$$\qquad\quad (1.9) \qquad\qquad (1.2) \qquad\qquad (3.7)$$

$$\qquad\quad .068\% \Delta S\&P_{-1} - 9.8\ D_1 + 2.5\ D_2 - 3.0\ D_3$$
$$\qquad\quad (2.2) \qquad\qquad (12.1) \quad\ (2.6) \qquad (4.1)$$

$$\overline{R}^2 = .958 \qquad SE = 1.31 \qquad \text{Interval: 1948-I to 1969-IV}$$

where $\% \Delta Y$ = quarterly percentage change in nominal GNP, $\% \Delta M_1$ = quarterly percentage change in M_1 (the narrowly defined money supply),

___

18. The t-statistics for the regression coefficients are shown in parentheses, and SE is the standard error of the estimate. Laffer and Ranson analyzed quarterly changes in the natural logarithms of the original data, but this is equivalent to using quarter-to-quarter percentage changes in the data without the logarithmic transformation.

$\% \Delta G$ = quarterly percentage change in Federal Government purchases of goods and services, ΔSH = quarterly change in a measure of industrial man-hours lost due to strikes, $\% \Delta S\&P$ = quarterly percentage change in Standard and Poor's Composite Index of Common Stock Prices (the "S&P 500"), D_1 = seasonal dummy variable for the first quarter,[19] D_2 = seasonal dummy variable for the second quarter, and D_3 = seasonal dummy variable for the third quarter. The variable SH is included to allow for the General Motors and similar work stoppages. The algebraic change in the index of stock prices of the previous quarter is included to serve as an efficient forecast of future income. The three dummy variables (D_1, D_2, and D_3) are used to allow for seasonal variation and to permit the optimal estimation of the seasonal factors under certain circumstances, notably where the seasonal pattern is constant over the entire sample period.

An important thing about the Laffer-Ranson model was that percentage changes in the money supply had virtually their full effect in one quarter. They contended further that the use of seasonal adjustments in analyses of data would obscure this effect and yield specious lag structures. Another aspect of the Laffer-Ranson model was a claim to superior forecasting properties. The model apparently became the basis for a White House forecast in early 1971 [316, pp. 13–14]. In any event, an unusually optimistic forecast for 1971 appeared in the *Economic Report of the President*, caused some consternation among forecasters, and later led to a statement by the president. He viewed it as a goal to be achieved rather than a forecast. In defending the forecast the Council of Economic Advisors, as reviewed by Samuelson [316, p. 14], saw it as consistent with the strength of rise in earlier postwar recoveries, noted that "forecasters generally tended to be overconservative in their estimate of numerical changes," and emphasized the target aspect of the GNP figure in question.

19. The present notation for three seasonal dummy variables contrasts with that for some equations in Sec. 10.4 above. The use of only three seasonal dummy variables suggests the representation of different seasonal effects as compared with a fourth. However, the restriction to only three dummy variables is important when using a program that automatically produces an intercept term, because there is a prospect of obtaining a singular matrix [213, pp. 178–80]. (The least-squares estimation of regression coefficients involves computations with an inverse matrix, and this is required to have a non-zero determinant, a corresponding non-singular matrix.) In the presence of other explanatory variables in a dummy variable treatment of seasonal influences with four dummy variables, one may obtain a matrix that is "nearly but not quite singular." In this case of the dummy variable trap, "the unwary investigator may not realize that anything is wrong."

Johnston discusses the larger role played by dummy variables in problems of seasonal adjustment [213, pp. 186–92].

The criticisms of the Laffer-Ranson equation are several. First, too much is made of the seasonally unadjusted data and dummy seasonals. Second, the time period chosen is largely responsible for the result obtained. To test this latter contention, Hamburger [180, pp. 294–95] re-estimated equation (4.2) and a modification of it with lagged values for the money variable, all for the subperiods 1948–I to 1952–IV and 1953–I to 1969–IV. (As with Laffer's and Ranson's estimates, Hamburger obtains his without the use of the Almon technique.) He found that "(a) the relationship between money and income in the 1948–52 period is not statistically significant . . . and (b) there is a significant lag in the effect of money on income during the most recent period."

Hamburger has also re-estimated equation (4.2) for the original sample period, only with lagged values for the money stock variable. He found that lagging the money stock variable did not alter the original estimate of the impact of the money stock in the first quarter. These re-estimations and split-sample results would seem to suggest that the lag is variable, as Warburton reported [365]. Furthermore, when equation (4.2) is re-estimated using lagged values for the money stock variable and the Almon technique for the 1953–69 period, little difference is found between the distributed lag implied by the Laffer-Ranson equations and that implied by Andersen's and Carlson's St. Louis equation (Sec. 14.4).

The Almon technique.—The use of the Almon technique can often make big differences. There are those where the degree of the constraining polynomial makes a big difference (as mentioned in note 17). R. G. Davis, an associate of Hamburger at the New York Federal Reserve, is reported as comparing some lag coefficients for a given equation, but obtained with and without the use of the Almon technique. As reported by Hamburger [180, pp. 296–97],

> Davis found that either 29 percent or 46 percent of the ultimate effect of money on income could be attributed to the current quarter. The lower number was obtained when the equation was estimated using the Almon technique . . . The explanatory power of the equation was essentially the same in both cases.

Substantial differences in the pattern of lag coefficients were obtained for the Laffer-Ranson model, with and without the Almon polynomial and with about the same $\bar{R}^2$. "In this model," Hamburger says [180, p. 297], "the estimates of the current-quarter effect of money on income are 31 percent with the Almon technique and 64 percent with unconstrained lags."

10.5 Summary

The outside lag for Federal Reserve policy is the lag between a change in policy and its effect. Such effect may be distributed in time, operating rather rapidly (or slowly) and then diminishing (or building up). It may be short or long, and in some instances its length will depend on the policy indicator selected. In fact, the short lags in policy reported by some monetarists in the late 1960s and early 1970s depend more on the selection of a policy variable than on the use of a structural or reduced form model.

In the lag framework and from a normative point of view, monetary authorities should select an intermediate target which they can change quickly, predictably, and with known effect. However, there are complications, including the possible desirability of distinguishing between defensive and dynamic operations. Dynamic operations may be conducted with some strategy of stabilizing business conditions overall for an entire cycle; not simply effecting a change in a target variable and expecting some pattern of effects to follow in time. The overall strategy, at least, is one that emerges in this book.

Among the major indicators of Federal Reserve or monetary policy that have been discussed are money market variables—such as free reserves and the Treasury bill rate—and monetary aggregates—such as the money stock variously defined, the monetary base, total reserves, and effective non-borrowed reserves. The Federal Reserve has traditionally favored the former. Some, Meltzer in particular, have argued that the money stock is a more reliable indicator. It is said to be more subject to control by the Federal Reserve, partly because it is less affected by feedback and other effects such as the expected rate of change in the level of prices. In focusing on interest rate changes as a target or indicator, it would appear that the actual thrust of policy as indicated by the rate of change in the monetary base of the money stock has been pro-cyclical at times. However, after allowance for lags in the effects such as those of the effective reserve measure, one finds covariation between business conditions and the effective reserve measures.

The question has arisen of the adequacy of control over the money base and the money stock. There is supporting analysis and evidence that the Federal Reserve can control these and related variables. There are other factors, such as gold flows and foreign and other Federal Reserve deposits in the case of reserves, and currency drains, time deposit drains, and Euro-dollars in the case of the money stock. Such factors, however, are thought to be predictable or manageable enough for the Federal Reserve to allow for them in conducting its own operations to achieve given targets for reserves and the money stock. There is also the prospect of a shift in the preference for excess reserves on the part of banks, so that a given change in reserves has one set of effects on at one time and another at another time. The effects and time lags of a change in reserves may be different at different times. In other words, lagged patterns are not necessarily fixed.

The presence of variable lag patterns is indicated by measures, as from peak (trough) rates of change in a monetary aggregate to the peak (trough) in business conditions. It is also indicated through the use of distributed lag, econometric models, where sample periods are split and different lag patterns are shown to follow. Such was the case for the Laffer–Ranson model, where sub-periods had different lags and the lag for the entire sample period showed the percentage change in the money stock as having its effect virtually in one quarter. But technique makes a difference, too. The presence or absence of Almon's constraining polynomial in a distributed lag model makes a substantial difference in the profile of lagged effects. On the other hand, some evidence suggests that the type of statistical model (structural or reduced form) is less important than other factors in explaining differences in results.

Despite the dependence of lags on the policy indicator selected, there is the prospect of interrelationships between different indicators such as free reserves, interest rates, and the money stock (or the demand deposit component). Evidence supports this prospect and the further prospect of translating a change in the rate of change in the money stock and other monetary aggregates into an interest rate change, and so on.

There is, finally, an apparent need to abstract from defensive Federal Reserve operations in considering its responsibilities and efforts to stabilize business conditions or vary the underlying rate of economic growth for the economy as a whole. In this case, the defensive aspects of Federal Reserve operations do not appear to have suffered from a traditional focus on the level of free reserves. The pre-1970 focus on money market variables including the Treasury bill rate mainly becomes a problem when the more dynamic aspects of Federal Reserve operations are brought under consideration.

11
Special Theoretical Discussions
of the Twenties and Thirties

11.1 INTRODUCTION

THE STUDY OF special events in the literature on the effects of monetary policy is important mainly because it focuses on an important prospect: the possibility that a given change in policy (however defined) may have different effects at different times. In particular, there is the notion that conditions underlying a change in the rate of change in the monetary base may have considerable influence on the differential effects and patterns of changes in bank credit, the money stock, and expenditures. An alternative and subtler version of this notion has arisen in discussions of splitting the sample (Appendix to Ch. 1, Sec. 5.2). Support for the prospect of effects differing according to changes in underlying conditions warns strongly against the use of the numerous analyses that have suggested fixed distributed lag patterns in the effects of policy changes (Secs. 10.4, 15.2, Appendix to Ch. 15).

One of the important dimensions in the controversy over differential patterns of effects is the possible existence of a liquidity trap or liquidity shift in the demand for bank reserves in the 1930s. Acceptance of the existence of a trap suggests that accelerating the growth of bank reserves will only increase excess reserves. One form of the trap argument centers about the metaphor "Pushing on a String." Acceptance of the existence of a liquidity shift instead of a trap suggests that acceleration of the growth of bank reserves will have expansionary effects on bank credit, only the acceleration must first satisfy the demand for liquidity.

Out of the 1930s grew an acceptance of the existence of a trap and the closely related notion that the Federal Reserve could control an expansion in business conditions but do little to bring about recovery. These arguments were especially questioned in their historical context by Friedman and

230

Schwartz [155] and Brunner and Meltzer [45]. They argued that the central bank's power to control bank reserves encompassed the power to determine the volumes of money and bank credit within close limits. Cloos [73] reviewed their positions and background conditions from the 1937–38 recession to Pearl Harbor. Later, Morrison [282], a doctoral student under Friedman, produced a University of Chicago Press publication on the trap and shift hypotheses, and Frost [159],[1] a doctoral student under Brunner at U.C.L.A., wrote a somewhat related dissertation. This chapter considers the works by Morrison and Frost and portions of Cloos' paper. It also deals with the paper by Brunner and Meltzer on the recessions of 1923–24 and 1926–27 and the 1929–33 depression.

11.2   CREDIT CONDITIONS IN THE LATE 1930s

BY INTEREST RATE and availability criteria, credit conditions were generally very easy throughout the 1930s and especially from the 1937–38 recession until the outbreak of World War II. The notions of faster growth in bank reserves and the money stock as means of combating a recession still awaited general acceptance.

Tables 11-1 and 11-2 depict these easy credit conditions by the interest rate criteria and the negative interest rates of the 1940–41 period. The ease was especially evident in 1935, as indicated by yields on money market instruments shown in Table 11-1. By the end of early 1940s, the average

TABLE 11–1

Money Market Yields: Yearly Averages

Year	3-Month Treasury Bills New Issues	4-6 Month Commercial Paper	90-Day Prime Bankers' Acceptances	90-Day Stock Exchange Loans
		(Percent Per Annum)		
1929	3.276[a]	5.85	5.03	7.75
1935	.137	.76	.13	.56

[a]December

Source of data: *Banking and Monetary Statistics*.

Source of table: George W. Cloos, "Monetary Conditions from the 1937–38 Recession to Pearl Harbor," *Financial Analysts Journal*, January-February 1966, p. 27.

---

1. The Frost paper [159] and subsequent article [160] bear the same title as Frost's Ph.D. dissertation, UCLA, 1966. The present references are to the Carnegie-Mellon paper [159]. The conclusions and general points of the latter are brought forward in the *J.P.E.* article [160].

TABLE 11–2

Yields on New Issues of 3-Month Treasury Bills

Year	Monthly Average High	Low	Yearly Average
1938	.099	.007	.053
1939	.101	.002	.023
1940	.042	a	.014
1941	.298	b	.103

aNegative in four separate months.

bNegative, one month.

Source of data: *Banking and Monetary Statistics.*

Source of table: George W. Cloos, "Monetary Conditions from the 1937–38 Recession to Pearl Harbor," *Financial Analysts Journal*, January-February 1966, p. 28.

yield was even lower as shown in Table 11-2. "With the exception of Treasury bills (first issued in December 1929)," as Cloos points out [73, p. 27], commercial banks traditionally had invested idle funds in the obligations presented in Table 11-1.

Noting the ease in the mid-1930s, as measured by the traditional criteria, the Board of Governors of the Federal Reserve System doubled reserve requirements in a series of steps in 1936 and 1937. As the records show, this was done under the authority to vary reserve requirements which was given to the Federal Reserve by the Banking Act of 1935. The purpose mentioned was "to reduce the inflationary potential created by large increases in excess reserves resulting from gold inflows." Cloos describes the conditions [73, p. 27]:

> Even so, money market conditions remained very easy by past standards. During 1937 excess reserves never were less than $750 million at month end, and member bank borrowings never exceeded $24 million. Rates on short-term instruments strengthened in 1937, but remained very low. The top rate on new bills that year was .74 percent, while peak rates on commercial paper, bankers' acceptances and stock exchange loans were 1.00, .56 and 1.25, respectively.

The recession of 1937–38 followed the actions taken in 1936 and 1937, and reserve requirements were reduced. In fact [73, p. 27], "From then until late 1941, the Federal Reserve System ceased its attempts to offset the tendency for continued inflows of gold to increase bank reserves." One argument in defense of expansionary efforts and their ineffectiveness, however, was (a) that the Federal Reserve could readily restrict credit and restrain an expansion in business conditions, but (b) that they could not induce a willingness of potential borrowers from banks to borrow and increase expenditures by increasing reserves. This is based on the metaphor that you can pull on a string but you can not push on it.[2]

Another question that has since arisen is whether the banks were experiencing an insatiable demand for liquidity in the form of excess reserves. That is, did a liquidity trap exist? As Frost notes, member banks increased their excess reserves from an average of 0.1 per cent of free assets (excess reserves and securities) in 1929 to 12.4 per cent in 1940. He says, "The most frequent explanation of excess reserves is that the banking system was caught in a liquidity trap." The existence of the trap has been discussed relatively extensively by Morrison and by Frost. Morrison's empirical evidence and some of Frost's is briefly reviewed later.

Both the Morrison study [282] and the Frost study [159] conclude that the trap did not exist. The Federal Reserve could have contributed positively to economic expansion by further increasing bank reserves. In the formal trap hypothesis, a schedule is envisioned similar to that for the liquidity preference demand for money. The trap hypothesis, in terms of Morrison's schedule, is that at low interest rates excess reserves (expressed as a ratio of excess reserves to deposits) are infinitely interest inelastic. In terms of Frost's analysis, the trap is the flat portion of the schedule relating the interest rate on the vertical axis to excess reserves on the horizontal axis. The idea in both instances is that along the flat portion of the schedule banks are completely indifferent to increases in reserves. Morrison's question is whether the trap existed in 1937–38 or whether there was a strong upward shift in the demand for excess reserves in relation to deposits (whether there was a shift in preference). An upward shift would ordinarily imply higher interest rates, but an earlier point (Sec. 5.4) is perhaps instructive: the trap depends on the strong prospect of a future rise in rates and cannot exist—even at low interest rates—if the normal or expected interest rate is

2. According to Cloos, the use of the metaphor appears to date from an exchange during hearings on the Banking Act of 1935. Cloos [73, p. 26], as have others [282, p. 5], quotes the following dialogue:

GOVERNOR ECCLES (of the Federal Reserve Board): Under present circumstances there is very little, if anything, that can be done.

MR. GOLDSBOROUGH (Congressman from Maryland): You mean you cannot push on a string.

GOVERNOR ECCLES: That is a good way to put it, one cannot push on a string. We are in the depths of a depression and . . . beyond creating an easy money situation through reduction of discount rates, and through creation of excess reserves, there is very little, if anything, that the reserve organization can do toward bringing about recovery.

equal to the market rate, in the case of Friedman, or equal or below the market rate, in the case of Keynes. Thus, the shift may not be in any carefully drawn schedule, but rather in the normal or safe interest rate.

Frost's analysis applies to the 1930s generally and to the prospect of an adjustment cost hypothesis, as defined later. In both Morrison's and Frost's analysis, policy depends on the answer: (1) the "trap" hypothesis leads to no increase in excess reserves and possibly to an increase in reserve requirements, and (2) the "shift" and "adjustment cost" hypotheses lead to substantial increases in excess reserves to satisfy demand and to stimulate the growth of bank credit.

Cloos himself appears to hold mixed views about the unwillingness of banks to expand credit. He raises some questions and suggests answers [73, p. 32]:

> What if the Federal Reserve System had purchased securities in the 1938–41 period to supplement the increase in reserves resulting from the inflow of gold? Would commercial banks have been willing to lower their credit standards to grant additional loans and make additional investments? Surely the effect would have been negligible. Banks did not hold large excess reserves because of a desire for liquidity but because they were unable to find suitable outlets for these funds.

In referring to an inadequate demand for bank credit by credit-worthy borrowers, Cloos emphasizes the presence of some demand for highly liquid securities. He ultimately explains the negative yields on Treasury bills, as shown in Table 11-2 and as follows [73, p. 29]:

> Why were investors prepared to offer more than face value for instruments that paid no interest and which would be redeemed at face value at maturity? There are a number of reasons. Exchange of cash for bills provided a means of avoiding personal property taxes in some states. In addition, some banks were said to have purchased bills at a premium at certain times of the year to reduce the excess reserves that otherwise would have appeared on their statements. It is probable, moreover, that individuals, including foreigners, held large denomination Treasury bills in preference to United States currency because of ease of transfer and storage. Federal deposit insurance was still new and untried in the late Thirties and, in any case, covered only deposits of $5,000 or less. Like currency, bills are payable to the bearer. Transfers are not recorded, repayment is assured and fluctuations in price are minimal.

> Obviously, the so-called "negative yield" on bills was not a true yield at all, but a premium or fee paid for certain attributes of the bills. Nevertheless, demand for these purposes would not have pushed the prices of bills above the face value if overall demand had not been very strong relative to supply.

Cloos appears at times to recognize a form of the trap hypothesis. According to his analysis and observations, banks did not purchase some long-term assets on the basis of their excess reserves because there were prospects of a future increase in interest rates (and, therefore, capital losses). It is also possible that banks had just not adjusted to the sharp decline in their commercial loan business in the 1930s. In any event, Cloos could be viewed as dealing with the difficulties of getting banks to expand credit under the dire conditions following the rapid expansion of business conditions and the boom of the late 1920s.

11.3 DEMANDS FOR EXCESS RESERVES

Morrison's [282] and Frost's [159] studies of banks' demands for excess reserves under the conditions of the 1937–38 recession or the entire 1930s, respectively, contain profit maximization models, seek to generate testable hypotheses, and introduce statistical results from analyses of data. Morrison's has interesting stochastic properties;[3] greater uncertainty about a withdrawal of cash and a drain on reserves results in an increased demand for excess reserves. Even so, the theoretical model is highly static.[4]

---

3. An example of the stochastic properties of Morrison's model is provided by the accompanying figure. There

$f(v), c \leq v \leq b,$

is a "uniformly distributed" probability density function (p.d.f.) for the expected change in cash reserves), and

$k = b\text{-}c, c \geq -1, k \geq 0,$

is expected dispersion of the distribution of cash drains or inflows.

Note that when there is greater uncertainty about cash drains (or inflows) k is large, and the probability of any particular change in cash is less—i.e., $f(v)$ declines. Note, too, that the function is not known or sought empirically. It is assumed to exist as a subjective probability in the mind of the bank's portfolio manager.

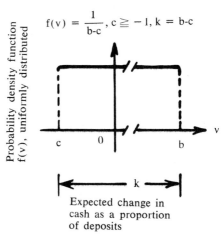

$$f(v) = \frac{1}{b\text{-}c}, c \geq -1, k = b\text{-}c$$

Expected change in cash as a proportion of deposits

Probability Density Function for the Expected Change in Cash (Reserves)

---

4. Morrison's theoretical model also contains some analytical flaws. For further

Frost's theoretical model is more traditional. Proceeding with two classes of assets—excess reserves and securities—he views a bank as faced with adjustment costs. These occur every time its reserves fall below the required level such that the bank may be faced with costs in selling securities to effect adjustments in the level of securities.[5] The model emphasizes adjustments via short-dated securities; the demand for excess reserves is independent of the rate on long-dated securities, "as long as the bank operates in a competitive market." The bank's demand curve for excess reserves is kinked, but it decreases as the interest rate decreases below the same minimum level. As the rate rises above this critical level, the desired level of excess reserves is zero; hence, a cost adjustment hypothesis for maintaining excess reserves. In the traditional sense of transactions costs models of the demand for money as mentioned in Section 4.2, the increase in yield on non-cash liquid assets pulls the balances into the earning assets category.

The shift hypothesis: "shock" and "inertia" effects.—In his 1966 book, Morrison deals with empirical results relating to the "trap" and "shift" hypotheses and with a theory of profit maximizing inventory policy as applied to banks' demands for excess bank reserves. On the empirical side, as presently emphasized in discussing the hypotheses,[6] Morrison's book deals with an instance where an untimely and inappropriate doubling of reserve requirements in 1936–37 produced a further increase in banks' desired short-run reserve position.

Quite simply, the shift hypothesis is that the liquidity preference schedule for excess reserves as a proportion of deposits changes position in response to "shock" and "inertia" effects. In terms of this hypothesis, strengthened preferences for excess reserves in the 1930s would have been due to the

comment on this aspect of the model, see Frazer [125, p. 301].

For another study employing a stochastic model and for further references to literature on security-loan portfolio choice and on expansion in response to changes in reserves, see Poole [294, pp. 769–91]. Poole's paper is primarily theoretical; it attempts to explore the theoretical implications of a stochastic model similar to Morrison's.

5. Frost describes his model as very similar to one presented by Miller and Orr for firm's demand for money [272, pp. 413–35]. The latter model proceeds in the tradition of models by Baumol and Tobin on transactions demands for money. Criticisms of these models have varied from criticism of the tendency to identify economies in transactions costs of trading in liquid securities with increases in sales to cash ratios, to criticism of the failure to recognize the relevance of the liabilities structure of firms in matters concerning cash management and the role of liquidity variously defined. In the former instance, see Section 4.2 of this book; in the latter, see Frazer [126, Chs. 7–8].

6. The theoretical side of Morrison's book—the side about profit maximizing policy—appears to be excessively static and to contain some serious flaws [125, n. 2]. Consequently, this aspect of the book is presently given only minor emphasis.

shocks of specific occurrences and to a failure, chargeable to inertia, to immediately readjust following the shocks. As Frost says [159], "the shock effect hypothesis attributes the accumulation to a shift in the bank's desired level of excess reserves that occurred because the bankers were shocked into expecting large reserve outflows due first to the runs on the banks and then to the reserve requirement changes." A key to the "inertia" effect, according to Frost, is found in the following expression:

$$\frac{d\,D_t^{p*}}{dt} = B\,(D_t^{p} - D_t^{p*})$$

where D_t^{p*} is permanent or "expected" deposit potential (an exponentially weighted average of "past deposit potential"), D_t^p is actual deposit potential ("total reserves plus vault cash divided by the average required reserve ratio against net deposits subject to reserves"), and B is a factor of proportionality.

Conceptually, Frost's expression seems to give no problem. In the next section, however, it must be pinned down empirically to specific time dimensions, and the matter comes out differently. Even so, in the present conceptual framework B decreases immediately after a "shock" (deposit potential is expected to be less permanent and more transitory), and then the inertia effect takes the form of a slow upward adjustment in B as the "shock" wears off. According to Frost, the inertia effect "causes reserve inflows to be viewed as transitory deposit potential [the difference between actual and expected deposit potential] during the period immediately following a shock."

For Frost the shock and inertia effects operate, but he attaches relatively more importance to an "adjustment cost hypothesis" (the hypothesis that bank holdings of excess reserves are determined by the desire to avoid the transactions cost of liquidating interest-bearing liquid assets). In any case, neither Morrison's nor Frost's analysis and empirical results would have led to a doubling of reserve requirements in the 1936–37 period when banks were maintaining unusually large ratios of excess reserves to deposits. In fact, they would have led to a further expansion of excess reserves by the Federal Reserve.

In the conflicting opinions and evidence with respect to whether a liquidity trap existed among banks during the middle and late 1930s, a "unifying thread" is reported by Morrison [282, Ch. 4]. It is [282, p. 34] "the view that banks held abnormal amounts of excess reserves not because of their passivity or indifference, but because it was the prudent thing to do under the circumstances." In Morrison's analysis, this means that their liquidity preference schedules shifted. (Or, more accurately, the normal interest rate shifted.)

The first part of Morrison's Chapter 4 contains reviews of preliminary evidence on the alternative hypotheses, exclusive of Frost's "adjustment cost" hypothesis. Applying the minimum requirement for the trap hypothesis —that interest elasticity increases as the interest rate falls—Morrison finds some evidence for the trap hypothesis, but his evaluation of the evidence mainly supports the shift hypothesis. For example, he concludes [282, p. 114] that "country member banks increased their ratio of total reserves to deposits, relative to that for nonmembers, by almost precisely the amount needed to restore their *excess* reserve ratio to the same relation with non-member banks' excess reserve ratio as existed before the reserve require-ment increase [the doubling of member bank reserve requirements in 1936–37]."

In his Chapter 5, Morrison seeks to reinforce the notion of a shift in the liquidity preference schedule by contrasting the experiences of Canadian and New York City weekly reporting member banks. He views Canada as a good case for comparison because of the similarities between changes in Canadian and United States business conditions, and because of the con-trast of an absence of a panic environment in Canada in the 1930s. The comparison is somewhat strained by the need to allow for differences in regulations and practices with respect to the composition and form of re-serves and by certain differences in deposit liabilities. Even so, Morrison concludes [282, p. 76] that "dissimilar response to Canadian and New York banks to increased bank reserves may be attributed to either the 'shock' effect or the 'inertia' effect."

Morrison's Chapters 6 and 7 review results from analyses of annual and monthly data, respectively. One chapter is confined to an examination of the national banking period from 1872–1914 and the other covers national banking and Federal Reserve periods. The results are unfavorable for the liquidity trap hypothesis.

The adjustment cost hypothesis.—Frost's adjustment cost hypothesis does not question the prospect of a shift in the desired level of reserves, but "substantial amounts of excess reserves will only be held at relatively low interest rates." The alternative hypotheses he was concerned with included the "trap," "shock," and "inertia" hypotheses.[7] With respect to the "trap" hypothesis, Frost brings forth some evidence that the absolute value of the

---

7. In this particular context, Frost attributes the shock effect hypothesis to Friedman and Schwartz [155, pp. 534–42] and the inertia hypothesis to Morrison [282].

interest elasticity for excess reserves is higher for high interest rates than for low, in contrast to the trap hypothesis. His analysis is rather complicated.[8]

In testing the inertia versus the adjustment cost hypothesis, Frost recognizes a special source of difficulty; the short-term interest rate reached extremely low levels during periods when there were large reserve inflows, so the excess reserves may be due either to an inertia in adjusting to the flows, to a tendency for excess reserves to increase as the interest rate falls below its critical value, or to some combination of both. In addition, Frost could have mentioned that both low interest rates and excess reserves may result from anticipated depression in business conditions and the condition of greater uncertainty about the future. In any event, Frost presents some simple correlation coefficients for Morrison's excess reserve ratio (ratio of excess reserves to deposits) and for the product of the adjustment coefficient and the transitory deposit potential [B $(D_t^p - D_t^{p*})$].[9]

What Frost finds is partly represented by the correlation coefficients for two-year periods from 1935 to 1941, as shown in Table 11-3. The excess reserves and the transitory deposit potential are positively and highly correlated during most of the two-year periods 1929–30 to 1934–35, as well as for those shown in Table 11-3. One might say this is to be expected—that banks would prefer excess reserves to match the reduced certainty concerning the buoyancy of business conditions. However, Frost goes further. He says, "the values of B that maximize the correlation between the excess reserve ratio and transitory deposit potential are surprisingly high during the crisis years from 1929 to 1933 and following the reserve requirement changes in 1936 and 1937." Using this as evidence to reject the hypothetical

8. In analyzing monthly data for 1929–41 and 1948–59 with a multiple regression model, he finds critical interest rates for different classes of banks. Hypothetical interest rate series are regressed on data for a given set of determinants but for different classes of banks, to estimate the interest rate at which the desired level of excess reserves becomes positive for the respective classes of banks. The critical interest rate (r^*) is estimated by picking the regression with the lowest standard error of estimate. Calculating interest rate elasticities for excess reserves at the means for the series provides the evidence in question.

Elasticities may be estimated by taking the product of the ratio of the mean values of two variables and the inverse of their corresponding regression coefficients. Elasticity coefficients also occur in loglinear regression models when the so-called independent variables are independent of one another and of the random error term.

9. In estimating "permanent" or expected deposit potential (D_t^{p*}) for these correlations, Frost's first observation is January 1919. This means that his exponentially declining weighted average is one for a ten year period. The period over which data are averaged could affect the role of B in the correlations reported in Table 11–3. Frost reports, however, that "transitory deposit potential is calculated the same way as in Morrison except that vault cash is excluded from total cash reserves."

TABLE 11-3

Simple Correlations Between Morrison's Excess Reserve Ratio
and Transitory Deposit Potential for Various Values of B

Years Value of B	1935 and 1936	1936 and 1937	1937 and 1938	1938 and 1939	1939 and 1940	1940 and 1941
.01	.9768*	.9700*	.9621	.9895	.9710*	.9979*
.02	.9745	.9686	.9744	.9956	.9357	.9974
.025	.9651	.9683	.9810	.9970	.8846	.9960
.033	.9469	.9680	.9896	.9977*	.7520	.9935
.05	.9142	.9672	.9974*	.9932	.3794	.9887
.10	.8621	.9520	.9834	.9175	−.2468	.9810
.15	.8407	.9017	.9527	.7441	−.3533	.9782
.25	.8104	.7230	.8865	.3103	−.3087	.9704
.50	.7184	.3984	.7532	−.1469	−.1185	.9302
1.00	.5793	.2322	.5984	−.2726	.0201	.8322

Data are for New York weekly reporting member banks.
*Denotes highest correlation coefficients in each two-year period.
Source: Peter A. Frost, "Banks' Demand for Excess Reserves," mimeographed,
Carnegie-Mellon University, Graduate School of Industrial Administration, 1968.

view that shock effects require downward shifts in B, he says that "there is
very little evidence that B falls sharply due to the traumatic effects of financial panics and reserve requirement changes and then rises slowly as time
passes. . . . B seems to vary directly with short-term interest rates which
tends to confirm our suspicion that the correlation is spurious [the correlation between the excess reserve ratio and transitory deposit potential]."

It is possible, however, that Frost's identification of shifts in B with the
shock hypothesis (given his method of measuring imbalances between expected deposit potential and actual deposit potential or, what amounts to
the same thing, imbalances between desired and actual excess reserves) is
too strenuous and lacks the sensitivity to discriminate between the refinements in question. If expected deposit potential is much less than actual as
a result of the shock effect, any increment in excess reserves may go entirely
into desired reserves (B may rise, and expected deposits may not be simply
affected by a small amount at the margin, say, as by the most recent data
on deposit potential). A seeming covariation between B and short-term
interest rates supports Frost's adjustment cost hypothesis. But, at the same
time, short rates are declining, actual deposit potential is greater than desired or expected, and so excess reserves increase. The former correlation,
however, does not imply that the latter is more spurious than the former,

unless the adjustment cost hypothesis is accepted as accounting in an explanatory sense for the change in excess reserves. The evidence is not clear that it does.

The "shock" hypothesis does not deny that interest rates have an effect on excess reserves. But to further compound the emphasis on the difficulty of distinguishing between the existence of a shock effect and an adjustment cost hypothesis as applied to banks, Frost reviews evidence presented by Morrison in his comparison of New York and Canadian banks [159]:

> Canadian banks did not accumulate large excess reserve balances during the 1930's despite the parallel movement in interest rates and economic activity in the two countries. Morrison attributes this difference to the absence of bank failures and any significant financial panic in Canada. The difference in behavior is also consistent with the adjustment cost hypothesis. Three things should be noted about the Canadian banking system during the 1930's. First, there were fewer than twenty banks in Canada, each having many branches and serving a wide area. Consequently, their adjustment costs should be similar in magnitude to those of the New York banks. Second, prior to 1935, the Canadian banks were not subject to legal reserve requirements. Instead, an informal reserve requirement of approximately 10 percent was enforced by the Canadian Bankers' Association. This was a very flexible requirement that apparently only had to be met on the last day of each month. Morrison notes that the banks "window dressed" their month end reports. The flexible reserve requirements in Canada certainly lowered the yield from holding excess reserves. This could easily explain why the Canadian banks did not accumulate excess reserves prior to 1935. Third, the Canadian Treasury first issued Treasury bills in 1934 and beginning in 1935 the Bank of Canada began to buy and sell these bills. Since the average annual rate on three month Canadian Treasury bills did not fall below .58 percent from 1934 to 1941, it is not surprising that the Canadian banks did not accumulate excess reserves. The New York banks did not accumulate excess reserves until the rate on United States Treasury bills fell well below .58 percent.

In introducing plausible evidence in support of the adjustment cost hypothesis, Frost proceeds along lines reminiscent of those suggested in Cloos' paper [73]. His discussion of the evidence also suggests a market segmentation theory of interest rates and the prospect of twisting the Treasury yield curve, as reviewed and rejected later in this book (Chs. 12, 13) and elsewhere [131]. The evidence and discussions are as follows [159]:

> The short-term interest rates reached record low levels because of the combined effect of a sharp reduction in the supply of interest bearing liquid assets and a very rapid increase in the banks' effective reserves. During the 1920's, call loans and interbank assets were the banks' major

source of interest bearing liquid assets. The 1933 regulation prohibiting the payment of interest on demand deposits shifted interbank assets from an interest bearing asset to a noninterest bearing asset. The turbulence in the stock market, along with the regulations prohibiting banks from making brokers loans for the account of others and giving the Federal Reserve the power to set margin requirements greatly reduced the importance of the call loan market as a source of interest bearing liquid assets. In addition, the depression reduced foreign trade and, thereby, reduced the supply of bankers acceptances. At the time that the supply of interest bearing liquid assets reached a minimum level, the banks were experiencing a record inflow of reserves primarily as a result of the inflow of gold. The change in effective reserves during each of the years from 1938 to 1940 was greater than the total combined supply of brokers loans, commercial paper, bankers acceptances, and Treasury bills outside of the Federal Reserve Banks. Apparently the commercial banks bid up the prices on these interest bearing liquid assets in an attempt to invest their new reserves, but because of the small supply of these assets they quickly drove the interest rates down to levels where they were willing to hold larger amounts of excess reserves.

In assessing the policy implications for the 1930s of the foregoing discussion, Frost suggests twisting the yield curve [159].

> If the goal was to eliminate excess reserves, it could have been done without any harmful side effects. One way to have done so would have been for the Treasury to have retired long-term debt and issued Treasury bills in their place. The short-term interest rates would have increased with the supply of Treasury bills and the level of excess reserves would have decreased rapidly. If the Treasury has issued enough Treasury bills to raise the bill rate to, say, .50 percent, excess reserves at the New York banks and the larger reserve city banks would have virtually disappeared and excess reserves at the smaller banks would have been significantly reduced. Two side effects of this policy should be noted. First, the money supply and bank credit would have increased rapidly because of the multiple expansion of reserves. This could have been offset, if desired, by either open market sales or a series of small reserve requirement changes. Second, long-term interest rates might have fallen due to the retirement of some of the long-term debt.

Since Frost definitely introduces the prospect of twisting the Treasury yield curve (the prospect of varying the spread between long- and short-dated securities by varying the relative supply of each), the evidence in the next two chapters of this book is relevant and perhaps unfavorable to the adjustment cost hypothesis. Terrell and Frazer [131] review data from the 1960s on maturity profiles of government security holdings that cast doubt on the transactions-cost, inertia effect notions bearing on the profiles [131, n. 19].

11.4   RECESSIONS: 1923–24, 1926–27, AND 1929–33

Much has been written about the monetary and banking history of the 1920s; the minor recessions and the Great Crash of 1929.[10] A common emphasis has been on the preoccupation of the Federal Reserve with international matters and the special events leading up and contributing to the 1929 crash. Friedman and Schwartz, in particular, have given a special interpretation to the 1929 episode and events contributing to it. Brunner and Meltzer [45] do not question the interpretation of these events so much, but they do argue that a common explanation can be found for the 1923–24 and 1926–27 recessions and the depression of 1929–33. In this common explanation, according to them, lie the main reasons for the failure of monetary policy following the peak in 1929.

As far as domestic aspects of monetary policy are concerned, the Federal Reserve is said to have operated in a very traditional policy framework; a decline in market rates reflects an "easy," even "expansive" policy. Given operations in such a framework, a decline in rates satisfied the requirements for monetary policy in the Great Depression. It was possible then, as in later years, for such monetary variables as bank reserves and the money supply to vary pro- rather than counter-cyclically. The empirical support for this thesis is suggested (1) by the cumulative changes indicating a decline in short-term interest rates following peaks in business conditions and (2) by the cumulative changes in the Federal Reserve's holdings of securities plus borrowing through the discount windows of the Federal Reserve banks following the peaks. The interest rate changes suggest ease in credit conditions traditionally viewed, and the changes in Federal Reserve credit reflect declines during the recessions designated. Brunner and Meltzer conclude [45, p. 347]:

> The failure of monetary policy to stop the contraction from 1929 to 1933 does not require a special explanation. It is the result of the same mechanism that produced the policy of 1922 to 1928 that has been so highly praised. Both can be explained as the result of a mistaken belief that low and/or falling interest rates were a sign of "easier" policy.

11.5   SUMMARY

Two episodes stand out in this chapter: (1) the depression of 1929–33 with declines reflected in Federal Reserve bank credit, and (2) the 1937–38

10. For a review of the period and a lengthy list of references, see Frazer and Yohe [133, pp. 142–55].

recession with a doubling of reserve requirements in a series of steps in 1936 and 1937. In the first instance, Brunner and Meltzer have examined the record and attributed the Federal Reserve's actions to constrain credit to member banks to their having focused on credit conditions traditionally viewed rather than on the growth of the reserve base. Brunner and Meltzer emphasize that recessions in 1923–24 and 1926–27 could also be attributed to the Federal Reserve's traditional attachment to credit conditions as a policy indicator.

The 1937–38 recession constitutes a rather unique period in several respects. There were low and in some instances negative interest rates, there were excess reserves at the banks, and the Federal Reserve raised reserve requirements. The latter action was taken with a twofold point of view: that liquidity would be excessive once expansion got under way, and that the Federal Reserve could constrain a boom but could not bring about recovery (could not "push on a string"). In some quarters there was the interpretation that a liquidity trap existed. Modern analysts such as Morrison reject this interpretation and point to a shift in liquidity preference in lieu of the trap (or, more accurately, shift in the normal or safe interest rate). The distinction is important because the shift hypothesis would simply call for further and further acceleration in the growth of reserves to combat the recession.

The accelerated growth rate needed to achieve given targets for bank credit and the money stock may be greater in the special 1937–38 situation than in more normal situations. Nevertheless, acceleration rather than deceleration is the prescription. This points to a further interpretation, particularly with respect to the distribution of lagged effects. Specifically, a given rate of change in bank reserves may exhibit one distributed pattern in relation to a target variable at one time and another at another time; the distributed lag pattern may vary.

Some analysts do not necessarily question the "shift" hypothesis with its "shock" and "inertia" effects but attach relatively more importance to the desire to maintain excess reserves and thereby avoid the transactions cost of holding low-yield securities. The evidence of the relative importance of transactions cost on excess reserves from the 1937–38 recession is not clear. In other contexts, such as that of the term structure of interest rates as in the succeeding chapters, its relatively great importance is questioned.

Part IV

Monetary Policy and the
Term Structure of Interest Rates

12

Theories of the Term Structure and the Decomposition of Expectations

12.1 INTRODUCTION

PREVIOUS SECTIONS have emphasized changes in "the" interest rate. Some (Secs. 3.4, 7.5) have also related this to changes in the term structure of interest rates (defined as the structure of yields on financial assets that differ mainly with respect to maturity), and even to changes in the income velocity of money and monetary policy. In the case of the interrelationship between changes in the interest rate and changes in the term structure, Meiselman notes [264, p. 85] "that one of the main findings of a large number of independent researchers in the last ten years [1958–68] has been that the only dependable way to change the relationship between short-term and long-term interest rates is to change the level of rates." Consequently, this chapter deals with the term structure of interest rates, possible relationships between monetary policy and the term structure, possible relationships between the real and financial sectors, and the decomposition of expectations with respect to interest rate data.

Explanations of the term structure of interest rates and statistical results concerning them have been widely discussed, especially since interest in the subject was reawakened through a study by David Meiselman [265]. Once again profuse analyses of readily available data have been made possible by the modern computer and, in the process, explanations have emerged relying on a predominant role for expectations. The literature on the term structure of interest rates is quite extensive, but this chapter and the next are, in effect, a survey of the more empirically oriented portion of that literature. If one wishes to go further, as in tree diagrams, to the references cited in chapters 12 and 13, then an exceedingly extensive bibliography may be compiled.

12.2   A CATALOGUE OF EXPLANATIONS

In very broad outline, the explanations of the term structure of interest rates tend to emphasize one or a combination of two points of view. One view holds that the market for securities consists of a group of separate, non-overlapping markets defined for different maturities. According to this view there is no tendency for the rates in the different markets to assume any particular relation to each other. Another view holds that the securities market is a collection of interrelated markets in which the term structure of rates is subject to some unifying principle involving expectations. Among the explanations centering about expectations, however, only one is released from a strong dependence on some supply-demand-quantity mechanism (whereby changes in the structure require some changes in the quantities either supplied to or withdrawn from the respective maturity sectors). This explanation is brought forward below as an alternative, and it is juxtaposed with explanations representing other points of view.[1]

Market segmentation.—A market segmentation theory represents the first point of view [81, p. 489]:

> The decisions of borrowers and of lenders as to the maturity of debt they create or hold, and the factors underlying them, determine the relative market valuation of debts of different maturities [and, thus, the relative market interest rates] in conjunction with government monetary and debt management policies.

In other words, the supply and demand conditions within the respective markets determine the relative interest rates. In the pure form, the respective cross elasticities of both demand and supply between maturity segments of the market are negligible. The market segmentation theory implies or asserts that a percentage change in the short-term interest rate ($d \ln i_S$) has negligible effect on the percentage change in the quantity of long-term bonds either supplied or demanded ($d \ln Q_L \approx 0$), and that a percentage change in the long-term interest rate ($d \ln i_L$) has negligible effect on the quantity of short-maturity bonds either supplied or demanded ($d \ln Q_L \approx 0$), that is,

$$\eta_{LS} = \frac{d \ln Q_L}{d \ln i_S} \approx 0; \; \eta_{SL} = \frac{d \ln Q_S}{d \ln i_L} \approx 0$$

1. A review of historical precedents to contemporary work on term structure appears in Culbertson [81, pp. 485–89]. He points to the attention paid to this area about the end of the 1920s, as does Leijonhufvud [249, pp. 149–57, 282–99].

The received expectations hypothesis.—The received (or Meiselman) expectations hypothesis [265, pp. 9–21] characterizes a second extreme of term structure theory—that expected return is the only relevant criterion for portfolio selection. This means, in contrast to the alternative mentioned below, that any preference for a particular maturity to meet a special or unforeseen need for funds at a future date is beyond consideration. The received theory may be outlined as follows [131, pp. 2–3]:

> Expected return—including a serialized stream of returns and/or appreciation (depreciation) in value—is derived from a series of single-period yields expected to prevail at various times in the future. An investor attempting to maximize expected return over some time period (t = 0 to t = n) chooses among debt instruments that mature at times $t = 1, 2, \ldots, n$. Given the expected single-period yield series, one can calculate the return expected over n periods no matter what the nominal time to maturity. For example, an investor might choose from a series of n consecutive single-period bonds and an n-period bond, depending on the greatest expected return over the entire period. This procedure (operating via a supply-quantity–demand-quantity mechanism and assuming no transactions costs) ultimately increases the price (reduces expected return) for securities purchased and reduces the price (increases expected return) for securities not purchased (sold) so that expected return over n periods is the same no matter which investment pattern is selected.

Meiselman added to this theory by making allowance for some inaccuracy in the implicit forecasting that is said to be embodied in the term structure. Meiselman recognized that market expectations may adjust imperfectly to errors in forecasting. His contributions were (1) to assume that a fictional "forward" interest rate was implicit in the term structure as represented by the yield curve, and to claim that the "forward" rate is the market expectation of the rate that will prevail in the future; (2) to set forth a known error learning model that was previously thought to have explained error learning as a part of the formation of expectations; and (3) to analyze term structure data to determine whether they behaved as if they represented forecasts.

Assuming a discussion of an interest rate per annum (a one year rate) to simplify the notation, Meiselman's error learning model may be denoted:

$$(1.0) \qquad {}_{t+n}r_t - {}_{t+n}r_{t-1} = a + b\,(R_t - {}_tr_{t-1}) + u$$

where r is a "forecast" or forward rate (r_t for forecast at period t) R is a spot rate (R_t for spot rate at period t), ${}_{t+n}r_t$ is the forecast made in period t (the right-hand subscript) of the rate expected in period $t+n$ (the left-hand subscript), and so on.

In other words, the forecast for the future period $(t+n)$ during the current period (t) is adjusted in relation to the last period $(t-1)$ forecast to compensate for the error of the previous forecast. This error is indicated by the difference between the period t spot rate (R_t) and the forecast of the spot rate made a period earlier $(_tr_{t-1})$. The error is the factor in parentheses in equation (1.0) and b is the coefficient reflecting the extent of the adjustment in response to the error.

Other studies have discussed expectations about the future and the way they may adjust to error in previous forecasts [350, pp. 151–56; 71, pp. 206–7]. Consequently, Meiselman's test of the expectations theory showed that adjustments in the yield-curve forecast of interest rates followed a pattern similar to that of other known forecasts.

The liquidity preference theory.—The liquidity preference theory—as attributed to Hicks and Keynes by Leijonhufvud [249, pp. 288–99] and others—asserts a preference for the certainty of capital over the certainty of income. It similarly asserts a preference for short- over long-term securities, on the grounds that changes in the interest rate have more effect on the value of securities when the time to maturity is longer. The market tendency for yield curves to slope upward more often than downward is typically offered as evidence to support the notion of a preference for liquidity and the need to pay extra interest (a higher yield or liquidity premium) to entice the market to hold long-term issues.

The tendency for yields on long-dated securities to exceed those on short-term securities gives rise to a reference to "normal backwardation" in the yield curve. The term "normal backwardation" is in fact equated to liquidity preference theory, but the latter is distinct from variants of Keynes' analysis of the liquidity preference demand for money as outlined earlier (Secs. 5.5, 8.5).

An alternative.—An alternative to received expectations theory of the term structure, as originally presented elsewhere [131], recognizes (1) an equality of foresight principle (mentioned in Secs. 2.1, 2.2), (2) the need for an explanation of turning points in interest rates (Sec. 8.5), and (3) the presence of a liquidity hedging motive for holding securities (a motive for holding particular maturities of securities for unanticipated needs for funds and in anticipation of a need for funds at specific future dates). The equality of foresight principle—according to which lenders and borrowers (traders, buyers, and sellers) of securities respond simultaneously to certain factors influencing expectations—releases expectational interest rate changes (and thus bond prices) from dependence on such intermediate steps as portfolio adjustments or supply-demand-quantity changes.

The theory then recognizes (1) that rates are determined at least partly by expected rates, and (2) that expectations are influenced considerably by current and past changes (Secs. 1.2, 8.5). The short rates are influenced predominantly by recent changes, and the longer rates by changes extending over a more distant past. The extent of the influence of the more distant past is related to the time horizon for forming expectations and to the time to maturity of the instrument. The extrapolative "push" of recent changes and the regressive "pull" toward normality operate for both short- and long-term rates; the relatively shorter time span for the rates on short-dated instruments provides an explanation of the tendency for such rates to vary over a wider range than the rates on long-dated instruments.[2] The earlier analysis (Ch. 8) of a coalescence of opinions, probabilistic slanting, and greater certainty is applicable. A coalescence of opinions and the accompanying greater certainty lead to a general lengthening of the time span being considered. Where the expectation is thought to be captured in a weighted average of past rates, with the weights declining exponentially, the greater certainty is captured through a shifting of the slants applied to the weights to favor the pull toward normality. As in the earlier chapter, this coalescing of opinions and shifting brings about the turn in interest rates, especially in the present case, where the turn concerns rates on relatively default-free securities of the type issued by the U. S. Government.

The hedging motive and (or including) the need for funds for dealing with unforeseen developments account for differences in time to maturity

2. This reasoning is supplemented by two additional pieces in Terrell and Frazer [131, n. 9]. "One is found in the received expectations theory where smaller fluctuations in long rates were said to result because the long rates are averages of the more widely varying short rates. This is accompanied by investors indifference between the two sets of yields and thus indifference about maturities. The second bit of reasoning, actually subsumed under the reading in the text, is that with a strengthened prospect of a decline (rise) in rates, the longer term rates will be lower (higher) because of greater anticipated appreciation (depreciation) in the value of long maturities for a given change in interest rates. The lower (higher) long-term yields are usually said to come about because of an increase (decrease) in the quantity of long-dated instruments demanded vis-à-vis short-dated ones. Actually an interest rate change of the same magnitude on the short- and long-dated securities would not be expected, either because of learning from the historical pattern of changes and/or because of the stronger pull toward normality for the rate on long-dated securities. Further, our explanation does not rule out taking into account appreciation (or depreciation) in the establishment of yields. What we add is that such prospects may be simply reinforcing to our view and, indeed, may be taken into account in the establishment of yields and the setting of security prices by traders without actual changes occurring in the quantity of long- vis-à-vis short-dated instruments flowing on the market at least without the quantity changes occurring over the same phase as the more volatile interest rate changes."

profiles of the securities held by various groups.[3] For example, the distribution of marketable government security holdings of nonfinancial corporations (Ch. 15) shows a relatively greater amount of short-dated holdings with a mean maturity of about fourteen months, as a hedge against the need for funds for meeting unforeseen needs and outlays, for discharging short-term liabilities, and for carrying out plans concerning capital expenditures. Life insurance companies, on the other hand, invest long and show a mean maturity of about seventeen and a half years; they can anticipate outlays far into the future or they require the income stability gained thereby.

Two prospects combine to suggest an impressionistic evaluation of the alternative explanation of the term structure just outlined. The prospects are (1) that the profiles exist and are determined as described, and (2) that the maturities are tailored by the Treasury to suit the market in the case of marketable government securities. Support for the alternative is provided against this background, if the profiles in question are relatively stable over periods in which the term structure is highly volatile, say as indicated by the spread between the yields on long- and short-dated assets. Such, in fact, were the findings from study of the decade of the 1960s [131].

12.3   THE POLICY IMPLICATIONS OF TERM STRUCTURE THEORIES

The policy implications of term structure theories concern three sets of prospects: (1) twisting the yield curve (varying the spread between the short- and long-term rates, $r_L - r_S$, as in the Federal Reserve's efforts at Operation Twist, beginning in early 1961) independently of changes in the level of interest rates; (2) changing the level of interest rates without changing expectations; and (3) simultaneously changing both the yield spread and the level of interest rates, via changes in expectations. All sets of prospects concern the financial markets, but the last two also involve theories about the interrelationships between the "real goods" and "financial" sectors of the economy.

Prospects and financial markets.—The first set of prospects is consistent with market segmentation theory, whereby the absolute level of rates in one

---

3. The profiles for various groups—as represented in the U.S. Treasury's survey of the ownership of marketable government securities—are obtained using the notion of a probability distribution (or relative frequency density) and viewing time to maturity on a horizontal axis and the relative frequency of the debt instruments held in the various maturity classes. Also, characteristics of the distributions such as mean and variance may be used to describe the distributions. Such distributions and their characteristics are shown and employed in Terrell and Frazer [131].

market sector can be determined simply by changing the supply-demand quantity of securities in that market. This is consistent with the use of Treasury debt management as an instrument for changing the term structure of interest rates, particularly as discussed in the next chapter (Ch. 13). The second set of prospects is consistent with the theory of "backwardation." The third set of prospects is consistent with expectations theories, both as in Meiselman's error learning model with some extrapolative push of past changes and as in the alternative explanation with emphasis on a weighted average of past rates, the slanting of weights, coalescing opinions, learning, and outside factors.

The weight of empirical evidence supports the predominance of expectations theories. Much of the variation in yields can be accounted for by expectations-forming mechanisms, as subsequent discussion reveals. Admitting the presence of both expectations-forming mechanisms and supply-demand, price-quantity mechanisms of the market segmentation type, however, the crucial question concerns which forces predominate. The ensuing analyses suggest that it is those operating via expectations.

Interrelationships: the "real goods" and financial sectors.—In earlier parts of this book (Chs. 4 and 8), the expectations of the managers of industrial corporations were said to be responding to the same factors that shape expectations in the financial markets. In applying theory to the non-financial business sector, two broad classes of assets have been distinguished —those with fixed claims and those with residual claims against future income. An important aspect of the analysis is the way factors—such as price level changes—exert differential effects on the respective streams of returns and alter the preference for one class over another at the margin. Here the important effect is the differential impact on expectations. As Leijonhufvud emphasizes [249, Ch. 3], Keynes related term structure theory to the real goods sector but proceeded along different lines. Keynes held expectations constant for the period over which he analyzed the effects of policy (for Keynes, the effects of a change in the long-term interest rate), and he emphasized interest insensitive assets (money and short-dated assets) and interest sensitive assets (assets with a long life, including bonds and capital goods). A lowering of the interest rate, given fixed expectations, raised the capital value (or mythical price) of long-dated assets and thereby stimulated capital investment.

In Keynes' framework there was a preference for capital certainty (interest insensitive assets). For instance, by buying short-dated securities the Federal Reserve could satisfy some of this preference related to the backwardation of the yield curve and this could effect a downward shift in the

yield curve (a decline in "the" interest rate). Leijonhufvud views this thinking as providing the basis for a "bills only" policy. In the Federal Reserve's
bills only doctrine of the post-accord decade (after March 4, 1951), the
interest rate could be lowered or raised by effecting open market transactions at the short end of the yield curve. According to Leijonhufvud,
Keynes was skeptical of the latter, but the question here is simply whether
the Federal Reserve has control over the interest rate through simple supply-
demand mechanisms and independent of the influence on expectations. To
concede that expectations are a predominating influence—as suggested in
various sections of this book—would reject the bankers' view of monetary
policy linkages (Sec. 3.4) and certain aspects of Keynes' and the Keynesian
models, as outlined earlier (Sec. 1.4).

12.4   MORE ON THE FORMATION OF EXPECTATIONS

Stanley Diller [95] presents an essay on the formation of expectations in
the context of a broader study of economic forecasts and expectations. A
general linear forecasting model with a weighted sum of current and past
values is presented [273, p. 85]:

$$_{t+1}y^*{}_t = \sum_{j=0}^{\infty} \beta_j Y_{t-1}$$

where the Ys with right-hand subscripts suggest time series, the βs are the
weights, and the forecast value is denoted by an asterisk with right-hand
subscript giving the date of the formation of the forecast and the left-hand
subscript denoting the date or target date of the forecast.

Error-learning and return-to-normality models.—Mincer [273] shows
that both an error-learning model of the Meiselman type and a return-to-
normality model may be deduced by algebraic manipulation as special cases
of the general model. The error-learning model was shown earlier as equation (1.0). The return-to-normality model may be denoted as

(2.0) $_{t+2}F_t - {}_{t+1}F_t = K (A_t - {}_N A_t), K < 0$

where Fs are forecasts (interchangeable with rs, forward rates), As are
actual values (interchangeable with Rs, spot rates), $_{t+2}F_t$ and $_{t+1}F_t$ are
forecasts made in period t with reference to periods $t + 2$ and $t + 1$ respectively, $_N A$ is the average or normal value, and $K < 0$ reflects inverse
relationship between change in the forecasts values over a given span
(change in $_{t+2}F_t - {}_{t+1}F_t$) and the deviation of actual spot value at period t
from the normal value ($A_t - {}_N A_t$). If the normal or average rate is treated

as a constant and if r and R are interchanged with F and A, then the above difference equation may be written as

(2.1) $$_{t+n}r_t - {}_{t+n-1}r_t = Q + K_N R_t + V_N$$

where Q is a constant term and V_N the error term.

Mincer has presented a linear extrapolative forecasting model where the forecast value for a future period $(t + n)$ is a weighted average of values ranging in sequence from the $t + n - 1$ period back to period t, and on back into the past. With algebraic manipulations on this, the linear extrapolations model has been shown to reduce revisions of the Meiselman type to a series of forecasts and to be consistent with Meiselman's error-learning model. Indeed, Mincer deduces an expression that relates the decline in coefficients of determination to Meiselman's revision coefficients (γ_is) whenever $\gamma_i \gtreqqless \gamma_{i+1}$,

(3.0) $$R_i^2 = \frac{1}{1 + \dfrac{(1-R_1^2)\,\gamma_i^2}{R_1^2\,\gamma_i^2}\,(1 + \gamma_1^2 + \ldots + \gamma_{i-1}^2)}$$

where R_i^2 is the coefficient of determination for the ith regression, and γ_i is the regression coefficient (or Meiselman adjustment or error-learning coefficient) for the ith regression.

Meiselman's original estimates for coefficients of determination and those obtained by Diller with the foregoing expression and using Durand data[4] are shown in columns (2) and (3) of Table 12-1. The consistency between these two sets of estimates is said to strengthen the interpretation of term

---

4. The data used to obtain the results in Tables 12–1 and 12–2 are referred to as "Durand data" or "Durand yields," a special set of yield curve data that have been computed by David Durand. In his more recent study, Diller updates these data, analyzes data read from the yield curves given in the Treasury Bulletin, and compares results from the respective sets of data.

Durand data are data on yields read from a yield curve. Curves may be fit to observations concerning maturities that are not spaced at regular intervals such as one year to maturity, five years to maturity, and so on. Data for such maturities can be read from a yield curve or computed from a formula as discussed by Telser [350]. The yield curve is referred to as a curve at a moment in time, such as December 31, 1969. It may also be a period of time, such as a year, in which case the scatter of observations about a curve would be greater due to changes in the period, but the curve could still be fit. The period in Durand data is a year.

In particular, Diller analyzes data read from Treasury yield curves at quarterly intervals from March 1945 to December 1964. "The maturities along the yield curve," however, "are read at annual intervals" and, consequently the forecast intervals are annual. Using these data the coefficients of determination are much lower than with Durand data, although the return-to-normality mechanism is still reflected in the statistical results.

TABLE 12–1

Comparison Between the Estimated and Predicted Coefficients of
Determinations for Regressions of the Error-Learning Model,
Durand Data, 1901–55

Span (1)	Estimated R^2 (adj) (2)	Predicted R^2 (adj) (3)
1	.9053	.9053
2	.7470	.7812
3	.5819	.6395
4	.4537	.5154
5	.4004	.4206
6	.3709	.3345
7	.4055	.3324
8	.3289	.2743

Note: Column (2) lists coefficients of determination that Meiselman computed and column (3) the ones predicted by equation (3.0).

Source: Stanley Diller, "Expectations in the Term Structure of Interest Rates," *Economic Forecasts and Expectations,* ed., Jacob Mincer (New York: Columbia University Press for the National Bureau of Economic Research, 1969), p. 123.

structure data as forecasts. The presence of "non-forecasting" components is said to be indicated by further analysis relating to the foregoing formula and by the tendency for predicted R^2s to decline more readily than the observed ones in Table 12-1.

As Table 12-1 suggests, Meiselman presented results for eight regressions. These corresponded to revisions representing eight spans of forecast (years between the date of forecast and the date to which the forecast applies). Meiselman found the adjustment to error "explained" less as the span between the spot and forecast rate increased. He also found that the adjustment coefficient declined with the coefficients of determination. With these results and other analysis, Meiselman concluded that term structure data behaved as though they were forecasts. The fact that Diller gets similar estimates using Mincer's equation (3.0) suggests that a moving average of past spot rates can predict a substantial part of the implicit forecast themselves.

Employing regressions in the form of equation (2.1), Diller reports the results in Table 12-2. The coefficient K has the correct sign, and the adjusted coefficients of determination rise and then decline, reaching a maximum for the forecast span for the third year in the future.

If the current normal value is treated as a declining weighted average of past normal values, and if a substitution is made in equation (2.0), then

TABLE 12–2

Statistics Computed From the Regression of the Expected
Change of Future Spot Rates on the Level of the
Current One-Period Spot Rate
(Durand data, annual observations, 1900–54[a])

Span of Forecast (1)	K (2)	t-Value of K (3)	Constant Term (4)	t-Value of Const. Term (5)	R^2 (adj) (6)
$_{t+1}r_t - R_t$	$-.1627$	-7.2109	$.6437$	7.8584	$.4904$
$_{t+2}r_t - {}_{t+1}r_t$	$-.1264$	-11.8510	$.4909$	12.6817	$.7246$
$_{t+3}r_t - {}_{t+2}r_t$	$-.0997$	-17.0387	$.3878$	18.2505	$.8452$
$_{t+4}r_t - {}_{t+3}r_t$	$-.0741$	-12.7946	$.2948$	14.0311	$.7543$
$_{t+5}r_t - {}_{t+4}r_t$	$-.0737$	-8.2939	$.3071$	9.5246	$.5612$
$_{t+6}r_t - {}_{t+5}r_t$	$-.0475$	-7.8774	$.1964$	8.9637	$.5353$
$_{t+7}r_t - {}_{t+6}r_t$	$-.0332$	-6.1131	$.1382$	7.0177	$.4070$
$_{t+8}r_t - {}_{t+7}r_t$	$-.0361$	-8.0801	$.1511$	9.3173	$.5481$
$_{t+9}r_t - {}_{t+8}r_t$	$-.0250$	-4.1018	$.0981$	4.4308	$.2299$

[a]The regressions were of the following form $_{t+n}r_t - {}_{t+n-1}r_t = Q + k_n R_t + V_n$.

Source: Stanley Diller, "Expectations in the Term Structure of Interest Rates," *Economic Forecasts and Expectations,* ed., Jacob Mincer (New York: Columbia University Press for the National Bureau of Economic Research, 1969), p. 132.

through further algebraic manipulation an equation with an estimate for the *K* coefficient and for Meiselman's error-learning coefficients may be obtained. Moreover, *K* may be shown to be negative when Meiselman's error-learning coefficients reflect declining values for the first and second forecast spans. By such means Diller shows that "the decline in Meiselman's coefficients as the span of forecast increases is algebraically identical to an inverse relationship between the expected change between two spans of forecast and the deviation of the current spot rate from the normal rate."

On the basis of such evidence and algebraic manipulation, Diller concludes that "as the span increases the market gives increasing weight to the more distant past and distinguishes less between the more immediate and the more distant past."

The decomposition of forecasts.—Diller's error-learning, extrapolative, and return-to-normality models have been considered and found to be three special models of a more general extrapolative model—the adaptive expectations model shown in Sections 1.2, 8.5, and on other occasions.

In the present analysis, both "extrapolative" or "induced" components and "non-extrapolative" or "autonomous" components (the part exclusive of the historical pattern of interest rate series) have been mentioned as parts of forecasts. Additional analysis directed at decomposition of forecasts assumes that the forward rates consist entirely of forecasts. Non-forecasting components include liquidity premia and errors of measurement. The decomposition of forecasts is said to be a method of analyzing market behavior. The isolation of the extrapolative component is attempted by regressing the forecast on the current and past spot rates. For example,

$$(4.0) \qquad _{t+n}F_t = b_1A_t + b_2A_{t-1} + \ldots b_8A_{t-7} + {}_{t+n}E_t$$

where—following earlier notations in part—F is the forecast, A is the spot rate, and E is the residual term. The residuals of such regressions measure "autonomous components," the part of the forecasts that is unrelated to the historical pattern of the series for interest rates. [In actually running regressions of the form of equation (4.0), the lagging process was stopped after seven lags to conserve data, to conserve the loss of degrees of freedom.]

The results for regressions of the form just given were obtained using both Durand and Treasury data. Those for Durand data with the time span varying from 1 to 9 years are shown in Table 12-3. The coefficients in the column labeled (2) indicate that the extrapolative component accounts for a large proportion of the variation of forecasts.

TABLE 12–3

The Percent Variation of the Forward Rates
Explained by Current and Lagged Spot Rates
(Durand data, annual observations, 1916–54)[a]

Span of Forecast[b] (year) (1)	R^2 Adjusted (2)	S^2_E (3)
1	.9878	.0346
2	.9735	.0601
3	.9597	.0733
4	.9447	.0798
5	.9196	.0868
6	.9091	.0760
7	.8890	.0748
8	.8727	.0647
9	.8015	.0805

[a]The general form of the regression is:

$$_{t+n}F_t = B_1A_t + B_2A_{t-1} \ldots B_8A_{t-7} + E_n$$

[b]Column (1) is the value of n, column (2) the adjusted coefficients of determination, and column (3) the squared standard errors of the estimate.

Source: Stanley Diller, "Expectations in the Term Structure of Interest Rates," *Economic Forecasts and Expectations*, ed., Jacob Mincer (New York: Columbia University Press for the National Bureau of Economic Research, 1969), p. 123.

Another method is also used to illustrate decomposition. It uses some standard business conditions indicators—the Federal Reserve's Index of Industrial Production and the Dow Jones' Index of Industrial Stock Prices. These are viewed as possible means of "autonomous" forecasting and facilitate a different decomposition of forward rates into extrapolative and autonomous components. The method requires dropping the notion of independence between extrapolative and autonomous components.

Many time series share a common historical process that should be extracted from the extrapolative component in some way. Such a common relationship between two of the time series in question is illustrated in Table 12-4. To accomplish a partitioning, regressions of the following form are run:

$$(5.0) \qquad {}_{t+n}F_t = B_1 \, {}_{t+n}F_t{}^* + B_2 I + u_n$$

where ${}_{t+n}F_t{}^*$ is computed from regressions in the form of equation (4.0), and I is the index of industrial production. Results are shown in Table 12-5. Diller concludes from a comparison of columns (2) and (4) of Table 12-5 "that the relation between the Index of Industrial Production and the forecasts of future rates stems largely from the common historical pattern in the variation of the spot rates and the index." He notes further, however, "a net relationship between the index and the forecasts after allowing for the common historical relationship." This grows with the span of the forecasts, as seen in column (4).

The evidence appears to indicate that the "induced" component accounts for a large part of variation of the forecasts. As Diller concludes, however,

TABLE 12–4

Coefficients of Determination Between Federal Reserve Boards Index
of Industrial Production and Forecasts of Future Interest Rates
(Treasury data, quarterly, 1949–64)

Span of Forecast (quarters) (1)	Coefficients of Determination (2)
1	.7159
2	.7806
3	.8107
4	.8176

Source: Stanley Diller, "Expectations in the Term Structure of Interest Rates," *Economic Forecasts and Expectations*, ed., Jacob Mincer (National Bureau of Economic Research, mimeographed, April 1968).

TABLE 12–5

Regression of Forward Rates on Estimated Induced Component
and Index of Industrial Production
(Treasury data, quarterly, 1949–64)[a]

Span of Forecast (quarters) (1)	Squared Partial Correl. Coef. of F* (2)	t-Value of Reg. Coef. Attached to F* (3)	Squared Partial Correl. Coef. of I (4)	t-Value of Reg. Coef. Attached to I_b (5)	Gross Coef. of Determination (adj) (6)
1	.8866	21.8365	.0078	.6909	.9667
2	.8075	15.9938	.1049	2.6743	.9564
3	.7343	12.9808	.1947	3.8404	.9480
4	.4705	7.3615	.2394	4.3817	.9003

[a]This table is based on equation (5.0) in the text.

[b]The t-values of the regression coefficients measure the significance of the relationship between a particular independent variable and the dependent variable given that the other independent variable is also in the regression. The t-values are therefore measures of *net* significance. A t-value exceeding 2 is indicative of a significant relationship about 95 per cent of the time.

Source: Stanley Diller, "Expectations in the Term Structure of Interest Rates," *Economic Forecasts and Expectations*, ed., Jacob Mincer (New York: Columbia University Press for the National Bureau of Economic Research, 1969), p. 147.

it may not reveal the actual extent of the market's reliance on past rates as distinct from other market indicators. A part of the common relationship between the forward rate and the indicator "will show up in the relation between the forward rates and the past spot rates."

One significant aspect of this last conclusion is that other sectors of the economy may rely on time series—rather than or in combination with interest rates—but still exhibit the same patterns of changes in expectations as those exhibited in the term structure of interest rates. This aspect of analysis and empirical findings is consistent with the expectational analysis of Chapter 8 and the alternative explanation of the interrelated term structure and real goods sectors (Secs. 12.2, 12.3). In that analysis, many time series shared common influences.

12.5 SUMMARY

Theories of the term structure of interest rates have been of several types; (1) market segmentation, (2) received expectations, (3) backwardation, and (4) an alternative with emphasis on a weighted average of past rates, the slanting of weights, coalescing opinions, learning, and outside factors. The first is consistent with the Federal Reserve's twisting the yield curve. The third is consistent with the Federal Reserve's changing interest rates without changing expectations and with the Federal Reserve's bills only doctrine of the decade following March 4, 1951. The other types are consistent with the Federal Reserve's changing simultaneously the level and the structure of rates via changes in expectations. The fourth is released from a strong reliance on some supply-demand-quantity mechanism. The trend in analyses of data in the 1960s, under the impact of the computer, increasingly favored the expectational theories, the "alternative" in particular, and the presence of interrelationships between the real and financial sectors of the overall economy.

In analysis of selected expectational models relating to the term structure, error-learning, return-to-normality ("pull" effect), and extrapolative ("push") effect, the models have been shown to relate to one another via algebraic manipulations of a general linear forecasting model. Analyses of interest rate data by Diller revealed the presence of the variety of effects and autonomous components. In dealing with the prospect that many time series simply share a common historical process, as posited in this text from time to time, Diller showed that some other business conditions indicators performed roles similar to term structure data, in that they revealed the presence of anticipations about future business conditions.

13

"Push" and "Pull" Effects and Changes in the Term Structure

13.1 Introduction

"Push" and "pull" effects have been mentioned before (Secs. 1.2, 5.3, 5.4, 7.4, 8.5, 12.2, 12.4). They were a basic part of the apparatus brought out in Chapter 12. Additional literature on term structure and these effects in particular is reviewed in this chapter. A paper by Modigliani and Sutch [280] (hereafter, on occasion, MS) was among the first to combine "push" and "pull" effects in analysis of term structure data.[1] Extensive controversy over analysis and methodology emanated from the MS paper and its fore-runner [281]. The methodology of MS's analysis, as reviewed in Section 13.3, focuses on important controversial points and sheds light on the changes occurring in term structure theory under the impact of the modern computer.

In addition to "push" and "pull" effects, the possibility of a fairly equal sensitivity with respect to anticipations on the part of the financial markets sector and the real sector (especially as represented by the large manu-facturing corporation) has been mentioned (Secs. 1.4, 2.2, 4.2, 4.3, 6.3, 7.4, 8.4, 12.2) and embodied in the "equality of foresight" principle (Secs. 2.1, 12.2). A state-of-mind variable frequently introduced to illustrate the principle has been the expected rate of change in prices. In this chapter the expected rate of change in prices, as dealt with by several authors [167, 171, 384], is again introduced as it relates to the term structure and possi-bly business conditions generally.

---

1. Malkiel [255, p. 562] notes that Frank de Leeuw and MS "have found ways of combining both the extrapolative 'push' of recent rate changes and the initial 'pull' of the normal level of rates into fabricated expectational variables."

13.2 "PUSH," "PULL," AND OTHER EFFECTS

Malkiel and Kane (hereafter, on occasion, MK) report on independent evidence from a sample survey concerning expectations. A description of their procedures and results is contained in two papers [221, 256]. One supports conclusions somewhat similar to those attributed to Diller (Sec. 12.4). Specifically, MK (1) support Meiselman's version of the expectations forming mechanism, (2) mention "shifts in expectations, unrelated to individuals previous forecast errors," and (3) state that the extrapolative "push" of recent changes dominates expectations formation in the short run and that the inertial "pull" of the normal level of rates becomes a more important force for rates more than six-to-nine months in the future. Malkiel comments [255, p. 562] that the latter evidence supports analysis along the lines of Modigliani and Sutch.

Major conclusions in MK's August 1967 paper [221], not mentioned in their August 1969 article [256], concern "backwardation," the policy implications of its presence, and the policy implications of the market segmentation theory. The conclusions are: (1) risk aversion does influence the behavior of investors in appraising the attractiveness of securities of different maturities; (2) the demands for various maturities of debt are not infinitely elastic at going rates, and therefore changes in the relative supplies of different maturities (as in the Federal Reserve's Operation Nudge or Twist) can alter the term structure.

The important policy question is not whether evidence indicates some degree of backwardation and market segmentation by some type of *ceteris paribus* approach as mentioned earlier (Sec. 1.2). It is rather whether the policy operation in question exerts its primary influence through some part of the expectations mechanism, considering the overall aspects of the operation. If the level of interest rates (and thus the yield spread) is affected mainly by, say, the prospective inflationary aspects of accelerated growth in the money supply, then the effects of efforts to alter the term structure via debt management or Federal Reserve purchases in different maturity sectors of the market may be overwhelmed by the expectational effects induced through simultaneous changes in the money stock. Abstracting from seasonal variations, defensive operations, and money market noise, the question is the net overall effect of stabilization operations on the structure of rates.

Modigliani and Sutch's theory.—MS present a "preferred habitat" theory—Kessel says this is another name for market segmentation [227, pp. 592–93]; "Modigliani and Sutch . . . have taken market segmentation seriously in the sense that they have attempted to produce evidence relevant for evaluating its validity." He says their findings are consistent with his own; market segmentation has little explanatory power. For the most part, MS find support for a variant of the expectations hypothesis, a combination of extrapolative "push" of recent rate changes and an inertial "pull" of the normal level of rates. Kessel concludes [227, p. 594]:

> I suspect that their a priori or pre-investigation beliefs in the existence of market segmentation were stronger than they should have been. Evidently, the experience during the war and the pre-accord period [pre–March 4, 1951] was interpreted as evidence that market segmentation exists. I believe this constitutes a misreading of history. This experience is consistent with both liquidity preference and expectations but contradicts market segmentation. During this period there were tremendous shifts in investor maturity preference; this contradicts the preferred habitat theory.

The early post–World War II period was one of "pegged" interest rates. One way of pegging the rates was for the Federal Reserve and the Treasury to vary maturities acquired or offered to the market, as Kessel implies. But there was also another way, by leading the market to expect certain rates through announcements about the maintenance of rates (induced effects operating via expectations).

The MS paper in question [280] is criticized by Neil Wallace [363] and by Terrell and Frazer [131]. Wallace [363, pp. 590–92] makes some critical points about the lag-structure model of MS, and in particular about the way changes in the maturity composition of the debt are introduced and evaluated. Terrell's and Frazer's criticism [131, Sec. III] finds MS's approach to be largely from the Treasury's side of the market at the expense of adequate emphasis on the demand side. This derives its importance in part from the earlier emphasis on the tailoring of the debt to suit the market (as in Sec. 12.2). The criticisms do not apply to the implications of the lag models for the extrapolation "push" and the inertial "pull" effects.

The lag structure.—Without going into the underlying theory or equations, the relationship dealt with by MS may be simply stated as

$$R_t - r_t = f \left(\sum_{i=o}^{n} \beta_i \, r_{t-i} \right)$$

where the spread between the long- and short-term rate ($R_t - r_t$) is some function of past short-term rates (r_{t-i}, $i = o, \ldots, n$), i represents the number of time periods prior to the current time (t), the β_i's reflect the shape of the lag structure, the weights for the more recent past reveal "push" effects, and those for the more distant past reveal "pulls" toward normality. Instead of treating the yield spread as the dependent variable, MS note that in actual estimation the short-term rate may be transferred from the left side to the right. The short-term rate appears in the distributed lag part of the relationship. There is the notion that "the long rate can finally be expressed as an average of short rates."

In effecting estimations, MS used the Almon lag technique described in the Appendix to Chapter 1 and Section 10.4. They were concerned with the effect of intercorrelation in the series representing the different lagged interest rates. As emphasized earlier, the Almon technique constrains the pattern of coefficients to fall on a curve, such as may be defined by a given polynomial. For their problem, MS decided on a fourth-degree polynomial. The idea was to find, for the given polynomial, the number of lagged terms that maximized the fit of the linear regression equation. The specific equation obtained using fifty-seven quarterly observations, I–1952 to I–1966, was

$$R_t = 1.491 + 0.259\, r_t + \sum_{i=1}^{16} \beta_i\, r_{t-i},$$
$$(0.063)\quad (0.036)$$

$$R^2 = 0.959 \qquad S_e = 0.124 \qquad D\text{-}W = 0.582$$

where the long-term rate (R) is the average yield on long-term government securities, the short-term rate is the average yield on three-month Treasury bills, and the estimates for the β_i and their standard errors (in the parentheses) are, from left to right [280, p. 574],

.014(.027), .022(.012), .030(.007), .038(.007),
.044(.007), .049(.006), .053(.005), .055(.005),
.054(.006), .052(.006), .049(.006), .043(.005),
.036(.006), .028(.007), .019(.007), .010(.006).

MS express the β's as percentages ($\times$ 100) and show their distribution graphically with the lags in quarters from one to sixteen shown on a horizontal axis. From the data for the β's one may observe that the lag structure begins with 1.4, rises to a peak of 5.5 for the eighth quarter, and then declines to 1.0 for the sixteenth quarter. MS also graphically show a band about the line just obtained. In addition, they show a comparison of the actual yield spread ($R_t - r_t$) with that estimated by the use of the distributed lag equation with r_t in the right hand member, and they show the difference between actual and estimated values. The band is obtained by adding and subtracting one standard error to each of the β's. The actual and estimated yield spreads compare favorably, with both increasing in recession periods such as 1953–54, 1957–58, and 1960–61. The residuals behave systematically and thus exhibit pronounced serial correlation, as also indicated by the Durbin-Watson statistic of 0.582. This, of course, suggests the presence of other influences. In terms of their model, MS say [280, p. 575], "these residuals would reflect in part the influence of variables other than the past history of rates on the market's expectations of the future of the long rate and, additionally, forces leading to variations in the size of the risk premium differential between the long and short market."

The good fit ($R^2 = 0.959$) of their equation is consistent with the presence of "push" and "pull" effects. Additionally it leaves little variation in the yield spread to be accounted for (or explained) by such forces as the relative quantities of government securities being placed on or withdrawn from the market. Modigliani and Sutch note this.

Turning points and "push" and "pull" effects.—The extrapolative "push" effect and the inertial "pull" effect became widely recognized in the late 1960s as a part of the expectations-forming mechanism [221, 256, 280]. A shortcoming of these effects is that they alone will not explain the timing of turning points in interest rates (and business conditions) and the duration of cycles, as mentioned earlier (Sec. 8.5).

The possibility of explaining turning points and the varying duration of expansion phases of different cycles was especially related—in Chapter 8 and again in Section 12.2—to the formation of expectations in group situations, the slanting of subjective probabilities in group situations, and the coalescing of opinions about the direction of change in business conditions.

13.3   SOME ADDITIONAL STUDIES ON THE TERM STRUCTURE AND DETERMINATION OF INTEREST RATES

In a publication more recent than the MS one, Hamburger and Latta [183] (hereafter, on occasion, HL) deal with the MS model and re-examine the relationship between short-and long-term interest rates as dealt with by Fand [110] and even earlier by Wood [378]. They report that the simple Wood model has more "explanatory power" than the MS model, and that the relationship between changes in the short- and long-term interest rates is more stable than Fand's results had indicated. Some other studies devoted specifically to interest rates and price level changes and to changes in the level of rates alone also hold implications for the term structure.

The Wood paper.—The Wood paper and the HL paper were both products to some extent of research at the Federal Reserve, at the Chicago and

New York banks. Wood himself later joined the Board's staff, before moving elsewhere.

In his paper [378] Wood had set out to develop the implications and present estimates of the "elasticity of expectations of future rates of interest with respect to current rates," concerning the responsiveness of the term structure to changes in current rates. He did not question how the current rates might be changed and a policy implemented to change the structure, except to say [378, p. 459], "the expectations hypothesis implies nothing with respect to the monetary authority's ability to influence the level of rates generally, only its ability to influence rates relative to each other." This of course was said before extensive speculation about the Federal Reserve's inability to control the level of interest rates directly (Sec. 1.4, 7.3, 7.4). In any event, if an interest rate could be changed, it could change the structure via a "push" effect and the prospect of an expected rise in rates, where the push effect has more effect on short-term rates.

In particular Wood wanted to "show that a Federal Reserve open market swap will cause the equilibrium structure of yields to be altered when expectations are not perfectly inelastic [not unresponsive to current interest rate changes]." He was actually dealing with the question of twisting the yield curve. By "swap" he meant "a simultaneous purchase and sale by the Federal Reserve of securities of different term-to-maturity such that total bank reserves are not changed." Finding a simple statistical relationship between changes in current short-term and longer-term securities, using Durand data (Ch. 12, n. 4) and government yields, he suggested that changes in the short-term rate would be followed by smaller changes in the long-term rate. This is what one may expect from the simple fact that short rates vary over a wider range than long rates and that their cyclical turning points tend to coincide.

One of Wood's conclusions [378, p. 470] was that "in a circumstance . . . where short-term rates rise as one of the immediate responses to the Federal Reserve induced disturbance, expectations of future short rates will rise, causing equilibrium long rates to rise relative to equilibrium short rates." As would follow from the fact that the yield spread widens as interest rates decline, the Federal Reserve could not, in Wood's framework [378, p. 469], "induce simultaneously a decrease in interest rates generally and a decline in the differential between long and short rates, $R_L - R_S$."

Hamburger and Latta on Modigliani and Sutch.—HL do not reject the MS and similar explanations of the formation of interest rate expectations. Rather, they look for better predictors or "explanatory" models in the computational or strictly statistical sense. Referring to the impressive results of the first MS study, HL say [183, p. 72], "Their model asserts that the yield on long-term bonds (R_t) may be expressed as a linear function of the short-term interest rate (r_t) and the expected capital gain on long-term bonds, which is inversely proportional to the expected change in the long-term interest rate. . . . this change is hypothesized to depend on both the speed with which the long rate is expected to return to its long-term 'normal' level and an extrapolation of the recent trend in the long-term rate." Since both the "pull" and the "push" effects can be expressed as a weighted average of past rates,

$$(1.0) \qquad R_t = A + B_1 r_t + B_2 \left(R_t - \sum_{i=1}^{m} C_i R_{t-1} \right)$$

where "m denotes the number of periods that investors look back in forming their expectations about the future; C_i denotes the weight attached to the rate in each period." This equation then leads to an equation for statistical analysis upon solving for R_t and substituting successively for R_{t-i}. The equation for empirical analysis is

$$(1.1) \qquad R_t \, \alpha = \beta_0 r_t + \sum_{i=1}^{m} \beta_i r_{t-i} + u_t$$

For comparison Hamburger and Latta use

$$(1.2) \qquad R_t = a + b_0 r_t + \sum_{i=1}^{3} b_i r_{t-i} + \sum_{i=1}^{3} c_i R_{t-i} + \epsilon_t$$

In making their comparison, HL modify both equations (1.1) and (1.2) to eliminate nonsignificant parameters and re-estimate them using some quarterly data. According to them [183, pp. 74–76], the modifications for the MS model "involved the use of two, rather than four, Almon variables to estimate the distributed lag weights," because two extra variables contribute less to explanatory power than they cost in degrees of freedom. Also, "the dependent variable used in these tests is the long-term bond rate as opposed to the differential between this rate and the short-rate which was used in the MS study." The modifications on equation (1.2) consisted of eliminating R_{t-2}, R_{t-3}, r_{t-2}, and r_{t-3} such that

$$(1.3) \qquad R_t = a_0 + c_1 R_{t-1} + b_0 r_t + b_1 r_{t-1} + \epsilon_t$$

Table 13-1 shows the comparison by HL of the HL and MS models. The equations in the table were estimated using monthly data for the first period shown and quarterly data for the others. As the table reveals, equation (1.3) has a smaller standard error of the estimate, S_e (Sec. 5.2), and a larger

TABLE 13–1

Parameter Estimates for Equation (1.3)
and Comparison with the Distributed Lag Model (1.1)

							Distributed Lag Model†	
			Equation (1.3)					
	a	c_1	b_0	b_1	S_e	R^2	S_e	R^2
May 1951–Dec. 1961	.0327	.9906** (.0174)	.1835** (.0272)	−.1800** (.0277)	.0703 DW=1.62	.985	.1038 DW= .53	.967
1951–III–1961–IV	.0672	.9737** (.0471)	.2342** (.0383)	−.2136** (.0423)	.1037 DW=2.05	.968	.0909 DW=1.34	.976
1962–I–1965–IV	1.8250	.4199 (.2406)	.3243* (.1119)	−.1658 (.1200)	.0558 DW=2.10	.848	.0633 DW=1.36	.805
1951–III–1965–IV	.1240	.9492* (.0384)	.2343** (.0333)	−.2059 (.0368)	.0937 DW=2.02	.977	.1213 DW= .62	.962

†Length of distributed lag is 46 months for regressions fitted to monthly data, 15 quarters for regressions fitted to quarterly data.

DW denotes Durbin-Watson statistics.

Standard errors in parentheses.

*Significant at the .01 level.

**Significant at the .0001 level.

Source: Michael J. Hamburger and Cynthia M. Latta, "The Term Structure of Interest Rates: Some Additional Evidence," *Journal of Money, Credit, and Banking.* February 1969, p. 75.

coefficient of determination in every comparison except the second. The second comparison covers the period most closely corresponding to the period originally used by MS. However, noting that the only significant differences in the standard errors of the regression coefficients (at the .05 level) were for equations fitted to monthly data for the MS period and to quarterly data for the complete period, HL say [183, p. 76], "the evidence is not clear-cut" and "the Durbin-Watson [DW] statistics indicate the presence of positive autocorrelation in the residuals of the MS equation."

The low DW statistics (Appendix to Ch. 3) suggest to them a re-estimation of the MS equation, after introducing an autoregressive transformation to improve the DW statistics, and a further comparison with the Wood equation. They also show that operations on the equation $R_t = a + b_o r_t + v_t$ and the application of an autoregressive transformation yield the Wood equation, stated subsequently as a first difference equation.

For HL the foregoing additional estimations and comparison supported the conclusion [183, p. 83] that "the case for including lagged rates in the term structure equation as suggested by Modigliani and Sutch would appear to be rather weak."

More evidence on the term structure.—The simple equation dealt with by HL and proposed by Wood was derived and denoted by HL as

$$(2.0) \qquad\qquad \Delta R_t = a^* + b \, \Delta r_t + \epsilon_t$$

where R_t is the yield on long-term government bonds, r_t is the rate on three-month Treasury bills, and a^* is the intercept parameter (assumed not significantly different from zero). Parameter estimates for this equation (including and excluding the intercept term) from analysis of monthly observations are shown in Table 13.2. As the table depicts [183, pp. 80–82], "the post–World War II period was divided into three sub-periods: the pre-Accord period (January 1947–March 1951); the post-Accord, pre–Operation Twist period (May 1951–December 1961); and the Operation Twist period (February 1962–December 1965)." To show that the relationship was relatively stable at business cycle turning points, "the periods January 1953–June 1954 and Jaunary 1957–June 1958 were singled out for special consideration."

Focusing on the results in Table 13-2, HL emphasize the stability of the regression coefficients, although they do change somewhat. The coefficient for the 1962–65 period of operation twist is higher than that for the pooled data, but higher estimates appear for other periods. In contrast to Wood, HL reject the prospect of twisting the curve. Emphasizing the stability of their regression coefficients, they conclude [183, p. 82] that "it appears that the effects of monetary operations undertaken in either Treasury bills or long-term bonds will be transmitted to the other end of the yield curve fairly promptly and in a predictable way." That is, the curve can be shifted if not twisted.

This last conclusion probably follows from no further evidence than that short- and long-term rates rise and fall together. If one combines the above analyses, in which Hamburger participated, with another study by Hamburger (Sec. 15.2), a banking view (Sec. 3.4) of the workings of monetary policy emerges. According to Hamburger's Federal Reserve studies, the Federal Reserve can intervene at either end of the yield curve to shift it, and following a lag in the change in the interest rate, investment expenditures will vary inversely.

Modigliani and Sutch on Hamburger and Latta.—In rebutting HL, MS [279, pp. 112–20] took issue with the questioning of "the usefulness of a distributed lag on past short-term rates as an indicator of expected future short-term rates." MS suggest another comparison of their own model, the

TABLE 13–2

Parameter Estimates for Equation (2.0)
Including and Excluding the Constant Term

Time Period	$\Delta R_t = a^* + b\Delta r_t + e_t$				$\Delta R_t = b\Delta r_t + e_t$		
	a*	b	R^2 S_e	DW#	b	R^2 S_e	DW
Pooled: Feb. 1920– Dec 1933 Feb. 1934– Dec. 1938 Feb. 1947– Dec. 1965	−.0000 (.003)	.181‡ (.015)	.254 .069	1.65	.182‡ (.015)	.256 .069	1.65
Feb. 1920– Dec. 1927	−.016 (.008)	.190‡ (.039)	.195 .079	1.64	.195‡ (.040)	.198 .080	1.58
Feb. 1928– Dec. 1933	.012 (.011)	.165‡ (.028)	.320 .092	1.86	.161‡ (.028)	.310 .093	1.83
Feb. 1934– Dec. 1938	−.011 (.007)	.501‡ (.099)	.297 .057	1.80	.524‡ (.100)	.314 .058	1.77
Feb. 1947– Mar. 1951	−.001 (.004)	.281† (.072)	.227 .026	1.23	.278† (.067)	.250 .026	1.23
May 1951– Dec. 1965	.008 (.005)	.184 (.023)	.260 .062	1.60	.187‡ (.023)	.264 .063	1.60
May 1951– Dec. 1961	.010 (.006)	.183‡ (.027)	.266 .070	1.63	.184‡ (.027)	.265 .071	1.59
Jan. 1953– Jun. 1954	.004 (.017)	.191 (.101)	.132 .071	1.27	.181 (.091)	.148 .071	1.25
Jan. 1957– Jun. 1958	.006 (.024)	.137 (.089)	.074 .101	1.44	.127 (.080)	.082 .102	1.43
Feb. 1962– Dec. 1965	−.002 (.005)	.256† (.070)	.212 .036	1.40	.248† (.064)	.237 .036	1.40

*Standard Errors in Parentheses.

#DW denotes the Durbin-Watson statistic.

†Significant at the .01 level.

‡Significant at the .0001 level.

Source: Michael J. Hamburger and Cynthia M. Latta, "The Term Structure of Interest Rates: Some Additional Evidence," *Journal of Money, Credit, and Banking*, February 1969, p. 80.

Wood model, and the "ad hoc lagged–dependent-variable equations" of HL.

Instead of a comparison of a first-difference form of the Wood model with the generalized form of the MS model, MS seek to compare models using the same dependent variable and employing data for the same time period. In their case, quarterly data for the sample period 1953–II to 1966–IV are used in a comparison of their model with their version of the Wood model [279, p. 113]:

(3.0)
$$R_t = 1.5791 + 0.24668r_t + \sum_{i=1}^{19} \beta_i\, r_{t-1}$$
$$\quad\quad (0.0740) \quad (0.03492)$$

$$\sum_{i=1}^{19} \beta_i = 0.5793$$
$$\quad\quad (0.0493)$$

$$R^2 = 0.951 \quad\quad SE = 0.141\% \quad\quad DW = 0.456$$

(3.1)
$$R_t = 2.290 + 0.484r_t$$
$$\quad (0.119) \quad (0.039)$$

$$R^2 = 0.749 \quad\quad SE = 0.308\% \quad\quad DW = 0.214$$

The pattern of coefficients for the first of these equations was constrained by a third-degree polynomial.

The MS description of the comparison is [279, p. 114]:

> Quite clearly the model we propose fits the sample data much more closely than Wood's model. The addition of the weighted average of past short-term rates reduces the standard error of estimate by more than 50 per cent, from 30.8 basis points to 14.1. Accordingly the R^2 is considerably improved. Of particular importance to the conclusion drawn by Hamburger and Latta is the fact that the distributed lag contributes significantly to the fit. The sum of the lag coefficients was 0.579 and the standard error of the sum implies a t-ratio of over 14.

MS note that HL compared a first-difference form of the Wood model with a version of their own. Their own model had been transformed by the use of a second-order autoregressive error model along lines suggested by Clifford Hildreth and John Y. Lu [204]. MS point out [279, p. 114] that "the justification for using an autoregressive transformation when estimating our model is the high degree of positive first-order serial correlation indicated by the low Durbin-Watson statistic." They point to the tradition of using the first-difference approach, as in the Wood model, to reduce the effects of serial correlation.

Using the Hildreth-Lu estimation technique, analyzing quarterly data for the period 1953–II to 1966–IV, and using a third-degree polynomial specification with the Almon distributed lag technique for their own model, MS bring forward the following:

(3.2) $R_t = 1.638 + 0.237 \, r_t + \sum_{i=1}^{20} \beta_i \, r_{t-i} + 0.802 \, \epsilon_{t-1}$
             (.0245) (0.032)

$$\sum_{i=1}^{20} \beta_i = 0.5653$$
$$(0.1057)$$

             $R^2 = 0.979 \qquad SE = 0.091 \qquad DW = 1.931$

(3.3) $R_t = 3.521 + 0.229 \, r_t + 0.970 \, v_{t-1}$

             $R^2 = 0.976 \qquad SE = 0.093 \qquad DW = 2.00$

(The use of the autoregressive technique is evidenced by the presence of coefficients and lagged error terms in place of the error terms.)

MS say such equations merely indicate that the autoregressive coefficient is able to absorb a great deal of the variance that the distributed lag was otherwise able to explain. They believe their model with its emphasis on "push" and "pull" effects is superior.

Interest rates and price level changes.—Earlier (Secs. 1.4, 4.3, Appendix to Ch. 1), theory and empirical results were introduced concerning a relationship between nominal interest rates and the expected rate of change in the price level. Two key studies in this area—one by Yohe and Karnosky [384] and one by Gibson [167][2]—imply at least partial theories of the term structure of interest rates. Following Fisher, both posit [384, pp. 25–26; 167, pp. 20–21] that the time horizon for the expected price changes should coincide with the time to maturity of the financial instrument in question. Gibson says [167, p. 21], "if the public expected deflation followed by inflation, then longer term rates would rise while shorter term rates would fall." In the distributed lag frameworks of these writers, this also means that potential buyers and sellers with longer time horizons will look into the more distant past in forming their expectations; the more nearly current rates of change in prices will have a predominating effect on short-term interest rates, partly since the effects of the current rates of change are less mitigated by changes in the more distant past.

What this means for the term structure is that expectations about the pattern of price changes over time twist the yield curve. Assuming a cyclical pattern of expected price level changes—or at least one in which prices are expected to rise in the expansion phase of business conditions—the yield curve would, in response to the prospects, take on less of an upward and

2. The Gibson paper [167] is an updated portion of an earlier study [169]. Yohe and Karnosky [384] had access to and cited the earlier study. Both papers are reprinted by Gibson and Kaufman in their readings book [170].

perhaps even a downward sweep in a later stage of accelerating prices. This is consistent with conventional notions about the behavior of the term structure.

Referring to their results from analysis of monthly data for the January 1952 to September 1969 period using the Almon lag technique with its constraint on the distribution of coefficients, Yohe and Karnosky conclude [384, p. 26] that

> Twelve months after the one per cent increase in prices, long-term rates would be 59 basis points higher than they were originally, as opposed to 72 basis points for short-term rates. The effect on long-term rates would be a total increase of 56 basis points after 48 months.

Using an unconstrained distributed lag model without the use of the Almon lag technique (without the use of a priori constraint on the time shape of the coefficients) and drawing on his overall results from annual observations, 1869–1963, and quarterly observations, 1948–63, Gibson concludes [167, p. 34]:

> There appears to be a cyclical factor in the formation of price expectations in the United States. . . . The second peak comes after three years, the average duration of a reference cycle, suggesting that price expectations also depend on the stage of the business cycle the economy is in. With this exception, however, expected price changes do appear to be related to past changes by a weighting scheme which gives lower weights to less recent past values.

Among other things, Gibson estimated coefficients for a first difference form of the functional relationship,

$$(4.0) \qquad i = f \left\{ \left(\frac{1}{P} \frac{dP}{dt} \right)_t, \left(\frac{1}{P} \frac{dP}{dt} \right)_{t-1}, \ldots, \left(\frac{1}{P} \frac{dP}{dt} \right)_{t-n} \right\}$$

He used four different interest rate series (i_c, i_{cp}, i_{L1}, i_{L2}) and the price deflator for annual net national product data (P = NNP deflator, 1929 = 100), 1869–1963, where i_c is the call money rate, i_{cp} is the commercial paper rate, i_{L1} is long term interest rate on American railroad bonds, and i_{L2} is index of yields on high grade industrial bonds, all expressed as annual averages.

Results from analyzing annual data before first differencing were less satisfactory in Gibson's case than those after taking first differences. His lags were much longer than Yohe's and Karnosky's, as the latter note in their study. In addition, Gibson notes that the coefficients for the short rates decline, rise, and decline again. He points to peaks in the coefficients for the short rates at three year intervals including the highest peak at the three year lag, which leads him to conclude [167, pp. 28–29]:

> Expected price accelerations are therefore apparently related to past accelerations not by a first-order weighting scheme but rather by a higher-order scheme that generates a cyclical pattern in the coefficients . . . the peak at the three year lag marks an interval which corresponds roughly to the average duration of a reference cycle, so that the peak in the coefficients may reflect responses to business cycles. The coefficients suggest that the weights do decline as the lag increases but that the decline shows a cyclical pattern. This suggests that people use knowledge about the current stage of the cycle in forming expectations. For example, if the economy is in the midst of an expansion phase, people remember what happened to prices in the last expansion and use this information in forming their price expectations. This seems reasonable, since at the same stage of different cycles we might expect roughly similar ratios of used to unused productive capacity and other determinants of the fraction of nominal income changes which take the form of price changes.

A difficulty with this interpretation of nominal interest rate changes is not the determination of expectations about prices (or the reliance on changes in prices as a surrogate for changes in business conditions), but the weight attributed to current and lagged prices as possibly the major causal factor contributing to interest rate fluctuations. As is well known, interest rates sometimes fluctuate widely when prices are relatively stable and prices are inclined to rise most rapidly only after productive capacity is most highly utilized. Interest rates moved in phase with business conditions in the 1950s as well as the 1960s but price level changes and the prospect of inflation were especially pronounced in the 1964–66 and 1967–70 periods. Splitting their sample of data into 1952–60 and 1961–70 periods, Yohe and Karnosky conclude [384, p. 29]:

> The total price expectations effect is much larger in the 1961–1969 period than in the earlier period. In the latter period the total effect on short-term rates is about 90 per cent of the annual rate of change in prices. The effect on long-term rates is about 80 per cent of the rate of price change. In the 1952 to 1960 period the sum of the coefficients range between 5 and 35 per cent of the price change for a lag of 36 months.

One may focus on the difficulty with the more formal aspects of the analysis of a relatively strict relationship between nominal interest rates and the current and lagged values of the rate of change in prices by (1) concentrating on certain aspects of analysis, and (2) juxtaposing the Modigliani-Sutch results in equations (3.0) and (3.2) with those concerning Gibson's relation (4.0).

In the basic Fisher equation, as set forth earlier (Sec. 1.3), the nominal interest rate is primarily the sum of a rate that would prevail in the absence of expected price changes and the expected rate of change in prices, possibly as indicated by the current and lagged values for rates of change in prices. However, as Gibson and other analysts note, nominal interest rates will be influenced by other determinants. Even so, to test relationships like (4.0), Gibson says that the analysis requires "that these other determinants [of interest rates] are not systematically related to rates of price change." The terms of equations (3.0) and (3.2) can be rearranged so that the yield spread ($R_t - r_t$) in each case is set equal to a sum of distributed lag terms and an error term. The equations then imply that changes in the term structure of interest rates are determined by the lagged values of the short-term interest rate.

Finally, juxtaposing the respective series of lagged variables,

$$\left(\frac{1}{P}\frac{dP}{dt}\right)_t, \left(\frac{1}{P}\frac{dP}{dt}\right)_{t-1}, \ldots, \left(\frac{1}{P}\frac{dP}{dt}\right)_{t-n}$$

$$r_{t-1}, \ldots, r_{t-n}, r_{t-(n+1)}$$

One might expect that there is a systematic relationship between the former so-called determinants of changes in the term structure of interest rates and the latter, at least to the extent that both sets of variables are emphasized by different analysts as determinants of changes in the spread between long- and short-term interest rates.[3] In addition, if there are "push" effects in both series, one might conclude that the series are affected by similar forces—current and expected business conditions, as possibly influenced by previous business conditions and their history. Such an interpretation would not be inconsistent with Gibson's use of the expected rate of price changes as a surrogate for business conditions.

Interest rate determination.—In papers by Friedman, as mentioned earlier (Secs. 1.4, 5.4), acceleration of the growth of the money stock has been said to contribute first to a decline in the interest rate and then to a rise as expenditures accelerated, partly in response to expected price level changes. Here there is an alleged tendency to "overshoot," referred to by

3. In a sense the juxtaposed series suggest that interest rates are a part of business costs and a determinant of the prices set by business firms. Such an interpretation is not uncommon [133, Ch. 16]. Yohe and Karnosky [384, n. 17] note the presence of mortgage costs in their measure of price level changes (the consumer price index) and the prospect that these might contribute to some degree of spurious correlation between interest rates and price movements. Of course, they do not find that it makes much difference.

some as a "whiplash" effect. In Section 4.2 the conventional IS–LM analysis was discussed. In other sections there appeared a covariation in the velocity of money and the interest rate, such that—for the manufacturing sector in particular—both were said to be responding to the same sets of factors, mostly operating via expectations of future returns from various classes of assets [Secs. 2.2, 7.4]. The factors include prospective price level changes, tax credit, accelerated depreciation, greater certainty about the future, and technological changes giving rise to increased productivity. Accelerated growth in the money stock might operate via prospective returns and prospective price level changes to increase interest rates and rates of return from additional capital expenditures with nominal lags as far as changes in business conditions are concerned. There were lagged patterns in the various time series involved in the analysis, but these may be attributed to some combination of the following: (1) a tendency for the rate of change in anticipatory series, such as planned capital outlays, to begin to change as opinions about the direction of future business conditions begin to coalesce, (2) the extent of imbalances between actual rates of change in stock and flow variables and sustainable rates of change in stock and flow variables (rates corresponding to full employment, secular growth patterns), and (3) lags in adjustments between actual and desired values for given stock and flow quantities.

In addition to the matters above, discussion has been introduced on single versus structural equations models and on reduced forms (Secs. 4.3, 5.2, 5.3), and more is to come (as in a discussion of the Federal Reserve–MIT model in Ch. 14). For the present, however, certain aspects of issues arise about the determination of the level of interest rates and about structural and reduced form equations—in a study by Hamburger and Silber [184] (hereafter, on occasion, HS) on interest rates determination and in a closely-related paper by Gibson and Kaufman [171] (hereafter, on occasion, GK).

Earlier (Sec. 2.2) a reduced form equation for a modified liquidity preference model was presented: $i = bY/(\gamma Y - cY)$ where i was the interest rate, $\gamma Y (= M_s)$ was the money supply, and so on. In the framework in question, shifts in b corresponded to shifts in the speculative demand for money, as might occur in anticipation of expected price changes. Thus some measure of price changes, such as $(1/P)(dP/dt)$, might be identified with shifts in b. Changes in the rate of change in the money stock might operate directly on the prospect of price level changes and the rate of return on investment goods such that the interest rate varies directly rather than inversely with the changes in the rate of change in the money stock, especially after abstracting from the seasonal or defensive operations of the Federal Reserve. Also, a doubling of the level of income leaves the interest rate unchanged, and deflating both the numerator and the denominator of the right-hand member of the reduced form leaves the interest rate unchanged. Thus, the reduced form with embellishments suggests a linear relationship such as

$$(5.0) \qquad i = \alpha + \beta_1 \frac{1}{M'}\frac{dM'}{dt} + \beta_2 \frac{1}{Y'}\frac{dY'}{dt} + \beta_3 \frac{1}{P}\frac{dP}{dt}$$

where P = price level, $M' = M/P$, $Y' = Y/P$, and $(1/P)\ (dP/dt)$ = rate of change in the price level.

Analyzing monthly observations from March 1952 through April 1966 for such a reduced form relationship as (5.0), GK report such results as

$$(5.1)$$
$$i = \text{const.} + 0.9\frac{1}{M'}\frac{dM'}{dt} + 4.5^*\ \frac{1}{Y'}\frac{dY'}{dt} + 0.17^*\frac{1}{P}\frac{dP}{dt}, R^2 = 72.8$$

$$(5.2) \qquad \Delta\, i = \text{const.} + 8.5\ \Delta\frac{1}{M'}\frac{dM'}{dt} + 4.9^*\ \Delta\frac{1}{Y'}\frac{dY'}{dt} +$$

$$0.07^*\ \Delta\frac{1}{P}\frac{dP}{dt}, R^2 = 20.5$$

*Significant at the 5 per cent level

where i is the three-month Treasury bill rate, M' is the money supply seasonally adjusted and deflated by the Consumer Price Index (CPI). The output measure is the Federal Reserve's index of industrial production (seasonally adjusted), $(1/P)\ (dP/dt)$ is "the net percentage change in the CPI over the preceding six months, expressed at an annual rate," and Δs indicate the first-difference forms for the variables. GK say [171, p. 474] that "Monthly observations are transformed into moving averages in which the current month is weighted 2 and the two previous months are each weighted 1." They also lag interest rates in relation to the other variables, obtain some results with a broad measure of the money supply (inclusive of time deposits at commercial banks), and present coefficients for simple and partial correlations between the interest rate and money and between the interest rate and the rate of change in prices.

The strength of the GK relationships, as indicated by R^2s, is not affected markedly by altering the definition of money or the lag time up to three months. Thereafter, the R^2s decline. On the simple and partial correlation coefficients they report [171, pp. 474–75]:

All simple correlations are strongly positive. The simple correlation between the three-month Treasury bill rate and industrial production is highest when the two variables are measured approximately concurrently. Correlation between interest rates and money tends to increase as rates are correlated with money in earlier months. Coefficients for M_1 are lower than for M_2 [for money broadly defined].

Because, however, income and money are closely related, simple correlation coefficients do not permit us to separate the influence of each on interest rates. Thus, we need to examine the partial correlation coefficients. The partial correlations between interest rates and output are positive but somewhat smaller than the simple correlation coefficients. These coefficients are highest when the two variables are observed synchronously, and they decline as output observations precede interest rates. In contrast, the partial correlation coefficients between interest rates and money differ markedly from the simple correlations. Coefficients for M_2 become strongly negative as predicted by a liquidity preference theory, while coefficients for M_1 decline sharply but remain positive. For either definition, the absolute values of the coefficients are substantially smaller than the corresponding coefficients for income. As with the simple coefficients, the partial correlation coefficients increase algebraically as money observations precede rate observations. The increase in algebraic value of the money coefficients as rate observations are progressively lagged occurs considerably faster than the comparable decline in the output coefficients.

Thus, while the correlation between rates and M_2 five months earlier is approximately zero, the correlation with output five months earlier is still positive and more than half its synchronous value. This suggests that interest rates are associated with output both more closely and for a longer period of time than with either measure of the money supply. Between the two measures of money supply, interest rates appear to be more closely related to M_2 than to M_1. The correlation between interest rates and price expectations is positive as expected, with very little difference between the simple and partial correlations.

On regression results for an equation such as (5.1), but with different lag times and definitions of money, GK say [171, pp. 474–76]:

Coefficients for output are consistently greater in absolute value than the coefficients for M_2, the only money measure with the expected negative coefficient. Positive output coefficients are also statistically significant at the .05 level for longer periods than are negative M_2 coefficients. Thus, a 1 per cent increase in M_2 is associated with a concurrent 6-basis-point decline in interest rates, while a 1 per cent increase in output is associated on the average with a 9-basis-point rise in rates. When rates are lagged three months, the impact of both money and output falls off, but more sharply for money. A 1 per cent increase in M_2 is then associated with only a 3-basis-point decline in interest rates and a similar increase in output with a 7-basis-point rise. Thus, interest rates appear to be influenced not only more closely and for a longer time span by output than by money, but appear also to be more sensitive to a given percentage change in output than to a similar change in money supply. The price change coefficients indicate a slow adjustment to price expectations. Nominal interest rates change during the month by about one-sixth of the expected rate of price change.

In their summary and concluding section, GK say [171, pp. 477–78] that "the results indicate that changes in interest rates in the postwar period reflect changes in the demand for funds somewhat more than changes in supply" and that "interest rates are also significantly influenced by expectations of price change based on recent experience." In their final paragraph [171, p. 478] they say:

> These findings do not deny that money or credit affects interest rates inversely. Rather, they suggest that the influence of money and credit may be too brief to be identified clearly in monthly observations. Thus, even in such short periods, the dominant influence on interest rates appears to come through the real sector . . . The results also help explain the (at first) surprising statements of some economists that high interest rates reflect easy monetary policy and low interest rates tight policy. These economists argue that while "expansionary monetary policy does lower interest rates in the shorter-run . . . the delayed effects working through expanding output and higher prices induce substantial increases in the demand for funds large enough to raise interest rates in the longer-run." The evidence provided in this study suggests that this "shorter-run" may be too short to be statistically observable in most, if not all, regular data series available.

HS [184] are somewhat critical of the GK analysis. They also wish to show that the sample period 1953–65 should be broken into two subperiods—1953–60 and 1961–65—at least as indicated by analysis of their model of interest rate determination. Further, they believe their model forecasts better than the financial sector of the Federal Reserve–MIT model, as cited earlier (Sec. 4.3).

With these objectives, HS analyze quarterly data and use a reduced form relation,

$$r_{TB} = (R_u, r_D, Y, GBT)$$

where r_{TB} is the yield on newly issued three-month Treasury bills, R_u is unborrowed reserves adjusted for changes in reserve requirements, r_D is the discount rate at the Federal Reserve Bank of New York, Y is *GNP*, and *GBT* is total U.S. Government bonds held by the public. The reduced form equation is said to be based on a structural system similar to the Federal Reserve–MIT model. (It is discussed in the next chapter.)

HS give these reasons for splitting off the pre-1961 period [184, p. 370]:

[1] In the pre-1961 period, under 'Eisenhower' economics, fiscal policy was based on the built-in flexibility approach. This implies that deficits, i.e., changes in the debt, can be explained to a relatively large extent by movements in income. . . . In the post-1961 period there is little doubt that an active discretionary fiscal policy was pursued under 'Kennedy-Johnson' economics.

[2] The CD-market [market for time certificates of deposits] emerged as a major financial institution.

[3] Analysts have observed that the 'seasonal' in the Treasury bill rate disappeared after 1960.

[4] The concern with the balance of payments became a major factor in all policy decisions [after 1960].

Using methods suggested by Chow [68, pp. 591–605; 126, pp. 44, 155], HS conclude that the coefficients generated by their analyses appear to be drawn from different universes.

For the 1961–65 period, HS get these results [184, p. 371]:

$$(6.0)\quad r_{TB} = 1.78 + 0.64\ r_D - 0.77\ R_u + 0.018\ Y + 0.022\ GTB$$
$$\phantom{(6.0)\quad r_{TB} = 1.78} (.12)\quad\ \ (.30)\quad\ \ \ (.005)\quad\ \ \ (.009)$$

$$R^2 = .98$$

They note their coefficients of the variables r_D and R_u "are significant and large in magnitude." Emphasizing the addition of lagged values of ΔR_u to an equation such as (6.0), they say [184, p. 372], "the results provide no evidence at all of a whiplash effect of unborrowed reserves on the bill rate." They also say [184, p. 372] that their "results cast some doubt on the assumption of long lags in both the demand function for money and the demand function for free reserves."

The HS results are somewhat difficult to compare with GK's. HS relate levels of income, debt, and unborrowed reserves to interest rates. They use unborrowed reserves as a major monetary variable rather than the money stock. They suggest that an increase in unborrowed reserves will lower the Treasury bill rate. In any event their equation predicts relatively well, but not outstandingly so.

They find that their equation corresponding to (6.0) above does the best job of predicting. They compare predictions for the period 1965–III through 1967–II with those obtained using the financial block of the Federal Reserve–MIT model, as reported in the de Leeuw and Gramlich paper cited earlier (Sec. 4.4). The only predictions that seem at all satisfactory are those generated for the quarters 1965–III through 1966–II.

Over the post–World War II years the velocity of money and interest rates have risen. Clearly, from the velocity ratio over these years, income has risen faster than the money stock or some closely related variable such as the level of commercial bank reserves. Thus if one computes simple algebraic money stock or reserve elasticities for interest rates [such as $(\Delta i/i)/(\Delta M/M)$ or, rearranging terms, $(\Delta i/\Delta M)\ (M/i)$] and a comparable income elasticity for interest rates [such as $(\Delta i/\Delta Y)(Y/i)$ where $\Delta i/\Delta Y$ is the coefficient from regressing the interest rate on income, and Y and i are mean values of the time series], then clearly the money stock or reserve elasticities are going to be higher. In this vein, HS say [184, p. 371], "evaluation of the elasticities at the sample means indicates that a change in unborrowed reserves has a greater impact on the bill rate than an equal percentage change in GNP" and "these results are not very different from those obtained by Gibson and Kaufman." Indeed they are not, except GK have examined coefficients resulting from analyzing quarterly data via regressions of the bill rate on the rates of change for money, income, and prices.

13.4 SUMMARY

The presence of "push" and "pull" effects in term structure data has been widely identified. Modigliani and Sutch report them, as do Malkiel and Kane. In an earlier study, Malkiel and Kane found some evidence of risk aversion among investors and some evidence to support the prospect of changing the term structure via changes in the relative supplies of different maturities. They viewed the former evidence as support for the "backwardation" theory. The latter they viewed as suggestive of the Federal Reserve's ability to twist the yield curve, all in contrast to Modigliani's and Sutch's findings. However, in reporting their findings, Malkiel and Kane did not indicate whether the twist could be affected independently of any Federal Reserve influence on expectations.

Rates of change in the price level have been shown to relate to interest rates, with short-term interest rates varying more than long-term rates and thus suggesting another relationship between term structure data and anticipations. The complications, however, are several: (1) the test of a causal relationship between expected price changes themselves and interest rates requires other determinants of interest rates to be independent of price changes; (2) the expected price changes can be viewed as a surrogate for expected business conditions; and (3) interest rates vary procyclically even in periods of relatively damped price level changes. With reference to some of his distributed lag results, Gibson says that "the peak in the coefficients may reflect responses to business cycles" and "this suggests that people use knowledge about the current stage of the cycle in forming expectations." All of this points to the sharing of common influences by time series.

Even in lagging interest rates in relation to measures of the money supply, Gibson and Kaufman conclude, as others have stated, "that changes in interest rates in the postwar period reflect changes in the demand for funds somewhat more than changes in supply." And, finally, they find that the influence of money and credit on interest rates (the so-called negative, expected sign influence) "may be too brief to be identified clearly in monthly observations." Hamburger and Silber are critical of the Gibson-Kaufman analysis. They show the need to split the sample, cast some doubts on long lags in the influence of money, and get high R^2s. However, their conclusion that a change in unborrowed reserves has a greater influence on interest rates than on income is simply a reflection of the fact that interest rates and the velocity of money increased (or that bank reserves and money increased less than in proportion to GNP) in the postwar years.

Part V

Special Purpose Models

14

The Federal Reserve - MIT Model

by William P. Yohe and William J. Frazer, Jr.

14.1 Introduction

LARGE SCALE, simultaneous equations models are a relatively new development in the field of economics. There were only a few, relatively small-scale quarterly econometric models in 1964. There were dozens by 1970, and there was an accelerated proliferation in their number and diversity. These models and the increases in their diversity were in large measure a product of the modern computer. Until the appearance of the computer of the 1960s, with large information storage capacity and fast operating time, the computations necessary for a large scale model were prohibitive.

To construct a structural equations model one may proceed in several directions. One may accept some corpus of economic theory, such as neo-Keynesian or monetarist theory, as a base and construct a structural equations model on it. The theory and the purpose of the model may affect its size. Models emphasizing forecasting alone—as distinct from assessment of causal forces—may be relatively small as to the number of equations. Those seeking to emphasize the determination of many variables—such as those resulting from policy actions as in the case of the several versions of the Federal Reserve–MIT model of the mid- to late 1960s as introduced earlier (Sec. 4.3)—may be quite large. The mid-year 1969 version was composed of 180 variables (111 labeled endogenous and 70

Note: The authors acknowledge assistance from Keith M. Carlson and Robert E. Williams. During the period in which this chapter was drafted, Carlson and Yohe were among those working on the St. Louis model [6], and Williams was writing a master's essay on the history of the Federal Reserve–MIT model [372].

A fairly extensive bibliography on the Federal Reserve–MIT model may be compiled by combining the references in this chapter with those in Williams' thesis [372].

labeled exogenous) related by 111 equations. The monetarist model produced at the St. Louis Federal Reserve in the late 1960s [6, pp. 7–25] was "designed to analyze economic stabilization issues within a framework which focuses on the influence of monetary expansion on total spending." It consisted of only eight equations.[1]

In contrast or in addition, proceeding along the foregoing lines, one may simply improve the theory or learn more of economic behavior through analysis and empirical study, either of the economy as a whole or of a sector. One may aim for the discovery of certain patterns or characteristics of change, learning, and so on, that may ultimately contribute to a structural equations model. Of course, all of this does not mean that economists have learned nothing from the plethora of structural equations models of the policy or explanatory type as distinct from the strictly forecasting models. For one thing, responses to the challenge of constructing a workable structural equations model have probably resulted in a higher degree of methodological sophistication and economic knowledge as reviewed earlier (Secs. 5.2, 5.3). The latter may have been somewhat negative in character—in constructing models on the basis of received economic theory, the main by-product may have been a revelation for some about the inadequacies of the theory and the definitions of key terms.

One of the main problems characterizing the structural equations models of the 1960s takes on two dimensions: (1) when the sample period for estimating the parameters of the model is split, the estimates based on the respective portions of the split sample differ; (2) the model may forecast developments relatively well when the forecasting is done for the period for which the parameters were estimated, but forecasts beyond the sample period have been less successful, particularly when some factor such as anticipated changes in the level of prices was operating in one but not the other of the periods.

Perhaps a main result of the evolution in the structural equations and some other models in the 1960s has been an increased recognition of the relevance of factors usually considered outside the realm of the usual economic calculus: the relevance of states of minds about inflation and governmental actions, varying degrees of certainty about the economic outlook, and the capacities of behavioral units to plan and anticipate the future differently after having experienced certain historical episodes or patterns of changes in business conditions.

---

1. Some would say nine equations, including a second interest rate equation. Also, an equation for stock prices was added later.

The relatively small St. Louis model [6] showed a fairly strong capacity for *ex ante* forecasting or simulating (forecasting or simulating changes beyond the period for which parameters are estimated, as distinct from *ex post* forecasting or the simulation of changes over the same sample period as that for which parameters are estimated). Such simulation consists of having a single equations model—or a structural model as a unit—generate a time series for a dependent or endogenous variable that may be compared with a corresponding series of actual (or observed) data, all as dealt with more fully in the Appendix to Chapter 14. The initial St. Louis *ex ante* simulations with the model as a unit were for nominal GNP, real GNP, and the implicit price deflator for GNP for the two year period 1968–69. A reason for its success in this period may very well have been the important role played by anticipated price level changes both in the model and the period in question. The anticipated price variable, moreover, may have served as a surrogate for anticipated business conditions generally (as in Sec. 13.3). By such a route, structural equations models may become increasingly capable of dealing with factors exclusive of those focused upon in the received economic calculus of the 1960s.

A great deal has been said in the less received economics of the 1960s about stabilizing the growth rate in the money stock to stabilize business conditions (as reviewed in Ch. 2). Monetarists have taken the forefront in this,[2] but once stability of the type monetarists discuss is achieved, there is still a task for the Federal Reserve in stabilizing business conditions. What remains to be stabilized is a more subtle phenomenon—of the same type that has posed difficulty for the structural equations models, as usually revealed by splitting sample periods.

Aspects of the structural equations models of the mid- to late 1960s—particularly those of the Federal Reserve–MIT model as represented by the mid-year 1967 and mid-year 1969 versions [3]—are reviewed in this

2. Andersen and Carlson express the matter as follows [6, p. 8]: "The general monetarist view is that the rate of monetary expansion is the main determinant of total spending, commonly measured by gross national product (GNP). Changes in total spending, in turn, influence movements in output, employment, and the general price level. A basic premise of this analysis is that the economy is basically stable and not necessarily subject to recurring periods of severe recession and inflation. Major business cycle movements that have occurred in the past are attributed primarily to large swings in the rate of growth in the money stock."
References on this monetarist view were to Brunner [42, pp. 9–24] and Fand [107, pp. 10–27; 106, pp. 275–89].

3. These are the versions that surfaced in two papers by de Leeuw and Gramlich [84, 85]. The June 1969 paper was also printed in the *Journal of Finance*, May 1969.

An earlier unpublished paper by Albert Ando and Stephen M. Goldfeld, "An

chapter. The St. Louis Model is introduced to a lesser extent. The review
should provide some perspective on the structural equations models and
their problems, as of the early 1970s. The methodological problems encountered in the construction of the models of the 1960s are emphasized,
and the mid-year 1969 version of the Federal Reserve–MIT model is
drawn upon to illustrate some of the model's features in greater depth.
There is some emphasis on investment and bank loans to business so that
Chapter 15 and its Appendix can focus on the behavior and financing of
mature manufacturing corporations, particularly those that are thought to
dominate the behavior of aggregate measures of investment in plants and
equipment. There is also the view that the effects of a monetary policy
implemented by an independent agency in a relatively free society are
especially in need of explanation.

In Chapter 15 the special analysis and neo-Bayesian methods of Chapter 8 are brought forward to provide improved insight into the financial
and investment behavior of firms. The analysis in Chapter 15 is not
presently carried to the structural equations level, though this may be
possible. The role of and need to incorporate so-called intangible factors,
state of mind variables, and so on is a difficult problem in the structural
equations method. An appendix to the present chapter deals with solutions to structural equations models and the Gauss-Seidel method used in
the Federal Reserve–MIT model in particular. Such methods are interesting, but they are relegated to the appendix partly because other problems
encountered in structural equations models in the 1960s are more significant.

14.2   LINKAGES AND LINKAGES RESEARCH

Under the original Federal Reserve Act, the Federal Reserve System was
viewed as operating automatically according to certain rules, as mentioned
later (Sec. 16.2). The primary tool at the disposal of the regional banks
and the board in Washington was the discount rates of the respective
banks. It was thought that, with adherence to certain standards in the

---

Econometric Model for Stabilization Policies," set forth the first model usually
associated with the Federal Reserve–MIT project, but it was already in existence
when the project was formed. It was a 50 equation model of the United States
economy designed to "evaluate short-run impacts of stabilization policies, both fiscal
and monetary." The Ando-Goldfeld model should be considered only as a very
primitive forerunner of the Federal Reserve–MIT model. Work on it was suspended
shortly after the Federal Reserve became involved.

discounting of commercial paper of a high quality and with variations in the rates, the amount of bank credit would be just right to accommodate the needs of business, commerce, and agriculture. There was more to the apparatus—the gold standard and all—and there were more detailed implications. Bank loans were the main source of funds for expanding inventories and for financing goods in transit (as implied by the Fisherian model in Sec. 1.4). As the economy grew and as business conditions changed, the amount of bank credit (and the money stock to which it gave rise) would be just right. There was in effect a one-to-one correspondence between bank credit, on one hand, and economic growth and business conditions, on the other.

The linkages in this scheme were fairly simple. An excess of credit brought on expansion in business conditions which would be automatically checked by rising prices and gold losses. Adherence to the criteria for discounting (or rediscounting) commercial paper was important, but the cost of credit to the commercial banks was thought to have some influence too. A reduction in the cost (in the discount rates) could bring about expansion in the short run. The linkage scheme was simple: lower the discount rate, increase bank reserves, increase bank credit (via credit multipliers), and hence increase expenditures. Another part of the early tradition was that central bankers should convey an air of confidence. Announcements about changes in the discount rate(s) were thought to have influence, even as they are thought to have in some quarters today, and an announced increase in the rate was often used to convey a determination to check increases in the level of prices and excessive credit expansion. The history is widely reviewed [133, Secs. 7.5, 8.1, 8.2], but things did not go well for the system in the late 1920s and early 1930s.

Following the Great Crash and unsuccessful or inadequate efforts to revive the economy, the banking acts of 1933 and 1935 were passed. These extended broad new powers to the Federal Reserve—control with limits over required reserve ratios and authority to conduct open market operations. Announcements and exhortation had few if any visible effects, and there were misdirected policies, as described in Chapter 11. In particular, the tie between bank loans and business expenditures was broken, as described in Chapter 15. The notion of linkages lingered on, albeit in more complicated form. The Federal Reserve was thought to be able to use one instrument or a combination of its instruments to transmit effects, via bank reserves and credit expansion, to the levels of prices and employment. The idea of a linked sequence emanating from specific Federal Reserve actions—say, a change in the discount rate or an open market purchase—seems to have been formalized in a research proposal as cited by Mitchell [275, pp. 4–5]. According to Governor Mitchell of the board, the research was to provide "quantitative information as to the many processes, linkages and relationships involved between specific Federal Reserve actions at one end of the line and the ultimate goals of economic stabilization at the other end." As Mitchell said [275, p. 3], "in a sense, the Fed has been doing linkage research all its life, just as Moliere's M. Jordain discovered that he had been writing prose for 40 years." What was new was the "system's first big entry into the wonderful world of econometric model building and large scale use of the computer."

Several research groups came into being, including in particular an "in-house staff of the board," mainly under the direction of Frank de Leeuw, and a subsequent university group jointly led by Franco Modigliani and Albert Ando. These groups were specifically oriented toward the construction of a structural equations model. One of the first formal presentations of what has since come to be called the Federal Reserve–MIT model appeared in January 1968 [85].[4]

The construction of econometric models with any sort of detailed financial sector had been feasible only since the appearance of quarterly income and product data in the late 1950s. With an observation period as long as a year, as was necessarily the case with earlier models, it was virtually impossible to capture any causal influence of financial variables on aggregate demand. A number of quarterly models with financial sectors were estimated from 1959 to 1965. By far the largest of these was the so-called Brookings model [96, 97, 158, 241, 285] (as initiated by the Social Science Research Council and subsequently transferred to the Brookings Institution). The financial sector of the model was actually supervised by de Leeuw and contained some nineteen equations to determine quantities and prices in seven financial markets.

Responsibility for monetary and fiscal policy simulations with the Brookings model was turned over to Gary Fromm. He first reported the results of simulating the late 1965 increases in the discount rate and Regulation Q ceilings [156] and subsequently produced a book with Paul Taubman [157] which made a number of important contributions to the methodology of policy simulations and reported the outcomes of extensive simulation experiments. The model was so large and its lag structure so

4. An early participant in the Fed–MIT project to leave and publish a paper on the research involving the structural equations type model was Hendershott [194]. Frank de Leeuw's departure was announced after the completion of the mid-year 1969 version of the Federal Reserve–MIT model [84].

complex that no one could have foreseen the difficulties that could arise with the monetary policy simulations.[5] This provided an important stimulus to the construction of the FRB-MIT model. As de Leeuw and Gramlich said [85, p. 11], a major purpose was "to be able to say more than existing models about the effects of monetary policy instruments—both in themselves and in comparison with other policy instruments."

The basic linkages in the model have been described [301, p. 146]:

> When Federal Reserve Credit is increased, the immediate reaction is an increase in reserves. This, through the supply function of demand deposits by commercial banks and its interaction with the demand for money, affects the short-term rate of interest. This process is modified by the activities in the commercial loan market. A change in the short-term rate of interest, through the term structure equation, affects the long-term rate with, of course, a time lag. The long-term rate will affect the cost of capital directly as one of its components, and indirectly through the dividend/price ratio which is also a component of the cost of capital. The cost of capital in turn enters the demand functions for the final outputs at three points.

From the mid-year 1967 version of the FRB-MIT model [85] others were to follow. There were even simultaneous versions of the model as the original "in-house" university group split up. Since the break-up of the original FRB-MIT group, Klein [230, p. 47] has referred to continuing official and "academic" versions of the original model. The latter is called the MPS (MIT–Pennsylvania–Social Science Research Council) model, where it came to be maintained by Warton Econometric Forecasting Associates. Klein [230, pp. 42, 47] has viewed it as the answer of professors Ando and Modigliani to the simple testing of crude quantity theory and multiplier equations, as reviewed in Section 5.2. There were also unrelated structural equations models with special emphasis on monetary and fiscal policy variables. The features of these models are reviewed, following some general discussion of econometrics and a textbook view of structural equations, policy-oriented models. There is some emphasis on the evolution of both the methods employed and the possible methods of dealing with the effects of policy. The models have some different emphases, particularly with respect to different sectors of the economy, such as the financial, banking, and non-financial corporate sector. To conserve space, however, the focus will be on the non-financial corporate

5. Stated simply, policy actions seem to operate in the wrong direction for several quarters, and discount rate changes turned out to be the most powerful instrument.

sector, capital investment and the like, at least as far as applied aspects of the models are concerned.

One might take various views about the structural equations models. The initial "linkages" research, with emphasis on structural equations models, seems to have advanced from rather specific prospects for tracing out the effects of so-called policy actions to a series of papers with "preliminary and tentative" conclusions, emphasizing "methodological problems" rather than "specific quantitative conclusions," "progress" reports, and "experimentation." A 1970 paper by Modigliani et al. [278] focussed on the impact of central bank actions on interest rates and the money stock. They concluded at that time that their methods needed refinements and that specifications of their model may be needed in the light of changes in institutions and emerging financial innovations. Nonetheless, they felt their results were sufficiently encouraging to justify their inclusion as a component of the FRB-MIT model. One might agree with Meltzer in his comment on an early version of the FRB–MIT model [269]:

> Few people would have attempted to construct a model of this size and complexity in so short a time. . . . None I venture to say would have done so much in so short a time as Franco Modigliani and the MIT–Federal Reserve Group. It is a tribute to them that there is a model to be⁣ discussed and that it is sufficiently rich and explicit that there is something of consequence to be discussed.

There must have been two points of view on the part of those underwriting the Federal Reserve–MIT group: (1) that fruitful results would follow from the use of the methods with a traditional Federal Reserve emphasis on a mass of detail, and (2) that the venture was more like travel in outer space, where possible side effects would follow from the research venture itself. In any event, the Federal Reserve entered "the wonderful world of econometric model building and large scale use of the computer." By 1972 they had shifted some emphasis to the construction of a smaller-scale model [352] for potential use in the monthly forecasting of money market variables. The monthly forecasting feature of the model was unusual and had as an objective the shedding of light on the structure of the market for large negotiable certificates of deposits (CDs). An additional distinguishing characteristic of the monthly model was the estimation of lagged relations using polynomial approximations (as in Appendices to Chs. 1, 15) to finite lag structures.

Carl Christ [69] has reviewed and catalogued differences in nine financial models, belonging to more complete models which include mainly the FRB-MIT model, but also the Brookings, Wharton, Office of Business Economics (OBE), and Michigan models. The first four of these are presently introduced. Christ reports favorably on their tracking ability and unfavorably on the completeness and adequacy of their underlying economic theories. This report leads him to conclude [69, p. 447] "That economic theory is not very useful for financial econometric models, and that once one gets a sufficiently large number of economic variables it is not difficult (though it may be expensive and time-consuming) to put together a system of econometric equations that will track their behavior reasonably well." Several comment on Christ's paper [105, 175, 386]. Fand [105] points to the relatively poor forecasting records in 1968–69 in the apparent presence of inflationary expectations (compare Sec. 3.2). He reports a need to revise the underlying theories of the price level and interest rates. Gramlich concedes the presence in the predominantly Keynesian-spirited models of an inadequate treatment of price expectations. He says [175, p. 467], "This may have been responsible for errors in our investment functions in the 1966–69 period." What has been said about underlying theoretical inadequacies may be extended to the Federal Reserve's monthly forecasting model too, especially in view of their reliance on the Baumol-Tobin transactions demand models, as reviewed and evaluated in Section 4.2.

14.3   ECONOMETRICS GENERALLY: SOME PRINCIPLES AND PROBLEMS

References to "econometrics" appear with increasing frequency since the modern computer came on the scene. From one point of view [24], much of economics may be viewed as econometrics, in the sense that it simply suggests "the application of mathematics and mathematical statistics to quantitative problems posed by economic theories and economic facts." From another view, econometrics may be viewed as the specialized study of methodology as it relates to economics and of the special methodological problems encountered in the use of mathematical and statistical methods in economics. In either case, a distinction is not carefully drawn in the literature of economics (or econometrics), and the reader is frequently left to draw his own conclusion about the meaning of the term "econometrics." Economics is a complicated subject, and this fact was made no less obvious by the rapid development and impact of econometrics, however defined, in the 1960s.

Economic models or equations are commonly viewed as nonstochastic (exact) and as stochastic (probabilistic). The stochastic models are characterized by the explicit or implicit introduction of an error term in each behavioral equation, and thus assumptions are made about the probability structures implied or stated. (Definitional identities, as distinct from equations with empirically estimated parameters, are not usually written with disturbances.) The so-called structural equations models with estimated coefficients are stochastic models. They are enormously complicated by the introduction and role of probability structures, especially if they contain nonlinearities.

To begin with, most simultaneous equations models, say of the common Keynesian type (Secs. 4.2, 4.3, 5.2), are not strictly susceptible to causal ordering (the ordering, as by the use of arrows, of a one-way chain of causation). To be so ordered, even in a "heuristic" sense, equations containing exogenous variables must be viewed as segmentable from the others, and statistically independent error terms must be assumed for all the behavioral equations of the model.[6] Thus, to proceed at all, one simply cannot be puristic. Indeed, models may be used for forecasting alone or for policy purposes, and the latter use invariably calls for some kind of causal sequence. A policy question, for example, may be framed as follows: if one changes the level or rate of change in this variable (or policy instrument), what will the effect be on the endogenous variables (goals or targets) of the system?[7]

The models may be single equation or structural, as reviewed earlier (Sec. 4.3). In the single equation model, all the so-called "independent" variables are exogenous in the sense that they are presumed to be independent of the random error term. Shifts in a simple consumption function ($C = \alpha + \beta Y + \mu$ for example) imply a shift in the mean of the error term (μ), and this may be associated with an upward shift in income (Y) such that the error term and income are not independent. Furthermore, a solution to a structural equation model is a reduced form equation, and there may be a solution in terms of parameters and exo-

6. On causal ordering, see Christ [71, Ch. 4]. Most large econometric models are "block recursive"—causally orderable from one block of equations to another but not necessarily within each block.

7. There are other policy questions, relating to the appropriateness of a policy model or analysis. For example, should the policy-making official adopt the simple linkages point of view in analyzing and interpreting conditions and effects of actions and inactions? Should developing changes and attempts to stabilize them be viewed broadly in the context of an overall pattern of interrelated developments? Would a given announcement or reported acceleration in a variable have one degree of effect at one time and a likely different degree at another, say, depending on different degrees of economic performance and refinements in relation to some optimal degree?

genous variables for each endogenous variable of the system.[8] In fact, single equations models themselves may be viewed as reduced form equations (Sec. 4.3), and one may simply proceed to estimate parameters for a reduced form equation (Sec. 13.3). A reduced form equation, independent of any mention of a structural equation background, implies the parameters of a structure. Ideally, when the relations of a structural equations model are "identified," as mentioned earlier (Ch. 5, n. 7), one should be able to obtain the parameter estimates for the structural equations by working back from the estimates for a reduced form equation, as discussed by Christ [71, Ch. 8]. This was doubtlessly nearly impossible as a practical matter, given the stage of econometric model-building at the close of the 1960s.

Some principles and practices.—In the textbook case for a structural equations model, the policy instruments or controlled variables enter as exogenous variables, or at least as exogenous to some distinct sector of the model. The ultimate goals or targets are endogenous variables. The result then is a solution for a target variable in terms of the controlled variable(s), the parameters of the model or a sector of the overall model,[9] and stochastic error terms. The economists advancing the model presumably should be able to give the policy-making official the effect on the target of a given change in the instrument. This is called a simulation with the model or a sector of the model. Of course, the resulting target value is probabilistic, since the random error of each behavioral equation in the model or sector gets translated into a random error for the reduced form equation.

In principle [71, Ch. 4, Sec. IV; 285, p. 349], the model or sector simulation is offered as independent of the endogenous variables and error terms entering into the structural equations. In practice, this is a remarkably unlikely condition if the economic system is subject to effects from

8. There are common algebraic methods of solution for linear models (the high school method of elimination and Cramer's rule). For nonlinear models, the Gauss-Seidel method is widely used; the equations are first causally ordered (as closely as possible) and successive "iterations" are made to grope toward a solution (see Evans [104, pp. 369–92]). On methods of solution and the Gauss-Seidel method as it was used in solutions for the mid-year 1967 version of the Federal Reserve–MIT model, see Appendix to Chapter 14.

9. Sectors play a special role in the solution to large structural equations models. A single solution in terms of the entire model may not be feasible, so the model is subdivided, as in the original Brookings model. It has been referred to as a "block recursive system." As described by Fromm and Klein [158, p. 349]: "Blocks of simultaneous equations feed into each other in a recursive causal chain. The endogenous values in each block are determined by the equation parameters, predetermined variables from lower order blocks, and exogenous variables."

outside factors and if it is characterized by a high degree of interdependence. In such a case, there will be a tendency for single equations' errors to be dependent on each other. The prospect of interaction in single equation error terms will be greater if estimated lagged values of "dependent" variables appear in single equations of the model or sector. Lagged variables are themselves estimated with some probability of error, possibly not even an independent probability.

One appraises a structural equations model and estimates of coefficients largely as one appraises single equations and estimates [71, Ch. 10] except for the additional complications just mentioned [10] and others mentioned in the appendix to this chapter. There are coefficients of determination, t-tests of statistical significance for coefficients, comparisons of estimated ("simulated") and actual values for endogenous variables, and comparisons of "estimated" values with and without hypothetical changes in a selected instrumental variable. Ando and Modigliani use the "root mean square error" (RMS) in appraising the basic measure of the reliability of their equations singly and jointly [12, pp. 297–98], as they did on an earlier occasion (Sec. 5.2). This method is also used with the St. Louis model and discussed in the Appendix to Chapter 14.

Linkages and lags.—A common view in many of the simultaneous equations models—suggestive of the "cruder" linkages approach—is "that a modern economy is a complex dynamic system with numerous and complex lags." As some would say [12], the response of the relevant variables to a given policy change will typically occur gradually in time and is best visualized as a time series, measuring the difference between two time paths: (1) the path the variable would follow without the change, and (2) the path it would follow as a result of the change in the policy variable. A serious difficulty with this type of statement is that all changes are presumed to follow in some causal order or neat sequence, whereas earlier (Ch. 13) there were extrapolative "push" effects common to certain time series, regressive "pull" effects, and "shock" effects

10. The inadequacies just mentioned concern the lack of knowledge about the probability structures of estimators in the structural equations context. Least squares and two-stage least squares are such estimators [71, Ch. 9]. Properties that appear only as the sample size tends to infinity are called asymptotic [71, p. 263]. They are commonly assumed in the testing of estimates for structural equations models. Basmann maintains in particular that the common tests in this context called "forecasting tests" are not statistically valid when based on finite samples. As reviewed by Murphy [284], Basmann suggests another form of testing, called "predictive testing." Murphy himself examines the feasibility and advisability of using predictive testing on the basis of reduced form estimates.

infringing on numerous series, possibly simultaneously. There was the proposition (Sec. 8.5) that "push" and "pull" effects alone will not account for the duration of cyclical phases and turning points of cycles, and one might presume that neither will fixed distributed lag relationships between time series. For policy and analytical purposes one might presume the following points: (1) cyclical changes in business conditions (the non-seasonal, non-secular, and non-random changes) might be envisioned as a whole; (2) once set in motion a boom sustains itself for a time and determines in some measure the extent of an ensuing adjustment in the time series: and (3) a number of outside factors affect time series simultaneously. Quite possibly, changes of this type and of the former distributed lag type are both at operation, but it may be difficult to determine which set predominates. Two points should be clear: (1) that economic time series tend to lead, lag, and follow one another in some pattern, and (2) that an econometric model may pick up lagged relationships between the series independently of their following in any "linked" or "causal" sequence.

There are many technical problems associated with the attempt to make meaningful policy recommendations based on econometric model simulations. Some of the major ones are:

1. The evaluation of alternative time paths in ultimate target variables. Different policy actions may produce responses with different time-shapes, different probabilities of success, and—depending on the nature of the "linkages"—different "side-effects."[11]

2. The identification of exogenous policy variables. To cite an example, most econometric models of the mid- to late 1960s specified nonborrowed reserves (with or without currency) as the appropriate proximate targets for open market operations. In real life, however, nonborrowed reserves may well require a model in which they are endogenous: the Federal Reserve may more or less automatically change nonborrowed reserves to offset member bank borrowings, for "defensive" purposes, to assist in treasury financing, or in response to "feedbacks" from the private sector.[12]

3. The interdependence of policy actions and balance sheet restraints. The problem has been succinctly stated by Christ [70, p. 102]: "(I)t is

---

11. For ways of handling the first and third of these problems, see Fromm and Taubman [157, pp. 92–106]. The second is discussed by Brainard [31].

12. On the merits of various reserve and monetary base targets, see de Leeuw and Kalchbrennor [83, pp. 6–11] and Andersen and Jordon [7, pp. 12–16]. On the influence of other than stabilization objectives on open market operations, see Keran and Babb [226, pp. 7–20] and Torto [357, pp. 40–49]. Without allowance for "feedbacks," the model may be seriously mis-specified.

impossible to change only one fiscal or monetary policy variable at a time. If one is changed, then at least one other must also change so as to satisfy the government budget restraint. (T)he effects of an increase in the high powered money stock depends upon how it is injected into the economy, and . . . the effects of increased government purchase of goods and services depend upon how they are financed." Apparently all econometric models existing by the early 1970s were under-specified with respect to both public and private sector balance sheets, and Christ [70, pp. 103–7] shows how this seriously limits the usefulness of policy simulations with the FRB-MIT model.[13]

4. The determination of the actual speed of adjustment to policy actions. There is some evidence that estimates of time lags in the response of targets to policy actions are not independent of the period of observation in a model: models using annual data produce long lags, those using quarterly data produce shorter lags, etc. [50, pp. 855–64]. If responses are quite short (a month), then aggregation of data over time into longer observation periods (a quarter) may produce a serious specification error which leads to results biased toward longer than true lags.

14.4   ADDITIONAL SPECIAL PURPOSE MODELS

As stated earlier, other models were to follow from the mid-year 1967 version of the FRB-MIT model. From the original Fed-University group, two interrelated models immediately followed: one by the university group of Ando and Modigliani [12, pp. 296–314], and another by the Federal Reserve group of de Leeuw and Gramlich [84, pp. 472–91].[14] The respective models continued to be somewhat interrelated, and there were subsequent developments. Even so, both papers draw heavily in their plant and equipment investment sectors on work by Charles Bischoff, as did the mid-year 1967 version of the FRB-MIT model. Ando and Modigliani say, "it is here that they would expect to find the strongest impact of financial factors."

There has also been considerable special work on structural equations models by other individuals and groups.[15] A model of the monetary sector was constructed at Duke University and used for a variety of simulations of financial responses to changes in monetary policy instruments [28, 29, 30]. The St. Louis model was another.

13. Similar arguments on the importance of implicit balance sheet adjustments are made by Brainard and Tobin [32, pp. 103–6].
14. Ando was involved at the same time with an up-dated version of Goldfeld's model [11].
15. For a survey of pre-1967 models, see Fand [109, pp. 380–400].

Investment expenditures.—Investment expenditures in the Ando-Modigliani paper [12], and in the de Leeuw–Gramlich mid-year 1969 version of the FRB-MIT model [84] include those on inventories, plants and equipment, and residential construction.[16] Chapter 15 deals only with capital outlays by manufacturing corporations, but the Appendix to Chapter 15 juxtaposes these with expenditures on housing. Chapter 15 is related nevertheless, although the focus in that chapter is on the narrower sector of expenditures. In addition, both the mid-year 1969 version of the FRB-MIT model and Chapter 15 are apparently related to analysis of a type due to Keynes or Keynesians, as distinguished by Leijonhufvud [249]. There is also a relation between the subsequent chapter and a discussion by Meiselman [262] of the Ando-Modigliani paper. In attempting to ferret out the essential analytical elements from the investment sector (s) of the Ando-Modigliani model, Meiselman concludes [262, p. 320]:

> Investment expenditures are also a function of what they term the "required yield," a weighted average of corporate bond yields [nominal market interest rates] and stock yields [the dividend to price ratio]. I find this rather puzzling, especially in the context of trying to explain investment expenditures during a period of anticipated inflation, because anticipated inflation clearly affects bond yields but not stock yields [presumably because dividends and stock prices are similarly affected]. . . . In general, the sequence seems to be a very traditional Keynesian one, to which I can make the by now very traditional comments that money can be spent for all kinds of assets and services including goods and services directly not merely for bonds, and here, only short-term claims at that.

The latter point is apparently the Leijonhufvud one noted earlier (Ch. 7) whereby Keynesians emphasize aggregation over two classes of assets, money and bonds, with emphasis on exchange between money and bonds.

Continuing with the problems posed for the Ando-Modigliani paper by inflation, Meiselman considers two cases—unanticipated inflation and a steady state of fully anticipated inflation. In the first he finds longer lags in the effects of accelerating the growth of the money stock on interest rates and expenditures than "recent monetary experience would indicate." In the second he finds that "the model predicts that investment expenditures would fall because nominal interest rates rise whereas price earnings ratios do not." This emphasis by Meiselman on the asset classification problem and the differential effects of price-level changes on different classes of assets (and/or yields) is clearly related to Keynes and Keynesian

16. Cf. Duesenberry, Fromm, Klein, and Kuh [97, Part II], and Jorgenson and Siebert [216, pp. 681–712].

analysis, as well as to Chapter 15. It is related also to the de Leeuw–
Gramlich discussion of capital investment, in that their rate of return (R)
for discounting future returns is "a linear function of a monetary interest
rate and the stock market yield." Their cost of capital is determined in
part by the rate of return (R). Further, de Leeuw and Gramlich introduce an interest-induced wealth effect, as defined earlier (Sec. 1.4) and
as dealt with by Leijonhufvud. They have changes in the rate on long-
term bonds exerting an inverse effect on both bond prices and stock prices.

Commercial loans.—In the unpublished appendix to the mid-year 1969
version, de Leeuw and Gramlich say that their equation defining the demand for bank loans is taken from work by Dwight Jaffee. They say that
the equation "embodies the notion that these short-term loans provide the
primary permanent source of financing inventory investment and a temporary means of financing all categories of net investment until the permanent long-term financing can be arranged." This sort of analysis
contrasts sharply with that in Chapter 15.

In the first place, in Section 15.4 bank loans are shown to increase
considerably less than in proportion to asset size, as firms increase in size.
The same type of analysis reported elsewhere reveals that inventories also
increase less than in proportion to asset size, but not as much less as bank
loans. Overall the ratio of bank loans to inventories (as a percentage)
declines as firms increase in asset size. Analytically, these findings from
cross-section data mean that over time some firms acquire more inventories than others and some more bank loans, all relative to size, and that
time series movements in bank loans and inventories do not mean what
they appear to mean.[17] A. G. Hart has commented [188, p. 234]:

> In the first edition of this volume, I noted the interesting relation between
> the time-shape of business loans of commercial banks and that of business
> inventories. Mr. William J. Frazer, Jr., points out that a large fraction of
> inventories is in lines of manufacturing where loans are relatively
> trifling. . . . There is still an interesting relation if we subtract most
> branches of manufacturing from both inventories and business loans; but
> the possibility of influencing inventories by moves toward stabilization of
> business loans is manifestly more remote than I had suggested.

In the second place, with respect to the de Leeuw–Gramlich bank loan
equation, bank loans may not follow the arrangement for permanent long-
term financing. In Chapter 15 bank loans are emphasized as a part of the

---

17. A chapter is devoted to this type of analysis in an unpublished dissertation
by Frazer [119, Ch. 5].

liquidity structure of firms. A reduction in such loans, as a part of a buildup in liquidity in anticipation of capital spending, is emphasized as a part of planning for the future by mature corporations.

The treatment of selected factors.—A number of factors, such as tax credits and accelerated depreciation, play similar roles in the mid-year 1969 version of the FRB-MIT model and in Chapter 15. There are, however, some major differences in the treatment of common factors. For example:

1. The cost of capital influences—particularly as affected by interest rate or time discount component—operate with a long lag and "it takes time for the open market operations to be reflected in long-term interest rates." In contrast, the lag in the effect of monetary policy is short in Chapter 15, but much of the difference turns on the definition of and perspective on monetary policy.

2. The interest-induced wealth effect exerts an inverse influence on both stock and bond prices. This effect is not mentioned in Chapter 15 because a secondary role is attributed to it in connection with other factors (compare Sec. 7.4).

3. Credit rationing by banks to business firms is found to have no effect on plant and equipment and inventory investment. In contrast, in Chapter 15 a form of rationing of loans to firms by banks is said to have a substantial effect on plant and equipment expenditures, particularly as indicated by the strong differential pattern of expenditures by large and small firms over phases of capital booms.

Some interesting features of the mid-year 1969 version of the FRB-MIT model that are not necessarily in conflict with Chapter 15 are (1) the allowance for a risk factor in the derivation of the "appropriate rate of interest," (2) the dynamic quality of the model implied by the emphasis on "the expected rate of capital gains" and expectations generally ("waves of optimism and pessimism that possibly influence both the stock market and capital expenditures"), and (3) the tie between the cost of capital formula and the production function.[18]

In Chapter 15 changes in monetary policy are identified with changes in the spread between yields on long- and short-term securities, changes in $d(i_L - i_s)/dt$. Such a policy is implemented through the acceleration and deceleration of the growth of bank credit and money. The concept is one of a policy over a cycle with the Federal Reserve exerting its influence via expectations about changes in future interest rates relative to prevailing rates. The emphasis is on classes of assets, notably those with

18. On all of these features, see Keran [225, pp. 16–31].

a fixed or contractual claim against future income (money and bonds) and those with a residual claim (stocks and instrumental capital). The analysis is readily distinguishable from Keynes' mode and Keynesian analysis as mentioned by Leijonhufvud [249, Ch. IV, Sec. 1].

Keynes emphasized money as one class of assets and debt and instrumental assets as a second class. He was interested in stabilization of the trade cycle, but as far as monetary policy was concerned, this was to be achieved in the short run as defined by Keynes [in the period over which long-term expectations were constant, as represented by $R_1, R_2, \ldots R_n$, where the demand price or capital value (CV) of a class of assets is equal to $R_1/(1 + i)^1 + R_2/(1 + i)^2 + \ldots + R_n/(1 + i)^n$]. Here interest rates and demand price vary inversely, and the central bank exerts an influence by lowering the long-term interest rate and providing an inducement for capital expenditures [via $r > i$ where the rate of return from additional expenditures (r) is the rate relating prospective returns to the supply price or cost, $C = R_1/(1 + r)^1 + R_2/(1 + r)^2 + \ldots + R_n/(1 + r)^n$]. Keynes questioned the Central Bank's ability to control the long-term interest rate—as Leijonhufvud indicates—and he thus favored fiscal policy, as did later "Keynesians" for different reasons, including assumed interest inelasticity of investment demand. Nevertheless, Keynes thought the Central Bank could influence the "normal" or "safe" interest rate (the average rate toward which the prevailing rate was expected to regress). If the prevailing rates were expected to rise, there would be a strengthened preference for money, a steady deflationary pressure, and recession.

In the analysis of Chapter 15, Keynes' short period vanishes for the purposes of stabilization and expectations are variable. The expected interest rate is also indicative of prospective returns on capital. Thus, a greater prospect of a future rise in rates—as indicated by a change in the yield spread $[d(i_L - i_s)/dt]$ and as controlled indirectly by the Central Bank—mitigates a recession or contributes to a boom. The effect is just the reverse of that following from Keynes' model, but some of the elements of Keynes' notion about Central Bank influence are present.

The St. Louis Model.—The St. Louis model is highly simplified in contrast to the various versions of the Federal Reserve–MIT model. It is in concept a linkages model; in keeping with its rationale, the Federal Reserve may vary the rate of change in the money stock and, after some time, anticipate given patterns of changes in total spending and hence movements in output, employment, and the general price level. In another sense the St. Louis model has a special purpose. The authors say [6, pp.

10–11] that "The purpose . . . is to estimate the response of output and prices to monetary and fiscal actions, not to test a hypothesized structure." The model with this special emphasis is reminiscent of the simple models and their uses, as reviewed in Chapter 5.

Since the model is relatively simple, it can readily be exhibited, as in Figure 14–1. Andersen and Carlson define and describe the equations in the model [6, pp. 9–10]: [19]

Equation (1) is the total spending equation. The change in total spending (ΔY) is specified as a function of current and past changes in the money stock (ΔM) and current and past changes in high-employment Federal expenditures (ΔE). This general specification represents the reduced form for that class of structures which has ΔM and ΔE as exogenous variables. In this form the total spending equation remains uncommitted as to structure; it is potentially consistent with both Keynesian and quantity theory models. (The magnitude and significance of the estimated parameters determine whether the data conform more closely to a Keynesian or a quantity theory).

Equation (2) specifies the change in the price level (ΔP) as a function of current and past demand pressures (D) and anticipated price changes (ΔP^A). Demand pressure is defined in equation (3) as the change in total spending minus the potential increase in output (X^F–X). The price equation is an alternative to the standard short-run Phillips curve relation generalized to include changes in total spending and anticipated prices.

Equation (4) defines a change in total spending in terms of its components, the part associated with changes in the price level (ΔP) and the part associated with changes in output (ΔX). With ΔY determined by equation (1), and ΔP by equation (2), ΔX can be derived from equation (4).

Equation (5) specifies the market rate of interest (R) as a function of current changes in the money stock (ΔM), current and past changes in output (ΔX), current price change (ΔP), and anticipated price change (ΔP^A). The price anticipations term is included to capture the Fisher effect. The anticipated price function is defined in equation (6). Antici-

---

19. There are numerous references to earlier articles in the St. Louis bank's *Review* that motivate the equation statements in various ways. For these, see Andersen and Carlson [6, pp. 9–10]. They refer to "Okun's Law" to which equations (7) and (8) pertain, and they indicate how it relates the GNP gap to the unemployment rate:

Arthur M. Okun, "Potential GNP: Its Measurement and Significance," *1962 Proceedings of the Business and Economic Statistics Section of the American Statistical Association*, pp. 98–104. Okun's Law relates the GNP gap to the unemployment rate as

$$X^F_t - X_t = .03(U_t - 4)X_t$$

The number .03 is a productivity factor and 4 is defined as the unemployment rate consistent with full resource utilization.

FIGURE 14-1. The St. Louis Model

Model in Algebraic Form

(1) Total Spending Equation
$$\Delta Y_t = f_1(\Delta M_t \ldots \Delta M_{t-n,} \Delta E_t \ldots \Delta E_{t-n})$$

(2) Price Equation
$$\Delta P_t = f_2(D_t \ldots D_{t-n}, \Delta P^A_t)$$

(3) Demand Pressure Identity
$$D_t = \Delta Y_t - (X^F_t - X_{t-1})$$

(4) Total Spending Identity
$$\Delta Y_t = \Delta P_t + \Delta X_t$$

(5) Interest Rate Equation
$$R_t = f_3(\Delta M_{t,} \Delta X_t \ldots \Delta X_{t-n}, \Delta P_t, \Delta P^A_t)$$

(6) Anticipated Price Equation
$$\Delta P^A_t = f_4(\Delta P_{t-1} \ldots \Delta P_{t-n})$$

(7) Unemployment Rate Equation
$$U_t = f_5(G_t, G_{t-1})$$

(8) GNP Gap Identity
$$G_t = \frac{X^F_t - X_t}{X^F_t}$$

Endogenous Variables	Exogenous Variables*
ΔY_t = change in total spending (nominal GNP)	ΔM_t = change in money stock
ΔP_t = change in price level (GNP price deflator)	ΔE_t = change in high-employment Federal expenditures
D_t = demand pressure	X^F_t = potential (full-employment) output
ΔX_t = change in output (real GNP)	
R_t = market interest rate	
ΔP^A_t = anticipated change in price level	
U_t = unemployment rate	
G_t = GNP gap	*Other than lagged variables.

Source: Leonall C. Andersen, and Keith M. Carlson, "A Monetarist Model for Economic Stabilization," *Review*, Federal Reserve Bank of St. Louis, April 1970, p. 9.

---

pated price change (ΔP^A) in the current period is assumed to depend on past price changes (ΔP).[20]

Equation (7) is the unemployment rate equation and is a transformation of the GNP gap (G), as defined in equation (8), into a measure of unemployment relative to the labor force. This transformation is based on "Okun's Law."

The authors illustrate the workings of their model, discuss estimation techniques, and exhibit their estimates. The parameters in the equations

---

20. The model actually contains two interest rate equations: one for the 4–6 month commercial paper rate, and one for the yield on Aaa bonds.

are estimated with ordinary least squares, and the lag structures—with one exception—were estimated with the Almon lag technique, (Appendix to Chapter 1, Sec. 10.4). The sample period was I–1953 to IV–1969 for the spending equation and I–1955 o IV–1969 for all the others. There were some *ex post* simulations for the entire 1959–69 period and some *ex ante* simulations for the 1968–69 period, as mentioned earlier (Sec. 14.1). To obtain the *ex ante* estimates, the equations of the model were re-estimated with data through 1967. "Root mean squared errors" for the simulation were shown. Andersen and Carlson concluded [6, pp. 18–19] that

> The success of the *ex ante* dynamic simulation can be assessed by comparing it with the tracking record of the *ex post* simulation for the same period. A comparison of the errors associated with the *ex ante* simulation with those of the *ex post* simulation (where the errors in both cases are computed with reference to actual values) suggests that any structural shifts that occurred in the 1968–69 period were not of such a magnitude that the *ex ante* tracking ability of the model was significantly different from that of *ex post* simulation.
>
> Any conclusions about the tracking ability of the model are necessarily tentative, because they are based on only one *ex ante* dynamic simulation experiment. Nevertheless, these results provide a tentative basis for confidence in the tracking ability of the model in estimating the economic response to monetary and fiscal actions. Unfortunately, it is difficult to conduct additional tests of this type for other subperiods in the sample, because degrees of freedom are severely reduced when the sample period is shortened further.

The St. Louis Model has been used and variously described as predictive [62, 114]. Carlson [62, p. 20], one of the developers of the model, brings out its special relevance as an "aid in the identification of fundamental determinants of economic trends over periods as long as a year or more," as distinct from quarter-to-quarter forecasting. In reporting on projections with the model, Carlson notes the three exogenous variables as listed in Figure 14–1, but he is actually concerned with annual rates of change in the money stock and federal expenditures. Projections are reported for the average annual rates of change in total spending, real product, and prices, on one hand, and the levels for the unemployment rate, the corporate Aaa bond rate, and the commercial paper rate, on the other. In making monetary policy recommendations, alternative steady growth rates of the money stock are assumed.

In evaluating the model, Carlson recognizes [62, p. 21] unexplained error (the difference between actual values and those yielded by *ex post* simulation) and two sources of explained error (error due to changes in the structure or regression coefficients from one sample period to another, and deviations of the monetary and fiscal variables from the assumed steady rates). In the light of his objectives, Carlson finds that the model succeeds in rounding out the time paths for the actual counterparts to the model's projections, at least for the period from late 1969 to mid-1971.

On a less complicated level, Francis points to the record of prediction beyond sample periods for key variables (GNP, rate of change in prices, and the unemployment rate) on an annual basis for the years 1969, 1970, and 1971. He points out [114, p. 35], as did Carlson, that the parameters of the model may shift from one sample period to another in response to external stocks (unforeseen natural, political, and economic events) but that the model is not adjusted or updated to take account of these shocks. The projections for the key variables are then compared with a "consensus" forecast, and with actual *ex post* values for the variables. Francis finds the model has performed well against the consensus forecast.

In contrast to the St. Louis group, some others such as Lawrence Klein [230] and Ronald Teigen [348] have questioned the forecasting record and methodological basis of its model. Klein does this especially in relation to the "academic" or MPS (MIT–Pennsylvania–Social Science Research Council) version of the original FRB-MIT model, and in relation to his own Wharton Model. He concluded [230, p 43] that they all fit the data fairly well. All have their strong and weak features.

Klein's own model has been quite prominent in the forecasting sphere. (Its results are commercially marketable, and the model's forecasts are published regularly in *Business Week*.) It has been in the Keynesian tradition with a primary emphasis on the real economy, fiscal changes, the interest rate as the control-transmission variable, and the short run. The model is a structural equations system, but allows for the use of a priori information that can be built into such a system [230, p. 44]. In part for this reason, one might object to a comparison of its forecasts with those of the St. Louis model.

Klein points out that the St. Louis Model is more mechanical in its forecasting "as a result of its being a reduced-form model," and [230, pp. 44–45] that "The monetarist theory need not be based on a reduced form econometric system, but until the practitioners come up with an explicit statement of the structural process by which monetary events are transmitted through the economy, they are in an awkward position for the strengthening of their system in application through the use of *a priori* information." Klein outlines the research strategy of the St. Louis Model [230, p. 45]:

The research strategy of the St. Louis Model builders and of monetarists generally is to determine GNP from a single-equation version of
the quantity theory and then to decompose it into segments of the economy
and separate market processes in other equations of the system. This is
in striking contrast to the usual approach of fiscal model builders, as in
the Wharton case, where GNP estimates result from adding up all the
separate components determined from individual equations. There is no
single dominant relation to the system as a whole.

A few additional points about the St. Louis Model may be made by
viewing estimates for its central relationship [(1) in Figure 14-1] for the
60 quarter period I–1955 to IV–1969 and the results of a "dynamic
simulation." The estimated relation is [230, p. 44]

$$\Delta Y = 2.84 + \sum_{i=0}^{4} m_i \, \Delta M_{t-i} + \sum_{i=0}^{4} e_i \, \Delta E_{t-i}$$
$$(3.73)$$

$\Sigma_{mi} = 5.02$ $\Sigma e_i = 0.055$ $R^2 = 0.65$ S. E. $= 3.84$ DW $= 1.71$
   (8.06) (0.17)

where—in addition to the variables defined for equation (1), Figure
14–1, and the usual R^2 and DW designations—m and e represent regression coefficients, $S.E.$ is the standard error of the estimate or the
root-mean-square error ($3.84 billion in one quarter forecast, in the
present case), and t-ratios are in parentheses. The error of $3.84 billion
in the one-quarter forecast is not considered impressive in comparison
with "true ex ante forecasting with fiscal type models such as the Wharton
Model." Klein compares it with a $2.5 billion error in his model.

Next, using levels of the money and government (federal, state, and
local) expenditures and goods and services (G), Klein obtains [230, p.
45]

$$Y_t = -115.66 + \sum_{i=0}^{4} m_i \, M_{t-i} + \sum_{i=0}^{4} g_i \, G_{t-i} + 0.765 \, Y_{t-i}$$
$$(-1.15)$$

$\Sigma \, m_i = 1.23$ $\Sigma g_i = 0.59$ $R^2 = 0.997$ S. E. $= 4.2$ D-W$=1.90$
   (1.23) (1.97)

Klein notes that the correlation statistic is not comparable with that of
the previous case, due to the use of levels rather than first differences,
"but the standard error statistic of $4.2 billion is only slightly higher than
the St. Louis version." A main point is that "Government expenditures
are just statistically significant while the money stock is not." Continuing,
Klein says, "the economic impact of the money stock is not significantly
greater in this form of the critical equation."

In examining the other relationships in the St. Louis Model, Klein does not find them distinctive as monetarist relationships. They are peculiar to the St. Louis position, he says, because [230, p. 46] they "are not structural equations based on explicit behavior patterns of particular groups of economic agents; they are more in the nature of empirical relationships that graduate sample data well and are in some sense reduced forms." Discussion of these "other relationships" is not carried much further, except to point to two interest rate equations [(5) in Figure 14–1 and an additional one].

Klein finds these interest rate relationships close to liquidity preference equations, as in the Keynesian building block, "except that money and income variables are expressed as rates of change, while interest rate is not." This point about liquidity preference is of interest to Klein because he finds an inconsistency in the elements of theory implicit in the St. Louis Model. "The liquidity preference theory of demand for money is the behavioral alternative to the quantity equation of the monetarist school." He points out that monetarists do not view velocity as dependent on interest rates, while "the Keynesian fiscal camp would claim that velocity is a function of the interest rate." Klein himsef [230, p. 47] wants to view evidence of the relationship between velocity and interest rates, as reviewed in Chapter 4, as support for the Keynesian liquidity preference theory.

In his evaluation of the St. Louis Model [348, pp. 3–27], Teigen makes many of the points variously reviewed above about the reduced form equations, some covered earlier about the exogeneity of the money stock (Sec. 2.2), and some about expenditure elasticities for specific expenditure categories (Sec. 3.2) and supply and demand functions for money. Somewhat along the same lines, he mentions portfolio effects, wealth effects, credit availability, and the need to deal with these in a structural equations model. He contrasts the so-called "effects" of a given increase in the money stock in the FRB-MIT and the St. Louis models. He does the same for given fiscal actions in the two models. He finds money has more "effect" than fiscal policy in the St. Louis model, and fiscal policy has more effect in the FRB-MIT model, somewhat along the lines of Klein's experience with the estimated relations given above. He concludes [348, pp. 26–27] that "The best evidence we have suggests the common-sense conclusion that changes in monetary variables certainly do affect income and employment substantially, although with a lag of several months; at the same time, expenditures and tax changes also unquestionably exert a significant and rapidly-felt effect."

14.5 SUMMARY

The modern computer with its large information storage capacity and fast operating time contributed to the proliferation of structural equations models in the 1960s. Examples of these models and the need for the computer's capacity include the Federal Reserve–MIT model with emphasis on structure and a mass of traditional details and the simpler St. Louis model with its computationally complicated Almon lag structures. The former type of research was especially ambitious, but it contributed to a greater methodological sophistication on the part of economists, pointed up inadequacies in received economic theory, brought renewed attention to the role of state-of-mind variables such as anticipated price changes, and revealed the difficulties in searching out a stable structure, particularly in view of the role of outside factors.

The St. Louis model emphasized the influence of monetary expansion on total spending. Such an interest characterized the monetarist's research. However, even with the achievement of stability of the type monetarists have discussed (stability without deep recessions and extreme swings in the money stock) there is still something to be stabilized in refining and improving the performance of the economy. The problems in analysis and structural equations models posed by outside factors seem especially challenging.

Two aspects of the Federal Reserve–MIT model in its 1960 versions stand out in relation to linkage mechanisms and stabilization, as reviewed in the present chapter. One is the role of short-term bank loans whereby funds are allegedly provided to finance inventories and to temporarily finance net investment. The second is the treatment of investment expenditures in an apparent Keynesian framework (one relying strongly on the level of interest rates and a strong relation between money and bonds, where an expansion of money lowers bond yields).

Emphasis on bank loans ignores their structural aspects whereby they increase considerably less than in proportion to asset size and even less than in proportion to inventories. Also overlooked is the planning of financing by the mature corporation. In planning, liquidity (a reduction in bank loans and an increase in non-cash liquid assets, both relative to asset size) is build up from a variety of sources in anticipation of a later need for funds. This is discussed further in the next chapter.

15

The Management and Financing
of the Mature Corporation

15.1 INTRODUCTION

MONETARY POLICY, as defined earlier (Ch. 2), may be thought of as implemented through the acceleration and deceleration of the growth of bank reserves, bank credit, and the money stock. There is also the historical view that the policy should be effected with minimum reliance on the more direct controls and mainly to achieve national economic goals, within the context of a relatively free, market-oriented economy. It would seem that such a policy should be directed, explained, and defended with reference to the relatively sizeable and volatile capital expenditures of manufacturing corporations. This would seem to be particularly true in view of the high social priorities associated with state and local government expenditures and with home construction [102].

With respect to the analysis of the effects of policy, there have been some incongruous tendencies, including (1) that of focusing on the effects of tight credit conditions on outlays by households for housing and then making the analogy between these effects and those on capital outlays by business firms (Sec. 3.4); and (2) that of focusing on the countercyclical nature of housing expenditures as distinct from the more procyclical behavior of capital expenditures by large manufacturing corporations. This chapter departs from these and other tendencies, assuming either the prospect of the sheltering of housing from tight credit [219] or that of improving their stability by stabilizing capital expenditures in the more industrialized sectors (Appendix to Ch. 15). The focus is on the mature corporation with emphasis on probabilistic views about anticipated

Note: This chapter is based on a paper that appeared in 1968 [121]. Some notions from Chapter 8 are added, along with some references.

312

events (as in Ch. 8) and particularly on planning to avoid the effects of tight credit traditionally defined (Sec. 2.3).

In the foregoing emphasis, firms are viewed less simplistically than in the mainstream of economics [197, Ch. 3],[1] and traditional mechanical relations—such as that between sales and the demand for inventories (Ch. 8, n. 24)—are subordinated to effects operating through expectations. Monetary policy is seen as working through expectations—through the term structure of interest rates (Chs. 12, 13) in the case of the financial markets, but through the expectations of the real goods or corporate manufacturing sector too, in view of assumed equality of foresight (Sec. 2.1) of participants in both these financial and real sectors in the formation of responses to factors concerning expectations.

With the subordination of certain of the received and mechanical aspects of the analysis of firms, there is also a departure from the emphasis by economists in the mid–1960s on fixed distributed lag structures and models. Lagged relations between time series doubtless exist, but the presence of judgment, leaning, shock effects, and probabilistic slanting as related to them introduces a less fixed and a more variable relation. In this chapter, the tendency for mature firms to plan more to reduce the uncertainty of the future availability of needed funds on prescribed terms concerns other interrelated tendencies, specifically for firms to rely more on a larger store of non-cash liquid assets and on unused bank credit as they increase in asset size [126, pp. 202–12]. Stronger prospects of a rise in interest rates—as embodied in the term structure of interest rates in the case of the financial markets—affect the planning of capital expenditures, their implementation, and the buildup of liquidity as a source of funds for effecting planned outlays. Liquidity in turn becomes a constraint on expenditures in a prolonged period of expansion in business activity, and bank loans to businesses are one ingredient of that liquidity. Changes in expectations therefore affect the flow of capital expenditures and the demand for bank loans.

In the post–World War II years, monetary policy has been intensely studied with reference to various economic aggregate and sector measures. There has been emphasis on the effects of changes in the availability of credit, as in the banking view and Keynesian analysis (Sec. 3.4), and on the demand for bank loans to business, as in Fisher's model (Secs. 1.4,

1. A simple version of a theory of the firm and even one without empirical relevance is adequate when the objective is a discussion of market structures, competition, and so on. But this objective is different from that of this chapter.

4.2, Appendix to Ch. 4). There has also been emphasis on the effects of
changes in the rates of change for the money stock and bank credit—in
some instances on interest rates and then on expenditures, and in
some fairly directly on the asset (and liability) position of economic units.
Difficulties in assessing the results from aggregate analyses arise, however,
from differences in sector responses to various measures. Major difficulties arise in efforts to trace direct linkages between business loans by
banks and firms' activities. They also arise in attempts to view direct
effects of absolute changes in interest rates on investment, as if there was
some stable, negatively-sloped schedule relating such rates to the flow of
investment. They arise in the case of bank loans because bank loans to
manufacturing corporations increase significantly less than in proportion
to firms' sizes and expenditures, and in the investment case because
changes in rates of return on the flow of investment vary directly though
roughly with market interest rates, as if they were responding to the same
sets of changes in the economy.

15.2   BUSINESS ENTERPRISES, FIXED LAG PATTERNS, AND ALTERNATIVES

A number of issues arise in specifying categories of expenditures and in
delineating economic sectors, particularly in relation to the analysis of
the behavior of firms. In one instance (Sec. 5.2), expenditures relating
to income are treated as consumption, and autonomous expenditures are
treated as investment. In another instance, as in a Friedman analysis of
the demand for money [136, p. 202], there is a distinction between "ultimate wealth holders, to whom money is one form in which they choose
to hold their wealth, and enterprises, to whom money is a producer's
good like machinery or inventories." This seems to suggest a utility
analysis [197, Ch. 2] in the case of households and an analysis centering
about production functions [197, Ch. 3] (the maximization of output
given cost, and the minimization of cost given output) in the case of firms.
   There is possible merit in identifying autonomous expenditures and
there is potential interchangeability between utility and production analyses. Even so, identifying the first by the criteria established in Section 5.2
leaves little to be analyzed, and probabilistic schemes concerning decision-
making have developed initially in combination with utility analysis. The
present chapter retains the emphasis on utility and simply points out
Friedman's distinct analysis of the demand for money by business enterprises. The various approaches may be judged by what they explain.

Friedman on the demand for money by business enterprises.—Friedman has symbolized his analysis of the demand for money by individual wealth holders by the following function [136, p. 204]:

$$\frac{M}{P} = f\left(y,\ w;\ r_m,\ r_b,\ r_e,\ \frac{1}{P}\frac{dP}{dt};\ u\right)$$

where *M* is the stock of money, *P* is the price index implicit in estimating national income in constant prices, and *y* is nominal income in constant prices. The other variables are defined as follows: "*w* is the fraction of wealth in non-human form (or, alternatively, the fraction of income derived from property). r_m is the expected nominal rate of return on money; r_b is the expected nominal rate of return on fixed valued securities, including expected changes in their prices; r_e is the expected nominal rate of return on equities, including expected changes in their prices; $(1/P)$ $(d\,P/dt)$ is the expected rate of change of prices of goods and hence the expected nominal rate of return on real assets; and *u* is a portmanteau symbol standing for whatever variables other than income may affect the utility attached to the services of money." Viewing changes in the distribution of income and wealth or their effects as constant or nearly so, Friedman's demand function may be applied to the community as a whole, with *M* and *y* referring to per capita amounts. As the term implies, the "portmanteau" variable is a "catch-all," and it may incorporate much of what one wishes to analyze (changes in the degree of certainty about anticipated returns and business conditions). It is reminiscent of the random error terms which, in Friedman's earlier work, stood for variables expected to affect tastes and preferences.[2] In applying the demand function to business enterprises, the *u* stands for a "set of variables other than scale affecting the productivity of money balances." Friedman says [136, p. 205], "at least one of these—namely, expectations about economic stability—is likely to be common to business enterprises and ultimate wealth holders."

Continuing in his discussion of business enterprises, Friedman says [136, p. 205] they "are not subject to a constraint comparable with that imposed by the total wealth of the ultimate wealth holder." He says that

2. The main difference between this demand function and its earlier counterpart in Friedman's framework as discussed elsewhere [126, pp. 8–9] is the introduction of expected nominal yield on money (r_m) and the treatment of the interest rates (or yields) on bonds and equities as expected rather than current. Friedman does not explain the shift, and the differences between current and expected yields may be important.

The total amount of capital embodied in productive assets, including money, is a variable that can be determined by an enterprise to maximize returns, since it can acquire additional capital through the capital market. Hence, there is no reason on this ground to include total wealth, or y as a surrogate for total wealth, as a variable in the business demand function for money.

There are several difficulties in this passage. One is the implication that individuals or households cannot vary total wealth by borrowing or re-paying debt or by participating in partnership ventures—such as group ownership of real property—where their own contribution to the capital in the venture is enlarged through borrowing by the group as a whole. Of course, most households are probably more constrained than are firms by their capacity to increase their total wealth through borrowing. A constraint employed in the subsequent analysis is total assets of the large firms, but this measure may be shown to substitute for sales, income, and net worth, to the extent that sales and GNP are highly correlated, to the extent that sales and total assets are highly correlated, and to the extent that percentage changes in net worth parallel percentage changes in total assets.[3]

In another instance there is closer agreement with Friedman [136, p. 205]: "The division of wealth between human and non-human form has no special relevance to business enterprises, since they are likely to buy the services of both forms on the market." But the difficulty is that house-holds can also buy the services of both forms of wealth. Total assets in the balance sheets of enterprises are clearly representative of assets in non-human form.

On rates of return, Friedman says [136, p. 205] that

Rates of return on money and on alternative assets are, of course, highly relevant to business enterprises. These rates determine the net cost to them of holding the money balances. However, the particular rates that are relevant may be quite different from those that are relevant for ulti-mate wealth holders. For example, rates charged by banks on loans are of

3. Regressing quarterly data for sales on GNP (both seasonally adjusted) for the years 1952–64 yields a coefficient of determination of 0.97. In a logarithmic transformation of the data, such a regression yields a slope parameter of 0.82.

Cross-section results from regressing sales on asset size for seven asset-size classes of manufacturing corporations with over 5 million dollars in assets include an average regression coefficient of 0.98 and a coefficient of determination of 1.00 for the 24 quarters 1959–64. Comparable results from regressing owners' equity (or net worth) on asset size include an average regression coefficient of 1.00 and a coefficient of determination of 1.00. The cross-section data are from FTC–SEC's *Quarterly Financial Report* as discussed below (Sec. 15.4).

minor importance for wealth holders yet may be extremely important for businesses, since bank loans may be a way in which they can acquire the capital embodied in money balances.

The meaning of the last sentence in this quotation is difficult to contemplate. The rate charged to (and the availability of funds for) a member of a household may determine whether he can obtain and carry a construction loan for home improvement or whether he can buy a new car or boat. As shown later, the role of bank loans is prominent for large and small firms alike. The role for small businesses and households may not be too different. Bank loans are especially important in the financial planning and capital expenditure programs of large firms.

Investment demand and some lagged relations.—The demand for capital goods (or the services of capital goods), its determinants, and especially the possibility of a lag between the changes in the demand for capital goods and the actual changes in capital goods have been widely studied [182, pp. 1–6; 215, pp. 35–92; 304, pp. 322–33; 217, pp. 16–17; 3, pp. 178–96]. Resek [304] outlined three principal types of theories for explaining investment behavior, and Hamburger surveyed portions of the investment demand literature with emphasis on the impact of monetary variables [182, pp. 1–6]. Neither of these authors, however, mentioned approaches of the type dealt with in this chapter. In addition to explaining the effects of a change in monetary policy, the present approach provides a basis for explaining differential rates of capital expenditures for large manufacturing firms and for expecting smaller firms to encounter special difficulty in increasing bank loans under increasingly stringent credit conditions.

In portions of the investment demand literature, expectations surveys serve as indicators of anticipated or desired investment expenditures [215, p. 37; 3, pp. 178–96] with actual expenditures expected to lag somewhat. In other instances, desired capital expenditures are indicated by some proxy measure such as a variable related to actual output [304, p. 323; 217, p. 17].

One lag scheme brought out in the context of a distributed lag model, where the overall lag in the sequence is fixed, is [215, pp. 38–41]

t_1	t_2	t_3	t_4	t_5
Initiation of Investment Project	Appropriation of Funds	Letting of Contracts	Issuing of Orders	Actual Investment

Here "anticipated investment expenditures" enter as a special kind of intermediate stage of the investment process, but investment expenditures are still assumed to lag behind "planned" or "anticipated" investment expenditures. Commenting on an overall sequence of "lags" in the investment process, Resek attributed them to a number of things [304, p. 326]:

> The need for new capital is likely to exist before it is recognized. After recognition of the need time will pass before the decision to invest is actually made. This decision can be thought of as occurring at the time the funds are appropriated. Finally, there is a lag between the appropriations and the actual investment. The last cause mentioned is likely to include most of the lag because of physical problems in ordering items and having them built and delivered.

Of course, there are technical problems such as serial correlation involved in the use of distributed lag models for dealing with possible "lagged" relationships between economic variables [178]. Hamburger mentioned the possible shortcomings of statistical techniques in estimating lags in both his first [182] and second (Sec. 10.4) survey of lagged models, but in the first survey he was favorably disposed toward the results from analyses with lagged variables when they supported the possibility of interest rate effects, with correct signs (presumably negative), on nonresidential investment (compare Sec. 13.3). Of course, this was before much of the experience with the Almon technique (Sec. 10.4) and before the ascendancy of the money stock and related aggregates as policy indicators vis-à-vis money market variables, such as occurred in the late 1960s and immediately succeeding Arthur Burns' appointment as Chairman of the Board (Sec. 2.1). Thus one may wonder whether in such a case Hamburger was not initially trapped as an economist at the Federal Reserve Bank of New York by the organization and the wish to find significant interest rate effects and short lags in the effects of the rate changes, all as would be favorable to a conventional assessment of monetary policy. In any event, he shows considerably more flexibility toward distributed lag models and policy indicators in the second survey (Sec. 10.4).

In his first selected survey [182, pp. 1–16] Hamburger emphasized the significance of interest rates with a correct sign (presumably negative), the increasing frequency with which interest rates have been found to be statistically significant, the consistency with which long-lagged relationships have been found, and the prospect of the introduction of bias in the estimates of lags because of the statistical procedures. Of course, he is aware that the change in the rate of change in capital expenditures by manufacturing firms and the interest rates vary directly, if very roughly, with phases of business conditions. Thus, the finding of inverse (negative sign) relation between the interest rate and capital expenditures should not be surprising, if the relationship is loosely viewed as lagged with interest rates rising as in an expansion phase and the rate of increase (or change) in capital outlays declining in an ensuing recession. This particular question about timing evidence is related to the controversy between Friedman and Tobin (Sec. 5.6).

Different analysts have viewed differently the significance of the increasing frequency with which interest rate effects with significant coefficient and "correct sign" are reported, particularly since the impact of the modern computer. Andersen said [10, p. 92], "it is altogether too easy to find 'significant' correlations and 'correct' signs in cyclical time series if one is sufficiently persistent in respecifying until he is satisfied with the results [if one is persistent in data mining]." Crockett, Friend, and Shavell elaborated on the same theme [78, p. 10]:

> Depending on the econometric model utilized, it is possible to point to significant interest rate effects on plant and equipment but not on inventories, on inventories but not on plant and equipment, on both, or on neither. Generally, the negative results seem more impressive than the positive results. The latter are frequently derived by testing a large number of models that turn out to have insignificant or even incorrect interest rate effects [presumably interest rate variables with positive coefficients] before models with nominally significant effects of correct [presumably negative] signs are obtained.

In addition to the methodological difficulties, there are operational shortcomings in the use of distributed lag models with fixed (as distinct from variable) lags between planned and actual outlays. Specifically, on occasion the backlog of planned capital expenditures has exceeded the desired level such that postponements of plans have taken place; on other occasions irreversible commitments have been made such that involuntary expenditures have occurred approaching an upper turning point of business conditions; and at times of less than average business conditions plants have operated at less than full capacity. These developments mean that at times more capital outlays have been planned than were needed and that the need for an enlarged flow of investment has not always led actual investment by any fixed time dimension, as assumed in the use of the distributed lag model. Furthermore, there is no special stage involving financial appropriations, as in the sequence of lags shown schematically above and as described by Resek.[4] As the subsequent outline of theory suggests, a buildup in liquidity may become a source of funds for future outlays, independent of any phase in a sequence of the type shown schematically.

It is interesting and meaningful to compare alternative views or to test alternative theories against one another. It is also of possible interest to note a contrast between the views of the effects of policy and lags in the effects in some of the research publications of the Federal Reserve, as cited above, and in some of the remarks by an official. In reference to the buildup in liquidity in the summer of 1967—following the liquidity squeeze of the summer of 1966—the Chairman of the Board, William McC. Martin remarked [121, pp. 71–72]:

> Market participants seem to feel that no matter how high interest rates may be pushed by their efforts to raise long-term funds now, the situation may be even worse before the end of the year. Borrowers, investors, and market professionals all are expecting a large Federal deficit in the fiscal year ahead. They fear that financing such a deficit will put additional heavy pressures on the market and that a deficit of this size, along with resurgence in private demands, harbors the potential or reviving inflationary pressures by the boost it will give to spending and to private incomes, in turn stimulating additional credit demands.

Here there is emphasis on the responses of interest rates, expenditures, and long-term financing to prospective price level changes—all in contrast to the views on interest rate effects and the appropriation of funds in the previously cited research publications of the Federal Reserve. This tendency for interest rates and returns to capital to be influenced by many of the same forces has been brought out on other occasions (Secs. 2.2, 14.4).

---

4. The notion that funds are actually appropriated when capital expenditures proposals enter as a part of the capital budget appears to be rather common. (See, as another example, Reynolds and Hart [314, p. 520].) In announcing its survey of planned and actual capital expenditures in 1956, however, the National Industrial Conference Board (NICB) did not mention "funds," as if "funds" were actually appropriated when authority was given to incur obligations for new plants and equipment [75, pp. 418–34], and Almon [3, p. 182] correctly defines appropriations in the latter survey: "Appropriations are thought of as the final stage of approval for expenditures, a confirmation of plans represented in the annual budget. They are data routinely tabulated by companies using formal capital budgeting procedures."

G. David Quirin, in an early 1967 publication [295, p. 22], mentioned the "appropriation of funds" in discussing capital appropriations. His views as revealed in correspondence are cited elsewhere [121, n. 1].

15.3   CAPITAL EXPENDITURES AND THE LIQUIDITY STRUCTURE OF FIRMS: SOME ELEMENTS OF THEORY

The interest rate may be viewed in various instances as the rate on long-term government bonds and as a rate for relating a prospective stream of returns to the present value of some assets. In either case, changes in the rate may be viewed as an upward or downward movement in the structure with some of the less flexible rates lagging the shifts somewhat and with relative rates also changing as the spread between long- and short-term rates varies indirectly with the movements in the structure (Ch. 13). The return to normality approach to liquidity preference analysis (Sec. 8.5) emphasizes shifts in the hyperbolic curve which relates the interest rate to the quantity of money balances demanded and which reflects a rising (declining) quantity demanded as the relation between a "normal rate" and "the rate" vary.

Along somewhat similar lines, the changes in the probability of a rise (decline) in future rates—in the liquidity preference model, a widening (narrowing) spread between long- and short-term yields on comparable debt securities—may be said to reflect an increasing (decreasing) subjective probability of a future rise in the interest rate. The short-dated securities provide some marginal protection from a loss in the event of a rise in the interest rate. The curve relating yields to time to maturity on comparable debt securities is, of course, the familiar yield curve. Changes in it reflect changes in anticipations, along lines reviewed in Chapters 12 and 13 of this book. It is subject to upward and downward shifts from changes in the conditions underlying possible changes, and its shape varies with the spread between long- and short-term yields.

The prospect of yield changes in response to anticipated price levels and business conditions was mentioned in Section 13.3, but the present interest is mainly in the outlook and decisions by behavioral units comprising the corporate manufacturing sector. Changes in the relevant expectations of the respective decision-making groups are viewed as responses to the same changes in the setting, including such responses as those concerning the prospect of rising prices for the output of goods and services and an enlarged flow of returns from a given capital expenditure.

To the extent that the yield spread remains constant and the level of interest rates varies a possible conventional approach to monetary policy is suggested with emphasis on the interest rate as a part of the linkages mechanism. To the extent that changing expectations about the future are introduced via the yield curve, however, an alternative approach by the monetary authorities to economic stabilization may be implied. The alternative is consistent with the use of the rate of change in the money stock as a policy variable that influences expectations about business conditions, and with the use of expected price level changes and interest rates in particular. Moreover, the notion that expectations of behavioral units in the corporate manufacturing and financial sectors are shaped by some common forces is consistent with conclusions from reviews of empirical work on the term structure of interest rates.

The changes in the yield spread are thought to be an adequate link in the influence of policy changes and to relate to planning by manufacturing corporations for interrelated reasons. The spread generally varies indirectly with the interest rate and therefore with changes in credit conditions—ease and tightness as traditionally defined. Also, changes in the long-term rate in relation to the short-term one are presently viewed as more relevant to capital expenditures than an absolute level of rates would be. Such changes readily fit into an earlier explanation of turning points in business conditions (Sec. 8.5).

The intensity of planning was introduced as a part of the analysis of changes in the liquidity structure of firms. These changes are now further discussed and related to the notion of equilibrium in investment demand. They are also related to the relatively greater independence from financial markets conditions that is achieved by some corporations through emphasis on planning. The latter is specifically related to differential patterns of reliance on bank loans by firms of different sizes and to differential patterns of capital outlays by relatively large firms, during a prolonged period of sustained growth in capital expenditures. The prospect of variable lags between the planning of expenditures in some form and actual expenditures is recognized.

Equilibrium and turning points.—One notion of equilibrium is that of a modified Keynesian investment demand model [127, pp. 193–99; 124]. The temporary equilibrium is specified by the equality of the interest rate and the rate of return on the flow of investment, after the allowance for risk premiums and liquidity elements in the respective rates. The respective rates vary directly over time, with allowance for imbalances. This allowance is somewhat fictional and more a matter of analytical convenience, as far as analysis of the effects of monetary policy is concerned. An excess of the rate of return over the interest rate simply aids in expressing a thrust in an expansionary direction.

In an expansion phase of business conditions, the temporary equilibrium shifts to give rise to an increased flow of investment; the rate of return tends to rise above the interest rate. In fact, in view of the possible response of behavioral groups in the debt instruments markets and the manufacturing sector, respectively, the point identified with the maximum probability of a future rise in interest rates is also roughly identified with a point in time at which a schedule relating the rate of return to the flow of investment begins to shift upward faster than the interest rate. The converse set of changes holds in the recession phase, and the direction of changes in the spread between short- and long-term yields indicates whether the temporary equilibrium is shifting upward or downward. Viewing a long-term yield net of a short-term one, the peak in business conditions coincides roughly with the minimum spread and the trough coincides roughly with the maximum.

Along lines introduced in Chapter 8, the probability of a change in the direction of business conditions and interest rates is a maximum at the turning points for the yield spread and business conditions. Here opinions coalesce and the slanting of probabilities applying to a given direction of change diminishes. There is a relative strengthening of pulls toward normality and the turning points occur. The normality has been variously viewed as a neutral position (Sec. 2.2) and as the equilibrium about which the economy has a tendency to overshoot (Sec. 5.4).

The liquidity of firms may be expected to vary directly with the spread between the long- and short-term rates, in view of variations in balance sheet accounts as proportions of total assets and as means of maximizing the value of firms. The maximum yield spread reflects the stronger probability of a future rise in the interest rate and therefore reflects a possibility of acquiring liquidity on relatively favorable terms through issuing bonds and using the proceeds for the purchase of non-cash liquid assets and for reducing the level of bank loans. This may be done to use the liquidity as a source of funds when future rates are higher. Acknowledging that policymaking personnel in the finance and capital budgeting areas may conceive of cyclical patterns of interest rates, rates of return, costs, and availability of funds, they could be thought of as maximizing the value of firms by building up liquidity when there is a relatively large probability of a future rise in rates. The funds could be increasingly reapportioned to plants, equipment, and inventories, as the rate of return on capital increases. On the other hand, liquidity is built up automatically from internal sources when the reverse set of prospects prevails—when rates are expected to decline as in a recession or adjustment phase of business conditions.

Viewing the spread between short- and long-term rates in conjunction with corporate liquidity and new issues of industrial bonds is related to efforts to explain the occasional buildup in corporate liquidity and the volume of new issues with reference to expectations as affected by conditions of the recent past and as reflected in the yield curve. A recurrence of the latter efforts in particular was widely evident in the financial press in the second quarter of 1967,[5] following the rather severe liquidity crisis in the late summer of 1966 [124, pp. 101–5]. Similar changes were evident during 1969 and 1970.

Liquidity, planning, and the "mature corporation."—There are shifts in liquidity—narrowly indicated by the ratio of government and similar non-cash liquid assets to bank loans—in accordance with phases of the cycle and the extent of planned capital expenditures in relation to total assets. The narrow measure of liquidity is introduced because other accounts making up the liquidity structure are thought to be relatively more stable or more mechanically determined. The cash account is viewed as relatively more stable than the principal accounts for adjusting changes in cash—government securities and bank loans. Changes in accounts receivable and accounts payable are viewed as offsets to one another or as determined primarily by purchases in the one instance and sales in the other, as well as by the terms of trade credit [124]. Changes in federal tax liabilities are thought to depend primarily on profits and the tax laws.[6] Liquidity and planned expenditures are related, and liquidity becomes a constraint with respect to expenditures over a given cyclical phase, although there is no absolute ceiling or trough to the measure of liquidity,

5. Specific references appear in Frazer [121, n. 3].

6. Miles [271] sets forth an interesting line of reasoning with respect to the effect of the speed-up of corporate tax payments (the acceleration of tax payments to a pay-as-you-go basis) in the 1960s. Emphasizing lines of credit at banks, he says, "corporations will depend on banks for lines of credit to a greater extent than in the past" and that "they must do this, or keep a larger cash balance against contingencies, for several reasons," including the greater difficulty of predicting next quarter's earnings than of predicting requirements for tax payments six to fifteen months after incurring the liability.

Miles' view may be translated to mean that, due partly to greater uncertainty, the acceleration of tax payments contributes to the need for more liquidity, primarily in terms of relatively larger amounts of non-cash liquid assets, and relatively smaller amounts of bank loans (including relatively larger unused lines of credit). Note that Miles' argument is in effect different from those emphasizing the holdings of governments as an offset of tax liabilities, although both Miles' contingency effect and the offset effect are probably working along with others.

despite its role as a constraint.[7] Large firms, however, are characterized by their greater demand for liquidity as a source of security and convenience in effecting future transactions [126, pp. 202–12].

Galbraith's characterization of the "mature corporation" and its reliance on planning would be consistent with such a view. The mature corporation—as described in the thesis on the new industrial state [162]—is related to the need to plan as a result of advanced technology and to the needs of the decision-making groups for autonomy from outside influences. A major means of achieving this and assuring independence from unforeseen developments is the planning of financing.[8]

Galbraith incorrectly emphasizes reliance on retained earnings by large firms [162, pp. 39, 168, 221], but his thesis need not depend on the outcome of a test of the retained earnings hypothesis implicit in his work.[9] Instead, planning need simply be more characteristic of the relatively large firms, as shown in this paper. The large firms plan their financing, achieve a more liquid financial structure than small firms, and achieve a degree of independence from the financial markets.

7. There may be secular shifts in liquidity of the type mentioned by Rousseas in discussing shifting ceilings to the income velocity of money [126, pp. 126–30].

8. "Advanced technology in combination with high capital requirements makes planning imperative," says Galbraith [162, p. 243] and "all planning seeks, so far as possible, to insure that what it assumes as regards the future will be what the future brings."

According to Galbraith, "no form of market uncertainty is so serious as that involving the terms and conditions on which capital is raised." He says [162, p. 39], "apart from the normal disadvantages of an uncertain price, there is danger that under certain circumstances no supply will be forthcoming at an acceptable price."

This comment on pricing may be compared with the discussions of price and quantity adjustments in Sections 5.4 and 7.2 of this book.

9. An hypothesis that retained earnings increase significantly more than in proportion to asset size is suggested by the role Galbraith attributes to retained earnings by the "mature" as distinct from the "entrepreneurial" firm. Retained earnings per firm (R), however, do not increase in such proportion. Instead, they increase roughly in proportion to assets per firm (A), as analyses of FTC–SEC data for year-end 1963 and for pooled data for the four quarters of 1963 show:

(1) $$\ln R = -2.18 + 1.03 \ln A$$
$$(0.0194)$$
$$r^2 = 0.9980$$

and

(2) $$\ln R^* = -2.15 + 1.02 \ln A^*$$
$$(0.027)$$
$$r^2 = 0.9818$$

The average coefficients of regression and determination resulting from analyzing cross-section data for the twenty quarters 1959–63, and from the FTC–SEC's *Quarterly Financial Report* (as discussed in Sec. 15.4 below) are 1.00 and 0.99, respectively.

The process of planning, implementing, and financing capital expenditures takes place against a background of cyclical and secular changes. A neutral position—about which unsustainable rates of changes occasionally occur—may be thought of for manufacturing firms as one in which all balance sheet accounts are changing at about the same rate (Sec. 2.2). This position yields exponential growth curves for capital expenditures, cash holdings, bank loans, and other forms of liabilities. Unsustainable changes occur about the implied and possible shifting growth curves. The changes about and in the slope of the implied curves represent changes in business conditions. These expand and contract in accordance with the common notion of a business cycle.

As part of the planning framework, there is a backlog of planned capital outlays for manufacturing firms, especially the larger ones accounting for most of the flow of investment. The capital budgeting process is relatively continuous, though characterized by definite seasonal dimensions—proposals are being prepared for inclusion in the capital budget, some proposals are being formalized as a part of the budget, some projects are being postponed, and capital expenditures are being made. In an early phase of expansion, the rate of change in capital expenditures may exceed that for the dollar volume of new items in the capital budget, but effecting an increase in the flow of investment does not depend on a sequence of time lags beginning with the initiation of new projects. In time a sizeable backlog of expenditures may result, but this need not necessarily mean that the level of actual investment is lagging the desired or needed level. In anticipation of an end to an unsustainable level of capital expenditures, the backlog of capital outlays may be reduced, especially in relation to asset size, and as the peak of the unsustainable level of expenditures is thought to approach, postponements increase. Indeed, if the peak is not anticipated with sufficient accuracy, some involuntary expenditures may take place. Adjustments to the excesses take place and constitute the adjustment or recession phase of a cycle.

On the financial side, planning takes place along with the planning of capital expenditures, and the developments on the financial side are complicated by additional considerations. Indeed, for a variety of reasons—including the publicity given to post–World War II patterns of changes in business conditions—the policymaking personnel of firms quite possibly conceive of changes in terms of these cyclical and growth patterns [78, p. 14] after allowance, of course, for the special role of their respective firms in such a context. In broad outline, cyclical phases may be thought of as phases in which variations in proportions of certain types of assets and liabilities occur after allowances for risk and liquidity considerations. These assets include those with a residual claim against future income such as inventories, plants, and equipment. The liabilities include accounts for debt instruments with fixed claims against future income. Increases (decreases) are sought in the latter accounts in the expansion (contraction) phases, but there are complications. As funds flow in from retained earnings and depreciation in a recession phase, they are used to achieve a preferred liquidity position—notably an increase in liquid assets and a reduction in bank loans. This buildup in liquidity becomes a source of funds for accelerating the acquisition of certain assets in the future, but the liquidity needs to be supplemented from outside sources when the large future drains on liquidity are anticipated. At such times the volume of debt instruments on the calendar of new issues increases, and proceeds from the sale of a portion of these new issues are used to build up liquidity. These proceeds are possibly identifiable with planned capital outlays. Thus, there are two classes of changes affecting liquidity—those coinciding with cyclical phases and those relating to planned capital outlays. Results from analyzing such data are examined later.

As firms increase in size, they acquire a stronger liquidity position. In the present context, this means that as manufacturing firms accelerate the flow of investment, the larger firms are more independent than are small firms of the need for bank loans over a protracted period of business expansion. As a boom progresses and its peak approaches, however, the large firms have a stronger preference for bank loans as a source of funds and as a means of reducing liquidity. The relatively smaller firms are more restrained by their weaker liquidity position. The liquidity of firms and the use of bank loans by manufacturing firms are related first to planned and then to actual capital expenditures.

Bank loans and tight credit.—The foregoing elements of theory suggest that firms' liquidity positions differ over time and on a cross-section basis with respect to size. The changes over time are related to changes in the yield spread between long- and short-term securities (as an indicator of credit conditions) and to changes in the backlog of planned capital outlays in relation to asset size. The cross-section or structural differences, in combination with the role of liquidity as a constraint on capital outlays, suggest differential effects on the capital outlays of firms. With bank loans as the denominator of the liquidity ratio being determined by changes in the yield spread, the theory suggests that the monetary officials contribute to an acceleration of the flow of bank credit in the form of loans to manufacturing firms by exerting a fairly direct influence on the relation between rates prevailing in the present and those expected to prevail in the future, rather than by exerting a relatively direct influence by simply increasing the growth of bank reserves and causing banks to seek to expand business loans. In other words, the volume of loans to manufacturing corporations is determined more by the shifting demand for bank loans than by the cost and availability of bank credit. The recognition of this source of influence is consistent with the Gibson-Kaufman statement (Sec. 13.3) that "the dominant influence on interest rates appears to come through the real sector." All of this means that certain developments are interposed between what would otherwise appear to be simple direct linkages between business expenditures and the changes in the flows of total bank credit in the form of bank loans.

The differential effects of tight credit (rising interest rates and the reduced availability of funds in relation to amount sought) have been studied before. In fact, developments during the capital boom ending with the 1957–58 recession were followed by a "high-water mark for legislation benefiting the nation's small business concerns" and by studies of the differential effects of tight credit [405; 20, pp. 52–80; 359, pp. 740–43; 21, pp. 743–45]. Bach and Huizenga noted specifically, as have others, that in the 1955–57 period commercial bank lending rose much more to large businesses than to small borrowers. They sought to explain the differential changes in terms of developments on the demand side of the market for bank loans [20, pp. 64–66, 79]: "Discrimination amongst borrowers was apparently largely on traditional banking standards of credit-worthiness and goodness of borrowers with differing changes in loans to various borrower groups reflecting primarily differences in loan demands, rather than discrimination by lenders on other grounds, once standards of credit-worthiness were met."

Analyses of balance-sheet data for manufacturing firms in the 1964–66 period also reflect the differential changes referred to by Bach and Huizenga, and they also reflect the tendency for bank loans to increase considerably less than in proportion to asset size as manufacturing firms increase in asset size [124]. This latter difference in firms' liquidity structures would appear to be consistent with the Bach-Huizenga explanation of why banks would be more willing to expand loans to larger firms under the relatively more stringent credit conditions. The differences in the liquidity of firms would provide some basis for expecting the smaller firms to encounter relatively greater difficulty in increasing bank loans under increasingly stringent credit conditions. Bach and Huizenga summarized developments suggested by their data as follows [20, p. 76]:

In summary, these data suggest that increasingly tight money during the 1955–57 period was reflected in significantly different increases of loans for different industry groups; and that especially at tight banks, as well as for the banking system as a whole, the loan expansion was greatest to those industries which were expanding most rapidly in terms of plant and equipment expenditures, inventory accumulation, and general levels of activity. Thus, broadly speaking, banks increased their loans most where the credit-worthy loans demand was greatest. This does not, of course, say that the rapidly expanding industries necessarily received the most credit *relative* to their loan demands.

The present emphasis is different from that of Bach and Huizenga; liquidity is viewed as a constraint on the capacity of firms of different asset size to effect expenditures on plants and equipment.

The theory and some survey results.—Crockett et al. reported the results of a special survey of the impact of credit or financial conditions (also referred to as "restrictive monetary measures") on business investment in 1966. They noted [78, p. 10] that "economists have generally assumed that such measures (acting through interest rates, credit availability, and perhaps directly through the money supply) have their most important impact on the demand for different types of investment and quasi-investment goods." Apparently they had in mind rather conventional notions held by economists, such that an increase in the interest rate (tighter credit conditions) has the effect of reducing expenditures, given a schedule relating the rate of return on the flow of capital expenditures to the latter flow, although Crockett et al. actually deal with deviations between anticipated and actual expenditures. They also attempted to design part of their questionnaire to get separate responses about effects in the latter context (so-called "direct effects"), independent of notions about changes in expected business conditions and the interrelationships between business and credit conditions.

Interestingly, Crockett et al. found relatively little support for the effects of tight credit on business expenditures. They encountered difficulty in getting respondents to distinguish "direct effects" from more general effects relating to changes in the general business outlook. Even in the instance where they found some effects, the effects seem to be mainly on relatively small firms which are constrained by less access to the financial markets [78, p. 18], as would be consistent with the notion about liquidity serving as a constraint on expenditures. In the instance dealing with the interdependence of credit and business conditions, Crockett et al. reported [78, p. 14] that:

Many firms indicated that financial market developments, by affecting the general business outlook, caused a reduction in investment and this presumably reflects an attempt by these firms to anticipate the resultant decline in their sales. The relatively high incidence of firms citing the changed business outlook as the basis for the financial market influence perhaps also indicates that, notwithstanding questionnaire instructions to exclude such cases, some companies attributed to financial market developments those reductions in investment resulting approximately from actual declines in sales and only indirectly from monetary stringency.

Crockett et al. reported earlier in their paper [78, Table 1] that changes in expectations about sales were the factor most frequently cited as responsible for deviations between anticipated and actual plant and equipment expenditures in 1966.

Some reductions in plant and equipment expenditures in 1966 were attributed to the impact of a rise in the interest rate as a cost factor, especially by large firms citing financial market developments as a cause of the reduction. The difficulty here is that the post–World War II secular rise in interest rates and the corresponding rise in the flow of capital outlays led to the questioning of the possible effect of any absolute interest rate level. The meaningful questions about the effect of the higher rate would seem to be: Higher rates with respect to what? With respect to rates expected to prevail in the future? Are the rates higher in relation to rates of return from discounting the streams of future returns from additions to plants and equipment?

Distinguishing factors affecting financial and investment decisions—as the Crockett et al. survey attempted—is a complicated matter. One may suggest that it is especially complicated by efforts to distinguish the effects of credit conditions from those of business conditions when in fact the two are simply different names for the same phenomenon or for very similar phenomena (Secs. 2.2, 2.3).

15.4   Data, Hypotheses, and Statistical Results

Elements of theory outlined above suggest a number of hypotheses about a variety of relationships between variables. Some of these are presented below with some results from analyses of data. Some are evaluated in terms of their consistency with others and with observations. Statistical results are examined to identify the primary balance sheet accounts for effecting adjustments in the cash account and storing temporarily idle funds for subsequent use in expenditures. One group of hypotheses—

referred to as a compound hypothesis—concerns changes in the liquidity structure of manufacturing corporations as they vary by asset size. These changes are related to an explanation of diverse flows of capital expenditures by "mature" and small manufacturing corporations. The second group of hypotheses concerns relationships between the sales-to-cash ratio and the interest rate and between liquidity and the interest rate. Theoretical elements of the preceding section are viewed in relationship to monetary policy and the demand for bank loans.

The data.—The data are discussed in greater detail elsewhere [121, Sec. IV; 124, pp. 99–101; 10, pp. 92ff.; 20, pp. 108ff.; 3, pp. 178, 195]. Those that have been analyzed include (1) the quarterly balance sheet and income statement data as reported by the Federal Trade Commission and the Securities and Exchange Commission (FTC-SEC) in their *Quarterly Financial Report for Manufacturing Corporations*; (2) quarterly capital expenditure estimates as reported by the National Industrial Conference Board (NICB) in *Investment Statistics* and expenditure data reported jointly by the Department of Commerce and the Securities and Exchange Commission; and (3) quarterly averages of marketable yields on Treasury bills, long-term government bonds, and Aaa corporate bonds, appearing in the *Federal Reserve Bulletin.*

In some analyses [126, pp. 203–13] the term "government securities" has been used generically as well as in a balance sheet account to mean essentially non-cash, marketable liquid assets. Until the reclassifications in 1964, the FTC-SEC account for "U.S. Government securities, including tax anticipation bills" included some negotiable certificates. With the rise in the importance of these certificates and other "non-cash, marketable, liquid assets" of manufacturing corporations in the 1960s, however, and with the practice of including state and local securities, commercial paper, and other marketable investments in "other current assets," the use of the balance sheet account for government securities as a generic classification has been viewed as potentially troublesome [121, Sec. IV]. To allow for the latter changes and to obtain some estimates for comparison, results from analysis of data for two sub-periods—1953–57 and 1958–63 inclusive—were reported in 1968 [121]. The first period encompasses a full cycle of activity, including the 1953–54 recession and the relatively extended 1954–57 capital boom. Economic developments in 1958–63 are less distinct. The expansion in business conditions in 1958–60 was relatively unpronounced, and the recovery following the mild 1960–61 recession was relatively slow through 1963. The differences in these periods should be reflected in the statistical results for the respective periods. The analyses of time-series data on capital outlays that are reported for 1953–63 are extended to encompass the capital booms of the mid- to late 1960s in the Appendix to Chapter 15. There housing expenditures are also considered and the Almon technique is used.

In addition to the emphasis on periods and sub-periods, time-series data have been arranged for analysis in several sets, as reported in this chapter. One includes all manufacturing corporations, another includes all manufacturing corporations with assets of 10 million dollars and over, and the third includes six industry groups—chemical products, paper products, electrical machinery, primary metals, transportation equipment, and motor vehicles. Firms with assets of 10 million dollars and over are treated separately because they account for a major portion of assets held by all manufacturing corporations [162, pp. 74–76], and because as firms increase beyond this size they appear to increase trading in marketable securities and to effect an increasing turnover of cash balances as indicated by sales-to-cash ratios [126, pp. 202–13]. The industry groups are considered to obtain a more detailed breakdown of results, but also because NICB data for the backlog of capital expenditures by the thousand largest manufacturing corporations appear by industry rather than by asset size groups. These particular industry groups, however, were selected because of the continuity of estimates and because of the relatively large size of the average firm for each of the groups [126, pp. 206–7].

These data are adequate for present purposes. There are errors in the data, no doubt, and variations in the quality of series for selected accounts. The present emphasis is on relatively large differences in results and repetitive patterns, which are probably not attributable to errors in the data.

Liquidity structure and capital expenditures.—The theoretical elements regarding the liquidity structure of firms suggest a compound hypothesis: first, money balances (M) increase less than in proportion to asset size (A); and second, liquidity—defined as the ratio of government securities to bank loans (G/B)—increases as bank loans (B) increase less than in proportion and government securities (G) more than in proportion to asset size (A). The maximum spread between long- and short-term interest rates is said (1) to coincide with the prospect of improved flows of returns from additional capital expenditures and (2) to relate to a buildup in liquidity as a future source of funds for effecting the expenditures. As prospects begin to change in relation to prevailing credit conditions, the liquidity becomes a constraint on expenditures.

To test this hypothesis and evaluate the possible effect of liquidity as a constraint on expenditures, cross-section data have been analyzed and time series have been examined for capital expenditures by large manufacturing corporations as percentages of capital expenditures by all manufacturing firms. Representative results from the cross-section data are: [10]

$$\ln M = -1.2255 + 0.8744 \ln A \qquad r^2 = 0.9991$$
$$(0.013)$$

$$\ln B = -1.6895 + 0.7148 \ln A \qquad r^2 = 0.9941$$
$$(0.086)$$

$$\ln G = -1.8427 + 1.1007 \ln A \qquad r^2 = 0.9747$$
$$(0.086)$$

These results are from data for the fourth quarter of 1963.[11] They are consistent with the compound hypothesis. The asset-size coefficients for

10. To indicate the representative character of these results, ratios of the respective regression and determination coefficients to the corresponding averages for 1959–63 were computed. They are: $0.87/0.87 = 1$ and $1.00/1.00 = 1.00$ for cash per firm; $1.10/1.11 = 0.99$ and $0.97/0.98 = 0.99$ for government securities per firm; and $0.71/0.73 = 0.97$ and $0.99/0.97 = 1.02$ for bank loans.

11. Illustrative diagrams for the bank loans and the governments appear as [121, Figure 1]:

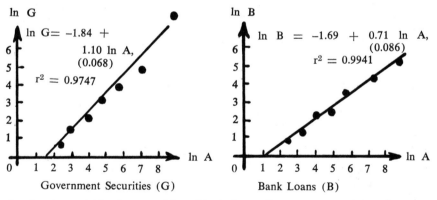

Government Securities (G)   Bank Loans (B)

Ln denotes variables in natural logarithmic form. Constants are added in the construction of the illustrations, however, to adjust for the presence of negative numbers resulting from the use of logarithms. The raw data are in millions of dollars and the logarithm of an amount less than one million yields a negative number.

Also, the raw data are converted to a per-firm basis. The results reported are from regression analyses of data for firms with assets over 5 million dollars. The data are those reported in the FTC–SEC's *Quarterly Financial Report for Manufacturing Corporations*.

money and bank loans are significantly less than one, and that for governments is significantly greater than one.[12]

Additional results for industry groups are also consistent with the compound hypothesis:

$$\ln M = 2.42 + \underset{(0.047)}{0.85 \ln A} \qquad r^2 = 0.9482$$

$$\ln B = 1.29 + \underset{(0.070)}{0.76 \ln A} \qquad r^2 = 0.8666$$

$$\ln G = 1.28 + \underset{(0.139)}{1.08 \ln A} \qquad r^2 = 0.7709$$

Once again, the results are from data for the fourth quarter of 1963.[13] The scatter of observations underlying these equations is greater than that for the earlier asset-size groupings, as indicated by the lower r^2s. This is probably due partly to the diversity of firm sizes in some industry groups.

12. As noted in the subsection on the data, the term "government securities" has been used in a generic sense to mean government securities and similar non-cash liquid assets. However, some other marketable securities have been included in the FTC–SEC account entitled "other current assets," and these have increased in importance in the liquid asset portfolios of manufacturing corporations. Even so, the introduction of "other current assets" into the analysis does not alter conclusions or results. "Other current assets" like "government securities" increase significantly more than in proportion to asset size. Results are shown elsewhere [121, p. 98].

13. Illustrative diagrams for the bank loans and the governments appear as [121, Figure 2]:

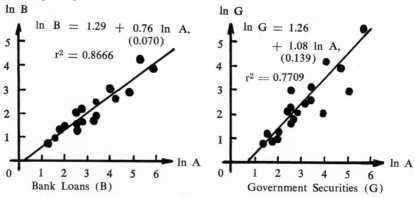

Bank Loans (B)   Government Securities (G)

Ln denotes a natural logarithm. Constants are added in the construction of the illustrations to adjust for the presence of negative numbers resulting from the use of logarithms. In any given parts of the illustrations the same constants are added

Increasing the number of observations by pooling data for four quarters does not weaken the fits for the relationships [121, n. 12].

The evidence of the predicted differential effects on capital expenditures is shown in Figure 15-1. The percentages there behave as posited for the extended capital booms ending in 1957, 1966, and 1969, respectively. Other explanations of the rise in the percentage of capital expenditures by the large concerns, as shown in Figure 15-1 for the 1955–57 capital boom, were given by Shirley Almon in her classical paper on distributed lags [3, p. 195]: "The explanation could be either that it was they who wanted to spend at the time, or that capital goods producers allocated scarce output to their larger customers."

Neither of the above explanations by Almon is consistent with the explanation given in this book. The latter of Almon's two possible explanations is inconsistent with some of the results in a special survey on business investment in 1966. Crockett et al. [78, p. 12 and Table 2] have reported on the basis of such a survey that "the net reduction in expenditures (decreases less increases) attributable to the capital goods supply situation was relatively more important for the largest firms." In fact, timing of deliveries and/or construction progress was cited 63.7 per cent of the time by nonfinancial firms with 50 million dollars and over in assets—as compared with 47.8 per cent for all firms, 12.5 for firms with assets under 1 million, and 26.1 for firms with assets of from 1 to 10 million—as the principal factor responsible for deviations between anticipated and actual plant and equipment expenditures in 1966.

Cash adjustments and variations in liquidity.—Theoretical elements in Section 15.3 recognize the role of cash in making payments and the prospect of effecting adjustments in the desired cash level primarily through changes in government securities and bank loans. Excess money balances may be temporarily employed in the purchase of non-cash liquid assets and the repayment of bank loans, and needed balances may be obtained for the individual firms from the sale of marketable assets or from bank loans. The latter accounts are considered the major means of effecting cash adjustments and storing temporarily idle funds. Other ac-

---

to intercept parameters to facilitate comparisons. A constant of two is added to the variable ln A in both instances.

The raw industry-group data are adjusted to a per-firm basis. The industry-group data are those reported in the FTC–SEC's *Quarterly Financial Report for Manufacturing Corporations*. To convert the data for 20 industry groups to a per-firm basis, however, Treasury Department estimates of the number of firms per industry groups were used (see U.S. Treasury's *Statistics of Income*).

FIGURE 15–1

Capital Expenditures by Large (and Large Durable Goods)
Manufacturing Firms as Percentages of Capital
Expenditures by all (and all Durable Goods)
Manufacturing Firms, during
Postwar Capital Booms

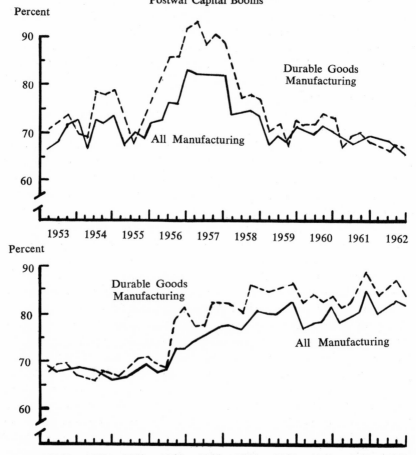

The percentages are computed from NICB estimates of expenditures by the
thousand largest manufacturing corporations (durable goods manufacturing corporations among them) and from Commerce-SEC estimates of expenditures by all
manufacturing firms (durable goods manufacturing firms among them). A similar
figure appeared in a 1968 Congressional Compendium. See "Statement by William J.
Frazer, Jr.," *Compendium on Monetary Policy Guidelines and Federal Reserve
Structure*, Subcommittee on Domestic Finance of the Committee on Banking and
Currency, House of Representatives (Washington, D. C.: U.S. Government Printing
Office, 1968), p. 195.

counts affecting the liquidity structure of firms are more mechanically determined: accounts payable depend primarily on the volume of purchases and on practices with respect to their repayment; federal tax liabilities depend primarily on corporate profits, rates of taxation, and the degree of acceleration of tax payments. Thus, viewing broadly the ratio of cash plus government securities to total current liabilities (L_3) as a liquidity measure and more narrowly the ratio of government securities to bank loans (L_1), one might examine the per cent variation in the broader measure that is accounted for by variation in the narrower measure. One might also consider statistical results concerning other measures—cash plus government securities to bank loans (L_2), government securities plus other current assets to bank loans (L_{1*}), and cash plus government securities plus other current assets to bank loans (L_{2*}).

Results from regressing the broader measure of liquidity on the narrower measure for all manufacturing firms indicate that the latter accounts for 84 per cent of the variation of the former for the 1953–66 period when the regression is linear, and 86 per cent when it is linear in the logarithms. For example, in the latter instance,

$$\ln L_3 = -0.63 + 0.59 \ln L_1 \qquad r^2 = 0.86$$
$$(0.01825)$$

Adding other current assets to the numerator of L_1 to get L_1* and regressing the latter on the former indicates that 75 and 63 per cent of variation is accounted for before and after logarithmic transformation of data. Adding money balances to the numerator of L_1 to get L_2 and regressing the broader L_3 measure on L_2 indicates that only nominal additional variation in the broader measure is accounted for by adding money balances. For the overall 1953–66 period, for example,

$$L_3 = 0.18 + 0.15 L_2 \qquad r^2 = 0.88$$
$$(0.00809)$$

$$\ln L_3 = -1.24 + 0.73 \ln L_2 \qquad r^2 = 0.89$$
$$(0.0357)$$

The use of seasonally adjusted data does not alter the results appreciably.[14] The results for the overall 1953–66 period reflect overwhelming support

14. Where seasonal adjustments in the data are noted and have not been available for the data in published form, a simple four-quarter moving average is used to adjust the data. As a result three observations are lost from adjusted series—for example seasonally adjusted data for the 1953–66 period run from the second quarter of 1953 to the second quarter of 1966 inclusive.

for the importance of government security holdings and the account for bank loans as means of effecting adjustments in the cash account and as means of building up liquidity.

Viewing such results for manufacturing corporations with assets over 10 million dollars and for six combined industry groups does not alter the latter conclusion. Results for the 1953–57 sub-period also support the conclusions, but a comparison of the 1953–57 results with those for the less ideal 1958–63 period reflects some differences.

Switching phenomena, interest rates, and rates of change.—Theoretical elements in Section 15.3 anticipate still further sets of changes. These are changes in balance sheet accounts as proportions of total assets or sales as interest rates vary, and the changes in proportions are analogous to differential rates of change in time series. In very broad outline, there is the prospect of decreases in fixed claim assets, such as money and government bonds, and of increases in fixed claim bank loans, all in relation to total assets or sales as interest rates rise. The reverse sets of shifts occur as interest rates decline, and the forward and reverse shifts lead to certain hypotheses: (1) the ratio of sales to cash (S/M) varies directly with the interest rate; (2) the ratio of sales to government securities (S/G) varies directly with the interest rate; and (3) the ratio of government securities to bank loans (L_1) varies inversely with the interest rate. A relatively weak relationship is expected in the latter instance, however, because the backlog of planned capital outlays is also viewed as a determinant of liquidity narrowly defined.

The foregoing prospects are well supported by results from analyses of data. For the overall 1953–66 period, such results as the following [15] are obtained for all manufacturing corporations:

unadjusted

$$\ln \frac{S}{M} = 0.43 + \underset{(0.065)}{0.95 \ln r} \qquad r^2 = 0.81$$

$$\ln \frac{S}{G} = 0.37 + \underset{(0.1455)}{1.20 \ln r} \qquad r^2 = 0.58$$

$$\ln L_1 = 2.05 - \underset{(0.186)}{1.55 \ln r} \qquad r^2 = 0.59$$

15. Equations of this simple two variable form, of course, may be written in multivariate form by taking logarithms of the ratios as quotients rather than as decimal fractions and by rearranging terms. Regression results for such equations

seasonally adjusted

$$\ln \frac{S}{M} = 0.41 + 0.96 \ln r \qquad r^2 = 0.85$$
$$(0.0578)$$

$$\ln \frac{S}{G} = 0.31 + 1.24 \ln r \qquad r^2 = 0.60$$
$$(0.1429)$$

$$\ln L_1 = 2.83 - 0.46 \ln r \qquad r^2 = 0.64$$
$$(0.1755)$$

As interest rates (r) rise, cash (M) and government (G) increase less than in proportion to sales (S), and liquidity (L_1) declines. There is even indication that the decline in government securities is more than that in cash.

The latter changes certainly suggest a decline in non-cash liquid assets in relation to sales and possibly even in relation to money balances as interest rates rise. Such a decline is evident for the critical group of large firms during the 1953–57 period:

$$\ln \frac{M}{G} = -0.60 + 0.49 \ln r \qquad r^2 = 0.26$$
$$(0.1982)$$

But for the same groups of firms in the less distinct 1958–63 period, the sign of the regression coefficient changes:

$$\ln \frac{M}{G} = 2.20 - 1.52 \ln r \qquad r^2 = 0.26$$
$$(0.2858)$$

And, when other current assets (O) are added to government securities because of a possible rise in the importance of marketable bond assets in that account during the 1958–63 period, the result is

$$\ln \frac{M}{G+O} = 2.56 - 2.05 \ln r \qquad r^2 = 0.63$$
$$(0.3456)$$

However, there are determinants of government securities in addition to money balances (M), as called for by the theory. These would include such factors as asset size (A), the backlog of planned capital expenditures (K_p), bank loans (B), and spread between yields on short- and long-term

---

for some of the ratios and for the strategic group of manufacturing firms with assets of 10 million dollars and over are reported elsewhere [121, n. 14].

government bonds ($r_L - r_S$). In fact, even for the relatively nondescript 1958–63 period, the latter variables account for 71 per cent of the variation in government security holdings by six combined industry groups, after a logarithmic transformation of the data. For six combined industry groups for which planned expenditures data are available, the result is:

$$\ln G = -5.07 + 1.51 \ln A - 0.06 \ln M +$$
$$(0.6128) (0.0467)$$

$$0.44 \ln K_p - 0.78 \ln B - 0.12 \ln (r_L - r_S)$$
$$(0.279) (0.5584) (0.0909)$$

$$R^2 = 0.71$$

Now changes in cash, government securities, and so on, in relation to sales or assets imply differential rates of changes in the respective series over time. A decline in cash in relation to sales or assets, for example, implies an increase in the rate of change in the sales or total assets variables in excess of the rate of change in the cash balances. In the present analysis, moreover, one is especially aided by the additional constraint of the balance sheet identity. The identity implies some amount of additional logic in dealing with numbers, and differential rates of change in, say, total current assets and total assets imply a differential rate of change in non-current assets. In other words, analyses of the liquidity structure of firms imply information about inventories and capital investment even though data for the latter are not explicitly analyzed. In these instances one could analyze time series data in the form of rates of change and examine broad averages of rates of changes for various series over time. Results are presented for the latter because postulated "causal" relationships between such variables should be the same over the cycle and as a secular matter.

The following are average growth rates (per annum) for the select group of corporations with 10 million dollars and over, for sales (S), total assets (A), and selected accounts, along with the equations defining exponential growth curves for the 1953–66 period from which the growth rates are derived:

$$S = (41,110) \ (1.058)^t, \ r^2 = 0.94$$
avg. growth rate = 5.8 per cent

$$M = (9,638) \ (1.022)^t, \ r^2 = 0.45$$
avg. growth rate = 2.2 per cent

$$G = (10{,}920) \ (0.993)^t, \ r^2 = 0.04$$
avg. growth rate $= -0.7$ per cent

$$B = (5{,}630) \ (1.059)^t, \ r^2 = 0.71$$
avg. growth rate $= 5.9$ per cent

$$A_c = (66{,}760) \ (1.059)^t, \ r^2 = 0.98$$
avg. growth rate $= 5.9$ per cent

$$G+O = (11{,}500) \ (1.041)^t, \ r^2 = 0.70$$
avg. growth rate $= 4.1$ per cent

$$A = (122{,}700) \ (1.068)^t, \ r^2 = 0.99$$
avg. growth rate $= 6.8$ per cent

The selected accounts are cash (M), government securities (G), bank loans (B), total current assets (A_c), and government securities plus "other current assets" (G+O). As the preceding growth rates show, sales, bank loans, total current assets, and total assets experienced high growth rates—5.8, 5.9, 5.9, and 6.8 per cent respectively—while cash balances and government securities experienced relatively lower rates of 2.2 and —0.7 per cent. Aaa corporate bond yields increased by about 62 per cent, from an average of 3.29 in the second quarter of 1953 to 5.32 in the second quarter of 1966. This information on trends reveals a broad pattern of rapid growth in inventories, plants, and equipment; rising interest rates and sales-to-cash ratios; declines in cash and non-cash liquid assets in relation to total assets or sales; and a rise in bank loans as a proportion of total assets.

This pattern of secular changes is what the theoretical elements of Section 15.3 would lead one to expect. It is consistent with the various explanations of post-World War II phenomena that are inherent in the theoretical elements. It implies that exogenous factors—such as accelerated depreciation, the tax credit, and especially those forces giving rise to greater certainty about the future—are major causes of the rise in sales-to-cash ratios and the rapid expansion of capital in the 1953–66 period. Apparently the distinction between accounts for cash and instruments with a fixed dollar claim against future income and those with a residual claim such as noncurrent assets is meaningful and useful. This would also be true of the idea that exogenous factors impinge on prospects and contribute to the switching from (to) cash and government securities into (out of) noncurrent assets in relation to total assets and to the related increment (decrement) in bank loans in relation to total assets.

Bank loans, "causal" relationships, and monetary policy.—The foregoing results are inconsistent with two broad and traditionally held notions: one whereby the rise in the interest rate contributes to a rise in
velocity (or the sales-to-cash ratio in the present instance) by causing
switching from money balances to non-cash liquid assets, as discussed in
Section 4.2; and another whereby a decline (rise) in the interest rate
"causes" the flow of investment to rise (decline), possibly after some lag,
with monetary authorities controlling the rate in a fairly direct way, also
as discussed earlier(Secs. 4.2, 7.4). Instead of the latter, there is an
abrupt break in any presumed close link between bank lending and business expenditures, and the effects of credit and money stock changes on
expenditures and thence on the demand for bank loans are indirect. The
break is most clearly indicated by the rise in the ratio of non-cash liquid
asset holdings to bank loans as firms increase in asset size. The ratio
varies as differential changes occur in the prospective flows of returns
from the broad classes of assets and as funds are temporarily set aside
for future expenditures.

Changes in monetary policy may be viewed as operating through expectations—as through the spread between long- and short-term interest
rates. There a maximum spread for a given cycle indicates an enlarged
flow of prospective returns on residual as distinct from fixed claim assets.
This creates a buildup in planned capital expenditures and liquidity. The
prospects and actions of the decision-makers with respect to capital expenditures do not directly relate to the expectations of participants in the
financial markets, as is implied by changes in the shape of the yield curve
and indicated by the spread in yields, but the two sets of expectations are
responses to the same factors or changes in the setting. The changes in
the outlook of the decision-makers of the manufacturing corporations,
however, are reflected directly in changes in sales-to-cash ratios, and the
latter's parallel movements with interest rates introduce some dynamics.
These suggest that accelerated growth in the money stock contributes at
such times to further increases in interest rates, the velocity of money
(sales-to-cash ratios), and capital spending. The accelerated growth in
bank credit and money stock has possible effects on expectations, and
the extra growth of money acts to maintain the imbalance between desired
and actual money stock in relation to the velocity increases.

Thus, as elements of theory from Section 15.3 suggest, monetary policy
changes operating via switching phenomena and financial planning determine liquidity (narrowly defined) as

(1.1) $\qquad L_1 = f(i_L - i_S, K_p, A)$

where L_1 is the ratio of non-cash liquid assets to bank loans, $i_L - i_S$ is the yield spread, K_p is the backlog of planned capital outlays, and A is asset size. With respect to relation (1.1),

$$(2.1) \qquad L_1 = k(i_L - i_S)^\alpha \left\{ \begin{array}{c} \text{planned} \\ \text{capital} \\ \text{outlays} \end{array} \right\} \beta \left\{ \begin{array}{c} \dfrac{1}{\text{total}} \\ \text{assets} \end{array} \right\} \gamma$$

Taking the logarithm of both sides of equation (2.1) and rearranging terms gives

$$(2.2)\ \ln\ (\text{bank loans}) = k + \alpha \ln\ (i_L - i_S) + \beta \ln \left\{ \begin{array}{c} \text{planned} \\ \text{capital} \\ \text{outlays} \end{array} \right\} -$$

$$\gamma \ln\ (\text{total assets}) -\rho \ln \left\{ \begin{array}{c} \text{non-cash} \\ \text{liquid} \\ \text{assets} \end{array} \right\}$$

Equation (2.2) relates bank loans to some of their determinants. However, theory does not lead us to expect the variables on the right side of the equation to enter regularly or continuously over time or from period to period. Asset-size and industry groups differ with respect to liquidity and emphasis on the planning and financing of capital and other outlays. Thus the time lags between the acquisition of funds for capital expenditures and the expenditures themselves vary for asset-size and industry groups. The duration of an expansion phase of business activity further contributes to differential patterns of capital expenditures by firms of various sizes and partly determines whether some variables enter at all or enter more or less than others in accounting for variations in bank loans.

As a consequence of the foregoing differential patterns and time lags, regression equations resulting from an analysis of quarterly data for the variables in equation (2.2) would reveal different regression coefficients for different periods or for industry groups with different liquidity structures. Some results along this line have been shown [121, p. 93]. Table 15-2 presents some coefficients of multiple determination (R^2s) from analyses of data for selected industry groups. Apparently some variables enter to "explain" variation in bank loans at one time and others do so at another time, so a fairly large percentage of variation is "explained."

Some Explained Variation: Equation (2.2)
(results from seasonally adjusted data)

Industry Group	Period	R^2
Six combined*	1953–66	0.92
	1953–57	0.85
Chemical and	1953–66	0.94
allied products	1953–57	0.94
Paper and	1953–66	0.93
allied products	1953–57	0.84
Electrical	1953–66	0.98
Machinery	1953–57	0.96

*The six industry groups include primary metals, transportation equipment, and motor vehicles in addition to the industries shown in the table.

Source of data: Federal Trade Commission and Securities and Exchange Commission, *Quarterly Financial Report for Manufacturing Corporations*; National Industrial Conference Board, *Investment Statistics*; and the *Federal Reserve Bulletin*.

Source of results: William J. Frazer, Jr., "Monetary Policy, Business Loans by Banks and Capital Outlays by Manufacturing Corporations," *Southern Journal of Business*, April 1968, p. 93.

15.5 SUMMARY

Assets may be viewed in broad classes—those with a fixed or contractual claim against future income and those with a residual claim. They have varying degrees of liquidity, a variety of factors may affect the respective classes differently, and assets of some behavioral units are liabilities of others. In one instance cash is highly liquid and is a means of coping with future uncertainties, such that greater certainty about the future may reduce the need for cash and strengthen the preference for, say, plants and equipment. In another instance, prospective changes in the price level adversely affect the purchasing power of cash and fixed claim assets and consequently contribute to a rise in interest rates and increases in the prospective returns from given outlays on plants and equipment. Factors such as a tax credit by the government for capital expenditures affect the relative rates of return from diverse classes of assets and the returns from capital expenditures, without necessarily altering the returns from cash and near-cash assets in the form of convenience and security. At times, some combination of the preceding factors may operate to contribute to differential growth rates for the various classes of assets and therefore to shifts in the various assets as proportions of total assets. The factors contributing to an acceleration of the flow of expenditures on inventories, plants, and equipment contribute to an expansion in business activity, in relation to some sustainable or stable level of activity.

The differential rates of change and shifts in response to factors, however, are complicated by the planning of expenditures and the planning of financing as the pattern of changing business conditions develops and as it is expected to develop. Anticipating an expansion—especially a relatively sustained expansion—liquidity may be built up beyond the level resulting from the flow of internal funds and the deceleration of growth in expenditures during a period of declining business activity. It may then serve as an additional source of future funds for carrying out planned capital outlays. Firms differ, however, in the intensity of their emphasis on planning as they vary in asset size.

Liquidity is related to some measure of cyclical change such as the spread between yields on long- and short-term securities and to the ratio of planned capital outlays to total assets. The measure of liquidity that is presently emphasized is narrow. Cash and other accounts reflect liquidity, but changes in non-cash liquid assets and in bank loans—both in relation to asset size—are the major means of effecting adjustments in the cash account, storing temporarily idle funds, and building up liquidity. As firms increase in size, the intensity of the emphasis on planning and liquidity increases. Planning, as outlined, involves the planning of capital expenditures and the planning of financing.

The planning of particular expenditures, as in the case of the formal introduction of plans in the capital budget, always leads the actual expenditure, and at times the planning may not adequately anticipate the need for new capital, but a series for capital expenditures need not always lag behind a comparable series for planned capital expenditures, especially by any fixed lag as some have suggested. Actual expenditures may be effected by drawing down on the backlog of planned expenditures so that at a lower turning point in business conditions there may be no lag in the series for actual expenditures. Moreover, actual expenditures may at times—for example, approaching an upper turning point in business conditions—exceed the need for new capital, so again there is no economically significant lag sequence with a fixed time dimension.

Causal sequences proceeding from changes in the absolute level of interest rates to capital expenditures do not appear to exist in the preceding framework. Instead, there is the possibility of direct but differential variation in the interest rate and a schedule relating the rate of return on the flow of investment to the flow of investment. The same sets of factors give rise to the prospect of profitable business, and investment conditions give rise to the prospect of rising interest rates and the sales-to-cash ratio. In the present framework, then, monetary policy influences capital expenditures through the relationship between the interest rate prevailing in the present and the probability of a future rise or fall, where the latter is also an indicator of the acceleration or deceleration of the growth of returns on capital outlays. Movements toward the maximum spread between the long- and short-term interest rate over a given cycle reflect an increasing probability of a future rise in rates, and movements toward the minimum spread over a cycle reflect the reverse.

Movements toward the extremes in the yield spread set the stage for the ensuing developments. In the case of the movement from the minimum to the maximum spread there is a buildup in liquidity, which is subsequently affected by the intensity of the prospect of a future rise in the rates. Firms differ in their liquidity structure, however, and liquidity subsequently becomes a constraint on capital expenditures with differential effects reflected in the pattern of the capital expenditures of large manufacturing firms in relation to those by all firms. Since liquidity is defined as the ratio of non-cash liquid assets to bank loans, and since it is related to the yield spread and the ratio of planned capital outlays to total assets, the demand for bank loans may be shown to depend on the yield spread, holdings of non-cash liquid assets, planned capital outlays, and asset size. In other words, the demand for bank loans is determined more from the demand than the supply side of the market for bank credit.

Monetary policy is implemented through changes in the rates of change in bank credit and the money stock. Even so, changes in policy are presently viewed as indicated by changes in the yield spread. The changes in the rates of change in bank credit and the money stock have their effect on the yield spread—as well as on the planning and financing of capital expenditures—via changing expectations about prices, interest rates, and the profitability of capital investment. Increasing rates of change in bank credit and the money stock have their effect on interest rates via the latter routes, and they contribute to the stronger prospect of rising interest rates and tight credit conditions rather than to lower rates, easier credit conditions, and—via a causal sequence—increases in capital expenditures.

Part VI

Rules Versus Discretion

16

Rules Versus Discretion
An Introduction

16.1 INTRODUCTION

WITH THE ADDITION of the "proviso" clause of the FOMC directive in mid-1966 (Sec. 2.1), with the arrival of Burns as Chairman of the Board of Governors in early 1970 (Sec. 1.1), and with the succeeding ascendency of aggregates for bank credit, the money stock, and bank reserves in the FOMC directive (Sec. 2.1), one might recognize some impact of the work of monetarists (Secs. 3.1, 3.2), especially in conjunction with the impact of the modern computer. Furthermore, many rules advocates— as discussed in this and the succeeding chapter—have tended to be monetarists, so in turn one might concede some partial success for the rules advocates' cause too. In the light of such success, their cause may be a vanishing one. Whatever the case, the controversy over the imposition of a fixed rule rather than discretion in the management of money has been historically important. The controversy possibly achieved its greatest visibility in the 1960s as the monetarists pushed their charges against the banking view of the workings of monetary policy (Sec. 3.4) and the closely related emphasis on discretion. This chapter introduces the controversy over rules, as at least a tangential aspect of the developments in the 1960s.

The long history of rules to eliminate administrative discretion in the management of money is introduced below (Sec. 16.2). The discussions of the 1960s, however, had their immediate roots in discussion initiated almost simultaneously by Edward S. Shaw [332][1] and Milton Friedman [139] in the late 1950s, and in what has come to be called Friedman's

---

1. A version of the essay by Shaw also appears in the revised volume edited by Jacoby [208, pp. 73–93].

fixed rule. They proposed that the money supply should grow at a fixed rate per annum, roughly the rate of growth in the full employment level of output at constant prices (Sec. 2.4). Friedman's estimate for this growth rate has varied between 3 and 5 percent and with reference to narrow and broad definitions of money (those without and with time deposits included). In the late 1960s he referred to this rule as the 5 percent rule to distinguish it from his 2 percent rule (Ch. 1, n. 18).

A central idea surrounding the 5 percent rule is that stabilizing the growth rate of the money stock is preferable to discretionary monetary management, regardless of what the rate is. As rules proponents argue (an example is mentioned in the next chapter) the rate is not fixed for all times and it may be reviewed and revised.

Other central ideas are: (1) the lags in the effects of monetary policy are so long and variable that policy cannot adequately offset or reinforce relatively unpredictable economic developments (given the status and accuracy of forecasts); (2) positive economic benefits would accrue from the greater certainties surrounding the fixed rule, given the unpredictable and erratic variability of monetary policy (as in the period leading up to congressional interest in monetary rules and guidelines in 1968 [395, 396], when the rate of change in the money stock was reported by Beryl Sprinkel as varying between —2 and +11 per cent); and (3) one may advocate a fixed rule for the same reason one buys insurance, even though the fixed rule performs no better than ordinary authorities (one pays a premium for the rule, but there is insurance against major mistakes by the discretionary authorities).

Friedman's 2 percent rule is offered to provide the optimum money stock. Its foundations concern long-run analysis, in contrast to that underlying the 5 percent rule. The analysis as advanced by Friedman is stated elsewhere [138, pp. 1–50]. For the present, two points are simply noted: (1) in accord with much professional opinion, the 5 percent rule implies that a stable level of prices for final production is a desirable policy objective; and (2) the 2 percent rule implies the desirability of a declining price level. With respect to the alternative rules, Friedman concludes [138, p. 48] that "The gain from shifting to the 5 percent rule would, I believe, dwarf the further gain from going to the 2 percent rule, even though that gain may well be substantial enough to be worth pursuing." The 5 percent rule would not eliminate all of the variation in the growth rate for the output of goods and services, with consequent variation in the income velocity of money, since the variation in velocity would reflect the variation in the growth of income, given the constant growth rate for the stock of money. Friedman and other proponents do not maintain that the rule would eliminate all of the variation in velocity. Some maintain that the rule should be modified to allow for major changes in velocity (or the "estimated growth rate of monetary velocity"). For example, as emphasized in several previous chapters, the post–World War II trend in velocity has been upward, and the forecast of such a trend would presumably lead to a revision downward in the growth rate for the money stock. Bronfenbrenner has broadened the rules proposal to allow for such changes [37, pp. 173–92; 36, pp. 98–100]. Congressman Ruess has also mentioned adjustments in the growth rate for the money stock to allow, for example, for "the extent to which time deposits in commercial banks, and in savings and loan associations, mutual savings banks, and credit unions, substitute for the narrowly defined money supply"; "the extent necessary to reflect the increase in dollar gross national product estimated to be attributable to cost-push inflation"; and balance of payments considerations. Modifications in the fixed rule to allow for changes in velocity and other such factors make the rule more realistic, more relevant to the real world. At the same time they open up rules proposals to the apparently unresolved controversies over the determinants of changes in velocity (as outlined in Chapter 4).

At one time the simple rules proposals seemed to require such modifications to make them more acceptable. In the second half of the 1960s, however, interest in the monetary rules extended even to certain congressional committees [395, 396]. At that time interest in a rules proposal swung toward keeping the rule simple, revising it on occasion, and stating a range within which the money stock may vary, partly to allow for errors by the Federal Reserve in achieving a target value for the money stock on a quarter-by-quarter basis.

Some mechanics and related changes underlying modification of the simple rule proposal are brought forward in Section 16.3. In particular, the adoption of a fixed rule is thought to restrict the role of Federal Reserve policy in dealing with balance of payments disequilibria—discussion of foreign exchange rates often accompanies discussions of monetary rules. Thus, Section 16.4 is devoted to the rules proposal, exchange rates, and the balance of payments objectives of the monetary officials. Chapter 17 contains an outline of two sorts of evidence concerning rules proposals (the opinions of those who have a most immediate interest in such proposals, and tests concerned with whether rules are superior to discretionary policy) and the views of some leading participants in the rules controversy.

The basic ideas of this chapter are: (1) some notions concerning reliance on rules as distinct from discretion have always been present in
discussion surrounding the Federal Reserve; (2) the rules proponents
gained support and practical interest in rules during the 1960s; (3) the
proposal of a range, such as 2 to 5 percent, for limiting changes in the
rate of change in the money stock had the most support and avoids some
of the objections and difficulties concerning fixed rules; and (4) analysis,
empirical evidence, and discussion supporting the need to limit variations
in the rate of change in the money stock and the need to explain extreme
variations may bring about such limited variations and explanations
without the formal adoption of a fixed rule or upper and lower limits on
changes in the rate of change in the stock of money.

16.2   AN HISTORICAL PERSPECTIVE [2]

The history of rules to eliminate administrative discretion in the management of money may be seen as being broadly based in doctrine generally opposing the centralization of power. The original Federal Reserve
Act and the notions surrounding it provide one such example. The system
was to operate automatically according to certain rules and related notions with the view to expanding bank credit (and presumably money)
to satisfy the needs of trade (and presumably income). The monetary
policy function of the system, such as it was, was decentralized. The rules
and the automatic functioning of the system centered about the "real
bills" doctrine, the gold-flows mechanism, and a simple quantity theory
of money. The only credit control instrument at the system's disposal in
the early years was the discount rate, or more generally the discount
mechanism, and changes in the rate were initiated at the regional bank
level, as they are today, with the approval of the Board. The system was
to be a "lender of last resort" and provide additional liquidity to commercial paper originating at the commercial banks as they extended credit.
This was done by the discounting of commercial paper ("real bills") or
by advancing credit in a properly secured form. The paper was real in
the sense that the credit originated in the extension of loans for the purchase of goods in shipment and inventories.

On a temporary basis, as in the case of a seasonal defense against
crisis, the Federal Reserve could serve as lender to the commercial banks

---

2. This section was originally published in a 1968 Congressional Compendium.
See "Statement of William J. Frazer, Jr." [395, Sec. IV].

and therefore satisfy a temporary need for credit and possibly avert the sort of recurring financial crisis of the pre–Federal Reserve (pre–1913) era. Moreover, a properly functioning gold-standard mechanism could serve as an overall regulator, both of the Federal Reserve System and of the growth of bank credit (and, therefore, the money supply). As trade, credit, and the money supply expanded excessively, the price level would rise in relation to price levels abroad and set in motion an outflow of gold. The latter would serve to constrain the growth of bank reserves and the money supply (and thus the level of prices, via the simple quantity theory of money). A decline in the domestic price level in relation to foreign price levels would have the reverse effects. All the Federal Reserve had to do was to adhere to the rules. There was little room for discretion. All was to work automatically. Economic stability was to be achieved, since it was thought to result from the malfunctioning of the financial system. In Keynes' work and later in the 1960s, economists came to emphasize the interrelationships between money and the financial and real good sectors in analyzing cyclical and other changes in output, employment, and prices.

Paradoxical as it may seem, however, the growth of monetary analysis in the 1930s was accompanied by a widespread emphasis on the ineffectiveness of monetary policy under alleged liquidity trap conditions, such as may have prevailed in the 1930s. The renewal of widespread belief in the effectiveness of monetary policy depended largely on post–World War II research and the large amount of empirical work since the advent of the modern computer. A large portion of this depended on certain reactionary souls, mainly at the University of Chicago, who maintained a rather militant faith in the efficacy of money, even when it was placed by some in a secondary position in relation to fiscal policy [141].

As time passed in the 1920s, the Federal Reserve System, the domestic economy, and the gold-flows mechanism did not work exactly as envisioned. The Federal Reserve Act had permitted the regional banks to buy some securities in the open market as a means of obtaining earnings for operating expenses, and soon this opened the door to the prospect of exercising control over bank reserves via open market operations. The opportunity for the exercise of discretion by bank officials was broadened, particularly at the Federal Reserve Bank of New York under the leadership of Benjamin Strong. The range for discretionary administration was further broadened and formally recognized in the banking acts of 1933 and 1935, following the catastrophic economic collapse of the early 1930s. Power in the Federal Reserve shifted to Washington;

general credit controls came to include open market operations and changes in reserve requirements.

Thus, observing the enhanced discretionary powers and the Federal Reserve's traditional emphasis on reserves and bank credit, observing an apparent loose link in the 1930s between bank reserves and the money stock, and embracing a quantity theory of money with emphasis on the level of prices—doing all of these things—Irving Fisher put forth his 100% reserve scheme in 1935.[3] Henry Simons also advanced proposals for monetary reform in the 1930s. He vacillated between a rule for the money stock and an instruction to the authorities to keep the price level stable [143]. And, finally, operating partly in the Fisher-Simon tradition and partly in the empirical tradition of the National Bureau of Economic Research, observing the economic consequences of the exercise of discretion by Federal Reserve authorities, and studying wide variations in the rate of change in the money stock—doing all of these things—Milton Friedman and his followers of the post–Word War II years were strong advocates of the need for some monetary rule. Their advocacy and research in support of the need for some monetary rule came to have widespread impact on economic thinking in the 1960s. Indeed, congressional hearings before the Senate–House Economic Committee in May 1968, as mentioned in Chapter 17, dealt essentially with a rules proposal and the possible need for constraint on Federal Reserve variations in the rate of change in the money stock [396]. William Proxmire, Chairman of the Economic Committee, later spoke of the need for the Federal Reserve "to adopt a constant and moderate monetary policy." He noted that the committee recommends reports by the Federal Reserve if during any quarter the increase in the money stock is less than an annual rate of 2 per cent or more than 6 per cent. Surveying the record Proxmire said, "the Federal Reserve has a record of deepening almost every recession or depression we have suffered in the last 30 years by reducing the money

3. Under the 100% reserve scheme, the Federal Reserve (or a special currency commission) would take over all of the assets of the commercial banks and the banks would in turn be required to hold 100% reserves against demand deposits. In this way fractional reserve banking would be eliminated and open market purchases would increase the money supply directly without any subsequent multiplicative effects resulting from increments in reserves and fractional reserve requirements. The banks, of course, would be compensated; they would charge their customers for service, or as later suggested by Milton Friedman, receive interest on their reserves. Also, the 100% plan, as noted by Bronfenbrenner [37], might require other changes in financial institutions, such as investment trusts "to supply funds to the traditional small-business customers of commercial banks." All of this, of course, was outside the mainstream of economic analysis in the 1930s.

supply. . . . it has often excessively increased the money supply to fan the flames of inflation when the economy has been booming."

Bronfenbrenner's review of monetary rules.—Bronfenbrenner ranges widely over the rules-versus-discretion literature [37]. In so doing, he refers to an irrelevant state reached by comparisons between economic performance under a fixed rule proposal and under discretionary policy. A main point he makes is that "even if, in ordinary times, a given rule performs no better than ordinary authorities, one may advocate it for the same reason he buys life insurance 'loaded' in the company's favor." Bronfenbrenner advances a proposal similar to Friedman's but includes a package of guideposts for adjusting the money supply target.

He proposes that the money stock grows at the same rate as income, including a labor force and an average productivity component. To compensate for adjustments in the money stock that may be called for by special developments, Bronfenbrenner introduces changes in velocity. Thus, before acting on the change in the rate of change in the money stock, the authorities can make corrections "for the effects of changing taste and financial innovations on the velocity of the monetary circulation." This broadens the policy discussion to include the whole host of analyses of the velocity-interest rate association [126].

Bronfenbrenner apparently thought that the introduction of guidelines for compensating changes in the money stock would make the rule proposal more acceptable, more relevant to the real world. In contrast, all of the invited participants in the May 1968 hearings on rules versus authority were opposed to the idea of guidelines for compensating changes, including in particular the guidelines suggested by Representative Henry S. Reuss [396, pp. 229–31]. Moreover, as Selden noted, such secular changes as the post–World War II rise in the income velocity of money could readily be compensated for in the framework of advocates of rules proposals. He said, for example, that "a simple procedure would be an annual review of the guidelines to determine whether they need revision." Continuing, he said, "the guidelines could be adjusted gradually to take care of long-run changes in the demand for money."

Hearings.—The May 1968 hearings before the Joint Economic Committee questioned whether the Federal Reserve should confine changes in the growth rate for the money stock within limits, such as 3 to 6 per cent per year. Much of the discussion centered about suggestions by Representative Reuss that were made available before the hearings.

In the form of a rule, Reuss stated simple limits for the rate of change in the money stock per annum. The membership of the Joint Economic

Committee generally subscribed to these,[4] but Reuss went further and stated specific qualifications to the rule as a basis for generating some discussion. Responses to the Reuss proposal and related discussion and interest on the part of the Joint Economic Committee have apparently brought out: (1) the inability of the Federal Reserve to state any specific and consistent criteria for monetary and credit policy; (2) a fairly widespread agreement among participants in monetary policy discussions over the desirability of having Congress set upper and lower limits to the growth rate per annum for the money stock, subject to the need to give explanations to the Joint Economic Committee for growth rates extending outside of the limits for any given quarter; and (3) the undesirability of listing specific exceptions to the limits on the rate of growth of the money stock.

Knowledge and the mystique.—A portion of the discussion of rules and discretion centers about knowledge or the lack of it. Most participants to the discussion agree that monetary and banking mechanics and phenomena are complicated, but then part over the question of knowledge. Traditionally the rules proponents have said that knowledge of the effects and lags in effects of policy is inadequate for the success of its use as the Federal Reserve has sought to use it. They conclude that in the absence of such knowledge some simple rule, such as stability in the growth rate for the money stock, is best. When one has the knowledge, one may make the departure. The proponents of discretion, on the other hand, have seemed to assume that the knowledge exists or that judgment about the need for a given policy was superior to any simple rule. Even so, one may simply note that central banking matters have often relied on a mystique.

Those invoking the mystique as a substitute for knowledge have often seemed to present as their best defense (1) an acquaintance with a frustrating array of facts and details, and (2) the attitude that study and research would confirm the validity of their view. This additional research is always in a promising future, despite all that has historically been completed. An example of the first characteristic is Mitchell's statement [396, p. 120] that "excessive concentration of our attention on any single variable, or even on any single group of related variables, would likely result in a potentially serious misreading of the course and intensity of monetary policy." An example of the second characteristic is the promise

---

4. For an outline of the background of the Committee's rules proposal, see Report of the Joint Economic Committee [397, pp. 16–18].

of the Fed-MIT, special-purpose policy model, as reviewed in Chapter 14.

The challenge to the mystique has come from an outpouring of results from statistical analyses as well as from other research and writing. Interestingly—at least with respect to the characteristic defenses of discretionary monetary policy—discussion in the form of the Joint Economic Committee has lead to the position that the rule can be abandoned when an explanation can be given for doing so. A course of developments with respect to the rules-discretion controversy seems to be indicated—to justify deviations from the simple rule with empirically verifiable explanations.

16.3   MECHANICS AND RELATED CHANGES UNDERLYING THE RULES PROPOSAL

A statement of mechanics underlying the simple rules proposal may proceed from a statement of the Cambridge equation and the related equation of exchange. These, however, have historical roots and relationships to more modern analysis. The Cambridge equation was especially familiar to economists and students in the lecture halls of Cambridge University before the days of Keynes' *General Theory* (1936). The equation of exchange was more prevalent in the United States. Both emphasized the relevance and importance of the price level (Sec. 5.4). In the 1950s and 1960s interest in the price level was renewed (Sec. 1.4, Appendix to Ch. 1).

The simple quantity theory relationship was written in the Cambridge form as

$$(1.0) \qquad Y = \frac{1}{k} \, M \text{ or, alternatively, } \frac{M^d}{P} = kQ$$

where Y is nominal income, $1/k$ is a substitute for the income velocity of money $(Y/M = 1/k)$, M (or M^d) is the demand for money, P is the weighted average of prices for the current output of goods and services, and k is a factor of proportionality relating the real money stock demanded (M^d) to real income (Q). By substituting income velocity for the reciprocal of the proportionality factor and by substituting the income components $(P \, Q)$ for income (Y) in equation (1.0), the equation of exchange follows, $MV = P \, Q$.

In Cambridge, Keynes was led to focus on explanations for changes in the demand for money, as mentioned earlier (Ch. 7), by focusing on the Cambridge k and giving it a highly behavioral interpretation. In the

United States, monetary study proceeded more directly from the equation of exchange, which symbolized the simple quantity theory. By introducing general equilibrium analysis and other elements, a more sophisticated sort of analysis was evolved, first in an oral tradition at the University of Chicago [5] and later in publications. Some have called it the new quantity theory, but as it evolved under Friedman's leadership its generality and empirical nature have been more heavily emphasized (Secs. 5.4, 5.5). The early Chicago influences receded some, but the influence of Burns as an empiricist and cyclical analyst came to the forefront (Sec. 3.5). Even so, the rules proposal evolved from the simple quantity theory and then took on special empirical dimensions in the hands of monetarists, a rather broad group. For example, there are Karl Brunner and Allan Meltzer whose roots evolved entirely independently of the Chicago School (Sec. 18.2).[6] But especially the emphasis extends to monetary economics

5. Friedman says in a 1956 essay [146, p. 3] that "at Chicago, Henry Simons and Lloyd Mintz directly and Frank Knight and Jacob Viner at one remove" taught and developed the notion that the quantity theory was connected and integrated with general price theory. He says it "became a flexible and sensitive tool for interpreting movements in aggregate economic activity and for developing relevant policy prescriptions."

6. Brunner has characterized the monetarists' thesis, approach and position [42, pp. 9–24]: "Monetary impulses are a chief factor determining variations in economic activity. . . . The monetarist approach accepted the general principle of applying relative price theory to monetary processes. . . . The monetarists' research strategy was concerned quite directly with the construction of empirical theories." The monetarist "view rejects the traditional separation of economic theory into parts: national income analysis (macroeconomics) and price theory (microeconomics)." Brunner distinguishes both a strong and a weak monetarists' position [42, pp. 18–20]. Moreover, there is an occasional assertion that the opponents of the monetarists reject the above positions and offer others instead.

Samuelson, a Keynesian (Secs. 1.1, 3.5), defines "monetarism" as [318, p. 7] "the belief that the primary determinant of the state of macroeconomic aggregate demand—whether there will be unemployment, whether there will be inflation—is money, M_1 or M_2; and more specifically, perhaps its various rates of change." He speaks of a spectrum of beliefs ranging from "money doesn't matter," on the left, to "only money matters," on the right. On the left he sees some men in England who haven't changed their minds since 1939 and whose views were embalmed in the Radcliffe Committee (Ch. 2, n. 2). On the right, he places Milton Friedman. He thinks the evidence fails to support the former view, and the latter to a lesser extent.

Samuelson further posits a velocity-interest rate association [318, pp. 11–12], such as that attributed to him earlier (Sec. 4.2). At the extreme left in this case, velocity is a systematic and increasing function of the interest rate. He says, "the minute you believe that, you have moved from the right of the spectrum—that of monetarism—to that noble eclectic position which I hold, the post-Keynesian position." The left of this spectrum is to the right of the Radcliffe Committee in the initial spectrum, as outlined.

generally and to the empirical study of the problems initially giving rise to rules proposals.

The quantity theory, the rules proposal, and changes in velocity.— Essentially, the simple quantity theory equation states—in either the Cambridge or the equation of exchange form—that the community demands to maintain, in the form of real money balances (or nominal balances), an amount in some proportion (k) to its real (or nominal) money income. The equation may be written as

$$(2.0) \qquad M^s = k\, QP$$

on the common assumption that the demand for nominal money balances (M^d) is equal to the supply of nominal money balances (M^s). The idea is that the public has no appreciable difficulty, as a first approximation, in (1) drawing its balances downward to a desired level in relation to expenditures by increasing expenditures, or (2) refraining from expenditures and increasing its balances in relation to expenditures. In other words, the lag in adjusting imbalances between "desired" and "actual" money balances is of a nominal or short duration. From equation (2.0) it is also apparent that

$$(3.0) \qquad \frac{\Delta M^s}{M^s} = \frac{\Delta k}{k} + \frac{\Delta Q}{Q} + \frac{\Delta P}{P}$$

Friedman's so-called 5 percent rule tries to make the rate of change in prices equal to zero ($\Delta P/P = 0$). On occasion Friedman has expressed the view that the long-run rates of change in k and Q were 1 and 3 per cent respectively. Here complexities—elements of the new quantity theory as some would say—are being introduced into the simple quantity theory. The idea in the case of k is that money is a luxury good (and thus increases more than in proportion to income). The 3 percent was to accord to the real growth of income. Since stating the 3 percent rate, the rate for real economic growth has been revised upward somewhat. Furthermore, the post–World War II change in velocity ($1/k$) has not worked out exactly as Friedman initially posited; [7] it rose instead of declining. The idea is clear in terms of the mechanics anyway.

7. The luxury goods hypothesis and papers relating to it are reviewed elsewhere [126, Ch. 6 and Appendix to Ch. 6]. One of the main papers reviewed in this source, "The Demand for Money: Some Theoretical and Empirical Results," is also reprinted by Friedman [138, Ch. 6]. On the luxury goods hypothesis see also Stroup and Frazer [132]. On the postwar rise in velocity see Chapter 6 of this book.

Bronfenbrenner's equation.—Bronfenbrenner [37, pp. 173–92; 36, pp. 98–100] suggests a slightly more complicated equation than (3.0):

(4.1)
$$\frac{\Delta M}{M} = \frac{\Delta k}{k} + \frac{\Delta N}{N} + \frac{\Delta \pi}{\pi}$$

or

(4.2)
$$\frac{\Delta M}{M} = -\frac{\Delta V}{V} + \frac{\Delta L}{L} + \frac{\Delta \pi}{\pi}$$

where $-\Delta V/V$ is equivalent to $\Delta k/k$ [as indicated by the relationship between the velocity of money and the reciprocal of the Cambridge k in equation (2.0)]; $\Delta N/N$ or $\Delta L/L$ is the percentage change in the labor force; $\Delta \pi/\pi$ is the percentage change in labor productivity ($\pi = Y/L$); and the price level is assumed stable ($\Delta P/P = 0$). Here the relationship of the size of the labor force and productivity of labor to income are explicitly brought out. There is still allowance for changes in the velocity of money. Equation (4.2) implies that the percentage change in the money supply should match the full employment income level for the economy plus allowance for changes in the demand for money.

Bronfenbrenner says [36, p. 99] that the rule implied by equation (4.2) "should be followed as closely as may be by the monetary authorities, with unavoidable errors in one period compensated by adjustments in the subsequent one rather than being permitted to cumulate. . . . the mechanism of following this rule should be primarily open market operations, and secondarily variations of commercial bank reserve requirements."

16.4   THE RULES PROPOSAL AND EXCHANGE RATES

Advocacy (or discussion) of a fixed monetary rule of the Friedman type has often been tied with advocacy (or discussion) of a system of flexible exchange rates.[8] It is noteworthy that the rule most commonly mentioned in the 1960s bears the name of the author of a classic essay on flexible exchange rates—Milton Friedman, "The Case for Flexible Exchange Rates" [147, pp. 157–203].[9] The relationship between the fixed monetary

8. See statements by Martin Bronfenbrenner, Karl Brunner, Meyer L. Burnstein, and Axel Leijonhufvud [395, pp. 99, 101–2, 104, and 412, respectively].

9. An abridged version of the essay on flexible exchange rates also appears as Chapter 25 in Caves and Johnson [65]. For a more recent statement of the case see Friedman and Roosa [150] and Johnson [211, pp. 12–24]. A portion of Friedman's contribution to the Friedman-Roosa debate is also reprinted as Chapter 9 of Friedman [142].

For the case against flexible rates see Annual Report [401, pp. 55–69], in addi-

rule and the notion of flexible exchange rates may be brought out through a brief review of the international role of a central bank under modified gold standard and related conditions.[10] Following the review, a suggestion by Brunner [41] is brought forward to the effect that with a slight weakening of the rule—say, to a 2 to 6 per cent range—it would not be necessary to abandon the traditional central banking role, as far as balance of payments adjustments are concerned.

Under gold standard conditions, including those of the 1920s, and under the administered international arrangements of the post–World War II years, exchange rates (the price of one national currency in terms of another) have for the most part been fixed or pegged within limits by exchange funds. As the supply of a currency becomes excessive or as its rate falls, it may be supported through purchases with a stronger currency; when the strong currency runs short an additional supply may be obtained through, say, a sale of gold by the weak currency country. A weak currency is usually associated with a deficit in the balance of payments. In such a case gold losses can be mitigated by attracting liquid funds from abroad, possibly by raising short-term interest rates in the deficit country's financial markets. This is one way of temporarily dealing with a deficit. Ultimately its correction under the arrangements outlined depends on an adjustment in the prices of the goods it exports relative to competing goods in the international economy, as partially reviewed earlier (Sec. 16.2). In a sense, the mechanism is thought to impose a discipline and force adjustments.

Under the conditions outlined, domestic economies are not entirely isolated from others in the international community, but some would like to conduct domestic policies as if they were isolated. One means of forcing domestic adjustments is thought to be a system of flexible exchange rates; exchange rates would be free to vary in response to supply and demand conditions, without government attempts to maintain fixed rates at which currencies exchange for one another.

In any event, central banks have traditionally been thought to play a role via the interest rate mechanism, in keeping with traditional international arrangements. There are questions about whether the ultimate

---

tion to the Roosa contribution to the book cited above.

Papers on flexible and fixed exchange rates also appear in Conference Proceedings [393].

10. For more detailed definitions, institutional descriptions, and analysis see Frazer and Yohe [133, Chs. 6, 21, 22, and 23].

relative price-level adjustments are not the main ones, and whether the central bank can actually control or "twist" the yield curve directly (compare Chs. 12 and 13). Even so, related to monetary rule is the idea that the short-term rate cannot be controlled if the stock of money must be varied at a constant rate, or even at a rate indicated by equation (4.2) in Section 16.2. Heller states the matter as follows [149, pp. 26–27]: [11] "Under the Friedman rule, market interest rates would be whatever they turned out to be. It would be beyond the pale of the Fed to adjust interest rates for balance–of–payments adjustments purposes. . . . Milton has heard all of this before, and he always has an answer—flexible exchange rates."

On an uncomplicated level, a fundamental argument for flexible exchange rates is [211, p. 12] "that they allow countries autonomy with respect to their use of monetary, fiscal, and other policy instruments, consistent with the maintenance of whatever degree of freedom in international transactions they choose to allow their citizens, by automatically ensuring the preservation of external equilibrium." An argument for fixed rates, advanced by Roosa and others, is that they provide the most hospitable environment for commerce and investment transactions between nations. The pros and cons imply complicated analyses and real world experiences. They are elaborated in the various references above.

More simply and with respect to the statement of the monetary rule— in terms of a 2 to 6 per cent range vis-à-vis the fixed rule—Karl Brunner says [41, pp. 101–2]:

Under the present circumstances broad indicators of economic activity closely associated with our ultimate goals offer poor guidance for the continuous adjustment of policy. It was stated above that the growth rate of the money stock is the most useful target at present. It would be inappropriate however, in the context of fixed exchange rates to impose a rigid constraint on the required growth rate of the money stock. Monetary growth should be maintained within a band (say 2–6 per cent p.a. for the exclusive money stock) without any sharp reversals and counter-reversals following in close succession as in the recent past. Adjustments of monetary policy to the conditions of the balance of payments does not require the pronounced short-run instability exhibited by past policies. A 6-month target between 2 per cent and 6 per cent without radical changes between successive 6-month periods should be sufficient to cope with balance-of-payments problems.

11. For a similar statement by President Johnson's Council of Economic Advisors, see *Compendium* [395, p. 76].

16.5 SUMMARY

Support for imposing some form of rule or money supply strategy upon the Federal Reserve gained considerable strength in the 1960s. The support was varied and came from different quarters, including congressional committees. Largely it surfaced as monetarists—primarily, but others also—pushed their charges against the banking view of monetary policy, brought forth empirical evidence, and pointed to errors of the past. Some had said that the lags in the effects of policy were too long considering the inadequacies of economic forecasting. There was emphasis on benefits from greater certainty centering about a fixed rule. Still others pointed out that in focusing on interest rates as a policy variable, the money stock fluctuated in destabilizing extremes.

The emphasis before the mid- to late 1960s had been on fixed rules like Friedman's 5 percent rule. Some thought this too unrealistic and sought a rule with special allowances, as for percentage change in the labor force and in productivity, for the role of so-called money substitutes, for possible cost-push inflation, and for balance of payments considerations. But, as support increased for a money supply strategy, there was the idea that too much concession to special factors departed from the rule concept and that the strategy should be simple. The idea of setting a range within which the money supply may vary and of considering departures from it brought compounded support for a money supply strategy. The range would leave room for errors in achieving target values for the money supply and especially would avoid having to tie the rule with a system of flexible exchange rates, as Friedman had advocated.

The proponents of a rules strategy met with some success in bringing about changes at the level of Federal Reserve policy and operations. No fixed rule was proposed, but the FOMC directive came to give greater emphasis to monetary aggregates and the desirable underlying growth rates for them.

17

Rules Proposals
Some Evidence and Views

17.1 INTRODUCTION

THE ACCELERATED FLOW of results from analyses of data in the 1960s contributed to the questioning of the basis for traditional approaches to policy by the monetary authorities. It also offered some support for claims about the importance of the money stock vis-à-vis short-term interest rates as an intermediate goal of Federal Reserve operations. At times the research results even offered some support to the prospect of a long lag in the effect of monetary policy. All of this, including the questioning, was directly or indirectly a product of the presence and increased availability of the computer. Without it the voluminous analyses of data would have been impossible.

Before the 1960s the prevalent emphasis on deductive and relatively static analysis, with a minimum of reference to empirical results, had contributed to dogma. Opinions changed, but not so much because of revelations from the empirical facts. Duesenberry has said [394, p. 83], as have others (Sec. 17.2), "Fashions in economic policy can change as rapidly as fashions in dress." But then the increased emphasis on empirical research in the 1960s at least provided a basis for questioning prevailing views. The questioning, in fact, was all that was needed to give ascendancy to the rules (and the rules advocates), to the extent that the case for rules could be based simply on an awareness of the inadequacies of the knowledge underlying the exercise of discretion (Sec. 16.2). So one may indirectly conclude that an initial impact of the modern computer in the 1960s was an ascendancy of interest in monetary rules.

In the closing years of the 1960s, the rules advocates experienced practical success to a degree previously unattained. They had persuaded the majority of the Joint Economic Committee of Congress, and the committee held hearings on a rules proposal. There was some sampling of professional opinion on the desirability of imposing a rule, and there were some efforts at testing the performance of selected rules vis-à-vis discretion in monetary management. Thus, there are two types of evidence bearing on the desirability of rules proposals, and both appear below (Sec. 17.2). The views of some of the protagonists participating in the May 1968 Hearings before the Joint Economic Committee (Senator William Proximire, Chairman) are reviewed in Section 17.3. These emphasize questioning the adequacy of the then prevailing knowledge underlying monetary policy and the occasional procyclical nature of monetary policy (as viewed from the money stock point of view). However, the success of studies by rules advocates cannot be judged entirely by the adoption or rejection of rules proposals. In response to the studies and opinions the Federal Reserve may simply adjust its ways, as emphasized in Section 2.1, and thereby reduce the need for additional constraint on Federal Reserve behavior.

There may even be incongruity in the course of events. In fact, the former teacher and long time associate of the foremost of the rules advocates and empiricists of the 1960s was named the new chairman of the Board of Governors by President Nixon in October 1969. Arthur Burns—the successor to William McChesney Martin, Jr.—assumed the chairmanship on February 1, 1970. He possibly ushered in a new era with greater emphasis on monetary aggregates; shortly after his appointment became effective, Burns provided some guidelines for monetary policy, in testimony and in a subsequent letter to Senator William Proximire of the Joint Economic Committee. As reported in the National City Bank's *Monthly Economic Letter* (April 1970), Burns agreed "That money supply expansion in 1970 should fall within the 'normal' range of 2–6 per cent." The average rate of growth thought possible for 1970 was 3–4 per cent. The letter continued, "The new money supply target suggests that the Federal Reserve will not repeat the mistakes of 1967–68, when it sponsored an inflationary 7 per cent average rate of growth in the money supply."

However, in the 1970–71 period the quarter-to-quarter money-supply growth was at the upper end of the 2–6 per cent annual rate, and the range of oscillation in 1971, on a quarter-to-quarter basis, was comparable to the widest in the whole postwar period, as emphasized in the *Monthly Economic Letter* (January 1972). In the record of FOMC actions for January 11, 1972, attention was directed to the nominal changes in the levels for member bank reserves and the money supply (narrowly defined) for the fourth quarter, "despite a progressive easing of money market conditions." In this context the committee voted to try harder and to be "guided more by the course of total reserves than had been customary in the past." There was continued provision for money market conditions. Three members (Brimmer, Hayes, and Kimbrel) of the FOMC dissented in their support for the FOMC directive for slightly different reasons—Hayes of New York because of preference for an interest rate target and Kimbrel because of risk of depressing short-term interest rates.

Changes in the orientation of the authorities can be effected without the need for statutory recognition of rules, as the shift from the primary emphasis on a money market target to one for monetary aggregates suggests. In 1969 rules advocate Meltzer had suggested the prospect of formalizing the directive for policy changes along more quantitative lines. The proposal concerns the proviso clause in the FOMC directive, as initially mentioned in Section 2.1. In discussion concerning monetary aggregates, Meltzer [394, p. 99] proposed "as a first step, that we reverse the present system, moving away from the use of free reserves, interest rates, or money market targets, all subject to a proviso clause, as in the announced policy of the Open Market Committee for the last several years. Instead, let the former proviso clause become the target. State the target as a growth rate of the quantity of money, or of the monetary base, or as an absolute change in the base (we can translate from one to the other). Set a range of fluctuations in interest rates as the new proviso clause."

In a paper on controlling aggregates in the mid–1969 period, Holmes notes [394, pp. 65–67] that the proviso clause explicitly referred to the "bank credit proxy" for the money stock. He mentions "specific instructions to modify open market operations if the proxy is tending to move outside a predicted or desired range," and leaves little question about (1) the difficulties surrounding the lag in the availability of data on the performance of monetary aggregates and (2) the usefulness of interest rate date in the very short run.[1]

---

1. Other statements by Holmes are brought forward later (Ch. 18). Wallich is also sympathetic with Holmes' point of view [394, p. 130]: "I would argue, therefore, that one should have a short-run interest rate target, for a few weeks or months, perhaps, and a money supply target over a longer period. Over time one should allow interest rates to vary sufficiently to achieve that money supply target. Of what that period of time is, I do not feel very certain. I hear by word of mouth that, in the money supply series, the cyclical trend begins to dominate the random elements only after 7 months. That would seem to say that for 7 you cannot really

17.2 SOME EMPIRICAL EVIDENCE

Empirical evidence on the desirability and performance of rules over discretion include (1) the evidence of professional opinion (the sort of evidence obtained, say, from a survey of the opinions of monetary economists), and (2) that of tests (of the performance of possible varying degrees of relevance and reliability). Some of both kinds of evidence is available. The first comes from fragments here and there, from congressional hearings [396], and from a December 1968 volume [395]. The second is found in papers by Bronfenbrenner [35, pp. 1–14; 34, pp. 621–25], Modigliani [277, pp. 211–45], and Argy [15, pp. 102–22].

Evidence on opinions.—When Shaw advanced a Friedman or Friedman-Shaw rules proposal in 1958, he recognized it [332, p. 49] as "a proposal regarding monetary policy that has been dismissed too often as an hallucination of the lunatic fringe of monetary theorists." There was no noticeable amount of discussion of the rules proposals before committees of the Congress or in bank newsletters. However, as the rules proposals were revived, as lags in monetary policy were researched (Sec. 2.4), and as evidence was brought out on occasional procyclical swings in the money stock, interest in rules was revived.

Following the May 1968 hearings [396], a report of the Joint Economic Committee concluded that "the rate of increase in the money supply should be determined to maintain a noninflationary balance between growth in the real productive capacity of the Nation and the expansion of aggregate purchasing power." [2] In September, the National City Bank's *Monthly Economic Letter* discussed the 2 to 6 per cent limits on the rates of change in the money stock [3] and quoted Chairman Proxmire's comments to Governor Mitchell of the Federal Reserve that "it might be wise to follow some kind of a general principle or rule rather than go by the seat of your pants."

---

tell what the 'true' money supply is, or what a given goal means. All one can do is to take a seven-months' moving average, then one knows what the money supply was 3½ months ago. It would seem then that one has to have a money supply target pretty far in the future."

2. Continuing in the 1969 Joint Economic Report, the committee reported that "Over the long run, the increase in the money supply should be roughly at the same rate as the growth of U.S. productive capacity . . . the expansion of the money supply should be somewhat above the long-run real growth rate during periods of high unemployment and excess capacity. On the other hand, monetary expansion should be below real growth in periods of inflation. We recommend a rate of increase ranging from 2 per cent to 6 per cent."

3. For additional discussion on the bank newsletter level, see Struble and Cacy [345, pp. 3–9].

In July 1968, the Chairman of the House Banking and Currency Committee addressed a questionnaire to Federal Reserve and government officials and to academic, bank, and research monetary economists. A result was the compendium mentioned earlier which includes a summary of questionnaire responses [395, pp. 7–27]. Of the 69 responses tabulated in Table 16-1, 20 per cent were reported as favoring the Federal Reserve regime as of the date of the questionnaire. Another 20 per cent favored constraining the Federal Reserve outright by a rule, and another 26 per cent also favored a rule strategy as a part of a larger program coordinating monetary and fiscal policies. In other words, 46 per cent of the respondents favored some kind of rules proposal. The type most commonly favored was a 2 to 6 per cent range setting upper and lower limits on the rate of change in the money stock.[4]

A majority of opinions about the superiority or desirability of rules over discretion is not itself strong evidence for one form of operation or another, at least not among economists. Recall, for example, the comment by Friedman and Meiselman in the early 1960s: "The striking thing about the intellectual history of economics in the past three or four decades, and it strongly suggests the flabbiness of the profession, is that so large a fraction of the profession shifted from one side to the other of the issue on the basis of essentially no evidence." In the case of rules proposals, however, the opinions of monetary economists may have shifted because of the empirical evidence generated in the 1960s on the results of discretionary monetary management. The question, moreover, is not entirely whether rules outperform discretionary management. As brought out earlier (Sec. 16.2), a case for rules may be based on the simple inadequacies of the knowledge thought to underlie the exercise of discretion.

Bronfenbrenner's tests.—Bronfenbrenner's tests of rules versus discretion (versus the "judgment" rule) are quite simple and straightforward. He proceeds with his equation (4.2) of Section 16.3, only with $Y = L\pi$, and gets

$$(4.3) \qquad \left(\frac{\Delta M}{M_0}\right) = \frac{dY}{Y} - \frac{dV}{V}$$

where the price level is stable ($\Delta P/P = 0$) as an ideal matter, and ($\Delta M/M_0$) is "the growth rate of M in any year which corresponds to

4. The finer points of interpretation cause some difficulties in classification. One may not agree in every instance with the tabulations reported by the committee's staff, as the report recognizes. A review of the views expressed, however, has not caused a revision in the percentages mentioned in the text.

TABLE 16–1. Tabulation of Views on Coordinating
Monetary and Fiscal Policies

Respondents' views	
Opposed to the present regime wherein the Federal reserve is neither guided by a program coordinating monetary and fiscal policies on a provisional basis, nor constrained by a monetary rule	In favor of the present regime

Favor a coordinated program		Favor a rule [1]	
Chairman Okun	Johnson [2]	Aschheim	Governor Martin
Arlt	Keiser	Bronfenbrenner	Secretary Fowler
Bach [2]	Kent	Brunner	Adams
Burstein	Keyserling [2]	Cagan	Eckstein
Chow [2]	Leijonhufvud [2]	Christ	Hester
Cohen	Luckett [2]	Crouch	Kane
Davidson	Mayer [2]	Culbertson	Madden
Dewald	McCracken	Friedman	Minsky
Earley	McDonald	Grossman	Ross
Fand	Morrison [2]	Harwood	Teigen
Fishman	Morton	Melitz	Walker
Frazer [2]	Noyes	Meltzer	Wallich
Gaines	Scott	Pesek	Whittlesey
Greenwald [2]	Sprenkel [2]		Wilde
Harris, S.	Stucki [2]		
Harriss, L.	Thompson [2]		
Hauge	Thorn		
Havrilesky [2]	Voorhis [2]		
Hoadley	Warburton [2]		
Horwich	Weintraub		
Hosek [2]	Yeager [2]		

[1]Dr. Harwood proposed adopting a full-bodied gold money. The others in this group favored a percent per annum monetary growth rule, or at least constraining the Fed to focus on money supply.

[2]However, also favor constraining Federal Reserve actions by imposing a clearly defined money supply strategy or alternatively, a monetary growth rule valid for the year.

Source of table: Staff Report, *Compendium on Monetary Policy Guidelines and Federal Reserve Structure*, Subcommittee on Domestic Finance of the Committee on Banking and Currency, House Representatives. (Washington, D.C.: U.S. Government Printing Office, 1968), p. 8.

this ideal pattern." As a consequence of the identity nature of the equation of exchange, the actual growth rate in the money supply is

$$(4.4) \qquad \left(\frac{\Delta M}{M}\right) = \frac{\Delta Q}{Q} - \frac{\Delta V}{V} + \frac{\Delta P}{P}$$

where $\Delta Q/Q$ is the growth rate for real national income ($\Delta Q/Q =$ $\Delta Y/Y$, when $\Delta P/P = 0$). The actual growth rate is also the one for which the monetary authorities were responsible. It is said to represent the "judgment" rule.

Other hypothetical growth rates are computed on the basis of other rules. The performance of the rules is tested by comparing the series they generate for the rates of change in the money stock with the ideal series obtained with equation (4.3), and evaluating the difference between the respective series. The notion of an ideal growth rate for the money stock, as in equation (4.3), is related to some of the more advanced research of the 1960s. For one thing, there is the notion that the rate of change in the money stock should vary countercyclically, to the extent that velocity moves procyclically. Otherwise the money stock is growing at the rate for the output of goods and services in constant prices.

The rules, in addition to the "judgment" rule, are

(4.5) $\left(\dfrac{\Delta M}{M}\right) = 3$ (or, alternatively 4 per cent per year)   (First and second variant of "inflexible" rule)

(4.6) $\left(\dfrac{\Delta M}{M}\right) = \left(\dfrac{\Delta N}{N} + \dfrac{\Delta \pi}{\pi} - \dfrac{\Delta V}{V}\right)_{t-1}$ (The Bronfenbrenner or "lag" rule)

Equation (4.5) corresponds to Friedman's so-called 5 percent rule as distinct from his 2 percent rule, as described in Section 16.3. Equation (4.6) is similar to (4.1) and (4.2), except the money stock is assumed to adjust to the changes in employment, labor productivity, and velocity in the period succeeding the changes.

For Bronfenbrenner's tests, annual data were first used for the entire period 1901–58, exclusive of the "price control" years of World War II, and for four sub-periods 1901–14, 1915–29, 1930–41, and 1947–58. Later, quarterly data were used for the postwar period 1947–59. In all instances both broad and narrow definitions of the money supply were used. The deviations (d_i, $i = 1, \ldots, n$) between each observation for the ideal series and each observation for the separate series computed for the respective rules were averaged in absolute form and algebraically

$$\left(\sum_{i=1}^{n} \frac{d_i}{n} \right) \text{ and } \left(\sum_{i=1}^{n} \frac{d_i}{n} \right)$$

The first form was to allow for irregularity, and the second to allow for inflationary or deflationary bias in the rule being tested.

In tests for the longer period and the subperiods, the 3 percent variant of the inflexible rule performed best [35, p. 13], although the lag rule performed best in the specific case involving algebraic values of the average deviations. The judgment rule ranked lowest [35, p. 13], "largely because of the pronounced inflationary bias of its algebraic deviations from the ideal pattern." However, in those tests using annual data the 3 percent rule was inferior for the postwar period. This was due to the large rise in the velocity of money during the postwar period (Chs. 4 and 6). In supplementary tests using quarterly data for the postwar period alone [34, pp. 622–24], "the judgment rule or status quo seems to do best . . . as regards absolute deviations from the ideal pattern." It was followed for these deviations by the 3 percent inflexible rule, the lag rule, and lastly the 4 percent inflexible rule. As regards algebraic fluctuations, the lag rule does best by a wide margin, then come the judgment rule and the variants of the inflexible rule.

Modigliani's tests of monetary management.—Prompted by dissatisfaction with Bronfenbrenner's procedures, Modigliani presented his own tests of monetary management and of rules versus discretion [277]. His target money supply was stated as

$$(5.1) \qquad M_t = \frac{Y_t}{m_t} \qquad m_t = \frac{Y_t}{M_t}$$

where the m_t is the target income velocity (as approximated by actual velocity in period t), and Y_t is target income (as approximated by the product of the target real income) and the target price level. The target real income is approximated by an empirical estimate of the real gross national product (Q) times the price level ruling at the opening of the period (P_t). The empirical estimate for the real gross national product is the product of real gross national product and a weight of 1 or more, depending on whether employment is at or above 96 per cent of the labor force, in the case of 1, or below 96 per cent, in the case of a larger weight.

The price level stability implied by Modigliani's formula for the target money supply is short-run price stability. "If prices have nonetheless changed in the period—whether through cost push and sellers inflation or from errors in the money supply—then the newly reached price level should be accepted as a *fait accompli.*" That is [277, p. 213], "it should become the new line to be held in the following period." Taking the natural logarithm of both sides of equation (5.1) and using earlier notation for velocity,

$$(5.2) \qquad \ln M = \ln Y - \ln V$$

implies that the money stock should grow at the same rate as income
minus the rate of change in velocity, all as suggested by equations (4.3)
and (4.4).

The main difference between Modigliani's target rate of growth and
Bronfenbrenner's is that for the latter the target income variable is
weighted upward in the case of unemployment in excess of 4 per cent of
the labor force. A fixed rule of the Friedman type is not actually tested.
Bronfenbrenner's rule calls for a steady expansion of the money supply,
whereas Modigliani tests variants of a "passive policy" (a series obtained
by applying a growth factor to the *"actual money supply outstanding at
the beginning* of the period"). Modigliani asserts [277, p. 219] that "it
is doubtful that such a test [an exact test of a pure Friedman-type rule]
can ever be performed from historical data." He does not say why, but
perhaps he has in mind the difficulty of choosing the proper base year
from which to begin computing the fixed-rule series.[5] He proceeds to test
a "switch" rule and various "passive rules" obtained by broadening the
definition of the target variable to ultimately include "Near Monies."

One may wonder about the tests of the "passive rules" since no interest has been shown in such rules. Even so, as reported, such test results
favor discretion over "passive policy." The time unit of analysis is two
quarters. Data are analyzed for the sixteen years beginning with the
second half of 1947. Four subperiods are recognized, but the main ones
are the "Pre-accord" period, 1947–II to 1950–I, and the "Post-accord"
period, 1952–I to 1960–I. The half year 1950–II to 1951–II covered the
acute phases of the Korean War, and the half-year 1960–II to 1962–II
covered the beginning of the "Gold problem" concerning deficits in the
U. S. balance of payments. Modigliani scores the performance of the
money authority by computing the relative error in the money supply
(the error estimated as a difference between the actual money supply and

---

5. Latané bases a journal comment on such a point [243, pp. 328–30]. "At the
present time both interest rates and the income velocity of money are very high.
There is strong evidence to support the prediction that velocity will come down if
and when interest rates fall. It also seems reasonable to assume that peace-time
full employment with stable prices cannot be maintained with present interest rates.
Hence it is entirely probable that during a transition period it will become advisable
to increase the money supply to compensate for the probably lower income velocity
of money in the future. In spite of this, apparently there is widespread and growing
political support for a monetary policy directed solely toward a steady rate of
growth in the money supply. Such a policy may possibly be reasonable if started
during a period when interest rates and monetary turnover are closer to long-range
norms than is the case at present but may well lead to a recession (or indeed, a
depression) if adopted now and persisted in."

the target money supply, relative to the target supply) for each half-year. The errors are averaged for the subperiods.[6]

Argy's test.—Suggesting dissatisfaction with the earlier tests of the possible results from the adoption of a simple Friedman-type rule, Argy [15] reviews some theoretical and empirical literature on the issue, carries out a simple empirical test of his own concerning a number of countries, and then, on the basis of a priori speculation, compares three rules in terms of their effects on the stability of income growth. In his review, Argy touches on the Friedman-Meiselman comparison of simple Keynesian and Quantity Theory models (as in Sec. 5.2), on lags in the effects of changes in monetary growth (as in Sec. 2.4, Chs. 9–10),[7] and on the empirical tests of rules vs. discretion by Bronfenbrenner and Modigliani [15, pp. 104–10]. He expressed the view that little light has been given by the rules tests.

Argy examined data for seventeen developed countries on the two velocity concepts (one with narrowly defined money supply, V_1, and one with broadly defined money supply, V_2) and on percentage changes in two money supply series, M_1 and M_2. His changes were annual for the years 1953–67, and he was particularly concerned with variances in them, denoted as V_{v1}, V_{v2}, M_{v1}, and M_{v2}. Performing a cross-section regression analysis, the following results were obtained [15, p. 112]:

$$V_{v1} = 4.96 + 0.70\, M_{v1} \qquad R^2 = 0.416$$
$$\phantom{V_{v1} = }(1.807) \quad\; (3.57)$$

$$V_{v2} = 5.93 + 0.84\, M_{v2} \qquad R^2 = 0.423$$
$$\phantom{V_{v2} = }(2.55) \quad\; (3.57)$$

6. In recognizing likely shortcomings and bias in the measure of error, Modigliani [277, n. 8] draws on literature of the velocity-interest rate association such as reviewed in Chapters 4 and 6 of this book. He follows the explanations whereby a rise in the interest rate increases velocity and so on, apparently via a form of switching from money balances to bonds, both in relation to income or assets.

7. In the review of the lags literature, Argy views Friedman's work as being marred by two weaknesses [15, p. 104]: "First, he relates the rate of change in the money supply series to the level of economic activity. If, on the other hand, first differences in the money supply are compared with first differences in production, the lag actually disappears. Second, his measure of the lag implies that the money supply is the most important determinant of income."

Argy's casual mention of the first weakness is due to an incomplete and incorrect reading of the particular rate of change controversy involving Kareken and Solow (as cited in Sec. 2.4). Friedman has simply not been interested in levels for stock and flow quantities (or their first differences). Instead, his notion of a level in economic activity or business conditions [274, Ch. 1] is ideally that of fluctuations

where the t-ratios are shown below the coefficients and where the ratios for the variance in the percentage change in the money stock are significant at the 1 per cent level.

These results are subject to a simple interpretation. Countries with high variance for the money stock tended to have high variances for velocity. There is the suggestion that a greater stability in the monetary growth rate would yield greater stability in the velocity of money, as Friedman has posited. Even in the presence of a simple monetary rule, however, there would be some variance in velocity.

Argy's results from the time series for the seventeen countries are possibly less interesting, as are his a priori speculations based on a simple Keynesian model [15, pp. 113–17]. In the case of the time series, the per cent changes in velocity are regressed on per cent changes in the money stock for each separate country. There are no lagged variables, but the regression coefficients are negative, as might result from a lag analysis à la Friedman—slower growth in the money stock occurs while business conditions are still expanding (as indicated by rising velocity) and faster growth occurs while conditions are still contracting. On the other hand, Argy says [15, p. 113], "Theory would suggest that the coefficient for money should be negative in that an acceleration in the money growth would tend to decelerate the rate of change in velocity and a deceleration in monetary growth would accelerate the change in velocity." He does not say which theory says this, but it appears consistent with the analogy attributed to the Radcliffe Report [57, p. 5] that velocity moves "balloon-like" as an offset to the effects of changes in the money stock. The Radcliffe Report (Sec. 2.1) was published in 1959 and approximately marks the end of the stagnation phase of Keynesian economics.

17.3 COMMITTEE HEARINGS, 1968

The Committee Hearings in May 1968 [396] centered about and were partly initiated by a proposal by Representative Henry S. Ruess in the 1968 January Economic Report. Among the participants in the discussion whose views are presently summarized, two opposed the idea of a monetary rule. These include the research staff of the Federal Reserve's Board [396, pp. 233–38] and Franco Modigliani [396, pp. 8–13]. Two other

---

about some secular growth pattern for stock and flow quantities such as production. As a practical matter he is using the National Bureau's reported peaks and throughs in measuring the particular lags in question. This point about levels in business conditions has been widely misunderstood. See "Statement by William J. Frazer, Jr." [395, pp. 173–74, esp. n. 12].

participants agreed in principle with the idea, Richard T. Selden [396, pp. 95–100] and Carl F. Christ [396, pp. 78–83].

The Ruess proposal, as reprinted in the May 1968 hearings, reads [396, pp. 228–29]:

> The Federal Reserve System, through open-market operations, reserve requirements, and discount policy, shall endeavor to accommodate a growing full-employment gross national product by expanding the money supply (narrowly defined to include commercial bank demand deposits and currency outside banks) by 3 to 5 per cent yearly, with the following qualifications:
>
> 1. The target figure should be adjusted up or down from the above band from time to time to reflect the extent to which time deposits in commercial banks, and in savings and loan associations, mutual savings banks, and credit unions, substitute for the narrowly defined money supply;
>
> 2. The target figure should be on the higher side of the band in periods of less than full use of resources, on the lower side in periods of full use of resources;
>
> 3. The target figure should be exceeded when resources are under-employed and simultaneously businesses are making exceptionally heavy demands on credit, not for current business expenditures, but for additional liquidity in anticipation of future needs or to replenish unexpected liquidity losses;
>
> 4. The target figure should be exceeded to the extent necessary to reflect the increase in dollar gross national product estimated to be attributable to cost-push inflation;
>
> 5. The target figure need be sought only over periods, such as 3-month periods, sufficient to allow the Federal Reserve System to accomodate large Treasury borrowings, with the averaging out to occur over the remainder of the period;
>
> 6. Balance-of-payments considerations should affect monetary policy only through varying the maturity of the Federal Reserve System's portfolio, so as to achieve to the extent possible appropriate interest differentials as between long-term and short-term securities;
>
> 7. The consequences of monetary policy for the homebuilding industry should be taken into account by including Federal National Mortgage Association and Federal Home Loan Bank Board securities in the Federal Reserve System's portfolio in meaningful amounts, and by lengthening its portfolio, whenever homebuilding finance is unduly retarded by overall monetary stringency.

The first qualification concerns variations in demand and time deposits as a proportion of total deposits, and the possible growth of money substitutes. These changes are dealt with in several chapters, including 4, 6, and 15. The second and third qualifications concern countercyclical as distinct from procyclical changes in the rate of change in the stock of money. Such changes were mentioned in Chapter 16. Demands for credit by business firms, as mentioned in the third qualification, were the subject of Chapter 15. The fourth qualification suggests that the Federal Reserve should validate price increases emanating from cost changes underlying supply prices rather than from demand conditions. This suggestion possibly results from the assumption that the Federal Reserve cannot stabilize cost-induced inflation without substantially affecting unemployment and production. Since the 1957–58 recession, the matter has at times been crucial [133, Ch. 16]. The fifth qualification concerns Treasury debt management and support operations by the Federal Reserve. Such operations were introduced in Chapters 12 and 13. The sixth qualification was dealt with in Section 16.3. The seventh qualification suggests that the housing industry should be more protected from the changes in credit conditions to which it is especially vulnerable. The subject was introduced in Section 15.1 and especially the Appendix to Chapter 15.

The Federal Reserve staff's defense of discretion.—The Federal Reserve's staff objected to the idea of a fixed rate of monetary expansion for several reasons. They mentioned the need to offset changes such as the postwar market rise in the velocity of money. They attribute this to innovations in financial technology, a tendency to economize in some sense on the holdings of cash, and the rise in interest rates. These explanations seem similar to the Gurley-Shaw and Baumol-Tobin explanations initially outlined in Sections 1.4 and 4.2. Such explanations conflict with others, as mentioned in Chapter 6.

Other reasons mentioned by the Board's staff for opposing the rules proposal include the possible need to stabilize economic changes resulting from fiscal operations, and the inadequacies of open market operations for twisting the yield curve and influencing the balance of payments.

Selden on rules.—Supporting Ruess' proposal in principle, Selden points to the benefits that such a rule would produce. First, it would minimize uncertainty and create a stable environment in which rational planning would be possible. This reflects his view that discretion increases uncertainty, rather than decreasing it. Second, the rule would minimize the power that control over our monetary affairs inevitably implies. Third, it would prevent the monetary authorities from pursuing a perverse policy. Fourth, he is persuaded that the lag in effect of monetary policy is both long and variable which means that frequently the impact of discretionary policy is perverse, notwithstanding that the discretionary action taken was appropriate when it was initiated.

With reference to the late- to mid-1960s phase of the guidelines debate and rules proposal, Selden says [396, p. 96]:

> It is probably fair to say that the contemporary phase of the guidelines debate grows out of Prof. Milton Friedman's work on lags in the effect of monetary policy, which has provided a fourth reason for adoption of a monetary rule. While by no means rejecting the arguments of Simons and Warburton, Friedman has argued that a flexible, that is, discretionary, monetary policy is likely to intensify business fluctuations rather than moderate them. The reason is that policy changes influence the economy only after very substantial time-lags. The policy initiated in May 1968 may not reach its maximum impact until, say, July 1969. But neither the Federal Reserve nor anyone else possesses dependable means of forecasting the state of the economy a year or more in advance; hence there is every likelihood that today's policy will turn out to be inappropriate by the time it matures. And to compound difficulties, Friedman believes that monetary lags are highly variable, and unpredictably so. Hence even if we could foresee the state of the economy a year or two from now there would be no assurance that the policy changes initiated today would blossom forth precisely when intended.

One may notice the emphasis on the long and unpredictable lag in the effects of policy, and thus on the inadequacy of information on which to conduct an active discretionary monetary policy.

Modigliani's defense of discretion.—Modigliani opens his paper by noting that the economic system is unstable. In contrast to assumptions he attributes to certain rules advocates, Modigliani emphasizes that population does not grow at constant rates,[8] that technological progress varies in its nature, and that experts behave irregularly in time (Sec. 16.3). Given such realities, Modigliani argues that discretion in Federal Reserve policy-making is essential. He also makes the point that the fiscal apparatus has a great deal of inertia so that it is ill-designed for economic "fine-tuning." Consequently, it would be foolhardy to yield up discretionary control of monetary policy as this is the only important stabilization technique which is capable of rapid and sensitive adjustment to changing economic circumstances.

Modigliani concedes that sometimes in the past discretion has been exercised unwisely. However, he expresses the view that the incidence of such mistakes is becoming less frequent as economic insight is acquired.

---

8. At one point in post-war discussions Friedman put strong emphasis on the stability of demand relations involving per capita money holdings, per capita income, and so on. Population was subsequently shown to be a poor predictor. This is reviewed elsewhere [126, Ch. 6].

Moreover, he suggests that by May 1968 economic knowledge was being acquired which will further reduce the likelihood of mistakes in the future. With respect to research and economic knowledge, Modigliani said [396, p. 13]

> I should finally like to stress that the Federal Reserve is deeply concerned with continuously improving understanding of the connections and lags between the tools at its command and economic activity. As evidence of this concern I should like to mention that the Federal Reserve is currently participating in a sizable research focusing on these issues and which involves jointly its research department and a group of universities including MIT, the Wharton School of the University of Pennsylvania and the University of Chicago, and with some cooperation of Harvard, Princeton, and Yale. We are trying to work to the best of our ability to try to put numbers into this process.
>
> I feel that the Congress should encourage the Federal Reserve in pursuing this line. The payoffs may not be immediate, but I think we are gradually learning. We are at least learning to ask the right questions. And I believe that the process can also be helped by the production of better data which, in some cases, are very much needed.

One may note here again the emphasis on research, particularly the prospect of improvement of understanding. Here, however, Modigliani refers to fairly speculative research, with its unique theoretical foundation, in which he has been an active participant. This work, as reviewed earlier (Ch. 14), probably contributed more to an awareness of the inadequacies of underlying methods and theory than it contributed to positive knowledge.

Modigliani concluded that the postwar exercise of discretion has led to smaller mistakes than would have been made if several alternative monetary rules had been followed (compare Sec. 16.3). About the only constraint that Modigliani would impose on the Federal Reserve's freedom of action is that it be enjoined from allowing the money supply to decline when economic activity is declining.

Christ on rules.—Like Selden, Christ supports Ruess' guidelines in principle.[9] He points to the record since World War I and notes that every decline in economic activity since then has been accompanied by a decrease in the supply of money [396, p. 79]:

> During 1941–45, the money stock grew at 22 per cent a year; everyone agrees that this was far too fast for stability. During the depressions of

---

9. The Christ presentation at the May 1968 Hearings is also reprinted in the 1968 Patman Compendium [395, pp. 109–15].

1921 and 1929–33, and all the recessions since 1921—they were in 1924, 1927, 1938, 1949, 1954, 1958, and 1961—the money stock actually declined in absolute terms, which in my opinion should not be· permitted.

I think that is a very important criticism of Federal Reserve policy in the past, that they have permitted the stock of money to decline during depressions.

The evidence so far is not persuasive in favor of the claim that small variations in the rate of growth of the money supply cause business cycles. But it is clear that an actual decline in the money stock, or a prolonged period of little or no growth, aggravates any recession that is in progress or that might develop. Similarly, a prolonged period of rapid growth in the money stock aggravates any overheating that is in progress or that might develop.

Furthermore, rapid changes in the rate of growth of money stock are themselves a disturbing factor.

Relevant information on the occasional procyclical nature of monetary policy (as viewed from the money stock point of view) was contained in one of the tables appended to Christ's paper [396, p. 82].

TABLE 17–1. Declines in the U.S. Money Stock (Demand Deposits and Currency, Seasonally Adjusted) During Depressions and Recessions Since 1921

Month during which the money stock reached its peak	Percentage decline on the money stock during recession	Number of months before the money stock regained its previous peak level
March 1920	15.0	53
December 1922	2.0	10
September 1925	3.0	26
October 1929	33.0	79
March 1937	6.0	20
January 1948	2.0	27
July 1953	.2	9
July 1957	1.0	9
July 1959	3.0	27

Sources: Milton Friedman and Anna Jacobson Schwartz, *A Monetary History of the United States, 1867–1960* (Princeton, N. J.: Princeton University Press for the National Bureau of Economic Research, 1963), pp. 709–715; and *Federal Reserve Bulletin*, June 1964, pp. 682–690.

Since Christ believes that a decrease in the supply of money contributed significantly to these declines in economic activity, he supports a rule which would make a decline in the supply of money impossible. However, Christ points out (Sec. 16.3) that a fixed rule of monetary expansion may be inconsistent with the balance of payments equilibrium. Thus, as in the case of some rules advocates, he would suggest the adoption of free exchange rates so that balance of payments adjustment can be independent of domestic economic policy. Although Christ has acknowledged advances in economic knowledge, he states that he knows of no extant econometric model that he would trust in formulating the country's stabilization policy.

17.4 SUMMARY

In the 1960s, the rules advocates made their points—about possible long lags in the effects of policy, about the inadequacy of the knowledge of the workings of policy, and finally about the occasional procyclical nature of monetary policy (as distinct from the countercyclical timing of credit conditions). One result of the research of the period was congressional interest in a rules proposal. A possible result of congressional testimony was the reversing of the order of priority in the FOMC directive with respect to the growth rate for the quantity of money (the bank credit proxy and/or total member bank reserves) and credit market conditions (or short-term interest rates).

Opinions shifted, as would be warranted by the evidence. Tests of the rules themselves—of the performance of rules versus discretion—did not provide much evidence, at least at a sufficiently early date to influence the shift. In the early 1960s stage of the rules versus discretion controversy, Bronfenbrenner and later Modigliani sought to test the performance of certain rules and the performance of the monetary authority against an ideal. The procedure was to generate series by certain rules, to let the actual observed series correspond to a discretionary policy of the authorities, and to test these against an ideal. The ideal was simple in both instances—that the money stock should grow at the same rate as income minus the rate of change in velocity—but Modigliani allowed for faster growth in the money stock when unemployment was in excess of 4 per cent of the labor force. Basically, the money supply should grow less when velocity is rising, and so Bronfenbrenner's test using annual data for 1901–58 favored fixed and special lag rules and Modigliani's test using semi-annual data for post–World War II years favored the continued exercise of judgment. Modigliani tested a "passive" rule rather than Friedman's fixed rule which he did not think could be tested. Bronfenbrenner viewed the fixed rule as a form of insurance against mistakes and thought one should pay some premium in terms of poorer routine performance in exchange for the insurance.

Whatever the case with the former tests, Argy's seventeen-country cross-section regressions for the variances in percentage changes in the velocity of money and the money stock suggested that countries with high variance in the money stock had tended to have high velocity variances. These suggested variances were direct and not of the Radcliffe Committee type where the velocity of money adjusts to offset any induced changes in money.

In 1968 hearings on a rules proposal there were those pro–Federal Reserve, including the Federal Reserve's Staff and Franco Modigliani, and rules advocates, including Richard Seldon and Carl Christ. The Federal Reserve proponents argued on the basis of some research that has not held up well: the Gurley-Shaw and Baumol-Tobin explanations of the post–World War II rise in the velocity of money and the Federal Reserve–MIT model as mentioned in Chapter 14. The first group also pointed to the conflict between a fixed rule and balance of payments objectives possibly relating to the international movement of short-term balances between international financial centers. Some rules advocates countered with a proposal about flexible exchange rates. The possibility of a range of rates for the money stock rather than a fixed rule avoided both the objection about the balance of payments objective and the possible need for flexible exchange rates, at least in relation to a rules proposal. The rules proponents carried the day, if only to the extent that the Federal Reserve altered the priority given to market conditions and the growth rate for monetary aggregates in the FOMC directive.

Part VII

Epilogue

18

Enclaves of Empiricism and Crisis

18.1 INTRODUCTION

ECONOMICS HAS experienced methodological controversies. In the United States these have mainly been identified with Thorstein Veblen (1857–1929) and later with the empirical movement at the National Bureau (Appendix to Ch. 8), but in American universities in the twentieth century, economics has mainly been characterized by the absence of empirical orientation. "Theory" was relatively pure by standards of economics, if not of mathematics, and it was treated separately from statistical study and from institutional and historical descriptions. Selection and indoctrination in graduate programs assured stability in the traditional approach. However, much that had been accomplished was torn asunder by analyses of data under the initial impact of the modern computer. Keynes' work had offered refreshing redirection, but this was in large measure suppressed by a tendency to construct a relatively static and parochial body of Keynesian economics.

Two arguments for the characteristic approach were the relative economy involved in arriving at conclusions in policy matters and the flexibility in claiming an objectively scientific case for one's special policy preferences. Whatever the arguments, the modern electronic computer changed the economies to favor the allocation of relatively more research resources to empirical work. The need for this new emphasis should be clear from the historical perspective and from the revealed weaknesses of the pre-computer orthodoxy in economic theory.

Keynes' and Keynesian economics provided early econometricians with the opportunity to research the consumption function, and the movements of the 1960s opened up even broader prospects. Econometric methods came to the forefront, yet there was still a tendency to accept overly simplistic approaches to behavioral phenomena. Whatever the case, the parties to the crisis in theory and the research controversies of the 1960s grew in methodological sophistication.

The crisis in economic theory extended to a number of the inherent attributes and tendencies of the received theory: (1) to the linkage mechanism and the relatively static quality of Keynesian theory (as indicated by its emphasis on levels rather than rates of change, on the liquidity trap, on the assumed absence of covariance between the interest rate and the marginal efficiency of capital, and on a short run with expectations constant); (2) to the tendency to construct a so-called macroeconomics with money unimportant (especially as a link between the past and the future) and with relative prices given (as distinct from an analysis of money in a relative price or general equilibrium framework); (3) to the structural equations method introduced in the 1960s, with an exaggerated emphasis on allocative detail, on its capacities to utilize existing theory in an empirical setting as distinct from an emphasis on forecasting, and on its being able to readily facilitate a distinction in the real world setting between endogenous and exogenous variables (such that the coefficients and parameter structures of related probability distributions were stable from one sample period to another); (4) to the theory of market structures (with its assumptions about perfect information and foresights); (5) to the idea of distributed lags with fixed distributions over time (rather than varying distributions and time profiles); (6) to the tendency to impound relevant expectational phenomena in ceteris paribus (rather than allowing relevant changes); (7) to the tendency for theory to emphasize a treatment of economic stabilization and policy actions (rather than to allow for defensive aspects of monetary operations and the role of inactions in the policy-making sphere); and (8) to the tendency to use distinct and unrelated languages in the discussion of "monetary theory," on the one hand, and "monetary policy," on the other (as also indicated by a tendency to consider formal models and to manipulate them with little or no attention to empirical content and range of relevant applicability).

But there were also positive aspects to the crises. The empirical onslaught facilitated by the computer revealed the need to deal more systematically with expectational phenomena, with the quality of information, and with uncertainties. Even Karl Brunner—who with Meltzer is viewed as attempting to avoid and suppress treatment of these phenomena (Appendix to Ch. 7)—after surveying aspects of the monetarist revolution [39, p. 26], could conclude that

> It seems probable that the information assessment process governing the anticipated inflation velocity [the rate of change in prices] is not con-

fined to actual price movements. This adoptive behavior absorbs much information bearing on the government sector's financial behavior and the political constraints imposed on that behavior. Experiences beyond the past evolution of prices are quite important for any useful analysis of the anticipated inflation velocity. Unfortunately, we know very little about the detail of these important informational processes.

The foregoing notions are recognized and related to analyses of data in this book. Probabilistic aspects of behavior and the improved prospects for treating them come to the forefront. There is emphasis on behavioral units with memories, in a world with a yesterday and a tomorrow (with money serving as a link between the two). Herein lies possible redirection.

J. K. Galbraith has said that "In economics there is no harm in a premature disclosure of the plot." Thus, summary statements of Keynesian and monetarist views were presented in Section 3.2. A similar statement of the particular contributions in this book was also provided there. They are not reproduced as closing remarks. However, Section 18.2 provides one summary of the rise in empiricism in the 1960s, especially in its relationship to the modern computer. Further, Section 18.3 re-examines some of the folklore about the antecedents of Friedman's approach, since much has been said about his ties with the National Bureau and about attributes of his work. Section 18.4 reviews parts of the Keynesian work that may be brought forward in the framework of economics. Section 18.5 reviews some strands of analysis bearing on policy and operations in particular. Section 18.6 closes with an overview of the related issues of inflation, unemployment, and controls as they confront economists and policy-makers.

18.2 ENCLAVES OF EMPIRICISM

A thesis of the book is that enclaves of empirical thinking existed in economics in the pre-computer, hand-calculator days (before the 1960s) when economists were still mainly oriented towards deductive method and only casual empiricism. The groups came to the forefront of economics in the 1960s under the impact of the modern computer, as judged by the professional attention and interest given to their work. One approach to this thesis is to attempt an identification of these groups under pre-computer conditions, and then to draw on the review of the work and issues of the 1960s in economics, as in the preceding chapters, to note whether in fact these pre-computer, empirically oriented groups did come to the forefront of economic research.

Pursuing this approach, the groups with some distinctive empirical orientation towards economics can apparently be identified in the Federal Reserve System, at the University of California (Los Angeles), at the National Bureau of Economic Research, at the University of Chicago, among Keynesians, and at the Survey Research Center of the University of Michigan. Independent researchers with empirical interest abound, and they also came to the forefront in the 1960s, but no comments will be directed toward them.

Of course, the Federal Reserve was not a homogeneous group, and the Board in Washington and the St. Louis and New York Federal Reserve banks may be singled out. Indeed, questions concerning informational detail and policy have interested officials in parts of the Federal Reserve System from its inception, and the issue of theory versus policy comes to reflect the research and interest of Karl Brunner and his former student Allan Meltzer, initially in the UCLA setting. The National Bureau's thrust and orientation has also been tied in with Milton Friedman's group at the University of Chicago (Chs. 3, 5, and Appendix to Ch. 8). The tie between empiricism and Keynesians is more subtle and actually concerns only a small proportion of Keynesians, or at least of the mass of economists who converted to the rather parochial Keynesian approach of the 1950s, as delineated earlier (Sec. 7.1).

Too many economists protected the sanctity of economic theory and, at the same time, appeased the policy-makers by making a distinction between theory and policy. The settlement was tenuous for two reasons: (1) because economics, from the days of Adam Smith at least, has been thought of as justifying itself by guiding economic policy; and (2) because theory so removed from the empirical realities confronting policy-makers could not stand for long, once large-scale, systematic efforts could be made in evaluation. The Federal Reserve has had a continuous interest in information, institutional detail, and the publication and discrimination of facts, as indicated by the various issues and statistical segments of the *Federal Reserve Bulletin* over the years. It enjoyed a flexibility of purpose and orientation that has doubtlessly contributed to the political survival and prominence of the institution. But the distinction between theory and policy was still tenuous.

Dissatisfaction over the theory and policy distinction [38, pp. 3–4, 112]

---

1. These have been reported with special reference to Rudolf Carnap, a philosopher and logical positivist (Appendix to Ch. 8), who conducted a seminar in Vienna (1926–31) and who came to UCLA during the early part of Brunner's tenure there.
Logical positivism, as formulated in Vienna in the 1920s, has been viewed as a

reflects Karl Brunner's early interest in scientific method.[1] The particular science orientation comes out strongest in his individual writing [38, 39, 43], and carries over to his work with his associate and former pupil, Allan Meltzer [49]. Its particular attribute is not the effort found in some quarters to impound troublesome aspects of expectations in ceteris paribus, as if economics was a laboratory science (Secs. 1.1, 3.1). Rather it seems to center about a conscious use of logic—a gymnastic described earlier (Appendix to Ch. 7)—to exclude appeal to "analytically extraneous sociological or psychological convolutions" [39, p. 4], even in the presence of psychological phenomena.[2] The effort is reminiscent of the use of the term "scientism" [330, pp. 17–18], to refer to an uncritical use or copying of the methods of the physical sciences. (Whatever the case, their particular approach gained the strong support of the National Science Foundation.)[3] On the other hand, the Brunner-Meltzer objection to a "gap" between economic theory and monetary policy (Sec. 10.1 [38, n. 1, pp. 3–4, 112; 49, p. 240]) appears to be a highly practical scientific interest in economics—that of the empirical questioning of the relevance of a theory that cannot serve as a guide to (or explanation of) monetary policy.

Darryl Francis, as president of the Federal Reserve Bank of St. Louis, has also focused on the theory versus policy issue in reviewing the research orientation of the Federal Reserve Bank of St. Louis [115, pp. 3–4]: "Those responsible for carrying out stabilization policies require considerable knowledge of the probable results of any particular course

---

critique of language, and "its result is to show the unity of science—that all genuine knowledge about nature can be expressed in a single language common to all the sciences." There is a role for empiricism, and it comes out in Brunner's work and his more philosophical writing [43]. In discussing rules for the market place for ideas, Brunner emphasizes the empirical content of theory [43, pp. 177–79]. He also draws on Carnap [43, n. 1] and semantic rules for relating "the (linguistic) entities of the formal structure [of a theory] with extra-linguistic entities of our observable world."

2. Brunner seems especially fearful of the possible use of expectations theories of the short-run volatility of capital investment. He says [39, p. 6], "They justify claims of innocence and achievement." In the former case, they justify a disclaimer when a tidal wave has engulfed the economy and made it intractable to monetary impulses. In the latter, they can claim that their intelligent adjustments moderated the impact of volatile investment on the pace of economic activity. Continuing, Brunner says, "This theory obviously maximizes the political survival possibilities of a Central Bank's bureaucracy." And, indeed, any theory with such vagueness would. Even so, both the possible relevance of such a theory and its current vagueness suggest the need for more precise study and formulation.

3. Brunner's and Meltzer's papers throughout the 1960s and early 1970s acknowledge support from the National Science Foundation.

of action . . . Development of this knowledge requires empirical substantiation of various economic theories."

Karl Brunner (often in work with Allan Meltzer), the Federal Reserve Bank of St. Louis, and Milton Friedman (often in work with Anna Jacobson Schwartz and especially in publication under a National Bureau imprint), came to emphasize "first approximation," special empirical relationships, and a search for regularity in the data, as distinct from a mass of detail in the form of a structure. In fact, Friedman's apparent Machian orientation—as described earlier and as related to comments by Samuelson (Appendix to Ch. 8, n. 4)[4]—and his particular National Bureau orientation concern the relatively ad hoc character and the broad, business conditions, leads-and-lags approach found in his work, as reviewed in Chapter 5 especially.

The foregoing groups have emphasized rates of changes in stock and flow quantities that gave a rather dynamic quality to their work. The particular approach led Friedman and the St. Louis bank especially to emphasize the demise of the interest rate as a determinant of the income velocity of money, in contrast to the Keynesian approach. Friedman's position was reviewed earlier (Chs. 4–6). The St. Louis bank's is summarized thus [115, p. 11]:

> One study in the mid-1960's found that interest rates have generally been high and rising during periods of rapid economic expansion and have been low and declining during periods of economic contraction. Although this behavior of interest rates appears to contribute to economic stabilization, the effect may not be great since the state of the economy itself appears to be the major influence on rates.

The St. Louis bank's research efforts began to move toward national policy matters and to extend beyond the traditional regional, public relations, data-collecting interests of Federal Reserve banks about 1960 [115]. These efforts were a challenge to the Board, and they coincided with the initial thrust given to empirical research by the computer. Homer

---

4. Samuelson also commented on the Machian view in his lecture in Stockholm, Sweden, on the occasion of his receiving the Nobel Prize in 1970 [315, pp. 250–51], "Seventy years ago, when the Nobel Foundation was first established, the methodological views of Ernst Mach enjoyed a popularity they no longer possess. Mach you will remember, said that what the scientist seeks is an 'economical' description of nature. By this he did not mean that the navigation needs of traders decreed that Newton's system of the world had to be born. He meant rather that a good explanation is a simple one that is easy to remember and one which fits a great variety of the observable facts. . . . Mach is not saying that Mother Nature is an economist; what he is saying is that the scientist who formulates laws of observable empirical phenomena is essentially an economist of economizer."

Jones, research vice president at the bank in the 1960s, provided direction. His empirical interests were colored by some years on the Board's staff and by training at the University of Chicago. Others who joined the St. Louis bank's staff and gave early direction to its research had exposure to Karl Brunner's and Chicago's influences.

The Board's own view, at least since the 1930s, can be described quite broadly as a "banking view" (as defined in Chs. 3, 4), with Keynesian attributes and with special interest in money market and institutional detail. This provided a natural tie with Keynesian interest and with the structural equations methodology—at least in the mid-1960s when that method was viewed as most promising (Ch. 14) for identifying structural detail, causal chains, and linkages between the interest rate (as a major control variable) and national economic goals, all without much interference from forces exclusive of those allowed for in the model. The Board's view in most of the 1950s and much of the 1960s was not different from that predominating at the Federal Reserve Bank of New York. The New York bank has always served as a foreign arm of the system and as the center for open market operations. Its money market interests have been pre-eminent, and the banking view suited them quite well. In the econometric sphere, papers by Hamburger in the late 1960s and early 1970s have characterized their research stance (Secs. 10.4, 13.2, 13.3, 15.1).

The Keynesian interest in structural equations and the special research approach to which the interest and method led in the 1960s are tied to the role of Lawrence Klein, as a Keynesian and an econometrician. Klein had written his dissertation on the Keynesian revolution [233] under Paul Samuelson in 1943–44. In a chapter added in the published dissertation, the essential nature of the Keynesian system as a simultaneous system of equations is stressed [233, Ch. IX]. Klein further drew on the pioneering work of Tinbergen in the 1930s [230, pp. 47–8; and 235] in his own work on multirelation models.[5] He became identified as a pioneer in the

5. Jan Tinbergen was co-recipient with Ragnar Frische of the first Nobel Prize in economics in 1969 (compare Ch. 1, n. 3). In reviewing Tinbergen's and Frische's contributions, Klein [231, pp. 715–17] especially takes note of Tinbergen's construction of a large-scale, mathematical, statistical model that "did inspire and lay the groundwork for today's models." Klein says these models "are in the tradition of Tinbergen's pioneering models of the U.S. economy. . . . They all pay substantial attention to money market phenomena, and this is one of Tinbergen's special contributions; he had tried to capture the influence of the security markets in the U.S. expansion and decline of the 1920's and 1930's in his League of Nations model." Tinbergen's introduction of the ideas of "targets" and "instruments" in policy models, as mentioned in Section 2.1, is also cited by Klein.

application of structural equations methodology [235]. He described [230, p. 42] his own Wharton model (Sec. 14.4) as "a product of the Keynesian tradition based on the theory of income and employment determination." The model places primary emphasis on the real economy, fiscal changes, the interest rate as the control-transmission variable, and the short run. Brunner says [39, p. 14] that Klein's view of economic fluctuations as conditioned by various events in many parts of the system actually motivates the construction of "ever larger models with more and more equations."

Probably because of Klein's particular interest and orientation, he offered little new in the 1960s in the realm of economic as distinct from methodological ideas. The computer impact in his case was more strictly that of forecasting with a structural equations model.

In the early 1960s, largely in response to Friedman's and Meiselman's use of simple models (Sec. 5.2), Ando and Modigliani became involved in rudiments of structural equations methodology. Both Ando and Modigliani were at MIT at the time, though Ando later joined Klein's department at the University of Pennsylvania (as reviewed in Ch. 14).

During this same period Frank de Leeuw took leave from the Board of Governors to return to Harvard. De Leeuw became involved in the Brookings model, as introduced by Klein [232]. He then became the main "in house" member at the Board, in the joint Federal Reserve–MIT model, with Ando and Modigliani serving as principal academic members, as reviewed in Chapter 14. Thus the tie and the Board's initial venture into econometric model building were established.

There were numerous independent and often young intellectuals involved in the exciting prospects for both old and new methods of research in the 1960s. But one who was not so young stood out in retrospect, as noted by Brunner. He has said [38, p. 3] that "Clark Warburton deserves substantial credit. . . . Throughout the 1940's he insisted on important questions and relevant issues." And so Warburton had written [336], but the present thesis helps explain his lack of impact on professional thinking—his research efforts paralleled the older pre-computer, hand-calcular days. As Samuelson said of his own initial rise as a Keynesian [324, p. 145], "To have been born an economist before 1936 was a boon—yes. But not to have been born too long before!"

Still another enclave of empiricism encompassed the Economic Behavior Program of the Survey Research Center at the University of Michigan, under the direction of George Katona since its establishment in 1946. Katona's work at the center has been supported by foundations and business firms. The Board of Governors of the Federal Reserve financed its survey of consumer finances from 1946 through the 1950s. Katona's group's special contribution was empirical study involving the survey research method [227; 385] and the introduction of an up-dated psychology.[6]

Katona's work also lacked any real impact on economics, broadly viewed, in part because it was offered without the hindsight of the experience with empirical research of the 1960s (without the results from the initial impact of the computer), and in part because it offered no specific tie with the structure of economic analysis.[7] Katona [223, p. 7] viewed economic psychology as non-axiomatic, almost as a "controlled observation," but he also recognized [223, p. 9] that it could be developed by studying economic behavior, and this broadened the field a bit. One might say that his was exactly the laboratory concept implicit in classical regression and structural equations models. A paradox in fact centers about his special interest in learning, for it is precisely a possible tendency for economic units to learn and respond to shocks that gets revealed as a source of inadequacy in the regression and structural equations approaches of the 1960s. One might say that notions of learning from the past and the non-repetitiveness of some events alone suggest the prospect of continuously sampling from a different universe. Hence, there is instability in the parameters of the characteristic economic models of the 1960s (Ch. 14).

To be sure, however pioneering Katona's work, it was superficial as far as the structure of economics was concerned. Views on learning, expectations, and uncertainty lacked the formal structure provided by Bayes' theorem and by related topics surfacing in modern economics (Ch. 8). There was early emphasis on expectations and inflation in statements of some principles [283]: (1) small price advances, initial perceptions of price advances, or large price advances stimulate advance buying; (2) when price advances persist, as during so-called "creeping inflation," consumers may react by reducing the flow of their discretionary purchases. These are precisely the sorts of notions one encounters in the 1960s when giving recognition to the role of an increase in the rate of change in prices as the source of stimulation for expenditures, rather than to a constancy of the rate of change (Ch. 1). Even so, it is difficult to accept such no-

---

6. The survey work was transferred to the Bureau of the Census in 1959 and changed from an annual to a quarterly survey, but only on an experimental basis.

7. Katona [223, p. 12] actually hedged against such charges and recognized the overwhelming nature of the interdisciplinary work he undertook.

tions, because they were offered without any structure, as would be provided by a general equilibrium framework, the Phillips curve (exclusive from the debate about whether the curve is a valid causal relationship or simply a reflection of short-run covariation in the percent of unemployment and the rate of change in prices), Fisher's equation for the nominal rate of interest and the real rates plus the expected rate of change in prices, or the adaptive expectations model relating an expected magnitude to the weighted average of magnitudes for recent and past changes (all with the prospect of changing weights.)

18.3   FRIEDMAN: AN ENIGMA

Friedman has been viewed as an empirical scientist, as one who rose to prominence in a highly organized professional setting (Sec. 3.2), and as a leader with a devoted and loyal following, especially among his students. A good bit of his special rise to prominence in the 1960s has been attributed to a combination of the presence of the modern computer and a pre-computer disposition toward empirical research, as represented by Arthur F. Burns and the National Bureau. Other influences are involved, especially in the area of monetary study, but controversy arises about preconceptions with respect to them [135; 292].

In the light of controversy over intellectual antecedents, in the light of the strong emphasis Friedman places on the differences in methodological points of view separating himself and his protagonists [135, pp. 906–8, 921, 925, 933], and in the light of a history of controversy concerning empiricism in economics (Appendix to Ch. 8), it is surprising that no attention has been given to the source(s) of Friedman's strong empirical interest. In this respect, Friedman himself [135, pp. 908, 920] mentions a Marshallian as distinct from a Walrasian approach in the use of economic theory. He identifies himself and Keynes more with the former, and some of his protagonists with the latter. He says [135, p. 908] that Keynes "was a Marshallian, an empirical scientist seeking a simple, fruitful hypothesis." He then views [135, pp. 908, 933] Patinkin and Tobin as Walrasian, as seeking "a general and abstract system of all-embracing simultaneous equations." [8] He also touches on the interest of members of

8. The labels "Walrasian" and "Marshallian" were used by Friedman in a 1949 paper, "The Marshallian Demand Curve," *JPE*, and later reprinted [147, pp. 47–93]. Although since dramatized by the empirical revolution of the 1960s, Friedman's main points in 1949, as in 1972, were methodological [147, esp. pp. 89–93]. The distinction between Marshall's analysis as "partial equilibrium" and Walras' as

the "Chicago" school in policy matters [135, pp. 932–33, 936–37], where their interest was particularly in the interpretation of fluctuations in business conditions ("short-run movements"). He even denies [135, p. 941] that details of his formal structure have counterparts in any tradition at Chicago, but nowhere are his early and strong ties with the bastion of American empiricism, the National Bureau, brought out. These must be so fundamental as to have been simply overlooked up to this time.

In the area of monetary study, the controversial and prevailing notion has been to associate Friedman with an early tradition at Chicago, in part an alledged "oral" one centering about the quantity theory of money and the teachings of Henry Simons, Lloyd Mintz, Frank Knight, and Jacob Viner. However, Patinkin, one of Chicago's products of the pre-Friedman period, says that Friedman has been responsible for unjustifiably perpetuating this notion of an "oral" Chicago tradition that preceded himself [292, p. 48]. In terms of Patinkin's examination of the tradition at Chicago before Friedman, and in terms of an examination of the main characteristics of Friedman's approach and an examination of its antecedents, the conventional and prevailing notion about Friedman's tie with the tradition simply does not always hold up. In some major respects, Friedman's Chicago was not the "other" Chicago (of Simons, Mintz, Knight, and Viner).[9]

Characteristics of the "other" Chicago, as viewed by Patinkin, may be summarized [292, pp. 50–51]:

1. "The quantity theory is . . . not a theory of the demand for money, but a theory which relates the quantity of money (M) to the aggregate demand for goods and services (MV), and thence to the price level (P) and/or level of output (T)"

2. The velocity of money is not constant, but reflects changes "due to

---

"general equilibrium" is spurious. Marshall had his system of n equations and m unknowns. The distinction rather lies in the purpose of theory. Marshall's, as stated, was to achieve fruitful empirical hypotheses. The Walrasians of Friedman's generation had altered this to give prominence to formal elegance and the treatment of detail.

The modern counterparts to Friedman's early distinctions would appear as the search for fruitful hypotheses (Ch. 5) as distinct from the Keynesians emphasis on structural equations models (Ch. 14) with their relatively static underpinnings. In the present discussion, detail is not disparaged as much as the relatively static attributes of the received theory.

9. Friedman joined the faculty at Chicago in 1946, the year he received a Ph.D degree from Columbia University. He was then thirty-four years of age. He received A.B. (Rutgers U.) and M.A. (U. of Chicago) degrees in 1932 and 1933 respectively.

anticipations of changing price levels, as well as to the changing state of business confidence as determined by earnings. . . . But the crucial point here is that these expectations will be self-justifying: for the very act of dishoarding [of money balances] will cause prices to rise even further, thus leading to further dishoarding, and so on." The processes of expansion or contraction feed upon themselves, without "natural limit."

3. The foregoing process may occur, even with the velocity of money constant. In any event, in the actual world the perverse behavior of the banking system is a source of instability.

4. The government should undertake a countercyclical policy, changing M to offset changes in V. The rule is: "If prices are downwardly flexible, the operational rule which will assure the proper variation in M is that of increasing M when P falls, and decreasing it when P rises."

5. There is an emphasis on open-market operations and fiscal policy. "The latter method is more efficient, and in some cases might even be necessary. Budget deficits, in turn, can be generated by varying either government expenditures or tax receipts . . . either method changes M; but from the viewpoint of the general philosophy of the proper role of government in economic life, the variation of tax receipts is definitely preferable. Hence, a tax system which depends heavily on the income tax is desirable not only from the viewpoint of distributive justice, but also from the viewpoint of automatically providing proper cyclical variations in tax receipts."

Of these characteristics elements, (2) and part of (3) are surely Friedman's, as he would point out [135]. The money stock is the control variable, and money is important, as in Friedman's work. This contrasts with the Keynesian emphasis on the interest rate as a crucial link in the transmission mechanism and on interest rate elasticities (notably the trap and inelasticity of investment demand), and again Friedman readily recognizes the fact [135, pp. 934–35, 944–45].

As brought out from time to time, Friedman's approach is primarily characterized by (1) a portfolio approach (the ideas of wealth and asset adjustments working through a general equilibrium framework, and associated changes in the velocity of money relating in turn to imbalances between desired and actual money balances), (2) a demand for money concept wherein the public adjusts its desired holdings of money in relation to income by varying the rate of expenditures and possibly the price level, (3) a liquidity approach to the demand for money with stress on the conditions of demand (in part as distinct from a medium of exchange or transactions demand approach with stress on conditions of supply),

(4) emphasis on underlying trends or permanent income as represented by an exponentially declining weighted average of current and past income measures, (5) the Fisherian equation with the money interest rate as the sum of the real rate and the expected rate of price inflation or deflation, and (6) a strong (even if at times disguised) interest in expectations in the permanent income notion and an emphasis on uncertainty. The historically perverse influences of monetary policy, the allegedly unpredictable influences of fiscal policy, and the prospect of greater certainty resulting from greater stability in the growth rate of the money stock are all additional aspects of Friedman's approach.

Friedman defends some of his early statements about his tie with a pre-Keynesian tradition at Chicago in several ways. He makes a distinction between an Austrian view of the quantity theory of money, as discussed at the University of London, and a view as discussed at Chicago and coincidently by Keynes. The former apparently led to a relatively austere policy [135, p. 936]; "the only sound policy was to let the depression [of the 1930s] run its course, bring down money costs, and eliminate weak and unsound firms." In contrast, the old Chicago group moved toward policy actions [135, p. 937–39]. In addition, Friedman says [135, p. 941] that "Keynes' discussion of the demand curve for money in the *General Theory* is for the most part a continuation of early quantity theory approaches, improved and refined but not basically modified."

By such a diverse route, but not going so far as to embrace the liquidity trap, Friedman is tied with Keynes' economics, if not the Keynesian economics of the early 1950s toward which he was somewhat "hostile" [135, p. 936]. Thus, as Patinkin has pointed out as best his evidence will permit (mainly written work, his lecture notes as a student at Chicago, 1943–45, and an examination of doctoral dissertations at Chicago in the monetary area from 1930 to 1950), some of the foregoing characteristics of Friedman's work have more direct antecedents in Keynes' work [10] than in a pre-Friedmanian, "oral" or written tradition at Chicago. The antecedents he emphasizes are the portfolio approach and the "Keynesian" theory of liquidity preference [292, pp. 47, 54, 57].

10. Patinkin [292] does not distinguish between Keynes' economics and Keynesian economics as in this book (Ch. 7). At times he stresses Keynes' *General Theory* and *Treatise*, but at times he clearly fails to distinguish a specific parochial Keynesian economics. He brings in the Keynesian proposition whereby the interest rate exerts special causal influence on the velocity of money and switching between money and bonds [292, pp. 60–61], without referring to Friedman's emphasis on the demise of the interest rate as a causal factor (Chs. 4, 6).

Why then would Friedman claim in his earlier work (mainly "The Quantity Theory of Money—A Restatement," 1956) that he followed a tradition at Chicago? Patinkin has suggested [292, p. 6] that initially Friedman simply did not recognize his intellectual indebtedness to aspects of Keynes' work. In fact, Friedman's reactions to his critics [135] do suggest that he had not sorted out the antecedents to his thinking from a history-of-doctrine point of view. Harry Johnson has further suggested the need to meet his second criterion for the success of revolutionary intellectual change (notably [210, pp. 4, 8–9] that a theory should appear to be new but should also appear to have roots in a valid orthodoxy). Friedman of course does not like this inference about his conscious or sub-conscious motives. He says [135, p. 941] that the "Chicago tradition" is clearly not something he invented "for some noble or nefarious purpose."

18.4   KEYNESIAN BUILDING BLOCKS: PROPOSITIONS BROUGHT FORWARD

Keynesian building blocks have been described (Sec. 1.3), variously embellished, and utilized. The liquidity preference block has been used by Friedman in his explanations of the tendency for the economy to overshoot in response to accelerated growth in the money stock. Accompanying interest rate changes could be viewed as in Fisher's equation for the sum of the real interest rate and the expected rate of change in prices (Sec. 1.4). The blocks were introduced into a general, portfolio choice framework (Sec. 2.2), with the secular or underlying condition that all stock and flow quantities were changing at the same rate, at least as a first approximation, and with the categories composing wealth or total assets yielding flows of returns. Tax and other factors were allowed to impinge on these, in a framework in which the condition for portfolio balance could be described as one in which the rates of return from additions to the various categories were equal. Liabilities have also been introduced in important respects (Ch. 15).

There was more detail concerning the building blocks but it need not be labored. Certain additional points simply stand out. In the light of the foregoing sorts of changes, consumption—as in the aggregate supply-demand block—is most meaningfully viewed as a function of permanent income, as in Friedman's theory of the consumption function. Yet the function can shift and the weights determining the relative influences of current and past income values may change. Thus, with minor modifications the following three propositions apply, as stated by Samuelson [316, p. 7]:

1. Even when the money supply [rate of change?] is held constant, any significant changes in thriftiness and the propensity to consume can be expected to have systematic independent effects on the money value of current output, affecting average prices or aggregate production or both.

2. Even when the money supply [rate of change?] is held constant, an exogenous burst of investment opportunities or animal spirits on the part of business can be expected to have systematic effects on total GNP.

3. Even when the money supply [rate of change?] is held constant, increases in public expenditures or reductions in tax rates—and even increases in public expenditure balanced by increases in taxation—can be expected to have systematic [if unknown] effects upon aggregate GNP.

The emphasis by Samuelson on "exogenous burst" and "animal spirits," however, is a return to Keynes. It contrasts somewhat with an earlier statement by Samuelson and with the relatively static use of the building blocks in the Keynesian tradition. Samuelson indeed minimized the role of expectations in Keynes work in the past and noted [324, p. 150] that "It paves the way for a theory of expectations, but it hardly proves one." Furthermore, in focusing on the IS-LM model as a summary statement by Keynesians of the building blocks, Brunner notes [39, pp. 4–5, 20–23] an important difference between Monetarist and Keynesian economics: Monetarists emphasize shifts in the schedules, whereas Keynesians emphasize slope properties.[11] Brunner says [39, p. 4]:

The relative price process involving the whole spectrum of assets and liabilities, connecting the production of new assets and liabilities with the existing assets and liabilities, introduced substitution and wealth adjustment channels which operate independently of the slope of the two curves and occur as shifts of the IS and LM curves. These shift properties supplement the slope properties in the transmission of monetary impulses.

18.5   STRANDS OF ANALYSIS: POLICY AND OPERATIONS

The strands of analysis bearing on policy matters and operations are varied. They include (1) a consideration of the business conditions at the

11. This distinction in emphasis is present in a variety of contexts, but it has been especially obvious in the discussion of the liquidity preference demand for

time of a policy change, (2) the interrelationships between normally distinct areas of analysis, (3) the various schemes and approaches to considerations of the role and effects of monetary policy, (4) the role of expectations, particularly in an explanation of turning points in business conditions, and (5) allowances for operational constraints and problems in efforts to stabilize growth rates for monetary aggregates. These strands all concern Keynesian building blocks or the tradition of attempting to separate the body of theory from policy discussions.

The point-of-entry aspect of analysis was introduced in Chapter 1 with the question of whether a variant of a static liquidity preference model should be used regardless of whether an analysis of the effect of a policy proceeded from an equilibrium or disequilibrium state. As suggested, the disequilibrium state was to be indicated by a change in income velocity or by an imbalance in the level of desired and actual balances relative to income. The weight of professional opinion, as indicated by authoritative analyses, would seem to favor proceeding from the static state. The present analysis, however, has tended to favor the evaluation of entry under the disequilibrium condition. The main reasons invoked to support it are that: (1) the disequilibrium state, as indicated by observed changes in velocity and interest rates, is the one characterizing the world in which monetary policy must be implemented; (2) there is an apparent need to abstract from defensive activities of the Federal Reserve, from the seasonal influences, and from the noise in the short-run data, all to focus on the "dynamic" stabilization aspects of Federal Reserve policy.[12] Not among these reasons but nevertheless of interest is Leijonhufvud's view of Keynes' economics as of concern for a disequilibrium state and changing ideas about the future (Ch. 7).

The relatively static role played by the liquidity preference building block in the Keynesian and banking orthodoxies of the 1950s and the

---

money (Sec. 5.4). The Keynesians emphasized the liquidity preference schedule and the liquidity trap in a relatively static context. Others have emphasized the pull toward normality (the normal or safe rate) with the prospect that the subjectively viewed norm could itself change rather than lead to the trap situation.

12. The need to abstract from the short run has been frequently emphasized. There have also been times when interpretations (Ch. 13) by Gibson and Kaufman could be pointed to: "These findings do not deny that money or credit affects interest rates inversely. Rather they suggest that the influence of money and credit may be too brief to be identified clearly in monthly observations. Thus, even in such short periods, the dominant influence on interest rates appears to come through the real sector." Discussing noise in the data, Maisel says [254, p. 152], "There are very few weeks—frequently even months—in which much of the reported movement in monetary aggregates is not primarily the result of statistical 'noise.'"

1960s is further related to the separation of interest rate control from that of the rate of return on additional investment. In the orthodoxy, an open market purchase could lower "the rate of interest" usually in the short dated sector of the yield structure. This would shift the structure of interest rates in relation to rates of return in the real sector and stimulates capital outlays. In contrast, however, an equality of foresight principle was introduced, expectations became an intervening variable, and factors impinging on expectations in the money and bond markets were viewed as less separable from those influencing the rates in the real goods sectors. Indeed, in considering the term structure of interest rates, evidence indicated that other sectors of the economy rely on time series other than and in combination with interest rates. They exhibit the same patterns of changes in expections as those exhibited in the term structure of interest rates (Ch. 12). Gibson pointed to further analysis and supporting evidence as he analyzed interest rate responses to expected price level changes and then changed to responses to expected business conditions more generally (Ch. 13).

In Chapter 14 the break was noted with an earlier linkage scheme. There influences emanated from a change in reserves to changes in bank loans and ultimately business conditions. Such linkages were said to have lingered on in analysis, as in the early versions of the Fed-MIT model, long after their presence in the real world was questioned, as revealed by the evidence. Perhaps there was the almost utopian desire that the wonderful world of econometric model-building of the 1960s would yield something to instruct the policy-makers. The instruction would say that if they did thus and so with a given instrument of policy, then they could achieve a prescribed target in terms of some aggregate indicator of economic performance.

In contrast, in Chapter 15 is outlined the prospect of the Federal Reserve exerting an influence on the prospect of changes in interest rates and business conditions, as indicated by the spread between long- and short-term rates. A narrowing (widening) spread is suggested as an indication of a decreasing (increasing) subjective probability of a future rise in the interest rate, when the anticipated change in rates is viewed as a surrogate for business conditions generally. Here the primary influence of the Federal Reserve is via the outlook for business conditions and on the volume of bank loans to business as influenced primarily from the demand side of the market for bank loans. Large corporations are characterized by planning and by the anticipations of their policy-making units. Financial planning is an important ingredient of overall planning. It centers about liquidity, and liquidity enters as a constraint on expenditures. A test of these theoretical speculations is said to be their ability to explain the differential patterns of capital expenditures by large and small firms.

In particular, the analysis underlying the investment sector of the Fed-MIT models included these features: (1) the Federal Reserve influences long-term interest rates, albeit with some time lag, through open market operations, and investment is supposed to vary inversely with the nominal interest rate; (2) an interest-induced wealth effect operates via both bond and stock prices; and (3) credit rationing by banks to business firms has no effect on plant and equipment and inventory investment. Other features of the investment analysis in the Fed-MIT models included allowances for risk in the appropriate interest rate and for the influence on capital expenditures of waves of optimism and pessimism.

In keeping with the spirit of the relevance of everything and with the complexity of linkages between policy actions and ultimate economic goals, there was apparently the need to bring such diverse groups of features into the FRB-MIT model. Nevertheless, the present volume has questioned the meaningfulness of attempts to separate—and, in effect, isolate—too large a variety of policy influences and to view them as operating independently of one another for the purposes of policy implementation. In discussing the term structure of interest rates, for example, the relevant question was posed (Sec. 13.2):

> The important question concerning policy, of course, is not whether evidence indicates some degree of backwardation and market segmentation. It is rather whether the policy operation in question exerts its primary influence through some part of the expectations mechanism, considering the overall aspects of the operation. If the level of interest rates (and thus the yield spread) are affected mainly by, say, the prospective inflationary aspects of accelerated growth in the money supply, then the effects of efforts to simultaneously alter the term structure via debt management or Federal Reserve purchases in different maturity sectors of the market may be overwhelmed. . . . The question is one about the net effects of stabilization operations overall.

In the discussions of interest-induced and price-induced wealth effects (Ch. 1), the prospect that the short-run effects would be swamped or overwhelmed by the expectation effects was brought out. Interest-induced wealth effects were said to recede to a secondary level of importance relative to revision of prospects about the future. Keynes' doubt about whether price-induced wealth effects could swamp the expectations effect was mentioned.

The role of expectations is often paramount in the assessment of the shortcomings of theory and methods in the increasingly empirically-oriented 1960s. This was particularly so in view of the number of different variables apparently responding, for example, to anticipated inflation. Further, it has been pointed out that the more mechanical constructs cannot explain turning points in business conditions and the varying duration of expansion phases of business conditions. An effect apparently common to many time series is the "push" effect—from the current and recent thrust of the movement in the series. It contributes to the prospect that the direction of the current and recent changes will continue in the near future. The "pull" effect is another—a pull toward normality, subjectively viewed and possibly as indicated by the long-run and trend influences underlying the short-run changes. There are also autonomous or "shock" effects.

In time the structural equations methods may be reoriented and improved as means of separating complex influences and interrelationships. The methods and their uses in the 1960s were simply not equal to the initial claims made for them. The same could be said of much of the economic theory underlying the more prevalent structural equations models.

The "push" and "pull" effects alone will not explain turning points in business conditions. To bring further to the forefront the subjective elements in decision-making, as viewed by positive economic theory, the following prospects were pointed out: (1) Keynes' analysis of disequilibrium and changing ideas about the future (Ch. 7); (2) the early ties of Keynes to modern decision theory (Ch. 8); and (3) the likely role of the slanting and discounting of probabilities of certain prospects, especially in the case of shaky beliefs and interpersonally controversial situations (Ch. 8). In the latter case, when opinions are almost equally divided, there is considerable slanting or discounting of probability because of the nature of allowances for controversial matters in group situations. As opinions about the anticipated changes coalesce, there is less uncertainty, opinions become reinforcing, and weights shift to favor "pull" relative to "push" effects. Turning points in business conditions may be explained in this fashion.

In this expectational, probabilistic context, the Keynesian building blocks are still parts of the analysis. The forces giving rise to shifts and differential rates of change in the various variables and schedules have simply been made explicit.

The expectational, probabilistic analysis and support for the presence of expectational phenomena pose certain difficulties for (1) common interpretations of distributed lag models, (2) the Federal Reserve, structural equation type of model (as reviewed in Ch. 14), and (3) simple linkage-scheme views of monetary policy. In the case of the distributed lag models, the relative size of the coefficients of lagged variables may vary, the length of the time lags may vary, and the impact of a given change—say, of accelerating the flow of bank credit—may vary at one time with that at another. This latter point was dramatized in the discussion of special monetary episodes (Ch. 11).

Discussion of such structural equation models with orientation toward money, as mentioned earlier, first came to the forefront in a classical controversy in the early- to mid-1960s, over an attempt to test a simple version of the quantity theory of money against a simple version of Keynesian income expenditure theory (Ch. 5). That controversy centered about speculation over the definition of autonomous expenditures or an autonomous variable. In the classical regression equation context, the definition was brought out that such a variable was uncorrelated with the random error term of the equation in which it appeared. It became synonymous with the notion of an exogenous variable in a stochastic model, as discussed elsewhere [116, p. 30]; "a variable whose value in each period is statistically independent of the values of all random disturbances in the model in all periods." In a later paper on the controversy [116, p. 30], Meiselman summarized the definition: " 'autonomous' spending is understood to originate outside of the usual economic calculus—a Vietnam . . . or a change in tax rates following a conversion to a new economic ideology."

In the structural equations context, the impact of outside forces and "shocks" was said to lead to an interdependence of so-called independent variables and to instability in the parameters of the models as estimated for different time periods. The interdependence in the variables and the unexplained forces reflected in the unstable parameters were said to lead to the need to add variables and equations to the models until they became extremely large, possibly too large.[13]

Analyses of expectational phenomena—shocks, common influences

13. In referring to structural equations methodology, from time to time there was the recognition that solutions to structural equations models implied reduced form equations and that single equation models could be viewed as reduced form equations. These in turn implied some underlying structure. These matters are summarized elsewhere as they relate to Federal Reserve policy [116, pp. 30–36].

shared by distinct variables, and so on—may be tricky. They may be further susceptible to misuse in justifying "claims of innocence and achievement" by policy-makers. Even so, the empirical onslaught of the 1960s and early 1970s suggests the relevance of expectational phenomena, extending to both theory and operations. The attention given to these phenomena in this book is consistent with many of the requirements and problems that operating officials of the Federal Reserve mention. In fact, there is a consistency with points made by Holmes, manager of the Federal Open Market Account since 1965, as he discusses the operational constraints and problems in stabilizing the monetary growth rate [206, pp. 65–67]:

[On interrelationships and expectations] Out of it all, there is bound to develop a better understanding of the relationships between monetary aggregates, interest rates, and the real economy. I suspect, however, that the underlying relationships are so complex that no simple formula can be found as an unerring guide to monetary policy. The psychology and expectations involved in private decision making are probably too complicated to compress into any such formula.

[On interest rates] One obvious problem with interest rates as either an indicator or target of monetary policy is that they may be measuring not only the available supply of money and credit but also the demand for money and credit. . . . But interest rates have the decided advantage of being instantaneously available. . . .

[On interrelationships and expectations] The moral of the story . . . is that Federal Reserve policy should not be judged exclusively in terms of interest rates or in terms of monetary aggregates but by the combination of the two—and by the resultant impact of this combination on market psychology and expectations about the future and, ultimately, on the real economy.

[On the short run] Not only are open market operations in the very short run unlikely to have a major impact on the real economy, but adequate measures of economic change are unavailable in the short time span involved. . . . I should add that we are fairly cautious about over-interpreting any short-run wriggle in the credit proxy [total bank credit as a proxy for the money stock]. While forecasts of the proxy have generally proved to be more stable than money supply forecasts—perhaps mainly because the proxy avoids the large and erratic shifts between Treasury deposits in commercial banks and private demand deposits—they, too, have proved to be somewhat unstable on a week-to-week basis.

[On "defensive operations"] Some of the proposals for moving to the money supply as a target and indicator have been coupled with complete abandonment of so-called "defensive" open market operations. . . .

It would appear wise to disassociate the debate over money supply from the problem of so-called defensive open market operations.

[On the short run and achieving a target rate of growth in the money supply] In my view, this [control over the rate of growth of the money supply] lies well within the power of the Federal Reserve to accomplish provided one does not require hair-splitting precision and is thinking in terms of a time span long enough to avoid the erratic, and largely meaningless, movements of money supply over the short periods.

[On expectations again] Psychology and expectations play too great a role in the operations of these [financial] markets to permit the monetary authority to ignore the interpretations that the market may place on current central bank operations.

18.6   INFLATION AND EXPECTATIONS: DIVERGENT VIEWS

A proposition of economic theory with emphasis on perfect competition as a useful first approximation to a long-run analysis of the price level and output may be stated thus: change all stock and flow quantities (money, income, output, wealth, total assets, total liabilities, and the various portions comprising these quantities) at the same rate (as by doubling each), and the average of prices (and interest rates) remains unchanged. In other words, as the stock and flow quantities grow over time, one is led to expect an underlying trend of constant prices (and interest rates) and a constant velocity of money (or ratio of income to money). Over the years since 1950, however, the average of prices for the output of goods and services has increased—but not decreased—at varying rates, and interest rates and the velocity of money have experienced parallel upward movements. Cycles have been imposed on these trends, and there are indeed complexities (such as when decision-makers look beyond the troughs and see government policies in their price-setting decisions) and special episodes.

The inflationary part of the foregoing changes in the 1965–72 period and the facts engendered in relation to them concern several aspects of received theory: (1) issues were provided that Keynesian theory could not cope with, (2) neither monetarist nor Keynesian theory could deal with the persistent and apparent expectations phenomena, and (3) both monetarist and Keynesian approaches offered non-competing and possibly overlapping explanations of downward inflexibility of prices during recessions. The Keynesians offered variants of the market-power explanation for the prices to adjust downward (Sec. 7.2) and some monetarists suggested an explanation in terms of uncertainty and imperfect information (Sec. 7.2, and Appendix to Ch. 7). Elements of the former explanation and analyses of expectations both seem necessary to explain the episodes leading to and motivating President Nixon's "new economic policy" in the second half of 1971. Elements of theory and divergent views come into focus through a brief consideration of the episodes and policy. The actions and issues are ominous for the future of theory and the economy.

Price changes in the post–World War II years were dramatized by the inflationary recessions of 1957–58 and 1970–71. The latter episode of persistent price increases and increasing percentage of unemployment appeared to have become especially deeply rooted since its beginnings in 1965. The apparent uniqueness of the 1970–71 recession led Arthur Burns [53, p. 656] to say that "The rules of economics are not working in quite the way they used to. Despite extensive unemployment in our country, wage rate increases have not moderated. Despite much idle industrial capacity, commodity prices continue to rise rapidly." In this context, Burns emphasized that the expectations of inflation "thus permeate the gamut of private decisions to spend and invest, and this is restraining the private efforts needed for vigorous and sustained economic recovery." The episode was referred to as "cost-push" inflation. The label arose out of the 1957–58 episode to describe a tendency for costs—mainly in the form of wages and in the more organized sectors of the labor market—to rise at excessive rates under slack conditions and to be passed on to ultimate consumers in rising prices. The "push" reference contrasted with a demand "pull" in which the pressure for rising prices was thought to originate on the demand side of the market.

The earlier argument continued thus [133, pp. 345–50]: Costs and prices would rise; with the government committed to the maintenance of full employment, the price rises would be validated by expansionary programs to avoid further unemployment. This could in fact go to a substantial level, if the unemployment was to serve as a check on rising wages and costs. The government's position has been referred to by some as "bail out"—the labor and management sides of industry make inappropriate decisions and the government bails them out. In the 1970–71 episode the matter was thought by some [53, pp. 660–62] to be compounded and by others [261] simply "incapable of explanation by textbook theories of classical economics."

The 1957–58 episode led to wage-price guideposts, as first published in the 1962 *Economic Report of the President* [133, pp. 344–45]. The guideposts were to make market participants behave as might be expected in a competitive economy—wage rates on the average could rise as fast as total (national) output per man-hour—and there were special allowances depending on whether an industry was in a rising or declining state, in need of more or less workers. The guidepost approach evolved from discussion to admonition by the president and finally to direct intervention by the government (in the case of a steel wage settlement in September 1965).

The early Nixon administration was committed to making the free market work with conventional measures along free market lines. One might say this followed the Chicago school.[14] However, in the light of the 1970–71 developments, a radical switch in policy occurred in mid-August 1971. The major new initiatives announced at that time included a 90-day freeze on virtually all prices and wages [390]. This "first" phase was followed by a "second" [391] with a more flexible price and wage policy, and the second phase was followed by an even more flexible "third," and then a "fourth." Under the new policy a Cost of Living Council was established, initially with the ancillary Price Commission and Wage Board. The controls were to be somewhat indirect, there were various subtle ways of enforcing them, and they were variously described as temporary, complicated in design, and weak in administration. These details need not be labored but two points are especially important: (1) among the four objectives of the "New Economic Policy," a principal one was "to slow sharply and at once the rate of inflation and thereby break the inflationary psychology gripping the Nation" [52, p. 123]; and (2) the controls and policies became especially directed at the more organized sectors of the labor and product markets. In other words, there was a clear commitment to the recognition and existence of special market power and its relevance to inflation and administered prices.

"Phase III" came in January 1973. It was ushered in with the abolition of the Pay Board and the Price Commission. The Cost of Living Council, however, was retained to manage the system of wages and prices, and a new labor-management advisory committee was established. The new system was more "self-administering and based on voluntary compliance," except in the special problems areas, including the health industry and food processing and retailing. Under Phase III, a 5.5 per cent wage-increase guideline from Phase II was to be taken as a guide to appropriate

14. George P. Schultz, a White House advisor and later Secretary of the Treasury, was principal White House spokesman in the free market phase of administrative policy. Schultz came to the administration in 1969 from the post of dean of the Graduate School of Business at the University of Chicago. He also had a hand in the use of the Laffer–Ranson monetary model discussed in Section 10.4.

maximum wage increases. There was reluctance to set a specific standard for fear that the collective bargaining process between the two sides of industry would be distorted, with the set maximum actually becoming a floor for wage increases. What was essential was the target for a reduced rate of inflation of 2.5 per cent by the end of 1973. As with the mechanics underlying the old wage-price guidepost of the early 1960s, the rate of inflation equaled a percentage increase in compensation per unit of output less the percentage increase in productivity. To be sure, there was speculation about escalating wage demands and inflation, and there were international overtones concerning the value of the dollar in foreign exchange markets and indeed even the system of fixed exchange rates, described earlier (Sec. 16.4). The domestic situation was compounded by developments abroad, even though domestic business conditions were expanding in 1973 with favorable inflationary rates and productivity gains relative to those in most of the developed world.

Indeed, on the domestic side the decline in the rate of inflation was short lived, following an initial jump at the end of Phase II. As the boom progressed in 1973, the inflation rate again accelerated. There was a strong foreign demand occurring as a part of a world-wide boom, and there was strong spending at home. The boom psychology was present again, so on June 13, 1973, the president announced a new 60-day freeze on prices. In this period they could go down but not up. New controls on wages and rents were avoided. The president in fact noted that wage settlements reached under Phase III had not been a significant cause of the increase in prices. A new phase, Phase IV, was scheduled to follow the second freeze. The administrative structure would continue—the Cost of Living Council with its advisors—but there were to be stronger controls, along the lines of Phase II, and again special sectors were to receive special attention. There was the prospect that with the passage of time the need to control the boom would decrease.

The policy stance with respect to controls and prices just described is ominous for a variety of reasons, including its relevance to future monetary policy. There is the greater potential for invoking wage-price controls in the future. There are conflicting explanations of the downward inflexibility of prices in dominant sectors of the factor and product markets. In Chapter 7, Keynesians were said to invoke the idea of market power to explain "sticky" downward adjustments in prices. This was said to lack theoretical elegance, and instead an analysis of price-setting affected by uncertainty and incomplete information was brought forward (Sec. 7.2, Appendix to Ch. 7). These notions themselves need not be in conflict, but Friedman [134] was quick to deny the possible effects of the controls and the claim for any uniqueness in the 1970–71 inflationary episode—as would be consistent with reviews often attributed to him on the singularity of the importance of money in the determination of the average of prices, and his commitment to the theory of perfect competition (Appendix to Ch. 8, Sec. 16.4). The developments with respect to the ideas of market power did not go his way. The international developments, in contrast, tended to give confirmation to his view.

On the domestic side, the New Economic Policy of 1971–73 suggests an administered price or Keynesian rather than monetarist, free-market approach. An administered price or Keynesian element of analysis then is retained and brought forward by those who accept such explanations. There are the usual arguments: monetary policy alone cannot achieve the national economic goals, mainly because a sufficiently stringent policy to check rising prices falls more on output and unemployment [261, 365]; practical politicans and voters are unwilling to accept the unemployment consequences of sole reliance on any sufficiently effective monetary-stabilization policy; tax policy, an improved matching of job skills with job vacancies, and improvements in the means of reducing frictional unemployment (due to the movement from one job to another), are all required. By the same token, the goals of economic policy are unattainable without the support of monetary policy. Any successful policy on the part of government with respect to the appropriate growth paths for prices and for incomes of the various sectors of the economy (any "incomes policy") will require Federal Reserve cooperation.

Analysis of stabilization matters and guidance in the attainment of economic goals call for a framework that recognizes a variety of prospects as fundamental: the large amount of seasonal and random movement and just plain noise in the data in the very short period; possible change in the secular and equilibrium growth paths underlying changes in business conditions; the presence of expectational, probabilistic phenomena (learning, uncertainty, and the role of information in reducing uncertainty); and the public's unwillingness to accept the consequences of almost exclusive reliance on monetary policy, even with its more modern emphasis on the underlying trends in monetary aggregates.

On the international side, the New Economic Policy was initially accompanied by a devaluation of the dollar from $35 to $38 per ounce of gold, in response to the further deterioration in the U.S. balance of payments in the 1960s and to speculation against the dollar. Fourteen months later, in Phase III, the dollar was again devalued to $42.22 in response to speculation against the dollar in foreign exchange and free gold markets. There were U.S. payments deficits contributing to an excess of dollars in foreign hands; there was rapid growth of economic strength in Japan and Western Europe (and Western Germany especially); and there was some realization of a narrowing of the U.S. lead in technology in many sectors of the economy. The role of the dollar as a store of value (Appendix to Ch. 8) seemed to be especially questionable. Even with some favorable conditions in real economic magnitudes, the two devaluations of the dollar had further removed the certainty and stability associated abroad with the dollar as a liquid asset. The overall change wrought by the developments was a more highly flexible system of foreign exchange rates, if not a system of freely floating rates. When the dollar's value could no longer be supported, especially against the German mark and the Japanese yen, the floating of some major currencies became necessary. European Common Market countries put together a "joint float" against the dollar (even while maintaining fixed exchange rates among themselves), and Japan floated the yen. What appeared to develop was a split into groups—a dollar area, the European bloc, and the yen bloc. Journalists could write (First National City Bank's *Monthly Economic Letter*, March 1973) about an "unplanned reform" of the international monetary system, an "absence" of agreed rules about the use of direct exchange controls, and the "politicized parities and exchange controls." And Milton Friedman could write ("The Crisis that Refreshes," *Newsweek*, March 12, 1973) about "the obsolete system of fixed exchange rates that has produced such crises repeatedly in the past few years." He wrote of "another step toward a system of exchange rates determined in free markets, the arrangement that is best for the U.S. and the world."

Appendices

Appendix to Chapter 1

Notation, Technical Points, and Econometric Problems

SOME TECHNICAL POINTS, terms, and notations have been introduced, and still others appear later. These concern mainly changes in series, measurement, and regression analysis. Their presence may prohibit the less initiated readers from proceeding in the monetary area. Thus, this appendix elaborates on the use of notation, some technical terms, and some econometric problems.

Notation.—Interest is often centered on percentage changes, elasticities, rates of change, and changes in the rates more than on levels for stock and flow variables. A variety of ways of denoting the latter measures have been introduced. To illustrate these and their interrelations further, the money stock (M), the interest rate (i), and time (t) will be used:

$(\Delta M/M) \times 100$ is a percentage change in the money stock and $\Delta M/M \approx dM/M$

$d \ln M \times 100$ is a percentage change in the money stock, where *ln* denotes a natural logarithmic transformation of the money stock, *ln M* is itself a variable, and *d ln M* is a change in the transformed variable *M*.

$\left| \dfrac{\Delta M/M}{\Delta i / i} \right|$ is a measure of interest elasticity of the demand for money (the percentage change in the money stock called forth by a percentage change in the interest rate) where *M* and *i* are coordinates of a point on a demand schedule for money, and where

$$\frac{\Delta M/M}{\Delta i / i} \approx \frac{dM/M}{d i / i} = \frac{dM}{d i} \frac{i}{M} = \frac{d \ln M}{d \ln i}$$

$$\left|\frac{d \ln M}{d \ln i}\right| \to \infty$$

is the liquidity trap (as illustrated in Sec 1.3, n. 9).

$M(t)$

denotes the money stock as a function of time.

$\ln M(t)$

denotes the logarithmic transformation of the money stock as a function of time.

$$\frac{d \ln M(t)}{dt}$$

denotes a rate of change in the money stock with respect to time, where

$$\frac{d \ln M(t)}{dt} = \frac{1}{M}\frac{dM}{dt} \quad \text{by}$$

rules of mathematical analysis. (Appendix to Ch. 15, n. 4)

$$\dot{M}$$

is notation for the rate of change in the money stock, thus

$$\dot{M} = \frac{1}{M}\frac{dM}{dt} \ .$$

$$\frac{d\,(\dot{M})}{dt}$$

is the change in the rate of change in the money stock over time, thus

$$\frac{d\,(\dot{M})}{dt} = \frac{d\,(\frac{1}{M}\frac{dM}{dt})}{dt}$$

$$\frac{d\,(\dot{M})}{dt} = 0$$

denotes that the rate of change in the money stock is not changing (it is constant or at a turning point) in that the rate of change has stopped moving in one direction and started moving in another direction.

The true regression coefficient.—To introduce econometric problems,[1] time series for the income velocity of money (Y/M) and the interest rate (r) may be used. These tend to move synchronously and directly over time. When one effects a logarithmic transformation of such data

1. For a survey of econometric problems in their applied context, and for a glossary of statistical terms appearing in the demand for money literature, see Frazer [126, pp. 34–56, 327–48]. The index to this book may also be helpful in locating definitions, as would some of the standard statistics textbooks. In introducing the methods of the multi-equation econometric models, the references will usually be to Christ [71].

on a quarterly basis (seasonally adjusted) for the period 1947–65, and regresses velocity on the interest rate, the following results are obtained:

(1.0) $\ln V_y = 0.11 + 0.81 \ln r$ $r^2 = 0.89$
                              (0.03)

where

r^2 is the coefficient of determination (a measure of the variation in *ln* V_y associated with variations in *ln* *r*),

r and i   are often used interchangeably as variables for the interest rate,

0.81   is the regression coefficient, such that 81 percent of a change in *ln* *r* becomes the change in *ln* V_y

                            thus $\dfrac{d \ln V_y}{d \ln r} = 0.81$, and

(0.03)   is the standard error of the regression coefficient.

In view of the high correlation (r^2s closeness to 1.00), equation (1.0) reflects a strong relationship between the variables. But a problem inherent in the use of classical least-squares regression analysis could cause difficulty in attempts to rely on regression coefficients in similar regression equations. In effect, equation (1.0) describes the fit of a line to a set of observations such that the vertical distances between the line and the observations are minimized, and all the error of measurement is assumed to be in the left-hand member of the equation. If one instead assumes the error to be in the variable in the right-hand member of the equation, then another estimate of the regression coefficient (0.81/0.89 = 0.91) is obtained by dividing 0.81 by r^2. Thus assuming that the regression line is fit by minimizing horizontal distances, the regression coefficient becomes 0.91 instead of 0.81. One may conclude that these coefficients are actualy upper and lower bounds, respectively, to the true value of the regression coefficient.[2] The foregoing classical problem causes no special difficulty in the present instance, because of the high co-

2. For a discussion of this classical problem in an applied context, see Stroup and Frazer [132].

efficient of determination (r^2), but it could in some contexts. One is simply warned to beware of reliance on specific values of regression coefficients.

In the analysis of time series, the standard error of the regression coefficient [(0.03), in equation (1.0)] is sometimes biased as a result of some dependence of current values in a series on lagged values. The econometric problem of autocorrelation, however, does not affect the estimate of the regression coefficient itself as distinct from the standard error of the estimate.

Multicollinearity.—Next, one may recognize that the left-hand member of equation (1.0) could be written as two variables. Recognizing this, one might then obtain from (1.0) an equation of the form

(1.1) $\ln M = \text{const.} + \alpha \ln r + \beta \ln Y, \ \alpha < 0$

This becomes a multiple as distinct from a simple regression equation. Such equations are frequently encountered. There may even be more variables in the right-hand member of the equation than shown here. In any event, there is a tendency to interpret such equations as mathematical (non-stochastic) and to conclude, for example, that the effect of a change in *ln r* on *ln M* is reflected in a precise way in α, and that the effect of a change in *ln Y* on *ln M* is reflected precisely in β, where α and β are regression coefficients. Such, however, is unlikely to be the case in the analysis of time series in economics, in part because of the high intercorrelation between variables. The econometric problem encountered here is multicollinearity. It is elaborated upon in Chapter 4, Section 10.4, and Appendix to Chapter 15.

In essence, the presence of intercorrelation in variables in the right-hand members of regression equations means that the separate effect of each variable cannot readily be isolated by simple procedures. Rather, the whole package of interrelationships must be considered. From one point of view, the difficulty is that the assumption of *ceteris paribus* is built into the computational mechanism of the regression model (as distinct from mathematics),[3] but, in fact, the assumption is not applicable to the world to which the analysis is being applied. The uninitiated reader is simply warned to beware of the use of the *ceteris paribus* assumption and of the presence of multicollinearity in interpreting statistical results.

---

3. In differential calculus there are variations of the chain or function-of-a-function rule, but there is no such exact counterpart in the general regression model, except possibly in the very restrictive case where a structure is identified as in Christ [71, p. 303] and where two-stage least-squares is applicable. See the discussion in Section 4.3.

This assumption is deeply engrained in economic reasoning, and it is often dangerously invoked. Economists often use the term when they wish to refer to the effect of one variable on another, independent of the effects of other variables, even when the latter assumption may not be warranted. In such cases the reasoning is sometimes improperly thought to be similar to that of differential calculus, where as an empirical matter $ln\ r$ and $ln\ Y$ would be directly related to the rate of change in prices (changes in $ln\ r$ and $ln\ Y$ are tied to some other variable and consequently to one another) and where the interrelationship between the variables needs to be allowed for in the reasoning, if not in explicit mathematical form.

The distributed lag model.—In economics one encounters some time series that lag relative to other series. For example, when the price level of the current output of goods and services is changing, it may lag in time behind changes in the growth rate of the money stock, and changes in an interest rate series may follow in time changes in a series for the price level. One method of presenting such lag relations is the distributed lag model, a regression equation model in which some current value such as a nominal interest rate (rn_t) is regressed on current and previous values for some series such as the rate of change in prices ($\dot{P}_t$, $\dot{P}_{t-1}$, $\dot{P}_{t-2}$, . . .). The regression coefficients resulting from such a regression are thought to give some clue to the behavior of the dependent-variable values relative to those in the right-hand member of the regression. (Discussions concerning distributed lag models appear throughout, esp. Secs. 10.4, 14.4, 15.4, Appendix to Chapter 15.)

The variables in the right-hand member of a distributed lag model are often interrelated and give rise to the problems of multicollinearity which make interpretation difficult. In fact, the regression coefficients are thought to fluctuate in the presence of multicollinearity. The Almon lag technique is suggested for dealing with this aspect of the analysis.[4] It constrains the coefficients to behave so as to provide a smoother pattern. Although the Almon lag technique does not adequately solve the problem of multicollinearity, it has the advantage of resulting in a smoother if constrained pattern of coefficients.

The fact that some series lead or lag in time relative to others is not in itself indicative of a causal relationship or of the complexity of possible linkage schemes and intervening factors (such as those governing the

---

4. The technique is referred to by the name of its author, Shirley Almon. Her primary paper on the technique [3] and her initial use of it is frequently cited in this book.

learning process and the formation of expectations as particularly emphasized in Chs. 7 and 8). However, one may choose an example of a lagged relationship that is thought to have plausibility. Its development is continued presently with reference to a paper by Yohe and Karnosky [384], and later in other contexts (Ch. 13).

Yohe and Karnosky were particularly interested in the Fisher equation (Sec. 1.3):

$$(2.0) \qquad rn_t = \dot{P}_t^e + rr_t$$

where, using their notation and symbols, rn_t is the nominal interest rate at time t for a particular debt instrument, $\dot{P}_t^e$ is the annual rate of change in prices expected to occur over the life of the debt instrument in question, and rr_t is the "real" interest rate. As is common in econometrics, they use a distributed lag equation to define expected price changes:

$$(2.1) \qquad \dot{P}_t^e = w_0\dot{P}_t + w_1\dot{P}_{t-1} + w_2\dot{P}_{t-2} + \ldots + w_n\dot{P}_{t-n}$$

The weights (w's) in relation to one another reflect the influence, say, of the more current price changes relative to the latter on the formation of expected price changes. Large weights for current and recent rates of changes in prices relative to the weights for more distant changes reflect the predominance of the influence of changes in the recent past. Nevertheless, the presence of weights for changes in the more distant past does reflect a pull or regression toward some possibly extrapolative norm in contrast to the "push" effect or thrust of the changes in the more recent past.

Substituting the right-hand member of equation (2.1) for the expected price changes in equation (2.0), one obtains the following for regression purposes

$$(2.2) \qquad rn_t = \sum_{i=0}^{n} w_i\dot{P}_{t-i} + rr_t$$

Since the real interest rate cannot be measured directly, the equation form for which Yohe and Karnosky choose to obtain estimates is, simply

$$(2.3) \qquad rn_t = a_0 + a_1\dot{P}_t^c + a_2\dot{P}_{t-1}^c + a_3\dot{P}_{t-2}^c + \ldots a_{n+1}\dot{P}_{t-n}^c$$

where the superscript c denotes their use of the consumer price index. Of course, this inability to empirically extract the influence of the "real" from the "nominal" interest rate is an unavoidable shortcoming of the analysis at the present state of the methodology.[5]

5. Two analysts have commented separately on the shortcomings of the analysis.

In estimating coefficients for equation (2.3) one may use ordinary least squares analysis and the regression analysis with the Almon technique.[6] In the latter case, Yohe and Karnosky experimented with various polynomials[7] which impose an a priori time constraint on the estimated coefficients. They chose a sixth degree polynomial because it "best approximated the unconstrained estimates, in that it minimized the sum of the squares of the differences between the unconstrained and Almon estimates." The idea both with and without Almon technique is to experiment with different numbers of lagged terms and choose the results giving the best fit (the highest coefficient of determination of R^2).

Representative Yohe-Karnosky results are shown in Figures A1-1 and A1-2, for ordinary least squares and for Almon technique, respectively. In both figures, patterns of coefficients are plotted against the time lags for their corresponding variables. Results are shown for both short- and long-term interest rates (rn^s and rn^L). In addition, there are results for lags of 24, 36, and 48 months. The data were monthly for the period 1952–69, short-term interest rates were approximated by the yield on

---

Gibson says [167, pp. 21–22]: "But the real rate, r [or rr in Yohe-Karnosky paper], is impossible to observe directly in the United States. If we could obtain a direct measure of r, we would have an equally good measure of the expected rate of price change, and we could examine the relationship between the expected rate and past actual rates of price changes. But as long as the market rates we observe are for payments in the form of money—a depreciating asset during inflation—all of these rates must include compensation for expected inflation. . . . We could only measure the real rate directly if we had observations on an asset whose yields were in the form of a commodity whose real value is unaffected by inflation."

Duesenberry says [98, p. 89]: "The target path for interest rates must, of course, reflect the policymakers' views about all the factors influencing investment decisions, including the effect of price expectations on investment decisions. It is fashionable nowadays to emphasize the distinction between real and nominal interest rates. I doubt whether the concept of real interest rates has any real usefulness in short-run policymaking. The difference between real and nominal interest depends in theory on the expected rate of price change. In a theoretical world in which all prices move together and price expectations respond only to past price movements, the real interest rate concept has a clear meaning. But when prices do not all move together and price expectations reflect interpretations of economic policy as well as price history, there is no well-defined empirical meaning to a real rate of interest."

6. As a third possibility, "geometrically decaying" lags are mentioned by Yohe and Karnosky [384] but they do not find their use as satisfactory as the other distributed lags.

7. An algebraic expression of the form

$$a_oX^n + a_1X^{n-1} + a_2X^{n-2} + \ldots + a_{n-1}X + a_n$$

is called a polynomial in the variable X of degree n. The degree of a term is the exponent of X, and the highest degree of any of the terms is the degree of the polynomial.

four-to-six month commercial paper, and long-term rates were approximated by the yield on Aaa-rated corporate bonds. In all cases, extending the number of lagged terms beyond two years did not appreciably increase the coefficients of determination (R^2s). This suggested that most of the total lagged effect worked itself out in a relatively short time. Finally, the pattern of the coefficients obtained with the Almon technique, as in Figure A1-2, is visibly smoother than that obtained with ordinary least squares alone, as in Figure A1-1.

The dummy variable and splitting the sample.—There are two commonly used methods for dealing with changes in conditions that are thought to underlie a posited relationship of the interest-rate, price-level type. The two methods include the use of the dummy variable and splitting the sample. In the case of the dummy variable, a variable is introduced into the regression equation. It is assigned either a zero or one value—zero when underlying conditions are thought to be normal and one otherwise. Presumably the dummy variable's coefficient captures the influence of the abnormal effect on a dependent variable. However, phenomena that are capable of taking on varying or three or more distinct states are not suited to the dummy variable technique. In the case of splitting the sample, one looks for changes in the estimated coefficients as evidence of distorting influences on some posited relation.

Yohe and Karnosky split their 1952–69 sample of quarterly data into samples for the 1952–60 and 1961–69 periods respectively. In doing so, they particularly want "to see whether there has been any apparent change in the mechanism relating past price changes to the formation of expectations of price expectations and any clues to the reasons for earlier findings of very long lags." Such changes could occur (1) in the increased sensitivity of behavioral units to the need to forecast and anticipate the future, (2) in the communications mechanisms for discriminating and interpreting information, and (3) in some institutional arrangements. Yohe and Karnosky point to the latter in their study, although this does not rule out other prospects.

Some of the Yohe-Karnosky results from splitting their sample are shown in Figure A1-3 and, indeed, differences are present. They reported little difference in the total price expectations effects from the use of different degree polynomials. Nevertheless, differences in the magnitude of the regression and determination coefficients (R^2s) are substantial. In the 1961–69 period, over 90 per cent of the variation in short- and long-term interest rates is explained in the computational sense by the current and lagged values for the rates of change in prices. In the 1952–60 period, in contrast, only 25.5 per cent and 16.4 per cent of the variation for the short and long rates respectively is accounted for. With further reference to the figure in question, Yohe and Karnosky report [384]:

The coefficients of the long-term rate were generated using a second-degree polynomial and 48 lags for 1961–69 and a sixth-degree with 36 lags for 1952–60. All of the coefficients estimated for the 1961–69 period are significant at the one per cent level. A mean lag of 16 months is implied by this result, meaning more than half of the adjustments in interest rates to price changes in the period were obtained in less than a year and a half.

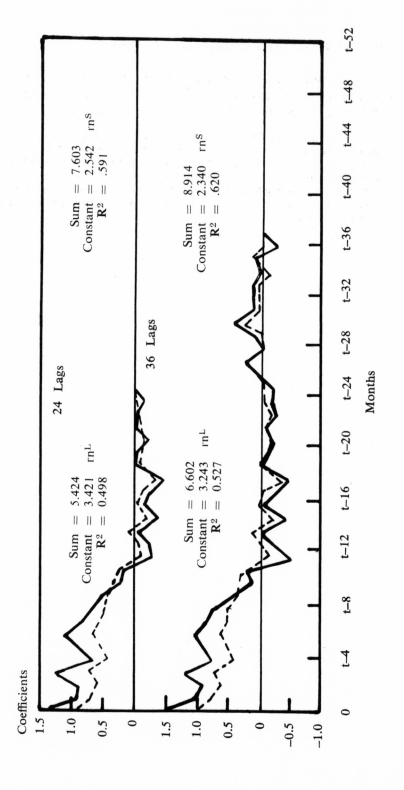

FIGURE A1-1 Summary of Regression Results—Ordinary Least Squares (1952–1969)

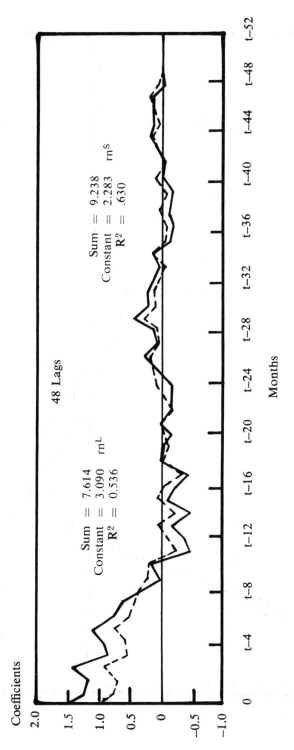

Coefficients

2.0

1.5

1.0

0.5

0

−0.5

−1.0

48 Lags

Sum = 7.614
Constant = 3.090 rn^L
R^2 = 0.536

Sum = 9.238
Constant = 2.283 rn^S
R^2 = .630

0   t–4   t–8   t–12   t–16   t–20   t–24   t–28   t–32   t–36   t–40   t–44   t–48   t–52

Months

Source of figure: William P. Yohe and Denis S. Karnosky, "Interest Rates and Price Level Changes, 1952–69," *Review,* Federal Reserve Bank of St. Louis, December 1969.

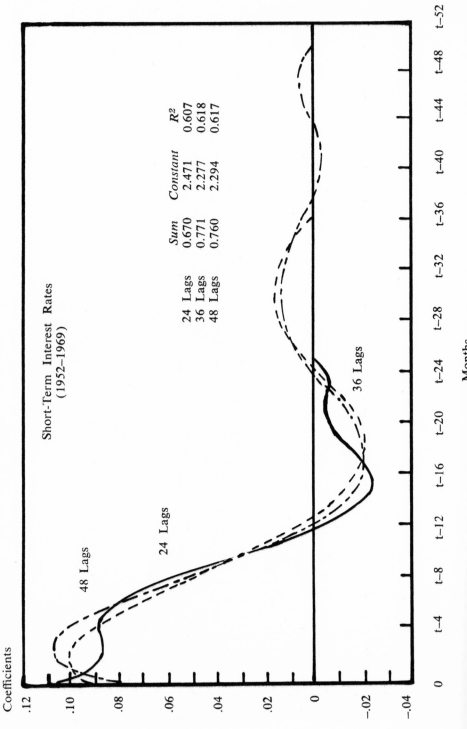

FIGURE A1-2. Summary of Regression Results (Almon Lag)—Short-Term Interest Rate (1952–1969)

Short-Term Interest Rates
(1952–1969)

	Sum	Constant	R^2
24 Lags	0.670	2.471	0.607
36 Lags	0.771	2.277	0.618
48 Lags	0.760	2.294	0.617

Coefficients

.12
.10
.08
.06
.04
.02
0
−.02
−.04

48 Lags

24 Lags

36 Lags

Months

0 t−4 t−8 t−12 t−16 t−20 t−24 t−28 t−32 t−36 t−40 t−44 t−48 t−52

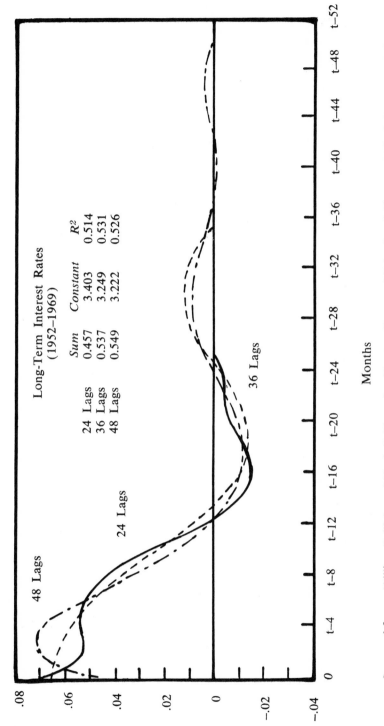

Coefficient

Long-Term Interest Rates
(1952–1969)

	Sum	Constant	R^2
24 Lags	0.457	3.403	0.514
36 Lags	0.537	3.249	0.531
48 Lags	0.549	3.222	0.526

48 Lags

24 Lags

36 Lags

Months

Source of figure: William P. Yohe and Denis S. Karnosky, "Interest Rates and Price Level Changes, 1952–69," *Review*, Federal Reserve Bank of St. Louis, December 1969.

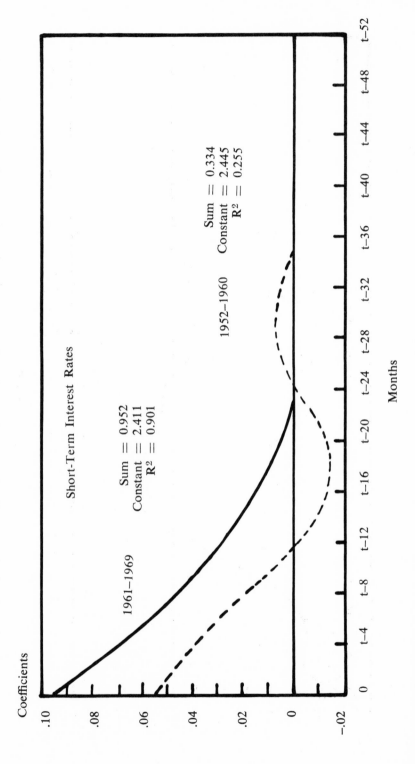

FIGURE A1-3 Summary of Regression Results

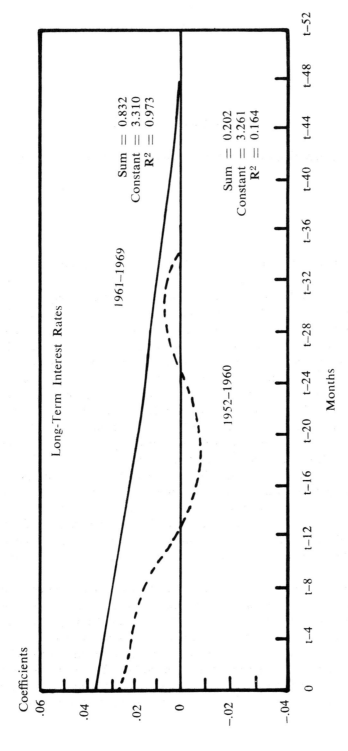

Source of figure: William P. Yohe and Denis S. Karnosky, "Interest Rates and Price Level Changes, 1952–69," *Review*, Federal Reserve Bank of St. Louis, December 1969.

Appendix to Chapter 3

Autocorrelation and the Durbin-Watson Statistic

A GOOD BIT has been said about multicollinearity (Appendix to Ch. 1), and more will be said from time to time (Secs. 4.3, 10.4, Appendix to Ch. 15), in view of its frequent presence in statistical analyses of time series. The study of auto or serial correlation of error terms for linear regression models (correlation between an error term and its leading or lagging values) is also related and important, for reasons that will be given. It is especially relevant to Chapters 5 and 6 and Parts IV and V.

The error $(\hat{v})$ in a regression analysis of time series data is an estimate of the random errors implied by the random error term in the linear regression model. It is the difference between the observed (X) and estimated or "predicted" values $(\hat{X})$ for the dependent variable at a given time. The estimated value $(\hat{X})$ is obtained by inserting actual values for the so-called independent variables in a regression equation for which coefficients have been estimated. It is the time series of errors $(\hat{v}'s)$ on which attention is focused. A useful procedure is to plot residuals or errors $(\hat{v}'s)$ on a vertical axis against time on a horizontal axis. If the plot of residuals shows an upward trend, they are almost certainly positively serially correlated. If the plot shows persistent alternations between negative and positive values, they are almost certainly negatively serially correlated.

The cause of both multicollinearity and autocorrelation is often thought to lie in the common trend in the respective series of data. It is thought that the trend represents some force common to the respective series. Such forces may be significantly deserving of attention in economic analyses of the real world, and indeed they may even be the overwhelming forces. Isolating or recognizing them is important, but economists sometimes seek to isolate causal sequences in relationships between time series using least-squares regression analysis, and to attach special significance

430

to the separate coefficients arising in such a context. Thus they seek to remove the common trend, as discussed in Chapters 4, 5, and 6. One measure of the possible absence, presence, or indeterminancy of serial correlation is the Durbin-Watson statistic[1] as reported in Tables 6–1 and 6–2 of Chapter 6 and on later occasions.

Autocorrelation.—The study of auto or serial correlation is important for the following reasons:

(1) The presence of correlation between the value of the error term at a given time and the leading or lagging value of the error term implies the presence of some unexplained systematic influence. This is analogous to saying that some omitted variable is included in the random error term.

(2) Assumptions or ordinary regression analysis include or imply an absence of correlation between the error term and one or more independent variables. If some omitted variable is the cause of the systematic variation in the error term, and if it is separated and included as an "independent" variable, then one encounters the presence of multicollinearity, as defined in Appendix to Chapter 1.

(3) In the presence of serial correlation one may obtain an unbaised estimate of a coefficient, but one is also likely to obtain an understatement of the sampling variance of the coefficient. This means further that the t-ratio may be overstated, as used in tests of statistical significance. Recall that

$$\text{t-ratio} = \frac{\hat{\beta} - \beta}{S}$$

where $\hat{\beta}$ is estimated coefficient, β is theoretical value of the coefficient, and S is the square root of the variance estimator. Then, as S is understated, t is overstated.

The Durbin-Watson statistic.—The Durbin-Watson statistic, d, is defined as:

$$d = \frac{\sum\limits_{2}^{T} (\hat{v}_t - \hat{v}_{t-1})^2}{\sum\limits_{1}^{T} (\hat{v}_t - \bar{v})^2}$$

1. On the Durbin-Watson statistic and the test of the significance of the difference between the computed and critical values for the statistic, see source works such as Durbin and Watson [100, pp. 409–28; 101, pp. 172–75]. Other references might include Frazer [126, pp. 46–54], Christ [69, pp. 521–31], and Kane [220, pp. 364–73].

where the time series of error terms is denoted $\hat{v}_1, \ldots, \hat{v}_T$, $\overline{v}$ is the mean value of the error term, $(\hat{v}_t - \hat{v}_{t-1})^2$ is the square of successive differences, and $\Sigma \, (\hat{v}_t - \overline{v})^2$ is a variance. On the assumption that the errors are randomly distributed, it has been worked out for a very similar ratio that the d's are distributed as indicated by the arc-shaped line in Figure A3-1. This is symmetrically distributed about the value 2, with a range for d of from 0 to 4.

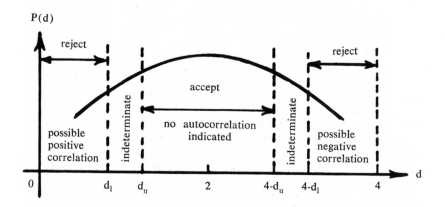

FIGURE A3–1. The Distribution of the Durbin-Watson Statistic for Test of Noncorrelation of Errors

At the intuitive level, one may note that the numerator of the ratio involves entire differences, whereas the denominator involves only half differences on the average or differences from the mean. Thus for large samples the ratio approaches the number 2. The statistic d and the correlation coefficient (r) for the successive differences are closely related: $d \approx 2[1 - r(1)]$. Herein, too, lies the implied rationale for the range of d. Note, that if there is no correlation (r = 0), then d = 2. If there is complete positive correlation (r = 1), then d = 0. If there is complete negative correlation (r = -1), then d = 4.

Unlike tests of significance (t-tests of the t-ratio), critical limits for accepting the hypothesis of no autocorrelation and for rejecting the alternatives of positive and negative autocorrelation do not coincide. The range for the statistic d is in fact divided into five sub-ranges or regions. Moving from left to right in Figure A3–1—where d is the dependent variable and P(d) is a probability density—the five sub-ranges are: (1)

reject the hypothesis of no autocorrelation (positive correlation indicated), (2) test is indeterminate, (3) tentatively accept hypothesis of no autocorrelation, (4) test is indeterminate, and (5) reject hypothesis of no autocorrelation (negative correlation indicated). The regions of indeterminacy arise because the sequence of estimated errors ($\hat{v}$'s) depends on the sequence of the random variables in the linear regression model (u's) and also on the sequence of the independent variable or variables. As Kane points out [220, p. 368], when d lies between d_l and d_u or between 4-d_l and 4-d_u, the apparent autocorrelation may or may not be due to the sequence of values assumed by the independent variable or variables.

As in the case of t-tests of significance, tests for autocorrelation may be either one- or two-tail tests, (for either positive or negative autocorrelation, or for both). Also as in t-tests, tables are used to obtain critical values. In the present case these are for d_l and d_u against which empirically estimated d's are tested. The critical values depend on the size of the sample and the number of independent or exogenous variables in the regression equation giving rise to the estimated or predicted values. This is, of course, in addition to allowance for the significance level for which one wishes to conduct the test.

The Durbin-Watson test is specifically designed for regression equations in which all the "independent" variables are strictly exogenous. The test is not strictly appropriate for equations belonging to a simultaneous equations system or for equations containing lagged values of dependent variables. If the equations to be estimated contain lagged values of dependent variables, then the D-W statistic is biased toward the value 2. When lagged dependent variables are used or when autocorrelation is indicated, various makeshift arrangements and corrective procedures are available. Christ discusses these for lagged dependent variables, and Kane discusses responses where residuals fail the test.

Appendix to Chapter 4

An Analysis of Adjustments

ZWICK OFFERS an analysis of adjustments [388]. It is horrendous because of the admixture of ingredients from monetary analysis and statistical problems. Here the ingredients are separated and examined.

Loanable funds and the IS–LM model.—In broad historical perspective, there are two simple models of the interest rate that are integrated into the Hicks-Hansen IS–LM model. They are the loanable funds model [185, pp. 140–53] and the liquidity preference model. In the loanable funds framework there are demand and supply schedules; a negatively sloping demand schedule relating the interest rate to the quantity of funds coming on the market, and a positively sloping supply schedule. The term "funds", as defined earlier (Ch. 1, n. 21), is a broader concept than money. From the financial markets point of view, funds are supplied—as through the acquisition of financial instruments as assets—and are obtained through the sale of such instruments and the incurrence of liabilities in the case of new issues. Money balances are used in effecting the latter transactions, as described elsewhere [120, n. 11], and all individuals and institutions other than commercial banks acquire assets by drawing down on money balances. The banks enter in a unique way. They are the only institutions that extend credit and increase assets without reducing cash, indeed by increasing the money stock. However, the banks do not supply the money stock in the loanable funds framework, as distinct from the liquidity preference framework.

In the liquidity preference framework, a rising velocity of money is usually equated with an excess of actual over desired money balances. Keynesians, proceeding from a static position, see an increase in the stock as spilling over into a demand for bonds, and then there is some rise in investment and income. But if the spillover is into expenditures on real goods rather than bonds and if velocity is already in motion with actual

434

exceeding desired balances, then accelerating the growth of balances may simply raise income further, as posited elsewhere [120]. Zwick [388, pp. 88–89] says only that "Unless people respond to the increased stock of money . . . by reducing the velocity of money in circulation . . . the product MV [M = money, V = velocity] must rise." [1]

A separation of effects.—Zwick says the effect of a monetary change on the interest rate can be separated into two components [388, p. 89]: (1) the direct effects of increasing bank credit (an inverse effect on the interest rate), as in the loanable funds framework, and (2) the indirect but positive effect of an increase in income on the demand schedule for funds (an outward shift in the schedule). His procedure entails supply and demand equations for bank credit in a simple structural equations model as introduced in the text (Sec. 4.3). There are so-called exogenous variables, and bank credit and the three-month Treasury bill rate are the endogenous variables. A reduced form equation is obtained for the interest rate (the bill rate), and there are methods of adjusting for the presence of autocorrelation of the residuals as indicated by the Durbin-Watson statistic (Appendix to Ch. 3). These are mentioned below.

The presumed presence of a laboratory situation—*ceteris paribus*, as discussed earlier (Sec. 1.2)—is exploited to the fullest. First, the structural equations and reduced form estimates permit an assessment of the direct effect of bank credit on the interest rate. A negative coefficient for the interest rate, bank credit relation is obtained as expected. Then— since *ceteris paribus* conditions are invoked or presumed present—this effect is said to be independent of allowance for the indirect effect of the money supply change on expectations and on the demand for bank credit. A series of a priori operations on variables and estimated coefficients follows [388, Sec. III] to illustrate how income (y) affects the demand for bank credit (E_p). In essence [388, p. 89]: "The Keynesian finding that interest rates fall in response to monetary expansion is obtained if the direct effect dominates; the Fisherian result that interest rates rise in response to a monetary increase is obtained if the indirect expenditures effect dominates."

Zwick's final interpretation [388, pp. 93–94] is that both direct and indirect responses are present.

The direct effect of a change in bank credit.—Zwick's structural equations model with emphasis on the direct effect is:

1. Zwick [388, n. 13] sees this as necessary unless one assumes that the demand for money is infinitely elastic.

Demand: $\ln E_p = \epsilon(s, W/P) \ln W/P + \epsilon(s, P) \ln P$

$\qquad + \epsilon(s, n) \ln N + \epsilon(s, S) \ln S + \epsilon(s, i) \ln i$

Supply:

$\qquad \ln E_b = \epsilon(a, B^a) \ln B^a + \epsilon(a, r^d) \ln r^d + \epsilon(a, r^t) \ln r^t$

$\qquad + \epsilon(a, k) \ln k + \epsilon(a, \phi) \ln \phi + \epsilon(a, i) \ln i$

Reduced form:

$$\ln i = \frac{-\epsilon(a, B^a) \ln B^a - \epsilon(a, r^d) \ln r^d}{\epsilon(a, i) - \epsilon(s, i)}$$

$$\frac{-\epsilon(a, r^t) \ln r^t - \epsilon(a, k) \ln k - \epsilon(a, \phi) \ln \phi}{\epsilon(a, i) - \epsilon(s, i)}$$

$$\frac{+\epsilon(s, W/P) \ln W/P + \epsilon(s, P) \ln P}{\epsilon(a, i) - \epsilon(s, i)}$$

$$\frac{+\epsilon(s, n) \ln n + \epsilon(s, S) \ln S}{\epsilon(a, i) - \epsilon(s, i)}$$

where E is bank credit (E_p demand, and E_b supply), W/P is wealth divided by the price level (P), n is ratio of current real income divided by permanent real income, S is stock of government debt, i is market interest rate, B^a is adjusted monetary base (currency plus member bank reserves less discounts and advances), $r^d (r^t)$ is weighted average reserve requirement ratios on member bank demand (time) deposits, k is ratio of currency to demand deposits, and ϕ is Federal Reserve discount rate.

Further, $a = E_b/B^a$ or a credit multiplier expressed as the ratio of bank credit to the reserve base, ln denotes a logarithmic transformation of the variable, and on the *ceteris paribus* assumption each of the coefficients denoted by epsilon (ϵ) is an elasticity measure, as ln d ln E_b/d ln B^a = $\epsilon(a, B^a)$. (On the *ceteris paribus* assumption and elasticity see Sec. 1.2 and Appendix to Ch. 1.)[2] Note that

$$\frac{d \ln E_b}{d \ln B^a} = \epsilon(a, B^a)$$

and

$$\epsilon(a, B^a) = E_b/B_a = a$$

2. Derivatives (d's) are used to denote elasticities rather than partial derivatives (∂'s) to emphasize that for each differentiation the other so-called independent

Also, commercial bank credit (E_b) is viewed as consisting of loans (L_b) and government securities (S_b), so that $E_b = L_b + S_b$. Zwick assumes [388, p. 83]

$$\frac{dL_p}{dW} > \frac{dS_p}{dW} > 0$$

and that

$$\frac{dE_p}{dW} > 0$$

This is probably a bad assumption as far as manufacturing corporations are concerned, for it may be shown (Ch. 15) that the demand for government securities by these firms increases more than in proportion to asset size (a surrogate for wealth) and that the demand for bank loans increases less than in proportion to asset size.

In the demand equation, $\epsilon(s, i) < 0$ and all other coefficients are greater than zero. The small s in the notation apparently suggests the ratio of government securities held by the public to the stock of government debt. In the supply equation $\epsilon(a, B^a)$ and $\epsilon(a, i) > 0$ and other coefficients are negative.

In utilizing data for the variables, Zwick uses the three-month Treasury bill rate for the interest rate. The expression KB^a combines the terms involving B^a, r^d, and r^t, so that KB embodies the monetary base and reserve requirements. The variables B^a, r^d, and r^t in the supply equation and the reduced form equation are replaced by KB^a. The stock of real wealth (W/P) is approximated by a distributed lag of net national product. Specifically,

$$.15 \sum_{i=0}^{20} (.85)^{\ i} (NNP/P)_{-i}$$

where i is raised by one each quarter. And, finally, because of seasonality in quarterly data for some variables, seasonal dummy variables, as discussed more fully on occasions (Sec. 10.4), are included (Q_1, Q_2, and Q_3,).

Against the foregoing background, coefficients for the supply, demand, and reduced form equations were estimated. Both ordinary (OLS) and two-stage least squares (2SLS) were used. The Durbin-Watson statistics

---

variables are impounded in *ceteris paribus*. Thus, there is no legitimate case for partial differentiation.

[388, p. 87] indicated "the presence of substantial autocorrelation of the residuals of both the reduced form and structural equations. To adjust for the autocorrelation, a variety of transformations of variables were estimated. In one case, each variable was replaced by the current level less .5 times the lagged value of the variable (where .5 denoted ρ), and this improved the D-W for the demand equation.

Among analysis of quarterly data from 1948 to 1963, Zwick emphasizes the following results [388, p. 88]:

	$\epsilon(i,KB^a)$	$\epsilon(i,k)$	$\epsilon(i,S)$	$\epsilon(i,P)$	$\epsilon(i,n)$	$\epsilon(i,W/P)$
Levels, $\rho = 0$:						
Reduced form estimates	-10.75	3.5	-0.01	4.04	8.9	6.3
Structural estimates	-14.0	-0.26	3.2	4.0	6.9	5.9
Transformation, $\rho = .5$:						
Reduced form estimates	-10.06	2.8	-0.11	3.9	7.8	5.97
Structural estimates	-14.1	-0.4	2.8	4.6	5.4	6.3

where estimates involved a direct use of the reduced form equation and involved first a substitution of 2SLS estimates for the structural equations and then a substitution of these in the reduced form equation.

Among the foregoing results the regression coefficients for KB^a, P, n, and W/P are said to possess high t-values in both reduced form and structural equations. These estimates are similar for both equations too, but other estimates are not. Even so, these results are said to reveal that "the interest rate falls in response to an increase in the monetary base (KB^a)."

Appendix to Chapter 7

Transactions Cost, the Demand for Money, and the Price System

THE DEFINITION of money since Keynes [133, Chs. 1–5; 154, Ch. 3–7][1] has been related to the functions performed by money (the medium of exchange, the standard of value, and the store of value functions) and the motives for using and holding money (the transactions, precautionary, and speculative motives). The medium of exchange property has been related to the transactions demand; to the indirect rather than coincidental satisfaction of wants in an exchange economy and to the need to make purchases with money because of the non-synchronous nature of the receipt and spending of income by separate behavioral units. The standard of value property has been related to the unit of account aspect of money; the reckoning and bookkeeping use of the dollar (or some other) unit in expressing the value of n-1 number of goods and services, all in relation to money. The store of value property has been related to precautionary and speculative demands; to the strength of the demand for an asset to hold so as to avoid the prospect of loss of purchasing power or principal (or to realize a gain) usually associated with either an anticipated rise (decline) in interest rates or the prices for goods and services expressed as an average.[2]

The store of value property was especially emphasized by Keynes in relating money to the tendency for the economy to persist at a dis-

---

1. The definition that follows is drawn from a wide variety of sources. Its statement has been influenced by observations and a reading of the relevant literature, but especially it has been influenced by Keynes' work and the efforts of various writers in clarifying that work.

2. Keynes, of course, held expectations constant in the short run, and a change in interest rates brought an inverse change in the price level (Chs. 1 and 7). In permitting the Keynesian short run to vanish, interest rates may vary directly with price changes, particularly anticipated ones.

equilibrium level of employment. In this store of value context, no asset
or group of assets could persistently serve as money in any fixed degree
because of the prospect of the loss (or even gain) of principal or purchasing power. Whatever the case, money has been thought the most
liquid of all assets, on balance and over-all. It has been associated with
low or negligible yield in dollar terms, negligible carrying cost from holding it, and a substantial return in the form of a liquidity element (a
symbol for the security and convenience associated with holding it). As a
matter of practical statistical research, some asset or group of assets could
be pointed to that served as money (as with currency plus demand deposits adjusted). In analysis with Anna Jacobson Schwartz, Friedman
[154, pp. 1–2, 76–77, 90–92] broadened the definition in this statistical
sense to include time deposits, partly because data sources do not distinguish between time and demand deposits at commercial banks in the
United States until 1914.

Friedman and Schwartz recognize the difficulty of choosing "an empirical counterpart to an abstract concept." In fact, they review some
literature in their 1970 publication with special attention to the choice
of the empirical counterpart to money by earlier writers [154, Ch. 2].
There is additional emphasis on and criticism of key a priori efforts to
define money that have been directed mainly at either the medium of
exchange function [154, pp. 104–26] or the liquidity function [154, pp.
126–36] separately. They say that both functions have relevance in deciding on the empirical counterpart, but they see no hard and fast formula for deciding what to call money.

With respect to the key approaches, Friedman and Schwartz note two
interesting features [154, pp. 136–37]: "The medium-of-exchange approach stresses conditions of supply, and the liquidity approach stresses
conditions of demand." They say the first tends to lead to a clearer empirical counterpart, but it becomes high-powered money rather than
currency and demand deposits. The second is less clear empirically, but
frequently treated as providing a reasonably unambiguous way of ordering assets. They stress the latter because they consider the emphasis on
demand to be more valid. They conclude that the definition should be
sought on grounds of usefulness in organizing knowledge of economic
relationships.

A review of a few numbers shows the importance of both the asset and
the medium of exchange roles [154, pp. 107–10]. For example, in the
United States in 1966 the total of currency plus demand deposits was
equal in value to "four months' personal disposable income, about one

month's in currency and three months' in demand deposits." Friedman and Schwartz say [154, p. 107]:

> Roughly two-thirds of the currency and two-fifths of the demand deposits was held by individuals and the rest by business. On the average, therefore, individuals held in currency about three weeks' income, in demand deposits about five weeks', or a total amount equal to two months' disposable income. Is it plausible that anything like this sum was held for the narrow medium of exchange function of money alone—that is, for mechanical transactions needs?

The liquidity emphasis is important in explaining matters of history, such as the acceptance of certain assets as money—whether gold, wampum, or liquor. There are, for example [133, Ch. 7], such matters of U.S. history to explain as the gradual extension by the bankers of the public's confidence in metallic money, specie, or bullion to paper note issues by the private banks. Beginning in the 1860s, there was a noticeable extension of this confidence to deposit liabilities. The private note issues had been taxed out of existence, and the survival of numerous state banks depended on the public's electing to hold their deposit liabilities.

There are some other matters of early and contemporary history that Brunner and Meltzer are able to explain while stressing the medium of exchange role of money and an integration of monetary analysis with the traditional theory of value.[3] They are perhaps over-critical of prior work on the definition of money when they say money's existence was accepted and its emergence unexplained [38, pp. 5–6].

Whatever the case, their special gymnastic is to drop the certainty axiom in "conventional" exchange theory [360, Ch. 3], to add two axioms on the marginal cost of acquiring information to reduce uncertainty as stated below,[4] and to bring in the notion of reducing uncertainty by purchasing information. In this way some behavioral matters often associated with the precautionary and speculative motives (though perhaps less so in Keynesian economics) can be associated instead with the transactional

3. Keynes, of course, suggested such an integration as a response to the neoclassical economist's tendency to separate monetary theory and the theory of relative prices, as stated earlier (Ch. 7), but in the hands of the Keynesians, Keynes' theory became a macroeconomics in which monetary policy did not matter very much. It is somewhat paradoxical that Samuelson, with his Keynesian classification (Secs. 1.1, 3.5), has reminded us how schizophrenic neoclassical economics really was in its distinct theories of money and value [319].
4. In an earlier paper [38, p. 9] Brunner introduced three axioms. For a review of some matters touching on the role of axioms in economic analysis, see the appendix to Chapter 8.

aspect.[5] By the axiomatic changes and related analysis, some additional explanations of phenomena are achieved, some are lost (the role of bankers in transferring the public's confidence to note issue and deposit liabilities), and the role of transactions costs is illuminated.[6] Special interest centers about the introduction of money into the standard theory of relative prices, about explanations of the continued use of existing monies in some countries (such as Brazil) even in the face of persistent inflation,[7] and about the emergence of specialized markets.

Brunner's and Meltzer's analysis.—In their treatment, Brunner and Meltzer extend the notion of the system of prices as a communications mechanism, one which enables traders with perfect foresight to detect and move to a new equilibrium (Sec. 7.2). In doing so, the assumption of perfect foresight is dropped and the standard theory of exchange (or price) is extended to include uncertainty, as defined below, and the costs of acquiring information, arranging payments, and scheduling purchases. They say [44, p. 786]:

> Shopping, budgeting, and planning expenditures are productive tasks that both absorb resources and yield benefits to the skilled or knowledgeable purchasers or sellers who make advantageous exchanges. The use of a medium of exchange permits the household to economize on the amount of resources absorbed by these activities and to enjoy a larger and more diversified basket of goods and more leisure.

It is difficult to explain why dominant mediums of exchange emerge. It is not enough to simply say there are a utility function and preferences,

5. There seems to be disguised a very special effort to avoid "appeal to analytically extraneous sociological or psychological convolutions" (even in their presence).

6. Several economists have reopened the question of the relationship between the real and monetary sectors and the reasons for holding money with special attention to transactions costs [38, 42, 44, 327]. Niehans [286] takes such an approach and shows that the neoclassical approach to monetary theory as stated by Samuelson [319] can be generalized to deal with some basic problems of monetary theory: the integration of monetary and value theory, and an explicit statement of the services of money, with the neutral money of the neoclassical theory as a limiting case.

This class of articles on transactions cost is of a different generation from those on the transaction demand for money (Sec. 4.3).

7. Brunner and Meltzer [44, p. 784] say that this continued acceptance "under conditions of ever-increasing holding cost calls into question the relevance of treating money as an asset that provides little or no return." Some have treated money as offering no return. However, notions about money yielding liquidity elements and focusing on acceptability and ease of disposal have not ignored even substantial return from holding money. This, however, does not nullify the importance of Brunner's and Meltzer's objective.

so attempts are made to provide an explanation of the preferences, in their case for a particular medium of exchange.

An effect of Brunner's and Meltzer's particular gymnastic is an additional model of the metastatic variety, despite the introduction of uncertainty. In effect, there is an endownment (undistinguished as to whether income or wealth) that can be used to maximize utility. The equilibrium is the common one (as discussed by Vickrey [360, pp. 118–23]), where the ratios of utilities from items to their respective prices are equal and also equal to the marginal utility of money:

$$\frac{U_x}{P_x} = \frac{U_y}{P_y} = \frac{U_z}{P_z} = \ldots = \lambda$$

The utility function (U) to be maximized may be denoted

$$U = f[E(Y),C] \qquad v(Y) = \text{const.}$$

where $E(Y)$ is the mean or expected value of goods acquired by trading in the market, C denotes resources reserved for various uses, and $v(Y)$ is the variance associated with the returns from the commodity bundle.

Such a function may be sketched in three-space. The utility surface in such a case takes on a greater slope as variance is reduced (reduced variance increases utility). Where the mean and variance concern probability distributions, they are conditional on investment in information and alternative transactions arrangements. In particular [44, p. 789], the mean or expected value of the acquired goods increases (though at a decreasing rate) as investment in information increases, and the variance decreases (though at a decreasing rate) as investment in information increases. Both changes increase utility, and the investment in information may be expected to continue until the gain in utility is equal to the loss from allocating resources to investment in information [44, p. 791].

The sort of probability introduced by Brunner and Meltzer is a probability distribution with a mean and a variance. The emphasis on variance also implies a relative frequency approach to probability theory, where repeated sampling from a universe leads to the concept of a variance for the mean value. In their framework, increasing the mean shifts the distribution to the right, and decreasing the variance gives more peakedness to the distribution. Their use of probability is more in the tradition of mean-variance analysis than that of neo-Bayesian analysis and decision theory as mentioned in Chapter 8. The subjectivists favor a personalistic interpretation, where weighted utilities reflect attitudes about risk and the confidence that can be placed in probabilistic beliefs. The probabilities of economic events are amenable mainly to personalistic interpretations.

The Brunner-Meltzer argument requires some probabilistic assumptions (as mentioned later) as well as two assumptions additional to those found in conventional exchange theory [44, p. 786]:

1. For each transactor in an exchange economy, the marginal cost of acquiring information, measured in units of consumption sacrificed, depends on the goods or services selected.

2. The marginal cost of acquiring information about the properties of any asset does not vary randomly within a social group and declines as the frequency with which the group uses a particular asset in-increases.

These assumptions are said to suffice as both necessary and sufficient conditions for explaining the use of a medium of exchange. They emphasize a main concern of Brunner and Meltzer, "That it is the uneven distribution of information, and not the existence of an undifferentiated uncertainty, that induces individuals to search for, and social groups to accept, alternatives to barter [an exchange of goods that results in a simultaneous satisfaction of wants or a 'double coincidence transaction,' rather than an indirect one where some good or medium of exchange is acquired for subsequent use in the satisfaction of wants]."

"Uncertainty" in Brunner and Meltzer's overall account is uncertainty about the quality of goods offered in exchange, about market conditions, and about prevailing market opportunities. Brunner and Meltzer say [44, n. 9] that uncertainty in their account differs from that about the price level, the timing of receipts, and the interest rates, as in past discussions of money. But this is not entirely clear, as pointed out later.

One way that money reduces uncertainty for Brunner and Meltzer [44, p. 787] is by providing a unit of account (a unit for reckoning in an accounting sense) in which prices are expressed. For example, in a barter economy with N commodities and excluding the price of each good in terms of itself, there are $(N \times N) - N$ barter prices and $N(N - 1)/2$ independent exchange ratios, where the unit of account is randomly selected. In contrast, there are simply $N - 1$ ratios if society selects a unit of account. Thus, every commodity need not have a separate price in terms of every other commodity, so "The cost of acquiring, processing and storing information falls."

Brunner and Meltzer say that there must be efficiency in having one unit perform both as a unit of account and as a medium of exchange, since the distinct functions frequently coincide. They relate the medium of exchange function to indirect or roundabout methods of exchange (exchange without a simultaneous satisfactions of wants, as in a barter economy), and they consider a transactor with an initial endowment of resources and some information about exchange ratios and quantities of commodities. There are several ways of transforming the initial endowment into a preferred bundle. First, in standard price theory, the endowment can be used for production, consumption, or exchange. In Brunner's and Meltzer's framework the transactor can invest in information (about the qualities of goods and opportunities for exchange), and engage in roundabout methods of exchange to obtain an optimal bundle by accepting goods relating to a low marginal cost of information, transformation, and storage.

The problem set by Brunner and Meltzer [44, p. 788] is for the individual consumer "to find the optimal sequence of transactions and the optimal investment in information while choosing an optimal bundle of goods or consumption plan." [8] A skilled trader has more information than an unskilled trader or infrequent participant. Further, greater certainty about quality and performance characteristics enables the trader to discern differences that enhance utility. But there is a tradeoff between consuming goods and acquiring more information. The latter can be used to reduce uncertainty.

The foregoing sort of optimizing behavior leads to an explanation of two observable phenomena [44, p. 793]: (1) the tendency for social choice to lead to a small number of medium-of-exchange assets, and (2) the emergence of specialists in various trading activities. The first instance relates to the second of Brunner's and Meltzer's additional assumptions [44, p. 793]: "(1) that the marginal cost of acquiring information does not vary randomly within a social group and (2) that the marginal cost declines as the frequency with which an asset is used increases." So there is economy in individuals using the same medium of exchange.

8. In standard price theory, maximizing utility subject to a budget constraint yields statements of equilibrium conditions, as stated earlier in the appendix. The same sort of maximization procedure may be engaged in, as in Section 2.2, where wealth or total assets serve as the constraint (rather than income). In this case, maximization is still a matter of the equality of ratios of marginal utilities to the respective prices, only now they are equal to the marginal utility of assets, total wealth, or Keynes marginal efficiency of capital (or simply the rate of return on additional investment). In a paper by Brunner on the monetarist position, relative prices are said to operate in reference to assets (liabilities) and stock quantities [42, pp. 18–19]. Consequently some adjustments need to be made to relate the Brunner-Meltzer analysis of transactions costs [44] to the price theory that Brunner introduces in discussing monetarism.

The tendency to economize by reducing the cost of information also leads to specialized trading functions. Specialists gain special information from being specialized and thus reduce the costs of acquiring information, at least as it relates to their specialty.

In summary, the use of an asset as a medium of exchange increases the part of wealth allocated to it. This follows because money as a medium of exchange is a substitute for costly information and the use of labor in searching for any optimal basket of goods. In other words, the use of money reduces uncertainty, the length of transaction chains, and the variance of price ratios (equated with greater certainty). It increases wealth and time available for leisure.

Some perspective.—Brunner and Meltzer's particular tie to decision theory (as introduced in more detail in Ch. 8) is unclear. But in combination with notions about the length of transactions chains and the broad spectrum of social evolution with respect to the selection of a small class of medium-of-exchange assets, some dynamic aspects of analysis are apparently present. There are shorter run dynamic elements, too [44, p. 800]. The net social product from having a limited range of assets serving as money varies with the degree of technological change and with large fluctuations in business conditions, since money is related to incomplete information about the quality of goods, exchange ratios, and market conditions; since the quality is thought to change more rapidly during periods of accelerated technological changes; and since large fluctuations in activity contribute to further uncertainty about quality.

Recognizing longer and shorter run elements of change, Brunner and Meltzer's analysis falls between that of the stationary state ("static" or "steady" state) and steady growth.[9] In fact, they view these as limiting cases in economics [44, p. 800].

Uncertainty, as it relates to the wider range of the services of money, has often been related to the demand for money (Ch. 6) and the wider range of the overlapping services of money. Brunner and Meltzer relate it to transactions costs with respect to information about exchange ratios and market conditions. In what appears to be simply a disguised precautionary demand for money—a demand to permit a transactor to take advantage of unknown future opportunities—they relate uncertainty to

9. In the former state, one is investigating an economic system at equilibrium, independently of its being continuously subjected to change. A simple and basic assumption is that everything keeps happening in the same way day after day. Uncertainty is absent. In the steady growth, all stock and flow quantities are presumably changing at the same rate. Uncertainty would again be absent.

transactions costs with respect to incomplete information and so on. They say [44, p. 800], "The longer the period of steady, gradual change continues, the lower the productivity of money and the smaller the demand for assets that reduce costs of acquiring information by serving as mediums of exchange."

A principal tie between the Brunner-Meltzer focus on money, relative prices, and the theory of exchange could be viewed as an extension of Brunner's interest in monetarism [42, esp. n. 8]. An attribute of monetarism brought out earlier by Brunner [42, pp. 11, 18] is the acceptance of "the general principle of applying relative price theory to the analysis of monetary processes." With reference to the transmission mechanism (Sec. 3.2) he says that "output and employment are explained by a suitable application of relative price theory [micro-economics]." This monetarist thesis as discussed by Brunner is divided into a weak monetarist thesis and a strong one [42, pp. 18–19].[10]

10. The weak thesis may be summarized thus [42, p. 18]:
    "Monetary impulses are transmitted to the economy by a relative price process which operates on money, financial assets (and liabilities), real assets, yields on assets and the production of new assets, liabilities and consumables. . . . The operation of relative prices between money, financial assets, and real assets may be equivalently interpreted as the working of an interest rate mechanism (prices and yields of assets are inversely related). Monetary impulses are thus transmitted by the play of interest rates over a vast array of assets. Variations in interest rates change relative prices of existing assets, relative to both yields and the supply prices of new production. Acceleration or deceleration of monetary impulses are thus converted by the variation of relative prices, or interest rates, into increased or reduced production, and subsequent revisions in the supply prices of current output."
    For Brunner these monetarist effects are said to be "direct," whereas in the analysis in this book effects are often "indirect" [via expectations]. Brunner does not seem to preclude these in his statement of the strong thesis.
    The strong monetarist thesis is obtained by supplementing the weak one with analysis concerning three sets of forces: monetary forces, fiscal forces, and others. According to Brunner [42, p. 19], "The latter include technological and organizational innovation, revisions in supply prices induced by accruing information and expectation adjustments, capital accumulation, population changes and other related factors or processes."
    "All three sets of forces are acknowledged by the strong thesis to affect the pace of economic activity via the relative price process previously outlined. . . . It is argued further that major variabilities occurring in a subset of the other forces (e.g., expectations and revisions of supply prices induced by information arrival) are conditioned by the observed variability of monetary forces."

Appendix to Chapter 8

A. Axioms and Empirical Relevance

MUCH HAS BEEN SAID about "crisis in economic theory," "counter-revolution," and the pace of change in economic thinking variously dated from the mid-to-late 1960s and early 1970s (Secs. 1.1, 3.1, 5.1, 5.2). The widespread availability of the modern computer and its related output has been pointed to as a source of the accelerated pace of change, revealing the inadequacies of the orthodox theory and giving rise to the use of both the labels "crisis" and "revolution." The rise of a form of empiricism—as would be consistent with the ascribed role of the modern computer—has been mentioned, and references have been made to Milton Friedman, a chief participant in the changes in question, as an empirical scientist. Friedman's ties with the pre-computer, empirical tradition in the United States have also been mentioned.

The early empirical tradition in the United States was rather casual by the standards of the 1960s. As with the crisis in theory—though at a less sophisticated level—it centered about describing and attempting to explain changes in business conditions.[1] In many respects, this early empiricism—along with the availability of data in the monetary area, the role of money as a link between the past and the future, and the relative absence of references to the past and anticipated states in the textbook exposition of the orthodoxy—foretold where the crisis in theory would occur. Johnson [210, pp. 2–3] speaks of a small empirical or econometric "revolution" in the late 1920s and early 1930s, "with its insistence initially on

---

1. The National Bureau's early tradition is presently viewed as a major movement in empirical economics. One also encounters simple econometric work on the theory of demand [239, p. 200], and the Keynesian economics with its consumption function offered a challenging relationship for empirical estimation [210, p. 5]. The rumblings of the structural equations models to come, as reviewed in Chapter 15, were on the scene in the early 1950s [239, pp. 201–12], in the work of Lawrence Klein, then at the University of Michigan.

the measurement of economic relationships and, subsequently and more ambitiously, on the testing of economic hypotheses." He says, though, that the testing of hypotheses "is frequently merely a euphemism for obtaining plausible numbers to provide ceremonial adequacy for a theory chosen and defended on *a priori* grounds."

Unfortunately there is too much support for Johnson's contention. Economics must deal with complicated and interrelated phenomena that are not as readily manageable in a laboratory context as much of the methodology of economics suggests. Some may point out, with reference to sciences generally [147, p. 10], that "the distinction between controlled experiment and uncontrolled experience is at best one of degree." But in any such continuum of degrees, economics must serve as a limiting case. A partial solution to the problem is for analysts to permit those things to change that do in fact change. Another is to seek consistency with a wider range of evidence.[2]

These topics have not attracted much attention. Nonetheless, the transformation from earlier to more recent opinions about empirical and theoretical work must have been affected by the accumulation of economic facts, by widespread efforts at testing in economics, and by the reduction in the cost of empirical work brought on by the modern computer. This appendix consequently sketches some of the opinions bearing on an assessment of the theories and facts, with attention to ties with early empiricism and the role of axioms (postulates or assumptions, to use some synonyms).

The National Bureau's early empiricism—The National Bureau of Economic Research was founded in reaction to an almost total emphasis by the main body of economics on deductive theory, a priori propositions. Wesley Mitchell, the Bureau's founder, thought that the systematic recording and publicizing of facts would influence economic theory. The Bureau was soon charged [239, p. 199] with placing priority on facts without theory. The measurement and recording of business conditions and the classification of business conditions indicators as leading, coincid-

---

2. This is a main point in work with Terrell [131] and in Chapter 4 on verification with respect to the notion of economy in the transaction demand for corporate cash balances. In work with Terrell, the theories of the term structure of interest rates and portfolio behavior are said to have developed in isolation from one another. Verification for term structure theory was related to interest rates alone but held implications for portfolio behavior. It was shown that some evidence on portfolio behavior was inconsistent with the behavior implied by the received theory. Similarly, the Baumol-Tobin analysis (Ch. 4) was said to focus on the velocity of cash balances for verification but to also hold implications for change in the balance sheet structure of corporations. The latter evidence was inconsistent with verification.

ing, and lagging, came to bear their hallmark under the leadership of Wesley Mitchell and Arthur Burns.[3]

The increasing need to impose discrimination in matters of classification and causation implied some theory, albeit only implicit. It fell to Milton Friedman, an early student and protege of Burns, to give some further emphasis to theory. It is more than coincidental that major papers and books attributed to Friedman in this volume carry the Bureau's imprint.

Friedman's positive economics.—Friedman's approach has been relatively ad hoc, as reviewed in Chapter 5. He was viewed as searching for regularity, first in one sphere and then in another as an empirical scientist. Rader [296, p. 10] relates such an approach to a disordered view of science, to an early essay by Friedman [147, pp. 3–43] with emphasis on the implications or predictive results of a theory as distinct from assumption, and to a Machian view (so named for a position stated in physics by Ernst Mach around the turn of the century).[4]

In his essay, Friedman distinguishes "normative" economics (how things should be) from "positive" economics (how things are).[5] The latter attracted his attention as an empirical scientist. Here the theory was to aid in classification, to predict, to be a body of "substantive hypotheses," and above all to be judged by the relation of its non-tautological implication with empirical facts. The postulates were to play a definite secondary role in judging the theory. There were modifications; some clarification is in order, but Friedman's position generated controversy [239, pp. 137–42; 296, pp. 9–11]. A review of it sheds some light on Friedman's monetarism and on the role of axioms, as introduced in Chapter 8 and in the Appendix to Chapter 7.

As widely recognized with respect to any logical system [239, p. 138; 147, p. 26], there is a certain amount of freedom as to which statements

3. Two collections of essays [54, 55], including one by Milton Friedman on Wesley Mitchell as a theorist and empirical scientist [55, pp. 237–82], provide background on Wesley Mitchell, on the National Bureau, and on empirical tradition in the United States.

4. Samuelson, in reflections on monetarism, refers to "a naive form of empiricism." He says [316, p. 10], "To call it 'positivism' would be to libel a doctrine that is already vulnerable to legitimate criticism." Continuing he refers [316, p. 11] to "the methodology of crypto-positivism," and asks "how big are your R^2s compared to mine?" He concludes by noting [316, p. 21] that "In none of the modern sciences would it be respectable to believe in the pseudo—positivism which prevails among the monetarists."

5. What he indirectly points out [147, p. 3] had been drawn by John Neville Keynes. The first edition of the latter's book, *The Scope and Method of Political Economy*, was published in 1890.

an analyst wishes to regard as premises and which as theorems or propositions. Friedman also recognizes [147, p. 17] that (1) of two theories,[6] an analyst might accept the theory in most agreement with the facts, given equal acceptability on other grounds, and (2) one theory may be accepted over another without its yielding the best predictions,[7] if the cost of achieving them is too great.

Continuing on assumptions, Friedman [147, pp. 23–30] recognizes a variety of roles. For one, they are often an economical mode of presenting a theory. For another, "they are sometimes a convenient means of specifying the conditions under which a theory is expected to be valid." Some evidence with respect to the assumption may also serve as indirect evidence on the acceptability of the hypothesis. This would apply "in so far as the assumptions can themselves be regarded as implications of the hypothesis, and hence their conformity with reality as a failure of some implications to be contradicted, or in so far as the assumptions may call to mind other implications of the hypothesis susceptible to casual empirical observations." The reason the assumptions concern only indirect evidence is that they may refer to a different class of phenomena from those the hypothesis is designed to explain [147, p. 28]. Furthermore [147, p. 28], a classification of theories by assumptions brings out a kinship between theories, and the one may benefit from the evidence on the other.

These statements are relevant enough. So why was Friedman so criticized for his assessment of the role of axioms? Two interrelated reasons appear to apply. First, he was defending the theory of perfect competition which he may have been attracted to on other than scientific grounds. Second, he placed his greatest confidence in some extreme statements about axioms, such as [147, pp. 14–15]:

> Truly important and significant hypotheses will be found to have "assumptions" that are wildly inaccurate descriptive representations of reality, and, in general, the more significant the theory, the more unrealistic the assumptions (in this sense). A hypothesis is important if it "explains" much by little, that is, if it abstracts the common and crucial elements from the mass of complex and detailed circumstances surrounding

6. In the essay [147, pp. 3–43], the term "hypothesis" is synonymous with "theory." It is also widely used, however, to mean a statement about a relationship. The stated relationship may be submitted to empirical verification.

7. Friedman uses the term "prediction" in his essay on method [147, pp. 3–43] to mean some outcome following from the theory, a stability and consistency of relationships following from the theory. He does not use it in the sense of the economic forecasting of business conditions, which may be little more than a crass extrapolation of the past into the future.

the phenomena to be explained and permits valid predictions on the basis of them alone. To be important, therefore, a hypothesis must be descriptively false in its assumptions; it takes account of, accounts for, none of the many other attendant circumstances, since its very success shows them [the assumptions] to be irrelevant for the phenomena to be explained.

The foregoing well defends the need for abstraction from the numerous details of reality in theoretical work. It could also serve as a slippery defense of unwarranted assumptions, and it was in fact tied in with some historical controversies [147, pp. 30–31; 239, pp. 38–39]. One centered about the assumption of utility maximization that was originally rooted in outmoded psychology, namely the pleasure-pain calculus of early economists [276, pp. 177–201]. Another controversy centered about the theory of monopolistic or imperfect competition, mainly as a response to dissatisfaction over the assumption of "perfect competition" or "perfect monopoly" in neoclassical economic theory.

To some extent Friedman's defense of utility maximization was tied in with a defense of an apparent crass maximization-of-return assumption from the theory of the firm. Friedman's defense of classical theory was also tied in with an absence of attributes that would make the theory of imperfect or monopolistic competition a truly general theory. The passage of time has favored Friedman in these controversies, but not necessarily because of his stand about the role of axioms. Instead, utility maximization was freed from the psychological trappings of pleasure-pain calculus, and the absence of a satisfactory logical structure of the theory of imperfect or monopolistic competition has been recognized.

Others on positive economics.—In reaction to Friedman, Koopmans [239, pp. 145–46] pointed out that postulates do matter. Since they were of the nature of conclusions, there must be some correspondence with facts. As Friedman would admit, systems of mathematics (calculus, matrix algebra, probability) contribute to an assurance of consistency within the structure of economic theory, especially where the reasoning becomes complicated. The purpose of theory is the "explanation" of economic phenomena and the "forecasting" of economic changes. Positivists identified with this point of view have been listed by Rader to include Karl Menger, Abraham Wald, and John von Neumann. He refers to them [296, pp. 10–11] as the "Vienna circle," because of their connection with a seminar in Vienna in the 1920s where the doctrine of logical positivism was first proclaimed. For this group, a particular valid theory has a permanent life, because theory deals with facts and facts are unlikely to change. A valid theory is stable over time. As stated by Rader [296, p.

11], "it [valid theory] is never superceded in its own sphere, and it is best supported or amended by further investigation."

This is a fairly idealistic view, especially as to what economics might accomplish. More limited aspirations might be accepted in the absence of satisfying ideal criteria, but the ideal goals are present. Ultimately there should be a consistency between a broad range of empirical facts and theoretical structure.

Adding axioms may add to explanatory power, as with cardinal utility analysis (Ch. 8). Adding axioms also imposes additional constraints on applicability. In some instances a more economical use of axioms may improve applicability and still provide a satisfactory explanation of particular phenomena.[8] By economic standards, much is accomplished if the theory explains and predicts the direction of changes with a high degree of consistency. More is accomplished when the theory predicts and explains the extent of the change, the cardinal magnitude of change.

B. Security Analysis, Technical Analysis, and an Explanation of Turning Points

TIME SERIES may be viewed as containing seasonal, cyclical, secular, and random components. Averages of stock market prices as time series are no different, and indeed such an average (Dow Jones' Industrial Stock Prices) has been cited as one of the National Bureau's seven selected leading indicators of business conditions. It is in this context that analysis of industrial stock prices is reviewed herein, as an extension of the analysis characterizing this book and Chapter 8 in particular.

Others [77] have moved in a different direction. As widely reviewed and popularized [335, Ch. 11], they sought to establish the behavior of stock market prices as a random walk: that successive price changes are independent and behave in a random fashion. There is even the prospect that they conform to some probability distribution. Cheng and Deets [67, pp. 11–30] have tested the independence part of the random walk hypothesis. They concluded that the assumption of mutual independence was probably incorrect and that the predominance of the signs of serial correlation coefficients among series tested by some researchers appeared to depend upon the particular differencing interval used.

---

8. A working rule is known as Occam's Razor: the simplest possible descriptions are to be used until they prove inadequate.

Some "noise" and "shock" effects apparently may be washed out by smoothing, as in the ensuing analysis, and "order" and "systematic" changes may be revealed. This analysis eschews the details of the random walk controversy but continues to apply probabilistic reasoning.

Probabilistic reasoning as applied to the direction of changes in stock prices has often characterized the background and foreground of security analysis. A 1970 volume by Latané and Tuttle [246] surveys the historical application of such reasoning as applied to common stock prices. The authors develop an approach to security analysis and the selection of securities by borrowing from "modern decision theory," theory involving the formation of probabilistic beliefs. This approach has long characterized Latané's interest [244] and special interest centered about his book with Tuttle.

Latané and Tuttle distinguish two historically emphasized schools of analysis about decisions with respect to purchasing or holding a stock, on the one hand, or selling and avoiding it, on the other [246, p. 260 and Part II]. The two forms are "fundamental analysis" and "technical analysis." The first is described as basically an economic approach to evaluation and the second as a trend-following approach. In the first instance, a basic decision rule is to purchase or hold a security when its "intrinsic" value is greater than its "actual" value and to sell or avoid a security when the "intrinsic value" is less than the actual value. In technical analysis the emphasis is on "momentum" in a stock's price either upward or downward, on convergence toward some more "realistic" or "intrinsic" value, and on turning points—points signified by a turn in price movement from an upward to a downward direction or vice versa, after some smoothing of the data. The two forms of analysis are inter-related and the use of both is recommended to analysts and portfolio managers. Even so, technical analysis is thought to be more relevant in the forecasting of turning point [246, p. 377].

There is no explanation of the occurrence of turning points inherent in the trend-analysis mechanisms, however, and the development of such an explanation in terms of modern (or neo-Bayesian) decision theory constitutes the contribution and objective of this appendix. To carry out this objective, aspects of technical analysis and neo-Bayesian decision theory are reviewed. The explanation of turning points follows.

The perspective for viewing the present analysis is "positive" rather than "normative"; the intent is explanation of market behavior rather than a prescription for successful management of securities and portfolios. In a securities and portfolio management work such as Latané and Tuttle's

[246], the exposition is constantly switching from an analysis of the environment to the prescription or tool needed for the proper decision. In the present approach the decision-makers and their tools and goals are still in the picture, but the focus is strictly on an explanation of behavior. In a work such as Latané and Tuttle's, moreover, one encounters discussions of the market, an industry, or a particular stock, whereas the present emphasis is on the behavior of the market as a whole as indicated by an average of the prices of the individual issues.

An overview of technical analysis.—Technical analysis, as reviewed by Latané and Tuttle [246, pp. 269–73 and Ch. 14], was originated by Charles Dow between 1900 and 1902. It was carried further by William Hamilton in a number of *Wall Street Journal* editorials from 1902 to 1929 and came to include technical devices and approaches such as filter techniques, exponentially smoothed price predictions, bar charting, point-and-figure charting, and the 200-day moving average.

An important part of Dow's and his associates' approach was a distinction between daily price fluctuations, those spanning a three-week to seven-month period, and major movements lasting from less than one year up to several years. The latter are of primary concern. A movement of this type may be expected to create a momentum and give rise to the prospect of a further change in the same direction. As the price changes cause further price changes in their set direction, relative to some future norm, there is a gradual loss or regaining of confidence, depending on whether a rise or decline in price is occurring. This norm may be subjectively and concretely viewed as a very long-run underlying trend—an upward sweeping, exponential trend line or growth curve. In effect, prices can rise or decline relative to the trend line, in such a way that as they change in one direction there is an increasing probability of a change in the other direction.

In the foregoing paragraph are exact counterparts to modern analysis of the term structure of interest rates (Chs. 12, 13). Only the terminology is different. The notion of an upward or downward momentum is referred to as a "push" (or extrapolative push) effect. The increasing probability of a return toward normality is referred to as a "pull" (or regressive pull) effect. Both "push" and "pull" effects have been widely discussed in the literature on the term structure of interest rates, and support for both has been found.

In the framework presently implied, there is room for expectational effects other than simply the "push" and "pull" ones. These forces may be accompanied and even reinforced by earnings, price level, and business-conditions prospects for the overall economy. In particular, there is a role for shock effects and learning from the past [131]. The shock effects refer to factors operating outside of the usual economic theory, such as announcements of important policy changes or events, a Vietnam, or changes in political administration. The learning enters clearly into the Bayesian framework of Section 8.3.

The "push" and "pull" effects as enumerated may be illustrated using the familiar relationship for expressing "adaptive expectations":

(1.0)

$$(\text{Price expectations})_t = f(w_oP_t + w_1P_{t-1} + w_2P_{t-2} + \ldots + w_nP_{t-n})$$

where price expectations at the current time (t) are said to depend on current and past prices, each multiplied by some weight (w_o, w_1, w_2, . . ., w_n). The correct price is closely related to the expected price, in the sense that the market is continuously adjusting to future prospects. The idea with reference to the relationship (1.0), and as reviewed on other occasions (Chs. 1, 8), is that "push" effects are expressed by the weighting of current and recent prices, and "pull" effects by the weighting of prices for the more distant past, in the sense that any norm for prices is also represented by them. "Push" and "pull" effects will not explain turning points in prices, and technical analysis is as much remiss in this as is economic literature generally. Of course, turning points would coincide with a downward re-evaluation of the weights for current and recent prices and an upward re-evaluation of the weights for prices in the more distant past. In other words, turning points would occur as weights shift to favor some anticipated norm or average, subjectively viewed and as possibly indicated by prices over a more distant past. The crucial question to be answered with respect to an explanation of turning points is this: What is it in the probabilistic mechanism that gives rise to a shifting of weights? The answer below, as in Chapter 8, centers about a coalescing of opinions or probabilistic beliefs as opinions reinforce one another. The propositional basis for this explanation is reviewed in Chapter 8.

A major use of technical analysis from the market participants' point of view is in detecting turning points. Several technical devices and approaches bear on this, including bar charting, point-and-figure charting, and the 200-day moving-average price-line analysis. Only the last technique is currently outlined to illustrate the relationship between technical analysis and the discussion accompanying relation (1.0).

The 200-day moving average price line analysis incorporates an average of stock prices (or values yielded by an index of prices) for the previous

200-day trading period. As each trading day passes a new price is added and an old one is dropped. This moving average may be plotted, with the average to coincide with the current trading day, and it may be compared as well with a series for current prices.

An upper turning point is signaled when the 200-day average flattens out or declines, and when, preceding a period of rising prices, the current price series penetrates the average from above. The situation could be turned upside down and a lower turning point would be signaled [246, p. 367]. There are two other events which also signal turning points. Periods of time other than 200 days could be used. In any case, in reference to the discussion surrounding relation (1.0), the message obtained with the technique is that a predominant regressive pull effect toward normality has been detected.

Some critics say that the forecast implicit in using technical analysis becomes self-fulfilling, especially as more investors follow it. For example, the identification of an upper turning point signals a future decline and flashes a signal to sell. Reacting to the signal will bring about the subsequent decline and validate the use of the technique. This may be true, but, it is of no special concern to the present analysis.

Neo-Bayesian decision theory with probabilistic slanting.—Modern decision theory is essentially probability theory encompassing the older objectivist approach as a special case. The Bayesian aspect enters when one introduces subjectivity (and the role of prior probabilities) via relationships inherent in Bayes' theorem. And the neo-Bayesian aspect enters when the probability is combined with utility analysis (Secs. 8.2, 8.3).

As stated earlier (Sec. 8.2), one may write, following Fellner

$$(2.0) \quad \underbrace{\frac{P_D(H_1)}{P_D(H_2)}}_{\substack{\text{ratio of} \\ \text{posterior} \\ \text{probabilities}}} = \underbrace{\frac{P_i(H_i)}{P_i(H_i)}}_{\substack{\text{ratio of} \\ \text{prior} \\ \text{probabilities}}} \cdot \underbrace{\frac{P(D|H_1)}{P(D|H_2)}}_{\substack{\text{represents} \\ \text{ratio of} \\ \text{likelihood} \\ \text{functions}}}$$

The ratio of posterior probabilities depends only on the ratio of prior probabilities and the ratio of the likelihoods. The modern Bayesians contend that prior probabilities should be assigned on the basis of initial guesses, hunches, and available information. So, once the likelihood ratio is found, the problem is solved. Additional steps can be taken toward further generalization of relation (2.0).

One could continue to gather information and continue to use the procedure just outlined. Especially relevant to changing initial beliefs is the following proposition of Fellner's:

> *Proposition (1.1).* If judgment is thought to be shaky in the sense of uncertain, "then it seems plausible to expect that in a good many cases the semiprobabilistic slanting inclinations will diminish (though they will not disappear) as the decison maker *gets used* to being faced with some specific type of decision."

Another plausible effect on judgments by decision-makers concerns its interpersonally controversial character, also as given earlier:

> *Proposition (1.2).* "Slanting inclinations will diminish . . . wherever large groups of *like-minded* individuals are formed."

There is here the suggestion that as opinions about changes coalesce the opinions of market participants and decision-makers generally become reinforcing.

Utility analysis, mathematical expectations, evaluation, and time enter as factors, as in Section 8.2. When certain or less certain prospects must be discounted for time preference, one gets the following:

$$(3.1) \qquad CV = \frac{R_1}{(1+i)^1} + \frac{R_2}{(1+i)^2} + \cdots + \frac{R_n}{(1+i)^n}$$

where i is the interest rate for discounting the returns, and where expected returns concern genuine economic expectations as distinct from mathematical expectations. For illustrative purposes, however, if one treats the time horizon as zero or nonexistent, the demand price relation (3.1) becomes

$$(3.2) \qquad\qquad CV = R + R + \ldots + R$$

and each of these R's could be treated in a simple mathematical expectation framework, with CV being the sum of their expected monetary values.

An explanation for turning points.—The explanation for turning points in stock prices is now straightforward. It requires the recognition of the presence of opinions (for example, about future stock market conditions). It also requires the recognition of interrelationships between even informed opinions about stock market conditions. For example, when opinions are almost equally divided on the immediate direction of change in market conditions, then there is considerable slanting of the probability of a change. This occurs along lines set forth in Fellner's semiprobabilistic approach and by the nature of allowances for controversial matters in group situations. As opinions about the anticipated change coalesce, there is less uncertainty, opinions become reinforcing, and weights shift to favor pull effects relative to push effects, as illustrated in the discussion surrounding relation (1.0). The final and principal proposition is in order.

Proposition (2.1). As opinions about a change in the direction of market conditions coalesce, turning points in market conditions occur.

The proof is straightforward, as suggested by the foregoing comments. By proposition (1.2), as opinions coalesce there would be diminished slanting of the probability of a change in the direction of market condition. Diminished slanting thus gives rise to a relative strengthening of pull effects. The turning point in market conditions occurs. The proposition follows. Proposition (2.1) and its related proof explain turning points in business conditions, because they are determined in the present framework by plans and actions based on the expectations themselves.

Heretofore the somewhat related disciplines of economic theory and security analysis have lacked the capacity to explain turning points in the stock market. This capacity now exists. The presence of probabilistic slanting of weights attached to possible outcomes in controversial situations and the diminution of slanting as opinions coalesce and reinforce one another combine to yield insights concerning the extent to which decision units are guided by the expectation of a return to normality or the expectation of continued and growing deviations from normal values.

Appendix to Chapter 13

Methodological Notes

ALMOST ALL of the methodological aspects of analysis introduced thus far appear in Chapter 13. For example, there is use of the Almon lag technique (Appendix to Ch. 1), the Durbin-Watson statistic (Appendix to Ch. 3), the notion of splitting the sample to determine changes in underlying conditions (Sec. 5.2 and Appendix to Ch. 1), the notion of a reduced form equation (Secs. 4.3, 5.2, 5.3). Not drawn upon before Chapter 13 is the survey-questionnaire method. In addition, Malkiel and Kane touch in their work on the presumption that least-squares conditions are met. Consequently, these latter topics are presently brought forward.

Survey-questionnaire method.—The survey-questionnaire method provides an important source of information, although information so obtained may be less than ideal. There are problems in communication with respondents. Some lack a perspective on the overall developments surrounding the matters being investigated. Some either consciously or subconsciously hold different frameworks for explaining the same phenomena, and some respondents may simply be unconscious of certain aspects of their own behavior. Indeed, in their first report on survey results, Malkiel and Kane mention two fundamental difficulties in the use of the survey-questionnaire in the study of the expectation formation governing market behavior [221, p. 350]:

1) The environmental influences and decision criteria which condition one's response to a questionnaire may be quite different from those which operate in the evaluation of securities at the time of investment.

2) The individuals filling out the questionnaire may not have been able to report the expectations of those who actually manage their firms' portfolios.

Malkiel and Kane report that they overcame the second difficulty.

Assumptions concerning the random error term.—In introducing one of their equations, Malkiel and Kane touch on another problem of data analysis, the presumption that standard least-squares conditions are met. Elsewhere, Kane conveniently catalogues assumptions regarding the random error term [220, p. 355]:

1. (*Randomness*) The individual errors of disturbances u_j are random variables with finite means, variances, and co-variances.

2. (*Zero mean independent of X*) Every disturbance u_j has zero expected value, irrespective of the value of X_j.

3. (*Homoscedasticity*) The variance of each u_j is the same for all j ($j = 1, \ldots, N$), and independent of X_j.

4. (*Non-autocorrelation of errors*) The error terms of different observations are distributed independently of each other:
$$E\,(u_j\,u_k) = E\,(u_j)\,E\,(u_k) = 0$$
$$\text{for all } j \neq k, j = 1, \ldots, N.$$

5. (*Normality*) The density function $f(u)$ is normal.

6. (*Properties of X*) The exogenous variable X is measured without error and has finite mean and variance.

The failure of results to conform to non-autocorrelation of errors receives repeated emphasis in Part IV.

Appendix to Chapter 14

Solutions to Systems of Equations

THE ECONOMISTS' early experience with equations systems involved non-stochastic equations. The methodology for estimating coefficients for equations of the stochastic type in the structural context was not introduced until the 1930s. For their introduction, Jan Tinbergen, a Dutch economist, received in 1969 the first Nobel Prize awarded in economics (compare Ch. 1, n. 3). This appendix deals briefly with the methods of solution of structural equations models, as distinct from the methods of estimation of coefficients. It does so by moving rapidly from a brief discussion of mathematical solutions to an iterative procedure for obtaining solutions to stochastic models. The emphasis is on the method of solution used for structural equations models of the Federal Reserve–MIT type, where the interest is in actually obtaining a solution for a relatively large model using the modern computer.

Solutions to large models were not feasible because so much labor was required before the advent of the modern computer, and large systems were dealt with mainly at a theoretical level. For example, there was interest in criteria for the existence of a solution rather than in the actual attainment of one.

The criterion emphasized by economists until quite recently was simply whether the number of equations correspond to the number of variables. The early theorists with interest in the general equilibrium of exchange set great store by it.[1] In reflecting on the supply-demand equality for a system of n items, they were concerned that markets would clear for given prices on n quantities. The n equations expressing the market clearing conditions for the n commodities yield a solution. Furthermore, special

---

1. Leon Walras (1834–1910) is credited with the discovery of general economic equilibrium.

concern was attached to the supply-demand equation for money. Fearing this might be a redundant equation and prohibit a solution, they concentrated especially on n-1 equations. Their fear was not adequately founded, as has been illustrated since the 1930s; if equilibrium is obtained in n-1 markets, then it is automatically attained in the nth. A budget constraint requires that the individual or economic unit shall buy and trade (exchange) commodities (or commodities and services) in competitive markets until the ratios of additional utilities from each to their respective prices are equal or, alternatively, until the ratios of utility-index increments for every pair of commodities equal their price ratios. This emphasizes relative prices and exchange ratios. The addition of the quantity theory of money brings in the relevance of the price level as reviewed elsewhere [133, pp. 88–93].

Solutions and Cramer's rule.—The main requirements for a solution are that the equations be non-singular and be linearly independent. Thinking of a system of n equations and n variables in matrix form, these requirements imply that there is no redundancy in the system, or that none of the n rows or n columns in the coefficient matrix is a linear combination (multiple or scalar multiple) of the other.

The equations in a system may be written with all the variables and their corresponding coefficients in the left-hand members of the equations and any constants in the right-hand members. In addition, the variables may be arranged for each equation so the ones common to each equation in the system appear in their respective columns. There may even be zero coefficients for some of the variables but they may be written out anyway. Then in matrix form such a system of n linear equations and n unknowns appears in general form as follows:

$$
\begin{pmatrix}
a_{11} \; a_{12} \; \ldots \; a_{1n} \\
a_{21} \; a_{22} \; \ldots \; a_{2n} \\
\ldots \ldots \ldots \ldots \\
a_{n1} \; a_{n2} \; \ldots \; a_{nn}
\end{pmatrix}
\begin{pmatrix}
x_1 \\
x_2 \\
\cdot \\
x_n
\end{pmatrix}
=
\begin{pmatrix}
b_1 \\
b_2 \\
\cdot \\
b_n
\end{pmatrix}
$$

matrix of coefficients where the first subscript is the row indicator and the second the column indicator	solution vector	vector of constant terms

The test of linear independence relates to the concept of a determinant. The one corresponding to the foregoing matrix is:

$$\begin{vmatrix} a_{11}\ a_{12} \ldots a_{1n} \\ a_{21}\ a_{22} \ldots a_{2n} \\ \cdots\cdots\cdots\cdots \\ a_{n1}\ a_{n2} \ldots a_{nn} \end{vmatrix} = \text{Det. A}$$

where the vertical bars indicate a determinant. A matrix is a collection of elements, but a determinant is a number. To get the number, one expands the determinant. Two methods of expansion are available,[2] but the important thing is that the determinant be non-zero.

There are also two mathematical methods for solving equations systems. One is the high school method of elimination. The other is Cramer's rule (determinants): the solution for x_j (x being the variable associated with the jth column) is given by the ratio of the determinant of coefficients with the jth column replaced by the column of constant terms (Det. A_j) to the determinant of coefficients for the entire equation system (Det. A.), or overall $x_j = $ (Det. A_j)/Det. A. (Note that if Det. A = 0 there is no solution since division by zero is undefined.) The solution to the entire system is a point in space with the coordinates x_j ($j = 1, \ldots, n$).

This method of solution is not pursued further, except to note two things: (1) Cramer's rule can be applied in theory to obtain solutions, but (2) the expansion of the determinants is enormously laborious for large equation systems.

The Gauss-Seidel method.—In the stochastic systems of the Federal Reserve–MIT type, the Gauss-Seidel method of solution has been the most commonly used.[3] It has the following advantages: (1) it is capable of giving very accurate answers; (2) it is relatively stable (the answer converges to the correct answer); (3) it does not introduce division errors, since it requires division by only one coefficient per equation;[4] and (4) it is very easy to program on the computer. The Gauss-Seidel method is iterative in that the procedure for estimating values for given variables is repeated. The original estimate of a value for a given variable

2. The two methods of expansion are (1) expansion by sets of products and (2) expansion by cofactors. One or the other and often both may be found in discussions of matrix algebra in some of the econometrics texts of the 1960s.

3. For a more detailed explanation of the method, see Conte [76, pp. 194–98]. For an example of how the method is programmed for a computer see Carnahan et al. [64, pp. 302–10]. For a discussion of the application of the method to the solution of the Federal Reserve–MIT model, see Norman [287].

4. Elimination procedures, such as the Gauss-Jordan procedure, introduce errors due to the large number of divisions required to set up the problem.

or an assumed value for the variable is improved as successive estimates for the values of other variables are substituted.

The present procedure may be illustrated using the following equation system:

$$a_{11} x_1 + a_{12} x_2 + \ldots + a_{1n} x_n = k_1$$

$$\ldots \ldots \ldots \ldots \ldots \ldots \ldots \ldots \ldots \ldots \ldots \ldots$$

$$a_{i1} x_1 + a_{i2} x_2 + \ldots + a_{in} x_n = k_i$$

$$\ldots \ldots \ldots \ldots \ldots \ldots \ldots \ldots \ldots \ldots \ldots \ldots$$

$$a_{n1} x_1 + a_{n2} x_2 + \ldots + a_{nn} x_n = k_n$$

where the a_{ij}'s are the known parameters (or estimated ones in the case of the econometric model), x_j's are the unknown variables (the endogenous variables), and the k_i's are linear combinations of known variables (exogenous or controlled variables). (Here one may note that the exogenous variables get impounded in what the mathematician views as constants. Exogenous variables are the creation of the economists or econometrician. They play no special role apart from constant terms in mathematics.) The equations given in the system are said to be in normal form (to be a set arrived at in estimation by the method of least squares).

The normal form equations must be transformed into a solution format —each equation has a different, but only one, unknown variable on the left hand side of the equation. This is accomplished by rearranging terms and thus expressing the x_ith variable in terms of other variables and parameters of the equation, where i corresponds to the equation number. In other words, the first equation is solved for x_1, the second for x_2, the third for x_3, and so on. The resulting set of equations may be denoted,

$$x_1 = (0 - a_{12} x_2 - \ldots - a_{1n} x_n + k_1)/a_{11}$$

$$\ldots \ldots \ldots \ldots \ldots \ldots \ldots \ldots \ldots \ldots \ldots \ldots \ldots \ldots$$

$$x_i = (- a_{12} x_1 - a_{12} x_2 - \ldots - a_{in} x_n + k_i)/a_{ii}$$

$$\ldots \ldots \ldots \ldots \ldots \ldots \ldots \ldots \ldots \ldots \ldots \ldots \ldots$$

$$x_n = (- a_n x_1 - a_{n2} x_2 - \ldots 0 + k_n)/a_{nn}$$

(Note that in rearranging terms each equation was divided through by the coefficient of the variable for which a solution was sought.) The system is now in a form suitable for solution.

The first step toward the solution of the latter system is the assumption of values for the n unknown x_i's. The assumed values form an initial solution vector. Next, the first equation is solved for the value for x_1, using the values of the remaining n-1 variables found in the solution vector. When the new value for x_1 is found, it replaces the old value for x_1, (the assumed value). The second equation is then solved for the value of x_2 which in turn replaces the old value of x_2. And so the solution proceeds. The ith equation is solved for the value for x_i, and so on. One pass is completed when all n equations have been solved for the respective x values. The next pass starts with the first equation again, but this time the updated solution from the first pass is used as the assumed solution. The total procedure is continued until the values in the solution vector do not change significantly from one pass to the next. When this occurs, the solution is said to have converged. The solution procedure is then stopped and the solution vector contains the solution to the system of equations.

This foregoing solution represents one time step in a structural equations model. To get a time series, for example for the variable x_1 as it may respond to changes in exogenous variables, k_1/a_{11} of the first equation would be recomputed for each time (t_2, t_3, . . .). In general, to get time series for x_ith variable, k_i/a_{ii} would be recomputed for each time, and so on.

The Gauss-Seidel method avoids the use of reduced form equations, as mentioned in the text on various occasions. Instead of a reduced form equation that facilitates the sketching of a series of estimated values as a given exogenous variable varies, there is the procedure as just outlined.[5]

Testing a model.—In testing hypotheses or parameters, a common reference is to the significance (or lack of it) of a difference between a parameter and some hypothesized value, as in the t-test of significance. Sometimes testing is implied with reference to an equation itself or to an entire model, but such testing comes after the testing of parameter values. First, each parameter in an equation may be checked to see if it is statistically significant. The equation may then be tested by observing the coefficient of correlation and testing for its significance. The equation, moreover, may also be tested in a dynamic sense involving a comparison of observed values of a dependent variable and values estimated using the regression equation and observed values of the so-called independent variables. The test of the observed and estimated values is usually carried out using a root mean square or loss function. Once individual equations

5. The Gauss-Jordan method mentioned in footnote 4 requires the use of reduced form equations.

are tested they may be incorporated into a sector model. This in turn may be tested dynamically, and observed series compared with estimated series. The estimated series may be viewed as responses to changes in exogenous variables and as being obtained through the use of reduced form equations or through the use of the Gauss-Seidel method.

Appendix to Chapter 15

Patterns of Capital Expenditures

THE TEXT has considered at various times business conditions and interest rates, often in association with leading rates of change in monetary aggregates. Two tendencies were brought out in Chapter 15: (1) for credit conditions to serve as a constraint on an enlarged flow of capital expenditures; and (2) for the larger firms to plan financing to avoid the more disturbing effects of tight credit. This suggestion—where the degree of planning varies directly with asset size—was said to impart a differential pattern to various classes of capital expenditures. Furthermore, attention was directed at the Keynesian's tendency to consider changes in housing expenditures as a primary example of the effects of credit conditions. All of this suggests some timing differences in broad classes of expenditures—say, those by large and small manufacturing firms and on new home construction—in contrast to a position enunciated by Brunner. Karl Brunner states the issue [38, p. 54] as

> The analysis of the transmission mechanism offered by the relative price approach [or Brunner, monetarist theory] denies in particular, systematic timing differences in the relative position of housing expenditures or even investment expenditures. The relative price theory implies that consumer expenditures are affected with equal speed as investment expenditures.

Continuing [38, p. 55], Brunner says "the instability of the housing industry over the recent decade is of course incontestable." But he says the instability resulted from variations in monetary and fiscal policies

Note: This appendix was initially presented at the 1971 meetings of the Econometric Society, New Orleans, Louisiana. The regression analyses were redone on later occasions, however, using different programs. The one with which the latest results were obtained was "Regression Analysis Program for Economists," by William J. Raduche, Harvard University.

During this 1971–73 period of experimentation with the data, my assistant in statistical matters was Derriel B. Cato.

combined with "a rigid price fixing in the form of ceiling rates on time deposits and share accounts of savings and loan associations [with changes affecting the mortgage purchasing institutions]."

In contrast to common explanations for timing differences [117, 338, 346, 389] as suggested by Brunner, this appendix focuses on a supplementary explanation for the differential patterns of investment expenditures. According to this explanation, the differential patterns arise mainly because of differences in the degree of planning on the demand side of the market to avoid some disturbing effects of credit conditions, as characterized by high interest rates. The degree of the planning of the financing of capital expenditures is shown to vary with large variations in asset size. This leads to the hypotheses that lags in the restraining effects of credit conditions on the different classes of expenditures will order themselves according to the extent of planning to avoid tight credit conditions (according to the average size of the expenditure units represented by the various time series).

In keeping with old and new themes, this appendix presents some further results from analysis of data for capital expenditures and for the money stock and interest rate variables. There is further experimentation concerning the presence of multicollinearity in the time series and the use of the Almon lag model (Appendix to Ch. 1, Sec. 10.4).[1]

In examining the various relations of classes of expenditures to monetary and credit measures, a pertinent question arises: What are the implications for monetary policy of sheltering housing expenditures from the effects of credit conditions, as in fact has been proposed [219] in consideration of the social priority attached to stability and growth in home construction? This would seem to bear on the question of expenditures

---

1. An outline of the mathematics of the Almon method may be found in Johnston [213, pp. 294–97]. However, as emphasized earlier (Appendix to Ch. 1), the Almon method for dealing with distributed lags is preferable in the presence of multicollinearity. Thus, the time series for the rate of change in the money stock and for the interest rate were tested for the presence of multicollinearity. The Farrar-Glauber test was used [213, pp. 163–64] "by considering the coefficients of multiple determination, R_i^2, between each X_i and the remaining (k-1) variables in X." This also involved the F statistic in testing the significance for each of the R^2s for the variables in question. These R^2s resulted from, say, regressing a variable at time t on its lagged values for each of the different time periods t-1, . . . , t-8. The null hypothesis of no collinearity was rejected at less than the 1 per cent level of significance in every case for the money stock when more than one lagged value was used, and it was rejected in every case for the interest rate. In other words, the R^2 ($\times$ 100) for the rate of change in the money stock with four lagged values was 66.10 per cent, and that for the interest rate with the same number of lagged values was 95.40 per cent.

by business units that are more like households in their financing than like mature corporations of the new industrial state, which may be characterized by "planning" particularly to avoid the destabilizing effects of tight credit conditions (traditionally defined) as described in Chapter 15 and elsewhere [122, Sec. III; 126, Ch. 7].

The net result of the appendix is especially suggestive of recommendations by the Board of Governors in this area of concern [389]. The Board has noted differential patterns of capital expenditures by firms and households. The more lasting effects of credit conditions are said to come from the demand side of the market [389, p. 216]. Ceilings on interest rates are acknowledged as having an historical role in affecting the patterns of capital expenditures [389, p. 217]. But, even with institutional reforms in this area and expanded government programs, there is the view that credit and business conditions must be stabilized to stabilize housing expenditures. To aid in the latter, a variable tax credit is recommended as an instrument for influencing business investment decisions [389, pp. 224–25]. This should stabilize home construction expenditures by stabilizing industrial expenditures, since industries are a main source of the competition for funds in the money, credit, and capital markets.

The classes of capital expenditures presently considered include expenditures on housing units [2] and industrial construction [3] (as reported by the U.S. Department of Commerce and the Bureau of the Census) and capital expenditures on plants and equipment (as reported by the U.S. Department of Commerce and the U.S. Securities and Exchange Commission, in one instance, and by the National Industrial Conference Board, in another). The Commerce-SEC data on capital expenditures encompass expenditures by U.S. manufacturers generally according to industry groups and durable and non-durable goods industries. The NICB data are more restricted. They represent outlays by large firms—approximately the thousand largest manufacturing corporations—again with a breakdown according to industry groups and durable and non-durable goods industries. Both the Department of Commerce and the Conference Board report anticipatory data on capital expenditures that relate to their respective expenditure series.

The monetary and credit measures to which the classes of expenditure

2. "Housing units" include new non-farm houses and apartments. The housing units classification includes housing at various levels of value and quality: prefabricated units, shell houses, and houses built of secondhand materials.
3. "Industrial construction" includes all buildings and structures at manufacturing establishments.

data are related are the rate of change in the money stock (currency plus demand deposits adjusted for interbank and government deposits) and the interest rate on long-term government bonds. Other interest rates could be considered, but the rate used is thought to be the relatively riskless component entering into other rates, to serve adequately as a measure of upward and downward movements in the structure of interest rates (as dealt with by Terrell and Frazer [131]), and to serve adequately in a first approximation as a measure of credit conditions and the availability of credit (Ch. 3, n. 7).

Rates of change were initially used for all stock and flow quantities in the present analysis and the level for the interest rate.[4] This was in keeping with notions about the homogeneity of relationships and the sort of analysis that is proper over time [126, Chs. 3–4]. Dealing with rates of change rather than levels for stock and flow quantities weakens the statistical relationships actually obtained, because the rates of change are based on terminal values ?nd reflect in an enlarged way the validity, errors, and noise in the underlying data. What may be lost in a plethora of high coefficients of determination was hopefully to be gained in the relevance of the results to the real world. In fact, in the case of the series for the rates of change in expenditures and the current and lagged values for the rate of change in the money stock, reasonably good fits to data were obtained. However results from regressing the rates of change on the level for interest rates were too fragile. Consequently, levels for capital expenditures were regressed on the current and lagged values for the interest rate, since the search for differential patterns could still be undertaken.

The methods and approach.—For illustrative purposes, a distributed lag equation for the rate of change in investment as regression on the rate of change in the money stock may be denoted as

$$\left(\frac{1}{I}\frac{dI}{dt}\right) = \text{const.} + \beta_0\left(\frac{1}{M}\frac{dM}{dt}\right)_t + \beta_1\left(\frac{1}{M}\frac{dM}{dt}\right)_{t-1} +$$

$$\ldots + \beta_n\left(\frac{1}{M}\frac{dM}{dt}\right)_{t-n}$$

4. The rates of chance were calculated using

$$\frac{X_t - X_{t-1}}{X_{t-1}} \approx \frac{1}{X}\frac{dX}{dt}$$

where X is the variable.
To convert the quarterly data to percentage terms at an annual rate,

$$\left(\frac{X_t - X_{t-1}}{X_{t-1}}\right) \times 400$$

As the reader will recall (Appendix to Ch. 1), the coefficients (β_s) may be constrained by a polynomial in the Almon model, and these coefficients may be plotted in line with a vertical axis and against time (t) and its lagged values (t-1, . . . , t-n) on the horizontal axis to reflect the distributed lag pattern. The degree of the polynomial and the number of lag periods may be varied to obtain the pattern that yields the best fit to the data (say, as measured by the coefficient of determination, R^2).[5] The sum of the regression coefficients (with sign attached), $\sum\limits_{i=0}^{4} \beta_i$, may be used to indicate the predominantly positive or negative sense of the relationship.

The approach has been to analyze data using four, eight, twelve, and sixteen quarter lags for second, third, fourth, fifth, and sixth degree polynomials.[6] With split sample periods, 1,280 distributed lag relationships were generated on each of several different occasions. Following such extensive analysis the results were scanned for the highest adjusted coefficients of multiple determination (R^2s).[7] These were expected to yield the most relevant time lags for the relationships involved. To conserve space, only representative results are shown here.

The overall sample period for which data were analyzed is 1953–70. This sample was also split into shorter periods for 1953–60, 1961–70, and 1964–70. Reasons for splitting the housing and other capital expenditure samples into the particular shorter periods include:

1. A tax credit amounting to 7 per cent of the expenditures on capital goods was in effect for the first time from January 1962 to April 1969, with a seven and one-half month suspension in 1966–67.

2. Yohe and Karnosky reported a special price expectations effect in the 1961–69 period in a study of price expectations and interest rates. Both of these factors may influence capital expenditures.

5. Using the maximization of R^2 (unadjusted for degrees of freedom) criterion for selecting the best fit yields the same selection as using a minimum standard effor of the estimate (SEE) criterion. For the variable Y,

$$R^2 = 1 - \frac{(SEE)^2}{\text{Variance of } Y}$$

Variance = constant, and min SEE = max R^2.

6. The main constraint on the degree of the polynomial is that it must be equal to or less than the number of lags in the distributed lag relation [3, p. 179]. The polynomials were not forced to zero at terminal points.

7. The coefficients in the Almon program employed are adjusted for degrees of freedom.

3. The possible relevance of a fiscal policy with emphasis on built-in flexibility in the Eisenhower years, 1953–60, in contrast to a more active discretionary fiscal policy in the Kennedy-Johnson years, has been mentioned by Hamburger and Silber [184, p. 370], and by Silber [333].

4. Any distorting economic effects of the military build-up in Vietnam would be most prevalent in the 1960, especially after 1964.

5. The inflation and an accompanying capital boom of the 1960s date primarily from 1964 onward.

6. As interest rates continued their post–World War II rise in the 1960s, the ceilings on savings deposits at commercial banks (with impact on home financing and savings at savings and loan associations [338, pp. 108, 124]) were more actively manipulated [122, pp. 182–83]. In addition, ceilings on FHA-insured and VA-guaranteed mortgages were more actively manipulated in the mid- to late 1960s [117]. Secondary support of the mortgage markets was expanded, especially after 1968 [117; 346, p. 63], with possible impact on the relationship between home construction and interest rates and a dramatic increase in household formations occurred in 1967–68 [346, p. 55] in conjunction with continued inflation and rising interest rates, so as to combine and give rise to the "equity kicker" and a shift toward multifamily housing units [117, p. 13; 346, pp. 58–59].[8]

The interest in splitting the sample was simply to determine whether such splits altered the ranking of expenditure groups, as hypothesized earlier. As the reasons for splitting the sample suggest, there are many factors influencing the various classes of capital expenditures and the indicators for monetary and business conditions. This has suggested to some economists that a structural equations approach with reduced form equations and all (as in the Federal Reserve–MIT model and its various versions) should be used in the study. However, the very limited approach is chosen for two reasons: (1) the structural equations method has its shortcomings in its present state, especially when one introduces shock effects and expectational phenomena that influence many variables simultaneously; and (2) the many other factors operating in an analysis of the present type are not expected to affect the ranking of expenditure groups as hypothesized earlier.

Results from analyses of data.—As a first approximation, the results from analyses of data for the overall and split sample periods fall into two

8. The inflation and other conditions led life insurance companies to virtually stop making mortgage loans, except in multifamily dwellings where they could obtain a share of equity (a share of the project's earnings) as a hedge against inflation. Hence the "equity kicker."

classes—those for the rate of change in the money stock and those for credit conditions. The current and lagged values for the rate of change in the money stock are most closely related to the selected classes of capital expenditures for the higher degree polynomials. Lags for four quarters do very well.[9] Eight quarter lags provide the best fits, when the degree of the polynomial is increased to six.

The results in Table A 15–1 are illustrative. There some distributed lag results from regressing selected classes of capital expenditures in rate of change form on the rate of change in the money stock are shown for the 1953–70 period. One may note the tendencies reflected in the results from analyses of the data for the period in question: the best results are for relatively short lag periods, and the coefficients of multiple determination decline as the number of lagged periods increases, but they increase as the degree of the constraining polynomial increases, such that the best fits to data are obtained with eight quarter lags and with a sixth degree polynomial. Except for the higher degree polynomials, there is a tendency for the regression coefficients to sum to a negative quantity for lags of eight to twelve quarters, while the coefficients for large manufacturing corporations never sum to a negative quantity. In other words, there is a tendency in some instances for the housing–money stock relation to be inverse, while that for large manufacturing corporations is generally direct. Between these somewhat limiting cases is that for small manufacturing firms. The capital expenditure–money stock relation is too fragile to be obtained by the method employed, as indicated by the presence of adjusted coefficients of determination with negative signs.[10]

The relatively strong relation for the rate of change in expenditures on new housing and the rate of change in the money stock lagged four quarters (with third degree polynomial) may be denoted in its fuller detail (for the 1953–70 period) as:

9. This result appears to be consistent with Silber's conclusion from his Almon lag analysis for changes in GNP and current lagged monetary and fiscal policy variables, although he does not experiment with polynomials beyond the third degree. Silber says [333, p. 365] that "The consistency of monetary policy effectiveness is quite clear."

10. Coefficients of determination are never negative, but adjusted ones may be so in the presence of a very poor fit to data [213, p. 130]. This prospect of a negative sign is apparent in the formula

$$\bar{R}^2 = R^2 - \frac{K\text{-}1}{n\text{-}K}\,(1 - R^2)$$

where $\bar{R}$ indicates an adjusted coefficient, n is sample size, and K is the number of explanatory variables. Note that $\bar{R}^2 \leqq R^2$.

$$(1.1) \quad \left(\frac{1}{I}\frac{dI}{dt}\right)_{Housing} = 9.6 + 5.6 \left(\frac{1}{M}\frac{dM}{dt}\right)_{t} - 4.2 \left(\frac{1}{M}\frac{dM}{dt}\right)_{t-1}$$
$$\phantom{(1.1) \quad \left(\frac{1}{I}\frac{dI}{dt}\right)_{Housing} = 9.6 + 5.6} (3.51) (5.17)$$

$$+ 1.9 \left(\frac{1}{M}\frac{dM}{dt}\right)_{t-2} + 6.2 \left(\frac{1}{M}\frac{dM}{dt}\right)_{t-3} - 9.4 \left(\frac{1}{M}\frac{dM}{dt}\right)_{t-4}$$
$$(2.59) (7.62) (5.86)$$

$$R^2 = 67.6 \qquad SEE = 44.6 \qquad \sum_{i=0}^{4} \beta_i = 0.17$$

Additional distributed lag results from regressing the flow of capital expenditures (by selected classes) on the interest rate are shown in Table 15–2 for the 1953–70 period. There one may note that the fits to the data are best for the large durable goods manufacturing corporations and weakest for the housing expenditures. Once again, the small firms (durable goods, in this case) exhibit an intermediate position. In the present case, moreover, a small number of lag periods provide fits that are not improved by increasing the number of lag periods, and variations in the degree of the polynomial do not improve the fits. Although not explicitly shown in Table A 15–2, the sum of the regression coefficients for the lagged relations are positive. In other words, when considering distributed lagged responses to the interest rate, the results show positive relations, rather than the inverse ones posited by Keynesian analysis. It is clear, however, that the relationship weakens as one moves from the larger firms to the households.

A more detailed statement of results may be shown for the relatively strong relationship obtained for large durable goods manufacturing firms with a second degree polynomial and a four quarter lag (1953–70):

$$(1.2) \qquad (I) \text{ Large Durable Goods Corp. } =$$

$$-1167.9 + 619.8\ r_t + 197.4\ r_{t-1} - 39.6\ r_{t-2} - 91.2\ r_{t-3} + 42.6\ r_{t-4}$$
$$(2.28) (1.39) (0.17) (0.66) (0.14)$$

$$R^2 = 66.2 \qquad SEE = 540.05 \qquad \sum_{i=0}^{4} \beta_i = 728.93$$

where the t-ratios are again shown in parentheses (in this case, the regression coefficient for the current term alone is significant at the 5 per cent level).

TABLE A 15–1

Rates of Change in Capital Expenditures
(Selected Classes) in Relation to the
Rate of Change in the Money Stock
(quarterly data, 1953–70)[1]

Coefficients of Determination (in percent)[2]

Degree of Polynomial	Lag in Quarters	New Housing Units[3]	Plant and Equipment Expenditures in Small Mfg. Firms[4]	Plant and Equipment Expenditures by Large Mfg. Corporations[5]
2nd	4	27.3	†	14.8
- -	8	12.7*	†	3.5
- -	12	10.0*	†	†
- -	16	11.7	†	†
3rd	4	67.6	†	18.5
- -	8	12.5*	†	3.9
- -	12	15.3*	†	3.7
- -	16	11.0	†	2.1
6th	4	n.a.[6]	n.a.[6]	n.a.[6]
- -	8	85.6	41.4	60.4
- -	12	45.0	†	12.7
- -	16	23.4	†	†

*The sum of the regression coeficients is negative.

†The relationship is too fragile to be captured by the method employed, as indicated by the presence of adjusted coefficients of determination with negative signs.

1. The money stock data are the revised ones reported in the *Federal Reserve Bulletin*, December 1970, pp. 887–909.

2. The coefficients of multiple determination are adjusted for degrees of freedom.

3. The new housing units series is in dollars. It is obtained from recent revisions in Commerce–Census Bureau construction data.

4. Small manufacturing firms are those reported by netting NICB data for expenditures by large corporations from Commerce-SEC data for capital expenditures by all manufacturing firms.

5. Large manufacturing corporations are those represented by NICB data.

6. Results are not available because of the constraint on the degree of the polynomial Almon lag program: the degree must be equal to or less than the number of lags.

Note: Rates of change in the stock and flow variables are percentage rates adjusted at an annual rate.

As samples of data for the 1953–70 period were split into sub-periods 1953–60, and 1961–70, similar patterns of signs and regression coefficients emerged. Some results for the 1961–70 for comparison with those in Tables A 15–1 and A 15–2 are shown in Tables A 15–3 and A 15–4.

TABLE A 15–2

Capital Expenditures (Selected Classes)
in Relation to the Interest Rate
(quarterly data, 1953–70)

Coefficients of Determination (in percent)

Degree of Polynomial	Lag in Quarters	New Housing Units	Plant and Equipment Expenditures by Small Durable Goods Mfg. Firms	Plant and Equipment Expenditures by Large Durable Goods Mfg. Corporations
2nd	4	30.0	57.7	66.2
- -	8	32.4	60.8	65.4
- -	12	37.9	71.3	64.9
- -	16	32.5	63.3	73.1
3rd	4	29.5	48.3	66.6
- -	8	31.2	61.8	65.0
- -	12	37.2	71.2	66.5
- -	16	32.8	63.0	72.7
6th	4	n.a.	n.a.	n.a.
- -	8	29.9	60.8	64.5
- -	12	35.2	69.7	66.5
- -	16	30.9	62.9	71.9

The notes to Table A 15–1 are also related to this table. In addition, the interest rate is the rate (per annum) on United States Government bonds (long-term) as reported in the *Federal Reserve Bulletin*.

As shown, the money stock still operates with a short lag with the apparently stronger effects on new housing expenditures and on plant and equipment expenditures by large manufacturing corporations.[11] This

11. Once again the results are consistent with Silber's analysis and results. He reports [333, p. 364] that "Monetary policy is also quite powerful in the second period [1960's], it is more powerful than in the 1950's."

The results mentioned, moreover, are possibly consistent with noticeably greater increases in the money stock in the 1960s, and with the presence of other factors affecting capital expenditures, particularly by manufacturing corporations. Such a factor would be expected inflation, especially when allowance is made for its simultaneous effect on interest rate, and the presently emphasized tendency for large manufacturing corporations to anticipate and avoid much of the effect of tight credit.

Bischoff and his discussants [25, pp. 127–33] emphasized expected inflation as a determinant of expenditures on plants and equipment in the capital boom extending over the late 1960s. Referring to inability of some simple and sophisticated models to shed light on the actual plant and equipment expenditures of 1969 and the anticipated ones for 1970, Bischoff asks [25, p. 132], "What other factors could be built in?" He notes the difficulty of dealing with the way in which businessmen

TABLE A 15-3

Rates of Change in Capital Expenditures
(Selected Classes) in Relation to the
Rate of Change in the Money Stock
(quarterly data, 1961–70)

Coefficients of Determination (in percent)

Degree of Polynomial	Lag in Quarters	New Housing Units	Plant and Equipment Expenditures by Small Mfg. Firms	Plant and Equipment Expenditures by Large Mfg. Corporations
2nd	4	23.9	†	18.9
- -	8	10.2	†	6.5
- -	12	15.9*	†	1.6
- -	16	17.5*	†	1.7
3rd	4	65.1	†	24.2
- -	8	8.7	†	6.1
- -	12	24.5*	†	9.6
- -	16	15.7*	†	2.9
6th	4	n.a.	n.a.	n.a.
- -	8	85.7	43.5	82.0
- -	12	38.0*	†	17.5
- -	16	16.2*	†	†

*The sum of the regression coefficients is negative.
†The relationship is too fragile to be captured by the method employed.
The notes to Table A 15–1 are also related to this table.

similarity of results is also reflected in individual equations for the split
sample periods. Some results from regressing the rate of change in housing
expenditures on the current and four lagged values for the rate of change
in the money stock, subject to the Almon constraint of a third degree
polynomial, are embodied in the following equation (1961–70 period):

$$(2.1) \qquad \left(\frac{1}{I}\frac{dI}{dt}\right)_{\text{Housing}} = 7.7 + 5.7 \left(\frac{1}{M}\frac{dM}{dt}\right)_t$$
$$(2.88)$$

$$- 4.2 \left(\frac{1}{M}\frac{dM}{dt}\right)_{t-1} + 2.0 \left(\frac{1}{M}\frac{dM}{dt}\right)_{t-2} + 6.6 \left(\frac{1}{M}\frac{dM}{dt}\right)_{t-3} - 9.3 \left(\frac{1}{M}\frac{dM}{dt}\right)_{t-4}$$
$$(4.39) \qquad\qquad (2.08) \qquad\qquad (6.45) \qquad\qquad (4.69)$$

$$\overline{R}^2 = 65.1 \qquad SEE = 48.3 \qquad \sum_{i=0}^{4} \beta_i = 0.44$$

TABLE A 15–4

Capital Expenditures (Selected Classes)
in Relation to the Interest Rate
(quarterly data, 1961–70)

Coefficients of Determination (in percent)

Degree of Polynomial	Lag in Quarters	New Housing Units	Plant and Equipment Expenditures by Small Durable Goods Mfg. Firms	Plant and Equipment Expenditures by Large Durable Goods Mfg. Corporations
2nd	4	17.4	17.6	68.6
- -	8	19.9	2.3	66.8
- -	12	21.4	10.2	73.3
- -	16	15.4	4.4	72.8*
3rd	4	16.7	17.4	69.2
- -	8	18.3	†	66.1
- -	12	19.3	9.0	74.4*
- -	16	12.9	2.6	74.9*
6th	4	n.a.	n.a.	n.a.
- -	8	14.8	†	66.1
- -	12	14.9	3.4	72.8*
- -	16	9.7	†	79.3*

*The sum of the regression coefficients is negative.

†The relationship is too fragile to be captured by the method employed.
The notes to the foregoing tables are also related to this one.

(in this case, all the regression coefficients are significant except that for the second lag term.) As may be expected, the coefficients show the same pattern of signs and relative order of magnitude as those for equation (1.1).

One important difference in Tables A 15–2 and A 15–4 that emerges in the analysis of data for the 1961–70 period of relatively volatile interest rate changes is the tendency for the interest rate to exhibit an apparent inverse effect on expenditures by large manufacturing corporations, at least after a lag of two to three years, as indicated by the asterisk attached to some coefficients of multiple determination in Table A 15–4. However, the interest rate bears its strongest relationship to capital ex-

---

form their expectations and the failures to allow for "the sort of expectations that might lead, for example, to hurried construction of a plant to avoid higher construction costs later on." In the discussion [25, p. 133], Terborgh also mentions this factor, especially with reference to 1969 and 1970.

penditures by large firms, and this is predominantly a direct rather than an inverse relationship for the early years of the apparent effects.[12]

To continue the comparison of results, an equation comparable to (1.2), but for the 1971–70 period appears as

(2.2)   (I) Large Durable Goods Corp. $=$

$$-2458.2 \; + \; 717.2 \; r_t \; + \; 56.3 \; r_{t-1} \; - \; 201.3 \; r_{t-2} \; - \; 55.8 \; r_{t-3}$$
$$(2.18) \qquad (0.32) \qquad\quad (0.70) \qquad\quad (0.33)$$

$$+ \; 493.1 \; r_{t-4}$$
$$(1.30)$$

$$\overline{R}^2 = 68.6 \qquad\qquad SEE = 545.63 \qquad\qquad \sum_{i=0}^{4} \beta_i = 1009.485$$

And, as in equation (1.2), only the regression coefficient for the current term is significant. As may be expected from what has been said about the overall comparison, the pattern of signs remains about the same, but some differences emerge in the relative order of the magnitudes of the regression coefficients.

To provide additional evidence on the differential patterns for the relationships, a simple method was also employed. Rates of change in capital

12. In fact, a positive overall credit conditions (interest rate) effect appears in the relationships with anticipated capital expenditures for the larger and more mature corporations. This effect may be further supported by the resulting $\overline{R}^2$s from regressing rates of change in planned capital outlays (by selected groups of manufacturing corporations) on the current and lagged values for the interest rate, again using the Almon technique. Such coefficients of determination for the large durable goods manufacturing corporations are (quarterly data, 1961–70 period)

Degree of Polynomial	Lag in Quarters	$\overline{R}^2$
4th	4	17.3
—	8	37.6
—	12	33.5
—	16	36.5
6th	4	n.a.
—	8	35.4
—	12	34.9
—	16	30.1

Planned outlays by all manufacturing firms are represented by the Commerce–SEC series for anticipated expenditures on plants and equipment (two quarters ahead). Large durable goods manufacturing firms are again those represented by NICB data.

Large non-durable manufacturing corporations, which tend to be smaller on the average than durable goods firms [126, Ch. 7] fail to yield the fits just reported.

outlays by large and small manufacturing corporations and in housing were first regressed separately on bond yields, and then regressed separately on rates of change for the money stock. For exampe, for the 1953–70 period and for the large firms,

$$\left(\frac{1}{I}\frac{dI}{dt}\right)_{\text{Large Mfg. Corp.}} = 3.27 + 3.21 \left(\frac{1}{I}\frac{dM}{dt}\right)_t$$

where t-ratio $= 2.11$ and $\bar{R}^2 = 0.084$

The simple regressions were run for lagged values of the policy variables (t-1, t-2, . . ., t-16) as well as for the current values (t). In the case of the interest rate (r), emerging signs for the regression coefficients for the 1953–1970 period were

	r_t,	r_{t-1},	r_{t-2},	r_{t-3},	. . .,	r_{t-14},	r_{t-15},	r_{t-16},
$\left(\frac{1}{I}\frac{dI}{dt}\right)_{\text{Large}}$	+	+	+	+	. . .	+	+	+
$\left(\frac{1}{I}\frac{dI}{dt}\right)_{\text{Small}}$	−	+	+	−	. . .	−	+	+
$\left(\frac{1}{I}\frac{dI}{dt}\right)_{\text{Housing}}$	−	−	−	−	. . .	−	−	−

These sign patterns are consistent with the differential patterns of responses discussed. The large firms accelerate capital outlays as interest rates increase, while housing tends to vary more inversely. Small manufacturing corporations are intermediate to these limiting cases. Although not shown, the responses to rate of change in the money stock are less distinct, but are predominantly positive for large manufacturing corporations.[13]

What has been said above about the changes and patterns reflected in the regression results—particularly the relatively pro-business conditions nature of plant and equipment expenditures on new housing units—is further illustrated in Figure A 15–1. There one may note (1) the tendency for plant and equipment expenditures by large durable goods manufacturing corporations to increase as a percentage of expenditures by all durable goods manufacturing corporations during sustained capital boom periods such as mid-1955 to mid-1957, 1963 to 1966, and through

---

13. The regression coefficients attached to the signs in the results as just discussed are predominantly insignificant at the one percent level of significance.

FIGURE A15–1   Selected Classes of Expenditures on Plants and Equipment and on Housing (as percentages of totals)

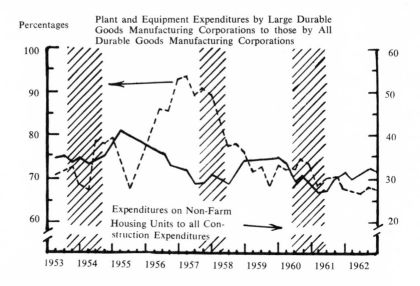

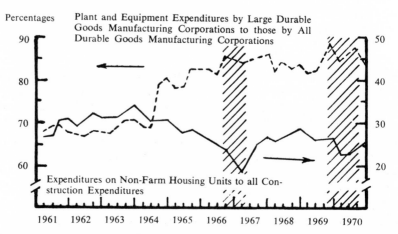

The shaded areas are (a) recessions as identified by turning points reported by the National Bureau of Economic Research in the upper part of the figure, and (b) the widely recognized mini-recession of 1966–67 in the lower part of the figure. The National Bureau's turning points are July 1953 (peak), August 1954 (trough), July 1957 (peak), April 1958 (trough), May 1960 (peak), February 1961 (trough), November 1969 (peak), and November 1970 (trough).

most of the late 1960s; (2) the tendency for expenditures on non-farm housing units as a percentage of all construction expenditures to turn upward during a recession or early in an expansion phase of business conditions, and to turn downward during the mid- to late stage of a recession or capital boom; and (3) the tendency for housing expenditures as a percentage of construction expenditures to maintain their lower (higher) levels, when plant and equipment expenditures by large durable goods manufacturing corporations as a percentage of all durable goods manufacturing corporations are maintaining their higher (lower) levels.

In other words, Figure A 15–1 reflects the varying proportions of expenditures and the out-of-phase character of two important classes of expenditures—one where the sector of large manufacturing corporations is characterized by planning the financing of its capital outlays to avoid the effects of tight credit, and one where the effects of tight credit are more or less unanticipated. The higher levels for expenditures by large durable goods manufacturing firms (as percentages) and the lower levels for non-farm housing units (also as percentages) in the 1960s (from 1964 onward) possibly reflect some of the inflationary impact of that period on capital expenditures and interest rates, in combination with the tendency for large firms to plan financing to avoid the effects of tight credit.

In the foregoing analysis, one can sense the increased complexity of the monetary policy problem if housing expenditures are sheltered from the effects of tight credit and if the monetary authorities accept the task of stabilizing capital expenditures by the larger manufacturing corporations.

Summary and conclusions. When the rate of change in the money stock increases, there are positive effects on the planned and actual expenditures. In the process of expanding business conditions, interest rates rise. With some lag these have constraining effects, particularly on expenditures on housing and plant and equipment outlays by small firms. In the case of the larger industrial concerns, however, these constraining effects are more or less avoided. In the modern industrial state these larger firms are characterized by planning, including the planning of the financing of capital expenditures to at least partially avoid the destabilizing effects of tight credit.

In broad outline the patterns of expenditures and effects suggest that initial effects of accelerating the rate of change in the money stock are fairly short, but that secondary effects require a longer time, especially in the case of mature corporations, which are most characterized by planning. In the case of housing the secondary effects exhibit themselves over a short time.

A question arises about the possible implications of sheltering expenditures on housing from the credit-conditions effects. Were this to occur, the lag time required for the overall primary and secondary effects of monetary policy would be longer. In the present context, the lagged patterns suggest that policy-making officials would need to anticipate more overall aspects of economic stabilization under either of two conditions: (1) when housing would be sheltered from the effects of monetary policy; or (2) when a greater emphasis would be placed on stabilizing expenditures by mature corporations. It would further seem that economists also need to place more emphasis in their theories on the planning and learning aspects of the behavior of mature corporations. In particular Brunner's thesis, as cited initially, does not hold.

Factors other than the rate of change in the money stock affect planned and actual expenditures on capital goods. Recognizing these and various behavioral aspects of mature firms as briefly introduced in this book suggests a policy emphasis on the overall aspects and phases of business conditions. This is in contrast to the received emphasis in the works of some economists on changing a policy variable at a current time and waiting for its effects to occur in a given direction as an offset to conditions occurring or unfolding at the current time.

Selected References

1. Ahmad, Syed, "Is Money Net Wealth?" *Oxford Economic Papers* (New Series), November 1970.
2. Allais, Maurice, "A Restatement of the Quantity Theory of Money," *American Economic Review*, December 1966.
3. Almon, Shirley, "The Distributed Lag Between Capital Appropriations and Expenditures," *Econometrica*, January 1965.
4. Andersen, Leonall C., "Federal Reserve Defensive Operations and Short-Run Control of the Money Stock," *Journal of Political Economy*, March/April 1968.
5. ————, "Seasonal Movements in Financial Variables—Impact of Federal Reserve and Treasury," *Business & Government Review*, University of Missouri, July–August 1965.
6. ————, and Keith M. Carlson, "A Monetarist Model for Economic Stabilization," *Review*, Federal Reserve Bank of St. Louis, April 1970.
7. ————, and Jerry L. Jordan, "Reply," *Review*, Federal Reserve Bank of St. Louis, July 1969.
8. ————, and Jerry L. Jordan, "The Monetary Base—Explanation and Analytical Use," *Review*, Federal Reserve Bank of St. Louis, August 1968.
9. ————, and Jules M. Levine, "A Test of Money Market Conditions as a Means of Short-Run Monetary Management," *National Banking Review*, September 1966.
10. Anderson, W. H. Locke, *Corporate Finance and Fixed Investment: An Econometric Study* (Boston: Graduate School of Business Administration, Harvard University, 1964).
11. Ando, Albert, and Stephen M. Goldfeld, "An Econometric Model for Evaluating Stabilization Policies," *Studies in Economic Stabilization*, Albert Ando, E. Cary Brown, and Ann F. Friedlaender, eds. (Washington, D.C.: The Brookings Institution, 1968).
12. ————, and Franco Modigliani, "Econometric Analysis of Stabilization Policies," *American Economic Review*, Proceedings, May 1969.
13. ————, and Franco Modigliani, "Rejoinder," *American Economic Review*, September 1965.
14. ————, and Franco Modigliani, "The Relative Stability of Monetary Velocity and the Investment Multiplier," *American Economic Review*, September 1965.
15. Argy, Victor, "Rules, Discretion in Monetary Management, and Short-Term Stability," *Journal of Money, Credit, and Banking*, February 1971.

485

16. Arrow, Kenneth J., and F. H. Hahn, *General Competitive Analysis* (San Francisco: Holden-Day, Inc., 1971).
17. Axilrod, Stephen H., and Ralph A. Young, "Interest Rates and Monetary Policy," *Federal Reserve Bulletin*, September 1962.
18. Bach, G. L., *Making Monetary and Fiscal Policy* (Washington, D.C.: The Brookings Institution, 1971).
19. ———, *Federal Reserve Policy-Making* (New York: Alfred A. Knopf, 1950).
20. ———, and C. J. Huizenga, "The Differential Effects of Tight Money," *American Economic Review*, March 1961.
21. ———, and C. J. Huizenga, "The Differential Effects of Tight Money: Reply," *American Economic Review*, September 1963.
22. Barger, Harold, *The Management of Money: A Survey of American Experience* (Chicago: Rand McNally & Company, 1964).
23. Bartholomew, David J., *Stochastic Models for Social Processes* (New York: John Wiley & Sons, 1967).
24. Basemann, R. L., "The Brookings Quarterly Econometric Model: Science or Number Mysticism?" unpublished paper (n. d.).
25. Bischoff, Charles W., "Plant and Equipment Spending in 1969 and 1970," *Brookings Papers on Economic Activity*, No. 1, 1970.
26. Bonomo, Vittorio, and Charles Schotta, "Federal Reserve Open Market Operations and Variations in the Reserve Base," *Journal of Finance*, June 1970.
27. ———, and Charles Schotta, "A Spectrial Analysis of Post-Accord Federal Open Market Operations," *American Economic Review*, March 1969.
28. Boughton, James M., Edward H. Brau, Thomas H. Naylor, and William P. Yohe, "A Policy Model of the United States Monetary Sector," *Southern Economic Journal*, April 1969.
29. ———, and Thomas H. Naylor, "Simulation Experiments with a Monetary Policy Model," a paper presented at the Econometric Society Meetings in Evanston, Illinois, December 30, 1968.
30. ———, "An Econometric Model for Monetary Policy," *Proceedings of the American Statistical Association*, August 1968.
31. Brainard, William C., "Uncertainty and the Theory of Policy," *Targets and Indicators of Monetary Policy*, Karl Brunner, ed. (San Francisco: Chandler Publishing Co., 1969).
32. ———, and James Tobin, "Pitfalls in Financial Model Building," *American Economic Review*, May 1968.
33. Brimmer, Andrew, "The Relevance of Monetary Theory to Monetary Policy," *American Economic Review*, Proceedings, May 1972.
34. Bronfenbrenner, Martin, "Statistical Tests of Rival Monetary Rules: Quarterly Data Supplement," *Journal of Political Economy*, December 1961.
35. ———, "Statistical Tests of Rival Monetary Rules," *Journal of Political Economy*, February 1961.
36. ———, "Statement of Martin Bronfenbrenner," *Compendium on Monetary Policy Guidelines and Federal Reserve Structure*, Subcommittee on Domestic Finance of the Committee on Banking and Currency, House of Representatives (Washington, D.C.: U.S. Government Printing Office, December 1968).
37. ———, "Monetary Rules: A New Look," *Journal of Law and Economics*, October 1965.
38. Brunner, Karl, "A Survey of Selected Issues in Monetary Theory," *Schweizerische Zeitschrift für Volkswirtschaft und Statistik*, March 1971.
39. ———, "The 'Monetarist Revolution' in Monetary Theory," *Weltwirtschaftliches Archiv*, March 1970.

40. ——, ed., *Targets and Indicators of Monetary Policy* (San Francisco: Chandler Publishing Company, 1969).

41. ——, "Statement of Karl Brunner," *Compendium on Monetary Policy Guidelines and Federal Reserve Structure*, Subcommittee on Domestic Finance of the Committee on Banking and Currency, House of Representatives (Washington, D.C.: U.S. Government Printing Office, December 1968).

42. ——, "The Role of Money and Monetary Policy—A Guest Article," *Review*, Federal Reserve Bank of St. Louis, July 1968.

43. ——, "The Controversy Between 'Quantity-Theory' and 'Keynesian-Theory': A Case Study on the Importance of Appropriate Rules for the Competitive Market in Ideas and Beliefs," *Schweizerische Zeitschrift für Volkswirtschaft und Statistik*, June 1967.

44. —— and Allan H. Meltzer, "The Uses of Money: Money in the Theory of an Exchange Economy," *American Economic Review*, December 1971.

45. ——, and Allan H. Meltzer, "What Did We Learn from the Monetary Experience of the United States in the Great Depression?" *Canadian Journal of Economics*, May 1968.

46. ——, and Allan H. Meltzer, *Some General Features of the Federal Reserve's Approach to Policy* (Washington, D.C.: U.S. Government Printing Office, 1964).

47. ——, and Allan H. Meltzer, *An Alternative Approach to the Monetary Mechanism* (Washington, D.C.: U.S. Government Printing Office, 1964).

48. ——, and Allan H. Meltzer, *The Federal Reserve's Attachment to the Free Reserves Concept* (Washington, D.C.: U.S. Government Printing Office, 1964).

49. ——, and Allan H. Meltzer, "Some Further Investigations of Demand and Supply Functions for Money," *Journal of Finance*, May 1964.

50. Bryan, William R., "Bank Adjustments to Monetary Policy: Alternative Estimates of the Lag," *American Economic Review*, September 1967.

51. Buehler, John E., and David I. Fand, "The Federal Reserve and Monetary Policy," *Michigan Academician*, Spring 1969.

52. Burns, Arthur F., "Statement by Arthur F. Burns before the Joint Economic Committee, February 9, 1972," *Federal Reserve Bulletin*, February 1972.

53. ——, "Statement by Arthur F. Burns before the Joint Economic Committee, July 23, 1971," *Federal Reserve Bulletin*, August 1971.

54. ——, *The Frontiers of Economic Knowledge* (Princeton, N.J.: Princeton University Press, for the National Bureau of Economic Research, 1954).

55. ——, ed., *Wesley Clair Mitchell: The Economic Scientist* (New York: National Bureau of Economic Research, Inc., 1952).

56. ——, and Samuelson, Paul A., *Full Employment, Guidepost and Economic Stability* (Washington, D.C.: Rational Debate Seminars, American Enterprise Institute for Public Policy Research, 1967).

57. Camp, A. B., "Two Views on Money," *Lloyds Bank Review*, July 1962.

58. Cagan, Phillip, "Interest Rates Versus the Quantity of Money—The Policy Issues," *Proceedings: 1968 Money and Banking Workshop*, Federal Reserve Bank of Minneapolis, May 1968.

59. ——, "Changes in Cyclical Behavior of Interest Rates," *Review of Economics and Statistics*, August 1966. Also published by the National Bureau of Economic Research as occasional paper 100.

60. Canterbery, E. Ray, *Economics on a New Frontier* (Belmont, California: Wadsworth Publishing Company, 1968).

61. ——, "A New Look at Federal Open Market Voting," *Western Economic Journal*, December 1967.

62. Carlson, Keith M., "Projecting With the St. Louis Model: A Progress Report," *Review*, Federal Reserve Bank of St. Louis, February 1972.

63. ———, "A Test of Money Market Conditions as a Means of Short-Run Monetary Management: A Comment," *National Banking Review*, March 1967.

64. Carnahan, Brice, H. A. Luther, and James O. Wilkes, *Applied Numerical Methods* (New York: John Wiley & Sons, Inc., 1969).

65. Caves, R. E., and H. G. Johnson, eds., *Readings in International Economics* (Homewood, Ill.: Richard D. Irwin, 1968).

66. Chandler, Lester V., Benjamin Strong, *Central Banker* (Washington, D.C.: The Brookings Institution, 1958).

67. Cheng, Pao L. K., and M. King Deets, "Portfolio Returns and the Random Walk Theory," *Journal of Finance*, March 1971.

68. Chow, Gregory C., "Tests of Equality Between Two Sets of Coefficients in two Linear Regressions," *Econometrica*, July 1960.

69. Christ, Carl F., "Econometric Models of the Financial Sector," *Journal of Money, Credit, and Banking*, May 1971.

70. ———, "Monetary and Fiscal Policy in Macroeconomic Models," *The Economic Outlook for 1969*, Proceedings of the 16th Annual Conference on the Economic Outlook, November 14–15, 1969 (Ann Arbor: University of Michigan Press, 1969).

71. ———, *Econometric Models and Methods* (New York: John Wiley & Sons, 1966).

72. Christian, James W., "A Further Analysis of the Objectives of American Monetary Policy, 1952–61," *Journal of Finance*, June 1968.

73. Cloos, George W., " 'Pushing on a String': Monetary Conditions from the 1937–38 Recession to Pearl Harbor," *Financial Analysts Journal*, January–February 1966.

74. Clower, Robert, "The Keynesian Counterrevolution: A Theoretical Appraisal," *The Theory of Interest Rates*, F. H. Hahn and F. P. R. Breachling, eds. (London: Macmillan & Co., Ltd., 1965).

75. Cohen, Morris, and Martin R. Gainsbrugh, "The Capital Goods Market: A New Survey of Capital Appropriations," *The Conference Board Business Record*, October 1956.

76. Conte, S. D., *Elementary Numerical Analysis* (New York: McGraw-Hill Book Company, 1965).

77. Cootner, Paul H., ed., *The Random Character of Stock Market Prices* (Cambridge, Massachusetts: M.I.T. Press, 1964).

78. Crockett, Jean, Irwin Friend, and Henry Shavell, "The Impact of Monetary Stringency on Business Investment," *Survey of Current Business*, United States Department of Commerce, August 1967.

79. Culbertson, J. M., "United States Monetary History: Its Implications for Monetary Theory," *National Banking Review*, March 1964.

80. ———, "The Lag in Effect of Monetary Policy: Reply," *Journal of Political Economy*, October 1961.

81. ———, "The Term Structure of Interest Rates," *Quarterly Journal of Economics*, November 1957.

82. Cyert, Richard, and James G. March, *A Behavioral Theory of the Firm* (Englewood Cliffs, N.J.: Prentice-Hall, Inc., 1963).

83. de Leeuw, Frank, and J. Kalchbrenner, "Monetary and Fiscal Actions: A Test of their Relative Importance in Economic Stabilization—Comment," *Review*, Federal Reserve Bank of St. Louis, April 1969.

84. ———, and Edward M. Gramlich, "The Channels of Monetary Policy," *Federal Reserve Bulletin*, June 1969.
85. ———, and Edward Gramlich, "The Federal Reserve–MIT Econometric Model," *Federal Reserve Bulletin*, January 1968.
86. Deming, Frederick L., "Monetary Policy Objectives and Guides," paper given at the Commercial and Central Banking Seminar, University of North Carolina, August 28, 1963.
87. DePrano, Michael, and Thomas Mayer, "Tests of the Relative Importance of Autonomous Expenditures and Money," *American Economic Review*, September 1965.
88. ———, and Thomas Mayer, "Rejoinder," *American Economic Review*, September 1965.
89. Dewald, William G., "Indicators of Monetary Policy," *Economic Papers* No. 25 issued by the N.S.W. and Victorian Branches of the Economic Society of Australia and New Zealand, 1967.
90. ———, "Money Supply Versus Interest Rates as Proximate Objectives of Monetary Policy," *National Banking Review*, June 1966.
91. ———, and William E. Gibson, "Sources of Variation in Member Bank Reserves," *Review of Economics and Statistics*, May 1967.
92. ———, and H. G. Johnson, "An Objective Analysis of the Objectives of American Monetary Policy, 1952–61," *Banking and Monetary Studies*, Dean Carson, ed. (Homewood, Ill.: Richard D. Irwin, 1963).
93. Dhrymes, Phoebus J., *Econometrics: Statistical Foundations and Applications* (New York: Harper & Row, 1970).
94. Dillard, Dudley, "The Theory of a Monetary Economy," *Post-Keynesian Economics*, Kenneth K. Kurihara, ed. (New Brunswick, N.J.: Rutgers University Press, 1954).
95. Diller, Stanley, "Expectations in the Term Structure of Interest Rates," *Economic Forecasts of Expectations: Analysis of Forecasting Behavior and Performance*, Jacob Mincer, ed. (New York: Columbia University Press for the National Bureau of Economic Research, 1969).
96. Duesenberry, James S., G. Fromm, L. R. Klein, and E. Kuh, eds., *The Brookings Model II: Some Further Results* (Chicago, Illinois: Rand McNally and Company, 1969).
97. ———, G. Fromm, L. R. Klein, and E. Kuh, eds., *The Brookings Quarterly Econometric Model of the United States* (Chicago, Illinois: Rand McNally and Company, 1965).
98. ———, "Tactics and Targets of Monetary Policy," *Controlling Money Aggregates: Proceedings of the Monetary Conference, June 1969* (Boston: Federal Reserve Bank of Boston, September 1969).
99. Dufey, Gunter, "Innovation in International Money and Capital Markets," *Michigan Business Review*, May 1970.
100. Durbin, J., and G. S. Watson, "Testing for Serial Correlation in Least Squares Regression, I," *Biometrika*, December 1950.
101. ———, and G. S. Watson, "Testing for Serial Correlation in Least Squares Regression, II," *Biometrika*, June 1951.
102. Eastburn, David P., "Federal Reserve Policy and Social Priorities," *Business Review*, Federal Reserve Bank of Philadelphia, November 1970.
103. ———, *The Federal Reserve on Record* (Federal Reserve Bank of Philadelphia, 1965).
104. Evans, Michael K., "Non-Linear Econometric Models," *The Design of Com-*

puter Simulation Experiments, Thomas H. Naylor, ed. (Durham, North Carolina: Duke University Press, 1969).

105. Fand, David I., "The Monetary Theory of Nine Recent Quarterly Econometric Models of the United States, Comment," *Journal of Money, Credit, and Banking,* May 1971.

106. ———, "A Monetarist Model of the Monetary Process," *Journal of Finance,* May 1970.

107. ———, "Some Issues in Monetary Economics," *Review,* Federal Reserve Bank of St. Louis, January 1970.

108. ———, "Keynesian Monetary Theories, Stabilization Policy, and the Recent Inflation," *Journal of Money, Credit, and Banking,* August 1969.

109. ———, "Some Implications of Money Supply Analysis," *American Economic Review,* May 1967.

110. ———, "A Time Series Analysis of the 'Bills Only' Theory of Interest Rates," *Review of Economics and Statistics,* November 1966.

111. Fellner, William, *Probability and Profit: A Study of Economic Behavior Along Bayesian Lines* (Homewood, Illinois: Richard D. Irwin, Inc., 1965).

112. Fels, Rendings, and C. Elton Hinshaw, *Forecasting and Recognizing Business Cycle Turning Points* (New York: Columbia University Press for the National Bureau of Economic Research, 1968).

113. Fisher, Irving, *Appreciation and Interest* (New York: Macmillan, 1896). Reprinted by Augustus M. Kelley (New York, 1961).

114. Francis, Darryl R., "Has Monetarism Failed?—The Record Examined," *Review,* Federal Reserve Bank of St. Louis, March 1972.

115. ———, "Money Supply Experience of the St. Louis Fed," unpublished paper delivered to Western Independent Bankers, San Francisco, California, March 15, 1971.

116. Frazer, William J., Jr., "Commentary: Monetary Analysis and Stabilization Policy," *Southern Journal of Business,* October 1970.

117. ———, "Instability in the Home Construction Industry and Monetary Policy," *Business and Economic Dimensions,* November 1970.

118. ———, "Monetary Analysis and Policy: An Exercise in Some Recent History of Economic Doctrine," *The Clemson Review of Industrial Management and Textile Science,* 1969.

119. ———, *The Liquidity Structure of Firms and Monetary Economics* (an unpublished dissertation at Columbia University, 1968).

120. ———, "Monetary Policy, Monetary Operations and National Economic Goals," *Schweizerische Zeitschrift für Volkswirtschaft und Statistik,* March 1968.

121. ———, "Monetary Policy, Business Loans by Banks, and Capital Outlays by Manufacturing Corporations," *Southern Journal of Business,* April 1968.

122. ———, "Statement of William J. Frazer, Jr." *Compendium on Monetary Policy Guidelines and Federal Reserve Structure,* Subcommittee on Domestic Finance of the Committee on Banking and Currency, House of Representatives (Washington, D.C.: U.S. Government Printing Office, December 1968).

123. ———, "The Demand for Money, Statistical Results and Monetary Policy," *Schweizerische Zeitschrift für Volkswirtschaft und Statistik,* March 1967.

124. ———, "Comments on 'Differential Effects of Monetary Policy on Firms of Various Sizes,'" *Southern Journal of Business,* July 1967.

125. ———, "A Review of Morrison's Liquidity Preference of Commercial Banks," *Southern Economic Journal,* October 1967.

126. ———, *The Demand for Money* (Cleveland, Ohio: The World Publishing Company, 1967).
127. ———, "The Financial Structure of Manufacturing Corporations and the Demand for Money," *Journal of Political Economy*, April 1964.
128. ———, "Monetary Analysis and the Postwar Rise in the Velocity of Money in the United States," *Schweizerische Zeitschrift für Volkswirtschaft und Statistik*, December 1964.
129. ———, "Some Comments on Professor Ritter's Interpretation of Keynes and Changes in Income Velocity," *Schweizerische Zeitschrift für Volkswirtschaft und Statistik*, March 1963.
130. ———, "Some Factors Affecting Business Financing," *Southern Economic Journal*, July 1958.
131. ——— (with William T. Terrell), "Interest Rates, Portfolio Behavior, and Marketable Government Securities," *Journal of Finance*, March 1972.
132. ——— (with Robert H. Stroup), "The Demand for Money by Households in South Vietnam: The Evidence from Cross-Section Data," *Journal of Political Economy*, July–August 1969.
133. ——— (with William P. Yohe), *Introduction to the Analytics and Institutions of Money and Banking* (Princeton, N.J.: D. Van Nostrand Company, Inc. 1966).
134. Friedman, Milton, "Have Monetary Policies Failed?" *American Economic Review*, Proceedings, May 1972.
135. ———, "Comments on the Critics," *Journal of Political Economy*, September–October 1972.
136. ———, "A Theoretical Framework for Monetary Analysis," *Journal of Political Economy*, March–April 1970.
137. ———, "Comment of Tobin," *Quarterly Journal of Economics*, May 1970.
138. ———, *The Optimum Quantity of Money and Other Essays* (Chicago: Aldine Publishing Company, 1969).
139. ———, *A Program for Monetary Stability* (New York: Fordham University Press, 1969).
140. ———, "The Role of Monetary Policy," *American Economic Review*, March 1968.
141. ———, "Factors Affecting the Level of the Rate of Interest," *Conference on Savings and Residential Financing: 1968 Proceedings* (Chicago, Ill.: United States Savings and Loan League, 1968).
142. ———, *Dollars and Deficits* (Englewood Cliffs, N.J.: Prentice-Hall, Inc., 1968).
143. ———, "The Monetary Theory and Policy of Henry Simon," *Journal of Law and Economics*, October 1967.
144. ———, *Price Theory: A Provisional Text* (Chicago, Ill.: Aldine Publishing Company, 1962).
145. ———, "The Lag in Effect of Monetary Policy," *Journal of Political Economy*, October 1961.
146. ———, "The Quantity Theory of Money—A Restatement," *Studies in the Quantity Theory of Money*, Milton Friedman, ed. (Chicago, Ill.: The University of Chicago Press, 1956).
147. ———, *Essays in Positive Economics* (Chicago, Ill.: University of Chicago Press, 1953).
148. ———, "A Monetary and Fiscal Framework for Economic Stability," *American Economic Review*, June 1948.

149. ———, and Walter W. Heller, *Monetary vs. Fiscal Policy* (New York: W. W. Norton & Company, Inc., 1969).

150. ———, and Robert V. Roosa, *The Balance of Payments: Free Versus Fixed Exchange Rates* (Washington, D.C.: American Enterprise Institute for Public Policy Research, 1967).

151. ———, and David Meiselman, "Reply to Ando and Modigliani and to DePrado and Mayer," *American Economic Review*, September 1965.

152. ———, and David Meiselman, "Reply to Donald Hester," *Review of Economics and Statistics*, November 1964.

153. ———, and David Meiselman, "The Relative Stability of Monetary Velocity and the Investment Multiplier in the United States, 1897–1958," *Stabilization Policies* (Englewood Cliffs, N.J.: Prentice-Hall, Inc. for the Commission on Money and Credit, 1963).

154. ———, and Anna Jacobson Schwartz, *Monetary Statistics of the United States: Estimates, Sources, Methods* (New York: Columbia University Press for the National Bureau of Economic Research, 1970). Pages 110–26 of this work are reproduced in Milton Friedman and Anna J. Schwartz, "The Definition of Money," *Journal of Money, Credit and Banking*, February 1969.

155. ———, and Anna Jacobson Schwartz, *A Monetary History of the United States, 1867–1960* (Princeton, N.J.: Princeton University Press for the National Bureau of Economic Research, 1963).

156. Fromm, Gary, "Recent Monetary Policy: An Econometric View," *National Banking Review*, March 1966.

157. ———, and Paul Taubman, *Policy Simulation with an Econometric Model* (Washington, D.C.: The Brookings Institution, 1968).

158. ———, and Lawrence R. Klein, "The Brookings–S.S.R.C. Quarterly Econometric Model of the United States," *American Economic Review*, Supplement, May 1965.

159. Frost, Peter A., *Banks' Demand for Excess Reserves*, mimeographed, Carnegie-Mellon University, Graduate School of Industrial Administration, 1968.

160. ———, "Banks' Demand for Excess Reserves," *Journal of Political Economy*, July–August 1971.

161. Gaines, Tilford, *Economic Report*, Manufacturers Hanover Trust, May 1969.

162. Galbraith, John Kenneth, *The New Industrial State* (Boston: Houghton Mifflin Company, 1967).

163. Galper, Harvey, "Alternative Interest Rates and the Demand for Money," *American Economic Review*, June 1969.

164. Garvey, George, "Money, Liquid Assets, Velocity and Monetary Policy," *Monetary Theory and Policy*, Richard A. Ward, ed. (Scranton, Penn.: International Textbook Company, 1966).

165. Georgescu-Roegen, Nicholas, "Utility," *International Encyclopedia of the Social Sciences*, Vol. 16, David L. Sills, ed. (New York: The Macmillan Company and the Free Press, 1968).

166. ———, "The Nature of Expectations and Uncertainty," *Expectations, Uncertainty and Business Behavior*, Mary Jean Bowman, ed. (New York: Social Science Research Council, 1958).

167. Gibson, William E., "Price-Expectations Effects on Interest Rates," *Journal of Finance*, March 1970.

168. ———, "Effects of Money on Interest Rates," *Staff Economic Studies*, No. 43, Board of Governors of the Federal Reserve System, January 1968.

169. ———, "The Effects of Money on Interest Rates," (an unpublished dissertation at the University of Chicago, 1967).

170. ——, and George G. Kaufman, *Monetary Economics: Readings in Current Issues* (New York: McGraw-Hill, Inc., 1971).

171. ——, and George G. Kaufman, "The Sensitivity of Interest Rates to Changes in Money and Income," *Journal of Political Economy*, May–June 1968.

172. Goldberg, Samuel, *Introduction to Difference Equations with Illustrative Examples from Economics, Psychology and Sociology* (New York: John Wiley & Sons, Inc., 1958).

173. Goldfeld, Stephen M., *Commercial Bank Behavior and Economic Activity: A Structural Study of Monetary Policy in the Postwar United States* (Amsterdam: North-Holland Publishing Company, 1966).

174. Goldstein, Elaine R., and Leonall C. Anderson, "1966—A year of Challenge for Monetary Management," *Review*, Federal Reserve Bank of St. Louis, April 1967.

175. Gramlich, Edward M., "Comments on the Discussion of the Carl Christ Paper," *Journal of Money, Credits, and Banking*, May 1971.

176. Gramley, Lyle E., "The Informational Content of Interest Rates as Indicators of Monetary Policy," *Proceedings: 1968 Money and Banking Workshop*, Federal Reserve Bank of Minneapolis, May 1968.

177. ——, and Samuel B. Chase, Jr., "Money Supply Versus Interest Rates: A Reply," *National Banking Review*, December 1966.

178. Griliches, Zvi, "Distributed Lags: A Survey," *Econometrica*, January 1967.

179. Guttentag, Jack M., "The Strategy of Open Market Operations," *Quarterly Journal of Economics*, February 1966.

180. Hamburger, Michael J., "The Lag in the Effect of Monetary Policy: A Survey of Recent Literature," *Monthly Review*, Federal Reserve Bank of New York, December 1971.

181. ——, "Alternative Interest Rates and the Demand for Money: Comment," *American Economic Review*, June 1969.

182. ——, "The Impact of Monetary Variables: A Selected Survey of Recent Empirical Literature," *Staff Economic Studies*, No. 34, Board of Governors of the Federal Reserve System, July 1967.

183. ——, and Cynthia M. Latta, "The Term Structure of Interest Rates: Some Additional Evidence," *Journal of Money, Credit, and Banking*, February 1969.

184. ——, and William L. Silber, "An Empirical Study of Interest Rate Determination," *Review of Economics and Statistics*, August 1969.

185. Hansen, Alvin H., *A Guide to Keynes* (New York: McGraw-Hill Book Company, Inc., 1953).

186. ——, *Business Cycles and National Income* (New York: W. W. Norton & Company, 1951).

187. Harris, Seymour E., "Monetary Policy Under Two Administrations," *Challenge*, February 1964.

188. Hart, Alber Gailord, "Making Monetary Policy More Effective," *United States Monetary Policy* revised ed., Neil H. Jacoby, ed. (New York: Frederick A. Praeger for the American Assembly, Columbia University, 1964).

189. Hastings, Delbert C., and Ross M. Robertson, "The Mysterious World of the Fed," *Business Horizons*, Spring 1962.

190. Havrilesky, Thomas, "A Test of Monetary Action," *Journal of Political Economy*, June 1967.

191. Heller, Walter W., *New Dimensions of Political Economy* (New York: W. W. Norton & Company, Inc., 1966).

192. Hendershott, Patric H., "The Full-Employment Interest Rate and the Neutralized Money Stock: Comment," *Journal of Finance*, March 1971.

494 Selected References

193. ——, "Neutralization of the Money Stock," *Review*, Federal Reserve Bank of St. Louis, May 1970.
194. ——, "Recent Development of the Financial Sector of Econometric Models," *Journal of Finance*, March 1968.
195. ——, "The Inside Lag in Monetary Policy: A Comment," *Journal of Political Economy*, October 1966.
196. ——, and Frank de Leeuw, "Free Reserves, Interest Rates, and Deposits: A Synthesis," *Journal of Finance*, June 1970.
197. Henderson, James M., and Richard E. Quandt, *Microeconomic Theory: A Mathematical Approach*, 2d ed. (New York: McGraw-Hill Book Company, 1971).
198. Hester, Donald D., "Keynes and the Quantity Theory: A Comment on The Friedman-Meiselman CMC Paper," *Review of Economics and Statistics*, November 1964.
199. ——, "Rejoinder," *Review of Economics and Statistics*, November 1964.
200. Hickman, Bert G., "Introduction," *Quantitative Planning of Economic Policy*, Bert G. Hickman, ed. (Washington, D.C.: The Brookings Institution, 1965).
201. Hicks, John R., "Automatists, Hawtreyans, and Keynesians," *Journal of Money, Credit, and Banking*, August 1969.
202. ——, *Critical Essays in Monetary Theory* (London: Oxford University Press, 1967).
203. ——, *Capital and Growth* (New York: Oxford University Press, 1965).
204. Hildreth, Clifford, and John Y. Lu, *Demand Relations with Auto-Correlated Disturbances* (East Lansing, Mich.: Michigan State University Press, 1960).
205. Hinshaw, C. Elton, "The Recognition Pattern of the Federal Open Market Committee," in Rendigs Fels and C. Elton Hinshaw, *Forecasting and Recognizing Business Cycle Turning Points* (New York: National Bureau of Economic Research, 1968).
206. Holmes, Alan R., "Operational Constraints on the Stabilization of Money Supply Growth," *Controlling Monetary Aggregates: Proceedings of the Monetary Conference, June 1969* (Boston: Federal Reserve Bank of Boston, 1969).
207. Jacoby, Neil H., "Introduction: Contemporary Monetary Issues," *United States Monetary Policy*, revised ed., Neil H. Jacoby, ed. (New York: Frederick A. Praeger for the American Assembly, Columbia University, 1964).
208. ——, ed., *United States Monetary Policy*, revised ed. (New York: Frederick A. Praeger, Publishers, 1964).
209. Jaffee, Dwight M., "The Structure of the Money-Expenditure Relationship: Comment," *American Economic Review*, March 1970.
210. Johnson, Harry G., "The Keynesian Revolution and the Monetarist Counter-Revolution," *American Economic Review*, Proceedings, May 1971.
211. ——, "The Case for Flexible Exchange Rates, 1969," *Review*, Federal Reserve Bank of St. Louis, June 1969.
212. ——, and John W. L. Winder, "Lags in the Effects of Monetary Policy in Canada," Working Paper prepared for the Royal Commission on Banking and Finance, November 1962.
213. Johnston, J., *Econometric Method*, 2d ed. (New York: McGraw-Hill Book Company, 1972).
214. Jorgensen, Dale W., "The Theory of Investment Behavior," *Determinants of Investment Behavior*, Robert Ferber, ed. (New York: Columbia University Press for the National Bureau of Economic Research, 1967).
215. ——, "Anticipations and Investment Behavior," *The Brookings Quarterly Econometric Model of the United States*, J. S. Duesenberry, G. Fromm, L. R. Klein, and E. Kuh, eds. (Chicago: Rand McNally & Company, 1965).

216. ———, and C. D. Siebert, "A Comparison of Alternative Theories of Corporate Investment Behavior," *American Economic Review*, September 1968.
217. ———, and James A. Stephenson, "The Time Structure of Investment Behavior in the United States, 1947–1960," *Review of Economics and Statistics*, February 1967.
218. Kahn, R. F., "The Relation of Home Investment to Unemployment," *Economic Journal*, June 1931.
219. Kaminow, Ira, "Should Housing be Sheltered from Tight Credit," *Business Review*, Federal Reserve Bank of Philadelphia, November 1970.
220. Kane, Edward J., *Economic Statistics and Econometrics: An Introduction to Quantitative Economics* (New York: Harper & Row, 1968).
221. ———, and Burton G. Malkiel, "The Term Structure of Interest Rates: An Analysis of a Survey of Interest-Rate Expectations," *Review of Economics and Statistics*, August 1967.
222. Kareken, John, and Robert M. Solow, "Lags in Monetary Policy," in Commission on Money and Credit, *Stabilization Policies* (Englewood Cliffs, N.J.: Prentice-Hall, Inc., 1963).
223. Katona, George, *Psychological Analysis of Economic Behavior* (New York: McGraw-Hill Book Company, Inc., 1951).
224. Keran, Michael W., "Neutralization of the Money Stock—Comment," *Review*, Federal Reserve Bank of St. Louis, May 1970.
225. ———, "Expectations, Money, and the Stock Market," *Review*, Federal Reserve Bank of St. Louis, January 1971.
226. ———, and Christopher T. Babb, "An Explanation of Federal Reserve Actions, 1933–68," *Review*, Federal Reserve Bank of St. Louis, July 1969.
227. Kessel, Reuben A., "Comment," *Journal of Political Economy*, Supplement, August 1967.
228. Keynes, John Maynard, *A Treatise on Money*, Vols. I and II (London: Macmillan and Co., Ltd., 1930).
229. ———, *The General Theory of Employment, Interest and Money* (New York: Harcourt, Brace and Company, 1936).
230. Klein, Lawrence R., "Empirical Evidence on Fiscal and Monetary Models," *Issues in Fiscal and Monetary Policy: The Eclectic Economist Views The Controversy*, James J. Diamond, ed. (Chicago: De Paul University, 1971).
231. ———, "Nobel Laurates in Economics," *Science*, Nov. 7, 1969.
232. ———, "Introduction: The Research Strategy and Its Application," *The Brookings Quarterly Econometric Model of the United States*, J. S. Duesenberry, G. Fromm, L. R. Klein, and E. Kuh, eds. (Chicago: Rand McNally & Company, 1965).
233. ———, *The Keynesian Revolution*, 2d ed. (New York: The Macmillan Company, 1966).
234. ———, "The Estimation of Distributed Lags," *Econometrica*, October 1958.
235. ———, *Economic Fluctuations in the United States, 1921–1941* (New York: John Wiley and Sons, 1950).
236. Klopstock, Fred H., "Money Creation in the Eurodollar Market—A Note on Professor Friedman's Views," *Monthly Review*, January 1970.
237. Kmenta, J., and P. E. Smith, "Autonomous Expenditures Versus Money Supply: An Application of Dynamic Multipliers," mimeographed, 1971.
238. Koch, Albert R., "An Approach to Monetary Policy Formulation," *Business Review*, Federal Reserve Bank of Philadelphia, February 1965.
239. Koopmans, Tjalling C., *Three Essays on the State of Economic Science* (New York: McGraw-Hill Book Company, 1957).
240. Kvansnicka, Joseph G., "Eurodollars—An Important Source of Funds for

496   Selected References

American Banks," *Business Conditions*, A Review of the Federal Reserve Bank of Chicago, June 1969.
241. Kuh, Edwin, "Econometric Models: Is a New Age Dawning?" *American Economic Review*, Supplement, May 1965.
242. Laffer, A. B., and R. D. Ranson, "A Formal Model of the Economy," *Journal of Business*, July 1971.
243. Latané, Henry A., "A Note of Monetary Policy, Interest Rates and Income Velocity," *Southern Economic Journal*, January 1970.
244. ———, "Criteria for Choice Among Risky Ventures," *Journal of Political Economy*, April 1959.
245. ———, "Statement of Henry Latané," *Compendium on Monetary Policy Guidelines and Federal Reserve Structure*, Subcommittee on Domestic Finance of the Committee on Banking and Currency, House of Representatives (Washington, D.C.: U.S. Government Printing Office, December 1969).
246. ———, and Donald L. Tuttle, *Security Analysis and Portfolio Management* (New York: The Ronald Press Company, 1970).
247. Lee, Tong Hun, "Alternative Interest Rates and the Demand for Money: A Reply," *American Economic Review*, June 1969.
248. ———, "Alternative Interest Rates and the Demand for Money: The Empirical Evidence," *American Economic Review*, December 1967.
249. Leijonhufvud, Axel, *On Keynesian Economics and the Economics of Keynes* (New York: Oxford University Press, 1968).
250. ———, "Keynes and the Effectiveness of Monetary Policy," *Western Economics Journal*, March 1968.
251. ———, "Keynes and the Keynesians: A Suggested Interpretation," *American Economics Review*, Proceedings, May 1967.
252. Lucus, Robert E., Jr., and Leonard A. Rapping, "Price Expectations and the Phillips Curve," *American Economic Review*, June 1969.
253. Lydall, H. F., "Income, Assets, and the Demand for Money," *Review of Economics and Statistics*, February 1958.
254. Maisel, Sherman J., "Controlling Monetary Aggregates," *Controlling Monetary Aggregates: Proceedings of the Monetary Conference, June 1969* (Boston: Federal Reserve Bank of Boston, 1969).
255. Malkiel, Burton G., "Comment," *Journal of Political Economy*, Supplement, August 1967.
256. ———, and Edward J. Kane, "Expectations and Interest Rates: A Cross-Sectional Test of the Error-Learning Hypothesis," *Journal of Political Economy*, August 1969.
257. Markowitz, Harry, "Portfolio Selection," *Journal of Finance*, March 1952.
258. Mayer, Thomas, "The Lag in Effect of Monetary Policy: Some Criticisms," *Western Economic Journal*, September 1967.
259. ———, "The Inflexibility of Monetary Policy," *Review of Economics and Statistics*, November 1958.
260. Mead, J. E., and P. W. S. Andrews, "Summaries of Replies to Questions on Effects of Interest Rates," reprinted in *Oxford Studies of the Price Mechanism*, T. Wilson and P. W. S. Andrews, eds. (Oxford: Oxford University Press, 1951).
261. Means, Gardner C., "The Administered-Price Theory Reconfirmed," *American Economic Review*, June 1972.
262. Meiselman, David, "Comment," *American Economic Review*, Proceedings, May 1969.
263. ———, "The Stock of Money or Autonomous Expenditures: Some Recent Evidence," *Business Economics*, June 1968.

264. ———, "The Policy Implications of Recent Research in Term Structure of Interest Rates," *Savings and Residential Financing: 1968 Conference Proceedings*, Donald P. Jacobs and Richard T. Pratt, eds. (Chicago: The United States Savings and Loan League, 1968).

265. ———, *The Term Structure of Interest Rates* (Englewood Cliffs, N.J.: Prentice-Hall, Inc., 1962).

266. Meltzer, Allan H., "Controlling Money," an unpublished paper presented for the meeting of Treasury Consultants, Washington, D.C., April 3, 1969.

267. ———, "The Appropriate Indicators of Monetary Policy," *Savings and Residential Financing: 1969 Conference Proceedings*, Donald P. Jacobs and Richard T. Pratt, eds. (Chicago, Ill.: United States Savings and Loan League, 1969).

268. ———, "Money Supply Revisited: A Review Article," *Journal of Political Economy*, April 1967.

269. ———, "Comments on the Federal Reserve–MIT Econometric Model," a paper read at the SSRC Conference on the Monetary Mechanism, Board of Governors of the Federal Reserve System, May 26, 1967.

270. ———, "Monetary Theory and Monetary History," *Schweizerische Zeitschrift für Volkswertschaft und Statistik*, December 1965.

271. Miles, Joseph E., "Tax Speedup and Corporate Liquidity," *Harvard Business Review*, July–August 1967.

272. Miller, Merton H., and Daniel Orr, "A Model of the Demand for Money by Firms," *Quarterly Journal of Economics*, August 1966.

273. Mincer, Jacob, "Models of Adaptive Forecasting," *Economic Forecasts and Expectations: Analysis of Forecasting Behavior and Performance*, Jacob Mincer, ed. (New York: Columbia University Press for the National Bureau of Economic Research, 1969).

274. Mintz, Ilse, *Dating Post-War Business Cycles* (New York: National Bureau of Economic Research, 1969).

275. Mitchell, George W., "Some Current Problems of Monetary Policy," *Southern Journal of Business*, July 1967.

276. Mitchell, Wesley C., *The Backward Art of Spending Money and Other Essays* (New York: Augustus M. Kelly, Inc., 1950).

277. Modigliani, Franco, "Some Empirical Tests of Monetary Management and of Rules Versus Discretion," *Journal of Political Economy*, June 1964.

278. ———, Robert Rasche, and J. Philip Cooper, *Journal of Money, Credit, and Banking*, May 1970.

279. ———, and Richard Sutch, "The Term Structure of Interest Rates: A Reexamination of the Evidence," *Journal of Money, Credit, and Banking*, February 1969.

280. ———, and Richard Sutch, "Debt Management and the Term Structure of Interest Rates: An Empirical Analysis of Recent Experience," *Journal of Political Economy*, Supplement, August 1967.

281. ———, and Richard Sutch, "Innovation in Interest Rate Policy," *American Economic Review*, Papers and Proceedings, May 1966.

282. Morrison, George R., *Liquidity Preferences of Commercial Banks* (Chicago, Ill.: University of Chicago Press, 1966).

283. Mueller, Eva., "Consumer Reaction to Inflation," *Quarterly Journal of Economics*, May 1951.

284. Murphy, James, "An Appraisal of Repeated Predictive Tests on an Econometric Model," *Southern Economic Journal*, April 1969.

285. Nerlove, Marc, "Discussion," *American Economic Review*, Supplement, May 1965.

286. Niehans, Jurg, "Money and Barter in General Equilibrium with Transactions Costs," *American Economic Review*, December 1971.
287. Norman, M. R., "Solving a Nonlinear Econometric Model by the Gauss-Seidel Iterative Method," a paper presented at the December 1967 meeting of the Econometric Society.
288. Noyes, Guy E., Hearings before the Joint Economic Committee, Congress of the United States, May 1968, *Standards for Guiding Monetary Actions* (Washington, D.C.: Government Printing Office, 1968).
289. Okun, Arthur, "Potential GNP: Its Measurement and Significance," *1962 Proceedings of the Business and Economic Statistics Section of the American Statistical Association.*
290. Peltzman, Sam, "The Structure of the Money-Expenditure Relationship: Reply," *American Economic Review*, March 1970.
291. ———, "The Structure of the Money-Expenditure Relationship," *American Economic Review*, March 1969.
292. Patinkin, Don, "The Chicago Tradition, the Quantity Theory, and Friedman," *Journal of Money, Credit, and Banking*, February 1969.
293. Pesek, Boris P., and Thomas R. Saving, *Money, Wealth, and Economic Theory* (New York: The Macmillan Company, 1967).
294. Poole, William, "Commercial Bank Reserve Management in a Stochastic Model: Implications for Monetary Policy," *Journal of Finance*, December 1968.
295. Quirin, G. David, *The Capital Expenditure Decision* (Homewood, Illinois: Richard D. Irwin, Inc., 1967).
296. Rader, Trout, *Theory of Microeconomics* (New York: Academic Press, Inc., 1972).
297. Raiffa, Howard, *Decision Analysis: Introductory Lectures on Choice Under Uncertainty* (Reading, Massachusetts, 1968).
298. ———, (with John W. Pratt and Robert Schlaifer), *Introduction to Statistical Decision Theory* (McGraw-Hill Book Company, 1965).
299. Rangarajan, C., and Alan K. Severn, "The Response of Banks to Changes in Aggregate Reserves," *Journal of Finance*, December 1965.
300. Rasche, Robert H., "Comments on the Monetarist Approach to Demand Management," *Review*, Federal Reserve Bank of St. Louis, January 1972.
301. ———, and Harold T. Shapiro, "The F.R.B.–M.I.T. Econometric Model: Its Special Features," *American Economic Review*, Supplement, May 1968.
302. Reagon, Michael D., "The Internal Structure of the Federal Reserve: A Political Analysis," *Monetary Management*, Frank M. Tamagna et al., eds. (Englewood Cliffs, N.J.: Prentice-Hall, Inc., 1963).
303. ———, "The Political Structure of the Federal Reserve System," *American Political Science Review*, March 1961.
304. Resek, Robert W., "Investment by Manufacturing Firms: A Quarterly Time Series Analysis of Industry," *Review of Economics and Statistics*, August 1966. This reference is also reprinted as *Staff Economic Study*, No. 28, Board of Governors of the Federal Reserve System, 1967.
305. Reuber, G. L., "The Objectives of Canadian Monetary Policy, 1949–1961: Empirical 'Trade-offs' and the Reaction Function of the Authorities," *Journal of Political Economy*, April 1964.
306. ———, "The Objectives of Monetary Policy," Working Paper prepared for the Royal Commission on Banking and Finance, December 1962.
307. Reuber, G. L., "The Objectives of Canadian Monetary Policy, 1949–1961,

Empirical 'Trade-Offs' and the Reaction Function of the Authorities," *Journal of Political Economy*, April 1964.

308. Ritter, Lawrence S., and Thomas R. Atkinson, "Monetary Theory and Policy in the Payments System of the Future," *Journal of Money, Credit, and Banking*, November 1970.

309. ———, and William L. Silber, *Money* (New York: Basic Books, Inc., 1970).

310. Robinson, Joan, "The Second Crisis of Economic Theory," *American Economic Review*, Proceedings, May 1972.

311. Romans, J. T., "Moral Suasion as an Instrument of Economic Policy," *American Economic Review*, December 1966.

312. Roosa, Robert V., *Federal Reserve Operations in the Money and Government Securities Markets* (New York: Federal Reserve Bank of New York, 1956).

313. Rossant, M. J., "Mr. Martin and the Winds of Change," *Challenge*, January 1964.

314. Sachs, Reynolds, and Albert G. Hart, "Anticipations and Investment Behavior: An Econometric Study of Quarterly Series for Large Firms in Durable Goods Manufacturing," *Determinants of Investment Behavior*, Robert Ferber, ed. (New York: Columbia University Press for the National Bureau of Economic Research, 1967).

315. Samuelson, Paul A., "Maximum Principles of Analytical Economics," *American Economic Review*, June 1972.

316. ———, "Reflections on the Merits and Demerits of Monetarism," *Issues in Fiscal and Monetary Policy: The Eclectic Economist Views the Controversy*, James J. Diamond, ed. (Chicago, Ill.: DePaul University, 1971).

317. ———, *Economics*, 8th ed. (New York: McGraw-Hill Book Company, 1970).

318. ———, "The Role of Money in National Economic Policy," *Controlling Monetary Aggregates: Proceedings of the Monetary Conference, June 1969* (Boston: Federal Reserve Bank of Boston, 1969).

319. ———, "What Classical and Neoclassical Monetary Theory Really Was," *Canadian Journal of Economics*, February 1968.

320. ———, *Economics*, 7th ed. (New York: McGraw-Hill Book Company, Inc., 1967).

321. ———, The Collected Scientific Papers of Paul A. Samuelson, Vol. I, Joseph E. Siglitz, ed. (Cambridge: Massachusetts Institute of Technology Press, 1966).

322. ———, The Collected Scientific Papers of Paul A. Samuelson, Vol. II, Joseph E. Siglitz, ed. (Cambridge: Massachusetts Institute of Technology Press, 1966).

323. ———, *Economics*, 2d ed. (New York: McGraw-Hill Book Company, Inc., 1951).

324. ———, "The General Theory (3)," *The New Economics*, Seymour E. Harris, ed. (New York: Alfred A. Knopf, 1950).

325. ———, *Foundations of Economic Analysis* (Cambridge: Harvard University Press, 1947).

326. ———, "Lord Keynes and the General Theory," *Econometrica*, July 1946.

327. Saving, Thomas R., "Transactions Costs and the Demand for Money," *American Economic Review*, June 1971.

328. ———, "Portfolio Choice and Monetary Theory," *Journal of Money, Credit, and Banking*, May 1970.

329. Sayers, R. S., "Monetary Thought and Monetary Policy in England," *Economic Journal*, December 1960.

330. Schumpter, Joseph A., *History of Economic Analysis* (New York: Oxford University Press, 1954).
331. Shapiro, Harold T., "Distributed Lags, Interest Rate Expectations, and the Impact of Monetary Policy: An Econometric Analysis of a Canadian Experience," *American Economic Review*, May 1967.
332. Shaw, Edward S., "Money Supply and Stable Economic Growth," *United States Monetary Policy*, Neil H. Jacoby, ed. (The American Assembly, Columbia University, 1958).
333. Silber, William L., "The St. Louis Equation: 'Democratic' and 'Republican' Versions and Other Experiments," *Review of Economics and Statistics*, November 1971.
334. Sims, Christopher A., "Money, Income, and Causality," *American Economic Review*, September 1972.
335. Smith, Adam (pseud.), *The Money Game* (New York: Random House, Inc., 1967).
336. Smith, Warren L., *Macroeconomics* (Homewood, Ill.: Richard D. Irwin, Inc., 1970).
337. ———, "A Neo-Keynesian View of Monetary Policy," *Controlling Monetary Aggregates: Proceedings of the Monetary Conference, June 1969* (Boston: Federal Reserve Bank of Boston, 1969).
338. ———, "Some Reflections on Interest Rates and Their Economic Implications," *Savings and Residential Financing: 1966 Proceedings*, Marshall D. Ketchum and H. Robert Bartell, Jr., eds. (Chicago: United States Savings and Loan League, 1966).
339. Snyder, Carl, *Capitalism the Creator* (New York: The Macmillan Company, 1940).
340. Sprenkle, Case M., "The Uselessness of Transactions Demand Models," *Journal of Finance*, December 1969.
341. Sprinkle, Beryl, "Monetary Growth as a Cyclical Predictor," *Journal of Finance*, September 1959.
342. Starleaf, Dennis R., "The Specification of Money Demand-Supply Models Which Involve the Use of Distributed Lags," *Journal of Finance*, Sept. 1970.
343. Stein, Jerome L., "The Optimum Quantity of Money," *Journal of Money, Credit, and Banking*, November 1970.
344. Stewart, Kenneth, "Government Debt, Money, and Economic Activity," *Review*, Federal Reserve Bank of St. Louis, January 1972.
345. Struble, Frederick M., and J. A. Cacy, "The Money Supply Rule and Countercyclical Monetary Policy," *Monthly Review*, Federal Reserve Bank of Kansas City, June–July 1968.
346. Swan, Craig, "Homebuilding: A Review of Experience," *Brookings Papers on Economic Activity*, No. 1, 1970.
347. Teigen, Ronald L., "A Critical Look at Monetarist Economics," *Review*, Federal Reserve Bank of St. Louis, January 1972.
348. ———, "The Keynesian-Monetarist Debate in the U.S.: A Summary and Evaluation," *Statsökonomisk Tidsskrift*, January 1970.
349. ———, "A Structural Approach to the Impact of Monetary Policy," *Journal of Finance*, May 1964.
350. Telser, L. G., "A Critique of Some Recent Empirical Research on the Explanation of the Term Structure of Interest Rates," *Journal of Political Economy*, Supplement, Part II, August 1967.
351. Theil, Henri, "Linear Decision Rules for Macrodynamic Policy Problems," *Quantitative Planning of Economic Policy*, Bert G. Hickman, ed. (Washington, D.C.: The Brookings Institution, 1965).

352. Thomson, Thomas D., James L. Pierce, and Robert T. Parry, "A Monthly Money Market Model," mimeographed, 1972.

353. Tobin, James, "Money, and Income: Post Hoc Ergo Propter Hoc?" *Quarterly Journal of Economics*, May 1970.

354. ——, "Rejoinder," *Quarterly Journal of Economics*, May 1970.

355. ——, "Commercial Banks as Creators of Money," *Banking and Monetary Studies*, Deane Carson, ed. (Homewood, Ill.: Richard D. Irwin, Inc. 1963).

356. ——, "Liquidity Preference as Behavior Towards Risk," *Review of Economic Studies*, February 1958.

357. Torto, Raymond G., *An Endogenous Treatment of the Federal Reserve System in a Macro-Econometric Model* (unpublished dissertation, Boston College, 1969).

358. Turgeon, Lynn, "The Crisis in Post-Keynesian Economics: A Revisionist Interpretation of Recent Economic History," *Quarterly Review of Economics and Business*, Winter 1971.

359. Tussing, A. Dale, "The Differential Effects of Tight Money: Comment," *American Economic Review*, September 1963.

360. Vickrey, William S., *Microstatics* (New York: Harcourt, Brace & World, Inc., 1964).

361. Vogel, Robert C., and G. S. Maddala, "Cross-Section Estimates of Liquid Asset Demand by Manufacturing Corporations," *Journal of Finance*, December 1967.

362. Wadsworth, George P., and Joseph G. Bryan, *Introduction to Probability and Random Variables* (New York: McGraw-Hill Book Company, Inc., 1960).

363. Wallace, Neil, "Comment," *Journal of Political Economy*, Supplement, August 1967.

364. Wallich, Henry C., "Discussion," *Controlling Monetary Aggregates: Proceedings of the Monetary Conference, June 1969* (Boston: Federal Reserve Bank of Boston, 1969).

365. Warburton, Clark, "Variability of the Lag in the Effect of Monetary Policy, 1919–1965," *Western Economic Journal*, June 1971.

366. ——, *Depression, Inflation, and Monetary Policy: Selected Papers, 1945–1953* (Baltimore: The John Hopkins Press, 1966).

367. Weintraub, Robert, "The Stock of Money, Interest Rates and the Business Cycle, 1952–1964," *Western Economic Journal*, June 1967.

368. White, William H., "The Flexibility of Monetary Policy," *Review of Economics and Statistics*, May 1961.

369. Whitlesey, C. R., "Federal Reserve Policy: Disclosure and Non-disclosure," *National Banking Review*, September 1963.

370. ——, "Power and Influence in the Federal Reserve System," *Economica*, February 1963.

371. Wicksell, Knut, "The Natural Rate of Interest," *Monetary Theory and Policy*, Richard A. Ward, ed. (Scranton, Pa.: International Textbook Company, 1966).

372. Williams, Robert Eugene, *Econometric Model Building: A Case History, The Federal Reserve–MIT Model* (unpublished master's thesis, University of Florida, 1970).

373. Willes, Mark H., "Lags in Monetary and Fiscal Policy," *Business Review*, Federal Reserve Bank of Philadelphia, March 1968.

374. ——, "The Inside Lags of Monetary Policy: 1952–1960," *Journal of Finance*, December 1967.

375. ——, *The Framework of Monetary Policy: A Staff Analysis of the Federal Open Market Committee in its Conduct of Monetary Policy* (Washington,

D.C.: U.S. Government Printing Office for the House Committee on Banking and Currency, 1967).

376. Wilson, J. G. S., "Some Reflections of the Radcliffe Committee's Report," *Monetary Policy and the Development of Money Markets* (London: George Allen & Unwin, Ltd., 1967).

377. Wood, John H., "A Model of Federal Reserve Behavior," *Monetary Process and Policy*, George Horwich, ed. (Homewood, Ill.: Richard D. Irwin, 1967).

378. ———, "The Expectations Hypothesis, the Yield Curve, and Monetary Policy," *Quarterly Journal of Economics*, August 1964.

379. Yohe, William P., "Federal Open Market Committee Decisions on a Markov Process," *Public Choice*, Fall 1971.

380. ———, "A Study of Federal Open Market Committee Voting, 1955–1964," *Southern Economic Journal*, April 1966.

381. ———, "The Open Market Committee Decision Process and the 1964 Patman Hearings," *National Banking Review*, March 1965.

382. ———, "A Model of Federal Open Market Committee Decision Processes," a paper presented to the Panel on Nonmarket Decision-Making, Southern Economic Association, November 10, 1966.

383. ———, and Louis C. Gasper, "The 'Even Keel' Decisions of the Federal Open Market Committee," *Financial Analysts Journal*, November/December 1970.

384. ———, and Denis S. Karnosky, "Interest Rates and Price Level Changes, 1952–69," *Review*, Federal Reserve Bank of St. Louis, December 1969.

385. Young, Ralph A., and Duncan McC. Holthausen, "Values and Limitations of Consumer Financial Surveys for Economic Research," *Federal Reserve Bulletin*, March 1947.

386. Zecher, Richard, "A Comment on Carl Christ's Paper," *Journal of Money, Credit, and Banking*, May 1971.

387. Zellner, Arnold, "The Bayesian Approach and Alternatives in Econometrics," a paper delivered at the Econometric Society Meeting, New York, December 1969.

388. Zwick, Burton, "The Adjustment of the Economy to Monetary Changes," *Journal of Political Economy*, January/February 1971.

389. Board of Governors of the Federal Reserve System, Report, "Ways to Moderate Fluctuations in the Construction Industry," *Federal Reserve Bulletin*, March 1972.

390. U.S. Congress, Hearings before the Joint Economic Committee, *The President's New Economic Program*, 92nd Cong., 1st Sess. (Washington, D.C.: U.S. Government Printing Office, 1971).

391. U.S. Congress, Hearings before the Joint Economic Committee, *Phase II of the President's New Economic Program*, 92nd Cong., 1st Sess. (Washington, D.C.: U.S. Government Printing Office, 1971).

392. Staff Editorial Committee, "Monetary Aggregates and Money Market Conditions in Open Market Policy," *Federal Reserve Bulletin*, February 1971.

393. *The International Adjustment Mechanism: Proceedings of the Monetary Conference, October 1969* (Boston: The Federal Reserve Bank of Boston, 1970).

394. *Controlling Monetary Aggregates: Proceedings of the Monetary Conference, June 1969* (Boston: Federal Reserve Bank of Boston, 1970).

395. U.S. Congress, House, Subcommittee on Domestic Finance of the Committee on Banking and Currency, *Compendium on Monetary Policy Guidelines and Federal Reserve Structure* (Washington, D.C.: U.S. Government Printing Office, December 1968).

396. U.S. Congress, Hearings before the Joint Economic Committee, *Standards for Guiding Monetary Actions*, May 1968 (Washington, D.C.: U.S. Government Printing Office, 1968).
397. U.S. Congress, Joint Economic Committee, *Report: Standards for Guiding Monetary Action* (Washington, D.C.: U.S. Government Printing Office, 1968).
398. Royal Commission, *Report of the Royal Commission on Banking and Finance* (Ottawa: Queen's Printer and Controller of Stationery, 1964).
399. "Opening the Books on Monetary Policy," *Morgan Guaranty Survey*, March 1965.
400. U.S. Congress, House, Subcommittee on Domestic Finance of the Committee on Banking and Currency, *Hearings, the Federal Reserve After Fifty Years* (Washington, D.C.: U.S. Government Printing Office, 1964).
401. *Annual Report of the Executive Directors for the Fiscal Year Ended April 30, 1962* (Washington, D.C.: International Monetary Fund, 1962).
402. Technical Staff, *The Federal Reserve System: Purposes and Functions*, 4th ed. (Washington, D.C.: Board of Governors of the Federal Reserve System, 1961).
403. Commission on Money and Credit, *Money and Credit: Their Influences on Jobs, Prices, and Growth* (Englewood Cliffs, N.J.: Prentice-Hall, Inc. 1961).
404. Radcliffe Committee, "Committee on the Working of the Monetary System," (London: Her Majesty's Stationery Office, 1959).
405. U.S. Congress, Committees on Banking and Currency and the Select Committees on Small Business, Report by the Federal Reserve, *Financing Small Business* (Washington, D.C.: U.S. Government Printing Office, 1958).

Index